FOR DUMMIES

The fun and easy way™ to travel!

U.S.A.

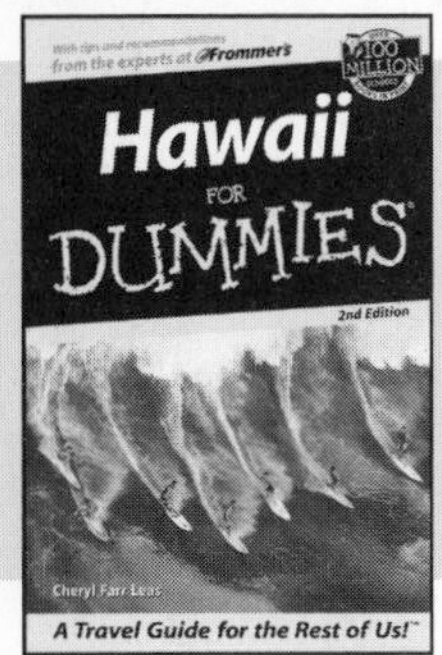

Also available:

America's National Parks For Dummies
Arizona For Dummies
Boston For Dummies
California For Dummies
Chicago For Dummies
Florida For Dummies
Los Angeles & Disneyland For Dummies
New Mexico For Dummies
New Orleans For Dummies
New York City For Dummies
San Francisco For Dummies
Seattle For Dummies
Washington, D.C. For Dummies
RV Vacations For Dummies
Walt Disney World & Orlando For Dummies

EUROPE

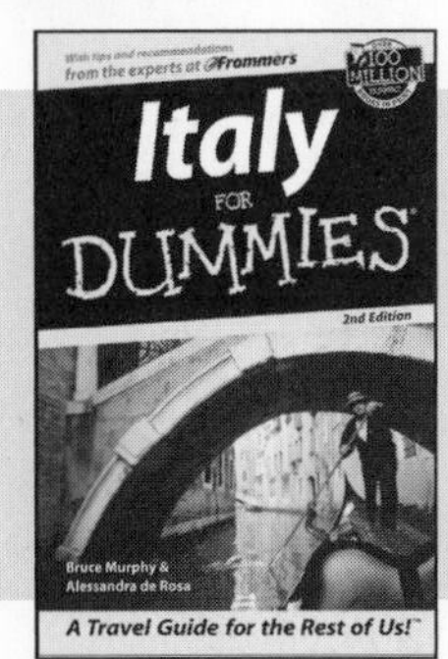

Also available:

England For Dummies
Europe For Dummies
Germany For Dummies
Ireland For Dummies
London For Dummies
Paris For Dummies
Scotland For Dummies
Spain For Dummies

OTHER DESTINATIONS

Also available:

Bahamas For Dummies
Honeymoon Vacations For Dummies
Mexico's Beach Resorts For Dummies
Vancouver & Victoria For Dummies

Available wherever books are sold.
Go to www.dummies.com or call 1-877-762-2974 to order direct.

England For Dummies®

2nd Edition

by Donald Olson

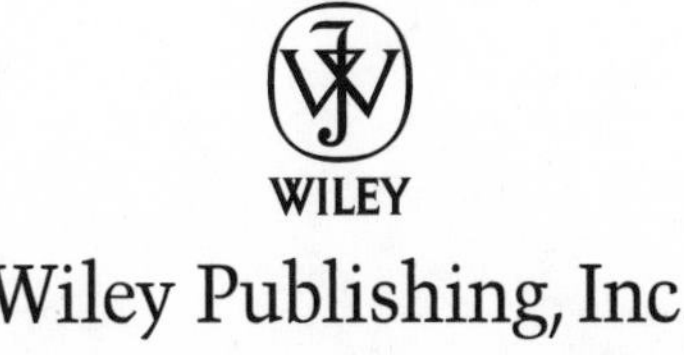

Wiley Publishing, Inc.

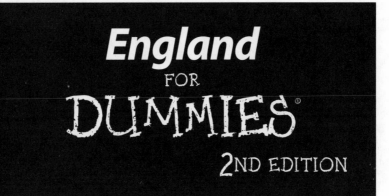

England For Dummies®, 2nd Edition

Published by:
Wiley Publishing, Inc.
111 River Street
Hoboken, NJ 07030
www.wiley.com

Published by Wiley Publishing, Inc., Indianapolis, Indiana

Published simultaneously in Canada

For general information on our other products and services or to obtain technical support, please contact our Customer Care Department within the U.S. at 800-762-2974, outside the U.S. at 317-572-3993, or fax 317-572-4002.

Wiley also publishes its books in a variety of electronic formats. Some content that appears in print may not be available in electronic books.

Library of Congress Control Number: 2003115748

ISBN: 0-7645-4276-1

Manufactured in the United States of America

10 9 8 7 6 5 4 3 2 1

About the Author

Donald Olson is a novelist, playwright, and travel writer. His newest novel, *My Three Husbands,* was published in 2003 under the pen name Swan Adamson. An earlier novel, *The Confessions of Aubrey Beardsley,* was published in the United Kingdom by Bantam Press, and his play, *Beardsley,* was produced in London. Donald Olson's travel stories have appeared in *The New York Times, Travel & Leisure, Sunset, National Geographic* books, and many other publications. He has also written guidebooks to Italy, Berlin, and Oregon; *Germany For Dummies* was published by Wiley in 2003. London is one of Donald's favorite cities, and England is one of his favorite countries. *England For Dummies* won a 2002 Lowell Thomas Travel Writing Award for best guidebook.

Dedication

This book is dedicated to Garen Robinson and Andrew Williams, with thanks for their generous hospitality in London and the Cotswolds, and to Deirdra Morris, a friend on stage and off.

Author's Acknowledgments

I would like to thank Rail Europe for helpful assistance while I was researching this new edition of *England For Dummies.* Thanks also go to Gary Larson and Stephen Brewer.

Publisher's Acknowledgments

We're proud of this book; please send us your comments through our Dummies online registration form located at www.dummies.com/register/. Some of the people who helped bring this book to market include the following:

Aquisitions, Editorial, and Media Development

Editors: Kelly Ewing, Lorraine Festa, Marie Morris

Copy Editor: Chad R. Sievers

Cartographer: Nicholas Trotter

Editorial Manager: Michelle Hacker

Senior Photo Editor: Richard Fox

Front Cover Photo: ©Kindra Clineff Photography

Back Cover Photo: © John Lawrence/ Tony Stone Images

Cartoons: Rich Tennant, www.the5thwave.com

Production

Project Coordinator: Maridee Ennis

Layout and Graphics: Lauren Goddard, Stephanie D. Jumper, Michael Kruzil, Kristin McMullan, Lynsey Osborn, Jacque Schneider

Proofreaders: Kathy Simpson, Charles Spencer, TECHBOOKS Production Services

Indexer: TECHBOOKS Production Services

Publishing and Editorial for Consumer Dummies

Diane Graves Steele, Vice President and Publisher, Consumer Dummies

Joyce Pepple, Acquisitions Director, Consumer Dummies

Kristin A. Cocks, Product Development Director, Consumer Dummies

Michael Spring, Vice President and Publisher, Travel

Brice Gosnell, Publishing Director, Travel

Kelly Regan, Editorial Director, Travel

Publishing for Technology Dummies

Andy Cummings, Vice President and Publisher, Dummies Technology/General User

Composition Services

Gerry Fahey, Vice President of Production Services

Debbie Stailey, Director of Composition Services

Contents at a Glance

Maps at a Glance

Table of Contents

Introduction

So you're going to England. Super! But what parts of England do you want to visit? The country stretches from the English Channel in the south to the Scottish border in the north, and from Wales and the Irish Sea in the west to the North Sea in the east. England isn't a huge country — you can drive its length in a day — but sightseeing possibilities pack the interior.

I have a hunch that London is on your itinerary, but what other cities, regions, or specific attractions do you want to see? The walled city of York? Stratford-upon-Avon, the birthplace of William Shakespeare? Are you interested in nightclubbing at a seaside resort, like Brighton, or strolling through an elegant 18th-century spa town, like Bath? Are there specific landscapes you want to see, such as the Yorkshire moors or the cliffs of Cornwall? What castles, cathedrals, and stately homes do you want to visit? And how about other historic sites? Do you want to visit Roman ruins, spend all day in the Tower of London, or walk around the field where the Normans and the Saxons fought the Battle of Hastings in 1066? England promises so much to see, do, and enjoy that planning a trip here can be a real challenge.

But don't worry, lucky traveler — in the following pages, I help you assemble your perfect itinerary from England's sightseeing riches. With a bit of planning and some useful information under your belt, you'll find that visiting England is easy.

About This Book

This is a selective guidebook to England. By definition, England is the southern part of Great Britain, excluding Wales. Wales and Scotland, although part of the United Kingdom of Great Britain and Northern Ireland, don't appear in this guide.

My goal throughout this book is to give you a good selection of the country's highlights, which means I exclude places that other, more exhaustive guidebooks routinely include. Birmingham, Manchester, and Bristol are important cities, but from the perspective of a first-time visitor to England, they don't have much to offer. So much is really worth seeing in England that you don't need to waste your time with the second-rate, the overrated, or the boring.

Use *England For Dummies,* 2nd Edition, as a reference guide. You can, of course, start at the first page and read all the way through to the end. Or, if you've already been to England and know the basics of international travel, you can easily flip to the specific part you need or hone in on one specific chapter.

Please be advised that travel information is subject to change at any time — this is especially true of prices. I suggest that you write or call ahead for confirmation when making your travel plans. The author, editors, and publisher can't be held responsible for readers' experiences while traveling. Your safety is important, however, so I encourage you to stay alert and be aware of your surroundings. Keep a close eye on cameras, purses, and wallets, all favorite targets of thieves and pickpockets.

Conventions Used in This Book

I recently tried to extract some information from a guidebook and felt that I needed training in hieroglyphics to interpret all the different symbols. I'm happy to report that user-friendly *England For Dummies*, 2nd Edition isn't like that. I keep the use of symbols and abbreviations to a minimum.

I do use the following credit card abbreviations to indicate which cards hotels, restaurants, and attractions accept:

- **AE** (American Express)
- **DC** (Diners Club)
- **MC** (MasterCard)
- **V** (Visa)

All local, U.K. telephone numbers in this guide are preceded by a zero followed by a city or area code. A slash divides the zero and city or area code from the local number. For information about calling U.K. numbers from within or outside of the United Kingdom, see the Appendix.

I divide the hotels into two categories — my personal favorites, and those that don't quite make my preferred list but still get my hearty seal of approval. Don't be shy about considering these runner-up accommodations if you can't get a room at one of my favorites or if your preferences differ from mine — the amenities that the runners-up offer and the services they provide make all these accommodations good choices to consider as you determine where to rest your head at night.

I also include some general pricing information to help you as you decide where to unpack your bags or dine on the local cuisine. In addition to giving you exact prices, I use a system of dollar signs ($) to show a range of costs for hotels or restaurants. The dollar signs for hotels correspond to *rack rates* (nondiscounted, standard rates), and reflect a hotel's low to high rates for a double room. For restaurants, the dollar signs denote the *average* cost of dinner for one person, including appetizer, main course, dessert, one nonalcoholic drink, tax, and tip (usually 10%, unless the bill already includes a service charge). The scale for hotels goes up to five $ signs; four $ signs indicate the priciest restaurants. Check out the following table to decipher the dollar signs:

Cost	***Hotel***	***Restaurant***
$	$150 and under	$25 and under
$$	$151 to $225	$26 to $35
$$$	$226 to $300	$36 to $50
$$$$	$301 to $400	$51 and up
$$$$$	$401 and up	

I always give prices in this guide first in British pounds sterling (£) followed by U.S. dollars ($) rounded off to the nearest dollar. (When prices are under $5, I don't round them off.) Although the exchange rate fluctuates daily, in this guide £1 = $1.60.

Foolish Assumptions

As I'm writing this book, I make some assumptions about you, dear reader, and what your needs may be as a traveler. Here's what I assume about you:

- Wondering whether to take a trip to England and how to plan for it, you may be an inexperienced traveler looking for guidance.
- Without much time to explore England in the past, you may be an experienced traveler who wants expert advice when you finally do get a chance to enjoy that particular locale.
- You're not looking for a book that provides all the information available about England or that lists every hotel, restaurant, or attraction. Instead, you're looking for a book that focuses on the places that will give you the best or most original experience in England.

If you fit any of these criteria, then *England For Dummies,* 2nd Edition, gives you the information you're looking for!

How this Book Is Organized

I break this book down into eight parts. The first two parts deal with trip planning and organization. They provide information, advice, and suggestions that can help you map out a wonderful vacation. I devote the other parts of the book to London and specific regions of the country. You find descriptions of the best towns and cities to visit, with hotel and restaurant choices, and the top attractions in the regions, including castles, stately homes, and gardens.

Part I: Getting Started

This first part introduces England and gives you some excellent reasons for going there. This section is an overview, a way for you to get the big picture. These chapters help you to decide when to visit and what to see, give you sound advice on planning a realistic budget, and provide tips for England-bound travelers with special needs: families, travelers with disabilities, and gay and lesbian travelers.

Part II: Ironing Out the Details

This part helps take some of the wrinkles out of the trip-planning stage. I talk about your options for airlines and airfares, how package tours can save you big bucks, and what kinds of guided tours are available. This part helps you to decide what form of transportation (train, bus, rental car) to use to get around the country, and it explains what kind of accommodations you can expect for your money. I also deal with some pre-trip loose ends, from passports to booking hotel rooms.

Part III: London and Environs

All you need to know about England's greatest city makes up this part. You find detailed information on London's airports and thumbnail descriptions of the city's diverse neighborhoods. Also, I help you get around like a Londoner on the Underground, on the bus, or in a taxi. You find a list of London's best hotels and an appetizing survey of London's best restaurants. I cover the top attractions in and around this exciting city, plus shopping and nightlife. Making side trips from London is easy, and I provide details on several possible destinations: Greenwich, Hampton Court Palace, Windsor Castle, Oxford, Blenheim Palace, and Cambridge.

Part IV: The Southeast

In this part, I outline the highlights of Kent and Sussex, counties close to London that border the English Channel. I also recommend overnight destinations, such as Canterbury, with its ancient cathedral, the swinging seaside resort of Brighton, and the cobblestoned town of Rye. I devote a chapter to Kent's greatest castles, stately homes, and gardens — including Knole, Hever Castle, Sissinghurst Castle Gardens, Dover Castle, and Leeds Castle.

Part V: The West Country

This part explores the West Country counties of Hampshire, Wiltshire, Devon, and Cornwall. Winchester is Hampshire's most historic city. Neighboring Wiltshire is the home of Salisbury, with its towering cathedral, and that great prehistoric monument Stonehenge. In Devon, you find the unique moorland landscape of Dartmoor National Park; Torquay, a laid-back seaside resort; and Plymouth, where the Pilgrims set sail for the New World. Mysterious Cornwall, which includes Land's End in England's southwesternmost corner, is a popular vacation destination with colorful seaside towns, such as Penzance and St. Ives.

Part VI: England's Heartland

I devote this part to central England. Stratford-upon-Avon in Warwickshire is famous as the home of William Shakespeare, and nearby Warwick Castle is one of the country's most popular attractions. Such an amazing collection of 18th-century buildings fills beautiful Bath that UNESCO (United Nations Educational, Scientific, and Cultural Organization) designated the city a World Heritage Site. The Cotswolds region, with its picture-perfect villages built of honey-colored stone, is one of England's premier touring destinations. Cheltenham and Cirencester make good bases for exploring the Cotswolds.

Part VII: Way Up North

Yorkshire and the Lake District are highly scenic areas close to England's northern border with Scotland. York is one of the most beautiful and historic cities in the North; Scarborough is a Yorkshire resort town on the North Sea; and amazing Castle Howard lies between them. North York Moors National Park and the Yorkshire Dales National Park protect Yorkshire's distinctive landscape of heather-covered moors, gentle dales, and rugged coastline. The Lake District, in Cumbria, is a spectacularly beautiful region of mountains and lakes, all within Lake District National Park. You can stay on Lake Windermere, England's largest lake, or in nearby Grasmere or Keswick.

Part VIII: The Part of Tens

The Part of Tens allows me to focus a little more attention on the extra-special places and sights I want you to know about. My "tens" include ten famous writers and how you can visit where they lived and worked, ten great English gardens, and ten magnificent churches and cathedrals.

You also find two other elements in this book. Near the back, I include an A-to-Z appendix — your Quick Concierge — containing plenty of handy information, such as how the telephone system works and what numbers to call in an emergency. You also find a list of toll-free telephone numbers and Web sites for airlines, car-rental agencies, and hotel chains serving England, plus Web sites where you can find additional information on specific cities or areas. Finally, I include a tear-out Cheat Sheet of useful language primers that can help you with unfamiliar English words.

I follow all this information with several worksheets that can help in your planning.

Icons Used in This Book

In this book's margins, you find five different icons, little pictures that clue you in on some important trip-planning matters and a few things that are just for fun.

This icon points out my report on the most newsworthy scandals — I mean stories — about people and places. I throw in these tidbits about English personalities and places just for the fun of it.

Bargain Alert is my favorite icon, and I suspect it may be yours, too. I'm not cheap, but I love to save money. You see this icon every time I tell you about something that can save you some dough.

I'm not an alarmist, so you won't find too many Heads Up icons. If you see one, I want you to be aware of something, like the double-tipping scam that you may encounter in a restaurant.

Traveling with children? Keep your eyes peeled for the Kid Friendly icon. If this icon is next to a hotel name, the hotel welcomes families with children. If I place it in front of a restaurant name, the icon means the kids may actually enjoy the food or atmosphere, and other diners or staff won't be upset by the presence of kids. If I place it before an attraction, the icon indicates that kids will (probably) enjoy it.

The Tip icon highlights useful bits of information that can save you time or enhance your travel experience. A Tip alerts you to something (such as a special guided tour) that you may not otherwise consider or even know about.

Where to Go from Here

To England, of course. How you want to use this guide is up to you. You can start from the beginning and read straight through, or you can start anywhere in between and extract information as you want or need it. Throughout the book, I hope you think of me as your guide or companion on this journey to England. However you choose to use the book, I want you to have a great time.

Part I

Getting Started

"This afternoon I want everyone to go online and find all you can about Native American culture, history of the old West, and discount air fares to England for the two weeks I'll be on vacation."

In this part . . .

Where to begin? If you've never been to England, you need advice and information to start planning your trip. This part helps to get you going. Chapter 1 is a brief overview that fills you in on the best England has to offer, from castles to cuisine. I also give you a brief outline of the main events in English history, right up to the latest royal scandals.

Chapter 2 offers more specific information to help you plan when and where you want to go. I include a calendar of events and a description of the seasons.

In Chapter 3, I suggest two possible itineraries: one for visitors who have one week in England, the second for visitors with two weeks. I also include itineraries for families, gardening enthusiasts, and history buffs. Even if you don't use them, the itineraries may give you some ideas for your own trip and how to budget your time.

In Chapter 4, I get into the nitty-gritty of money. Having an approximate idea of what things cost is essential for any first-time traveler who's trying to come up with a workable budget.

And finally, in Chapter 5, I offer some specific information and tips for visitors with special needs or interests: You can find advice for families (traveling with children), senior travelers, travelers with disabilities, single travelers, and gay and lesbian travelers.

Chapter 1

Discovering the Best of England

In This Chapter

- Experiencing the great landmarks of modern and ancient England
- Enjoying glorious gardens and the English countryside
- Exploring England's retail therapy outlets
- Eating and drinking, English-style
- Brushing up on English history

England claims a special place in the hearts and minds of many people. English speakers (and readers) in the United States, Canada, Australia, and New Zealand often feel a kinship with the land of their mother tongue. England shares many cultural ties and hundreds of place names with those countries. So, for some people, a trip to England is like going home. The country's great age, and the sheer weight of its history, can induce a sense of awe and wonder. England is a land of ancient cities, royal palaces, massive cathedrals, and legendary sites. The layers of its long history are visible everywhere you look. And travelers can enjoy the country in so many different ways. Mighty castles, stately homes, glorious gardens, and tiny picturesque villages enhance the countryside's natural beauty. The cooking is unique, and so is the English pub.

This chapter introduces you to some of the things that make traveling in England so much fun and so endlessly fascinating. I present a broad overview so that you can begin to identify those aspects of England that interest you as you start to plan your trip. Consider this chapter a rundown of the best England has to offer.

Checking Out the Scene in Legendary London

London (Part III) is one of the world's great cities, and I give it plenty of coverage in this guidebook because almost every visitor to England heads here first. London is exciting, historic, cultured, cutting-edge, and romantic. London is where you can visit truly world-class museums. **The British Museum,** the **National Gallery,** the **Tate Modern,** the **Tate Britain,** the **Victoria & Albert Museum,** and the **Natural History Museum** — to name the best known — display a mind-boggling array of artwork and unique treasures. The **Tower of London, Westminster Abbey,** and **Buckingham Palace** are just three of the famous historic places you can visit. **Hyde Park, Kensington Gardens, Green Park,** and **St. James's Park** form a vast network of green space shared by Londoners and visitors to the capital of the United Kingdom. London's dining scene is phenomenal, and the entertainment choices — theater, music, dance, opera, film — are almost limitless. The shopping opportunities are endless, too.

Exploring England's Fascinating Cities, Towns, and Villages

England isn't that large, so you can base yourself in London and take day trips to many historic cities and towns in other parts of the country. Or you can make them part of an itinerary that showcases the country's best cities. One of the most elegant is the former spa town of **Bath** (Chapter 20), with its amazing Georgian *crescents* (row houses built in a long curving line) and 18th-century architecture. Two other destinations are **Oxford** and **Cambridge** (Chapter 13), famous university towns where centuries-old colleges cluster around quadrangles. For some laid-back fun beside the sea, you can visit **Brighton** (Chapter 14) on the south coast or head up north to **Scarborough** (Chapter 21) on the North Sea in Yorkshire. **Cornwall** (Chapter 18) has several picturesque towns, many of them former fishing villages with colorful histories of smuggling and pirates: **Penzance** is the largest, but you also find **St. Ives,** an artist's colony with a beautiful beach, **Mousehole,** and **Fowey. Rye** (Chapter 14), in Sussex, is one of the best-preserved and most attractive towns in England, full of Elizabethan homes and buildings. **York** (Chapter 21), two hours north of London by train, is still surrounded by its medieval walls, has narrow, medieval lanes, and is home to York Minster, one of the largest churches in the world. The scenic **Cotswolds** (Chapter 20) region is dotted with charming villages — **Broadway, Bourton-on-the-Water, Chipping Campden,** and **Cirencester** — that all grew rich on wool during the Middle Ages. The **Lake District** (Chapter 22), too, is an area where you find picturesque villages, such as **Grasmere,** and lakeside towns, such as **Keswick,** in stunning countryside.

Marveling at England's Castles, Palaces, and Stately Homes

Step into one of England's castles, palaces, or stately homes, and all you can do is marvel at the way people used to live. *Some* people, I should say, because these enormous estates belonged to an elite minority with royal connections or private fortunes. Usually set amidst spectacular grounds, these places are treasure troves of history and art, packed with rare paintings and beautiful furniture.

In London, you can visit **Buckingham Palace,** the queen's official residence, and **Kensington Palace,** once the home of Princess Diana (both, Chapter 12). Henry VIII's **Hampton Court Palace** is a short train ride from London, as is 900-year-old **Windsor Castle,** another official residence of Queen Elizabeth II (both, Chapter 13).

Knole, which has 365 rooms (some with their original 17th-century furnishings) and moated **Hever Castle,** birthplace of Anne Boleyn, are just two of the many castles and stately homes you can visit in Kent (both, Chapter 15).

One of the most dramatically sited castles in England is **St. Michael's Mount** (Chapter 18), on its own rocky island in Mount's Bay, Penzance. **Castle Drogo** (Chapter 17), in Dartmoor National Park, is the last private castle to be built in England (it was completed in 1930). **Blenheim Palace** (Chapter 13), near Oxford, was the palatial childhood home of Winston Churchill, who later moved to **Chartwell** (Chapter 15), a house in Kent that is filled with Churchill memorabilia.

Farther north, just a few miles from Stratford-upon-Avon, is mighty **Warwick Castle** (Chapter 19), surrounded by thick stone walls and towers. The wax artisans at Madame Tussaud's have "peopled" the castle with its former owners and some of their famous guests. **Castle Howard** (Chapter 21), in Yorkshire, is one of the most beautiful stately homes in England, an enormous domed wonder set amidst landscaped grounds with classically inspired buildings.

History's building blocks

When identifying the period in which a building was constructed (or reconstructed), look for details of architecture and decoration. In a country like England, where the age of buildings can span a thousand-year period (a few Anglo-Saxon churches are even older than that), many different styles evolved. The architectural periods are often named for the monarch or royal family reigning at the time.

(continued)

(continued)

You can enhance your enjoyment of England's abundance of historic buildings if you know a few key features of the different styles. The following is a brief primer in English architectural history from Norman to Victorian times.

Norman (1066–1189): Round arches, barrel vaults, and highly decorated archways characterize this period's *Romanesque* style.

Early English Gothic (1189–1272): The squat, bulky buildings of the Norman period gave way to the taller, lighter buildings constructed in this style.

Decorated Gothic (1272–1377): Buildings in this style have large windows, *tracery* (ornamental work with branching lines), and heavily decorated gables and arches.

Perpendicular Gothic (1377–1483): Large *buttresses* (exterior side supports) allowed churches to have larger windows than ever before. Tracery was more elaborate than in previous Gothic buildings, the four-centered arch appeared, and *fan vaulting* (a decorative form of vaulting in which the structural ribs spread upward and outward along the ceiling like the rays of a fan) was perfected.

Tudor (1485–1553): During this period, buildings evolved from Gothic to *Renaissance* styles. Large houses and palaces were built with a new material — brick. England has many *half-timbered* Tudor and Elizabethan domestic and commercial buildings. This method of construction used brick and plaster between visible wooden timbers.

Elizabethan (1553–1603): The Renaissance brought a revival of *classical* features, such as columns, *cornices* (prominent rooflines with brackets and other details), and *pediments* (a decorative triangular feature over doorways and windows). The many large houses and palaces of this period were built in an E or H shape and contained long galleries, grand staircases, and carved chimneys.

Jacobean (1603–1625): In England, Inigo Jones used the symmetrical, classically inspired *Palladian* style that arrived from Italy. Buildings in this style incorporate elements from ancient Greek and Roman.

Stuart (1625–1688): Elegant classical features, such as columns, cornices, and pediments, are typical of this period, in which Sir Christopher Wren was the preeminent architect.

Queen Anne (1689–1714): Buildings from the English *baroque* period mix heavy ornamentation with classical simplicity.

Georgian and Regency (1714–1830): During these periods, elegant terraced houses were built; many examples survive in Brighton and Bath. Form and proportion were important elements; interior decoration inspired by Chinese motifs became fashionable.

Victorian (1830–1901): A whole range of antique styles emerged — everything from Gothic and Greek Revival to pseudo-Egyptian and Elizabethan. Hundreds of English churches were renovated during the Victorian era.

Viewing England's Great Cathedrals and Churches

England's mighty cathedrals, still in use 800 years and more after they were built, dominate the heart of England's cities. Their stupendous size never fails to impress, and some of their architectural details are stunning. I include several of my favorite cathedrals and churches in this guide.

English monarchs have been crowned in London's **Westminster Abbey** (Chapter 12) since the time of William the Conqueror. **St. Paul's Cathedral** (Chapter 12) is the masterpiece of Sir Christopher Wren, who rebuilt London after the Great Fire of 1666. Chaucer's pilgrims in *The Canterbury Tales* were headed toward **Canterbury Cathedral** (Chapter 14), and tourists still flock there in droves. Massive **York Minster** (Chapter 21), the largest Gothic building in northern Europe, contains more medieval stained glass than any other cathedral in England. The west front of **Exeter Cathedral** (Chapter 17) is remarkable for its rows of sculptured saints and kings, the largest surviving array of 14th-century sculpture in England.

A brief history of England

England's history is an inexhaustible subject. Huge tomes have been written on individual monarchs, colorful personalities, architectural styles, and historical epochs. But I'm going to be as brief as a bikini and give you a history of England that covers only the bare essentials.

Beginning about 5,000 years ago, a **Neolithic civilization** was cutting and hauling mega-ton slabs of stone over dozens of miles and erecting them in elaborate geometric configurations. Stonehenge is an example of their work. When the **Romans** conquered England in A.D. 43, they suppressed or subdued the local **Celtic tribes.** The legendary Queen Boudicca (or Boadicea) was a Celtic warrior queen who fought back the invading Romans. You can see a statue of her on Westminster Bridge in London. The Romans brought their building and engineering skills to England, and you can see the remains of Roman walls, roads, forts, temples, villas, and baths throughout the country.

With the Roman Empire's breakup in A.D. 410, Jutes, Angles, and Saxons from northern Europe invaded England and formed small kingdoms. For the next 600 years or so, the **Anglo-Saxon kingdoms** fought off Viking raiders. In the north, *Eboracum,* a Roman settlement, became Jorvik, a Viking city, and eventually York.

(continued)

(continued)

The next major transitional period in England started in 1066, when William of Normandy fought and killed Harold, the Anglo-Saxon king of England, at the **Battle of Hastings.** William and his French nobles took over the land and built castles (Windsor Castle and the Tower of London are two of them) and cathedrals that still stand today. Every monarch up to the present day claims descent from **William the Conqueror.**

King John, a Plantagenet, signed the ***Magna Carta*** in 1215, granting more rights to the nobles. What about the common man and woman? As serfs and vassals in a closed, hierarchical, class-ridden society, their lot wasn't an easy one. **Geoffrey Chaucer** (1342–1400) was the first writer to give us some recognizable portraits of folks who lived during the medieval period, in *The Canterbury Tales.*

At home and abroad, war and bloodshed tore England apart for more than 300 years. The **Hundred Years' War** between France and England began in 1337. There was also the **War of the Roses,** fought between the Houses of York and Lancaster.

Henry VIII, the Tudor king famous for taking six wives, brought about the next great shift in what had been Catholic England. In 1534, he dissolved all the monasteries and became head of the Church of England. His daughter, **Elizabeth I,** ruled during a period of relative peace, power, and prosperity. The Elizabethan period was England's Golden Age, the time when Shakespeare's plays were being performed at the Globe Theatre in London.

In 1603, James VI of Scotland became **King James I** of England, uniting the crowns of England and Scotland. But conflicts between monarchs and nobles were endless. **Charles I,** seeking absolute power, dissolved Parliament in 1629. He was beheaded in 1649 after **Oliver Cromwell** led a bitter civil war between Royalists and Parliamentarians. Cromwell's armies destroyed churches and royalist strongholds throughout the country. Cromwell was elevated to Lord Protectorate of the Realm, but by 1660 a new king, **Charles II,** was on the throne. This time, however, his powers were limited. Five years later, London, which had been growing steadily, was devastated by two back-to-back catastrophes, the **Great Plague of 1665** and the **Great Fire of 1666.**

England reached its zenith of power and prestige during the reign of **Victoria** (1837–1901), who ruled over an empire so vast that "the sun never set" on it. The **Industrial Revolution** spawned another major change during this period, moving England away from its agrarian past and into a mechanized future. **Charles Dickens** and other social reformers exposed the wretched working conditions in Victorian England, where children as young as 6 were forced to labor in mines and factories, and families lived in wretched slums. The late Victorian age was the time of **Sherlock Holmes,** a fictional detective created by Arthur Conan Doyle, and **Jack the Ripper,** a real-life serial killer who terrorized London's West End.

England suffered terrible losses during **World War I** (1914–1918), but emerged victorious. During **World War II,** from the fall of France in 1940 until the United States entered the war in 1941, England stood alone against Hitler. **Winston Churchill** was the country's prime minister during the war years. With strictly rationed food, mandatory blackouts, and terrible bombing raids that destroyed cities and killed tens of thousands of civilians, life in wartime England had a profound effect on its citizens. Shortages continued for many years afterward. Another major societal shift occurred in 1945 when the **Labour Party** began to dismantle the empire and introduced the welfare state. Under the National Health System, every citizen in the United Kingdom can receive free health care (how good the care is is another story). It wasn't until **Margaret Thatcher** and the **Tory Party** came into power during the 1980s that England began privatizing formerly state-run agencies, such as the railroad (with what some would say are disastrous results).

Queen Elizabeth II ascended the throne in 1952. The fairy-tale wedding of her son Prince Charles to Lady Diana Spencer was the last high point for the **House of Windsor.** Charles and Diana's subsequent divorce seemed to unleash a floodgate of royal scandals, with the result that the popularity of the British monarchy is at an all-time low. In 2002, the queen celebrated her 50th anniversary on the throne. A poll in 2001 revealed that Cherie Blair, the super-charged lawyer wife of Prime Minister **Tony Blair,** was perceived to be the most powerful woman in England. This marked the first time that the queen lost the power sweepstakes to a "commoner." Queen Elizabeth has also lost her standing as the richest woman in England: J. K. Rowling, the author of the Harry Potter books, has usurped that title.

In 2001, Blair was elected to a second term as prime minister. *New Labour,* with its centrist approach, was in control of the government, but the turnout for the elections was the lowest in history. The big question now is whether the country will eventually change its pounds and pence currency to euros. If that happens and England moves toward full partnership with the European Union, it will represent another major shift in English society, which has never really viewed itself as European.

Looking at England's Landmarks of History

England markets its history big time, and with good reason: No soap opera can beat the stories associated with its most famous historic sites. In southern England, at a place called **Battle** (Chapter 14), you can walk around the battlefield where in 1066 William of Normandy fought Harold, the Saxon king of England. The battle changed the course of English history. When you visit the **Tower of London** (Chapter 12), you can walk on a piece of ground where the great dramas and terrors of a turbulent kingdom were played out, where Elizabeth I was held captive while still a princess, and where Sir Thomas More and Anne Boleyn were beheaded. The Tower and the site of the Battle of Hastings represent almost *1,000 years* of history. The great historical landmarks of England stir the imagination because they've witnessed so much — from glorious triumphs to bloody tragedies.

Visiting the Mysteries of the Past

England's "recent" history stretches back some 2,000 years, to a time when Latin-speaking Roman soldiers built forts, roads, and temples from Kent to Northumberland. In this guidebook, I point out some of the most interesting Roman sites and museums in England. But England was inhabited for thousands of years before the Romans arrived. Long-vanished peoples erected mysterious monuments that still fill the country. The most famous is **Stonehenge** (Chapter 16), a massive stone circle on the plains of Wiltshire. Was it really an advanced astronomical calculator, as some have claimed? In **Cornwall** (Chapter 18), you can visit other tantalizing prehistoric sites, including **Chysauster,** the remains of an Iron Age village. In northern England, up in the Lake District, **Castlerigg Stone Circle** (Chapter 22), near Keswick, is another enigmatic reminder of early human presence in England; the circle is thought to be about the same age as Stonehenge, that is, approximately 5,000 years old.

Strolling through England's Great Gardens

In England, gardening has been raised to an art form. Chalk it up to a temperate climate that can support (especially in the southeast and southwest) all kinds of rare and exotic plant species, including azaleas and rhododendrons. I include several great English gardens in this book because gardens are a growing (pardon the pun) interest for visitors from around the globe. The gardens usually surround a stately home or castle that you can also visit.

Perhaps the most famous garden in England is at **Sissinghurst Castle** (Chapter 15) in Kent. The plantings there, and at equally beautiful **Hidcote Manor** (Chapter 20) in Gloucestershire, form living "rooms" of shape, color, scent, and texture. **Stourhead** (Chapter 16), in Wiltshire, was laid out in 1741 and is one of the oldest landscape gardens in England. In **Cornwall** (Chapter 18), **Cotehele** and **Lanhydrock** are estates known for their superb riverside gardens. Cornwall is also the site of England's newest garden, a massive world-environment learning center called the **Eden Project.** Immaculately landscaped grounds, where every shrub and blade of grass is clipped to perfection, are at **Hever Castle** (Chapter 15) in Kent, **Warwick Castle** (Chapter 19) near Stratford-upon-Avon, and **Castle Howard** (Chapter 21) up north in Yorkshire. Closer to London, you find historic gardens at **Hampton Court Palace** and the Royal Botanic Gardens at **Kew** (both, Chapter 13).

Enjoying England's Natural Beauty

England has been settled for thousands of years, and truly wild places are rare in this densely populated country where 46,382,000 people inhabit 50,357 square miles of land. Yet travelers always comment on the countryside's beauty, a domesticated blend of farms, enclosed fields, and small villages that seem to snooze under a blanket of history. The way humans have interacted with the environment for thousands of years — leaving behind grand monuments, such as Stonehenge, humble country churches, thatched cottages, and hedgerows — contributes to the enduring charm of the English countryside. Many visitors respond to the sense of human continuity. Touring the **Cotswolds** (Chapter 20), for example, you see picturesque villages of honey-colored stone that date back to the Middle Ages interspersed with lightly forested valleys and high open fields where sheep graze as they've done for a thousand years. If you explore **Cornwall** (Chapter 18), you encounter rocky coastal headlands, windswept *moors* (areas of wild, treeless countryside where only heather and scrubby shrubs and ferns grow), and Celtic crosses left by Irish missionaries 14 centuries ago.

Luckily, the country's wildest and most unique landscapes are protected as national parks. Unlike national parks in the United States, the national parks in England are both publicly and privately owned and include working farms and villages. Limiting commercial development and opening the countryside to walkers, the parks preserve the regions' essential character. Places like **Dartmoor National Park** in Devon (Chapter 17), **North York Moors** and **Yorkshire Dales** national parks in Yorkshire (Chapter 21), and **Lake District National Park** in semi-remote Cumbria (Chapter 22), are all great places for you to experience the beautiful landscapes of England.

Shopping in London and Beyond

London (Chapter 12) is one of the world's greatest shopping cities, and my credit cards aren't doing all the talking. From mighty Harrods to the super-chic boutiques of Bond Street, from the 200-year-old shops on Jermyn Street to the wonderland of bookstores on Charing Cross Road, London offers a seemingly endless array of goods and goodies. Custom-made shirts, hand-tooled leather shoes, high-quality woolens — in London, you can still find such things. You can hunt for an old engraving, paw through bric-a-brac at an outdoor market stall, or wander through the London silver vaults in your quest for a Georgian soup ladle.

London's abundance of shopping opportunities simply can't be matched elsewhere in the country. Outside the capital, however, small shops and one-of-a-kind places draw the shopper's eye. The **Cotswolds** (Chapter 20) has more antique stores than anywhere else in England. **Exeter** (Chapter 17) is a good place to look for silver. Antiquarian bookstores abound in **Cambridge** and **Oxford** (both, Chapter 13). Many areas of the country feature locally made handicrafts. Look for pottery in **Devon** (Chapter 17), **Cornwall** (Chapter 18), and the **Lake District** (Chapter 22). You may also stumble across some treasure at a rural *car-boot* sale or *jumble* sale. (At these informal sales in school or church buildings or in parking lots, you can buy secondhand odds-and-ends.) And, of course, every major historic attraction in England — from Sissinghurst Castle Garden in Kent to Castle Howard in Yorkshire — has a gift shop.

Dining English Style from Traditional to Modern

Once upon a time, you could always count on getting lousy meals in England. English "home cooking" — all too often dull, insular, and uninspired — was the joke of Europe. That began to change in the 1980s, with the influx of new cooking trends that favored foods from France and Italy. Since then, London has become a major food capital, and the rest of the country has raised its food consciousness considerably. London is certainly the easiest place to find restaurants serving inventive Modern British cuisine, but you also encounter the new cooking style in smaller towns and even in some pubs. And don't forget that spicy Indian cooking is England's second "national" cuisine. You find thousands of Indian and other ethnic restaurants throughout the country.

But traditionalists have nothing to worry about. All those wonderful Old English faves — eggs, kippers, beans, and fried tomatoes for breakfast; bubble and squeak; roast beef and Yorkshire pudding; meat pies; fish and chips; cottage pie; sticky toffee pudding; and trifle — are still around. (See the Cheat Sheet at the front of this book for a glossary of English food terms.) When traditional, nonfancy English dishes are done well, they're super-satisfying and delicious. If you travel around the country, look for local and regional specialties, such as sausage, lamb, cheese, and desserts.

While you're in England, you can also look forward to the world of afternoon tea. In the West Country, you get a cream tea, which consists of tea, homemade scones, strawberry jam, and thick, rich, clotted cream from Devon or Cornwall. (The cream is put on your scones, not in your tea, and then topped with the jam.) Elsewhere, whipped cream may be substituted for the clotted cream. Teas can be as simple or fancy as you want.

Quenching Your Thirst

The pub (short for *public house*) is an English institution. England is awash with historic pubs where you can sit all evening with a pint of ale, bitter, stout, or cider and soak up the local color. No matter how tiny the village or town, you always find at least one pub. In London and larger towns, you can do a *pub crawl,* walking (upright) from pub to pub and sampling the incredibly diverse brews on tap. Although you can get a hard drink at both bars and pubs, when you're in a pub, you're better off confining yourself to beer.

Parliament has instituted the strict hours that most pubs adhere to: Monday through Saturday from 11 a.m. to 11 p.m., and Sunday from noon to 10:30 p.m. Americans, take note: No service charge is asked for or expected in a pub, and you *never* tip the bartender; the best you can do is offer to buy him or her a drink — an acceptable practice in England. Ten minutes before closing, a bell rings, signaling that the time has come to order your last round.

A beer primer: Are you bitter or stout?

Most of the pubs in London and throughout the United Kingdom are "tied" to a particular brewery and sell only that brewery's beers (you see the name of the brewery on the sign outside). Independent pubs can sell more brands than a tied pub. Either way, you still have to choose from what may seem like a bewildering variety. The colorful names of individual brews don't provide much help — you can only wonder what Pigswill, Dogs Bollocks, Hobgoblin, Old Thumper, Pommies Revenge, or Boondoggle taste like. Depending on all sorts of factors — the water, the hops, the fermentation technique, and so on — the brewery crafts the taste of any beer, whether on draught or in a bottle. You can get a few U.S. and international brands, but imports are more expensive than the homegrown products.

When ordering beer in a pub, specify the type, the brand, and the amount (pint or half-pint) you want. Asking the bartender to recommend something based on your taste preferences is perfectly okay. Just remember that most English beer is served at *room temperature.* The following brief descriptions of beer will come in handy in a pub:

- **Bitter** is what most locals drink. It's a clear, yellowish, traditional beer with a strong flavor of hops. *Real ale* is a bitter that's still fermenting ("alive") when it arrives from the brewery; it's pumped and served immediately.
- **Ale** isn't as strong as bitter and has a slightly sweeter taste. You can order *light* or *pale ale* in a bottle; *export ale* is a stronger variety.
- **Lager,** when chilled, is probably the closest you can come to an American-style beer. Lager is available in bottles or on draught.
- **Shandy** is equal parts bitter and lemonade (sometimes limeade or ginger beer); it's for those who like a sweet beverage that's only partially beery.
- **Stout** is a dark, rich, creamy version of ale. Guinness is the most popular brand. A *black and tan* is half lager and half stout.

Chapter 2

Deciding When and Where to Go

In This Chapter

- Exploring England's main points of interest
- Getting a grip on the seasons: Tourism and the weather
- Checking out the country's calendar of events

So, when and where do you want to go in England? In a country full of options, I help you narrow your focus. This chapter tells you the highlights of each region and gives you the rundown on the seasons so that you can determine the best destinations and time of year for your visit.

Everywhere You Want to Be: What This Book Covers and Why

England For Dummies, 2nd Edition, is a selective book, geared to first-time travelers who want to know more about England's leading sights. I don't cover every county and region, but only the country's essential highlights — including the best of the cities, castles, cathedrals, gardens, and countryside. (Wales and Scotland, although part of the United Kingdom, aren't included in this book.) To help figure out which regions to visit during your trip, check out the following thumbnail sketches. For locations, see "The Regions in Brief" map in this chapter.

Looking at London: From Buckingham Palace to the British Museum

The Romans founded **London,** the capital of the United Kingdom, 2,000 years ago. London is the largest, fastest, and most important city in England. Over the centuries, this seat of power has accrued an unrivaled collection of treasures, from historic cathedrals and royal palaces to matchless museums and parks. London's top sights include the **British Museum, Buckingham Palace,** the **Tower of London, Westminster Abbey,** the **Houses of Parliament, St. Paul's Cathedral,** the **National Gallery,** the **National Portrait Gallery,** the **Tate Modern,** the **Victoria and Albert Museum,** the **Natural History Museum, Kensington Palace,** and **Kensington Gardens.**

London could easily consume all your time, but you can make many easy day trips from the city. In less than an hour, you can reach **Hampton Court Palace, Windsor Palace, Kew Gardens, Greenwich** (site of the Prime Meridian, the line from which the world measures longitude), and the ancient college towns of **Cambridge** and **Oxford.** Close to Oxford is another excellent destination, **Blenheim Palace,** one of the greatest country estates in England.

London offers all the delights of a great international city. It has more than its share of revered monuments and historic sites, but it's not a city that dozes in the past. London is both traditional and trendsetting. It's a crowded, fast-paced, multiethnic metropolis. If you love art, culture, and people watching, you'll probably love London.

Exploring Southeast England: Canterbury, castles, and historic towns

East and **Southeast England** includes the counties of Kent and Sussex, with their abundance of fascinating castles, famous gardens, and picturesque towns. **Canterbury,** in Kent, is one of the most beautiful and historic cathedral towns in England. Tourists (formerly called pilgrims) have been visiting Canterbury's magnificent cathedral since before Chaucer wrote *The Canterbury Tales,* more than 600 years ago. Many people want to visit the Kentish coastal town of **Dover** to see the famous white cliffs. To be honest with you, I wouldn't make Dover a special destination. **Dover Castle,** with its 1,000 years of history (the castle was in use right through World War II), is well worth visiting, but the town of Dover contains little else.

Rye, on the other hand, is a Sussex town whose charms are irresistible. More historic buildings (the earliest dates to 1250) line the cobblestone streets and time-warped lanes than any other town in England. With its fine restaurants and cozy inns, Rye makes a good base for further exploration of this area along the Channel coast. If the date 1066 means anything to you, you may want to visit nearby **Battle,** where William the Conqueror defeated King Harold at the Battle of Hastings and thus gained control of England. Walk around the famous battlefield and explore the ruins of the abbey William erected to commemorate his victory. You can't get much closer to English history than that!

The Regions in Brief

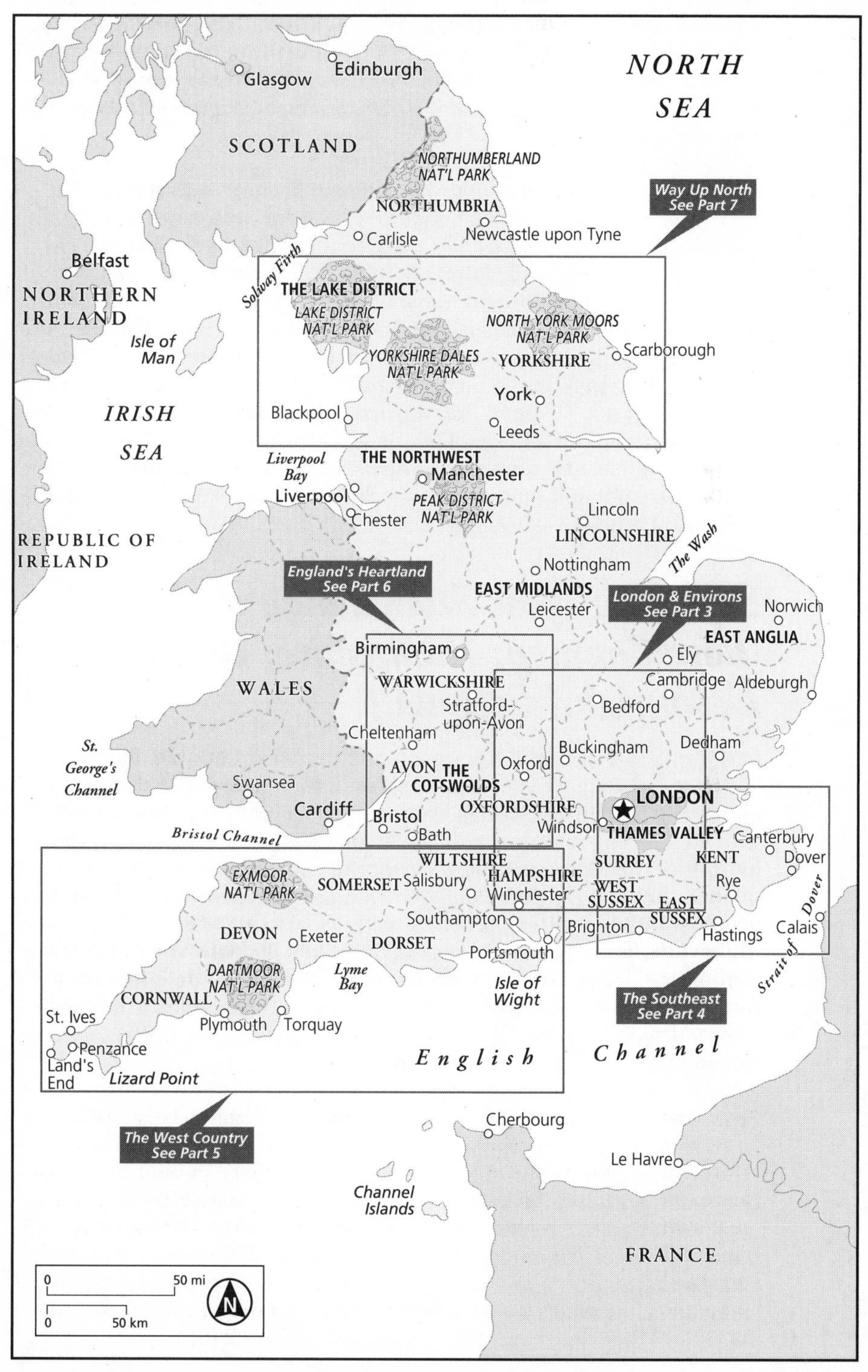

Brighton is a popular resort town on the south coast, within commuting distance to London (the town makes for an easy day trip). Brighton has been a seaside destination since the early 19th century, when the Prince Regent built the remarkable **Royal Pavilion,** now the town's major tourist attraction. With its long beach, amusement pier, promenades, and late-night club scene, Brighton remains a favorite weekend getaway spot.

In addition to the preceding towns, I devote a chapter to the castles, stately homes, and magnificent gardens of **Kent,** which are all special places that you can visit as day trips from London or as part of a car tour. The American Astor family purchased, restored, and lived in **Hever Castle,** the childhood home of Anne Boleyn, second wife of Henry VIII. **Knole,** with 365 rooms and many of its original Elizabethan furnishings, is the largest and one of the most splendid country homes in England. Knole was the birthplace of Vita Sackville-West, who later created, with her husband Harold Nicholson, the world-famous gardens at **Sissinghurst,** now a place of pilgrimage for garden lovers from around the world. Kings and queens who spent time at **Leeds Castle,** sitting in a lake-size moat and built more than 900 years ago, added to the castle over the centuries.

Sightseeing at Stonehenge and in the West Country: Hampshire, Wiltshire, Devon, and Cornwall

Part V of this book, which is devoted to the **West Country,** fills you in on the feast of sightseeing possibilities in Hampshire, Wiltshire, Devon, and Cornwall. **Winchester,** in Hampshire, is a graceful, genteel town with an amazing history (in Anglo-Saxon days, Winchester was more important than London) and a wonderful cathedral. Jane Austen, who penned the "Eng Lit" hits *Pride and Prejudice* and *Sense and Sensibility,* is buried in Winchester Cathedral; you can also visit her modest home in nearby **Chawton.** Bare, brooding Salisbury Plain in Wiltshire, west of Hampshire, is the setting for **Stonehenge,** the stone circle that is one of the world's most famous ancient monuments. A few miles from this Neolithic wonder is **Salisbury.** The soaring spires of its Gothic cathedral dominate this busy country town.

Thrusting out into the Atlantic, Devon and Cornwall occupy the southwesternmost corner of England. The cathedral town of **Exeter** is a good starting place for a tour of these two counties surrounded by the sea. **Dartmoor National Park** lies a few miles west of Exeter. If you want to explore this open, treeless moorland with its gray stone fences and tunnel-like lanes winding beneath tall hedgerows, the area around **Chagford** is a good place to stay. Devon's southern coastline boasts sandy beaches and comfortable, old-fashioned resort towns, such as

Torquay, clustered in a mild-weather zone called the English Riviera. Many people want to visit **Plymouth** because, in 1620, the Pilgrims set sail from Plymouth for the New World, but after you've seen the Mayflower Steps (the departure point for the Pilgrims), not much else will detain you.

Thousands of years ago, Cornwall was a Celtic land known for its tin mines. Ancient mysteries still cling to Cornwall's rocky coastline in the form of stone circles. You find some of these *cromlechs,* as they're called, in the vicinity of **St. Ives,** a beautiful Cornish seaside town that became famous as an artists' colony. South of St. Ives, overlooking the island-castle of **St. Michael's Mount** on Mount's Bay, is the bustling market town of **Penzance.** A five-hour train ride from London, Penzance is the last station before windy **Land's End,** where you can walk along the headlands that face the Atlantic. The Land's End Peninsula, with its tiny, stone-built fishing villages, such as **Mousehole** (pronounced *Muz-zle*) and the lovely town of **Fowey** (pronounced *Foy*) farther along the coastline to the east, is best explored by car.

Discovering England's heartland: Stratford-upon-Avon, the Cotswolds, and Bath

William Shakespeare, whose plays still enchant, grip, amuse, and move audiences 400 years after his death, was born in **Stratford-upon-Avon,** a small Warwickshire village. This highly commercialized town located in central England, only 1½ hours northwest of London by train, is one of England's top tourist destinations. If you're a Shakespeare fan, you can easily spend a day visiting the various shrines. Consider staying overnight if you want to see a play performed by the Royal Shakespeare Company. From Stratford, local train service runs to Warwick, whose top attraction is mighty **Warwick Castle.** Behind its thick stone ramparts, this imposing hilltop fortress features beautiful Victorian-era living rooms (with wax figures by the artisans at Madame Tussaud's), a creepy dungeon, and beautifully landscaped grounds.

The **Cotswolds** is a mostly rural area of bare rolling hills, river valleys, and woodlands south of Stratford-upon-Avon and west of Oxford. The region is known for its small, beautiful villages built of honey-colored stone during the prosperous years of the medieval wool trade. Although they have inevitably lost some of their soul to the flourishing tourist trade that now supports them, Cotswold villages, such as **Broadway, Chipping Campden, Bourton-on-the-Water,** and **Cirencester,** are still worth a visit. Tour the villages by car because public transportation to the small villages is spotty. In these villages, you can shop for hours (the Cotswolds has more antiques shops than anywhere else in England) and then relax in an old-fashioned tea shop for an afternoon cream tea.

Hidcote Manor, one of the greatest of English gardens, is a must for flower lovers visiting this region. You may want to make **Cheltenham,** a lively county town laid out as a spa in the early 19th century, your headquarters in the Cotswolds. You also find beautiful **Bath,** the queen of spa towns and a picture of Regency elegance. Located at the southern edge of the Cotswolds, Bath, with its superb Georgian terraces and renowned **Roman Baths Museum,** deserves at least a full day.

Heading north: Yorkshire and the Lake District

Northern England has a different character (and a different accent) from softer, greener southern England. The North is where you find the walled city of **York,** with its Viking heritage, medieval buildings, and glorious cathedral — the largest Gothic cathedral in Europe. Crammed with museums, restaurants, and plenty to do day and night, York is a great place to make your headquarters for exploring England's northern climates. With a car, you can make the easy drive to **North York Moors National Park** and **Yorkshire Dales National Park,** two areas of haunting beauty where the heather-covered moors and winding river valleys draw walkers and nature lovers. Emily Brontë's novel *Wuthering Heights* or Charlotte Brontë's equally beloved *Jane Eyre* may have formed your images of bleak, windswept Yorkshire moors. The Brontë homestead in the village of **Haworth** is a place of literary pilgrimage year-round. East of York, in a vast, landscaped park, sits the greatest country house in Yorkshire: **Castle Howard.** This castle was used in the television series *Brideshead Revisited* and is open to visitors year-round. **Scarborough,** on the Yorkshire coast, is a fun-loving seaside resort with a wide, curving beach and plenty of gaudy seaside arcades. Getting from Scarborough to **Whitby,** a small, attractive fishing village, is easy.

Cumbria, the northern county west of Yorkshire, offers some of the most beautiful and unusual countryside in England. Here you find the high, bare hills (or small, bare mountains, if you prefer), numerous lakes, and villages nestled in the unspoiled countryside that characterizes the **Lake District,** a national park area. **Bowness,** one of the region's resort centers, sits on 10-mile-long **Lake Windemere,** the largest lake in England. The Lake District is associated with the poet William Wordsworth, whose homes in **Grasmere** and **Rydal** you can visit, and with Beatrix Potter, the author and illustrator of children's classics such as *The Tale of Peter Rabbit.* Potter's home in **Far Sawrey,** on the north side of Lake Windemere, is open to the public. **Hawkshead,** a short distance away, is a charming village constructed of the distinctive gray Lakeland stone. **Keswick,** a few miles north, is a country town (a large, important town) on the shores of Derwentwater. Like the rest of the Lake District, Derwentwater buzzes with visitors from Easter to October.

Figuring Out the Secret of the Seasons

How do you decide what time of year to travel to England? This section presents the pros and cons of each season, so you can choose the best time for your visit.

Traveling during high and low seasons

Roughly speaking, the high season for travel in England lasts from Easter to the end of September. The country is most crowded, and the prices are highest, during the peak summer months of June, July, and August. October to Easter is considered the low season, when tourism dwindles, prices drop, and attractions shorten their opening hours.

During your trip, you probably want to visit London, a destination on almost every English itinerary. London is popular year-round. In fact, London is one of the world's most popular tourist destinations.

Arriving in the capital at any time of year without hotel reservations is unwise. However, planning ahead is *essential* if you want to travel to England in high season.

In the winter months, generally from October through March, you find that castles, museums, and tourist offices outside of London have shorter hours and may be closed certain days of the week. Hours and open days increase during the crowded months of June, July, and August. During the summer tourist season, in popular cities like Cambridge or York, you can choose from three daily walking tours instead of the one that's offered in the winter. If you're a garden lover, time your visit to fall between Easter and September — peak tourist months, but also peak garden months. You can visit most castles and palaces year-round, but in summer, when lines are longest, you may find yourself waiting to get in and feeling rushed after you are. Long-distance train and bus schedules don't change much between winter and summer. However, local public transportation options in regions, such as the Lake District or the Cotswolds, are curtailed during the less touristy months.

Watching those unpredictable skies

England's weather is what you might call "changeable." Except in the most general terms, predicting just what the weather will be like in any given season is difficult. Remember that England is part of an island, and the surrounding seas, as well as its northerly location, determine its weather patterns. In general, however, London and the south of England remain fairly mild year-round, rarely dipping below freezing or rising above 80° F/27° C (at least for extended periods). Table 2-1 gives you an idea of London's temperature and rainfall variations. But don't rely on these figures too much: In 2001, London and the rest of England (and Europe) experienced the coldest and wettest winter and spring since written records originated in the 18th century. And then, in August 2003, the mercury soared to the mid-90s for several days and even reached 100°F.

Table 2-1 London's Average Temperatures and Rainfall

	Jan	Feb	Mar	Apr	May	Jun	Jul	Aug	Sept	Oct	Nov	Dec
Temp (°F/°C)	40/4	40/4	44/7	49/9	55/13	61/16	64/18	64/18	59/15	52/11	46/8	42/6
Rainfall (in.)	2.1	1.6	1.5	1.5	1.8	1.8	2.2	2.3	1.9	2.2	2.5	1.9

Wherever you're in England, the weather can be drizzly, brisk and windy, still and muggy, dry and hot, clammy, or even glorious. Some days you get a combination. But whatever the weather, whatever the season, England is well worth seeing.

Spring comes earliest to Cornwall and Devon in the southwest, where camellias, azaleas, and rhododendrons start to bloom in March. Northern counties, such as Yorkshire and Cumbria, take longer to warm up. Anyone who's spent a winter's day trying to enjoy a walk on the windswept moors of Yorkshire will tell you to postpone a walking tour there until spring is well advanced or summer has arrived. The Lake District in Cumbria tends to be rainy year-round, so expect sudden squalls even in summer.

Blooming in spring

England is at its greenest, blooming best in April and May. Highlights of the season may include the following:

- The great English parks and gardens, such as Sissinghurst in Kent or Hidcote Manor in Gloucestershire, are at their peak of lushness. Bright yellow fields of *rape* (a European plant in the mustard family) brighten the countryside. Daffodils blooming along the lovely River Cam in Cambridge and throughout the Lake District form an unforgettable image of an English spring.
- In London, the Chelsea Flower Show is the quintessential spring event.
- Airfares are lower than in summer.
- The sky stays light well into the evening.

But keep in mind these springtime pitfalls:

- During the half-term school holidays in late February and for three weeks around Easter, visitors pour into London. As a result, the major attractions have longer lines (*queues* in Britspeak), and hotel rooms may be harder to find. During Easter week, towns and major attractions outside of London can be crowded as well.
- The weather is always unpredictable.
- Public transportation thoughout England is reduced during holiday periods.
- Many museums, stores, and restaurants close on Good Friday, Easter, and Easter Monday.

Shining (and raining) in summer

Notoriously chilly England becomes irresistible under the sun. Unfortunately, many tourists flock to England to enjoy the fine weather, which can often turn into rain in July and August. The crowds descend to enjoy the following:

- Everyone moves outdoors to take advantage of the fine weather with alfresco theaters, concerts, and festivals. Tables sit outside cafes, pubs, and restaurants all over the country.
- Roses and colorful plants bloom in the great English gardens and in front of small cottages.
- Summer evenings are deliciously long and often cool, even if the day has been hot.
- The evening stays light past 10 p.m.

But keep in mind:

- July and August are the months of highest rainfall in London and the midsection of England, so skies can stay gray and cloudy.
- Occasional summer heat waves can drive the mercury into the 80s and even 90s, making July and August hot and muggy. Many businesses and budget-class hotels in London don't have air-conditioning.

- Most overseas visitors converge on London and the rest of England from July to September. Lines for major attractions can be interminably long.
- Hotels are more difficult to come by, especially on weekends, and high-season rates apply.

- The beach resorts along the southern coast and up into Yorkshire are crowded with vacationers.
- Roads in the beautiful Lake District, which receives millions of visitors annually, are clogged in July and August.

Glowing in autumn

Autumn's golden glow casts a lovely spell over England. This is my favorite time of year here, and I can think of only one disadvantage to counteract the many advantages:

- In Kent, apples and pears ripen in the orchards and roadside stands sell fresh produce. Country farms harvest hay. Falling leaves skitter down ancient streets and through town squares, and the heather and *bracken* (a type of fern) on the moors and hillsides turn russet and gold. A crispness is in the air, and the setting sun gives old stone buildings and church spires a mellow patina.
- After mid-September, fewer tourists are around, so everything feels less crowded, and you may encounter more natives than visitors.
- With the drop in tourism, hotel rates and airfares may go down as well.
- London's cultural calendar springs to life in the fall.
- Although you may experience rain at this time of year, you're just as likely to encounter what Americans call *Indian Summer.*

But autumn has one drawback:

- Like every season in England, autumn can bring rain.

Welcoming in winter

The English love to be cozy, and English winters are the perfect time for some coziness. Although most overseas visitors to London arrive in July and August, the number of visitors from *within* the United Kingdom is highest between January and March. What do they know that you should know? Consider the points that make winter wonderful:

- The season has a cozy feeling. Country inns welcome guests with crackling fires in ancient stone fireplaces. Game appears on restaurant menus. A sprinkling of snow gives a sparkling new charm to parks, cathedrals, gardens, and old towns.

- London and the rest of England is a bargain. The country's off-season is November 1 to December 12 and December 25 to March 14. Winter off-season rates for airfares and hotels can sometimes be astonishingly low — airline package deals don't get any cheaper (see Chapter 6). At these times, hotel prices in London and throughout England can drop by as much as 20%.

- Although the winter winds may blow, nothing in London stops — in fact, everything gets busier. The arts — theater, opera, concerts, and gallery shows — are in full swing.
- London and many other cities and towns throughout England develop a lovely buzz during the Christmas season: The stores decorate, lights glow, carolers sing, pantomimes perform special holiday scenes, and, in London, the giant Norwegian spruce goes up in Trafalgar Square. On Christmas Day, the boys' choir of King's College Chapel in Cambridge performs the Festival of Nine Lessons and Carols, a traditional Christmas service with music that is broadcast throughout the world.

Naturally, winter has its downside:

- Although the Yuletide holidays are always jolly, they also add up to another peak London tourist season from mid-December to Christmas. You know what that means: bigger crowds and higher prices.
- The entire country virtually shuts down on December 25 and 26 and January 1. Stores, museums, and other attractions close, and public transportation is severely curtailed. On December 26 (Boxing Day, so called because in Victorian times, service workers, such as postmen, received Christmas boxes on this day), finding any open restaurant is difficult.

- Wintertime England may be gray and wet for weeks on end; in midwinter, the skies get dark by about 3:30 p.m. The English usually keep their thermostats set rather low (about 10° F lower than do Americans). Rather than turn up the heat, the English don their *woollies* (long underwear). You should do the same — or be prepared for a chronic case of goose pimples.

England's Calendar of Events

England hums with festivals and special events of all kinds, some harking back to centuries past. If London is going to take up all or part of your trip, write or call **VisitBritain,** the country's official tourist agency (see the Appendix at the back of this book for the address and phone number), and request a copy of its monthly *London Planner,* which lists major events, including theater and the performing arts. Do this at least a month before your departure date. Another good resource for checking England-wide events and dates before you go is the VisitBritain Web site: `www.visitbritain.com`.

For recorded information on weekly London events while in London, call the London Tourist Board's 24-hour **London Line** at ☎ **09068/66-33-44;** calls cost 60 pence (about 90¢) per minute. You can't call the London line from outside the United Kingdom. To find out what's going on while you're traveling throughout the rest of England, stop in at the tourist information centers. (I list street addresses, phone numbers, and Web addresses of these centers throughout this guide and in the Appendix.) You may just happen upon some unique local event.

January

In January, the **London New Year's Day Parade** features marching bands, floats, and the Lord Mayor of Westminster traipsing in a procession from Parliament Square to Berkeley Square. Call ☎ **020/8566-8586** for more details. January 1 (noon to 3 p.m.).

Late January brings in the **Chinese New Year,** marked by colorful street celebrations on and around Gerrard Street in Soho, London's Chinatown. Date varies.

February

In mid-February, the **Jorvik Viking Festival** in York features a combat event and parade to celebrate this Yorkshire city's thousand-year Viking heritage. For more information, call ☎ **01904/621-756** or check the Web: `www.york-tourism.co.uk`. February 13 to 22 in 2004; dates vary from year to year.

March

Bath hosts its highly regarded **Literature Festival,** with new and established writers giving readings and leading seminars. For more information, contact the Bath Festivals Box Office (☎ **01225/463-362)** or check out the city's Web site at `www.visitbath.co.uk`. Early March.

St. Patrick's Day is a big to-do in London, which has the third-largest Irish population after New York and Dublin. There are no parades, but you see plenty of general merriment. March 17.

The **Chelsea Antiques Fair** draws antiques lovers to London's Chelsea Old Town Hall (King's Road) for ten days. For more information, call ☎ **01444/482-514.** Mid-March (also held in mid-September).

At the **Oxford and Cambridge Boat Race** between Putney Bridge and Mortlake Bridge, rowers from the two famous universities compete for the Beefeater Cup. A good viewing spot is the Hammersmith Mall. Last Saturday in March or first Saturday in April (check local press or `www.theboatrace.org` for exact date).

April

The **London Marathon** was first held in 1981 and has become one of the most popular sporting events in the city. Some 30,000 men and women, from champion athletes to first-timers, take part. The 26.2-mile race begins in Greenwich, winds its way past the Tower of London and along the Thames, and finishes in The Mall in front of Buckingham Palace, one of the best viewing spots. For more information, call ☎ **020/7620-4117** or visit `www.london-marathon.co.uk`. Mid-April.

May

The **Brighton International Festival** brightens up venues all over the resort town of Brighton on the Sussex coast with a wide array of drama, literature, visual art, dance, and concert programs ranging from classical to hard rock. Call ☎ **01273/292-950** for more information or check `www.tourism.brighton.co.uk`. Most of May.

The **Football Association FA Cup Final** takes place at Wembley Stadium or another venue. Remember that *football* in the United Kingdom is soccer, and tickets are difficult to obtain given the sport's popularity. Contact the Box Office, Wembley Stadium Ltd., Wembley HA9 0DW; ☎ **020/8900-1234.** Mid-May.

Bath's 18th-century buildings provide wonderful settings for performances during the **International Music Festival.** For more information, contact the Bath Festivals Box Office at ☎ **01225/463-362** or check out the city's Web site at `www.visitbath.co.uk`. Mid-May.

One of London's most famous spring events, the **Chelsea Flower Show,** held on the grounds of the Chelsea Royal Hospital, draws tens of thousands of visitors from around the world. Ordering tickets in advance is a good idea; in the States you can order them from Keith Prowse at ☎ **800/669-7469.** For more information, call the Royal Horticultural Society at ☎ **020/7834-4333** or check out the Web site, `www.rhs.org.uk`. Third week in May.

June

April 21 is Queen Elizabeth II's birthday, but her official birthday parade, **Trooping the Colour,** takes place on a Saturday in June. The Horse Guards celebrate "Ma'am's" birthday in Whitehall with an equestrian display full of pomp and ceremony. For free tickets, send a self-addressed envelope and International Reply Coupon (or U.K. stamps) from January 1 to February 28 to Ticket Office, Headquarters, Household Division, Chelsea Barracks, London SW1H 8RF; ☎ **020/7414-2279.** Mid-June.

The most prestigious horseracing event in England is **Royal Ascot,** held at the Ascot Racecourse (near Windsor in Berkshire, about 30 miles from London) in the presence of the Royal family. For information, call ☎ **01344/876-876** or visit the Web site at www.ascot.co.uk. You can order tickets online for this event. Mid- to late June.

The world's top tennis players whack their rackets at the **Wimbledon Lawn Tennis Championships,** held at Wimbledon Stadium. Getting a ticket to this prestigious event is complicated. From August 1 to December 31, you can apply to enter the public lottery for the next year's tickets by sending a self-addressed envelope and International Reply Coupon to All England Lawn Tennis Club, P.O. Box 98, Church Rd., Wimbledon, London SW19 5AE. For more information, call ☎ **020/8944-1066** or 020/8946-2244 (recorded information) or visit www.wimbledon.com. Late June to early July.

The **City of London Festival** presents a series of classical concerts, poetry readings, and theater in historic churches and buildings, including St. Paul's Cathedral and the Tower of London. For more information, call ☎ **020/7377-0540** or visit www.colf.org. Late June to mid-July.

Living artists from all over the world present more than 1,000 works of art at the juried **Royal Academy Summer Exhibition.** For more information, call the Royal Academy at ☎ **020/7300-8000** or visit www.royalacademy.org.uk. Early June to mid-August.

Kenwood, a lovely estate at the top of Hampstead Heath, is the bucolic setting for the **Kenwood Lakeside Concerts,** a summer season of Saturday-night open-air concerts. For more information, call ☎ **020/8233-7435.** Mid-June to early September.

July

Cheltenham hosts the **International Festival of Music,** which brings in soloists and ensembles from around the world. For more information, call ☎ **01242/227-979** or check out the festival Web site: www.cheltenhamfestivals.co.uk. Early July.

The **Henley Royal Regatta**, one of England's premiere sporting and social events, is a championship rowing event with a long tradition. The regatta takes place on the Thames just downstream from Henley, an Oxfordshire town 35 miles west of London. For more information, call ☎ **01491/572-153** or visit the regatta Web site at www.hrr.co.uk. First week in July.

The **Hampton Court Flower Show,** held on the palace grounds in East Molesey, Surrey (part of Greater London), shows off one of the loveliest gardens in England. For more information, call Hampton Court Palace

☎ **0870/752-7777** or visit the palace Web site at www.hrp.org.uk. Second week in July.

In July, you can attend the much-loved **BBC Henry Wood Promenade Concerts.** Known as "The Proms," this series of classical and popular concerts takes place at London's Royal Albert Hall. To book by credit card, call the box office at ☎ **020/7589-8212.** Mid-July to mid-September.

August

Buckingham Palace opens to the public August through September. For details and to charge tickets, call ☎ **020/7321-2233.** For more information on visiting the palace, see Chapter 12 or the palace Web site, www.royalresidences.com. August 1 to October 1 (dates vary by a day or two every year).

The **Houses of Parliament** open for guided tours in late summer. You can reserve tickets by phone at ☎ **0870/906-3773,** or order tickets online at www.firstcalltickets.com. July 26 until the end of August.

During London's **Notting Hill Carnival,** steel bands, dancing, and Caribbean fun take over the streets of Notting Hill (Portobello Road, Ladbroke Grove, All Saints Road). This enormous street fair is one of Europe's largest. For more information, call ☎ **020/8964-0544.** Bank Holiday weekend in August (last Monday in August).

September

The **Thames Festival** celebrates the mighty river, with giant illuminated floats. For more information, call ☎ **020/7401-2255.** Mid-September.

The **Chelsea Antiques Fair** draws antiques lovers to Chelsea Old Town Hall (King's Road) for ten days. For more information, call ☎ **01444/482-514.** Mid-September (also held in mid-March).

October

Rural towns and villages all over the country hold **harvest festivals**. Contact the tourist office in the region you want to visit for details. (Refer to the regional chapter in this book for tourist office phone numbers.) Weekends throughout the month.

Cheltenham hosts the **Cheltenham Festival of Literature,** showcasing the talents of internationally known writers. For more information, call ☎ **01242/227-979** or click on the Web site www.cheltenhamfestivals.co.uk. Early to mid-October.

November

Although based at the National Film Theatre on the South Bank, the **London Film Festival** presents screenings all over town. Call ☎ **020/7928-3232** in November for recorded daily updates on what's showing and where. Throughout November.

The Lord Mayor of London goes on the grand **Lord Mayor's Procession** through The City from Guildhall to the Royal Courts of Justice in his gilded coach; festivities include a carnival in Paternoster Square and fireworks on the Thames. For more information, call ☎ **020/7971-0026.** Early November.

For the **State Opening of Parliament,** Queen Elizabeth II, in all her finery, sets out from Buckingham Palace in her royal coach and heads to Westminster, where she reads out the government's program for the coming year. (This event is televised.) For more information, call ☎ **020/7971-0026.** First week in November.

On **Guy Fawkes Night,** throughout England, bonfires and fireworks commemorate Guy Fawkes's failure to blow up King James I and Parliament in 1605. For the locations of celebrations in London, check *Time Out* magazine, available at newsstands around the city. (For a brief history of Guy Fawkes, see Chapter 14.) November 5.

December

Christmas lights go on in London's Oxford Street, Regent Street, Covent Garden, and Bond Street. Mid-November to early December.

The **lighting ceremony** of the huge Norwegian spruce Christmas tree in London's Trafalgar Square officially announces the holiday season. Check with the Britain Visitor Centre or Tourist Information Centre for the time. First Thursday in December.

Trafalgar Square is the focus of **New Year's Eve** celebrations. December 31.

Chapter 3

Presenting Five Great Itineraries

In This Chapter

- Seeing England's top attractions in one or two weeks
- Visiting England with kids
- Hitting the highlights for garden lovers and history buffs

Every visitor to England faces the same questions: How can you see as much as possible in a limited amount of time? How can you sort out what's really worth seeing and fit those attractions into a realistic itinerary? This chapter provides the answers. If you budget your time wisely and choose your sights carefully, you can enjoy a satisfying and manageable trip from beginning to end.

Start with a couple of basic premises. The first is that you probably have a limited amount of time. You have to be selective, because you simply can't see everything. The second premise is that you want to see England's highlights without turning your trip into a test run for the London marathon.

The secret to any "successful" trip is to be well organized yet flexible. If you travel by train in England, for example, you need to be aware of train schedules. Call the train information number I provide and get exact departure times. But don't pack your schedule so tightly that a late train ruins your day. Even with limited time, you can see more if you organize your days efficiently and use common sense. Disorganized travelers waste plenty of time, show up at the museum on the day it's closed, and end up in the nether regions of Tooting Bec (a suburb of London) because they hopped on the wrong Underground line. Don't assume that every museum or sight is open every day, all day. Take a moment to look at the details I provide for each attraction later in the guide.

On average, England's top attractions take about two hours to visit, after you're actually there and inside. Some, such as the Tower of London or Warwick Castle, take more time, while others, such as Westminster Abbey, take less. A local museum outside of London may take as little as 15 to 30 minutes to visit. But other variables enter in: whether you're taking a guided tour (usually about 60 to 90 minutes, no matter where) and if crowds make lines move slowly. Another variable is the difficulty of allotting a certain amount of time to a great institution, such as the British Museum, which is loaded with so many treasures you can easily spend a full day or more there, or to a great English garden that beguiles you into dawdling.

This chapter offers five itineraries for people with limited time or special interests. The daily itineraries are commonsense, limited-time suggestions only. Maybe you prefer to spend all day in the British Museum rather than the couple of hours that I suggest. Maybe shopping and cafe-hopping in York is more appealing to you than visiting York Minster. Or your real desire is to get outdoors and go walking in the Lake District. Whatever your preference, go for it! You can enjoy England in countless ways, depending on your own individual interests. See Chapter 1 for some preliminary information on what the country offers.

Seeing England's Highlights in One Week

Spend at least three days of a weeklong trip to England in **London.** You may, in fact, want to stay in London for the entire week, making easy day trips from the city and returning to your hotel at night (that's the premise I use in this itinerary). This saves you the wear and tear of lugging your baggage around. Plus, you can often get special rates for a weeklong stay.

To maximize your sightseeing time, try to book flights that arrive in the morning and depart in the evening.

To avoid wasting time in lines (*queues,* in Britspeak), try to hit the top London sights early in the day, preferably right when they open, or late in the afternoon. I mean, in particular, Buckingham Palace (when it's open to the public during August and September), the Tower of London, Westminster Abbey, and Madame Tussaud's wax museum. Westminster Abbey, to cite just one example, can receive upwards of 15,000 visitors a day!

For information on all the London attractions mentioned in this itinerary, see Chapter 12 unless noted otherwise.

Spend part of **Day One** settling into your London hotel, getting your bearings, and fighting jet lag. Don't make it a big day, but make walking part of your itinerary. Walking gets you into the swing of London and helps your body to adjust to the new time. Start your trip with a visit to majestic **Westminster Abbey,** visiting the Royal Tombs and Poets' Corner. Afterward, because they're right next door, stroll around **Big Ben** and the **Houses of Parliament.** Unless you queue up to hear a debate, or come in August when guided tours are offered, you can't get inside, but you get a great riverside view from Westminster Bridge. On the opposite side of the Thames is the **British Airways London Eye,** a 450-foot-high Ferris wheel. Reserve in advance for the trip up and over London; otherwise you may spend at least a half-hour waiting in line for a ticket and another hour before your scheduled ride. You're not far from the **Tate Modern,** so if you're in the mood to look at modern art, walk along the Thames to London's newest museum (open until 6 p.m. Monday through Thursday, 10 p.m. Friday and Saturday). If you'd rather look at 18th- and 19th-century masterpieces of British painting, head over to **Tate Britain** in Pimlico instead. Have dinner in the Covent Garden area, or on the Thames (see the listing for R.S. *Hispaniola,* passenger boat turned quaint restaurant, in Chapter 11).

Greet **Day Two** with a walk through **Green Park.** You're on your way to **Buckingham Palace** to witness the pageantry of the **Changing of the Guard** (check beforehand to make certain it's taking place that day). For details on touring Buckingham Palace's **State Rooms** during August and September, see Chapter 12. Reserving tickets so you know your specific entry time is a good idea; otherwise you may have to wait in line for an hour or more to get in. If you're not touring the palace itself, visit the **Royal Mews** (the stables that surround the palace) or the newly renovated **Queen's Gallery.** From Buckingham Palace, you can stroll down The Mall, through **St. James's Park,** passing **Clarence House,** the home of the Queen Mother until 2002 and now the official London residence of the Prince of Wales, and St. James's Palace.

Trafalgar Square, London's grandest and certainly most famous plaza, is your next stop. You can have lunch or tea at the National Gallery's restaurant or in the restaurant in the crypt of St. Martin-in-the-Fields church on the square's east side. Spend your afternoon viewing the **National Gallery**'s treasures. Renting one of the self-guided audio tours helps you to hone in on the collection's most important paintings. You can, instead, spend your afternoon in the **National Portrait Gallery,** next door to the National Gallery. The fascinating portrait gallery offers a concise but comprehensive display of famous Brits, from the Tudors to the Spice Girls. If you haven't already reserved a seat for a West End show, you may want to stop by the half-price ticket booth in nearby **Leicester Square** to see what's available. Have dinner in **Soho** before the show (see Chapter 11 for my restaurant recommendations).

On **Day Three,** arrive as early as you can at the **Tower of London** and immediately hook up with one of the one-hour tours led by the Beefeaters, the tower guides in the distinctive red coats. Later, you can explore the precincts on your own, making certain that you allot enough time to see the Crown Jewels. From the Tower, head over to nearby **St. Paul's Cathedral,** which you can see in about a half-hour if you're not on a tour. The **British Museum,** your next stop, has enough to keep you occupied for several days; if you want to see only the highlights, allow yourself a minimum of two hours. Later in the afternoon, explore **Piccadilly Circus,** the teeming epicenter of London's West End. Regent Street, Piccadilly, and Jermyn Street offer great shopping.

On **Day Four,** hop on a train from Waterloo Station and make the half-hour trip to **Hampton Court Palace.** Or, for a much longer but far more scenic alternative, take a boat. Boats usually depart Westminster Pier at 10 a.m. from April to September for the four-hour journey to the palace; you can also take the train there and the boat back. Give yourself a minimum of three unhurried hours at Hampton Court. Touring the various staterooms and apartments with an audio guide can give you a good historical perspective. The gardens can easily take up an hour. Have lunch or tea on the premises and be back in London in plenty of time for dinner and a show. (For information on Hampton Court Palace, see Chapter 13.)

On **Day Five,** take an early train from King's Cross Station and head up north to Yorkshire, where you can spend the day in the walled city of **York.** The train trip takes two hours, making York a relatively easy day trip from London. Or you may want to stay overnight. For an overview of York, considered northern England's most beautiful city, hook up with a guided walking or bus tour — several options exist. Give yourself at least an hour to visit spectacular **York Minster,** the largest Gothic church in northern Europe. The stained glass is marvelous, and a fascinating museum lies beneath the church where excavations have revealed Roman-era buildings. Two other attractions in York are definitely worth seeing: The **National Railway Museum** has royal train cars used by Queen Victoria and Queen Elizabeth II, and the **Jorvik Viking Centre** lets you time-travel back to York in the Viking era. Set aside some time for wandering down York's winding medieval lanes. You may also want to walk along the circuit of amazingly preserved medieval walls. (For details on visiting York, see Chapter 21.)

For **Day Six,** take your pick: **Cambridge** (trains from King's Cross) and **Oxford** (trains from Paddington Station) are both easy-to-reach destinations for day trips from London. If you spent the night in York, you can take the train down from there. Oxford and Cambridge are fascinating university towns with medieval colleges built around quadrangles. (See Chapter 13 for more details on both cities.)

If you opt for Oxford, sign up for the two-hour walking tour that leaves at 11 a.m. and 2 p.m. from the Tourist Information Centre. This tour is the best way to gain an overall perspective on the town and get in to some of the major colleges, which may otherwise be closed. Later, you can spend an hour in the **Ashmolean Museum,** famed for its antiquities, coins, and porcelain and painting collections.

A two-hour walking tour is also available in Cambridge, or you may prefer the open-top bus tour. **King's College Chapel,** one of the most beautiful churches in England, is a must-see in Cambridge; hearing the famous boys' choir sing *Evensong* (an evening church service in which part of the liturgy is sung) is an unforgettable experience. Set aside an hour to tour the **Fitzwilliam Museum;** its fine and varied collection includes Egyptian, Greek, and Roman antiquities and some modern British paintings. **"The Backs"** — so named because some of the colleges back onto the River Cam — is a beautiful place for strolling. If you feel adventurous, you can rent a *punt* (small boat) and pole yourself down the Cam; you can also pay to have someone do the punting for you.

Day Seven is your last day in London. Hopefully you booked your return flight for the evening, so you can have at least a few morning hours for more sightseeing, shopping, or both. Checkout time is probably no later than noon, so ask the hotel front desk if the hotel can store your luggage. Alternatively, if you plan to take a fast airport train from Victoria (Gatwick) or Paddington (Heathrow) station, you can check in with your luggage early in the day (airline counters are in the train stations) and ask that your luggage go on to the airport; you can then take a later train. (See Chapter 11 for detailed information on getting to and from London airports.) If you haven't made it to **Harrods** department store yet, do that first, or check out the other shopping options in Knightsbridge. Instead of shopping, you may want to squeeze in one last museum. Several major South Kensington museums aren't far from Harrods, including the **Natural History Museum** with its famous dinosaur exhibits and the **Victoria & Albert Museum,** renowned for its superlative art and design collections. Instead of visiting a museum, you can visit **Kensington Palace** in Kensington Gardens, but allow yourself at least two hours if you do so. Following your morning activities, grab a quick lunch or snack, and then make your way to the airport to catch your plane.

Touring the Best of England in Two Weeks

Lucky you. With two weeks, you can explore so much of the country.

For the first week, follow the first itinerary in this chapter, but because you don't have a plane to catch, **Day Seven** for you begins at **The National Portrait Gallery,** if you haven't visited it yet. From the portrait gallery you can easily walk to **Covent Garden Market,** where you find scores of interesting shops. Covent Garden Piazza, a perfect spot for lunch, is a lively hub filled with restaurants. Alternatively, spend your seventh morning in one of the famous South Kensington museums, such as the **Natural History Museum** or **Victoria & Albert Museum.** From there you can easily stroll to **Kensington Gardens** and visit **Kensington Palace,** the former home of Princess Diana. In the evening, go for a traditional English dinner at **Rules,** London's oldest restaurant, or **Simpson's-in-the-Strand.** Other options for the evening include a play or concert, or maybe a stop in a couple of good pubs. (See Chapter 11 for information on restaurants and Chapter 12 for attractions and nightlife.)

On **Day Eight,** hop a train from Paddington Station to **Exeter,** in Devon. In Exeter, you can rent a car and drive into nearby **Dartmoor National Park** and other parts of the West Country. (Renting a car in Exeter makes more sense than renting one in London.) **Chagford** is a good place to stay overnight. Before you leave Exeter, though, give yourself an hour to explore beautiful **Exeter Cathedral.** If you don't want to rent a car, you can explore the town on foot, and continue by train to Penzance or St. Ives in Cornwall. (See Chapter 17 for information on Exeter and Chagford.)

Devote **Day Nine** to **Cornwall,** the southwestern tip of England. From Exeter or Chagford, make the fairly short drive to **Penzance,** where you need at least two hours to visit the fabulous island-castle of **St. Michael's Mount.** If you have a car, you can easily drive from Penzance to **Land's End,** stopping at the picturesque fishing village of **Mousehole** on the way. Don't waste your time with the theme-park attractions at Land's End; go for the stupendous views westward out over the Atlantic, and then head on to St. Ives. If you're without a car, skip Land's End and take the train from Penzance to **St. Ives,** an artist's colony that's become a seaside resort town. Loaded with charm, good restaurants, and hotels, St. Ives makes a good place to stay overnight. The town's big draw is **Tate St. Ives,** a museum that exhibits artists who lived and still work in Cornwall. More interesting is the **Barbara Hepworth Museum** and sculpture garden, located in and around the great sculptor's former studio. On a beautiful summer evening, when the sun lingers late in the sky, you may want to drive (if you have a car) to **Chysauster,** a prehistoric site near St. Ives. (I describe Cornwall, including Penzance, Land's End, and St. Ives, in Chapter 18.)

From St. Ives or Penzance, you can reach **Bath** on **Day Ten** in about four hours by car or train (depending on connections). Bath deserves as much time as you can spare, so I suggest that you spend the night there. Bath is a wonderfully walkable city, filled with outstanding examples of Regency-era architecture, including the **Royal Crescent** and the **Pump Room,** a charming place to have your afternoon tea. Set aside at least two hours for the wonderful **Roman Baths Museum.** (Check out Chapter 20 for Bath's many attractions.)

You need a car for **Day 11**'s tour of the nearby **Cotswolds.** (If you've been traveling by train until now, you can rent a car in Bath.) You can visit several lovely villages, all built of mellow, honey-colored Cotswold stone. **Broadway** and **Bourton-on-the-Water** are no longer dependent on the wool trade, as they were in the Middle Ages, but now depend on visitors who come to stroll, shop, and have cream teas. Near Broadway is **Hidcote Manor,** one of England's great gardens. If you're a garden lover, don't miss it; plan on spending at least two hours here. Overnight in **Cheltenham,** a small but lively spa town, or **Cirencester,** a beautiful Cotswolds market town with a noteworthy church and the **Corinium Museum,** full of Roman mosaics and artifacts from the area. Both towns are full of good restaurants and hotels. (See Chapter 20 for information on the Cotswolds.)

From Cheltenham or Cirencester on **Day 12,** drive (or take the train) northeast to **Stratford-upon-Avon,** a good place to spend the night. The drive takes about two hours. In Stratford, you want to spend at least three hours visiting the **Shakespeare sites.** If you're a theater lover, see a production at one of the **Royal Shakespeare Festival** theaters. Reserving tickets in advance is best; if you haven't, head directly for the box office before doing anything else. In the afternoon, you may want to drive or take the local train from Stratford to nearby **Warwick Castle.** The castle, nearly 1,000 years old, is one of England's premiere tourist attractions and can easily keep you occupied for several hours. (For details on Stratford-upon-Avon and Warwick Castle, see Chapter 19.)

From Stratford on **Day 13,** drive south to **Stonehenge,** a few miles outside Salisbury. If you're without a car, take the train to **Salisbury** and hop on a local bus to Stonehenge. This great stone circle, believed to be about 5,000 years old, is the most famous prehistoric site in England. Afterward, take a couple of hours to wander through Salisbury, with its magnificent Gothic **cathedral.** You can spend the night in Salisbury, or you may want to head back to London. (See Chapter 16 for details on Salisbury and Stonehenge.)

The task at hand on **Day 14** is to return your rental car and get to the airport. You may be able to return your car in Salisbury, even if you rented it in Exeter. If so, I recommend doing that and taking a train (a 1½-hour trip) back to London. Otherwise, see if you can drop the car directly at Heathrow or Gatwick, the most likely departure points for your flight. From Salisbury, just to be on the safe side, give yourself at least three hours to drive back to London.

Discovering England with Kids

So you want to spend five days in England and bring along your kids? No problem. Perhaps this trip will be your kids' introduction to the country, or their first experience of a foreign country. You may know what *you* want to see, but where do you take *them?* I have a few suggestions to keep you and your kids excited and entertained.

Much, of course, depends on your children's ages and their interests. Teens are going to be bored out of their minds with what the toddlers and pre-teens find enthralling.

Try to get their interest up before you buckle your seat belts for the transatlantic flight. A visit to your local library can yield some real treasures in this regard: children's books set in England (the *Harry Potter* series), children's travel books with maps, even travel videos that the whole family can watch. For more tips on traveling with kids, see Chapter 5.

For this itinerary, I assume that you want to spend at least three of your five days entirely in London, which is a good decision because the capital city is jam-packed with sights that kids of all ages can enjoy. Plus, staying in London and making day trips means that you don't have the additional hassle of a car. You can get everywhere on public transportation.

For information on all the London attractions in this itinerary, see Chapter 12 unless noted otherwise.

Don't schedule too much on **Day One.** Exercise helps ward off jet lag. After sitting in a plane for several hours, take smaller children to one of London's great parks so they can run and let off steam. Depending on where your hotel is located, your destination may be Hyde Park, Kensington Gardens, Green Park, St. James's Park, or Regent's Park. During your stay, you may want to visit them all. If you're traveling with a teen, a stroll through London's four royal parks following the **Princess Diana Commemorative Walk** (see Chapter 11) is a great introduction to the city.

More focused sightseeing can begin on **Day Two.** Consider a guided bus tour that helps orient everyone and gives you at least a glimpse of all the major sights. Several outfits provide tours on double-decker buses — always a treat for kids — and Frog Tours uses amphibious vehicles to show you the main sights on land and from the Thames. More expensive guided tours may include the **Changing of the Guard** at **Buckingham Palace,** a bit of pageantry that children and adults find exciting. After the tour, make the **British Airways London Eye** your first stop. This giant, high-tech Ferris wheel revolves on the South Bank, beside the Thames, across from the Houses of Parliament. Reserve your ticket beforehand to avoid waiting in a long line. All ages enjoy the half-hour "flight." Afterward, cross Westminster Bridge and stroll over to view the **Houses of Parliament** and **Big Ben** (hopefully the clock strikes the hour while you're in the vicinity). And because it's close at hand, use this opportunity to visit **Westminster Abbey.** Younger children may not get much out of the place, but you will. Later in the afternoon, take a ferry ride down the Thames to the **Tower of London;** you can catch the ferry at Westminster Pier near the Houses of Parliament. After you're inside the Tower, hook up with one of the Beefeater tours; the red-coated custodians of the Tower have plenty of dramatic tales to tell. If you're with a child age 10 to 17, you may want to have dinner at the **Hard Rock Cafe** in Mayfair (see Chapter 11).

Begin **Day Three** at the **Natural History Museum** in South Kensington, where the dinosaur exhibit, complete with life-size animatronic raptors and a T-Rex, captures the imaginations of both young and old(er). If your child's a budding Einstein, the **Science Museum,** with its many hands-on, interactive exhibits, may be a better choice. Afterward, if you have small children in tow, stroll over to **Kensington Gardens** for a look at the famous statue of Peter Pan. The **Princess Diana Memorial Playground** in the northwest corner of Kensington Gardens enchants little ones. You can have lunch in **The Orangery** of adjacent Kensington Palace, or make your way to **Café-in-the-Crypt** in St. Martin-in-the-Fields church in Trafalgar Square. If you're with a teen, you may want to spend the morning or afternoon in **Madame Tussaud's wax museum** or the **London Dungeon** on the South Bank; some of the gorier exhibits are unsuitable for young children. In the evening, older kids and teens may also enjoy one of the West End's razzmatazz musicals.

Make **Day Four** a day trip to **Brighton,** on the Sussex coast. The quick trip takes less than an hour. There you can visit the **Royal Pavilion** and take the kids over to **Palace Pier,** a spot filled with games and souvenir stands. If the weather's warm, rent a deck chair and sit on the beach. Brighton is a fun place just to stroll around, with plenty to keep you and the family entertained. (For details on Brighton, see Chapter 14.)

On **Day Five,** head out to **Hampton Court Palace,** another quick train ride of less than an hour. (You can also take a boat, but the trip takes about four hours.) Hampton Court offers much to explore, so give yourself at least four hours. Small children may not get much out of the visit, but they will probably find the staff members who wear period costumes intriguing. You can eat on the premises. Save the best part for last: The famous Maze in the gardens brings out the kid in everyone. (For information on Hampton Court, see Chapter 13.) Following your visit to Hampton Court Palace, you can depart from London on a flight that leaves later in the evening; however, that may require too much rushing for most families. A better plan may be to fly out the next morning.

Strolling through England's Greenery: An Itinerary for Garden Lovers

England is a paradise for gardeners. In London and throughout the country, you find superb gardens created in a variety of styles. You can reach many of England's great gardens by train and taxi, but a car definitely comes in handy if you're intent on seeing several gardens in different parts of the country. Serious garden lovers may want to consider a guided garden tour. (See Chapter 6 for information on the garden tour offered by Maupintour.)

If you want to tour English gardens at their best, you need to travel between May and August. Although a great garden is interesting at any time of year, spring to late summer are the peak blooming seasons, when English gardens are at their best, showing off with a blazing dazzle of color.

The gardens in England are often part of a stately home, which you may also want to visit. Touring a house and its gardens usually takes a minimum of three hours. If you're a gardener, you'll want to make these excursions the focal point of your day, and plan other activities accordingly.

If you have one week in England and want to spend part of your time in London, what gardens can you see? Well, you have many beautiful options.

Spend **Day One** strolling around London's magnificent royal parks (St. James's Park, Green Park, Hyde Park, Kensington Gardens). Former hunting grounds, they've been landscaped over the centuries to accommodate millions of visitors each year. Visit the lovely formal gardens around Kensington Palace in **Kensington Gardens.** If you're going to be in London in May, you may want to attend the famous **Chelsea Flower Show,** which kicks off the gardening season. I recommend that you reserve tickets in advance for this yearly event. (See Chapter 2 for details on the flower show and Chapter 12 for information on the gardens in this paragraph.)

On **Day Two,** take a half-day to visit the **Royal Botanic Gardens** at Kew, which include wonderful Victorian-era glass conservatories. You can reach Kew by Underground or by boat. Charming Kew Palace and an 18th-century Chinese pagoda are part of this once-royal pleasure garden. (See Chapter 13 for details on visiting Kew.)

Devote **Day Three** to the gardens at **Hampton Court Palace,** Henry VIII's extravagant showplace beside the Thames. In addition to viewing formal plantings in the geometric Tudor style, you can visit the ancient greenhouse, see a 300-year-old grapevine, and wind your way through the famous maze. You may want to time your visit to coincide with the **Hampton Court Flower Show** in July. (See Chapter 2 for details on the flower show and Chapter 13 for information on Hampton Court Palace.)

Reserve **Day Four** for your visit to **Sissinghurst Castle Gardens** in Kent. Sissinghurst is a major highlight of any garden tour of England. From London, you can ride the train. Laid out and planted by Vita Sackville-West and Harold Nicholson in the 1930s, Sissinghurst is one of the greatest and most romantic gardens in the world. Now a National Trust property, the gardens are so popular that they use a timed-entry system at peak periods during the spring and summer. A restaurant and tea shop are on the premises. (See Chapter 15 for information on Sissinghurst.)

If you have a car and get an early start, you can combine a visit to Sissinghurst with a visit to **Hever Castle,** Anne Boleyn's childhood home. Surrounding the moated castle are remarkable Italianate gardens that were designed for William Waldorf Astor in 1903. (See Chapter 15 for details on Hever Castle.)

If you're without a car, you can travel to Hever Castle by train and taxi on **Day Five.** If you visit both Sissinghurst and Hever Castles on Day Four, use Day Five to visit those royal parks you may have missed on Day One.

Among the hundreds of gardens in England, two more unforgettable ones await garden lovers. In order to see them as part of your weeklong trip, however, you need to rent a car.

Spend part of **Day Six** at **Stourhead,** located a few miles west of Salisbury, in Wiltshire. Laid out in 1741, Stourhead is one of the oldest landscape gardens in England. A lake, a bridge, and classically inspired buildings serve as focal points in a graceful landscape. (See Chapter 16 for details on Stourhead.)

You may want to spend the night in Salisbury, or continue north to Bath or one of the Cotswolds towns that I describe in Chapter 20.

Day Seven belongs to **Hidcote Manor** in the Cotswolds. The plantings at this remarkable garden in Gloucestershire form living "rooms" of shape, color, scent, and texture. The gardens at Hidcote, begun in 1907, have influenced gardeners from around the world. Strolling through this magnificent creation, patiently fashioned from inhospitable terrain, is a perfect way to end your weeklong garden tour of England. (For information on Hidcote Manor, see Chapter 20.)

Visiting England's Past: An Itinerary for History Buffs

Many travelers thrill at the experience of standing in a place where history was made. England, as you probably know, is loaded with these hallowed spots. In this ancient realm, you can see places that span roughly 5,000 years of human history. My suggested itinerary covers only a fraction of the sites you can visit. Using London as a base for several day trips, this itinerary is geared for an eight-day stay in England. With this itinerary, you don't need a car.

On **Day One,** you arrive in London, a city that's hardly lacking in historic monuments. Start off with a trip to the granddaddy of them all, the 900-year-old **Tower of London.** Join one of the guided tours led by the Beefeaters and wander around afterward on your own. Tower Green is the spot where political prisoners, such as Anne Boleyn and Sir Thomas More, were beheaded during the reign of Henry VIII. The Crown Jewels, housed in a high-security armory, are a must-see.

From the Tower, travel by boat (you find a ferry pier right outside) to Westminster Pier, the stop for the **Houses of Parliament** and your next destination, **Westminster Abbey.** This ancient Gothic edifice, where almost every British monarch since William the Conqueror has been crowned, resonates with history. In the chapels, you find the tombs of Queen Elizabeth I; her half-sister, Mary Tudor ("Bloody Mary"); and her onetime rival, Mary Queen of Scots. Great English statesmen, war heroes, and writers are commemorated throughout. Have dinner at **Rules,** London's oldest restaurant, to cap off your history-filled day. (For details on the sights in this paragraph, see Chapter 12; for the restaurant Rules, see Chapter 11.)

On **Day Two,** head over to **Buckingham Palace,** hopefully on a day when the historic pomp and pageantry of the **Changing of the Guard** is taking place (daily from April 1 through early June, on alternate days the rest of the year). The palace itself, Queen Elizabeth's official London residence, is open to the public in August and September. If you can't get into the palace, stop in at the **Royal Mews,** where you can view the amazing gilded coach in which the queen rides to open Parliament. After your royal tours, make your way to the **Imperial War Rooms** in Westminster. The fascinating underground bunker was the World War II headquarters for Prime Minister Winston Churchill and his War Cabinet. The bunker has been preserved exactly as it was during England's "darkest hour" in the 1940s. Your last major stop of the day is **St. Paul's Cathedral,** site of the famous fairy-tale wedding of Prince Charles and Princess Diana in 1981. (Information on all these London attractions is in Chapter 12.)

Day Three, if you're up for it, can be your day to compare and contrast a royal palace and a royal castle. Start the day early at **Kensington Palace,** used by monarchs from William and Mary to Queen Victoria, who was born there. An audio guide fills you in on the history. On display in the historical dress collection are gowns worn by Queen Victoria, Queen Elizabeth, and Princess Diana. (For details on Kensington Palace, see Chapter 12.) Afterward, travel to **Windsor Castle,** less than an hour by train from London. Another one of the queen's official residences, the historic castle set in its Great Park is open to visitors most of the year. The sumptuous interior was redone in the 19th century. (You find information on Windsor in Chapter 13.)

Treat yourself to a full-day trip to **York,** one of England's most historic cities, on **Day Four.** Get an early start, because the train takes two hours to get there. You find a wealth of historic attractions in York. Start your explorations at awe-inspiring **York Minster,** the largest Gothic structure in northern Europe. Its enormous windows shimmer with medieval stained glass. Then head over to **Jorvik Viking Centre** for a ride back to York of a thousand years ago, when the city was a Viking settlement called Jorvik. York is wonderfully walkable, although its ancient lanes can be confusing. Stroll through the **Shambles,** a medieval street where butchers had their shops, and make a full or partial circuit of the medieval city walls. You can have dinner in York, on the train ride back, or in London. (See Chapter 21 for details on York and its attractions.)

Day Five is another day trip, this time to **Winchester,** the ancient Anglo-Saxon capital of Wessex under King Alfred. By train from London, the trip takes about 1½ hours. Winchester is a small, delightful town and a pleasure to explore. Begin at mighty **Winchester Cathedral,** which houses the remains of some of the Anglo-Saxon kings of England. You also can see the grave of Jane Austen, the brilliant author of *Pride and Prejudice* and other early-19th-century classics. Making a circuit of the town, passing Winchester College (founded in 1382), and following the River Itchen, is easy. The famous King Arthur's Round Table hangs in **Castle Hall,** the largest medieval hall in England after Westminster. Sir Walter Raleigh heard his death sentence in Castle Hall in 1603. In the small **City Museum,** you can see Roman mosaics from the period when Winchester was a Roman settlement. You can be back in London in time for dinner at **Ye Olde Cheshire Cheese,** the onetime hangout of Dr. Johnson and Charles Dickens. (See Chapter 16 for information on Winchester; see Chapter 11 for the restaurant Ye Olde Cheshire Cheese.)

Day Six is another day trip, this time to **Canterbury,** about 1½ hours east of London in Kent. In terms of England's religious history, few places are more important. More than 700 years ago, pilgrims began flocking to the shrine of St. Thomas à Becket, who had been murdered by King Henry II's henchmen in **Canterbury Cathedral.** Becket's shrine was destroyed during the reign of Henry VIII, but the site is marked near the high altar. The poet Geoffrey Chaucer wrote about a group of those Old English-speaking pilgrims in *The Canterbury Tales,* and you may want to step into **The Canterbury Tales,** an entertaining museum and exhibition on nearby St. Margaret's Street, to renew your acquaintance with them or discover more about them.

For a glimpse of how the locals lived 2,000 years ago, when Canterbury was a Roman settlement called Cantuaria, spend some time in the small but informative **Canterbury Roman Museum.** Then make your way to the ruins of **St. Augustine's Abbey,** a Christian site that predates the cathedral by about 600 years. You can take an audio-guided tour of this

UNESCO World Heritage site, one of the oldest Anglo-Saxon monastic sites in the country. Nearby is another ancient treasure: **St. Martin's Church,** perhaps the oldest church in England. It was already in existence when St. Augustine arrived to convert the natives in 597. (You can find more information on Canterbury and its sights in Chapter 14.)

On **Day Seven,** go prehistoric and visit **Stonehenge,** possibly the world's most famous ancient monument. Ride a bus from Salisbury, about 1½ hours west of London. The ancient stone circle retains its mystery even in the face of thousands of daily tourists. Was the circle used as an astronomical laboratory, as one popular theory holds? Even the date is uncertain — it's estimated to be at least 5,000 years old. In Salisbury, before heading back to London, visit beautiful **Salisbury Cathedral,** a masterpiece of English Gothic. Its spire is the tallest in England. (Details on Stonehenge and Salisbury are in Chapter 16.)

On **Day Eight,** go into **Battle** — Battle, Sussex, that is. In this small town just north of Hastings, you find one of the most historically hallowed spots on English soil: the battlefield where in 1066 William of Normandy fought King Harold for the throne of England. William won and became known as William the Conqueror. His defeat of Harold spelled the end of Anglo-Saxon rule and marked the beginning of a new French culture imposed upon the country. At **The 1066 Battle of Hastings Abbey and Battlefield,** you can walk on the battlefield. A clever audio guide that tells the story from three different perspectives enhances your experience. William the Conqueror built the Battle Abbey, now in ruins, on the spot where Harold was slain, and where English history moved into a new phase. The town of Battle, about 90 minutes south of London by train, has several good restaurants for lunch or tea. (See Chapter 14 for information on Battle.)

Chapter 4

Planning Your Budget

In This Chapter

- Planning a realistic budget for your trip
- Pricing things in England
- Uncovering hidden expenses
- Considering money-saving tips

Okay, you want to go to England. You're excited and eager to pack, but can you really afford it? At this point, a financial reality check is in order. You may have heard that London is an expensive city, but just how expensive? And what about destinations outside of London? What does it cost to stay overnight in romantic Cornwall, for example, and how much is the train fare from London? This chapter helps you answer all these questions and assemble a budget.

Adding Up the Elements

You can easily budget for your England trip, but holding down costs while you're there may be another matter. (The goods in shop windows are so enticing — and expensive, if you're in London.) You can use the worksheets at the back of this book to get an approximate idea of what you'll spend throughout your trip. A good way to get a handle on costs is to walk yourself mentally through your trip as follows:

1. **Begin with the cost of transportation to the airport.**
2. **Add the cost of your flight and the price of getting from the London airport to your hotel.**
3. **Add the total cost of hotel rooms for your trip's duration.**
4. **Factor in a daily allowance for meals and snacks.**

   Exclude breakfast if the hotel rate includes it.
5. **Figure in transportation costs.**

6. **Add admission prices to museums, the theater, and other entertainment expenses.**

   Don't forget the cost of film and processing.

7. **Determine what you want to spend on souvenirs.**

8. **Add the cost of getting back to the London airport and of traveling from your originating airport to your home.**

After you've done all that, tack on another 15 to 20% for good measure.

Budgeting for your biggest expense: Lodging

The biggest bite from your budget is the cost of your accommodations. And that cost is going to be higher in London than anywhere else in England. If you book your rooms in advance, especially for the London part of your trip, you'll know this expense before you leave on vacation.

Chapter 8 discusses what kind of lodgings you can expect for your money and how to get the best rate. After you get a firm handle on prices and locations, peruse Chapter 11 for my recommendations of top-notch London B&Bs (bed-and-breakfasts) and hotels in all price ranges and locations. You also find recommended hotels and B&Bs in the regional chapters of the book.

In London, rates vary considerably from B&B to B&B, and from hotel to hotel, so giving a reliable average is difficult. For the recommendations in this guide, however, the rates for a double room are *generally* between £83 and £100 ($125 to $160) for an inexpensive property, between £100 and £150 ($160 to $240) for a moderately priced one, and between £150 and £200 ($240 to $320) for an expensive one. After that, you hit the stratosphere of £200-plus ($320-plus) for a luxury B&B or hotel. Keep in mind that all B&Bs, and many midrange London hotels, include at least a continental breakfast as part of the room rate, so you can save a few pounds there.

In other parts of England, the rates for accommodations are more uniform and much lower, generally from £25 to £30 ($40 to $48) *per person* per night. Overall, prices are lower for everything after you leave London. However, you still find plenty of opportunities to drop a king's ransom for a room, especially in some of those truly elegant country-house hotels. Check for special deals when you're outside of London. Many country-house hotels offer bed, breakfast, and a full dinner at bargain prices. Throughout England, properties offer special price breaks for stays of two nights or a full weekend (Friday and Saturday night).

Saving with trains: Transportation

I have some good news that can save you a bundle: You may not need to rent a car in England, because you can tour London using public transportation and reach many destinations outside of the city by train.

Within London, you can take advantage of the fast, convenient, and easy- to-use subway system, the Underground (called the "Tube"). Special reduced-price transportation passes, **Visitor Travelcards** (see Chapter 11), make getting around the city relatively inexpensive.

A train can take you to many of England's castles and other destinations. If you plan to do much traveling in the countryside, consider getting a **BritRail pass** (see Chapter 7 for details). You must buy these passes, which offer enormous savings over individual fares, before you arrive in England. In England's smaller towns and cities, you can walk almost everywhere, because the city centers are so compact. Or you can hop on a bus, as the locals do. Sometimes you may need to take a taxi, which can get expensive depending on the distance from the rail stations to your destinations in the towns.

In some areas, a car makes exploration of the countryside much easier. However, renting a car can be a very expensive proposition. You may find a great rate, but gasoline (*petrol* in Britspeak) costs more than twice what it does in the States. See Chapter 7 for more details on renting a car in England.

Eating cheaply or splurging: Restaurants

The food in England used to be the butt (or shank) of many a joke, but in recent years, London has emerged as one of the great food capitals of the world. You find superb restaurants in the rest of the country, too. Of course, eating at the top restaurants, no matter where you are, is going to cost you. However, in London and in every town and village throughout England, you can find countless pubs and restaurants where you can dine cheaply and well — and where you can enjoy your meal along with the locals. In addition, many of the best restaurants in London and elsewhere offer special fixed-price meals that can be real bargains.

Again, everything is going to be more expensive in London. If you eat lunch and dinner at the moderately priced London restaurants recommended in Chapter 11, you can expect to pay £25 to £40 ($40 to $64) per person per day for meals, not including wine (assuming that your hotel rate includes breakfast). Outside of London, unless you splurge on really high-class restaurants, your daily food cost will be about £20 to £30 ($32 to $48). In the countryside, you'll find that many hotels offer full board — that is, bed, breakfast, and dinner. In most cases, full board adds up to considerable savings.

If you have breakfast at a cafe instead of your hotel and are content with coffee and a roll, expect to pay about £3.50 to £5 ($6 to $8) in or out of London. Depending on the restaurant, an old-fashioned English breakfast with eggs, bacon or sausage, toast, and tea or coffee can run anywhere from £7 to £10 ($11 to $16) in London, about half that outside London — but remember, your hotel cost nearly always includes breakfast. Likewise, a simple afternoon tea at a cafe in London sets you back about £4.50 to £7 ($7 to $11), but a lavish high tea (a light supper with a hot dish and dessert) at one of the great London hotels may total £25 ($40) or more. Elsewhere, expect to pay about £5 ($8) for a scrumptious cream tea (with scones, jam, and Cornish or Devon clotted cream).

Paying as you go: Attractions

Your budget for admission fees depends on what you want to see, of course. But don't cut costs with your sightseeing. After all, the sights are what you came all this way to see. Sure, an adult ticket to the Tower of London is £11.50 ($18), but do you really want to miss seeing this historic landmark and the extraordinary Crown Jewels housed there? Keep in mind that if you're a senior or a student, you can often get a reduced-price admission. Plus, many attractions offer reduced family rates that are good for two adults and two children.

Check out the London sights in Chapter 12 and determine which are on your list of "must sees." Then add them to the worksheet at the back of this book. All the top national museums — the British Museum, National Gallery, National Portrait Gallery, Tate Britain, Tate Modern, Victoria & Albert Museum, Natural History Museum, and Science Museum — are free. And it costs nothing to stroll through London's great parks or to view Buckingham Palace (okay, from the outside) and see the Changing of the Guard.

You encounter must-see sights in the rest of England, too. As a general rule, expect to pay about £10 ($16) for admission to famous castles and palaces, such as Castle Howard in Yorkshire and Warwick Castle near Stratford-upon-Avon. Some of the great English cathedrals, such as Salisbury, now charge admission fees or ask for donations of £3 to £5 ($4.80 to $8) to help defray the enormous cost of upkeep. You rarely pay more than £5 ($8) for museums and local attractions outside of London.

Unless they're students with valid identification, those 16 and up must usually pay the adult admission charge at attractions.

If your plans call for visiting castles, such as Windsor or Warwick; palaces, such as Hampton Court or Blenheim; historic properties, such as Shakespeare's Birthplace in Stratford-upon-Avon; and gardens, such as Sissinghurst in Kent, you can save money by purchasing a **Great British Heritage Pass.** The passes are good for 4 days ($36), 7 days ($54), 15 days ($75), and one month ($102). They include almost all major historic properties in England, and you get 50% off the admission price at the Tower of London. You can order one by phone at ☎ **888/ BRITRAIL** in North America; from a travel agent in Australia or New Zealand; or online at `www.britrail.net`. In London, you can buy the Heritage Pass at the Britain Visitor Centre, 1 Regent St, SW1. For more information, check VisitBritain's Web site, `www.visitbritain.com/heritagepass`.

Controlling costs: Shopping and nightlife

Shopping and entertainment are the most flexible parts of your budget. You don't have to buy anything at all, and you can hit the sack right after dinner instead of seeing a play or dancing at a club. You know what you want. Flip through the London shopping options and the London entertainment and nightlife venues in Chapter 12. If anything strikes you as something you can't do without, budget accordingly. Keep in mind that a pint in a pub sets you back about £3 ($5), while a London theater ticket can go for anywhere between £12 and £70 ($13 and $112). Stratford-upon-Avon is another place where you may want to budget for a theater ticket; seats are between £8 and £42 ($13 to $67). Coastal resort towns, like Brighton, are big with club-goers, so you may want to check out the scene while you're there; club cover charges are rarely more than £5 ($8), but drinks are always expensive, about £3 to £5 (roughly $5 to $8) for nonpremium alcohol.

Table 4-1 and Table 4-2 give you an idea of what things typically cost in London and the rest of England, so you can avoid some culture shock.

Table 4-1 What Things Cost in London

Item	*Cost in U.S. $*
Transportation from airport to Central London	
From Heathrow by Underground	$6
From Gatwick by train	$16
One-way Underground fare within Central London	$2.60
Double room at the Cadogan Hotel	$360–$448
Double room at Hazlitt's 1718	$328–$408
Double room with breakfast at Aster House	$200–$264
Double room at Astons Apartments	$144–$200
Double room with breakfast at Hotel 167	$144–$158

(continued)

Table 4-1 *(continued)*

Item	*Cost in U.S. $*
Dinner for one at Asia de Cuba, excluding wine	$50
Set-price dinner for one at Rules, excluding wine	$32
Pub dinner for one at Devonshire Arms	$14
Pizza at Gourmet Pizza Company	$10
Afternoon tea for one at the Lanesborough	$39
Coffee and cake at Pâtisserie Valerie	$8
Pint of beer at a pub	$3.50
Admission to the Tower of London (adult/child)	$18/$12
Admission to Madame Tussaud's (adult/child)	$24/$17
Theater ticket	$25–$90
Theater program	$4

Table 4-2 What Things Cost Outside of London

Item	*Cost in U.S. $*
Round-trip train ticket London-Cambridge	$25
Round-trip train ticket London-Bath	$53
Admission to Roman Baths Museum, Bath	$12
Combined ticket price for all Shakespeare sights in Stratford	$21
Lunch for one at Opposition Restaurant, Stratford	$18
Theater ticket, Stratford-upon-Avon	$13–$67
Admission to Warwick Castle	$18
Double room with private bath and breakfast, Hamlet House B&B, Stratford	$72–$90
Double room with private bath and breakfast at Thistle Hotel, Stratford	$205–$246
Room, dinner, and breakfast for two, Mt. Prospect Hotel, Penzance	$160
Admission to St. Michael's Mount Castle, Cornwall	$8
Admission to Tate St. Ives art museum	$7

Item	*Cost in U.S. $*
Cornish cream tea	$6
Room, dinner, and breakfast for two, Miller Howe Hotel, Lake District	$272
Tank of unleaded gas, economy car	$60

Keeping the VAT and Hidden Costs in Check

Allow me to introduce you to Britain's version of sales tax — the *value-added tax (VAT).* Brace yourself: The tax amounts to 17.5%. The VAT is part of the reason prices (particularly in London) are so high. The tax is added to the total price of consumer goods (the price on the tag already includes the tax) and to hotel and restaurant bills. The VAT isn't a hidden expense, but not all quoted room rates, especially in the luxury tier, include the tax. Make sure to ask whether your quoted room rate is inclusive or exclusive of VAT. (In the hotel listings in this book, I tell you if the rate doesn't include the VAT.)

If you're not a resident of the European Union, you can get a VAT refund on purchases made in the United Kingdom — not including what you spend at hotels and restaurants. See Chapter 9 for details.

On top of the VAT, a few restaurants add a service charge of 12.5 to 15% to your bill. If they do so, the menu must state this policy. ("A 15% service charge has been added to your bill.") This charge amounts to mandatory tipping, so if your charge receipt comes back with a space for you to add a tip, put a line through it.

As a general rule, except for tips in restaurants (12.5 to 15%) and to cab drivers (10%), London isn't a city where you tip excessively. An exception is if you stay in an expensive hotel with porters who carry your bags (£1 per bag) and doormen who hail you a cab (£1 per successful hail). In fancier country-house hotels, like Gidleigh Park, where the service is extremely attentive, tipping is left to the discretion of the guests. In such cases, I suggest that you leave a minimum of £20 ($32) per guest for the staff.

The telephone in your hotel is convenient, but don't use it if you're on a budget. A local call that costs 20 pence (32¢) at a phone booth may cost you £1 ($1.60) or more from your hotel phone. If you plan to make a number of calls during your trip, get a phone card (see the Appendix for more details) and use a phone outside the hotel.

Cutting Costs

BARGAIN ALERT

Throughout this book, Bargain Alert icons highlight money-saving tips and great deals. Check out some additional cost-cutting strategies:

- **Go in the off-season.** If you can travel at nonpeak times (October to mid-December or January to March), hotel prices can be as much as 20% less than during peak months.
- **Travel on off days of the week.** Airfares vary depending on the day of the week. If you can travel on a Tuesday, Wednesday, or Thursday, you may find cheaper flights to London. When you inquire about airfares, ask whether you can obtain a cheaper rate by flying on a specific day.
- **Try a package tour.** For popular destinations like London, you can make just one call to a travel agent or packager to book airfare, hotel, ground transportation, and even some sightseeing. You'll pay much less than if you tried to put the trip together yourself (see Chapter 6).
- **Reserve a hotel room with a kitchen** (in England these are called *self-catering units*) and do at least some of your own cooking. You may not feel as if you're on vacation if you do your own cooking and wash your own dishes, but you'll save money by not eating in restaurants two or three times a day. This strategy is often useful to parents traveling with children.
- **Always ask for discount rates.** Membership in AAA, frequent-flier programs, trade unions, AARP, or other groups may qualify you for discounts on plane tickets and hotel rooms booked before you go. When you're in England, there is usually a lower admission rate for seniors and students with ID.
- **Try expensive restaurants at lunch instead of dinner.** At most top London restaurants, prices at lunch are considerably lower than those at dinner, and the menu often includes many of the dinnertime specialties. Also, wherever you travel in England, look for fixed-price menus.
- **Travel off-peak, standard class.** A train ticket always costs more if you travel at peak commuter times (before 9:30 a.m.). A first-class train ticket generally costs about one-third more than a standard class.
- **Walk.** London is large but eminently walkable, and every historic English town or city is compact. A good pair of walking shoes can save you money on taxis and other local transportation. As a bonus, you get to know the city and its inhabitants more intimately, and you can explore at a slower pace.

Chapter 5

Planning Ahead for Special Needs or Interests

In This Chapter

- Bringing the family
- Discovering discounts and special tours for seniors
- Locating wheelchair-accessible attractions
- Traveling alone
- Finding lesbian and gay communities and special events

Many of today's travelers have special interests or needs. Parents may want to take their children along on trips. Seniors may want discounts or tours designed especially for them. People with disabilities need to ensure that their itineraries offer wheelchair access. Solo travelers have special considerations about safety. And gays and lesbians may want to know about welcoming places and events. In response to these needs, this chapter offers advice and resources.

Bringing the Brood: Advice for Families

Traveling with children, from toddlers to teens, is a challenge — no doubt about it. Bringing the brood can strain the budget and influence your choices of activities and hotels. But in the end, isn't sharing your experiences as a family great?

Look for the Kid Friendly icon as you flip through this book. I use it to highlight hotels, restaurants, and attractions that are particularly family friendly. Zeroing in on these places can help you plan your trip more quickly and easily.

In addition, the following resources can help you plan your trip:

- **About Family Travel** (3555 S. Pacific Hwy., Medford, OR 97501; ☎ **541/535-5411;** Fax: 541/488-3067; www.about-family-travel.com) can tailor a tour specifically for families traveling to London. Its services include arranging airfare, hotel rooms, transportation, and theater tickets, as well as providing tips on sights and other destinations in England.
- **Family Travel Forum** (☎ **888/FT-FORUM** or **212/665-6124;** Fax: 212/665-6136; www.familytravelforum.com) offers a call-in service for subscribers. To order a subscription ($3.95 per month), write FTF, Cathedral Station, P.O. Box 1585, New York, NY 10025, or call to request a free information packet.

Admission prices for attractions in London and throughout England are reduced for children 5 to 15 years old. Under-5s almost always enter free. If you're traveling with one or two children ages 5 to 15, always check to see whether the attraction offers a money-saving family ticket, which considerably reduces the admission price for a group of two adults and two children.

Locating family-friendly accommodations and restaurants

Most hotels can happily accommodate your family if you reserve your rooms in advance and make the staff aware that you're traveling with kids. The establishment may bring in an extra cot or let you share a larger room; these types of arrangements are common. Smaller bed-and-breakfasts (B&Bs) may present problems, such as cramped rooms and shared toilet facilities, and some places don't accept children at all. Ask questions before you reserve.

London and many of England's midsize cities have plenty of American-style fast-food places, including Burger King, McDonald's, Pizza Hut, and KFC. You don't find these chains in smaller villages and towns, however. If you need a family-friendly spot, consult the pages of this book. I point out plenty of places where you can take the kids.

Expensive, high-toned restaurants in England aren't particularly welcoming to young children. The menus aren't geared to the tastes of American youngsters, the prices are high, and the staff can be less than accommodating.

To keep costs down, rent a hotel room with a kitchen (in England, these rooms are called "self-catering units") and prepare your own meals, as long as you don't mind cooking while on vacation. Another option, when the weather cooperates, is to take the family on a picnic. London's

Kensington Gardens (see Chapter 12) or the parks of **Windsor** and **Warwick castles** (Chapters 13 and 19, respectively) are great outdoor destinations. When in London you can also take advantage of pre-theater fixed-price menus (usually served 5:30 to 7 p.m.), which are usually a good deal.

Younger teens traveling in London probably want to check out the **Hard Rock Cafe** (see the listing in Chapter 11) or the scene at the **Trocadero** in **Piccadilly Circus** (see Chapter 11 for information on this neighborhood), which offers theme restaurants, such as **Planet Hollywood** and the **Rainforest Cafe.** For adventurous teens and younger children, London may be a good place to introduce them to Chinese or Indian cuisine.

Planning your trip together

Your children may be more excited about their trip to England if they know about some of the special sights and events in store for them. Before you leave, sit down with your kids and make a plan. Go over the sights and activities in this book and let your children list a few of the things they want to see and do, in order of preference. Make a similar list of your own. Older children may want to do some research on the Internet. (See the Appendix for the best Web sites.) Together, plot out a day-by-day schedule that meets everyone's needs.

Letting your younger children read *Peter Pan* or *Peter Pan in Kensington Gardens* and telling them about his statue there can generate excitement about the trip. Slightly older children may enjoy the *Harry Potter* series, which takes place in real and fictional settings in London and around the country. (If your kids have already read the series, they know that Harry shops in Diagon Alley in London before he goes off to school at Hogwarts.) Older children may enjoy the thought of traveling around London in the Underground (called the "Tube") or taking a boat trip down the Thames. With the information in this book and some online investigating, you can also incite your kids' curiosity about historic sites, such as the **Tower of London** (see Chapter 12), **Stonehenge** (Chapter 16), and **Warwick Castle** (Chapter 19).

Some kids and adult activities can easily overlap. You may want to spend one afternoon in **Kensington Gardens.** After your entire family visits **Kensington Palace,** the kids can blow off steam in the new **Princess Diana Memorial Playground.** Many kid-oriented activities in London and throughout England are just as interesting for parents. For example, from the dinosaur exhibit in the **Natural History Museum** to the animatronic robots re-creating historic scenes in **Madame Tussaud's wax museum,** you *and* your kids have plenty you can experience and enjoy together. (See Chapter 12 for the attractions in this paragraph.)

Don't overschedule your days with your children. You can't enjoy your trip if both you and they are worn out.

Preparing for a long plane trip

The shortest international trip to London (from New York) is about six hours; compare that to the 25 hours to Australia, which is a lot of time for kids to sit still and be quiet. Although children can spend some of the journey watching a movie (or two) on the plane, come prepared with extra diversions: games, puzzles, books — whatever you know will keep your kids entertained. Request a special kids' menu at least a day in advance from the airline. If your child needs baby food, bring your own and ask a flight attendant to warm it. Dealing with jet lag can be hard on adults but even harder on small children. Don't schedule too much for your first day in London. Get everyone comfortably settled and take it from there.

Hiring a baby-sitter while on your trip

What you really need is a relaxing evening at the opera and a romantic late dinner. But you can't take Junior along on this special evening. What are your options? Ask your hotel staff if they can recommend a local baby-sitting service. Most of the hotels marked with a Kid Friendly icon in this book can help arrange baby-sitting. London also has several respected and trustworthy baby-sitting agencies that provide registered nurses and carefully screened mothers, as well as trained nannies, to watch children. Check the London Yellow Pages. One old and trustworthy baby-sitting service is **Universal Aunts** (**☎ 020/7386-5900**), which charges £6.50 ($10) per daytime hour, £5 ($8) after 6 p.m. (4-hour minimum) plus a £3.50 ($6) agency fee. In Chelsea, **Pippa Pop-ins** (165 New Kings Rd. SW6; **☎ 020/7385-2458**) provides a lovely toy-filled nursery staffed by experienced caregivers where you can safely park the little ones during the day (open Monday through Friday 8 a.m. to 7 p.m.).

Going Gray: Suggestions for Seniors

England won't present any problems for you if you're a senior who gets around easily. If not, when you plan your trip, be aware that not all hotels — particularly less expensive B&Bs — have elevators. The steep staircases in some places are a test for *anyone* with luggage. When you reserve a hotel, ask whether you'll have access to an elevator (or *lift,* as they're called in England).

Although some sections of London are very crowded, people are generally polite and courteous. The British *queue* (stand in line) for buses and expect everyone else to do the same. And you don't need to be overly concerned about crime. Yes, crime does occur, but it happens with far less frequency than in many other major cities.

Being a senior may entitle you to some terrific travel bargains, such as lower prices for BritRail passes and reduced admission at theaters, museums, and other attractions. Always ask, even if the reduction isn't posted. Carrying ID with proof of age can pay off in all these situations. ***Note:*** You may find that some discounts, such as public transportation reductions in London, are available only to U.K. residents.

The following sources can provide information on discounts and other benefits for seniors:

- **AARP** (formerly the American Association of Retired Persons; 601 E St. NW, Washington, DC 20049; ☎ **800/424-3410;** `www.aarp.org`), offers member discounts on car rentals and hotels. AARP offers $12.50 yearly memberships that include discounts of 12 to 25% on Virgin Atlantic flights to London from eight U.S. cities.
- **Elderhostel** (11 Ave. de Lafayette, Boston, MA 02110-1746; ☎ **877/426-8056;** `www.elderhostel.org`) offers people 55 and over a variety of university-based education programs in London and throughout England. These courses are value-packed, hassle-free ways to travel. Travel packages include airfare, accommodations, meals, tuition, tips, and insurance. And you'll be glad to know that no grades are given. Tours focus on London's legal, music, and art scenes; the gardens of the Cotswolds, Kent, or the Lake District; literary sights in Wessex and Yorkshire; or a number of other topics and locations.
- **Grand Circle Travel** (347 Congress St., Boston, MA 02210; ☎ **800/597-3644;** `www.gct.com`) is another agency that escorts tours for mature travelers. Call for a copy of its publication *101 Tips for the Mature Traveler* or order online.

Most of the major U.S. domestic airlines, including American, United, and Continental, offer discount programs for senior travelers — be sure to ask whenever you book a flight.

Accessing London: Information for People with Disabilities

A disability needn't stop anybody from traveling; more options and resources are available than ever before. Most hotels and restaurants are happy to accommodate people with disabilities. London's top sights and many of the attractions in other towns and regions are wheelchair accessible. (Call first to make arrangements and get directions to special entrances and elevators.) Theaters and performing-arts venues are usually wheelchair accessible as well (again, call first).

If you use a travel agent, discuss with him or her the means of travel (train or plane, for example) that can accommodate your physical needs; special accommodations or services you may require (transportation within the airport, help with a wheelchair, and special seating or meals); and the type of special assistance you can expect from your transportation company, hotel, tour group, and so on.

Persons with disabilities are often entitled to special discounts at sightseeing and entertainment venues in Britain. These discounts are called *concessions* (often shortened to "concs").

Before departing on your trip, contact **VisitBritain** (see the Appendix for addresses and phone numbers) and request a copy of its *Disabled Traveler Fact Sheet,* which contains some helpful general information. The **British Travel Book and Shop** (128 Ebens Rd., Bloomfield, NJ 07003; ☎ **866/338-6867;** www.btb-books.com) sells *Access in London* ($15.95), the best and most comprehensive London guide for people with disabilities and anyone with a mobility problem. The book provides full access information for all the major sites, hotels, and modes of transportation.

The United Kingdom has several information resources for travelers with disabilities. The best of these resources include the following:

- **Artsline** (☎ **020/7388-2227**) provides advice on the accessibility of London arts and entertainment events. The **Society of London Theatres** (32 Rose St., London WC2E 9ET; www.officiallondontheatre.co.uk) also offers a free guide called *Access Guide to London's West End Theatres.*
- **Holiday Care Service** (Sunley House, 4 Bedford Park, Croyden, Surrey CR0 2AP; ☎ **0845/124-997**; www.holidaycare.org.uk) offers information and advice on suitable accommodations, transportation, and other facilities in England.
- **The National Trust** (☎ **020/7447-6742;** www.nationaltrust.org.uk) is a British organization that owns and operates hundreds of historic properties (castles, gardens, and more) throughout England. The free booklet *Information for Visitors with Disabilities* provides details on accessibility at each site. Contact The National Trust Disability Office, 36 Queen Anne's Gate, London SW1H 9AS, to obtain a copy. Although not all National Trust sites are accessible, the organization provides powered four-wheeled vehicles free of charge at more than 50 properties; you can drive yourself or have a companion or volunteer drive for you.
- **RADAR** (Royal Association for Disability and Rehabilitation, 12 City Forum, 250 City Rd., London EC1 8AF; ☎ **020/7250-3222;** www.radar.org.uk) publishes information for travelers with disabilities in Britain.

- **Tripscope, The Courtyard** (Evelyn Road, London W4 5JI; ☎ **08457/585-641** or 0117/939-7782; www.tripscope.org.uk) provides travel and transport information and advice, including airport facilities.

Some other helpful information resources in the United States include the following:

- **American Foundation for the Blind** (11 Penn Plaza, Suite 300, New York, NY 10001; ☎ **800/232-5463;** www.afb.org) offers information on traveling with seeing-eye dogs; the foundation also issues ID cards to the legally blind.
- The **Society for Accessible Travel & Hospitality** (347 Fifth Ave., Suite 610, New York, NY 10016; ☎ **212/447-7284;** Fax: 212/725-8253; www.sath.org) is a membership organization with names and addresses of tour operators specializing in travel for people with disabilities. You can call to subscribe to its magazine, *Open World.*
- **Travel Information Service** (☎ **215/456-9603** or 215/456-9602 [TTY]; www.mossresourcenet.org) provides general information and resources for travelers with disabilities.

Considering the benefits of escorted tours

You can find tours designed to meet the needs of travelers with disabilities. Organizations that offer trips to England are as follows:

- **Accessible Journeys** (☎ **800/846-4537;** www.disabilitytravel.com) offers tours of Britain and London in minibuses or motorcoaches.
- **The Guided Tour** (☎ **800/783-5841;** E-mail: gtour400@aol.com) has one- and two-week guided tours for individuals, with one staff member for every three travelers.
- **Undiscovered Britain** (☎ **215/969-0542;** www.undiscoveredbritain.com) provides specialty travel and tours for individuals, small groups, or families traveling with a wheelchair user.

Dealing with access issues

The United Kingdom doesn't yet have a law like the Americans with Disabilities Act. By 2004, some form of legislation may be in place, and more and more businesses will become accessible.

Not all hotels and restaurants in Britain provide wheelchair ramps. Most of the less expensive B&Bs and older hotels don't have elevators, or they have elevators that are too small for a wheelchair. Ask about this issue when you reserve your room or table.

England's better-known museums and attractions are accessible, but in some cases, you must use a different entrance. Call the attraction to find out about special entrances, ramps, elevator locations, and general directions.

Trains throughout the United Kingdom now have wide doors, grab rails, and provisions for wheelchairs. To get more information or to obtain a copy of the leaflet *Rail Travel for Disabled Passengers,* contact The Project Manager (Disability), British Rail, Euston House, Eversholt Street, London NW1 1DZ; ☎ **020/7922-6984.** You can also check out the Web site www.nationalrail.co.uk, which has a section on travel by people with disabilities and contact details for the various train operating companies.

Travelers with disabilities will want to keep the following in mind when traveling in London:

- Although London's streets and sidewalks are in good repair, you don't find as many modern curb cuts as in younger cities. (In other historic towns, such as Rye, you have to deal with cobblestones.)
- Not all the city's Underground ("Tube," or subway) stations have elevators and ramps.
- Most public buses aren't wheelchair accessible.
- London's black cabs are roomy enough for wheelchairs.
- Victoria Coach Station in Central London has Braille maps.

The following organizations provide access information and services for travelers with disabilities in London:

- **London Transport** (☎ **020/7941-4600** Access and Mobility line; www.londontransport.co.uk) publishes a free brochure called *Tube Access*, available in Underground stations. The organization also provides information on the wheelchair-accessible minibus service (called Stationlink) between all the major BritRail stations.
- **Wheelchair Travel** (1 Johnston Green, Guildford, Surrey GU2 6XS; ☎ **1483/233-640;** Fax: 01483/237-772; www.wheelchair-travel.co.uk) is an independent transport service for the traveler with disabilities arriving in London. The organization offers self-drive cars and minibuses (although I strongly discourage anyone, with a disability or not, from driving in London) and can provide wheelchairs. Drivers who act as guides are available on request.

Taking health precautions

Before you leave on your trip, talk to your physician about your general physical condition, prescriptions needed for the time you're traveling, medical equipment you should take, and how to get medical assistance when you're away. Carry all prescription medicines in their original bottles with the contents clearly marked, along with a letter from your doctor.

Make a list of the generic names of your prescription drugs in case you need to replace or refill them during your visit. Pack medications in your carry-on luggage. If you're in a wheelchair, have a maintenance check before your trip and take some basic tools and extra parts if necessary. If you don't use a wheelchair but have trouble walking or become easily tired, consider renting a wheelchair to take with you as checked baggage.

Flying Solo: Tips for Travelers on Their Own

Traveling alone in England isn't unusual and presents no special difficulties. Single travelers regularly and safely explore all parts of the country. Women travelers should exercise the usual common-sense precautions. A few tips for both men and women are as follows:

- If you plan to arrive in an unfamiliar town after dark, book your hotel ahead and ask how to get from the train or bus station to the hotel. If the trip involves a taxi ride, ask the hotel owner for the number of a local taxi company. Don't assume that local bus service is always available; get exact information from the hotelier before you arrive. Remember, too, that trains don't always arrive on time, so you may be arriving later than you anticipated.
- If you require assistance during the day, head to the tourist information center, usually located near the train station or in the center of town. These centers keep daytime business hours.
- If you experience any difficulty in the evening, head for the nearest pub, where you can always find a telephone and someone who can give you local information.

Stepping Out: Resources for Gay and Lesbian Travelers

London has always been a popular destination for gays and lesbians, even in the days (up to 1967) when homosexuality was a criminal offense in Britain. Today, with a more tolerant government at the helm, gay pride is prominent. The government has actually *spent money* to promote gay tourism. Click the "Gay and Lesbian" bar on the Visit Britain Web site at www.visitbritain.com for information on gay venues and events throughout England.

In London, you can find gay theaters, gay shops, more than 100 gay pubs, famous gay discos, and gay community groups of all sorts. The gay-friendly resort town of Brighton is also known for its pub and club scene. Elsewhere in the country, at least in the larger cities, you can usually find a gay pub or two, and clubs with at least one night a week for gays.

Old Compton Street in Soho is the heart of London's Gay Village. The area has dozens of gay pubs, restaurants, and upscale bars and cafes. The **Earl's Court area,** long a gay bastion, is where you find the gay **Philbeach Hotel** (www.philbeachhotel.freeserve.co.uk) and many gay-friendly restaurants.

Lesbigay events in London include the **London Lesbian and Gay Film Festival** in March, the **Pride Parade** and celebrations in June, and the big outdoor bash known as **Summer Rites** in August. You can obtain information and exact dates from **London's Lesbian and Gay Switchboard (☎ 020/7837-7324;** www.llgs.org.uk).

Brighton (which I describe in Chapter 14) is one of the gayest seaside resort towns in Europe. From London, you can get there on the train in under an hour.

As you plan your trip, you may want to check out the following Web sites; all are specifically geared to gay and lesbian travelers to England:

- www.pinkpassport.com
- www.demon.co.uk/world/ukgay
- www.gaytravel.co.uk
- www.gayguide.co.uk
- www.gaybritain.co.uk
- www.timeout.com, the online edition of *Time Out* magazine, with a gay and lesbian section

The newest and most useful gay and lesbian travel guide — covering London, Brighton, and many other hot European destinations — is *Frommer's Gay & Lesbian Europe* (Wiley Publishing Inc.), available at most bookstores. In addition, several gay magazines and publications, useful for their listings and news coverage, are available in London's gay pubs, clubs, bars, and cafes. The most popular are *Boyz* (www.21stcenturyboyz.com), *Pink Paper* (www.pinkpaper.com), and *QX* (*Queer Xtra;* www.qxmag.co.uk).

Gay Times (www.gaytimes.co.uk), which covers all England, is a high-quality monthly news-oriented mag available at most news agents. *Gay to Z* (www.freedom.co.uk/gaytoz) is the United Kingdom's "pink telephone directory." Indispensable for its citywide listings (including gay listings), *Time Out* (www.timeout.com) appears at news agents on Wednesdays.

Gay's the Word (66 Marchmont St., WC1; ☎ **020/7278-7654;** www.gaystheword.co.uk; Tube: Russell Square) is the city's only all-around gay and lesbian bookstore. The store stocks a wonderful selection of new and used books and current periodicals.

Part II

Ironing Out the Details

"And how shall I book your flight to England – First Class, Coach, or Medieval?"

In this part . . .

This part helps you with the practical details of planning your trip to England. Throughout this part, I try to anticipate and answer the questions that first-time visitors most frequently ask.

In Chapter 6, I go over the transportation options for getting you to England. Before booking a flight, you may want to think about consulting a travel agent. I let you know some of the advantages of doing so. I also discuss the various types of escorted and package tours. If you're an independent traveler and want to do your own planning, this chapter gives you the rundown on what airlines fly to England, where to find special deals, and how to book your flight online.

After you're in England, you may want to get out of London and travel around the rest of the country. In Chapter 7, I tell you about traveling by train, bus, and car.

An Englishman's home may be his castle, but a traveler's home is his hotel room. Booking your accommodations ahead of time is wise, and Chapter 8 tells you how to do so. I explain what hotel rack rates are and give you some pointers to help you find the best room for the best rate. I also give you some tips on how to land a hotel room if you happen to arrive without a reservation.

You'll be dealing with British money every day of your trip, so Chapter 9 is all about pounds and pence. I also help you to decide whether you want to bring traveler's checks, credit cards, or cash, or use ATMs.

Chapter 10 is devoted to last-minute details. I discuss getting a passport, buying travel and medical insurance, and making advance reservations for London shows, sightseeing, and restaurants. If you're wondering what to pack, look at the end of this chapter for my recommendations.

Chapter 6

Getting to England

In This Chapter

- Evaluating the benefits of using a travel agent
- Deciding whether to travel on your own or take an escorted tour
- Discovering the advantages of package tours
- Planning the trip on your own
- Traveling by plane, train, or ferry

You just wanted to take a nice little trip to London and spend a few days traveling around England. But now, trying to make all the necessary decisions, you're overwhelmed. Do you need a travel agent? Do you want to travel with a tour group and have all the decisions made for you, or do you want to venture out on your own? How do you find the best airfares to England? This chapter helps you find the answers.

Consulting a Travel Agent: A Good Idea?

A travel agent can help you find a bargain airfare, hotel room, or rental car. The best travel agents can tell you how much time to budget for a destination, find you a cheap flight that doesn't require you to change planes in off-the-beaten-path airports, get you a better hotel room for about the same price, and even give recommendations on restaurants.

Word of mouth is the best way to find a good travel agent. Check with family members, neighbors, coworkers, or friends who've had experiences with travel agents. Make sure that you pick an agent who knows England.

To ensure that your travel agent meets your needs, find out all you can about the destinations in England that you want to visit. (You've already made a sound decision by buying this book.) Pick out some hotels and attractions you think you'll like. If you have access to the

Internet, check prices on the Web in advance so that you can compare them with those offered by the travel agent. Then bring your guidebook and Web information with you to the travel agency. If the agent offers you a better price, ask him or her to make the arrangements for you.

Because travel agents have access to more resources than even the most complete travel Web site, they should be able to get you a better price than you can get by yourself. And an agent can often issue your tickets and vouchers on the spot. If the agent can't get you into the hotel of your choice, ask for an alternative recommendation; then look for an objective review in your guidebook while you're still at the travel agency. Remember, too, that a travel agent can take care of BritRail passes (see Chapter 7), airport-to-city transfers, Visitor Travelcards for the London bus and Underground system (see Chapter 11), sightseeing tours, and the Great British Heritage Pass, which is good for admission to castles and other historic sites throughout England (see Chapter 4).

Travel agents work on commission. The good news is that *you* don't pay the commission; the airlines, accommodations, and tour companies do. The bad news is that you may run into some unscrupulous travel agents who will try to persuade you to book the vacations that bring them the highest commissions.

Some airlines and resorts have begun limiting or eliminating travel agent commissions altogether. The immediate result has been that agents don't bother booking certain services unless the customer specifically requests them. If more airlines and companies throughout the industry lower commissions, travel agents may have to start charging customers for their services.

Considering Escorted Tours

Do you like letting a bus driver worry about traffic while you sit in comfort and listen to a tour guide explain everything? Or do you prefer renting a car and following your nose, even if you don't catch all the highlights? Do you like having events planned for each day, or would you rather improvise as you go along? The answers to these questions determine whether you should choose the guided tour or travel à la carte.

Some people love escorted tours. The tour company takes care of all the details and tells you what to expect at each attraction. You know your costs upfront, and you don't have many surprises. Escorted tours can take you to the maximum number of sights in the minimum amount of time with the least amount of hassle.

Other people need more freedom and spontaneity. They prefer to discover a destination by themselves and don't mind getting caught in a thunderstorm without an umbrella (*brolly* in Britspeak) or finding that a recommended restaurant is no longer in business — that's just part of the adventure.

If you decide to go with an escorted tour, purchase travel insurance, especially if the tour operator asks you to pay upfront. But don't buy insurance from the tour operator! If the tour operator doesn't fulfill its obligation to provide you with the vacation you paid for, you have no reason to think it'll fulfill its insurance obligations either. Get travel insurance through an independent agency. (I give you more about the ins and outs of travel insurance in Chapter 10.)

Talking with tour operators

If you decide to take an escorted tour, ask a few simple questions before you make a commitment. Along with finding out whether you need to put down a deposit and when final payment is due, ask the following questions:

- **What is the cancellation policy?** How late can you cancel if you can't go? Do you get a refund if you cancel? Do you get a refund if the operator cancels?
- **How jam-packed is the schedule?** Does the tour schedule try to fit 25 hours into a 24-hour day, or does it give you ample time to relax or shop? If getting up at 7 a.m. every day and not returning to your hotel until 6 or 7 p.m. sounds like a grind, certain escorted tours may not be for you.
- **How big is the group?** The smaller the group, the less time you spend waiting for people to get on and off the bus. Tour operators may be evasive about this because they may not know the group's exact size until everybody has made their reservations, but they should be able to give you a rough estimate.
- **Does the tour require a minimum group size?** Some tour operators require a minimum group size and may cancel the tour if they don't book enough people. If a quota exists, find out what it is and how close they are to reaching it. Again, tour operators may be evasive in their answers, but the information may help you select a tour that's sure to take place.
- **What exactly is included?** Don't assume anything. You may be required to get yourself to and from the airport at your own expense. The excursion may include a box lunch, but drinks may be extra. Beer may be included, but not wine. How much flexibility does the tour offer? Can you opt out of certain activities, or does the bus leave once a day, with no exceptions? Are all your meals planned in advance? Can you choose your entree at dinner or does everybody get the same chicken cutlet?

Finding escorted tours

Dozens of companies offer escorted tours to London and destinations throughout England. Many escorted-tour companies cater to special interests, such as theater or history buffs, and others are more general. A good travel agent can help you find a tour that suits your particular interests. You may also want to scan the travel section in your local paper for more tour possibilities or check the Web sites of the major airlines (see the Appendix for their Web addresses), some of which offer escorted tours.

A few companies that offer escorted tours to London and the rest of England (with prices per person, based on double occupancy) are

- **Globus and Cosmos** (`www.globusandcosmos.com`) are well-known budget tour companies working in partnership. Current offerings include an eight-day tour of the scenic and historic highlights in southern England starting at $1,122, airfare included.
- **Maupintour** (`www.maupintour.com`) has an eight-day garden tour that includes the Chelsea Flower Show, the great gardens at Kew, Sissinghurst, Leeds Castle, and Hever Castle; prices start at $3,925, including airfare. Other tours go to Yorkshire and the Lake District and the West Country.
- **Trafalgar Tours** (`www.trafalgartours.com`) provides more upscale choices; prices for the 15-day "Best of Britain" tour start at $1,699, airfare included.

Weighing the Benefits of Package Tours

Package tours are different from escorted tours. Package tours are only a way of buying your airfare and accommodations at the same time. And for popular destinations, such as London, they can really be the smart way to go, because with a package tour, you can save a *ton* of money.

A package tour to England that includes airfare, hotel, and transportation to and from the airport may cost less than the hotel alone if you book the room yourself. That's because tour operators buy package tours in bulk and resell them to the public. Each destination usually has one or two packagers that offer better deals than the rest because they buy in even greater volume.

Package-tour costs vary greatly. Prices differ according to departure city, hotel, and extras, such as car rental and optional tours. Timing is as important as other options in determining price. Adjusting your travel dates by a week (or even a day) can yield substantial savings.

Shop around and ask plenty of questions before you book your trip. The time you spend doing research will be worth the bucks you save.

Locating package tours

Information about package tours is available from a variety of sources. A few companies that offer packages to England are

- **British Travel International** (☎ **800/327-6097;** `www.britishtravel.com`) is a good source for discount packages.
- **Liberty Travel** (☎ **888/271-1584;** `www.libertytravel.com`), one of the biggest packagers in the northeastern United States, offers reasonably priced packages.
- **Trailfinders** (`www.trailfinders.com`), another good source for discount packages, has several offices in Australia: Sydney (☎ **02/9247-7666**), Melbourne (☎ **03/9600-3022**), Cairns (☎ **07/4041-1199**), Brisbane (☎ **07/3229-0887**), and Perth (☎ **08/9226-1222**).

Good places to look for additional package tours include

- **Local newspapers:** Look in the travel section of your local Sunday paper for advertisements. One reliable packager that you may see is **American Express Vacations** (☎ **800/346-3607;** `http://travel.americanexpress.com/travel`).
- **National travel magazines:** Check the ads in the back of magazines, such as *Arthur Frommer's Budget Travel, Travel & Leisure, National Geographic Traveler,* and *Condé Nast Traveler.*
- **Online at `www.vacationpackager.com`:** At this Web site, you can plug in your destination and interests, and the site makes several suggestions of companies that you can contact on your own or through a travel agent.

Checking out airline and hotel packages

Airlines are good sources for package tours, especially to London, because they package their flights together with accommodations. When you pick an airline, you can choose the one that has frequent service to your hometown and on which you accumulate frequent-flier miles.

Although disreputable packagers are uncommon, they do exist. By buying your package from an airline, you can be fairly sure that the company will still be in business when your departure date arrives.

The following airlines offer packages to England:

- **American Airlines Vacations (☎ 800/321-2121;** www.aavacations.com)
- **British Airways Holidays (☎ 800/AIRWAYS;** www.britishairways.com/holiday)
- **Continental Airlines Vacations (☎ 800/525-0280;** www.continental.com)
- **Northwest Airlines World Vacations (☎ 800/800-1504;** www.nwaworldvacations.com)
- **United Airlines Vacations (☎ 800/328-6877;** www.unitedvacations.com)
- **Virgin Atlantic Vacations (☎ 888/YESVIRGIN;** www.virgin.com/vacations)

To give you an idea of cost, look at these sample airline package prices — based on per person, double occupancy. (Single supplements are available for solo travelers, but they increase the price considerably — aggravating, isn't it?) These packages don't include airport taxes and surcharges, which typically amount to about $100. All hotels have private bathrooms (with tubs or shower stalls), and rates include breakfast. The following London packages were available at press time; they may not be available when you travel, but they can give you an idea of typical offerings. The package prices are for the summer season (the price drops considerably between October and March), with midweek flights from JFK or Newark, airport transfers, taxes, and six nights in a hotel with breakfast:

- **Virgin Atlantic** had a $1,429 "Spotlight on Family" deal that included admission to the Tower of London, a bus tour, and tickets to a West End show.
- **United** offered a good bare-bones air and hotel package for $1,011.
- **British Airways** was charging about $1,200 for a package.
- **Continental** offered a package for $1,157.
- **American** had a package for $1,095.

The biggest hotel chains also offer packages, most of them for London only. The following are among large hotel groups with properties in London and throughout England; telephone numbers (except for Moat House Hotels) are U.S. reservation lines:

- **Comfort Inn (☎ 800/654-6200**; www.comfortinn.com)
- **Crowne Plaza (☎ 800/227-6963**; www.crowneplaza.com)
- **Grand Heritage Hotels International (☎ 888/934-7263**; www.grandheritage.com)

- **Hilton Hotels (☎ 800/HILTONS;** www.hilton.com)
- **Holiday Inn (☎ 800/465-4329;** www.holidayinn.co.uk)
- **Hyatt Hotels & Resorts (☎ 800/228-3336;** www.hyatt.com)
- **Inter-Continental Hotels & Resorts (☎ 800/327-0200;** www.interconti.com)
- **Le Meridien (☎ 800/543-4300;** www.lemeridien-hotels.com)
- **Macdonald Hotels (☎ 888/892-0038**; www.macdonaldhotels.co.uk)
- **Moat House Hotels (☎ 0870/225-0199** in the U.K.; www.moathousehotels.com)
- **Radisson Hotels (☎ 888/201-1718**; www.radisson.com)
- **Sheraton Hotels & Resorts (☎ 800/325-3535;** www.sheraton.com)
- **Thistle Hotels Worldwide (☎ 800/847-4358;** www.thistlehotels.com)

If you already know where you want to stay, call that hotel and ask whether it offers land/air packages.

Making Your Own Arrangements

Are you a totally independent traveler? Maybe you're a control freak and can't stand even a single detail being out of your hands; or you're into spontaneity and hate having anything prearranged except for what's absolutely essential (like, say, your flight). Or perhaps you just like to be on your own. Whatever your reason, I'm happy to supply some basic transportation data for those who want to make their own arrangements.

Finding out who flies where

Where you arrive depends on the city you're flying from and your airline. Most regularly scheduled international flights from the United States, Canada, Australia, and New Zealand arrive at London's Heathrow and Gatwick airports. Flights from the Continent land at Heathrow, Gatwick, Stansted, or London City. A destination for charter flights from the Continent is Luton, the smallest of London's airports. International airports are also in Birmingham and Manchester, but I wouldn't recommend flying into either place unless you plan to skip London entirely. Here's a brief description of each of the five London airports, who flies to them, and how to travel from them to Central London (see the Appendix for the contact information of the airlines mentioned):

- **Heathrow,** the main international airport, is 15 miles west of Central London. It's served by Air Canada (flights from Calgary, Montreal, Ottawa, Toronto, Vancouver, and St. John's); Air New Zealand (flights from Australia and New Zealand); American (flights from Boston, Chicago, Los Angeles, New York, and Miami); British Airways (U.S. flights from Boston, Chicago, Detroit, Los Angeles, Miami, Newark, New York JFK, Philadelphia, San Francisco, Seattle, and Washington Dulles; Australian flights from Brisbane, Melbourne, Perth, and Sydney; New Zealand flights from Auckland); Continental (flights from Los Angeles, New York JFK, Newark, San Francisco, and Washington Dulles); Icelandair (flights from Baltimore, Boston, Minneapolis/St. Paul, and New York JFK); Qantas (flights from Melbourne, Perth, and Sydney, Australia, and Auckland, New Zealand); United (flights from Boston, Chicago, Los Angeles, Newark, New York JFK, San Francisco, and Washington Dulles); Virgin Atlantic (flights from Chicago, Newark, New York JFK, San Francisco, and Washington Dulles)

  From Heathrow, you can get into London on the Underground (the Tube) in about 40 minutes for £3.70 ($6). The Heathrow Express Train travels between Heathrow and Paddington Station (in 15 minutes) for £11.70 ($18), and the Airbus runs to Victoria and Euston rail stations (in about 75 minutes) for £8 ($11).

- **Gatwick** is a smaller airport about 25 miles south of London. It's served by American (flights from Boston, Dallas/Ft. Worth, and Raleigh/Durham); British Airways (flights from Atlanta, Baltimore, Charlotte, Dallas/Ft. Worth, Denver, Houston, New York JFK, Miami, Orlando, Phoenix, and Tampa); Delta (flights from Atlanta and Cincinnati); Continental (flights from Boston, Cleveland, Houston, Miami, Newark, and Orlando); Northwest (flights from Detroit and Minneapolis/St. Paul); Qantas (flight from Sydney, Australia); and Virgin Atlantic (flights from Boston, Las Vegas, Miami, Newark, Orlando, and San Francisco).

  Gatwick Express trains travel from the airport to Victoria Station in Central London in about half an hour for £11.20 ($18).

- **Stansted,** 50 miles northeast of London, handles national and European flights. The Stansted Sky Train to Liverpool Street Station takes 45 minutes and costs £13 ($21).

- **London City,** only 6 miles east of Central London, services European destinations. A bus charges £5 ($8) to take passengers on the 25-minute trip from the airport to Liverpool Street Station.

- **Luton,** 28 miles northwest of London, services mostly charter flights. Travel by train from the airport to King's Cross Station for £9.50 ($15); the trip takes about an hour.

Snagging the best airfare

If you need flexibility, be ready to pay for it. Full-price fare usually applies to last-minute bookings, sudden itinerary changes, and round trips that get you home before the weekend.

You pay far less than full fare if you book well in advance, can stay over Saturday night, or can travel on Tuesday, Wednesday, or Thursday. A ticket bought as little as 7 or 14 days in advance costs only 20% to 30% of the full fare. If you can travel with just a couple days' notice, you may also get a deal (usually on a weekend fare that you book through an airline's Web site — see the section "Getting away on the weekend," later in this chapter, for more).

Airlines periodically lower prices on their most popular routes (such as London). Restrictions abound, but the sales translate into great prices — usually no more than $400 for a transatlantic flight to London from the East Coast. You may also score a deal when an airline introduces a new route or increases service to an existing one.

Watch newspaper and television ads and airline Web sites, and when you see a good price, grab it. These sales usually run during slow seasons (in England, November 1 to December 12 and December 25 to March 14) and rarely coincide with peak travel times (late April to mid-October in England), when people often fly regardless of price.

See the next three sections for information on how consolidators and airline Web sites can save you big money.

Using consolidators to cut ticket cost

Consolidators, also known as bucket shops, are good places to find low fares. Consolidators buy seats in bulk and resell them at prices that undercut the airlines' discounted rates. Be aware that tickets bought this way are usually nonrefundable or carry stiff cancellation penalties (as much as 75% of the ticket price). *Note:* Before you pay, ask the consolidator for a confirmation number and then call the airline to confirm your seat. Be prepared to book your ticket through a different consolidator if the airline can't confirm your reservation.

Consolidators' small ads usually appear in major newspapers' Sunday travel sections at the bottom of the page. **STA Travel** (☎ **800/781-4040;** `www.statravel.com`) caters to young travelers. Other reliable consolidators include **1-800-FLY-CHEAP** (☎ **800/359-2432;** `www.flycheap.com`); **TFI Tours International** (☎ **800/745-8000** or 212/736-1140) serves as a clearinghouse for unused seats; and *rebaters,* such as **Travel Avenue** (☎ **800/333-3335** or 312/876-1116; www.travelavenue.com), rebate part of its commissions to you.

Surfing for deals on the Web

Use the Internet to search for deals on airfare, hotels, and car rentals. Among the leading Web sites are **Frommers.com** (www.frommers.com), **Travelocity** (www.travelocity.com), **Lowestfare** (www.lowestfare.com), **Microsoft Expedia** (www.expedia.com), **The Trip** (www.thetrip.com), **Smarter Living** (www.smarterliving.com), and **Yahoo!** (http://travel.yahoo.com).

Each site provides roughly the same service, with variations that you may find useful or useless. Enter your travel dates and route, and the computer searches for the lowest fares. Several other features are standard, and periodic bell-and-whistle updates make occasional visits worthwhile. You can check flights at different times or on different dates in hopes of finding a lower price, sign up for e-mail alerts that tell you when the fare on a route that you specified drops below a certain level, and gain access to databases that advertise cheap packages and fares for those who can get away at a moment's notice.

Remember that you don't have to book online; you can ask your flesh-and-blood travel agent to match or beat the best price you find.

Getting away on the weekend

Airlines make great last-minute deals available through their Web sites once a week, usually on Wednesday. Flights generally leave on Friday or Saturday (that is, only two or three days later) and return the following Sunday, Monday, or Tuesday. Some carriers offer hotel and car bargains at the same time.

You can sign up for e-mail alerts through individual Web sites or all at once through **Smarter Living** (www.smarterliving.com). If you already know what airline you want to fly, consider staying up late on Tuesday and checking the Web site until the bargains for the coming weekend appear. Book right away and avoid losing out on the limited number of seats.

Arriving Via the Channel or Chunnel

If you're traveling to London from another destination in Europe, flying isn't the only way to get there. Train and car ferries and high-speed hovercrafts cross the English Channel throughout the year from ports in France, Holland, and Belgium. And the Eurostar high-speed train zips beneath the channel through the Chunnel, a tunnel beneath the English Channel.

Taking the train

London has several train stations, and the one you arrive at depends on your point of departure from the Continent. The three-hour Eurostar service connecting Paris and Brussels to London via the Chunnel arrives at **Waterloo International Station.** Trains from Amsterdam arrive at **Liverpool Street Station.** Other London train stations include **Victoria, Paddington, King's Cross,** and **Euston Station.** Every London train station has an Underground link.

The trains in England and the rest of the United Kingdom are separate from those in continental Europe, so a Eurail pass isn't valid in the U.K. If you're going to travel within England or the rest of the United Kingdom, check out the various **BritRail passes** available by calling **RailEurope** at ☎ **877/272-RAIL** in the U.S., or 800/361-RAIL in Canada, or by going online to `www.raileurope.com`. (For more on BritRail passes, see Chapter 7.)

Several types of Eurostar fares are available. Senior fares for those over 60 and youth fares for those under 26 can cut the price of a first-class fare ($279 at press time) by 20% or more. The same reductions apply for passengers traveling with validated Eurail and BritRail passes. To check out current and special promotional fares for Eurostar, visit RailEurope's Web site at `www.raileurope.com`.

Riding a ferry or hovercraft

Crossing time for the car, train, and passenger ferries that regularly crisscross the English Channel can be anywhere from 90 minutes to 5 hours, depending on the point of departure. Various hovercrafts (high-speed ferries with propellers that lift them off the surface of the water) skim over the water in as little as half an hour. The price of any European train ticket that has London as its final destination includes these channel crossings. Frequent train service to London is available from all the channel ports. The following is a list of the major ferry and hovercraft companies:

- **Hoverspeed UK Limited** (☎ **08705/240-241** in the U.K.; `www.hoverspeed.co.uk`) operates hovercrafts that zip across the channel between Calais and Dover in 35 minutes; the SuperseaCats (jet-propelled catamarans) run between Newhaven and Dieppe in 55 minutes.

- **P&O European Ferries (☎ 561/563-2856** in the U.S. or 870/242-4999 in the U.K.; www.poportsmith.com) offers daily ferry/car crossings between Cherbourg and Portsmouth (crossing time is five hours) and Le Havre and Portsmouth (5½ hours).
- **P&O Stena Line (☎ 561/563-2856** in the U.S. or 0870/600-0600 in the U.K.; www.posl.com) operates ferries between Calais and Dover (crossing time is 75 minutes).
- **Sea France Limited (☎ 01304/212-696** in the U.K.; www.seafrance.co.uk) runs ferries between Dover and Calais (crossing time is 90 minutes).

Chapter 7

Getting around England

In This Chapter

- Traveling through England by train
- Seeing the country by bus
- Deciding whether driving is for you
- Renting a car

Because of England's small size and easy access to train and road networks, the country is a joy to explore. Many cities and sites are workable as day trips from London. You can reach Bath, Brighton, and Canterbury from London in 90 minutes or less by train and in about two hours by car or bus. The trip to Stratford-upon-Avon or to Salisbury (the closest large town to Stonehenge) is about two hours by train and about three hours by car or bus. If London is your home base and you get an early start, you can explore any one of these places, have lunch, and be back in London in time for dinner.

I strongly recommend that you explore at least a portion of England that has nothing to do with London. Out of the city and in the countryside or an ancient village, the quiet magic of this country comes over you like a spell.

This chapter helps you decide whether train travel, bus travel, or automotion is for you.

Riding the Rails

In England, people still take trains to travel around the country. I do, too. I recommend traveling by train over all other forms of transportation — especially if you're a first-time visitor to England. Traveling by train is fun, safe, and convenient. In smaller cities, the train stations are never more than a few minutes' walk or a simple bus ride from the town center. If you want to explore the countryside, taking a train to a new city and then renting a car is easy.

The current state of English trains

Prime Minister Margaret Thatcher privatized the entire railway system in the 1980s. Twenty-five companies now operate trains to specific parts of the country. (Virgin, Connex, and Great Western are three of the major companies.) But following what many Brits consider an unacceptable standard of service (primarily concerning delayed and cancelled trains), some Brits are once again talking about re-nationalizing the railroads.

The sleek, high-speed **Intercity trains** that run between London and heavily traveled main-line routes are the most dependable and comfortable trains you can take. You can ride these fast trains to York, Stratford-upon-Avon, Bath and Cheltenham (both good bases for exploring the Cotswolds), Oxenholme (closest station to the Lake District), Exeter (in Devon), and Penzance (in Cornwall). For shorter trips, such as to Brighton and Cambridge, you can take a **commuter train.** In some cases, you may need to transfer to a **local train** to reach your destination.

The local trains connect larger towns to smaller ones and are very basic. Unlike all other trains, local trains don't have toilets or food service. Smoking isn't permitted on local trains, and it's confined to strictly designated areas on commuter and Intercity trains. The local stations are small; sometimes (particularly on Sunday) no one is available to help with information or ticket sales. You always find train schedules posted in the local stations, and if no window service is available, you can buy your ticket on the train.

For the most current train schedules and fares, call **National Rail Enquiries** at ☎ **08457/484-950** in the United Kingdom. You can also find timetable information online at `www.nationalrail.com`, but always call National Rail Enquiries to verify schedules.

An announcement is made before the train arrives at each station. Station stops are short, so be ready to disembark when the train comes to a halt. In newer trains, you push a well-marked button to open the door automatically. In older trains, you need to open the door yourself. It may open from the inside, or you may have to open the window and reach outside to turn the door handle.

Buying your train ticket

You can purchase your train ticket with cash or credit card at a ticket window in the train station. If the windows are closed, you must buy your ticket on the train with cash. If you have a BritRail pass (see "Saving with BritRail passes," later in this chapter), you don't have to bother with buying tickets; just board the train.

In England, a one-way train ticket is a *single*. A round-trip ticket is a *return*. If you go on a day trip, ask for a *day return*.

When you buy your ticket, you must choose between first and standard (second) class. First-class tickets cost about one-third more than standard class. The first-class cars have roomier seats, but you can travel quite comfortably in standard class. If you want a first-class ticket, you must request one — otherwise, the agent will probably sell you a standard-class ticket.

First-class service on some Intercity train routes includes free coffee, tea, beverages, and snacks served at your seat, plus a free newspaper and a higher standard of personal service. Standard-class passengers can buy sandwiches and drinks in a cafe car. On some lines, an employee comes through with a food and beverage trolley.

Local trains don't offer first-class service or food service.

Negotiating the rail system

The British rail system is currently in something of a crisis. It has seriously deteriorated since being privatized in the 1980s and is in the midst of a multibillion-pound, five-year restoration plan. Hopefully, things will improve by 2008. In the meantime, management frequently cancels trains, departure tracks change without notice, service can be slow and sporadic (especially on Sunday), maintenance can be poor, and railway employees don't always have the correct information to help you on your journey.

For all these reasons, I urge you to keep your wits about you when traveling by train in England. Keep the following in mind:

- Always call **National Rail Enquiries (☎ 08457/484-950)** the night before your train trip to verify departure times and departure stations.
- Whenever possible, **choose a direct train** over one that requires a change along the way. In some cases, trains going to the same destination (such as Canterbury or Dover) depart from different London stations. Ask National Rail Enquiries or information agents at the station for the quickest and most direct routes to a destination.
- Tracks can change without an announcement, so always **verify with a railway employee** *before you board* that the train is going to your destination.
- On some lines, **Sunday is one of the worst days to travel** because there are fewer trains and they tend to be slow. Track work often takes place on Sunday, sometimes causing long delays or requiring that you complete part of the journey by bus.

Getting to know London's train stations

One of the busiest transportation hubs in the world, London has 11 major stations, so getting to the right station to catch your train is important. (Throughout this book, I always tell you which London station serves the destination that I'm describing.) The Underground (subway) serves all London's train stations. In every station, a large overhead display, usually near the platforms, lists the departing trains and platforms.

If you travel around England or the rest of the United Kingdom from London, you'll depart from one of the following stations:

- **Charing Cross Station:** Trains from here travel southeast to Canterbury, Hastings, Dover, and English Channel ports that connect with ferry service to the Continent.
- **Euston Station:** Trains from this station head north to the Lake District and up to Scotland.
- **King's Cross Station:** Trains from here travel to destinations in the east of England, including Cambridge and York.
- **Liverpool Street Station:** Trains from this station head to English Channel ports with continuing service to the Netherlands, northern Germany, and Scandinavia.
- **Paddington Station:** Trains from Paddington travel southwest to Bath, Plymouth, and Penzance in Cornwall, stopping at cities along the way.
- **St. Pancras Station:** Currently being renovated, this station will eventually provide expanded Eurostar service to Paris and Brussels from the Midlands.
- **Victoria Station:** Head here for trains traveling to the south and southeast of England, including Canterbury, Brighton, and Gatwick Airport.
- **Waterloo International:** Primarily for trains going to the south of England, Waterloo International, which is connected to Waterloo Station, is the place to catch Eurostar trains to and from Paris and Brussels.

Saving with BritRail passes

If you plan to travel around England by train, consider purchasing a **BritRail pass** before you arrive. BritRail passes are really convenient because you don't have to stand in line to buy train tickets; if a train is in the station, you can just hop on. In peak summer travel months, you may want to reserve your seat, which you can do for a small fee.

BritRail passes are sold only outside the United Kingdom; therefore, you must purchase them *before* you arrive in England. You can order the passes through a travel agent or by contacting **RailEurope** (☎ **877/272-RAIL** in the U.S., or 800/361-RAIL in Canada; `www.raileurope.com`). The various kinds of BritRail passes are

- The **BritRail Days Out from London Pass** covers a large area around London and gets you to Cambridge, Oxford, Canterbury, Dover, Winchester, Salisbury, and as far west as Exeter in Devon. With this pass, the cost for first-class travel for any two days in an eight-day period is $89 for adults and $31 for children (5 to 15 years); standard class is $59 for adults and $21 for children. Four- and seven-day Days Out from London Passes are also available. The first-class, round-trip full fare between London and Exeter is approximately $334, so with this pass you save money the farther you travel from London (within the allowed area). If you take day trips only to Hampton Court Palace and Windsor, for example, you're better off paying the regular train fares.
- A **BritRail Flexipass** allows you to travel any 4, 8, or 15 days within a two-month time period. A four-day, first-class Flexipass is $355 for adults, $305 for seniors over 60, and $177.50 for children (5 to 15 years). In standard class, the four-day pass is $239 for adults and $119 for children (there's no standard-class senior rate). The Flexipass allows you to visit Wales and Scotland.
- A **BritRail Classic Pass** is good if you're going to be on the go, visiting all of England, over a specific number of consecutive days. An eight-day, first-class Classic pass is $405 for adults, $345 for seniors over 60, and $202.50 for children 5 to 15. An eight-day standard-class pass costs $269 for adults, $134 for children (standard class is not available for seniors). The Classic Pass allows you to wander into Wales and Scotland.

- The **BritRail Family Pass** makes traveling with kids cheaper and easier. Buy any adult or senior pass, and you get a free youth pass (ages 5 to 15) of the same type and duration. Children under 5 travel free at all times.

Hopping a Coach: Bus Travel

A long-distance touring bus in England is a *coach.* (Buses are what you take for local transportation.) The main long-distance coach company is National Express. Its routes cover the entire country, and its comfortable coaches are equipped with reclining seats and a toilet; they often have food and beverage service. Tickets are usually half of what the train costs, and even cheaper if you buy a return ticket. The one drawback, at least for the busy traveler without much extra time, is that coaches take at least one or two hours longer than the train.

If you travel around England by coach from London, you'll depart from **Victoria Coach Station,** Buckingham Palace Road (☎ **020/7730-3466;** Tube: Victoria), located just two blocks from Victoria Station. Coach stations in cities outside of London are always close to the city center, often next to the train station. For information on travel by coach, contact **National Express** (☎ **0990/808-080**); you can view schedules and fares online at www.nationalexpress.co.uk.

National Express offers a **Tourist Trail Pass** for unlimited travel on its extensive network, which covers all England. A two-day pass costs £49 ($78) adult and £39 ($62) child 5 to 15 years; a five-day pass for use within any 30 consecutive days costs £85 ($136) for adults and £69 ($110) for kids. An eight-day pass is also available.

Driving on the Left, Passing on the Right: Car Travel

I always suggest that people travel through England by train instead of car. Much of a long-distance car trip can be spent on motorways without much scenery, so what's the point? But some people want to drive, no matter what. And having a car opens up whole regions of the English countryside for exploration. In areas, such as the Cotswolds, where trains don't serve villages and local bus service is sporadic or infrequent, having a car is almost a necessity. Additionally, parts of Cornwall and the Lake District aren't accessible by train or bus.

If you're a nervous driver at home, in your own car, don't put yourself through the ordeal of driving in England. Before you even consider renting a car, ask yourself whether you'd be comfortable driving with a steering wheel on the right-hand side of the vehicle while shifting with your left hand. (You can get an automatic, but it costs considerably more money.) Remember, you must drive on the left and pass on the right.

Renting a car in London — or not

Having a car in London is far more of a hassle than a help for the following reasons:

- Finding your way through the city in heavy traffic while driving on the *left-hand side* of the road can turn even the best American driver into a gibbering nut case.
- Maneuvering through London's congested and complicated maze of streets can be an endurance test even for Londoners.
- Parking is difficult to find and expensive. (Street meters cost £1/$1.60 for 20 minutes.)

- Just entering central London on weekdays will set you back £5 ($8); for details, see the box "Cough up for the congestion charge," later in this chapter.
- Paying for gas (*petrol* in Britspeak) costs almost £3 (over $4.50) a gallon.
- Riding public transportation — especially the Underground — gets you everywhere you want to go at a fraction of the cost.

Do yourself a favor: Forget about renting a car in London. If you want to be with Londoners on their own turf (or in their own tunnels), the Tube (Underground) is a great way to do it. Even if you plan excursions outside London, the trains are a better option than a car. If you need a car to explore the countryside, you can rent one in a hub city or town after you arrive by train.

Renting a car in England

Although the car-rental market in Britain is highly competitive, renting a car in England costs more than in the United States — unless, that is, you can find a special promotional offer from an airline or a car-rental agency. When I last rented a car in England, in 2002, without benefit of any special offers, the total cost was more than $300 for a four-day rental of a compact car with manual transmission. That price included unlimited mileage and all the insurance but not gas *(petrol),* which added another $60.

Car-rental rates vary even more than airline fares. The price depends on a host of factors, including car size, the length of time you keep it, where and when you pick the car up and drop it off, and how far you drive it.

If you decide to rent a car while you're in England and you haven't made a reservation, look in the local Yellow Pages under *Car Hire.* Smaller local companies are usually less expensive than large, international ones. However, the larger companies usually offer newer cars and some give you the option of picking up the car in one location and returning it to another.

Asking a few key questions can save you hundreds of dollars. What follows are factors to keep in mind when renting a car:

- You can often get a lower car-rental rate if you reserve seven days in advance using a toll-free reservations number. (See the Appendix for a list of international car-rental firms that rent cars in England.)
- Find out whether the quoted price includes the 17.5% value-added tax (VAT). (See Chapter 9 for more on this tax.)
- If you plan to do much driving, a rental package with unlimited mileage is your best option.

- Weekend rates may be lower than weekday rates.
- If you keep the car for five or more days, a weekly rate may be cheaper than the daily rate.
- The rate may be cheaper if you pick up the car at a central town office rather than at an airport.
- Don't forget to mention membership in AAA, AARP, frequent-flier programs, and trade unions. These affiliations usually entitle you to discounts ranging from 5 to 30%. Check with your travel agent about any and all of these rates.
- Most car rentals are worth at least 500 miles on your frequent-flier account.
- Some airlines offer package deals that include car rental. (See Chapter 6 for more on package tours.)

In addition to the standard rental prices, other optional charges apply to most car rentals. Many credit-card companies cover the *Collision Damage Waiver* (CDW), which requires you to pay for damage to the car in a collision. Check with your credit-card company before you go so you can avoid paying this hefty fee (as much as $15 per day).

The car-rental companies also offer *additional liability insurance* (if you harm others in an accident), *personal accident insurance* (if you harm yourself or your passengers), and *personal effects insurance* (if your luggage is stolen from your car). If you have insurance on your car at home, you're probably covered for most of these unlikelihoods. If your own insurance doesn't cover you for rentals, or if you don't have auto insurance, consider the additional coverage.

Although not as common a practice as in the United States, some international companies also offer *refueling packages,* in which you pay for an entire tank of gas upfront. The price is usually fairly competitive with local gas prices, but you don't get credit for any gas remaining in the tank. If you reject this option, you pay only for the gas you use, but you have to return the car with a full tank or face costly per-gallon charges for any shortfall. If you think that a stop at a gas station on the way back to the airport will make you miss your plane, then take advantage of the fuel purchase option. Otherwise, skip it.

Americans renting a car in England need a valid U.S. driver's license that they've had for at least one year. The same holds true for Canadians, Australians, and New Zealanders. In most cases, depending on the agency, you must be at least 23 years old (21 in some instances, 25 in others) and no older than 70. (Some companies have raised this to 75.)

As with other aspects of planning your trip, using the Internet can make comparison-shopping for a car rental much easier. The major booking Web sites — **Travelocity** (`www.travelocity.com`), **Expedia** (`www.expedia.com`), and **Yahoo Travel** (`http://travel.yahoo.com`), for example — have search engines that can dig up discounted car-rental rates. Just enter the car size you want, the pickup and return dates, and the city where you want to rent, and the server returns a price. You can even make the reservation through these sites.

Hitting the road: Motorways, dual carriageways, and roundabouts

What is commonly known as a freeway in some countries, the Brits call a *motorway*. England has a good motorway network. Don't stop on a motorway (indicated as *M* plus a number on maps) unless you have an emergency. No toll is charged to drive on British motorways if you're going to any of the places described in this guide.

The English call a two-way road a *single carriageway* and a four-lane divided highway (two lanes in each direction) a *dual carriageway*. Country roads, some of them paved-over tracks dating back centuries, are full of twists and turns and often barely wide enough for two cars to pass. One element of British roads that invariably throws non-native drivers is the *roundabout* — traffic junctions where several roads meet at one traffic circle. On a roundabout, the cars to your right (that is, those already on the roundabout) always have the right of way.

Before you arrive in England, or before you leave on your car journey, find and purchase a good quality, large-scale road map. I recommend one with a scale of 3 miles to 1 inch or 2 kilometers to 1 centimeter.

On certain sections of the motorway, where speeding is especially dangerous, speed cameras have been installed. The cameras take a photograph of any car exceeding the speed limit so that the police can trace the culprit. You'll see a camera symbol on entering these areas. Surveillance cameras have also been installed at some traffic lights to catch anyone who doesn't stop for the red.

Cough up for the congestion charge

Traffic in central London was such a snarl that in February 2003, a new congestion charge went into effect. Drivers must now pay £5 ($8) to enter central London from 7 a.m. to 6:30 p.m. Monday through Friday. Payment is made online (`www.cclondon.com`), at retail outlets, or by phone (☎ 0845/900-1234). There are no tollbooths, but high-tech cameras read the plate numbers of all cars entering the charge zone and match them to a database; if you haven't paid by 10 p.m., you'll be fined. The Inner Ring Road forms the boundary for the congestion charge.

Following the rules of the road

You need to know some general facts if you're going to drive in England:

- All distances and speed limits are shown in miles and miles per hour (mph). If you need to translate from the metric system, a kilometer is 0.62 of a mile, and a mile is 1.62 kilometers. Speed limits are usually
  - 30mph (48kph) in towns
  - 40mph (65kph) on some town roads where posted
  - 60mph (97kph) on most single carriageway (2-way) roads
  - 70mph (113kph) on dual carriageways and motorways
- Road signs are usually the standard international signs. Buy a booklet (available at many shops and in airports) called *Highway Code* for about £1 ($1.60) before you set out. The information in this book is essential for driving in England.
- The law requires you to wear a seat belt. If you have children, make sure that you ask the car-rental agency about seat belts or car seats before you rent.
- At roundabouts, traffic coming from the right has the right of way.
- You can pass other vehicles only on the right.
- Parking in the center of most big towns is difficult and expensive. Make sure that you read all posted restrictions, or park in a lot.
- You must stop for pedestrians in cross walks marked by striped lines (called *zebra crossings*) on the road. Pedestrians have the right of way.

Coping with emergencies on the road

All motorways have emergency telephones stationed a kilometer apart. Markers at every tenth of a kilometer point to the nearest phone. The phone operator can obtain emergency or automotive services if you require them. If you must pull over to the side of the motorway, park as near to the far edge of the shoulder as possible. Motorway service stations are usually about 25 miles apart and occasionally as far as 50 miles apart.

Filling up the tank

Petrol (gasoline) stations are self-service. The green filler pipe is for unleaded petrol, the red filler pipe is for leaded petrol, and the black filler pipe is for diesel fuel.

The royal fast lane

In 2001, Princess Anne, the 50-year-old daughter of Queen Elizabeth, was found guilty of driving her Bentley at 93 mph in a 70 mph zone on a two-lane road in rural Gloucestershire. The princess had a unique defense: She claimed that she thought the police cars flashing their lights behind her were offering an escort, so she didn't slow down. A local magistrate fined her $700.

Making the mistake of filling up a car with diesel fuel instead of petrol is easy. Make sure that you use the green gas pump.

Petrol is often cheapest at supermarkets. (Yes, they may have pumps outside.) But going to a motorway service station is more convenient. Petrol is purchased by the liter (3.78 liters equals one gallon). Expect to pay about 84p ($1.35) per liter (approximately $4.80 per gallon) for unleaded petrol.

Chapter 8

Booking Your Accommodations

In This Chapter

- Checking out the options
- Getting the best room for the best rate
- Surfing for cyberdeals
- Landing a room without a reservation

Chant this as your mantra: "I will not arrive in London without a hotel reservation. I will not arrive in . . ." Reserving a room is especially important if you plan to be in London from mid-April to early October (high season). If you arrive in London with a hotel reservation, you don't have to waste your precious time trying to find a place to stay.

Booking ahead isn't quite as important in the rest of England, but I recommend that you do it — particularly if you're going to spend a Friday or Saturday night in a major tourist spot like Stratford-upon-Avon, or in a resort town like Brighton. Hotels in popular tourist areas, such as the Cotswolds, Cornwall, and the Lake District, also fill up fast in July and August. Off-season, and especially in the middle of winter, you won't have a problem booking a room on the spot, wherever you are. In a small village, finding a room may be as simple as seeing a "room-to-let" sign in the front window of a house.

You find tourist information centers in all the larger towns and in the national parks, and they can always help you find a room. In most cases, tourist information centers charge 10% of the first night's hotel rate, but you get that back at the hotel, so the service ends up costing nothing.

Finding the Place That's Right for You

Accommodations in England are available in varying price ranges and degrees of luxury. Places to stay generally fit into one of two categories: hotels and bed-and-breakfast inns (B&Bs).

The situation in London — one of Europe's most visited cities — is different from the rest of England. The selection of hotels is far greater than you'll find elsewhere in England, and they cost considerably more money. But London does offer good budget hotels and plenty of B&Bs that won't render you unconscious when you see the bill. If you have a few more dollars (*pounds,* that is) to throw around, you can choose from unique boutique hotels, large chain hotels, and several ultra-luxurious places. Other options include self-catering hotels (where the rooms come equipped with small kitchens) or a fully equipped flat (apartment).

Outside London, prices generally drop by half for small B&Bs and by about one-third or more for hotels. The distinction between B&B and hotel is less obvious outside of the capital because most places, even large hotels, include breakfast with the room, which isn't the case at most high-end hotels in London. In small towns and rural villages, you can also experience a "real" B&B — a home where a family resides and rents out maybe one or two bedrooms. You can also find marvelous country-house hotels, where the service is impeccable and the prices astronomical. Away from the big city, many hotels also offer dinner to guests for a special *half board* rate.

Brits and Europeans in general aren't as committed to smoke-free environments as Americans are. But this attitude is beginning to change. More and more hotels and B&Bs in England reserve special rooms or an entire floor for nonsmokers. In my hotel descriptions, I always note completely smoke-free hotels.

The following sections provide a rundown on the quirks and perks of each type of accommodation.

Understanding the pros and cons of B&Bs

Bed-and-breakfast inns (B&Bs) in England are different from what you may have experienced elsewhere. Most are former — usually old — homes, and the comfort and service vary widely. (Some are current homes where you stay with the family.) The plumbing can be unpredictable, as can the water temperature. Space is often scarce. But they do offer a slice of domestic life that you can't get in a larger, more anonymous hotel.

Because B&Bs are often private homes and not hotels, typical amenities can also vary widely, especially in the bathroom facilities. Nearly all B&B rooms contain washbasins, but you may have to share a bathroom down the hall. The facilities are usually kept scrupulously clean, but many travelers prefer private bathrooms. Keep in mind, however, that *en-suite* (in the room) bathrooms are generally so small that you feel as if you haven't left the airplane, and squeezing into the super-tiny showers can be a trial.

The decor in many of the lowest priced B&Bs is fairly unimpressive. Coming back to a small room with mismatched furniture, avocado walls, and a tiny bathroom down the hall with no hot water may be an inconvenience you're willing to suffer for saving money, but I don't recommend any such places in this guide. The more popular and well-appointed B&Bs are, of course, more expensive, but their comforts and conveniences are worth the price.

What about the breakfast part of the B&B? Well, gone are the days when the staff of every B&B cooked you up a *full English breakfast* (also known as a *fry-up*) of eggs, sausages, bacon, fried tomatoes, and beans. Many still do — especially outside London — but others put out a *continental buffet,* which consists of cereals, fruits, and breads. The B&B descriptions in this book say "rate includes English breakfast" or "rate includes continental breakfast," so you know what to expect.

Licensed B&Bs, like hotels, are inspected regularly, and the quality of B&Bs has improved greatly over the years. I recommend them for people who don't require many extras, although the most successful B&Bs continually upgrade their services or offer some enticing amenities. For example, many B&Bs now provide cable TV and direct-dial phones in the rooms.

If you're physically disabled or infirm in any way, B&Bs may not be the choice for you. B&Bs usually don't have elevators, so you may have to carry your luggage up steep, narrow stairs. Be sure to check how accessible the B&B is before making reservations.

Exploring hotel choices

England boasts a wide choice of hotels. Some inexpensive ones provide breakfast with a room rental; others charge an additional fee for the most important meal of the day. At a four- or five-star hotel, you pay a hefty price to eat breakfast on the premises. The guest rooms at a self-catering hotel (see the section "Self-catering options," later in this chapter, for more on these rooms) are equipped with small kitchens so that you can make breakfast in your room.

Boutique and deluxe hotels

London offers a few *boutique hotels,* which you won't really find outside of the city. These hotels, such as the **Covent Garden Hotel** (see Chapter 11), are midrange in size but not price; sumptuously furnished, they offer state-of-the-art amenities and full service.

Older deluxe hotels, full of charm and character, offer a distinctly English style. Older London hotels, such as **The Gore** or **Hazlitt's 1718,** have been around for a century or more (see Chapter 11). Outside London, you can routinely find hotels (such as **The Mermaid Inn,** in Rye; see Chapter 14) that served as coaching inns 400 years ago. Perhaps the most atmospheric hotels in England, they're full of twisting stairways and oak-beamed bedrooms (the bathrooms are always modern, however).

Chain properties

Maybe you *always* stay at one of the chain hotels — a **Hyatt,** a **Sheraton,** a **Best Western,** or a **Marriott.** These newer places are basically the same no matter where they are: They rely on their brand name and a no-surprise approach to win customers. London is chock-full of chain hotels, if that's what you fancy. Outside the capital, you also find chain hotels in most medium-size towns and in tourist-heavy areas (such as the Lake District), but the names may be unfamiliar to you. **Thistle** is one reliable British chain to look for. Its hotels aren't always new; some are in historic properties. Most chain hotels cater to large groups, and you may feel rather anonymous in them. On the other hand, these hotels are usually well equipped for people with disabilities and families with children. For a list of chain hotels in England, see the Appendix.

Landmark and country-house hotels

At the top of the hotel spectrum, in both price and prestige, are the landmark hotels and country-house hotels. In London, the **Dorchester, Claridge's,** the **Park Lane Sheraton Hotel,** and the **Savoy** (see Chapter 11) rank among the world's best hotels. You can expect glamorous public salons (and glamorous fellow guests), a generously proportioned and well-decorated room with a large private bath, an on-site health club or access to one nearby, and top-of-the-line service.

Country-house hotels are a world onto themselves. Former private estates, set within landscaped gardens, they typify a world of privilege and tradition and work hard to make their guests feel pampered and comfortable. You can always expect fine gourmet cooking and a full range of amenities, including room service and an on-site health club. **Gidleigh Park** in Devon and **Middlethorpe Hall** in Yorkshire are two outstanding country-house hotels (see Chapters 17 and 21, respectively).

Self-catering options

In London, you can also consider staying at a *self-catering hotel,* where *you* do the cooking in your own hotel room. (**Aston's Apartments** in London [see Chapter 11] is the only self-catering hotel I list in this guide.) For short stays and for one or two people, self-catering hotels don't always beat the competition's price. But for families and people who can't afford or don't want to eat every meal out, self-catering hotels can be a budget-saver. Outside of London, you find few self-catering hotels; instead, you find self-catering flats (apartments) or holiday homes that you can rent for a week or more.

Getting the Best Room Rate

The rate you pay for a room depends on many factors, the most important being the way you make your reservation. The strategies in this section will help you get the best rate available.

Beating the rack rate

The maximum rate that a hotel charges for a type of room is the *rack rate.* If you walk in off the street and ask for a room for the night, the hotel may charge you this top rate. Be aware that you don't always have to pay the rack rate in big and some medium-size hotels! Hardly anybody does. Just ask for a cheaper or discounted rate. The result is often favorable when savvy travelers make this request at larger hotels. Prices aren't quite so negotiable at smaller hotels and bed-and-breakfasts (B&Bs), but asking never hurts. Many B&Bs offer special rates for longer stays or if you're there off-season.

Calling around

Call your prospective hotel's toll-free number (if there is one) and the local number. Calling both sources takes time and money, but the quoted rates can vary so widely that you may save a bundle.

Asking about discounts

If you make your reservation with a large chain hotel, mention membership in AARP, frequent-flier programs, and any other corporate rewards program. Budget hotels and small B&Bs rarely offer these organization discounts, but you never know unless you ask.

Traveling in the off-season and on weekends

Room rates change as occupancy rates rise and fall. You're less likely to receive discount rates if a hotel is close to full, but if it's close to empty, you probably can negotiate a significant discount. Expensive hotels catering to business travelers are most crowded on weekdays and usually offer discounts for weekend stays.

You may be able to save 20% or more by traveling *off-season,* which is mid-October to mid-December and January to March.

Choosing a package tour

The best rates of all hotels and B&Bs are probably with a package tour that includes airfare and hotel (see Chapter 6). With these packages, which are sometimes astonishingly cheap, you have to choose a hotel that's part of the package. The hotels included in packages offered by airlines tend to be larger chains. So what? The money you save may amount to hundreds of dollars.

Using a travel agent

Checking with travel agents is wise, too. A travel agent may be able to negotiate a better room rate than you can. (The hotel gives the agent a discount in exchange for steering his or her business toward that hotel.)

Agents can usually find you a good package deal. To give you an example: In 2003, through a travel agent, friends of mine booked a two-week package in May that included airfare from Portland, Oregon, to London via Seattle (the closest international hub); ten nights in a four-star London hotel; a seven-day Travelcard for London bus and Underground; a trip to Paris on the Eurostar train; three nights in a fine Paris hotel; and flight back from Paris. The cost was $2,200 per person for everything except meals. And this package was in two of the world's most expensive cities. I'm not saying you can duplicate this trip or pricing with your travel agent, but I'm recommending that you see what kind of bargain a travel agent can find for you.

Surfing the Web for Hotel Deals

Another great source for finding hotel deals is the Internet. Although the major travel-booking Web sites (`Frommers.com`, Travelocity,

Microsoft Expedia, Yahoo!, and Smarter Living; see Chapter 6 for details) offer hotel booking, try using a Web site devoted to lodging, because more general sites don't list all types of properties. Some lodging sites specialize in a particular type of accommodation, such as B&Bs, which aren't on the more mainstream booking services. Other services, such as TravelWeb (see the following list), offer weekend deals on major chain properties that cater to business travelers and have more empty rooms on the weekends. Some good all-purpose Web sites that you can use to track down and make online reservations at hotels in England are

- **All Hotels on the Web** (www.all-hotels.com) doesn't actually include *all* the hotels on the Web, but it does have tens of thousands of listings throughout the world, including England. Bear in mind that each hotel in the list has paid a small fee ($25 and up) for placement, so the listings aren't objective, but more like online brochures.
- **Bed & Breakfast (GB)** (www.bedbreak.com) is an excellent search engine that can set you up in an inexpensive B&B anywhere in England. One click on a region lets you view the available choices; another click gives you information on the individual B&B. You can also call this service toll-free from the U.S. at ☎ **800/454-8704.**
- **British Hotel Reservation Centre** (www.bhrc.co.uk) lists current and seasonal specials at selected London and U.K. hotels.
- **Hotel Discount.Com** (www.180096hotel.com) lists bargain rates at hotels in the U.S. and international cities, including London. If you click "London" and input your travel dates, the site provides a selection of hotels in various neighborhoods. The toll-free number is printed all over this site, so call if you want more options than the Web site lists.
- **Independent Traveler** (www.gowithit.co.uk) lists hundreds of self-catering accommodations in London. These are private flats, not hotels, and are available for a one-week minimum period; they can be a fantastic bargain.
- **London Bed & Breakfast** (☎ **800/872-2632** in the U.S. or 020/7351-3445 in the U.K.; www.londonbandb.com) can provide inexpensive accommodations in select private homes.
- The **London Tourist Board** (www.londontown.com) hotel Web site has a long list of London properties from which to choose. Some properties on the list offer special low rates.
- **SeniorSearch U.K.** (www.ageofreason.com) is a site for seniors looking for special hotels and other forms of accommodation, including home and apartment exchanges.

- **TravelWeb** (www.travelweb.com) lists more than 16,000 hotels worldwide, focusing on chains, such as Hyatt and Hilton. You can book almost 90% of the properties online. Its Click-It Weekends, updated each Monday, offers weekend deals at many leading chains.
- **Uptown Reservations** (www.uptownres.co.uk) provides listings for dozens of B&Bs in private homes in London.

Reserving the Best Room

After you know where you're staying, asking a few more questions can help you land the best possible room:

- Ask about staying in a corner room. They're usually larger, quieter, and brighter, and may cost a bit more.
- Ask about staying in a room in the back of the building. In London, especially, traffic noise can be loud and annoying. In the back, you may get a room that looks over a quiet garden.
- Ask whether the hotel is renovating. If the answer is yes, request a room away from the renovation work and make sure that you ask again when you check in.
- If you have any physical impairments, ask whether the hotel has a *lift* (elevator). Many small and older hotels in London and throughout England don't have elevators. If the hotel lacks a lift, ask whether a *ground-floor* (first floor) room is available.
- Inquire about the location of restaurants, bars, and meeting facilities, which can be noisy.
- If you aren't happy with your room when you arrive, return to the front desk right away. If another room is available, the staff should be able to accommodate you, within reason.

If you need a room where you can smoke, request one when you reserve. If you can't bear the lingering smell of smoke, tell everyone who handles your reservation that you need a smoke-free room. Hotels in England usually have nonsmoking rooms; some establishments are entirely smoke-free.

Paying for Your Room

Hotels almost never consider a room reservation confirmed until they receive partial or full payment. (This policy varies from hotel to hotel.) You can almost always confirm your reservations immediately with a credit card; otherwise, you must mail in your payment (generally using an International Money Order, available at most banks). Before booking, always ask about the cancellation policy. If your plans change, you don't want to pay for a room you've never slept in. At some hotels, you can get your money back if you cancel a room with 24 hours' notice; in others, you must notify the hotel five or more days in advance. After you book a room, request a written confirmation by fax, e-mail, or postal mail and be sure to take it along on your trip.

Smaller guesthouses and B&Bs outside London, especially those in country villages, don't always accept credit cards. If you're going to ramble through the Cotswolds and choose B&Bs as they strike your fancy, make sure that you have enough cash in pounds sterling.

Sorry, but you can't escape the annoying 17.5% *value-added tax (VAT).* In general, the quoted room rate includes the VAT (except for rooms at the upper end of the price scale). Be sure to ask, though, so you don't get an unpleasant surprise when you're checking out. Unless otherwise noted (that is, unless the listing reads, "Rates don't include 17.5% VAT"), the rates for my recommended hotels include the VAT.

Unfortunately, VAT refunds for those who live outside the European Union are only for store purchases and not for VAT paid at hotels and restaurants.

Arriving without a Reservation

If your trip to England includes a stay in London, I want to remind you again: *Booking ahead is important.* However, if you do arrive without a reservation, your first option is to start calling the hotels directly — try to get into town in the morning, so you can begin your room search early.

In London, you can also book rooms through the following trustworthy agencies, but the first two don't have phone service, so you must show up in person (in high season, expect long lines at both):

- The **Britain Visitor Centre,** 1 Regent St. (Tube: Piccadilly Circus), is open Monday through Friday 9 a.m. to 6:30 p.m. and Saturday and Sunday 10 a.m. to 4 p.m. (Saturday June through September from 9 a.m. to 5 p.m.) In addition to booking rooms for London, reserve hotels in cities and regions throughout the country.
- The **Tourist Information Centre,** in the forecourt of Victoria Station (Tube: Victoria), is open Easter through May, Monday through Saturday from 8 a.m. to 8 p.m., and to 9 p.m. June through September. Sunday and every day during the winter, it's open from 8 a.m. to 6 p.m.

- The London Tourist Board's **Accommodation Bookings Hotline** at ☎ **020/7932-2020** is open Monday through Friday 9:30 a.m. to 5:30 p.m.; with this service, you must book with a credit card.

The following private agencies can also help you find a room in London and elsewhere in England:

- **British Hotel Reservation Centre** (☎ **020/7340-1616**) offers a 24-hour phone line. The center provides free reservations and discounted rates at all the leading hotel groups and the major independents. This agency operates a reservations desk (open daily between 6 a.m. and midnight) at the Underground station of Heathrow Airport.
- **First Option Hotel Reservations** (☎ **0345/110-011**) is another hotel booking service. This agency operates kiosks at the following Central London rail stations: Victoria, by Platform 9 (☎ **020/7828-4646**); King's Cross, by Platform 8 (☎ **020/7837-5681**); Euston (☎ **020/7388-7435**); Paddington (☎ **020/7723-0184**); and Charing Cross (☎ **020/7976-1171**).
- The London office of **Worldwide Bed & Breakfast Association** (☎ **020/8742-9123**) can arrange a B&B room for you.
- **The London Bed and Breakfast Agency Limited** (☎ **020/7586-2768**) also offers inexpensive accommodations in private homes.

Of course, you can't be as choosy about price or location when you literally arrive on the fly without a reservation. To keep all your options open, remember to book ahead.

Chapter 9

Minding Your Pounds and Pence

In This Chapter

- Getting a primer on pounds and pence
- Deciding whether to bring cash, traveler's checks, or credit cards
- Changing your dollars into pounds after you arrive
- Finding and using ATMs
- Dealing with theft and loss
- Preparing for (and recouping) the British sales tax

Money makes the world go around, but dealing with an unfamiliar currency can make your head spin. Travelers to foreign destinations, especially first-time travelers, often have big money worries. They don't worry so much about having enough money as they do about the difference between money in their home country and money abroad. What are the conversion rates? Where can they change one currency into another at the best rate? Are traveler's checks better than credit cards or ATM cards? Will their home PIN work in a foreign country? Travelers have a seemingly endless list of money matters to consider.

You can't avoid these questions because you'll spend money every day of your trip. You'll often spend it on items that you don't buy at home. Although British currency is different, getting the hang of it is easy. In this chapter, I explain the basic money matters you'll encounter.

The immigration authorities may ask you how much money you have with you when you arrive at the London airport. In order to enter the United Kingdom, you must have sufficient means (in the form of cash, traveler's checks, or credit cards) to maintain and accommodate yourself and any dependents without recourse to public funds. Then again, they may not ask you this question at all.

Euro-free zone, for now

The fate of British currency in its pounds-and-pence form is one of the most hotly debated topics in the United Kingdom today. You may have heard about the single European currency, the euro, which 11 European countries adopted on January 1, 1999. Cautious, contentious Britain has opted out from switching over to the euro. Consequently, you don't use the euro while you travel in England.

Making Sense of Pounds and Pence

Britain's unit of currency is the *pound sterling (£)*. Every pound is divided into *100 pence (p)*. Coins come in denominations of 1p, 2p, 5p, 10p, 20p, 50p, £1, and £2. Notes are available in £5, £10, £20, and £50 denominations. As with any unfamiliar currency, British pounds and pence take a bit of getting used to. The coins have different sizes, shapes, and weights according to value. Each banknote denomination has its own color and bears a likeness of the queen. The Bank of England draws all the currency.

Choosing Traveler's Checks, Credit Cards, ATMs, or Cash

In England, you pay in pounds and pence, so you have to convert your own currency into British pounds sterling. When getting cash in England, should you bring traveler's checks or use ATMs? What about paying with credit cards? Check out this section to see what you need to know so that you can decide.

Toting traveler's checks: Safer than cash

Today, traveler's checks (*cheques* in the U.K.) are something of an anachronism from the days before credit cards and ATMs. These days, you don't really need traveler's checks in England. Throughout the country and just about everywhere in London, 24-hour ATMs are linked to an international network that most likely includes your bank at home (see "Using ATMs: How did we live without them?" coming up in the next section). Still, if you want the security of traveler's checks and don't mind the hassle of showing your passport every time you want to cash one, you can get them at almost any bank before you leave home.

Your home bank issues traveler's checks in your local currency. You generally pay a 1% commission fee to buy the checks. After you arrive in England, you need to convert them to pounds and pence. (See the section "Exchanging Your Currency," later in this chapter.) The good thing about carrying traveler's checks instead of cash is that you can get a refund if your checks are lost or stolen. Keep the checks separate from the official receipt that you receive for buying them and note each check number as you cash it. You need this record for any refund.

Never pay for hotels, meals, or purchases with traveler's checks denominated in any currency other than British pounds. You get a bad exchange rate if you try to use them as cash.

Using ATMs: How did we live without them?

In less than ten years, ATMs (sometimes called *cashpoints* in England) have revolutionized the money side of travel. You can fly to England with as little as $20 in your pocket and use your bank card to withdraw the cash you need, in pounds, on arrival. ATMs offer a fast and easy way to exchange money at the bank's bulk exchange rate, which is better than any rate you can get on the street. If you withdraw only as much cash as you need every couple of days, you won't feel the insecurity of carrying around a huge wad of bills.

If you plan to use ATMs, make certain you have a four-digit PIN (personal identification number) *before* you arrive. You need a four-digit PIN to use ATMs in England — if you have a six- or an eight-digit PIN, you need to have a new one assigned. (You can also use ATMs to get credit-card cash advances, but you need a PIN suitable for overseas use. Check with your bank or credit-card company for details.)

In London, you find 24-hour ATMs all over the place: outside banks, in large supermarkets, and in some Underground (Tube) stations. In other cities and towns, you find ATMs in local banks. (Look for banks on a town's main street, often called High Street.) Obviously you find fewer ATMs away from London. **Cirrus (☎ 800/424-7787;** `www.mastercard.com`) and **Plus (☎ 800/843-7587;** `www.visa.com`) are the most popular networks; check the back of your ATM card to see which network your bank uses. The toll-free numbers and Web sites give you locations of ATMs where you can withdraw money in England.

Many U.K. banks impose a fee of 50¢ to $3 every time you use an ATM. Your own bank may also charge you a fee for using another bank's ATM. Obviously, you need to think twice about the amount you're withdrawing to keep bank fees low by limiting your need to use an ATM.

If you try to withdraw cash from an ATM and get a message saying that your card isn't valid for international transactions, most likely the bank just can't make the telephone connection to check your account. Don't panic. Try another ATM or wait until the next day.

Paying with plastic: Classy and convenient

Credit cards are invaluable when traveling — they're a safe way to carry money and provide a convenient record of all your travel expenses. American Express, Diners Club, MasterCard, and Visa are widely accepted throughout England. A Eurocard or Access sign displayed at an establishment means it accepts MasterCard.

When traveling, I've come to rely more and more on credit cards to pay for hotel rooms, meals, theater and concert tickets, and many other purchases. I don't do this because I'm a chargeaholic. I just find it much easier than carrying around a wad of pound notes, stopping to cash traveler's checks, or using ATMs all the time.

Credit-card purchases are usually translated from pounds to dollars at a favorable rate and show up on your monthly statement, so keeping track of expenditures is easy.

Your credit-card company may charge a "conversion fee" of up to 3% of the price of goods purchased in foreign currencies.

You can also use credit cards to get cash advances at any bank or from ATMs (see the preceding section, "Using ATMs: How did we live without them?"), although you start paying interest on the advance the moment you receive the cash. You won't receive frequent-flier miles on an airline credit card, either.

In smaller towns and villages outside London, you may have trouble paying for B&Bs and restaurants with credit cards. Many B&Bs with one to three guest rooms operate on a cash-only basis, as do some small tearooms. If the town is large enough to support a bank, you can find an ATM or currency-exchange window there. Additionally, you can usually exchange cash or traveler's checks at a post office.

If your bank debit card is compatible with one of the international credit card systems (such as Cirrus), you can use it in England. There is one major difference in using debit cards, however: In England, you can't get extra cash back. The debit card is good only for the exact amount of the purchase.

Bringing cash: Always appropriate

Britain has no exchange controls, so you can bring as much cash and as many traveler's checks into the country as you want. Some folks like to change a small amount (say $100) of currency into pounds before leaving. This small emergency fund is always enough to cover transportation from the airport to the hotel. You can do this at currency exchanges in airports offering international flights to the United Kingdom.

Nowadays, though, waiting until you arrive in England before changing money may be simpler. The currency-exchange windows at London's Heathrow and Gatwick airports (see Chapter 11) will almost certainly be open when your flight arrives, or you can use one of the airport's ATMs. Getting and changing money in England has never been so convenient.

Exchanging Your Currency

The *exchange rate,* which fluctuates every day, is the rate you get when you use your own currency to buy pounds sterling (see Table 9-1). In general, $1 = 65p (or £1 = $1.60). These are *approximate* figures, but they're what I use for all prices in this guide (rounded off to the nearest dollar). Just before you leave on your trip, check with your bank or look in the newspaper to find out the current rate.

Table 9-1 Simple Currency Conversions

U.S.	*U.K.*	*U.K.*	*U.S.*
$1	63p	£1	$1.60
$5	£3.15	£2	$3.20
$10	£6.30	£5	$8
$20	£12.60	£10	$16
$50	£31.50	£20	$32
$100	£63	£50	$80

Changing money (either cash or traveler's checks) into a foreign currency makes many people nervous, especially if they're changing money for the first time. You needn't fear. Changing money is really a simple and straightforward operation. Just remember that every time you exchange money, you need to show your passport.

Visiting a bureaux de change or a British bank

By using a currency-exchange service called a *bureaux de change,* you can easily change cash or traveler's checks. These services are available at major London airports, any branch of major banks (throughout the country), all major rail and Underground stations in Central London, post offices countrywide, many Tourist Information Centres, and American Express or Thomas Cook offices. Bureaux de change in airports and rail stations are generally open daily between 8 a.m. and 9 p.m.

Almost every major bank in Central London and in cities throughout England has a foreign-currency window where you can exchange traveler's checks or cash. Weekday hours for banks are generally 9:30 a.m. to 3:30 p.m. Some banks (usually based in busy shopping areas) are open from 9:30 a.m. to 1 p.m. on Saturday. All banks close on public holidays, but many branches have 24-hour banking lobbies with ATMs, ATMs on the street outside, or both. Banking is a volatile business, with mergers, acquisitions, and name changes occurring all the time. The big names in England currently include **Barclays Bank** (☎ **020/7441-3200**), **Midland Bank** (☎ **020/7599-3232**), and **NatWest** (☎ **020/7395-5500**). These companies have branches throughout England.

Reputable British banks and bureaux de change exchange money at a competitive rate but charge a commission (typically 1% to 3% of the total transaction). Some currency-exchange services now guarantee you the same exchange rate when you return unspent pounds for dollars. (Remember to keep your receipt if you want to use this service.)

All U.K. bureaux de change and other money-changing establishments are required to clearly display, with equal prominence, exchange rates and full details of any fees and commission rates. They must display rates at or near the entrance to the premises. Rates fluctuate from place to place, and so do fees, so shopping around sometimes pays.

Steer clear of bureaux de change that offer good exchange rates but charge a heavy commission (up to 8%). You find them in major tourist sections. (Some are open 24 hours.) Some hotels also cash traveler's checks, but their commission is considerably higher than at a bank or bureaux de change. Before exchanging your money, always check the exchange rate, the commission rate, and additional fees.

You can avoid paying a second commission fee by using American Express traveler's checks and cashing them at an **American Express** office. The main office is in London at 6 Haymarket, SW1 (☎ **020/7930-4411;** Tube: Piccadilly). Its foreign exchange bureau is open Monday through Friday from 9 a.m. to 5:30 p.m., on Saturday from 9 a.m. to

6 p.m., and on Sunday from 10 a.m. to 5 p.m. For the addresses of other American Express offices in London and throughout England, see the Fast Facts sections of Chapter 12 and the Appendix.

Gaining pounds from ATMs

You can find ATMs throughout London. For convenience, they can't be beat. For more information, see the section "Using ATMs: How did we live without them?" earlier in this chapter.

Foreign banks in England tend to be for corporate business accounts rather than personal banking, so be prepared to use the ATM of another bank (such as Barclays Bank, Midland Bank, or NatWest) and pay a fee.

Citibank customers using ATMs at **Citibank International** (☎ **0800/005500**) — with branches at 332 Oxford St., W1 (Tube: Marble Arch), 16 Eastcheap, EC3 (Tube: Monument), and 336 Strand, WC2 (Tube: Charing Cross) — pay no transaction fee.

Traveling Smart: Handling Loss or Theft

Oh, no! You reach for your money and find that it's missing. Or you've fallen afoul of a thief. England is a very safe country, but crime happens. If you follow four basic rules, you can minimize the risk of a crime happening to you:

- Keep your wallet or purse out of sight, but *not* in your back pocket or in your backpack.
- Never leave your purse, briefcase, backpack, or coat unattended in any public place.
- Ladies: Don't hang your purse over the back of your chair in crowded or outdoor cafes or restaurants, particularly in London.
- Don't flash your money or credit cards around.

In the unlikely event that someone steals your wallet or purse, you'll need to cancel all your credit cards. Canceling your credit cards is probably a wise thing to do even before you call the police. (Call **directory assistance** at ☎ **192,** free from public pay phones, or look under *Police* in a phone directory for the police station nearest you.) The same advice applies if you lose a credit card. If you can think back to where you had the card last, call that place. Some good soul may have found the card and turned it in. If it's a lost cause, however, cancel your card so that no one else can use it.

The royal payroll — and payoff

Are you curious about how much the government pays the queen and other members of the royal family every year? Queen Elizabeth II's yearly Civil List income is £7.9 million ($12.6 million). Prince Phillip, the queen's hubby, is paid £359,000 ($574,400). Princess Anne gets £228,000 ($364,800) from the Privy Purse. Prince Charles takes home close to a cool £11 million ($17 million) from the Duchy of Cornwall (he's the Duke of Cornwall) and investments; he voluntarily pays 40% tax. In 2003, after a scandal-ridden year, Charles released a detailed accounting of his income and expenses for the first time. It was a public-relations gesture meant to counteract embarrassing public disclosures that his aides regularly sold unwanted gifts received by the prince, splitting the proceeds with him; that he relied upon a valet to squeeze toothpaste on his toothbrush; and that he insisted that the hospital room where he stayed during a minor operation be redecorated with his own furniture and that his hospital meals be served on his own china.

Almost every credit-card company has an emergency toll-free number that you can call if your card is lost or stolen. The company will cancel the card immediately and may also be able to wire you a cash advance; in many places, you can get an emergency replacement card in a day or two. If your credit card(s) gets lost or stolen while you're in England, immediately call the following U.K. number that applies to you:

- **American Express ☎ 01273/696-933**
- **Diners Club ☎ 0800/460-800**
- **MasterCard ☎ 01702/362-988**
- **Visa ☎ 01604/230-230**

If you carry traveler's checks, keep a record of their serial numbers separate from the checks. Write down the numbers of the checks as you cash them. If the checks are stolen, you need to be able to report exactly which checks are gone in order to get them replaced. The check issuer will tell you where to pick up the new checks.

If your purse or wallet is gone, the police aren't likely to recover it for you. However, after you cancel your credit cards, call to inform the police. You may need the police report number for credit card or insurance purposes later.

Taxing Matters: So Just Where Is This Added Value?

No discussion of money matters in England would be complete without a reference to the *value-added tax (VAT),* Britain's version of a sales tax. It amounts to 17.5% and is added to the total price of all consumer goods (the price tag already includes it), as well as hotel and restaurant bills. If you're not a resident of the European Union, you can get your VAT refunded on purchases made in England (but not the VAT paid at hotels and restaurants).

Every store requires a minimum purchase — of at least £50 ($80) — to qualify for a VAT refund. The exact amount varies from store to store: The minimum is £100 ($160) at Harrods in London, for example. But qualifying for a tax refund is far easier in Britain than in almost any other country in the European Union.

To get the refund, you must obtain a VAT refund form from the retailer, and the retailer must complete the form at the time of purchase. Don't leave the store without a completed refund form. Don't let any merchant tell you that you can get refund forms at the airport.

You can get back about 15% of the 17.5% VAT you pay on your purchases. To do so, follow these steps:

1. **Ask the store whether it does VAT refunds and how much the minimum purchase is.**
2. **If you spend the minimum amount, ask for the VAT refund paperwork with the retailer's portion completed.**
3. **Fill out your portion of the form (name, address).**
4. **Present the form — along with the goods — at the VAT Refunds counter in the airport.**

Remember: You're required to show the goods at your time of departure, so don't pack them in your checked luggage; put them in your carry-on instead. (I say this even though the authorities didn't ask to see anything the last time I went through this procedure.) After the paperwork is stamped, you have two choices:

- You can mail in the papers and receive your refund in a British check (no!) or a credit-card refund (yes!).
- You can go directly to the Cash VAT Refund desk at the airport and get your refund in cash.

The bad news: If you accept cash other than sterling, you lose money on the conversion rate. Many stores charge a flat fee for processing your refund, so £3 to £5 ($4.80 to $8) may be automatically deducted from the total refund. Even so, you may still be saving a bundle.

If you travel from England to other countries in the European Union, don't apply for your VAT refund at the airport. Apply for all your European VAT refunds at one time at your final destination, prior to departure from the European Union.

VAT isn't charged on goods shipped out of the country, no matter how much you spend. You can avoid VAT and the hassle of lugging large packages back with you by having stores ship your purchases for you; many are happy to do so. However, shipping charges can *double* the cost of your purchase, and you may also have to pay duties when the goods arrive. Instead of this costly strategy, consider paying for excess baggage (rates vary with the airline).

Chapter 10

Tying Up Loose Ends

In This Chapter

- Reading the fine print: Passports, visas, and insurance
- Taking care of your health: Medications and emergencies
- Making reservations: Restaurants and theater
- Packing light: What to take and what to leave

Before you depart for England to visit the British Museum in London or Shakespeare's birthplace in Stratford-upon-Avon, tie up some of your loose ends. Do you have an up-to-date passport? Have you taken steps to meet your health needs while you're on your trip? Have you made reservations for the London restaurant you have to try, and do you have your tickets for the play you just can't miss? Do you know what to pack? This chapter helps you wrap up these and other last-minute details.

Dealing with Passports

A valid passport is the only legal form of identification accepted around the world. You can't cross most international borders without it. Getting a passport is easy, but the process takes some time.

The **U.S. Department of State's Bureau of Consular Affairs** maintains `www.travel.state.gov`, a Web site that provides everything you ever wanted to know about passports (including a downloadable application), customs, and other government-regulated aspects of travel.

Applying for a U.S. passport

Apply for your passport at least a month, preferably two, before you plan to leave on your trip. The processing takes an average of three weeks, but can run longer during busy periods (especially in spring). For people older than age 15, a passport is valid for ten years; for those 15 and under, a passport is valid for five years.

If you're a U.S. citizen applying for a first-time passport and are 14 or older, you need to apply in person at one of the following locations. (See "Applying for Australian, Canadian, and New Zealand passports," later in this chapter for info on how to apply in other countries.)

- One of the 13 passport offices throughout the United States — in Boston, Chicago, Honolulu, Houston, Los Angeles, Miami, New Orleans, New York City, Philadelphia, San Francisco, Seattle, Stamford, Connecticut, and Washington, D.C. Check the telephone directory or call the **National Passport Information Center** at ☎ **877/487-2778** for the addresses of these offices.
- A federal, state, or probate court.
- A major post office. (Not all accept applications; call the phone number in the following paragraph to find the post offices that do.)

To apply for your first passport, fill out *form DSP-11*. To renew your passport, you need *form DSP-82*. You can obtain these applications at the locations in the preceding list, on the Web at `www.travel.state.gov`, or by calling the **National Passport Information Center** at ☎ 877/487-2778.

For first-time passports, travelers 14 to 18 years of age must apply in person and fill out form DSP-11. Parents or guardians of children under 13 can obtain passports for them by presenting two photos of each child. Children's passports are valid for five years.

Bring the following when you apply for your first passport or to renew an old one:

- **Application fee:** For people older than 15, a passport costs $85 ($55 plus a $30 handling fee); for those 15 and under, a passport costs $70 total.
- **Completed passport application (form DSP-11 or form DSP-82):** You can fill out this form in advance to save time. However, don't sign the application until you present it in person at the passport agency, court, or post office.
- **Proof of identity:** Among the accepted documents are a valid driver's license, a state or military ID, a student ID (if you're currently enrolled), an old passport, or a naturalization certificate.
- **Proof of U.S. citizenship:** Bring your old passport if you're renewing; otherwise, bring a certified birth certificate with registrar's seal, a report of your birth abroad, or your naturalized citizenship documents.
- **Two identical 2-x-2-inch photographs with a white or off-white background:** You can get these taken in just about any corner photo shop; these places have a special camera to make the photos identical. Expect to pay up to $10 for them. You can't use

the strip photos from a photo vending machine, but high-quality digital photos are acceptable. (See the State Department Web site for details.)

If you're 18 or older and renewing an undamaged passport issued when you were 16 or older, within the last 15 years, you don't have to apply in person; you can renew the passport by mail. Include your expired passport, pink renewal form DSP-82, two identical photos (see the preceding bulleted list), and a check or money order for $45 (no extra handling fee). Send the package (registered, just to be safe) to one of the agencies listed on the back of the application form. Allow at least four to six weeks for your application to be processed and your new passport to be sent.

Do you need your passport in a hurry, perhaps to take advantage of that incredibly low airfare to London? To expedite your passport (for receipt in five business days), visit an agency directly or go through the court or post office and have the application sent by overnight mail. This process costs an extra $60. For more information, call the **National Passport Information Center** at ☎ **877/487-2778.**

Applying for Australian, Canadian, and New Zealand passports

The following list offers more information for citizens of Australia, Canada, and New Zealand:

- **Australians** can visit a local post office or passport office, call toll-free ☎ **131-232** (from Australia), or log on `www.dfat.gov.au/passports` for details on how and where to apply. Adult passports cost $128, and passports for travelers under 18 are $64.
- **Canadians** can pick up passport applications at the central **Passport Office** (Department of Foreign Affairs and International Trade, Ottawa, ON K1A 0G3; ☎ **800/567-6868**), at one of the 28 regional passport offices, at most travel agencies, or from `www.dfait-maeci.gc.ca/passport` (which has downloadable forms). Children under 16 may be included on a parent's passport, but they need their own passport to travel unaccompanied. Applications must include two identical 2-x-2-inch (37-x-37cm) photos and a birth certificate or Certificate of Canadian Citizenship. Passports are valid for five years and cost $60. Processing takes five to ten days if you apply in person or ten days to three weeks by mail.
- **New Zealanders** can pick up passport applications at any travel agency, online at `www.passports.govt.nz`, or at the **Passport Office,** P.O. Box 10–526, Wellington (☎ **0800/225-050**). Adult passports cost $80, and passports for travelers under 16 are $40. Mail the completed form, along with a pair of identical 50-x-40-mm photos and proof of citizenship, to the Wellington office.

Understanding passport rules

European Union (EU) citizens supposedly don't need a passport to visit other EU countries, but in reality they do need one if their country doesn't issue identity cards. If you're a citizen of the United States, Canada, Australia, or New Zealand, you must have a passport with at least two months remaining until its expiration to enter the United Kingdom.

You need to show your passport at the customs and immigration area when you arrive at a U.K. airport. After your passport is stamped, you can remain in the United Kingdom as a tourist for up to three months.

Keep your passport with you at all times, or be certain it's in a safe place. You only need to show it when you're converting traveler's checks or foreign currency at a bank or currency exchange. However, a hotel clerk may ask to see it when you check in; after examining it, the clerk will return the passport to you. If you're not going to need your passport for currency exchanges, ask whether the hotel has a safe where you can keep it locked up.

Dealing with a (gulp) lost passport

Don't worry; you won't be sent to the Tower of London if you lose your passport in England, but you need to take steps to replace it *immediately.* First notify the police. Then go to your consulate or high commission office (they're all located in London). Bring all available forms of identification, and the staff will get started on generating your new passport. For the addresses of consulates and high commissions, see the Appendix. Always call first to verify open hours.

Getting Visas and Health Certificates

No *visa* (a stamp on a passport showing that a person has official permission to enter a country) is required if you're going to stay in England or the rest of the United Kingdom for less than three months. The **U.S. Department of State's Bureau of Consular Affairs** operates a phone line for current visa information: ☎ **202/663-1225** (Monday through Friday 8:30 a.m. to 4 p.m.). Or you can check its Web site at `www.travel.state.gov`.

Likewise, you don't need an International Certificate of Vaccination to enter the United Kingdom (as you would if traveling to Southeast Asia or parts of Africa).

Deciding Insurance Needs

When you travel, unfortunate occurrences sometimes happen. A company may cancel an escorted tour, you may get sick, or the airline may lose your luggage. In order to prepare for these misfortunes, the following types of insurance can help:

- **Trip-cancellation insurance** is a good idea if you signed up for an escorted tour and paid a large portion of your vacation expenses upfront (for information on escorted tours, see Chapter 6). Trip-cancellation insurance covers three emergencies
  - If a death or sickness prevents you from traveling
  - If a tour operator or airline goes out of business
  - If some kind of disaster prevents you from getting to your destination
- Buying **medical insurance** for your trip doesn't make sense for most travelers. Your existing health insurance should cover you if you get sick while on vacation (although if you belong to an HMO, check to see whether you're fully covered while in the United Kingdom).
- **Lost-luggage insurance** isn't necessary for most travelers. Your homeowner's or renter's insurance usually covers stolen luggage if you have off-premises theft coverage. Check your existing policies before you buy any additional coverage. If an airline loses your luggage, the airline is responsible for paying $1,250 per bag on domestic flights and $635 per bag (maximum of two bags) on international flights. If you plan to carry anything more valuable than that, keep it in your carry-on bag.

Some credit cards (American Express and some gold and platinum Visa and MasterCards, for example) offer automatic flight insurance against death or dismemberment in case of an airplane crash. If you still feel you need more insurance, try one of the following companies:

- **Access America,** 6600 W. Broad St., Richmond, VA 23230 (☎ **800/284-8300**)
- **Travelex Insurance Services,** P.O. Box 641070, Omaha, NE 68164-7070 (☎ **800/228-9792**)
- **Travel Guard International,** 1145 Clark St., Stevens Point, WI 54481 (☎ **800/826-1300;** `www.travelguard.com`)
- **Travel Insured International, Inc.,** P.O. Box 280568, East Hartford, CT 06128 (☎ **800/243-3174;** `www.travelinsured.com`)

Don't pay for more insurance than you need. For example, if you only need trip-cancellation insurance, don't buy coverage for lost or stolen property. Trip-cancellation insurance costs about 6% to 8% of the total value of your vacation.

Taking Care of Your Health

Getting sick may ruin your vacation, so I strongly advise against it. (Of course, the last time I checked, the influenza bugs weren't listening to me any more than they probably listen to you.)

Talk to your doctor before leaving on a trip if you have a serious or chronic illness. If you have a serious condition, such as heart disease, epilepsy, or diabetes, wear a Medic Alert identification tag, which immediately alerts any doctor to your condition and gives him or her access to your medical records through Medic Alert's 24-hour hot line (a worldwide toll-free emergency response number is on the tag). Membership is $35, plus a $20 annual renewal fee. Contact the **Medic Alert Foundation International,** 2323 Colorado Ave., Turlock, CA 95382 (☎ **888/633-4298;** `www.medicalert.org`).

Bring all your medications with you, as well as prescriptions for more medications (in generic, not brand name, form) if you worry that you may run out. Also, pack your medications in a carry-on that you always keep with you. If you have health insurance, carry your insurance card in your wallet. Write down your insurance information and keep a copy in another secured location just in case your wallet is lost or stolen. If you worry about getting sick away from home, buy medical insurance (see the preceding section on insurance), which may cover you more completely than your existing health insurance.

If you fall ill while traveling, ask the concierge at your hotel to recommend a local doctor. If you can't locate a doctor, contact your country's embassy or consulate (see the Appendix for addresses and phone numbers). If the situation is serious, dial ☎ **999** (no coins required), the number for police and medical emergencies in England. If the situation is life-threatening, go to a local hospital's emergency or accident department. Any taxi driver can take you there.

Under the United Kingdom's nationalized health care system, you're eligible only for free *emergency* care. If you're admitted to a hospital as an *in-patient,* even from an accident and an emergency department, you must pay unless you're a U.K. resident or European Union resident. This financial obligation is true for follow-up care as well. See the Appendix for the names, addresses, and phone numbers of hospitals offering 24-hour emergency care in London.

Most U.S. health insurance plans and HMOs cover at least part of the out-of-country hospital visits and procedures if insurees become ill or are injured while out of the country. Most require that you pay the bills upfront at the time of care, issuing a refund after you return and file all the paperwork.

Before leaving home, you can obtain a directory of U.K. doctors from the **International Association of Medical Assistance to Travelers.** Its address in the United States is 417 Center St., Lewiston, NY 14092 (☎ **716/754-4883**); in Canada, 40 Regal Rd., Guelph, Ontario N1K 1B5 (☎ **519/836-0102**); and in New Zealand, P.O. Box 5049, Christchurch 5 (no phone). IAMAT is on the Web at `www.iamat.org`.

Getting Reservations and Tickets Before You Leave Home

You're going to England, your time is limited, and you don't want to miss specific plays, concerts, or top restaurants — what do you do? Just make your reservations or buy your tickets in advance.

Your finest table, please: Dinner reservations

For dinner reservations, call the restaurant directly from home. Restaurant listings throughout this book include phone numbers. (Don't forget to keep the time change in mind. England is five hours later than Eastern Standard Time, so when the clock strikes noon in New York, it's 5 p.m. in London.) You can also ask your hotel concierge to make the reservation for you after you arrive, but be sure to do so far enough ahead — you may have to reserve a couple of days or even a month in advance for some trendy places in London. You probably don't need to reserve a table more than a day or two in advance for a restaurant outside London. But keep in mind that the best restaurants, wherever they are, generally require reservations.

If you plan on enjoying a high tea at the Ritz or one of the other elegant London hotels that serve legendary afternoon teas (I list them in Chapter 11), you may have to book that reservation in advance as well.

Two on the aisle: Theater tickets

Seeing a play in London or Stratford-upon-Avon is a must for many visitors to England. Your chances of getting a seat to a sold-out show are good if you go directly to the theater box office. But you should definitely purchase a ticket in advance if attending a specific play, concert, or opera will make or break your trip. To book in advance (and pay an additional commission) before you leave home, contact one of the following:

- **Albemarle:** This respected booking agency (74 Mortimer St., London, W1N 8HL; ☎ **020/7637-9041** in the U.K.; Fax: 020-7631-0375; E-mail: sales@albemarle-london.com; Internet: www.albemarle-london.com) maintains a definitive London Theatre Web site with listings of all current West End shows, opera, ballet, and rock and pop concerts. If you find a performance you want to attend, you can purchase a ticket by e-mail. The prices include a booking fee of 23% plus tax. Albemarle sells the best seats to most West End shows for about £50 to £60 ($80 to $96), including commission. Time permitting, the company mails tickets worldwide; otherwise, you can pick them up at the theater or have them delivered to your hotel.
- **Keith Prowse:** The New York office of this London-based ticket agency (☎ **800/669-7469** or 914/328-2357; www.keithprowse.com) handles West End (commercial) shows, the English National and Royal Opera, pop concerts, and events such as the Chelsea Flower Show (see Chapter 2 for details) and the British Open. After payment is received, the agency sends you a voucher to be exchanged for tickets at the box office.

If you want to attend an opera or a ballet at the **Royal Opera House,** reserve weeks, not days, in advance. Check out the performing arts venues in Chapter 12 (London) and Chapter 19 (Stratford-upon-Avon) for more details.

In the know: What's playing and where

The Web sites for the ticket-booking agencies in the preceding section can tell you what's currently happening in London. The following Web sites are also useful:

- **The Society of London Theatre** (www.officiallondontheatre.co.uk) offers a comprehensive listing of plays, opera, and dance.
- **Electronic Telegraph** (www.telegraph.co.uk), the online version of the *Daily Telegraph*, reviews theater and other performance events in its "Arts & Books" section.
- The Net edition of the ***Sunday Times*** (www.sunday-times.co.uk) offers reviews and listings of West End shows and other events. Look under "Arts" and "Culture."
- The online version of the ***Evening Standard*** newspaper (www.thisislondon.co.uk) has listings of current theater and music events.

Packing It Up and Taking It on the Road

If you ask me, packing is a spiritual exercise that teaches you a great deal about yourself and your basic needs. Packing is about lightening your load.

Before you start packing, think realistically about what you need for the length of time you'll be gone. And think practically. A sauce stain makes a white silk dress or dress shirt unwearable (I hope). Pack *non-white* clothing. In general, plan to dress in *layers*. And unless you're going to England in the height of summer (perhaps even then), consider that the temperature will probably be between *45° F and 70° F*, and the climate is often damp.

The English favor woolens because the fabric is warm and practical, and holds its shape even after a drenching downpour. Many hotel rooms are equipped with trouser presses, which can get out the wrinkles and save you the hassle of toting along a travel iron. If you base yourself in London, remember that some of the best shopping in the world surrounds you. If you forget a critical item, you can buy it in London.

Deciding what to bring

To start packing, compile everything that you think you'll need on your trip. Then get rid of half of it. You don't want to injure yourself as a result of lugging half your house around with you. Getting from the airport and your hotel can be difficult; if you're staying in a B&B without an elevator, lugging a heavy load of suitcases up and down narrow London stairways can be a royal pain in the gluteus max.

Weather patterns

According to 18th-century writer Dr. Samuel Johnson (1709–1784), "When two Englishmen meet, their first talk is of the weather." Things haven't changed much since then. The unpredictability of the English climate has led to another sound British maxim: There is no such thing as bad weather; there is only inappropriate clothing. For an Englishman (and woman), appropriate foul-weather gear includes a *mac* (short for mackintosh, a raincoat), a *brolly* (umbrella), and *Wellingtons* (rubber boots).

Some essentials for your trip include

- Comfortable walking shoes
- A versatile sweater (gray or dark colored); make this a heavy sweater if visiting in late fall or winter
- A waterproof jacket or coat (preferably one with a hood); select outerwear that's lined if visiting in late fall or winter
- Something to sleep in (London thermostats are often set rather low)
- A collapsible umbrella (or *brolly,* as the Brits call them)
- Gloves and a scarf if visiting in late fall or winter

Nowadays, England is as casual in its dress as the United States — although if you go to London, you'll find that it's a clothes-conscious capital. You need a formal suit or fancy dress only if you plan to attend a board meeting, a funeral, or a wedding, or you want to dine in one of the city's finest restaurants. For daily wear around the city, a pair of jeans or khakis works fine. You may want to consider a couple of cotton pullovers you can wear under a sweater or sweatshirt.

Dressing like a native

London — like Paris, Milan, and New York — is a fashion-conscious city. This doesn't mean that you *must* be fashionable, only that you *can* be, and that if you *are*, other fashionable people may notice you. If you plan to eat in any upscale restaurants (in London or anywhere else in the country), you'll encounter a smart-casual dress code. You won't be let in if you try to enter the dining room wearing jogging shoes, sweatpants, or blue jeans. A very few classy places require you to wear a shirt, tie, and jacket at dinner.

Smart-casual men need to bring along a pair of dressy but comfortable trousers and a sports jacket (or a suit if you like), a shirt and tie (or dressy sweater), and leather shoes (preferably with a nice shine). Smart-casual women can wear a dress, a skirt and blouse, a suit with skirt and jacket, or a pantsuit.

Packing smart

Before you choose a suitcase for your trip, decide what kind of traveling you intend to do. My personal preference for a suitcase is one with wheels. A foldover garment bag is a nuisance if you pack and unpack often, but it can help keep dressy clothing wrinkle-free. Hard-sided luggage protects breakable items better but weighs more than soft-sided bags.

Traveling with carry-on bags

You no longer have to leave your eyelash curler at home, but the federal Transportation Security Administration (TSA) continues to bar from airplane cabins sharp items and anything else that may be used as a weapon, which includes utensils with an edge, such as straight razors and scissors, and larger items like golf clubs and ski poles. Airlines limit passengers to one carry-on bag and one personal item (such as a laptop computer) onto the aircraft. These items must fit in the overhead compartment or beneath the seat in front of you. For more information on restrictions, check the TSA Web site at www.tsa.gov, or contact your airline.

Each airline defines its own dimension limits for carry-ons, but the limits usually average around 60 inches total (10 x 14 x 36 inches). Your carry-on should contain your valuables, such as jewelry, a book (this one, of course), any medications you use, breakable items that you don't want to put in your suitcase, a change of clothes, film, and your vital documents (such as return tickets and passport).

Select a backpack or shoulder bag as one of your carry-ons and then put it to use on your trip as an all-purpose carry-along bag for your guidebooks, maps, and camera when you leave your hotel and go out exploring.

Leaving electronics at home

When I'm on an exciting trip, the last thing I want is to tune myself *out* of what is going on around me. I want to enjoy the sights and atmosphere. People today think that they need to haul along every new electronic toy or gadget wherever they go. Trust me, doing so won't add anything to your trip — it'll detract from it. Even the mobile phone that's glued to your ear at home can be turned off and left behind, which is a good idea because your calling plan probably doesn't include international locales. (You'll notice, though, that every other Londoner now seems to be talking while walking.)

If you think that you won't enjoy your trip without a few electrical gadgets, you can't plug an appliance from the United States or Canada into a British outlet without frying your appliance, blowing a fuse, or both. North American current runs 110V, 60 cycles; the standard voltage throughout Britain is 240V AC, 50 cycles. You need a current converter or transformer to bring the voltage down and the cycles up. Two-pronged North American plugs won't fit into the three-pronged square British wall sockets, so you also need a three-pronged square adapter and converter if you use North American appliances in Britain. Plug adapters and converters are available at most travel, luggage, electronics, and hardware stores. Some plug adapters are also current converters. Most contemporary laptop computers automatically sense the current and adapt accordingly (check the manual, bottom of the machine, or manufacturer first to make sure that you don't destroy your data or equipment).

The standard voltage in Australian and New Zealand is 240V, the same as in England, but the plugs are different. If you're coming from one of these countries, bring an adapter with you.

Travel-size versions of hair dryers, irons, shavers, and so on are dual voltage, which means that they have built-in converters (usually you have to turn a switch to go back and forth). If you insist on lugging your own hair dryer or electric shaver, make sure that it's dual voltage or that you carry along a converter. Small hotels and B&Bs black out on a regular basis when someone from North America plugs in a 110V hair dryer, and the appliance explodes in an impressive shower of sparks or melts in his or her hands. To avoid voltage issues, use a straight-edge razor for shaving, unless you have a battery-operated electric shaver. However, most hotels have a special plug for low-wattage shavers *and shavers only.*

Count down: Ten things to do before you leave

For peace of mind on your trip, make sure that you take care of some housekeeping details before you leave. Although most are fairly obvious, they're easy to overlook in the excitement of getting ready for a trip:

- Get someone to look after your pets (or kennel them) and water the plants.
- Put a hold on your mail and newspaper deliveries.
- Empty/defrost your refrigerator.
- Put several lights in the house on timers (dining room at dinner time, TV room during prime time, and so on).
- Lock all windows and doors (don't forget the basement and garage).
- Arrange for a friend or taxi to take you to the airport (this method is cheaper and better than leaving your car in the airport garage).
- Reconfirm your plane's seat reservation and your hotel bookings.
- Call the airline to double-check that your flight is on time.
- Get to the airport at least two hours before your flight.
- Sit back on the plane, take a deep breath, and tell yourself: "I'm on my way to England!" Cheerio! Have a great time.

Part III
London and Environs

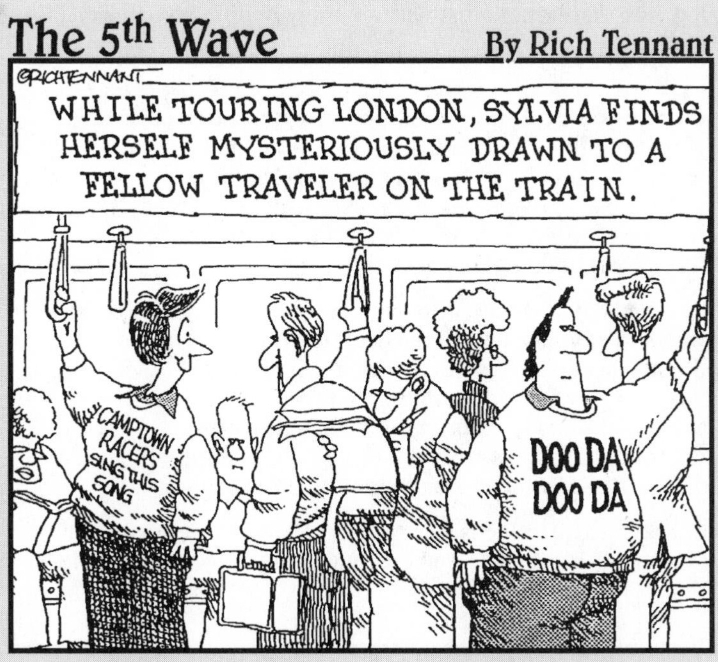

The 5th Wave
By Rich Tennant
©RICHTENNANT
WHILE TOURING LONDON, SYLVIA FINDS HERSELF MYSTERIOUSLY DRAWN TO A FELLOW TRAVELER ON THE TRAIN.
CAMPTOWN RACERS SING THIS SONG
DOO DA DOO DA

In this part . . .

For many travelers, a trip to England begins and ends in London. That's why I devote an entire part of this guide to the United Kingdom's capital. Chances are you'll fly into one of London's airports and use the city as your major transportation and cultural hub. London is one of the world's major tourist magnets. After you start exploring, you understand just why so many people love this city.

In Chapter 11, I help you settle into this exciting metropolis. I explain how to get into the city from the airport, and then I describe Central London's neighborhoods and tell you about the transportation options available. Next, I list my recommended hotels and give advice for finding a room if you arrive without a reservation. And finally, I give you selected restaurants in all price categories that feature different kinds of cuisine.

Chapter 12 is dedicated to exploring London in your own way and at your own pace. I describe the top attractions — those places you absolutely don't want to miss — and a host of other intriguing sights that may interest you. I explain options for touring by bus, boat, or foot. Next, I delve into London's truly mind-boggling shopping scene and its array of theater and nightlife possibilities.

Chapter 13 introduces you to several great side trips from London — places you can easily visit in a day, returning in time for dinner and a show.

Chapter 11

Settling into London

In This Chapter

- Arriving in London
- Getting from the airport into the city
- Orienting yourself to the neighborhoods
- Traveling by Underground, bus, and taxi
- Choosing your hotel
- Picking a good restaurant
- Enjoying a scrumptious tea

As the oft-quoted Dr. Samuel Johnson observed more than 200 years ago, "When a man is tired of London, he is tired of life." Year-round, millions from all corners of the globe visit the United Kingdom capital. London is famed for its venerable monuments, splendid museums, royal palaces, magnificent parks, literary associations, exciting nightlife, and super shopping. For many visitors, a trip to England begins and ends in London.

This city may be old and full of quaint corners and age-old traditions, but London isn't a stodgy place. Trend-setting London is to the United Kingdom what New York City is to the United States: The spot where everything happens first (or ultimately ends up). This ancient metropolis is now as high-tech as a hyperlink, with mobile phones, cybercafes, and e-communications part of everyday life. In this city, you can see the traditional and the cutting edge on the same street corner. An enormous city with more than 7 million inhabitants, London harbors a diversity of sights, sounds, and experiences that make it as fascinating today as it was for Dr. Johnson.

Londoners, accustomed to sharing their city with international visitors, tend to be friendly, open, and polite. Tourism is a big business in England, and visitors can expect to be treated with courtesy and helpfulness throughout the country.

Getting There

As the capital and largest city in the United Kingdom, London doesn't lack transportation options. The city acts as a huge international hub, which makes travel to London from overseas and the Continent easy.

Flying to London

London has five airports, but chances are you'll fly into Heathrow or Gatwick, which handle the bulk of London's international flights. The airports manage tens of thousands of visitors per day and are geared to moving people efficiently from point A to point B.

Arriving at Heathrow

About 15 miles west of Central London, **Heathrow (☎ 02087/594-321;** www.baa.co.uk) is the largest of London's airports. In fact, Heathrow is the world's busiest airport, with four passenger terminals serving flights from around the globe. The corridors are surrealistically long, but moving walkways make the trek easier. And everything is sign-posted so you won't get lost.

Your first stop after deplaning is **Passport Control and Customs,** which involves a fairly routine procedure. On the plane, you receive a landing card to fill out. You must provide your name, your address, your passport number, and the address where you're staying in the United Kingdom. Present this completed form and your passport to the passport official. After the passport is stamped, you proceed to pick up your luggage. From there, you wend your way out through the Customs Hall.

At the Customs area, you have two choices: "Nothing to Declare" and "Goods to Declare." Chances are you won't be declaring anything, in which case you walk right through. You may be stopped for a random luggage search. Don't take it personally. Unless you're smuggling contraband, you have nothing to worry about.

After clearing Customs, you enter the terminal's main concourse. All sorts of services are available, including ATMs, hotel-booking agencies, theater-booking services, banks, and *bureaux de change* (currency exchange) windows, where you can swap your dollars or traveler's checks for pounds and pence. (See Chapter 9 for information about changing money.) If you want to pick up a free map and general info, go to the London Tourist Board's **Tourist Information Centre** in the Underground station for Terminals 1, 2, and 3 (open Monday through Friday 6:15 a.m. to 5 p.m., Saturday and Sunday 7:15 a.m. to 4 p.m.).

You have several options for getting into the city from Heathrow. You can travel by train, bus, or shuttle as follows:

- The **London Underground** (☎ **02072/221-234**), a subway system that's called the Underground or the Tube, is the cheapest mode of public transportation to Central London destinations. All terminals at Heathrow link up with the Tube system. Follow the Underground signs to the ticket booth. The **Piccadilly Line** gets you into Central London in about 45 minutes for a fare of £3.70 ($6). Underground trains run from all four Heathrow terminals every five to nine minutes, Monday to Saturday, 5:30 a.m. to 11:30 p.m., and Sunday 6 a.m. to 11 p.m.

  The one potential hassle with the Underground is that the trains don't have luggage racks. You have to stash your bags as best you can — behind your legs, on your lap, or to one side of the center doors where the cars have more space. To reach your hotel on the Underground, you may have to change trains or take a taxi from the Underground station closest to your destination.

  If the Underground is closed when you arrive, the N97 night bus connects Heathrow with Central London. Buses (located in front of the terminals) run every 30 minutes, Monday to Saturday from midnight to 5 a.m., and Sunday from 11 p.m. to 5:30 a.m. The trip takes about an hour; the one-way fare is £1.50 ($2.40) before 4:30 a.m. or £1 ($1.60) after 4:30 a.m.

- **National Express** buses (☎ **08705/747-777;** `www.gobycoach.com`) may be a better alternative to the Underground if you're loaded down with heavy luggage. Two buses — the Express bus and the A2 Airbus — provide service from the airport to Central London. The Express bus goes from Heathrow to Victoria Station, making stops at Cromwell Road, Knightsbridge, and Hyde Park Corner. The A2 Airbus goes to King's Cross Station, stopping at Bayswater, Marble Arch, Euston, and Russell Square. Travel time for both is about 75 minutes, and the fare is £8 ($13), payable on the bus. Up to three buses an hour depart daily between 4 a.m. and 11:23 p.m. from the front of Heathrow's terminals.

- The fastest way into London is the **Heathrow Express train** (☎ **08456/001-515;** `www.heathrowexpress.co.uk`), which runs from all four Heathrow terminals to Paddington Station in just 15 minutes. The trains have air-conditioning, ergonomically designed seating, and plenty of luggage space. The standard-class fare is £11.70 ($19) one-way. You can buy tickets at the airport or on the train for a small extra charge. Service runs every 15 minutes, Monday to Saturday 5:07 a.m. to 11:32 p.m. and Sunday 5:03 a.m. to midnight. All the major airlines have check-in counters right at Paddington, so when you're returning from London to the airport you can conveniently check your luggage *before* boarding the train; when you arrive at Heathrow, you can go directly to your departure gate without further check-in.

- **Taxis** from Heathrow into Central London are cost effective if two or three people are traveling together. You can order one at the Taxi Information booths in Terminal 3 (☎ **02087/454-655**) or Terminal 4 (☎ **02087/457-302**). Expect to pay about £40 ($64) plus tip for a trip of about 45 minutes. Taxis are available 24 hours a day.

Arriving at Gatwick

Gatwick (☎ **012933/535-353;** www.baa.co.uk), located about 28 miles south of Central London, is considerably smaller than Heathrow. International flights arrive at the South terminal. Gatwick provides the same services Heathrow does, except that the London Tourist Board doesn't have an office there. You find fewer transportation options for getting into Central London.

The highway system from Gatwick into London is far less efficient than from Heathrow, so buses, minivans, or cabs can end up taking two to three hours if traffic is in a snarl. Your best bet for getting into Central London is the handy **Gatwick Express train** (☎ **0990/301-530;** www.gatwickexpress.co.uk), right in the South terminal. The train serves airport passengers only, and offers plenty of room for luggage and a flight check-in option at Victoria Station (convenient when you're returning to the airport from London). The train whizzes you from the airport to Victoria Station in half an hour for £11 ($18) express class, £16 ($24) first class. Trains run daily every 15 minutes 5:20 a.m. to midnight, and hourly (1:30, 2:35, 3:35, 4:35 a.m.) throughout the night.

The local **Connex South-Central train** (☎ **01332/387-601**) also runs to Victoria Station in half an hour and costs £8.20 ($13). Older than the Gatwick Express, these trains are regular passenger trains. Four trains run an hour during the day; they run every half-hour from midnight to 5 a.m.

Hotelink (☎ **01293/552-251;** www.hotelink.co.uk) is a minibus service that charges £20 ($32) to take you directly to your hotel. Minibuses are available at the terminal on the half-hour in the summer or on the hour in winter.

Checker Cars provide 24-hour taxi service between Gatwick and Central London. You find cars outside the terminals, or you can order a taxi from the South terminal (☎ **01293/502-808**) or the North terminal (☎ **01293/569-790**). Fares are £65 ($104) plus tip for the 90-minute journey.

Arriving at another London airport

If you fly from North America, you'll arrive at Heathrow or Gatwick. European travelers have three other airport options in London:

- About 33 miles northeast of Central London, **Stansted** (☎ **08700/000-303**) is a single-terminal airport used for national and European flights. The **Stansted Express** (☎ **08457/444-422;** www.stanstedexpress.com) to Liverpool Street Station takes 45 minutes and costs £13 ($21). Trains run every half-hour daily 6 a.m. to 11:59 p.m. A taxi fare into the city averages about £60 ($96) plus tip.

- A mere 6 miles from the city center, **London City Airport** (☎ **0207/646-000**) services European destinations only. A **blue shuttle bus** (☎ **02076/460-000**) takes passengers from the airport to Liverpool Street Station in 25 minutes for £5 ($8). The buses run every ten minutes daily 6 a.m. to 9:30 p.m. A taxi to the vicinity of Marble Arch costs about £25 ($40) plus tip.
- A small independent airport 33 miles northwest of the city, **Luton** (☎ **01582/405-100**) services European charter flights. The **Greenline 757 Bus** (☎ **08706/087-261**) runs from the airport to the Victoria Coach Station on Buckingham Palace Road daily every hour from 5:30 a.m. to midnight; the trip takes about 75 minutes and costs £8 ($13). The 24-hour **Railair Coach Link** also runs to Luton Station (3 miles away), where it connects with the Thameslink City Flyer train to King's Cross Station in Central London. The fare is £9.50 ($15); trip time is one hour. Taxis into the city cost about £50 ($80) plus tip.

Taking the train

If you travel to London by train from the Continent, you'll probably get off the train near the English Channel and take a ferry or hovercraft (a high-speed ferry) across the water. You'll disembark at one of the United Kingdom's Channel ports. The ports closest to London are Dover, Ramsgate, and Folkestone to the east, and Southhampton, Portsmouth, and Newhaven to the south. From there you take another train into London. Trains connecting with ferries on the U.K. side of the Channel generally go to Liverpool Street Station, Victoria Station, or Waterloo International. Waterloo is also where the Eurostar Chunnel trains arrive from Paris and Brussels. (The Chunnel is the tunnel beneath the English Channel.) On the super-convenient Eurostar, you don't have to make any train-boat-train transfers along the way.

London's train stations are bustling beehives of activity. In them you find restaurants, bookstores, news agents, bureaux de change, and many of the services you would find at an airport. London's main **Tourist Information Centre,** in the forecourt of Victoria Station, is open Monday through Saturday 8 a.m. to 7 p.m. in January and February, 9 a.m. to 8 p.m. from Easter through May and October through Easter, and 8 a.m. to 9 p.m. from June through September; Sunday year-round from 9 a.m. to 6 p.m. The agency offers booking services and free maps and brochures on London attractions and entertainment. Tourist information centers are also located in the Liverpool Street Underground station (open Monday through Friday from 8 a.m. to 6 p.m., Saturday from 8 a.m. to 5:30 p.m., and on Sunday from 9 a.m. to 5:30 p.m.) and the Arrivals Hall of the Waterloo International terminal (open daily 8:30 a.m. to 10:30 p.m.).

London's train stations link to the Underground system. Just look for the Underground symbol (a circle with a horizontal line through it). Waterloo links to the Northern and Bakerloo lines; Victoria is on the District, Circle, and Victoria lines; Liverpool Street is on the Circle, East London, Metropolitan, and Central lines. (See "Getting Around London," later in the chapter, for more information about the Underground.) There are taxi ranks outside all the train stations.

Orienting Yourself in London

From its beginnings as a Roman garrison town called *Londinium* nearly 2,000 years ago, London has grown steadily and in a somewhat pell-mell fashion, swallowing up what were small villages. Today, Greater London encompasses a whopping 622 square miles, an area larger than some of England's national parks. The main tourist portion of London is only a fraction of that (25 square miles at the most).

London's size, along with its confusing and sometimes oddly named streets and its seemingly endless plethora of neighborhoods, confounds many visitors — and Londoners as well. To help you find your way around, I strongly suggest that you buy a copy of *London A to Z* (*z* is pronounced "zed"). You can pick up this indexed street map at just about any bookstore or from any news agent. You may want to get it at the airport.

Introducing the Neighborhoods

London grew up along the north and south banks of the **River Thames,** which snakes through the city in a long, loose S curve. This great tidal river has played a major role in London's growth and prosperity through the ages. London's major tourist sights, hotels, and restaurants are on the river's **north bank,** while many of the city's famous performing arts venues are on the **south bank.**

Central London, on the north bank of the Thames, is considered the city center. Londoners think of this district as roughly the area covered by the Circle Line Underground route, with Paddington Station anchoring the northwest corner, Earl's Court at the southwest corner, Tower Hill at the southeast corner, and Liverpool Street Station at the northeast corner. Central London is divided into three areas: **The City of London,** the **West End,** and **West London.**

All London street addresses include a designation, such as SW1 or EC3. These are **postal districts,** like ZIP codes in the United States. When you actually hit the streets, the postal district designations aren't as important as the nearest Tube stop.

For the locations of the districts in the following sections, see the "London's Neighborhoods" map in this chapter.

The City of London

The City of London is a self-governing entity extending south from Chiswell Street to the Thames. The area is bounded to the west by Chancery Lane and to the east by the Tower of London, its most important historic monument. Fleet Street, the former heart of newspaper publishing, cuts through the center of the district to Ludgate Circus, where it becomes Ludgate and leads to St. Paul's Cathedral. Built on top of the original 1 square mile the Romans called *Londinium* is an area called The City. Today, this is the Wall Street of England, home to the Bank of England, the Royal Exchange, and the Stock Exchange. The major Tube stops are Blackfriars, Tower Hill, St. Paul's, Liverpool Street Station (the main rail terminus in this area), Bank, Barbican, and Moorgate.

West End

The West End (that is, west of The City) may be loosely called "downtown" London. For most people, the West End is synonymous with the theater, entertainment, and shopping areas around Piccadilly Circus and Leicester Square. But the West End actually includes a host of neighborhoods:

- **Holborn:** Abutting the City of London to the west is the old borough of Holborn, the legal heart of London. Barristers, solicitors, and law clerks scurry to and fro among the Inns of Court, Lincoln's Inn Fields, and Royal Courts of Justice and Old Bailey. This in-between district is bounded roughly by Theobald's Road to the north, Farringdon Road to the east, the Thames to the south, and Kingsway, Aldwych, and Lancaster Place to the west. The major Tube stops are Holborn, Temple, and Blackfriars.
- **The Strand and Covent Garden:** The northern section of The Strand, the area west of Holborn, is Covent Garden, with Shaftesbury Avenue as its northern boundary. The Strand, a major street running from Trafalgar Square to Fleet Street, is the principal thoroughfare along the southern edge, with Charing Cross Road to the west and Kingsway, Aldwych, and Lancaster Place to the east. The major Tube stops are Covent Garden, Leicester Square, and Charing Cross.
- **Bloomsbury:** Just north of Covent Garden, New Oxford Street and Bloomsbury Way mark the beginnings of the Bloomsbury district. Home of the British Museum and several colleges and universities, this intellectual pocket of Central London is bounded to the east by Woburn Place and Southampton Row, to the north by Euston Road, and to the west by Tottenham Court Road. The major Tube

London's Neighborhoods

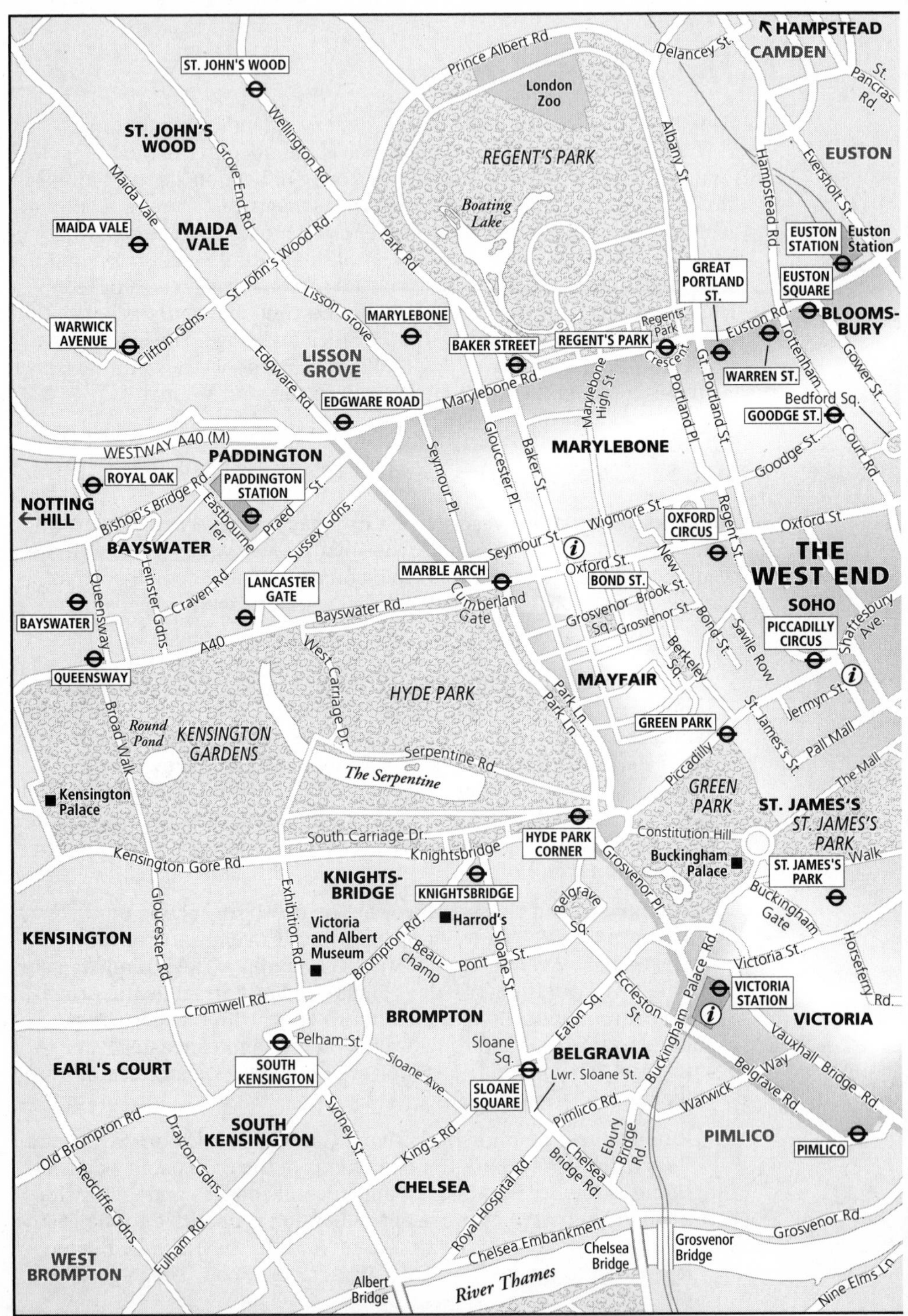

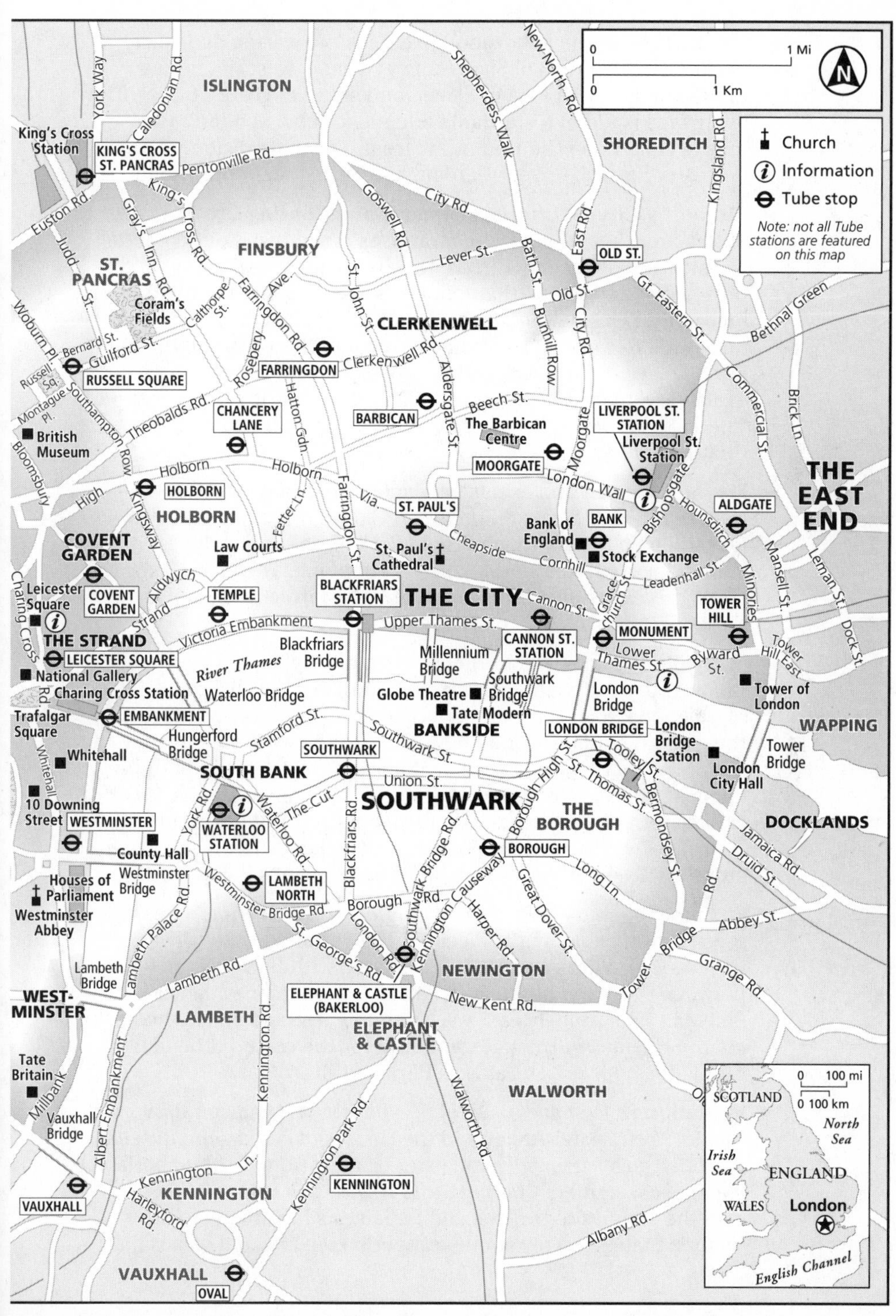
ISLINGTON
SHOREDITCH
FINSBURY
CLERKENWELL
ST. PANCRAS
HOLBORN
COVENT GARDEN
THE STRAND
THE CITY
THE EAST END
BANKSIDE
SOUTH BANK
SOUTHWARK
THE BOROUGH
DOCKLANDS
WAPPING
NEWINGTON
LAMBETH
WESTMINSTER
ELEPHANT & CASTLE
WALWORTH
KENNINGTON
VAUXHALL
King's Cross Station
KING'S CROSS ST. PANCRAS
RUSSELL SQUARE
FARRINGDON
BARBICAN
CHANCERY LANE
HOLBORN
ST. PAUL'S
MOORGATE
LIVERPOOL ST. STATION
Liverpool St. Station
OLD ST.
BANK
ALDGATE
TOWER HILL
MONUMENT
CANNON ST. STATION
BLACKFRIARS STATION
TEMPLE
COVENT GARDEN
LEICESTER SQUARE
EMBANKMENT
SOUTHWARK
LONDON BRIDGE
WATERLOO STATION
WESTMINSTER
LAMBETH NORTH
BOROUGH
ELEPHANT & CASTLE (BAKERLOO)
KENNINGTON
VAUXHALL
OVAL
Coram's Fields
British Museum
Law Courts
St. Paul's Cathedral
The Barbican Centre
Bank of England
Stock Exchange
Leicester Square
National Gallery
Charing Cross Station
Trafalgar Square
Whitehall
10 Downing Street
County Hall
Houses of Parliament
Westminster Abbey
Tate Britain
Millennium Bridge
Southwark Bridge
Globe Theatre
Tate Modern
London Bridge
London Bridge Station
Tower of London
Tower Bridge
London City Hall
River Thames
Blackfriars Bridge
Waterloo Bridge
Hungerford Bridge
Westminster Bridge
Lambeth Bridge
Vauxhall Bridge
York Way
Caledonian Rd.
Pentonville Rd.
Euston Rd.
King's Cross Rd.
Gray's Inn Rd.
Judd St.
Woburn Pl.
Bernard St.
Guilford St.
Russell Sq.
Montague Pl.
Southampton Row
Bloomsbury
Calthorpe St.
Farringdon Rd.
Rosebery Ave.
Theobalds Rd.
Hatton Gdn.
Holborn
High
Kingsway
Fetter Ln.
Holborn Via.
Farringdon St.
St. John St.
Goswell Rd.
City Rd.
Lever St.
Bath St.
Old St.
Bunhill Row
Aldersgate St.
Beech St.
Clerkenwell Rd.
Shepherdess Walk
New North Rd.
East Rd.
City Rd.
Kingsland Rd.
Gt. Eastern St.
Bethnal Green
Commercial St.
Brick Ln.
Moorgate
London Wall
Bishopsgate
Houndsditch
Cheapside
Cornhill
Leadenhall St.
Cannon St.
Gracechurch St.
Minories
Mansell St.
Leman St.
Dock St.
Tower Hill East
Byward St.
Lower Thames St.
Upper Thames St.
Victoria Embankment
Aldwych
Strand
Charing Cross Rd.
Stamford St.
Southwark St.
Union St.
Borough High St.
Tooley St.
St. Thomas St.
Bermondsey St.
Jamaica Rd.
Druid St.
The Cut
Waterloo Rd.
York Rd.
Blackfriars Rd.
Southwark Bridge Rd.
Kennington Causeway
Long Ln.
Great Dover St.
Harper Rd.
Westminster Bridge Rd.
Borough Rd.
London Rd.
St. George's Rd.
Lambeth Palace Rd.
Lambeth Rd.
Kennington Rd.
New Kent Rd.
Tower Bridge Rd.
Abbey St.
Grange Rd.
Walworth Rd.
Kennington Park Rd.
Albert Embankment
Millbank
Kennington Ln.
Harleyford Rd.
Albany Rd.
0 1 Mi
0 1 Km
N
Church
Information
Tube stop
Note: not all Tube stations are featured on this map
SCOTLAND
0 100 mi
0 100 km
North Sea
Irish Sea
ENGLAND
WALES
London
English Channel

stops are Euston Square, Russell Square, Goodge Street, and Tottenham Court Road.

- **Soho:** The Soho neighborhood occupies the warren of densely packed streets north of Shaftesbury Avenue, west of Charing Cross Road, east of Regent Street, and south of Oxford Street. This lively area is full of restaurants and nightclubs. London's Gay Village centers on Old Compton Street. The major Tube stops are Leicester Square, Covent Garden, and Tottenham Court Road.
- **Piccadilly Circus, Leicester Square, and Charing Cross:** Think of this area, just west of The Strand, as downtown London or Theatreland. Piccadilly Circus, the area's major traffic hub and best-known tourist destination, feeds into Regent Street and Piccadilly. Leicester Square and Shaftesbury Avenue, a few minutes' walk to the east, are home to most of the West End theaters. From Leicester Square, Charing Cross Road runs south to Trafalgar Square, the National Gallery, and Charing Cross Station. The Tube stops are Piccadilly Circus, Leicester Square, and Charing Cross.
- **Mayfair:** Elegant and exclusive Mayfair nestles comfortably between Regent Street on the west, Oxford Street on the north, Piccadilly on the south, and Hyde Park on the west. This is the land of luxury hotels and luxurious shopping. The major Tube stops are Piccadilly Circus, Bond Street, Marble Arch, and Hyde Park Corner.
- **Marylebone:** The neighborhood north of Mayfair and west of Bloomsbury, Marylebone (*Mar*-lee-bone) abuts giant Regent's Park. Marylebone Road runs south of the park. Great Portland Street is the eastern boundary and Edgware Road the western. You may call this "Medical London," because it has several hospitals and the famous Harley Street Clinic. But perhaps the most famous street is Baker Street, home of the fictional Sherlock Holmes. Madame Tussaud's wax museum is on Marylebone Road. The major Tube stops are Baker Street, Marylebone, and Regent's Park.
- **St. James's:** Considered "Royal London," St. James's is a posh green haven beginning at Piccadilly and stretching southwest to include Green Park and St. James's Park, with Buckingham Palace between them and St. James's Palace across from St. James's Park. Pall Mall runs roughly east-west into the area and meets the north-south St. James's Street. Regent Street is the eastern boundary. The Tube stops are St. James's Park and Green Park.
- **Westminster:** East and south of St. James's, Westminster draws visitors to Westminster Abbey and the Houses of Parliament, the seat of British government. Westminster extends from Northumberland Avenue just south of Charing Cross to Vauxhall Bridge Road, with the Thames to the east and St. James's Park to the west. Victoria Station, on the southwest perimeter, is a kind of axis for

Westminster, Belgravia, and Pimlico (see the next two listings). The Tube stops are Westminster, St. James's Park, and Victoria.

- **Pimlico:** The pie-shaped wedge of London extending west from Vauxhall Bridge Road to Buckingham Palace Road is Pimlico. Crowning it to the north is Victoria Station, and here you also find the Tate Britain gallery. The Tube stops are Pimlico and Victoria.
- **Belgravia:** A posh quarter long favored by aristocrats, Belgravia begins west of Victoria Station and Green Park and extends south to the river and west to Sloane Street; Hyde Park bounds the area to the north. Belgravia is where many foreign embassies are located. The Tube stops are Victoria, Hyde Park Corner, and Sloane Square.

West London

West London — still considered part of Central London — has several distinctive neighborhoods filled with hotels, restaurants, great shopping, and major tourist attractions.

- **Knightsbridge:** West of Belgravia is the fashionable residential and shopping district of Knightsbridge, bounded to the north by Hyde Park and to the west by Brompton Road, where you find Harrods, the neighborhood's chief shopping attraction. The Tube stops are Knightsbridge and Sloane Square.
- **Chelsea:** Below Knightsbridge and west of Belgravia, Chelsea begins at Sloane Square and runs south to the Thameside Cheyne Walk and Chelsea Embankment. King's Road, a bustling shopping artery, acts as its northern boundary and Chelsea Bridge Road its eastern border. To the west, Chelsea extends as far as Earl's Court Road, Redcliffe Gardens, and Edith Grove. The Tube stop is Sloane Square.
- **South Kensington:** Forming the green northern boundary of South Kensington are Kensington Gardens and Hyde Park. Frequently referred to as Museumland, South Ken hops with hotels, restaurants, and tourists flocking to the Natural History Museum, Science Museum, and Victoria & Albert Museum. The district is bounded to the west by Palace Gate and Gloucester Road, to the east by Fulham Road, and to the south by busy Brompton Road. The Tube stops are Gloucester Road and South Kensington.
- **Kensington:** The residential neighborhood of Kensington fills the gap between Kensington Gardens and Holland Park, with Notting Hill Gate and Bayswater Road marking its northern boundary. Kensington Church Street runs north-south between Notting Hill Gate and Kensington High Street. Kensington Palace, formerly the home of Princess Diana, sits on the western side of Kensington Gardens. The Tube stop is High Street Kensington.

- **Earl's Court:** Beginning south of West Cromwell Road and extending down to Lillie Road and Brompton Road is the down-to-earth Earl's Court neighborhood. Its western boundary is North End Road and its eastern boundary is Earl's Court Road. You won't find any major tourist attractions in Earl's Court, which has long been a haven for budget travelers (particularly Australians — hence its nickname "Kangaroo Court") and for gays and lesbians. The area is gradually being spruced up, but many streets still look a bit frayed. The Tube stop is Earl's Court.
- **Notting Hill:** Beginning north of Holland Park, Kensington Gardens, and Hyde Park (Holland Park Avenue and Bayswater Road run along the northern perimeter of the parks) are Notting Hill and the rising subneighborhood of Notting Hill Gate. The area is bounded by Clarendon Road to the west, Queensway to the east, and Wesbourne Grove to the north. The most famous street, Portobello Road, runs north-south through the center. The super-hip neighborhood was a backdrop for the 1999 movie *Notting Hill,* starring Julia Roberts and Hugh Grant. The Tube stops are Notting Hill Gate, Bayswater, and Queensway.
- **Bayswater and Paddington:** Picking up where Notting Hill ends, Bayswater runs east to meet Marylebone at Edgware Road. The roaring A40 (Westway) highway acts as its northern boundary. Paddington Station is in the northwestern corner of Bayswater. This area is fairly commercial and not particularly attractive. Here you find no major tourist attractions and plenty of budget B&Bs. The Tube stops are Paddington, Lancaster Gate, Marble Arch, and Edgware Road.

The South Bank

You probably won't stay on the South Bank, but you may be going to the South Bank Centre for a play or a concert at one of its internationally known arts and performance venues, all clustered beside the river

The royal rap sheet

Thanks to a dog named Dotty, Princess Anne, otherwise known as the princess royal, became the first member of the modern royal family to have a criminal record. On April 1, 2003, Anne and her husband were walking their three English bull terriers in the park around Windsor Castle (see Chapter 13). Dotty, one of the dogs, bolted away, knocked over two boys on bicycles, and bit them. In court, Anne pleaded guilty to charges of losing control of her dog and was required to pay a £500 ($800) fine, £250 ($400) to the boys, and £148 ($237) in court costs. Dotty escaped destruction but was ordered to undergo retraining and be leashed and muzzled in public.

within easy walking distance of Waterloo Station. Closer to Westminster Bridge is the city's newest high-rise attraction: the British Airways London Eye observation wheel. For a scenic route to the South Bank, take the Tube to Embankment, on the north bank, and walk across the Thames on the newly glitzed-up Hungerford pedestrian bridge. The Jubilee Walkway, a breezy riverside path, extends east from the South Bank Centre to the new Tate Modern art gallery, the Globe Theatre, the new London City Hall, and Tower Bridge. The new pedestrian-only Millennium Bridge spans the Thames from the Tate Modern to St. Paul's Cathedral. The Tube stops are Waterloo, London Bridge, and Southwark.

Finding Information After You Arrive

The **Britain Visitor Centre,** 1 Regent St., Piccadilly Circus, SW1 (Tube: Piccadilly Circus), provides tourist information to walk-in visitors; phone assistance isn't available. The office is open Monday to Friday 9 a.m. to 6:30 p.m. and Saturday and Sunday 10 a.m. to 4 p.m. (Saturday until 5 p.m. June through October). You can find hotel- and theater-booking agencies, a currency exchange, and plenty of free brochures on river trips, walking tours, and day trips from London.

The main **Tourist Information Centre,** run by the London Tourist Board, is in the forecourt of Victoria Station (Tube: Victoria). Hours are Monday through Saturday 8 a.m. to 7 p.m. in January and February, 9 a.m. to 8 p.m. from Easter through May and October through Easter, and 8 a.m. to 9 p.m. from June through September; it's also open Sunday year-round from 9 a.m. to 6 p.m. The center offers booking services and free literature on London attractions and entertainment, as well as an excellent bookshop. Other Tourist Information Centres are in the following locations (please note that these locations don't have telephone numbers):

- **Heathrow Airport Terminal 1, 2, and 3 Underground station** (open Monday through Friday 6:15 a.m. to 5 p.m., Saturday and Sunday 7:15 a.m. to 4 p.m.).
- **Liverpool Street Underground station** (open Monday through Friday from 8 a.m. to 6 p.m., Saturday from 8 a.m. to 5:30 p.m., and on Sunday from 9 a.m. to 5:30 p.m.).
- **Waterloo International Terminal Arrivals Hall** (open daily from 8:30 a.m. to 10:30 p.m.).

LondonLine at ☎ **09068/663-344** provides 24-hour information, updated daily, on everything that's going on. At 60p (95¢) per minute, this service isn't cheap, but it's reliable, providing information about the Changing of the Guard, guided walks, special attractions (such as the summer opening of Buckingham Palace), and tours.

For current listings and reviews of everything that's going on, buy a copy of *Time Out.* This publication hits the newsstands on Wednesday and costs about £2 ($3.20).

Getting around London

You can choose many ways to get around London. If you travel for any distance, the fastest mode of transportation in this enormous city is the Underground or Tube (the subway system). Many of the slower but more scenic buses are double-deckers. Most convenient (unless you're stuck in a traffic jam) is to go by taxi. But walking is the most fun of all. When you're on foot, you see more and can explore some of the leafy squares and cobbled lanes that contribute to London's enduring charm.

For general London travel information, call ☎ **02072/221-234.** You can get free bus and Underground maps and buy Travelcards and bus passes (see the next section, "Scurrying around with the new Oyster card") at any major Underground station or at the London Travel Information Centres in the stations at King's Cross; Liverpool Street; Oxford Circus; Piccadilly Circus; St. James's Park; Victoria; and Heathrow Terminals 1, 2, and 3.

Scurrying around with the new Oyster card

Just as this edition of *England For Dummies* was going to press, the London transportation system announced a big change. Beginning in 2004, a new plastic "smart card" called **Oyster** will allow Tube and bus riders to prepay and save money on fares. Prepaying by credit or debit card at machines in Underground stations will also reduce long queues at ticket windows (or so it's hoped).

Tube and bus fares will be frozen at 2003 levels for anyone using the Oyster card. Paper tickets will remain available, but non-Oyster Underground fares in Zone 1 will jump to £2 ($3.20), and the non-Oyster cash-only bus fare for Central London will climb to £1 ($1.60). Other changes include allowing children under 11 to travel free on buses and allowing children to travel free on weekends with the Family Travelcard. (See the section "Saving with Travelcards," later in this chapter.) For more information on the new Oyster card, visit its Web site at `www.oyster.com`. For general London public transportation updates, visit `www.londontransport.co.uk`.

Taking the Underground (subway)

London has the oldest and most comprehensive subway system in the world. The Tube is fast and convenient, and just about everyone but the royals use it. Everywhere you'll want to go is near a Tube stop, each of which is clearly marked by a red circle with a horizontal line through it. For an Underground map, see the inside back cover of this book.

Using the Underground

Thirteen Underground lines crisscross the city and intersect at various stations where you can change from one train to another. On Underground maps, every line is color-coded (Bakerloo is brown, Piccadilly is dark blue, and so on), which makes planning your route easy. All you need to know is the name of your stop and the direction you're heading. After you figure out which line you need to take, look on the map for the name of the last stop in the direction you need to go. The name of the last stop on the line appears on the front of the train and sometimes on electronic signboards that display the name of the arriving train. (The one exception to this is the Circle Line, which runs in a loop around Central London.) Inside all but the oldest trains are electronic signs, recorded voices, or both, which announce the name of each approaching stop. Easy-to-read route maps, with each station marked, are in every car.

Most of the Underground system operates with automated entry and exit gates. You feed your ticket into the slot and the ticket disappears and pops up again like a piece of toast, the gate bangs open, and you remove your ticket and pass through. At the other end, you do the same to get out, but the machine keeps the ticket (unless your ticket is a Travelcard, which the machine returns to you). Ticket collectors are located at some stations outside of Central London.

Traveling to your destination by Underground may require transferring from one Underground line to another. All Underground maps clearly show where various lines converge. Signs in the stations direct you from one line to another. To get from one line to another, you go through tunnels (which the Brits call "subways"), and you may have to go up or down a level or two.

Underground service stops around midnight (a little earlier on less-used lines). Keep this in mind when you're out painting the town red. If you miss the last train, you have to take a taxi or one of the night buses.

Buying tickets

You can purchase Underground tickets at the ticket window or from one of the automated machines found in most stations. Machines can change £5, £10, and £20 notes. Fares to every station are posted.

For fare purposes, the city is divided into zones. **Zone 1** covers all Central London. **Zone 6** extends as far as Heathrow to the west and Upminster to the east. Make sure your ticket covers all the zones you're traveling through (no problem if you're staying in Central London), or you may have to pay a £10 ($16) penalty fare.

A **single-fare one-way ticket** within one zone costs £1.60 ($2.40) for an adult and 60p (95¢) for a child from 5 to 15 years of age. You don't have to pay more than this to reach any sight in Central London (provided you're also staying in Central London). Tickets are valid for use on the day of issue only.

If you're going to travel by Underground, you can save time and money by buying a book of 10 tickets, called a "carnet." **Carnet tickets** are valid in one zone only. Each ticket is good for a single ride on any day. The price is £11.50 ($18) for an adult and £5 ($8) for a child. With a carnet you save £4.50 ($7) over single fares and don't have to wait in line to buy tickets. With a Travelcard (see the next section), you can save even more.

Saving with Travelcards

To make the most of London's public transportation system, consider buying a **Travelcard,** which allows unlimited travel by Underground *and* bus. You can purchase these cards in the following increments:

- A **one-day Travelcard for Zones 1 and 2** (everything in Central London) costs £4.10 ($7) for an adult and £2 ($3.20) for a child; the card is valid after 9:30 a.m. weekdays and all day Saturday and Sunday.
- The **weekend Travelcard for Zones 1 and 2,** good for a consecutive Saturday and Sunday, costs £6.10 ($10) for an adult and £3 ($4.80) for a child. *Note:* This Travelcard isn't valid between midnight and 4:30 a.m.
- A **seven-day Travelcard for Zone 1** (all Central London) costs £16.50 ($26) for an adult and £6.80 ($11) for a child.
- The **Family Travelcard** is good for families or groups of one or two adults traveling with one to four children; to use it, you must travel together as a group. The Family Travelcard is valid after 9:30 a.m. Monday to Friday and all day Saturday and Sunday. Rates for one day of travel in Zones 1 and 2 are £2.70 ($4.30) for an adult and 80p ($1.30) for a child.

  Note: This Travelcard isn't valid after midnight — long after most families are asleep.

If you travel by Tube or bus before 9:30 a.m. and still want a bargain day pass, buy a **one-day all-zone LT Card** for £8 ($12) adults, £3.50 ($6) children.

Another great way to save money on London transportation is the **Visitor Travelcard,** which you can buy in the United States and Canada before leaving home (they aren't available in London). You can choose from two kinds of Visitor Travelcards, the All Zone and the Central Zone (good for Zone 1 only); both allow unlimited travel on the Tube and bus and are available in three-, four-, or seven-day increments. Prices for the Central Zone card are $22 for adults and $10 for children for 3 days; $27 for adults and $11 for children for 4 days; and $33 for adults and $14 for children for 7 days. (Buying a 7-day Travelcard in London costs less but requires a photo.) You can buy Visitor Travelcards by contacting a travel agent, by calling **RailEurope** from the United States at ☎ **877/272-RAIL,** from Canada at ☎ 800/361-RAIL, or by going online to www.raileurope.com.

Riding a bus

Distinctive red double-decker buses are very much a part of London's snarled traffic scene, but not all London buses are double-deckers, and some aren't red. The one drawback to bus travel, especially for first-timers, is that you need to know the streets of London so you can get off at the correct stop. Get a free bus map at one of the Travel Information Centres (see "Finding Information After You Arrive," earlier in this chapter), or you may overshoot your destination. On the plus side, riding the bus is cheaper than taking the Tube; you don't have to contend with escalators, elevators, or tunnels; and you get to see the sights as you travel.

A concrete post with a red or white sign on top reading "London Transport Bus Service" clearly marks each bus stop. Another sign shows the routes of the buses that stop there. If the sign on top is red, the stop is a request stop, meaning you must hail the approaching bus as you would a taxi (don't whistle, just put up your hand). If the sign is white, the bus stops automatically. Be sure to check the destination sign in front of the bus to make certain that the bus travels the entire route. Have some coins with you, because the driver won't change banknotes.

The bus network is divided into two fare zones to simplify cash transactions. **Zone 1** covers all Central London, including all the main tourist sites. **Zone 2** is everything beyond Zone 1. If you travel by bus into, from, within, and across Central London (Zone 1), the bus fare for adults is £1 ($1.60). For any bus journey you take in outer London (Zone 2), the fare is 70p ($1.10). Children pay a 40p (65¢) flat rate good for both zones. *Note*: Child fares aren't available 10 p.m. to 4:30 a.m. Children 14 and 15 years old must have a **Child Photocard** to obtain the child rate; you must supply your own passport-size photo for this free ID card, which is available at a Tube station or one of the Travel Information Centres.

A **one-day bus pass** is a good thing to have if you plan to do much traveling by bus. The pass can be used all day but isn't valid on N-prefixed night buses (see the next paragraph). You can purchase this and bus passes good for longer periods at most Underground stations, selected news agents, and the Travel Information Centres. A one-day bus pass for all Central London costs £2 ($3.20) for an adult and £1 ($1.60) for a child age 5 to 15. A **seven-day bus pass** for Central London costs £8.50 ($14) for an adult and £4 ($6) for a child 5 to 15. *Note*: Children must have a **Child Photocard** ID in order to buy and use any of these passes; the card is free at major Tube stations and Travel Information Centres but requires a passport-sized photograph.

At the witching hour of midnight, buses become **night buses** ("N"), their routes change, and Central London fares increase to £1.50 ($2.40). Your one-day bus pass and family or weekend Travelcard won't be good on a Night Bus. Nearly all Night Buses pass through Trafalgar Square, Central London's late-night magnet for insomniacs.

Hailing a taxi

Taking a taxi is a safe and comfortable way to get around the city. Riding in the old-fashioned, roomy black taxis is a pleasure. Today, there are also many smaller and newer-model taxis. London cabs of any size or color aren't cheap. The fare starts at £1.40 ($2.25) for one person, with 40p (65¢) for each additional passenger. Then you have to deal with the surcharges: 10p (16¢) per item of luggage; 60p (95¢) weeknights 8 p.m. to midnight; 90p ($1.50) from midnight until 7 a.m.; 60p (95¢) Saturday and Sunday until 8 p.m. and 90p ($1.50) after that. The meter leaps 20p (32¢) every 111 yards or 90 seconds. Tip your cabbie 10% to 15% of the total fare.

You can hail a cab on the street. If a cab is available, the yellow or white FOR HIRE sign on the roof is lit. You can order a **radio cab** by calling ☎ **02072/720-272** or 02072/535-000. Be aware that if you call for a cab, the meter starts ticking when the taxi receives notification from the dispatcher.

London is one city where you don't have to worry about whether the cabdriver knows where he's going. When it comes to finding a street address, London cabbies are among the most knowledgeable in the world. Their rigorous training, which includes an exhaustive street test called "The Knowledge," gives them an encyclopedic grasp of the terrain.

Walking on your own two feet

Sure, you can hop from one place to the next using the Tube, a bus, or a cab. But if you really want to get acquainted with the charming hodgepodge and monumental grandeur of London, bring along a good pair of walking shoes and explore on foot. Everywhere you turn, you see enticing side streets, countrylike lanes, little *mews dwellings* (former stables converted into homes), and picturesque garden squares. London's great parks are as safe to walk in as its streets. (In fact, crime is less prevalent in London than in many other major cities, and all the neighborhoods included in this book are safe.)

If you want to follow a detailed stroll or two around the city, perhaps of Dickens's London or of Westminster and Whitehall, check out the 11 tours in *Frommer's Memorable Walks in London* by Richard Jones (Wiley Publishing, Inc.).

A 7-mile walk commemorating the life of Princess Diana opened walk passes through four of London's royal parks — St. James's Park, Green Park, Hyde Park, and Kensington Gardens. Along the way are 90 plaques that point out sites associated with Diana, including Kensington Palace (her home for 15 years), Buckingham Palace, St. James's Palace (where she shared an office with Prince Charles), and Spencer House (her family's mansion, now a museum).

When you walk in London (or anywhere in England), remember:

- **Traffic moves on the opposite side of the street from what you're accustomed to.** This sounds simple enough on paper, but in practice you need to keep reminding yourself to look in the "wrong" direction when crossing a street. Throughout London, you see LOOK RIGHT or LOOK LEFT painted on street crossings.
- **Pedestrian crossings are marked by striped lines (called *zebra crossings*) on the road.** Flashing lights near the curb indicate that drivers must stop and yield the right of way when a pedestrian steps out into the zebra to cross the street.

Staying in Style

As you'd expect, London's hotels are the most expensive in England. Accommodations come in all shapes, sizes, and prices. Nothing is going to be as inexpensive as that roadside motel on the freeway back home, but you do find a few good budget hotels and plenty of B&Bs that won't cost you an arm and a leg. Sliding up the scale, you come to unique boutique hotels, older traditional hotels, large chain hotels, and several ultra-luxurious places known the world over. Basically, though, you find only two categories of accommodations: hotels and bed-and-breakfast inns.

Arriving in London without a hotel reservation is unwise, which is especially true if you visit from mid-April to early October (high season). If you do arrive without a reservation, you can book rooms through the agencies listed in Chapter 8.

If you stay in London over a weekend, ask if your hotel has a special weekend rate. Larger hotels that cater to business travelers often drastically reduce their rates and throw in a few extra perks for Friday-to-Sunday-night stays. Special weekend rates generally aren't available at smaller, less expensive hotels and B&Bs.

London's Top Hotels

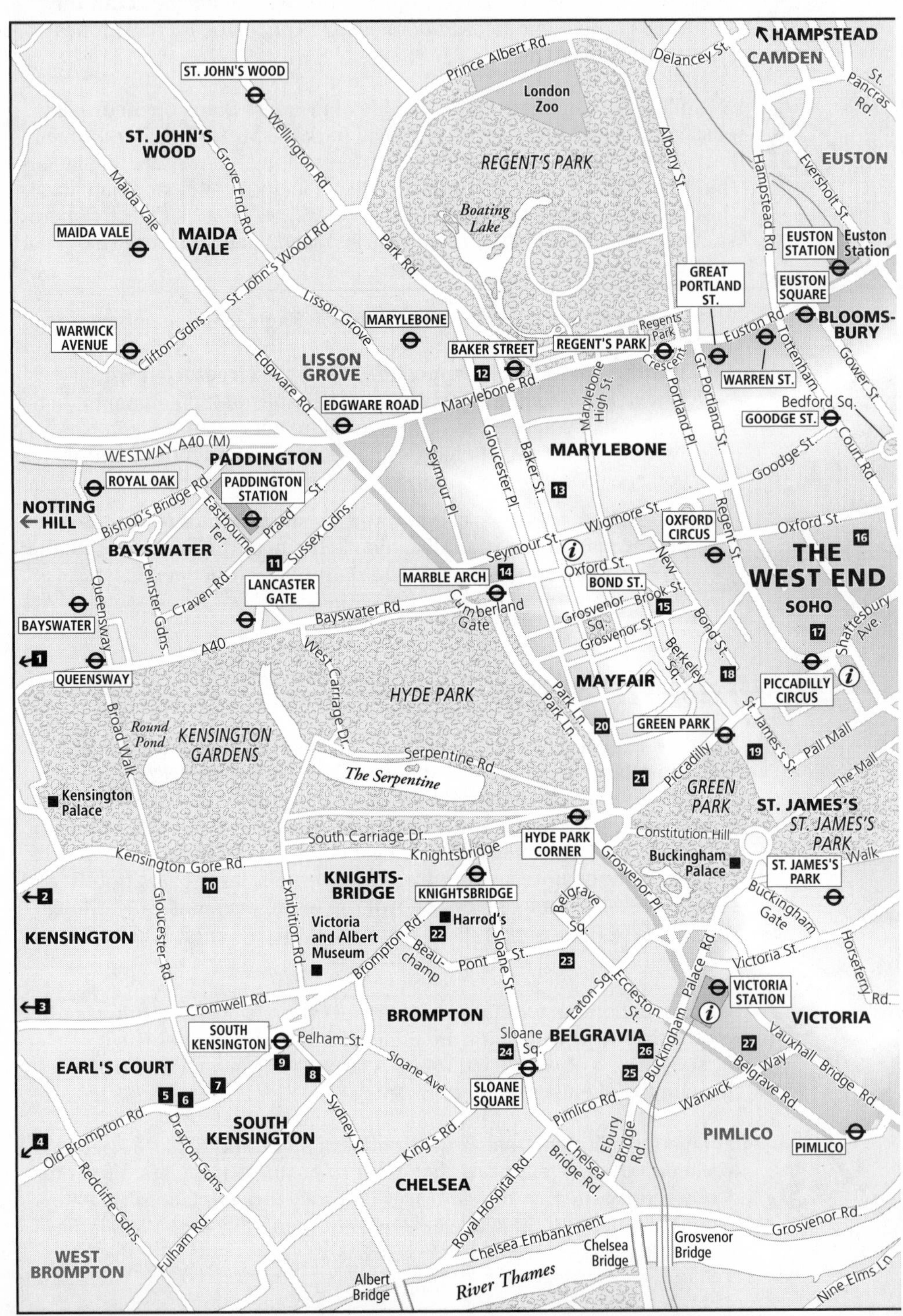

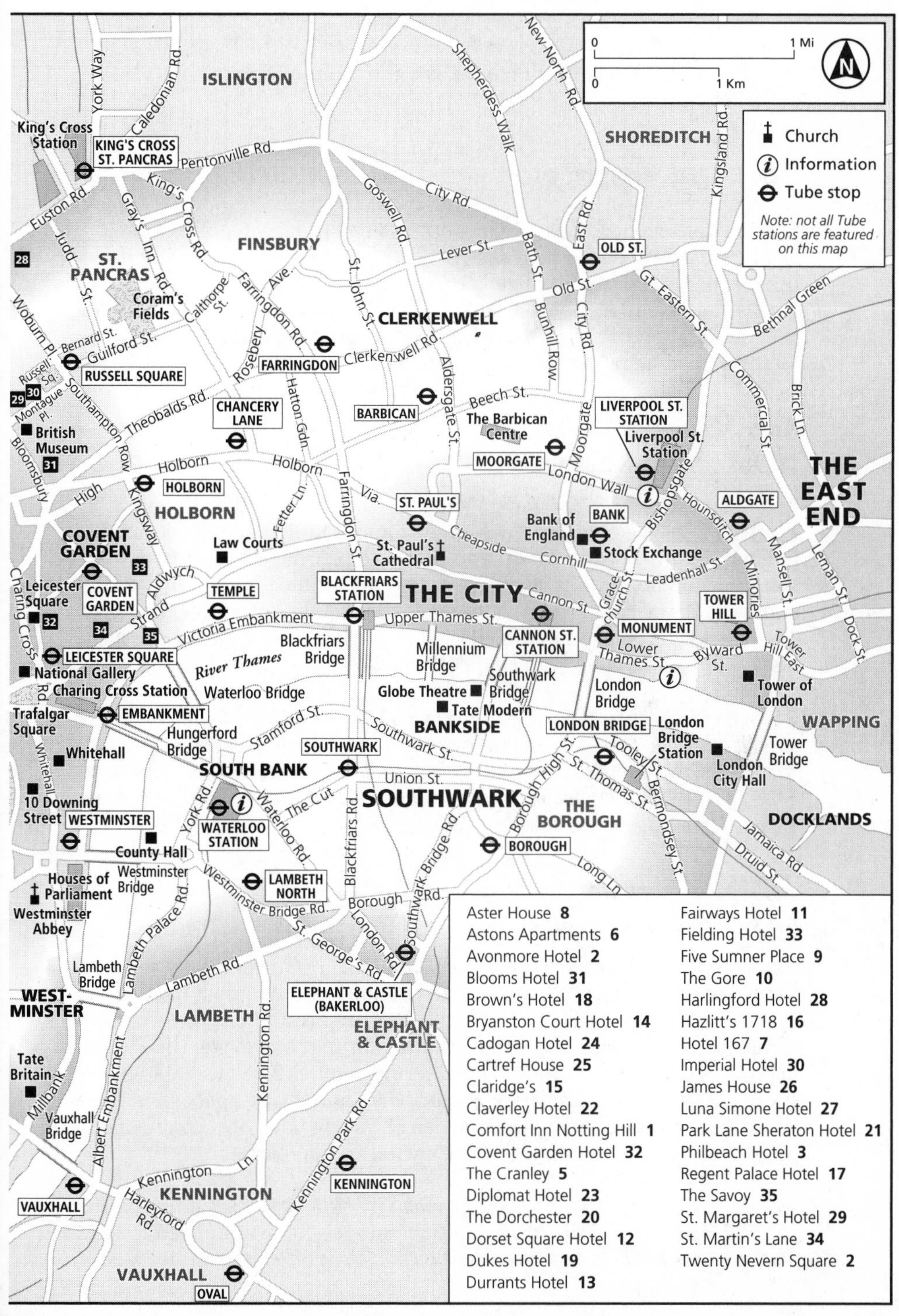
0 1 Mi
0 1 Km
N
Church
Information
Tube stop
Note: not all Tube stations are featured on this map
ISLINGTON
SHOREDITCH
FINSBURY
CLERKENWELL
ST. PANCRAS
HOLBORN
COVENT GARDEN
THE CITY
THE EAST END
WAPPING
BANKSIDE
SOUTH BANK
SOUTHWARK
THE BOROUGH
DOCKLANDS
WEST-MINSTER
LAMBETH
ELEPHANT & CASTLE
KENNINGTON
VAUXHALL
King's Cross Station
KING'S CROSS ST. PANCRAS
RUSSELL SQUARE
FARRINGDON
CHANCERY LANE
BARBICAN
OLD ST.
LIVERPOOL ST. STATION
Liverpool St. Station
MOORGATE
HOLBORN
ST. PAUL'S
BANK
ALDGATE
TEMPLE
BLACKFRIARS STATION
CANNON ST. STATION
MONUMENT
TOWER HILL
COVENT GARDEN
LEICESTER SQUARE
EMBANKMENT
SOUTHWARK
LONDON BRIDGE
WESTMINSTER
WATERLOO STATION
LAMBETH NORTH
BOROUGH
ELEPHANT & CASTLE (BAKERLOO)
KENNINGTON
VAUXHALL
OVAL
York Way
Caledonian Rd.
Pentonville Rd.
King's Cross Rd.
Euston Rd.
Judd St.
Gray's Inn Rd.
Woburn Pl.
Bernard St.
Guilford St.
Russell Sq.
Montague Pl.
Southampton Row
Bloomsbury
Calthorpe St.
Farringdon Rd.
Rosebery Ave.
Theobalds Rd.
Hatton Gdn.
Clerkenwell Rd.
St. John St.
Goswell Rd.
City Rd.
Lever St.
Shepherdess Walk
New North Rd.
East Rd.
Bath St.
Bunhill Row
City Rd.
Old St.
Kingsland Rd.
Gt. Eastern St.
Bethnal Green
Commercial St.
Brick Ln.
Beech St.
Aldersgate St.
Moorgate
London Wall
Bishopsgate
Houndsditch
Holborn
High Holborn
Kingsway
Fetter Ln.
Farringdon St.
Holborn Via.
Cheapside
Cornhill
Leadenhall St.
Gracechurch St.
Minories
Mansell St.
Leman St.
Dock St.
Tower Hill East
Byward St.
Lower Thames St.
Cannon St.
Upper Thames St.
Aldwych
Strand
Victoria Embankment
Charing Cross Rd.
River Thames
Blackfriars Bridge
Millennium Bridge
Southwark Bridge
London Bridge
Waterloo Bridge
Hungerford Bridge
Stamford St.
Southwark St.
Union St.
Tooley St.
St. Thomas St.
Borough High St.
Bermondsey St.
Jamaica Rd.
Druid St.
Long Ln.
The Cut
York Rd.
Waterloo Rd.
Blackfriars Rd.
Southwark Bridge Rd.
Borough Rd.
London Rd.
St. George's Rd.
Westminster Bridge Rd.
Lambeth Palace Rd.
Lambeth Rd.
Kennington Rd.
Kennington Park Rd.
Kennington Ln.
Harleyford Rd.
Albert Embankment
Millbank
Whitehall
Coram's Fields
British Museum
The Barbican Centre
Law Courts
St. Paul's Cathedral
Bank of England
Stock Exchange
Tower of London
Leicester Square
National Gallery
Charing Cross Station
Trafalgar Square
Whitehall
10 Downing Street
Globe Theatre
Tate Modern
London Bridge Station
Tower Bridge
London City Hall
County Hall
Westminster Bridge
Houses of Parliament
Westminster Abbey
Lambeth Bridge
Tate Britain
Vauxhall Bridge
28
29
30
31
32
33
34
35
Aster House 8
Astons Apartments 6
Avonmore Hotel 2
Blooms Hotel 31
Brown's Hotel 18
Bryanston Court Hotel 14
Cadogan Hotel 24
Cartref House 25
Claridge's 15
Claverley Hotel 22
Comfort Inn Notting Hill 1
Covent Garden Hotel 32
The Cranley 5
Diplomat Hotel 23
The Dorchester 20
Dorset Square Hotel 12
Dukes Hotel 19
Durrants Hotel 13
Fairways Hotel 11
Fielding Hotel 33
Five Sumner Place 9
The Gore 10
Harlingford Hotel 28
Hazlitt's 1718 16
Hotel 167 7
Imperial Hotel 30
James House 26
Luna Simone Hotel 27
Park Lane Sheraton Hotel 21
Philbeach Hotel 3
Regent Palace Hotel 17
The Savoy 35
St. Margaret's Hotel 29
St. Martin's Lane 34
Twenty Nevern Square 2

For a key to the dollar-sign ratings used in the hotel listings, see the Introduction. For general information on U.K. accommodations and for definitions of such terms as "value-added tax" (VAT), "self-catering rooms," and "English breakfast," see Chapter 8. For the locations of all the hotels I discuss in this chapter, see the "London's Top Hotels" map in this chapter.

The top hotels

London has an enormous range of hotels in all price categories and in all parts of town. I list a fair range of accommodations; if you want more options or have particular needs that my picks don't meet, the London Tourist Board's main **Tourist Information Centre** (☎ **020/7932-2020** for accommodation bookings), in the forecourt of Victoria Station (Tube: Victoria), can help you find what you need.

Aster House

$$–$$$ **South Kensington**

At the end of a street of early Victorian townhouses, this 12-unit, non-smoking B&B is a charmer. Each guest room is individually decorated in English country-house style, and many rooms have four-poster, half-canopied beds and silk wallpaper. The bathrooms come with power showers. Every room has a dataport for plugging in a laptop computer. The breakfasts, served in the glassed-in garden conservatory, are more health-conscious than you'd expect from an English B&B.

3 Sumner Place (near Onslow Sq.), London SW7 3EE. ☎ ***02075/815-888.*** *Fax: 02075/844-925. Internet:* `www.AsterHouse.com`. *Tube: South Kensington (then a five-minute walk west on Old Brompton Rd. and south on Sumner Place). Rack rates: £125–£165 ($200–$264) double; special winter rates posted on Web site. Rates include buffet continental breakfast. MC, V.*

Astons Apartments

$–$$ **South Kensington**

Astons offers value-packed accommodations in three carefully restored Victorian red-brick townhouses. Each studio has a compact kitchenette (great for families on a budget), a small bathroom, and bright, functional furnishings. (Because you can cook on your in-room stove, the English call these accommodations "self-catering" units.) The more expensive designer studios feature larger bathrooms, more living space, and extra pizazz in the decor. If you like the idea of having your own cozy London apartment (with daily maid service), you can't do better.

39 Rosary Gardens (off Hereford Sq.), London SW7 4NQ. ☎ ***800/525-2810*** *in the U.S. or 02075/906-000. Fax: 02075/906-060. Internet:* `www.astons-apartments.com`. *Tube: Gloucester Rd. (then a five-minute walk south on Gloucester Rd. and west on*

Hereford Sq.; Rosary Gardens is 1 block further west). Rack rates: £90–£125 ($144–$200) double. Rates don't include 17.5% VAT. AE, MC, V.

Avonmore Hotel

$$ **Kensington**

In 2000, the British Automobile Association awarded this small hotel four diamonds (out of a possible five) for its high standards of service. The property is in a quiet neighborhood easily accessible to West End theaters and shops. Each of the nine tastefully decorated guest rooms has an array of amenities (such as hairdryers, minibars, tea- and coffee-making facilities, and color televisions) not usually found in this price range. An English breakfast is served in a cheerful breakfast room, and a bar and limited room service are available. The staff can arrange babysitting if necessary.

*66 Avonmore Rd. (northwest of Earl's Court), London W14 8RS. ☎ **02076/034-296**. Fax: 02076/034-035. Internet:* `www.avonmorehotel.co.uk`*. Tube: West Kensington (then a five-minute walk north on North End Rd. and Mattheson Rd. to Avonmore Rd.). Rack rates: £95 ($152) double without bathroom, £105 ($168) double with bathroom; discounts for longer stays. Rates include English breakfast. AE, MC, V.*

Bryanston Court Hotel

$$ **Marylebone**

In a neighborhood with many attractive squares, three houses were joined to form the 200-year-old Bryanston Court, one of Central London's finest moderately priced hotels. Family owned and operated, the freshly refurbished 54-room hotel has small guest rooms (and equally small bathrooms) that are comfortably furnished and well maintained. You find a comfy bar with a fireplace in the back of the lounge.

*56–60 Great Cumberland Place (near Marble Arch), London W1H 7FD. ☎ **02072/623-141**. Fax: 02072/627-248. Internet:* `www.bryanstonhotel.com`*. Tube: Marble Arch (then a five-minute walk north on Great Cumberland Place to Bryanston Place). Rack rates: £110–£120 ($176–$192) double. Rates include continental breakfast. AE, DC, MC, V.*

Cadogan Hotel

$$$$–$$$$$ **Chelsea**

Memories of the Victorian era pervade this beautiful 65-room hotel, which is close to the exclusive Knightsbridge shops. The main floor includes a small, wood-paneled lobby and sumptuous drawing room (good for afternoon tea). The Cadogan (pronounced Ca-*dug*-en) is the hotel where Oscar Wilde was staying when he was arrested. (Room 118 is the Oscar Wilde Suite). The large guest rooms, many overlooking Cadogan Place gardens, are quietly tasteful and splendidly comfortable, with large bathrooms. The sedate Edwardian restaurant is known for its excellent cuisine.

75 Sloane St. (near Sloane Sq.), London SW1X 9SG. ☎ ***800/260-8338*** *in the U.S. or 02072/357-141. Fax: 02072/450-994. Internet:* www.cadogan.com. *Tube: Sloane Sq. (then a five-minute walk north on Sloane St.). Rack rates: £225–£280 ($360–$448) double. Rates don't include 17.5% VAT. AE, MC, V.*

Claverley Hotel

$$$–$$$$ **Knightsbridge**

On a country-quiet cul-de-sac a few blocks from Harrods and the best of Knightsbridge shopping, this cozy place is one of London's best B&Bs. Georgian-era accessories, 19th-century oil portraits, elegant antiques, and leather-covered sofas accent the public rooms. Most of the 29 guest rooms have wall-to-wall carpeting, upholstered armchairs, and marble bathrooms with tubs and power showers. The hotel offers an excellent English breakfast and great value for this tony area.

13–14 Beaufort Gardens (off Brompton Rd.), London SW3 1PS. ☎ ***800/747-0398*** *in the U.S. or 02075/898-541. Fax: 02075/843-410. Internet:* www.claverleyhotel.co.uk. *Tube: Knightsbridge (then a two-minute walk south past Harrods on Brompton Rd. to Beaufort Gardens). Rack rates: £120–£190 ($192–$304) double. Rates include English breakfast. AE, DC, MC, V.*

Comfort Inn Notting Hill

$ **Notting Hill**

Comfort Inn is a franchise, but you'll get a rate at least 10% lower than the official one if you book directly with the hotel instead of through central reservations (the lower "direct booking" rates appear in this listing). On a quiet, pretty street off Notting Hill Gate, the Comfort Inn stretches across five terrace houses and has 64 fair-sized rooms on the three upper floors (there's an elevator). Rooms have been redecorated with a nice traditional look and equipped with firm new beds; a few newly redone rooms face a charming interior courtyard. Standard amenities include dataports, coffeemakers, and hairdryers. The bathrooms are also newly renovated. Breakfast is a self-service buffet, or you can pay £5.95 ($10) for a full English breakfast.

6–14 Pembridge Gardens (near Pembridge Square), London W2 4DU. ☎ ***02072/296-666****. Fax: 02072/293-333. Internet:* www.lth-hotels.com. *Tube: Notting Hill Gate (then a two-minute walk north on Pembridge Gardens). Rack rates: £58–£94 ($93–$150) double. Rates include continental breakfast. AE, DC, MC, V.*

The Cranley

$$$–$$$$ **South Kensington**

On a quiet street near South Kensington's museums, the Cranley occupies a trio of restored 1875 townhouses. Luxuriously appointed public rooms and 39 high-ceilinged, air-conditioned guest rooms — with original plasterwork, a blend of Victorian and contemporary furnishings, and up-to-the-minute in-room technology — make this property a standout. The bathrooms are large and nicely finished, with tubs and showers. Rates include tea with scones in the afternoon and champagne and canapes in the evening. Several new rooms in an adjacent building will be ready in 2004.

10–12 Bina Gardens (off Brompton Rd.), London SW5 OLA. ☎ ***800/448-8355*** *in the U.S. or 02073/730-123. Fax: 02073/739-497. Internet:* `www.thecranley.co.uk`. *Tube: Gloucester Rd. (then a five-minute walk south on Gloucester Rd., west on Brompton Rd., and north on Bina Gardens). Rack rates: £180–£190 ($288–$304) double. AE, DC, MC, V.*

Diplomat Hotel

$$–$$$ Belgravia

Part of the Diplomat's charm is that it's a reasonably priced small hotel in an otherwise prohibitively expensive area. The lobby area features a partially gilded circular staircase and a cherub-studded chandelier from the Regency era. The 27 high-ceilinged guest rooms are tastefully done in Victorian style. Not exactly state-of-the-art, the property is nevertheless very well maintained and a cut above the average for this price range.

2 Chesham St. (just south of Belgrave Sq.), London SW1X 8DT. ☎ ***02072/351-544.*** *Fax: 02072/596 153. Internet:* `www.btinternet.com/~diplomat.hotel`. *Tube: Sloane Sq. (then a five-minute walk northeast on Cliveden and north on Eaton Place, which becomes Chesham St.). Rack rates: £125–£170 ($200–$272) double. Rates include English buffet breakfast. AE, DC, MC, V.*

Dorset Square Hotel

$$$–$$$$ Marylebone

This sophisticated 38-room luxury hotel occupies a beautifully restored Regency townhouse overlooking Dorset Square, a private garden surrounded by graceful buildings. Aggressively gorgeous inside and out, the hotel is the epitome of traditional English style. Each guest room is unique, but all are filled with a superlative mix of antiques, original oil paintings, fine furniture, fresh flowers, and richly textured fabrics. The bathrooms are marble and mahogany.

39–40 Dorset Sq. (just west of Regent's Park), London NW1 6QN. ☎ ***800/553-6674*** *in the U.S. or 02077/237-874. Fax: 02077/243-328. Internet:* `www.dorsetsquare.co.uk`. *Tube: Marylebone (then a two-minute walk east on Melcombe to Dorset Sq.). Rack rates: £164–£240 ($256–$384) double. Rates don't include 17.5% VAT. AE, MC, V.*

Durrants Hotel

$$$ Marylebone

Opened in 1789 off Manchester Square, this 92-room hotel makes for an atmospheric London retreat. Durrants is quintessentially English, with pine- and mahogany-paneled public areas, a wonderful Georgian room that serves as a restaurant, and even an 18th-century letter-writing room. Most of the wood-paneled guest rooms are generously proportioned and nicely furnished, with decent-size bathrooms. Some rooms are large enough for families with children.

George St. (across from the Wallace Collection), London W1H 6BJ. ☎ ***02079/358-131.*** *Fax: 02074/873-510. Internet:* `www.durrantshotel.co.uk`. *Tube: Bond St. (then a five-minute walk west on Oxford St. and north on Duke St. and Manchester St.). Rack rates: £145–£165 ($232–$264) double. AE, MC, V.*

Fielding Hotel

$–$$ Covent Garden

The Fielding is on a beautiful old street (now pedestrian only) lit by 19th-century gaslights, just steps from the Royal Opera House. The hotel doesn't have an elevator, and the stairways are steep and narrow. The 24 rather cramped guest rooms have showers and toilets but aren't particularly memorable. However, this quirky hotel is an excellent value for such a central location. A small bar is on the premises, and the area is loaded with cafes, restaurants, and fab shopping.

4 Broad Court, Bow St., London WC2B 5QZ. ☎ ***02078/368-305.*** *Fax: 02074/970-064. Internet:* `www.the-fielding-hotel.co.uk`. *Tube: Covent Garden (then a five-minute walk north on Long Acre and south on Bow St.). Rack rates: £100–£115 ($160–$184) double. AE, DC, MC, V.*

Five Sumner Place

$$ South Kensington

Winner of the English Tourist Board's "Bed & Breakfast of the Year" award for 2000, this 14-room charmer occupies a landmark Victorian terrace house that has been completely restored in elegant English style. The guest rooms are comfortably and traditionally furnished, and all have bathrooms (a few have refrigerators as well). The B&B offers a full range of services, including breakfast served in a Victorian-style conservatory, and welcomes families.

5 Sumner Place (just east of Onslow Sq.), London SW7 3EE. ☎ ***02075/847-586.*** *Fax: 02078/239-962. Internet:* `www.sumnerplace.com`. *Tube: South Kensington (then a three-minute walk west on Brompton Rd. and south on Sumner Place). Rack rates: £130 ($208) double. Rates include English breakfast. AE, MC, V.*

The Gore

$$$$ South Kensington

Lovers of true Victoriana love the Gore, which is on a busy road near Kensington Gardens and South Kensington museums. More or less in continuous operation since 1892, this hotel has loads of historic charm. Each of the 54 guest rooms is unique, filled with high-quality antiques and elegant furnishings. Even old commodes conceal the toilets. Bistro 190, the hotel restaurant, is hip and popular.

189 Queen's Gate (south of Kensington Gardens), London SW7 5EX. ☎ ***800/637-7200*** *in the U.S. or 02075/846-601. Fax: 02075/898-127. Internet:* `www.gorehotel.com`. *Tube: Gloucester Rd. (then a five-minute walk east on Cromwell Rd. and north on Queen's Gate). Rack rates: £190–£210 ($304–$336) double. Rates don't include 17.5% VAT. AE, DC, MC, V.*

Hazlitt's 1718

$$$$–$$$$$ Soho

Staying in this intimate, 23-room gem (built in 1718) is a delight, thanks in part to its old-fashioned atmosphere and location in the heart of hip Soho. The Georgian-era guest rooms are charming, with mahogany and pine furnishings and antiques as well as lovely bathrooms, many with clawfoot tubs. Every room is equipped with dataports for laptop computers; the hotel lacks an elevator, however. Rooms in the back are quieter; the front rooms are lighter, but restrictions on historic properties don't allow for double-glazed windows.

6 Frith St., Soho Sq. (just west of Charing Cross Rd.), London W1V 5TZ. ☎ ***02074/341-771.*** *Fax: 02074/391-524. Internet:* `www.hazlittshotel.com`. *Tube: Tottenham Court Rd. (then a five-minute walk west on Oxford St. and south on Soho St. to Frith St. at the south end of Soho Sq.). Rack rates: £205–£255 ($328–$408) double. Rates don't include 17.5% VAT. AE, DC, MC, V.*

Hotel 167

$ South Kensington

Hotel 167, one of the more fashionable guest houses in South Ken, attracts both young visitors who like the price and businesspeople who like the central location. Every guest room has a decent-size bathroom (some with showers, others with tubs), and the overall ambience is bright and attractive. The 16 rooms are furnished with a mix of fabrics and styles. Have fun exploring this busy neighborhood.

167 Old Brompton Rd., London SW5 OAN. ☎ ***02073/730-672.*** *Fax: 02073/733-360. Internet:* `www.hotel167.com`. *Tube: South Kensington (then a ten-minute walk west on Old Brompton Rd.). Rack rates: £90–£99 ($144–$158) double. Rates include continental breakfast. AE, DC, MC, V.*

James House and Cartref House

$ Westminster and Victoria

One of the top ten B&Bs in London, James House and Cartref House (across the street from each other, with a total of 20 rooms) deserve their accolades. Each guest room is individually designed; some of the larger ones contain bunk beds, which makes them suitable for families. Fewer than half have private bathrooms. The English breakfast is extremely generous, and everything is in tip-top order. Neither house has an elevator, but guests don't seem to mind. Both are completely smoke-free. It doesn't matter which house you're assigned; both are winners.

*108 and 129 Ebury St. (near Victoria Station), London SW1W 9QD. James House ☎ **02077/307-338;** Cartref House ☎ **02077/306-176.** Fax: 02077/307-338. Internet:* `www.jamesandcartref.co.uk`. *Tube: Victoria Station (then a ten-minute walk south on Buckingham Palace Rd., west on Eccleston St.,). Rack rates: £70 ($112) double without bathroom, £85 ($136) double with bathroom. Rates include English breakfast. AE, MC, V.*

Luna Simone Hotel

$ Westminster and Victoria

The outside of this big, stucco-fronted, family-run hotel gleams bright white, and each freshly renovated guest room has a newly tiled private bathroom (with shower). The 36 rooms vary widely in size, but with their blue carpeting and cream-colored walls, they beat all the dowdy, badly designed hotels and B&Bs for miles around. The beechwood and marble-clad reception area is all new, too, as is the smart-looking breakfast room, now totally nonsmoking. The look throughout is refreshingly light, simple, and modern.

*47–49 Belgrave Rd. (just west of Warwick Way), London SW1V 2BB. ☎ **02078/345-897.** Fax: 02078/282-474. Internet:* `www.lunasimonehotel.com`. *Tube: Victoria (then a five-minute walk east on Belgrave Rd.). Rack rates: £60–£80 ($96–$128) double. Rates include English breakfast. MC, V.*

St. Margaret's Hotel

$ Bloomsbury

The welcome here inspires devoted loyalty. Mrs. Marazzi is the second generation of her family to run this nonsmoking B&B, which rambles over four houses. The 64 rooms are simple and immaculate, and no two are alike. Only about 10 rooms have private bathrooms, but the Marazzis recently created some beautiful extra public bathrooms, so it's easy to survive the sharing experience. Some rooms look out onto the quiet communal garden, which all guests may use. Baby-sitting can be arranged.

*26 Bedford Place (south side of Russell Square), London WC1B 5JL. ☎ **02076/364-277.** Fax: 02073/233-066. Internet:* `www.stmargaretshotel.co.uk`. *Tube: Russell Sq. (then a five-minute walk to Bedford Place). Rack rates: £64.50 ($103) double without bathroom, £78–£95 ($125–$152) double with bathroom. Rates include English breakfast. MC, V.*

The big splurge

If you're looking for the crème de la crème of luxury, here are a few more five-star, $$$$$ suggestions:

- **Brown's Hotel,** 29–34 Albemarle St., London W1X 4BP. ☎ **02074/936-020.** Fax: 02074/939-381. Internet: www.brownshotel.com.
- **Claridge's,** Brook Street, Mayfair, London W1A 2JQ. ☎ **800/223-6800** in the U.S. or 02076/298-860. Fax: 02074/992-210. Internet: www.savoy-group.co.uk.
- **The Dorchester,** 53 Park Lane, London W1A 2HJ. ☎ **800/727-9820** in the U.S. or 02076/298-888. Fax: 02074/090-114. Internet: www.dorchesterhotel.com.
- **Park Lane Sheraton Hotel,** Piccadilly, London W1Y 8BX. ☎ **800/325-3535** in the U.S. or 02074/996-321. Fax: 02074/991-965. Internet: www.sheraton.com/parklane.
- **The Savoy,** The Strand, London WC2R 0EU. ☎ **800/63-SAVOY** in U.S. or 02078/364-343. Fax: 01712/406-040. Internet: www.savoy-group.co.uk.

St. Martin's Lane

$$$$–$$$$$ **Piccadilly Circus**

An Ian Schrager hotel, St. Martin's Lane opened in 1999 and is one of the "in" places to stay if you have the bucks and are into trendy high design. This formerly nondescript office block has become a haven for the hip, boasting an ultracool, almost surreal lobby, three restaurants, and 204 beautifully minimalist, all-white guest rooms designed by Phillipe Starck. The bathrooms are roomy and luxurious, and the windows run floor-to-ceiling. Every room has its own color-lighting panel, so you can control the mood. Weekend rates are available.

45 St. Martin's Lane (next to the English National Opera), London WC2N 4HX. ☎ ***02073/005-500.*** *Fax: 02073/005-501. Internet:* www.schragerhotels.com. *Tube: Leicester Sq. (then a two-minute walk east on Court to St. Martin's Lane). Rack rates: £210–£255 ($336–$408) double. Rates don't include 17.5% VAT. AE, DC, MC, V.*

Runner-up accommodations

Here are some further hotel suggestions if your top choices are booked.

Blooms Hotel

$$$$ **Bloomsbury** A luxurious country-house atmosphere prevails in this appealing hotel with a walled garden next to the British Museum. *7 Montague St., London WC1.* ☎ ***02073/231-717.*** *Fax: 02076/366-498.*

Covent Garden Hotel

$$$$$ **Covent Garden** This small, stylish boutique hotel is beautifully designed and wonderfully situated in Theatreland. *10 Monmouth St., London WC2H 9HB.* ☎ ***800/553-6674*** *in the U.S. or 02078/061-000. Fax: 02078/061-100. Internet:* www.firmdale.com.

Dukes Hotel

$$$$ **St. James's** At Dukes you get charm, style, and tradition in a 1908 townhouse hotel; baby-sitting services can be arranged. *35 St. James's Place, London SW1A 1NY.* ☎ ***800/381-4702*** *in U.S. or 02074/914-840. Fax: 02074/931-264. Internet:* www.dukeshotel.co.uk.

Fairways Hotel

$ **Paddington** This large late-Georgian house from the 1820s exudes charming English ambience. *186 Sussex Gardens, London W2 1TU.* ☎ ***02077/234-871.*** *Fax: 02077/234-871. Internet:* www.fairways-hotel.co.uk.

Harlingford Hotel

$ **Bloomsbury** In the heart of Bloomsbury, this wonderfully personable, immaculately maintained hotel occupies three 1820s town houses. *61–63 Cartwright Gardens (north of Russell Square), London WC1H 9EL.* ☎ ***02073/871-551.*** *Fax: 02073/874-616. E-mail:* book@harlingfordhotel.com.

Inperial Hotel

$$ **Bloomsbury** This large, full-service hotel isn't particularly glamorous, but it's well run and a terrific value right on Russell Square. *Russell Sq., London WC1B 5BB.* ☎ ***02072/787-871.*** *Fax: 02078/374-653. Internet:* www.imperialhotels.co.uk.

Regent Palace Hotel

$$ **Piccadilly Circus** One of Europe's largest hotels, the 920-room Regent Palace provides affordable accommodations in the heart of the West End. *12 Sherwood St. (just north of Piccadilly Circus), London W1A 4BZ.* ☎ ***08704/008-703.*** *Fax: 02077/346-435. Internet:* www.forte-hotels.com.

Twenty Nevern Square

$$–$$$ **Earl's Court** This sumptuously refurnished boutique hotel is plush and glamorous, with individually designed rooms and decor that emphasizes natural materials. *20 Nevern Square, London SW5 9PD.* ☎ ***02075/659-555.*** *Fax: 02075/659-444. Internet:* www.twentynevernsquare.co.uk.

Dining Out

For the past two decades or so, London has been in the grip of a gastronomic revolution. The "Modern British" cuisine many London restaurants now serve takes old standards and deliciously reinvents them with foreign influences and ingredients, mostly from France (sauces), the Mediterranean (olive oil, oregano, garlic), and northern Italy (pasta, polenta, risotto). Besides Modern British cuisine, London foodies continue to favor classic French and Italian cuisines. Indian cooking has been a favorite ethnic food for decades. London abounds with Indian restaurants (about 1,500 of them) serving curries and dishes cooked in clay tandoori pots.

At the same time, you find a renewed interest in and respect for traditional English fare. In the past, English cooking was often maligned as dull and tasteless. But when done well, this country's cuisine is both hearty and delicious. The best traditional dishes are game, lamb, meat and fish pies, and the ever-popular roast beef with Yorkshire pudding (a crispy concoction made with drippings and served with gravy). At the lower end you find fish and chips, steak-and-kidney pie, and *bangers and mash* (sausages and mashed potatoes) with a side of peas and carrots.

Neighborhoods for ethnic eats

London has more than 5,000 restaurants, so chances are that you can find something to suit your tastes and your pocketbook. Unlike in some other large cities, ethnic restaurants aren't really confined to one particular area of London. You do find a few exceptions, however: Several Chinese restaurants cluster along Lisle, Wardour, and Gerrard streets in Soho's Chinatown; Notting Hill has long been a standby for low-price Indian and Caribbean restaurants; and a number of Middle Eastern (especially Lebanese) restaurants line Edgware Road. But otherwise, ethnic restaurants are scattered all over. In terms of sheer variety, Soho and neighboring Covent Garden offer the most choices in the West End, with British, African, Caribbean, Mongolian, American (North and South), French, Italian, Spanish, Thai, Korean, Japanese, Middle Eastern, Eastern European, Modern European, Turkish, and vegetarian all represented. South Kensington is another grab bag of culinary choices.

Strategies for budget dining

Eating out in London can be pricey. So where do you go for lower-cost meals? Try pubs, cafes, sandwich bars, pizza places, and fast-food restaurants — places where you're not paying for custom cooking and personal service. If you opt for a pricier establishment, always see if

London's Top Restaurants

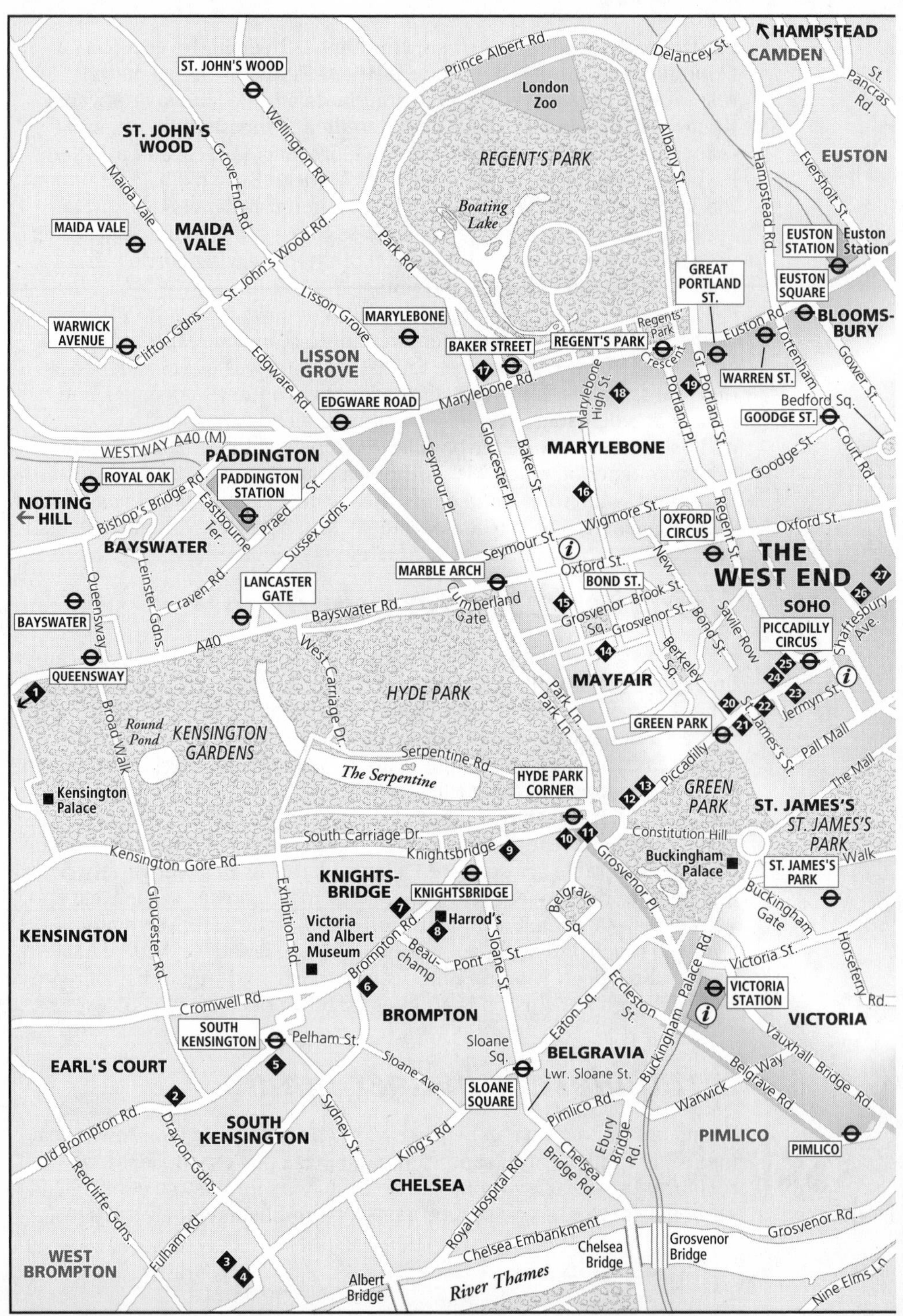

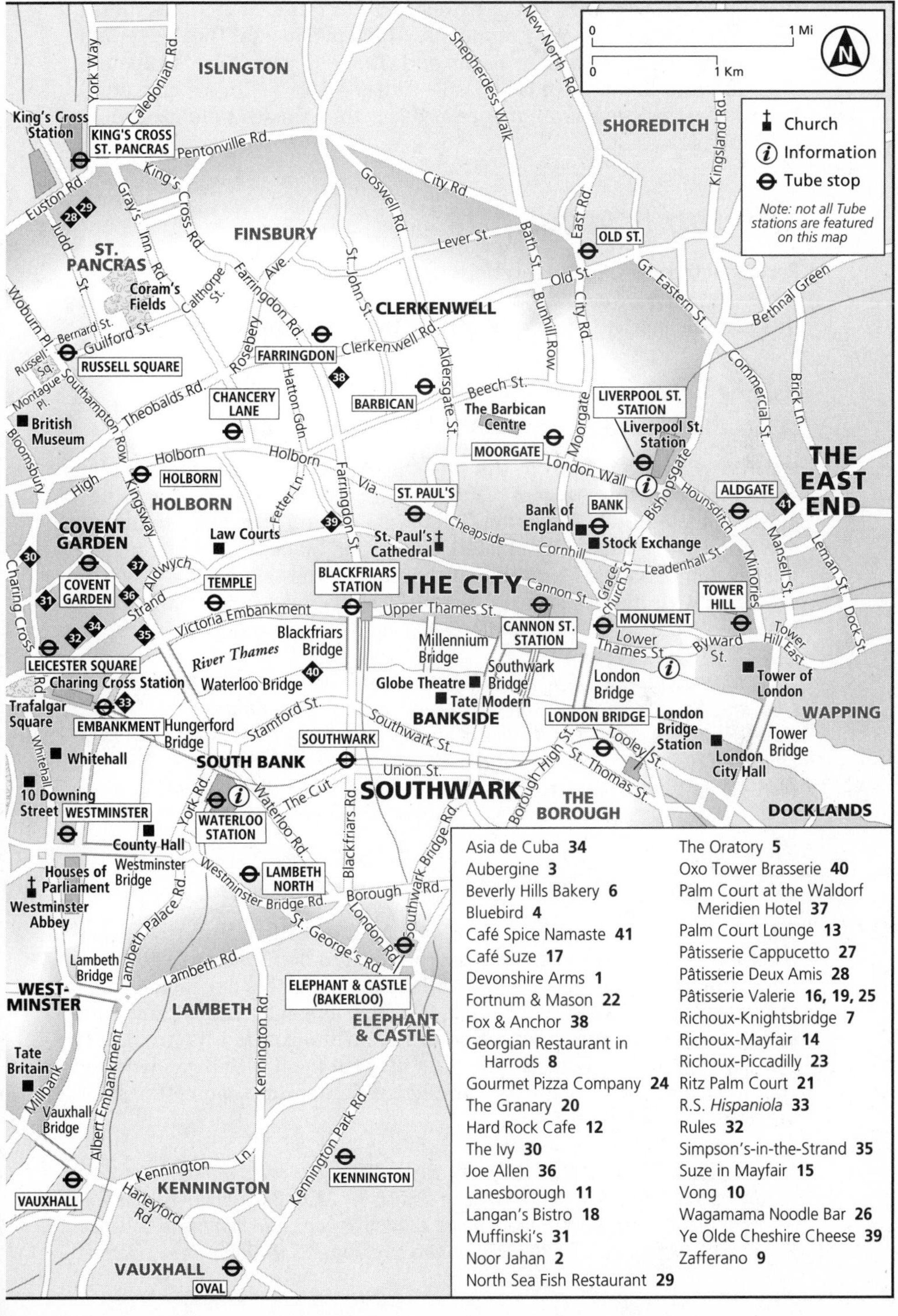

0
1 Mi
0
1 Km
N
Church
Information
Tube stop
Note: not all Tube stations are featured on this map
ISLINGTON
SHOREDITCH
FINSBURY
ST. PANCRAS
CLERKENWELL
HOLBORN
COVENT GARDEN
THE CITY
THE EAST END
WAPPING
BANKSIDE
SOUTH BANK
SOUTHWARK
THE BOROUGH
DOCKLANDS
WEST-MINSTER
LAMBETH
ELEPHANT & CASTLE
KENNINGTON
VAUXHALL
KING'S CROSS ST. PANCRAS
King's Cross Station
OLD ST.
RUSSELL SQUARE
FARRINGDON
CHANCERY LANE
BARBICAN
MOORGATE
LIVERPOOL ST. STATION
Liverpool St. Station
HOLBORN
ST. PAUL'S
ALDGATE
BANK
TEMPLE
BLACKFRIARS STATION
COVENT GARDEN
CANNON ST. STATION
MONUMENT
TOWER HILL
LEICESTER SQUARE
EMBANKMENT
SOUTHWARK
LONDON BRIDGE
WESTMINSTER
WATERLOO STATION
LAMBETH NORTH
ELEPHANT & CASTLE (BAKERLOO)
KENNINGTON
VAUXHALL
OVAL
Coram's Fields
British Museum
The Barbican Centre
Law Courts
St. Paul's Cathedral
Bank of England
Stock Exchange
Millennium Bridge
Globe Theatre
Tate Modern
Southwark Bridge
London Bridge
Tower of London
London Bridge Station
London City Hall
Tower Bridge
Blackfriars Bridge
River Thames
Waterloo Bridge
Charing Cross Station
Trafalgar Square
Hungerford Bridge
Whitehall
10 Downing Street
County Hall
Houses of Parliament
Westminster Bridge
Westminster Abbey
Lambeth Bridge
Tate Britain
Vauxhall Bridge
York Way
Caledonian Rd.
Pentonville Rd.
King's Cross Rd.
Euston Rd.
Judd St.
Gray's Inn Rd.
Woburn Pl.
Bernard St.
Guilford St.
Russell Sq.
Montague Pl.
Southampton Row
Bloomsbury
Theobalds Rd.
Calthorpe St.
Farringdon Rd.
Rosebery Ave.
Hatton Gdn.
Goswell Rd.
Shepherdess Walk
New North Rd.
City Rd.
Lever St.
St. John St.
Bath St.
East Rd.
Kingsland Rd.
Old St.
Bunhill Row
City Rd.
Gt. Eastern St.
Bethnal Green
Commercial St.
Brick Ln.
Clerkenwell Rd.
Beech St.
Aldersgate St.
Moorgate
London Wall
Bishopsgate
Houndsditch
High Holborn
Holborn
Kingsway
Fetter Ln.
Farringdon St.
Via.
Cheapside
Cornhill
Leadenhall St.
Minories
Mansell St.
Leman St.
Dock St.
Aldwych
Strand
Charing Cross Rd.
Victoria Embankment
Upper Thames St.
Cannon St.
Gracechurch St.
Lower Thames St.
Byward St.
Tower Hill East
Stamford St.
Southwark St.
Union St.
Tooley St.
St. Thomas St.
Borough High St.
Whitehall
York Rd.
Waterloo Rd.
The Cut
Blackfriars Rd.
Southwark Bridge Rd.
Westminster Bridge Rd.
Borough Rd.
London Rd.
St. George's Rd.
Lambeth Palace Rd.
Lambeth Rd.
Kennington Rd.
Albert Embankment
Millbank
Kennington Park Rd.
Kennington Ln.
Harleyford Rd.
Asia de Cuba 34
Aubergine 3
Beverly Hills Bakery 6
Bluebird 4
Café Spice Namaste 41
Café Suze 17
Devonshire Arms 1
Fortnum & Mason 22
Fox & Anchor 38
Georgian Restaurant in Harrods 8
Gourmet Pizza Company 24
The Granary 20
Hard Rock Cafe 12
The Ivy 30
Joe Allen 36
Lanesborough 11
Langan's Bistro 18
Muffinski's 31
Noor Jahan 2
North Sea Fish Restaurant 29
The Oratory 5
Oxo Tower Brasserie 40
Palm Court at the Waldorf Meridien Hotel 37
Palm Court Lounge 13
Pâtisserie Cappucetto 27
Pâtisserie Deux Amis 28
Pâtisserie Valerie 16, 19, 25
Richoux-Knightsbridge 7
Richoux-Mayfair 14
Richoux-Piccadilly 23
Ritz Palm Court 21
R.S. Hispaniola 33
Rules 32
Simpson's-in-the-Strand 35
Suze in Mayfair 15
Vong 10
Wagamama Noodle Bar 26
Ye Olde Cheshire Cheese 39
Zafferano 9

the restaurant of your choice has a set-price menu. More and more of London's top restaurants offer two- and three-course fixed-price meals that can slash an a la carte tab by one-third or more. Sometimes these are called pre- or post-theater menus, which means that they're served only from about 5:30 p.m. to 7 p.m. and after 9:30 p.m. Wine is expensive, so forgo that if price is an issue. And try your splurge dining at lunch, when prices are often one-third less than those at dinner and the food is the same.

The top restaurants

For a key to the dollar-sign ratings used in the following listings, see the Introduction. For the locations of all the restaurants I discuss in this section, see the "London's Top Restaurants" map in this chapter.

Asia de Cuba

$$$$ Piccadilly Circus CUBAN/ASIAN

If you're dying to check out the scene at one of London's ultracool hot spots, call now to reserve a place at Asia de Cuba in Ian Schrager's St. Martin's Lane hotel. The Asian-Cuban fusion food is usually shared by everyone at the table. For starters, try Cuban black-bean dumplings or foie gras empanadas. Then move on to miso-glazed salmon satay (fish on skewers) with juniper-scented *jus*, or Cuban spiced chicken. Be aware that the volume of the music increases as the night wears on.

45 St. Martin's Lane, WC2 (in the St. Martin's Lane hotel). ☎ ***02073/005-588.*** *Tube: Leicester Sq. (then a two-minute walk east on St. Martin's Court to St. Martin's Lane). Reservations essential; book at least two to three weeks in advance. Main courses: £14.50–£32 ($23–$51). AE, DC, MC, V. Open: Mon–Sat 11:30 a.m.–2:30 p.m.; Mon–Wed 6 p.m. to midnight, Thurs–Sat 6 p.m.–1 a.m.; Sun 6–10:30 p.m.*

Aubergine

$$$$ Chelsea FRENCH

This is one of London's top "name" restaurants, with celebs, royals, and commoners vying to get a table, so you need to book weeks in advance. Chef William Drabble has earned a Michelin star for his delicate delivery of French haute cuisine. Every dish, from fish and lighter-Mediterranean-style choices to pigeon with foie gras and quail salad, is a culinary achievement of the highest order. Cap off your meal with the celebrated cappuccino of white beans with grated truffle. Service is sometimes perfunctory rather than polished.

11 Park Walk, SW10. ☎ ***02073/523-449.*** *Tube: Sloane Sq. (then a ten-minute walk southwest on King's Rd. to Park Walk; or bus 11, 19, 22, or 211 southwest on King's Rd. from the Tube station). Reservations essential; book two months in advance. Fixed-price menus: lunch £20 ($32) for two courses, £25 ($40) for three courses;*

dinner £48 ($77) for three courses, £65 ($104) for five courses. AE, DC, MC, V. Open: Mon–Fri noon to 2:15 p.m.; Mon–Sat 7–10:15 p.m.

Bluebird

$$$ Chelsea MODERN EUROPEAN

Sir Terence Conran transformed a car-repair garage into this sleek white-and-blue place with a gleaming chrome bar, central skylights, and an open kitchen with a wood-burning stove. The result is upscale but still comfortable and unpretentious. The menu emphasizes cooked-to-the-minute hearty cuisine. Fish and fresh shellfish (oysters, clams) and crustaceans (lobster, crab) are stand-outs, as are grilled meats (veal, lamb, pigeon, organic chicken). A cafe and food store are on the first floor.

350 King's Rd., SW3. ☎ ***02075/591-000.*** *Tube: Sloane Sq. (then a ten-minute walk south on King's Rd.; or bus 19, 22, or 49 from the Tube station). Reservations recommended. Main courses: £11–£30 ($17–$48). Fixed-price menus: lunch (12:30–3 p.m.) and pretheater (6–7 p.m.) £15.50–£20 ($25–$32). AE, DC, MC, V. Open: Mon–Fri noon to 3:30 p.m., Sat–Sun 11 a.m.–3:30 p.m.; Mon–Sat 6–11:30 p.m., Sun 6–10:30 p.m.*

Cafe Spice Namaste

$$ The City INDIAN

The competition among London's Indian restaurants is stiff, but this one remains a perennial favorite for the consistently high quality of its food. The homemade chutneys alone are worth the trip. Housed in a landmark Victorian hall near Tower Bridge, this cafe has a kitchen that concentrates on spicy southern and northern Indian dishes with a strong Portuguese influence (such as pork vindaloo). It offers excellent chicken, duck, lamb, and fish dishes, served mild to spicy-hot. All dishes come with fresh vegetables and Indian bread.

16 Prescot St., E1. ☎ ***02074/889-242.*** *Tube: Tower Hill (then a five-minute walk north on Minories St. and east on Goodman's Yard, which becomes Prescot St. after you cross Mansell St.). Reservations required. Main courses: £8–£15 ($12–$24). AE, DC, MC, V. Open: Mon–Fri noon to 3 p.m. and 6:15–10:30 p.m., Sat 6:15–10:30 p.m.*

Devonshire Arms

$ Kensington BRITISH

A good place for lunch if you're shopping on Kensington High Street, this mid-19th-century establishment serves upmarket pub food in pleasant surroundings. The offerings change frequently, but you might find spinach ricotta ravioli, Mediterranean salad with feta cheese, a Thai stir-fry, ribeye steak, or good ol' sausage and mash.

37 Marloes Rd., W8. ☎ ***02079/370-710.*** *Tube: High St. Kensington (then a five-minute walk west on Kensington High St. and south on Wright's Lane to Marloes Rd.). Main* *courses: £4.50–£10.90 ($7–$17). AE, MC, V. Open: pub daily 11 a.m.–11 p.m.; food served Mon–Sat noon to 11 p.m., Sun noon to 10 p.m.*

Fortnum & Mason

$$ St. James's BRITISH

Fortnum & Mason, a posh London store famous for its food section, also has three restaurants: the lower-level Fountain (breakfast, lunch, tea, and dinner), the mezzanine-level Patio (lunch), and the fourth-floor St. James's (lunch and afternoon tea). Although crowded with tourists, these remain pleasant places where you can get a good meal and a glimpse of the fading Empire. The Fountain serves sandwiches and daily specials. The Patio's lunch menu offers an assortment of pricey sandwiches and main courses, especially hot and cold pies (steak and kidney, curried fish and banana, chicken, and game) and Welsh *rarebit* (thick melted cheese poured over toast) prepared with Guinness stout. The well-heeled dine at the St. James's, where the menu is even more traditionally British: For starters, try the *kipper* (smoked herring) mousse or potato and Stilton brûlée; main courses include pies and roast rib of Scottish beef. The more informal Fountain and Patio are good places to dine with a family, although St. James also welcomes children.

*181 Piccadilly, W1. ☎ **02077/348-040.** Tube: Piccadilly Circus (then a five-minute walk west on Piccadilly). Reservations accepted for St. James's only. Main courses: £7.95–£15.95 ($11–$24). Fixed-price menus: £14.95–£19.50 ($24–$31). AE, DC, MC, V. Open: St. James's and the Patio, Tues–Sat 10 a.m.–6:30 p.m.; the Fountain, Mon–Sat 9 a.m.–7:45 p.m.*

Fox & Anchor

$ The City BRITISH

For an authentic taste of early-morning London, this unique pub is tops. Fox & Anchor has been serving gargantuan breakfasts to butchers from the nearby Smithfield meat market since 1898. Here you also rub elbows with nurses coming off night shifts and city clerks and tycoons. The "full house" breakfast plate comes with sausage, bacon, kidneys, eggs, beans, black pudding, and a fried slice of bread, along with unlimited tea or coffee, toast, and jam. If you're in a festive mood, order a *Black Velvet* (champagne with Guinness) or a *Bucks fizz* (orange juice and champagne — what Americans call a mimosa). Fox & Anchor serves breakfast, the reason to go here, until 3 p.m. If you come for lunch, skip the sandwiches and salads and go for steak and kidney pie or steak with vegetables. Meat is what this place is all about.

*115 Charterhouse St., EC1. ☎ **02072/535-075.** Tube: Barbican (then a five-minute walk north on Aldersgate and west on Charterhouse St.). Reservations recommended. Breakfast: "full house" £7 ($11). Lunch: £6.50–£15 ($10–$24). AE, DC, MC, V. Open: Mon–Fri 7 a.m.–9 p.m., but food served only to 3 p.m.*

Gourmet Pizza Company

$ St. James's PIZZA/PASTA

If you're in the West End and want an economical lunch or dinner or need to please some pizza-loving kids, stop here. The area's shop and office workers frequent this large, bright, pleasant place. You can choose from 20 pizzas (this is pizza as in pie, not slice). Everything from a B.L.T. version to one with Cajun chicken and prawns is available; about half the choices are vegetarian, and some are vegan. The crusts are light and crispy, and the toppings fresh and flavorful. Instead of pizza, you may want to try ham and tomato tortellini with cream.

7–9 Swallow Walk (off Piccadilly), W1. ☎ ***02077/345-182.*** *Tube: Piccadilly Circus (then a five-minute walk west on Piccadilly and north on Swallow St.). Pizzas: £5.55–£8.95 ($9–$14). Pastas: £7.75–£9.25 ($12–$15). AE, DC, MC, V. Open: daily noon to 3 p.m. and 5–10:30 p.m.*

The Granary

$ Piccadilly Circus/Leicester Square BRITISH

This affordable country-style restaurant has had the same owners and many of the same staff for more than 25 years. The Granary serves a simple but flavorful array of home-cooked dishes, listed daily on a chalkboard. Specials may include fresh pan-fried fish; lamb casserole with mint and lemon; steak and mushroom pie; or avocado stuffed with prawns, spinach, and cheese. Vegetarian meals include meatless versions of *paella* (a Spanish rice dish), lasagna, and *korma* (curried vegetables with Greek yogurt). The most tempting desserts are bread-and-butter pudding and brown Betty (both served hot). Large portions guarantee you won't go hungry. Kids enjoy the casual atmosphere and simple food.

39 Albemarle St., W1. ☎ ***02074/932-978.*** *Tube: Green Park (then a five-minute walk east on Piccadilly to Albemarle) or Piccadilly Circus (then a five-minute walk west on Piccadilly). Main courses: £8.60–£9.60 ($14–$16). MC, V. Open: Mon–Fri 11:30 a.m.–7:30 p.m., Sat 11:30 a.m.–3:30 p.m.*

Hard Rock Cafe

$$ Mayfair NORTH AMERICAN

This is the original Hard Rock, now a worldwide chain of rock-and-roll/American-roadside-diner-themed restaurants serving up food and service with a smile. Teenagers like the rock memorabilia and loud music as well as the juicy burgers and shakes. Vegetarian dishes are available too. The portions are generous, and the price of a main dish includes a salad and fries or baked potato. Fajitas are always a good choice, and homemade apple pie is one of the better desserts. Be prepared to stand in line on weekend evenings.

*150 Old Park Lane, W1. ☎ **02076/290-382.** Tube: Hyde Park Corner (take the Park Lane exit; Old Park Lane is just east of Park Lane). Main courses: £7.75–£15 ($12–$24). AE, MC, V. Open: Sun–Thurs 11:30 a.m.–12:30 a.m., Fri–Sat 11:30 a.m.–1 a.m.*

The Ivy

$$ Soho BRITISH/FRENCH

The Ivy, with its 1930s look, tiny bar, glamour-scene crowd, and later-than-usual hours, is one of the hippest places to dine after the theater. The menu is simple and the cooking notable for skillful preparation of fresh ingredients. Popular dishes are white asparagus with sea kale and truffle butter; seared scallops with spinach, sorrel, and bacon; salmon fish cakes; and Mediterranean fish soup. Try one of the wonderful English desserts, such as sticky toffee pudding and caramelized bread-and-butter pudding.

*1–5 West St., WC2. ☎ **02078/364-751.** Tube: Leicester Sq. (then a five-minute walk north on Charing Cross Rd.; West St. is at the southeastern end of Cambridge Circus). Reservations required; book at least a month in advance. Main courses: £9.50–£21.75 ($15–$35). Fixed-price menu: Sat–Sun lunch £18.50 ($30). AE, DC, MC, V. Open: daily noon to 3 p.m. and 5:30 p.m. to midnight.*

Joe Allen

$$ Covent Garden NORTH AMERICAN

With its checkered tablecloths and crowded dining room, Joe Allen is the sort of gabby place where actors often come after a performance to wolf down chili con carne or gnaw on barbecued ribs. This spot keeps a low profile on a back street in Covent Garden. The food, American classics with some international twists, is sturdy and dependable, and the set menu is a real value: After a starter (maybe smoked haddock vichyssoise), you can choose main courses, such as pan-fried parmesan-crusted lemon sole, Cajun chicken breast, and grilled spicy Italian sausages. If you're feeling homesick, console yourself with a burger, a brownie, and a Coke. Come before the show for the best prices; come after for potential star-gazing.

*13 Exeter St., WC2. ☎ **02078/360-651.** Tube: Covent Garden (then a five-minute walk south past the Market to Burleigh St. on the southeast corner of the Piazza and west on Exeter St.). Reservations recommended. Main courses: £9–£15 ($14–$24). Fixed-price menus: lunch and pretheater dinner Mon–Fri £14–£16 ($22–$26);. AE, MC, V. Open: Mon–Fri noon to 12:45 a.m., Sat 11:30 a.m.–12:45 a.m., Sun 11:30 a.m.–11:30 p.m.*

Langan's Bistro

$$ Marylebone BRITISH/FRENCH

Clusters of Japanese parasols, rococo mirrors, paintings, and old photographs cover this busy bistro's dining room, which is behind a brightly colored storefront. The menu is English with an underplayed (some may say underdeveloped) French influence. Depending on the season, the fixed-price menu may start with asparagus risotto or chicken liver vol-au-vent (in a pastry shell) and move on to chargrilled sirloin of Scottish beef, grilled trout fillets, or red onion and wild mushroom quiche. The dessert extravaganza known as "Mrs. Langan's chocolate pudding" is a must for chocolaholics.

*26 Devonshire St., W1. ☎ **02079/354-531.** Tube: Regent's Park (then a five-minute walk south on Portland Place and west on Devonshire St.). Reservations recommended three days in advance. Fixed-price menus: lunch or dinner £17.50 ($28) for two courses, £21 ($34) for three courses. AE, DC, MC, V. Open: Mon–Fri 12:30–2:30 p.m.; Mon–Sat 6:30–11 p.m.*

Noor Jahan

$$ South Kensington INDIAN

Small, unpretentious, and always reliable, Noor Jahan is a neighborhood favorite. The marinated chicken and lamb dishes cooked tandoori style in a clay oven are moist and flavorful. Chicken tikka, a staple of northern India, is one specialty worth trying. So are the biriani dishes — chicken, lamb, or prawns, mixed with basmati rice, fried in *ghee* (thick, clarified butter), and served with a mixed vegetable curry. If you're unfamiliar with Indian food, the waiters will gladly explain the dishes.

*2A Bina Gardens (off Old Brompton Rd.). ☎ **02073/736-522.** Tube: Gloucester Rd. (then a five-minute walk south on Gloucester Rd., west on Brompton Rd., north on Bina Gardens). Reservations recommended. Main courses: £6.50–£11.50 ($10–$18). Fixed-price menu: £18.50 ($30). AE, DC, MC, V. Open: daily noon to 2:45 p.m. and 6–11:45 p.m.*

North Sea Fish Restaurant

$$ Bloomsbury SEAFOOD

If you get a craving for "real" fish and chips — not the generic frozen stuff that often passes for it — definitely try this unassuming "chippie" where the fish is *always* fresh. With its sepia prints and red velvet seats, the place is pleasant, comfortable, and popular with adults and kids. You may want to start with grilled fresh sardines or a fish cake before digging into a main course of cod or haddock. The fish is most often served battered and deep-fried, but you can also order it grilled. The chips are almost as good as the fish.

*7–8 Leigh St. (off Cartwright Gardens), WC1. ☎ **02073/875-892.** Tube: Russell Sq. (then a ten-minute walk north on Marchmont Place and east on Leigh St.). Reservations recommended. Main courses: £8.30–£16.95 ($13–$27). AE, DC, MC, V. Open: Mon–Sat noon to 2:30 p.m. and 5:30–10:30 p.m.*

The Oratory

$$ South Kensington MODERN BRITISH

Named for the nearby Brompton Oratory, a famous late-19th-century Catholic church, and close to the Victoria & Albert Museum and Knightsbridge shopping, this funky bistro serves up some of the best and least expensive food in tony South Ken. The high-ceilinged room is decorated in what I call Modern Rococo, with enormous glass chandeliers, patterned walls and ceiling, and wooden tables with wrought-iron chairs. Take note of the daily specials on the chalkboard, especially any pasta dishes. Homemade fish cakes, roasted field-mushroom risotto, and grilled calves' liver with bacon and deep-fried sage are all noteworthy. For dessert, the sticky toffee pudding with ice cream is a melt-in-the-mouth fave.

232 Brompton Rd., SW3. ☎ ***02075/843-493.*** *Tube: South Kensington (then a five-minute walk north on Brompton Rd.). Main courses: £7–£14.50 ($11–$23). Fixed-price menu: lunch specials £3.50–£6.95 ($5–$11). MC, V. Open: Daily noon to 11 p.m.*

Oxo Tower Brasserie

$$$ South Bank FRENCH

Book well in advance and insist on a window table at this sleek and stylish brasserie perched atop the landmark Oxo Tower on the South Bank. The Brasserie is less chi-chi than the adjacent Oxo Tower Restaurant, but the food is marvelous and costs about half of what you pay next door. Plus, the river and city views are just as sublime. Order such tasty dishes as roast lamb cutlets, roast salmon, or porcini mushroom tortellini. The fixed-price lunch and pre-theater menu makes this an affordable extravagance.

Oxo Tower Wharf, Barge House St., SE1. ☎ ***02078/033-888.*** *Tube: Waterloo (the easiest foot route is to head north to the South Bank Centre and then follow the Thames pathway east to the Oxo Tower, about a ten-minute walk). Reservations essential; book at least one or two weeks in advance. Main courses: £15–£18.50 ($24–$30). Fixed-price lunch and pretheater menu: £15–£18.50 ($24–$30). AE, DC, MC, V. Open: daily noon to 3 p.m. and 5:30–11 p.m.*

R.S. Hispaniola

$$$ The Strand BRITISH/FRENCH

Permanently moored in the Thames, this comfortably outfitted former passenger boat provides good food and spectacular views of the river traffic. The frequently changing menu offers a variety of sturdy and generally well-prepared dishes. On any given night you may find flambéed Mediterranean prawns with garlic, fried fish cakes with tartar sauce, poached halibut with prawn sauce, rack of lamb flavored with rosemary and shallots, and several vegetarian dishes, such as linguini with chili and basil oil. Most nights feature live music, and the place can be fun and romantic, if a bit touristy.

*River Thames, Victoria Embankment, Charing Cross, WC2. ☎ **02078/393-011.** Tube: Embankment (the restaurant is a few steps from the station). Reservations recommended. Main courses: £9.95–£16.95 ($16–$27); £15 ($24) minimum per person. AE, DC, MC, V. Open: Mon–Fri noon to 2:30 p.m. and 6:30–11 p.m.; Sat 6–11:30 p.m.; closed Dec 24–Jan 4.*

Rules

$$$ Covent Garden BRITISH

If you want to eat classic British cuisine in a memorable (nay, venerable) setting, put on something dressy and head for Maiden Lane. London's oldest restaurant, Rules was founded in 1798, and two centuries' worth of prints, cartoons, and paintings decorate the walls. The restaurant is completely nonsmoking, a rarity in London. If you're game for game, go for it, because that's what Rules is famous for. Ptarmigan, widgeon, partridge, and snipe — game birds shot at the restaurant's hunting grounds — are roasted to order from September to February. In recent years the restaurant has added fish and a few vegetarian dishes.

*35 Maiden Lane, WC2. ☎ **02078/365-314.** Tube: Covent Garden (then a five-minute walk south on James St. to Southampton St. behind Covent Garden Market and west on Maiden Lane). Reservations recommended. Main courses: £16.95–£22.50 ($27–$36). Fixed-price menu: pretheater Mon–Thurs 3–5 p.m. £19.95 ($32). AE, DC, MC, V. Open: Mon–Sat noon to 11:30 p.m., Sun noon to 10:30 p.m.*

Simpson's-in-the-Strand

$$$ The Strand BRITISH

Simpson's, open since 1828, boasts an army of formal waiters serving the best of staunchly traditional food. You find an array of the best roasts in London: sirloin of beef, saddle of mutton with red-currant jelly, and Aylesbury duckling. (Remember to tip the tailcoated carver.) For a pudding (dessert course), you may want to order treacle roll and custard or Stilton with vintage port. That's the downstairs restaurant. Simply Simpson, a brighter, lighter dining area on the second floor, is actually (gasp) nouvelle. This is also a great place to come for a real English breakfast. A jacket and tie are required for men downstairs; Simply Simpson has a smart-casual dress code (leave your tennis shoes and sweatpants or jeans in your hotel room).

*100 The Strand (next to the Savoy Hotel), WC2. ☎ **02078/369-112.** Tube: Charing Cross (then a five-minute walk east along The Strand). Reservations required. Main courses: downstairs, £10.50–£22.95 ($16–$34); Simply Simpson, £9.70–£15.50 ($16–$29). Fixed-price menus: lunch and pretheater dinner £22–£26 ($35–$42); breakfast £15.50 ($25). AE, DC, MC, V. Open: Mon–Fri 7:15–10:15 a.m., 12:15–2:30 p.m., and 5–10:45 p.m.; Sat–Sun noon to 2:30 p.m. and 5–9 p.m.*

Suze in Mayfair

$–$$ **Mayfair PACIFIC RIM/INTERNATIONAL**

Suze Wine Bar, in Marylebone, was so successful that the New Zealand owners opened this charming counterpart with a comfortable bistro-like ambience in Mayfair. The food is Australasian with some international crossovers and always simply and well prepared. Try the succulent New Zealand green-tipped mussels, a house specialty, or New Zealand scallops. You can also get New Zealand rack of lamb. There are several sharing platters to choose from: Italian antipasti, vegetarian, Greek, seafood, and cheese. A favorite dessert is Pavlova, a light meringue covered with kiwi fruit, strawberries, passionfruit, and mangoes. And, of course, you can get a fine glass of wine. The original Suze Wine bar is at 1 Glentworth St., NW1 (☎ **02074/868-216**).

41 North Audley St., W1. ☎ ***02074/913-237.*** *Tube: Marble Arch (then a five-minute walk east on Oxford Street and south on North Audley Street). Reservations recommended. Main courses: £5.95–£13.50 ($10–$22); platters to share £5.95–£10.95 ($10–$18). AE, DC, MC, V. Open: Mon–Sat 11 a.m.–11 p.m.*

Vong

$$$ **Knightsbridge FRENCH/THAI**

This artily minimalist restaurant is a chic hangout for food groupies who can't get enough of chef-owner Jean-Georges Vongerichten's food. The cooking is subtle, innovative, and inspired, as you can see (or taste) if you order the "black plate" sampler of six starters. You can dine on perfectly roasted halibut or sublime lobster-and-daikon roll with rosemary-and-ginger sauce. Other temptations: crab spring roll with vinegary tamarind dipping sauce, and sautéed foie gras with ginger and mango, which literally melts in your mouth. The exotic desserts include a salad of banana and passion fruit with white-pepper ice cream. You may get a same-day table if you dine early; the place starts filling up after 8 p.m.

In the Berkeley Hotel, Wilton Place, SW1. ☎ ***02072/351-010.*** *Tube: Knightsbridge (then a three-minute walk east on Knightsbridge and south on Wilton Pl.). Reservations required; book seven days in advance. Main courses: £14.50–£20.95 ($23–$34). Fixed-price menus: tasting £50 ($80); lunch, pre- and post-theater dinner £21 ($34). AE, DC, MC, V. Open: Mon–Sat 11:30 p.m.–2:30 p.m. and 6–11:30 p.m., Sun 6–10:30 p.m.*

Wagamama Noodle Bar

$ **Soho JAPANESE**

If you're exploring Soho and want a delicious, nutritious meal in a smoke-free room, try this trendsetting noodle bar modeled after the ramen shops of Japan. You pass along a stark, glowing corridor with a busy open kitchen and descend to a large open room with communal tables. The specialties are ramen, Chinese-style thread noodles served in soups with various toppings, and the fat white noodles called *udon*. Rice dishes, vegetarian dishes, dumplings, vegetable and chicken skewers, and tempura are also on the menu. Your order is sent by radio signal to the kitchen and arrives the moment the food is ready, which means that not everyone in a group is served at the same time. You may have to stand in line to get in, but it's worth the wait. Teens especially love the loud, hip, casual atmosphere. There are several other Wagamamas scattered all over London.

10A Lexington St., W1. ☎ ***02072/920-990.*** *Tube: Piccadilly Circus (then a five-minute walk north on Shaftesbury Ave. and Windmill St., which becomes Lexington St.). Reservations not accepted. Main courses: £5.35–7.95 ($9–$13). MC, V. Open: Mon–Thurs noon to 11 p.m.; Fri–Sat noon to midnight; Sun 12:30–10 p.m.*

Ye Olde Cheshire Cheese

$$ The City BRITISH

Opened in 1667 and a one-time haunt of Dr. Johnson, Charles Dickens, and Fleet Street newspaper scandalmongers, Ye Olde Cheshire Cheese is London's most famous chophouse. You find six bars and two dining rooms in this place, which is perennially popular with families and tourists looking for some Olde London atmosphere. The house specialties include "ye famous pudding" (steak, kidney, mushrooms, and game), Scottish roast beef with Yorkshire pudding and horseradish sauce, and Dover sole. If those choices put the kids off, they can choose sandwiches and salads.

Wine Office Court, 145 Fleet St., EC4. ☎ ***02073/536-170.*** *Tube: Blackfriars (then a ten-minute walk north on New Bridge St. and west on Fleet St.). Main courses: £7.25–£12.95 ($12–$21). AE, DC, MC, V. Open: pub Mon–Sat noon to 11 p.m., Sun noon to 10:30 p.m.; bar snacks and hot food daily noon to 10 p.m.*

Zafferano

$$$$ Knightsbridge ITALIAN

If you want perhaps the best Italian food in London, served in a quietly elegant, attitude-free restaurant, head to Zafferano (but only after you've made reservations weeks in advance). The semolina pastas are perfectly cooked and come with various additions; chestnut *tagliatelle* (wide noodle pasta) with wild mushrooms is sometimes available. The deliciously simple main courses may include roast rabbit with Parma ham and polenta, venison with polenta, tuna with rocket and tomato salad, and pan-fried prawns. For dessert, try ricotta and lemon cake with rum raisin ice cream.

15 Lowndes St., SW1. ☎ ***02072/355-800.*** *Tube: Knightsbridge (then a five-minute walk south on Lowndes St., two streets east of Sloane St.). Reservations essential. Fixed-price menus: lunch £21.50–£26.50 ($34–$42), dinner £29.50–£37.50 ($47–$60). AE, MC, V. Open: daily noon to 2:30 p.m. and 7–11 p.m. (Sun until 10:30 p.m.).*

Treating Yourself to a Tea

The stereotype is true: Brits do drink tea. In fact, they drink 171 million cups per day (give or take a cup). Teatime is traditionally from about 3:30 to 5 p.m. Your afternoon tea can be a lavish affair served by a black-coated waiter in a hotel lobby, or a quick "cuppa" with a slice of cake or a sandwich at a corner tea shop or *pâtisserie* (a bakery where you can sit down or get pastries to take away). Tea may be served fast-food style in paper cups, homestyle in mugs, or more elegantly in bone china.

So what exactly, you ask, is the difference between afternoon tea and high tea?

- **Afternoon tea** is tea with cakes, sandwiches, or both, served between 3 and 5 p.m.
- **High tea,** served from about 5 to 6 p.m., is a more elaborate affair, including a light supper with a hot dish, followed by dessert and tea.

Casual tea rooms and pâtisseries

In the following comfortable neighborhood tearooms and pâtisseries, you can get a good cup of tea along with a scone or other pastry or a plate of tea sandwiches for about £4 to £10 ($6 to $15):

- **Beverly Hills Bakery** (3 Egerton Terrace, SW3; ☎ **02075/844-401;** Tube: Knightsbridge) is noted for its muffins and serves light lunches from noon on. The bakery is open Monday through Saturday from 7:30 a.m. to 6 p.m. and Sunday from 8 a.m. to 5:30 p.m.
- **Muffinski's** (5 King St., WC2; ☎ **02073/791-525;** Tube: Leicester Sq.) offers great homemade muffins, including lowfat and vegetarian. Hours are Monday through Friday from 8 a.m. to 7 p.m., Saturday from 9 a.m. to 7 p.m., and Sunday from 10 a.m. to 6 p.m.
- **Pâtisserie Cappucetto** (8 Moor St., W1; ☎ **02074/379-472;** Tube: Leicester Sq.) serves breakfast, sandwiches, soups, and superb desserts Monday through Thursday from 8 a.m. to 11:30 p.m. and Friday and Saturday from 8 a.m. to 12:30 a.m.
- **Pâtisserie Deux Amis** (63 Judd St., WC1; ☎ **02073/837-029;** Tube: Russell Sq.) is a good choice for a quick bite. Hours are Monday through Saturday from 9 a.m. to 5:30 p.m. and Sunday from 9 a.m. to 1:30 p.m.
- **Pâtisserie Valerie** (44 Old Compton St., W1; ☎ **02074/373-466;** Tube: Leicester Sq. or Tottenham Court Rd.) has been around

since 1926 and serves a mouthwatering array of pastries, but expect to stand in line night or day. Hours are Monday through Friday from 7:30 a.m. to 8 p.m., Saturday from 8 a.m. to 6:30 p.m., and Sunday from 9 a.m. to 6 p.m.

Pâtisserie Valerie also has two branches in Marylebone. One is at 105 Marylebone High St., W1 (☎ **02079/356-240;** Tube: Bond St. or Baker St.); the other is near Regent's Park at 66 Portland Place, W1 (☎ **02076/310-467;** Tube: Regent's Park). The Marylebone branch is open Monday through Saturday 7:30 a.m. to 6 p.m., and Sunday 9 a.m. to 6 p.m. The Regent's Park branch stays open until 7 p.m. and opens at 8 a.m. on Sundays.

- **Richoux** has three old-fashioned tearooms in choice London locations. They serve food all day long, and they're kind to your budget: **Richoux-Knightsbridge** (215 Brompton Rd., SW3; ☎ **02078/239-971;** Tube: Knightsbridge); **Richoux-Mayfair** (41a South Audley St., W1; ☎ **02076/295-228;** Tube: Bond St. or Green Park); and **Richoux-Piccadilly** (172 Piccadilly, W1; ☎ **02074/932-204;** Tube: Piccadilly Circus). All keep the same hours: Monday through Friday 7 a.m. to 7 p.m., Saturday 7:30 a.m. to 7 p.m., and 8 a.m. to 6 p.m. on Sunday.

Elegant spots for high tea

A traditional afternoon English tea has cakes, sandwiches, and scones with clotted cream and jam, and is "taken" in a posh hotel or restaurant. These rather lavish affairs are expensive but memorable. At any one of the following places, you can get a proper traditional afternoon or high tea (a smart-casual dress code is in effect — tennis shoes and jeans are inappropriate):

- **Fortnum & Mason** (181 Piccadilly, W1; ☎ **02077/348-040;** Tube: Piccadilly Circus) serves tea in the **St. James's Restaurant,** Monday through Saturday 3 to 5:30 p.m. for £18 ($29). Reservations aren't necessary.
- **Georgian Restaurant,** on the fourth floor of Harrods (87–135 Brompton Rd., SW1; ☎ **02072/256-800;** Tube: Knightsbridge), serves high tea Monday through Saturday from 3:45 to 5:30 p.m. It costs £18 ($29) per person, and you don't need reservations.
- **Lanesborough** hotel (Hyde Park Corner, SW1; ☎ **02072/595-599;** Tube: Hyde Park Corner) requires reservations for high tea daily 3:30 to 5:30 p.m. The cost is £24.50 ($39); the price goes up to £32 ($51) if you add strawberries and champagne.
- **Palm Court** at the Waldorf Meridien Hotel (Aldwych, WC2; ☎ **02078/362-400;** Tube: Covent Garden) serves afternoon tea Monday through Friday from 3 to 5:30 p.m. at a cost of £18 to £21 ($29 to $34); reservations are required.

- The **Palm Court Lounge,** in the Park Lane Hotel (Piccadilly, W1; ☎ **02074/996-321;** Tube: Hyde Park Corner or Green Park), requires reservations. Teatime is daily from 3 to 6 p.m., and afternoon tea runs £19 ($30), £25 ($40) if you want strawberries and champagne.
- **Ritz Palm Court,** in the Ritz Hotel (Piccadilly, W1; ☎ **02074/938-181;** Tube: Green Park), requires reservations at least one month in advance for weekday teas, and three months in advance for weekend teas. Men must wear jackets and ties. Teatime is daily from 2 to 6 p.m., and afternoon tea is £29 ($46).

Chapter 12

Exploring London

In This Chapter

- Visiting London's top attractions
- Choosing a tour that's right for you
- Finding London's hot shopping spots
- Discovering London theater and nightlife

Two millennia ago, London was *Londinium,* a walled colony of the Roman Empire. Today, this dazzling metropolis, home to more than 7 million people, is one of the most historic, cultured, and exciting cities on earth. London is a big city built (mostly) on a human scale, with charming old streets, bustling modern thoroughfares, plenty of greenery, plenty of traffic, and a vitality that spills over into the night. When the sun goes down and floodlights bathe London's historic buildings and monuments, all kinds of new possibilities spring up.

History-laden London can stir the imagination like few other cities. No matter how often you've heard or read about places such as Westminster Abbey, Buckingham Palace, and the Tower of London, nothing can beat the thrill of actually visiting them. And although you'll no doubt be busy trying to see the important sights, save a little time for just wandering around London's streets. You find a wealth of architectural styles, curious reminders of days gone by, and blue famous-person-lived-here plaques on houses all over the city. On some streets you can almost hear the horses' hooves clopping on the cobblestones as they did until about 1915. London grew from a series of villages, and that villagelike character survives in many London neighborhoods.

Discovering the Top Attractions

Where do you begin? If you're a dedicated museum maven, London's museums could keep you going for days, weeks, months, and even years. But the city is also loaded with famous monuments, fascinating historic buildings, and flower-filled parks. In this treasure trove of possibilities, you have to make some decisions. The sights in this section

London's Top Attractions

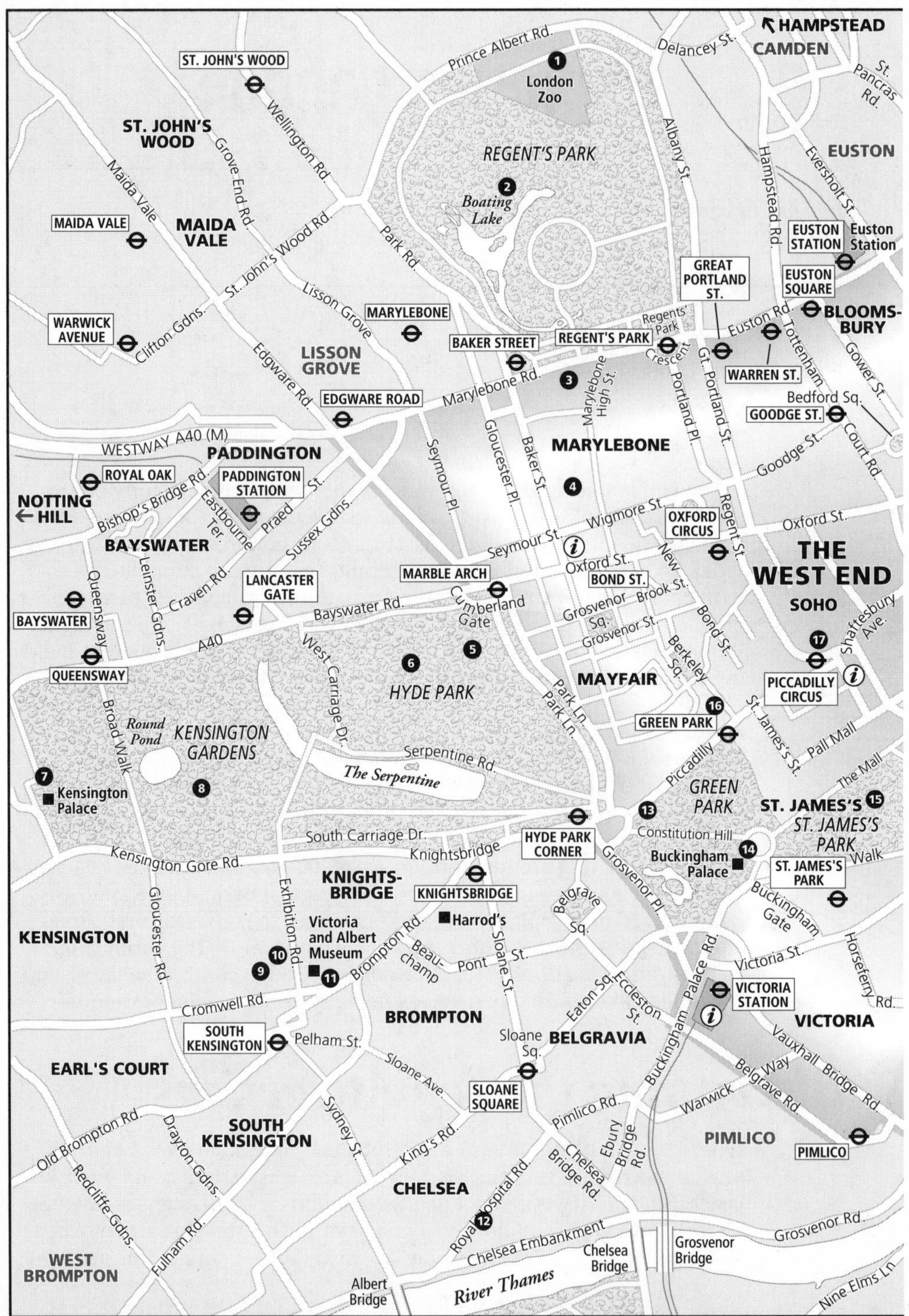

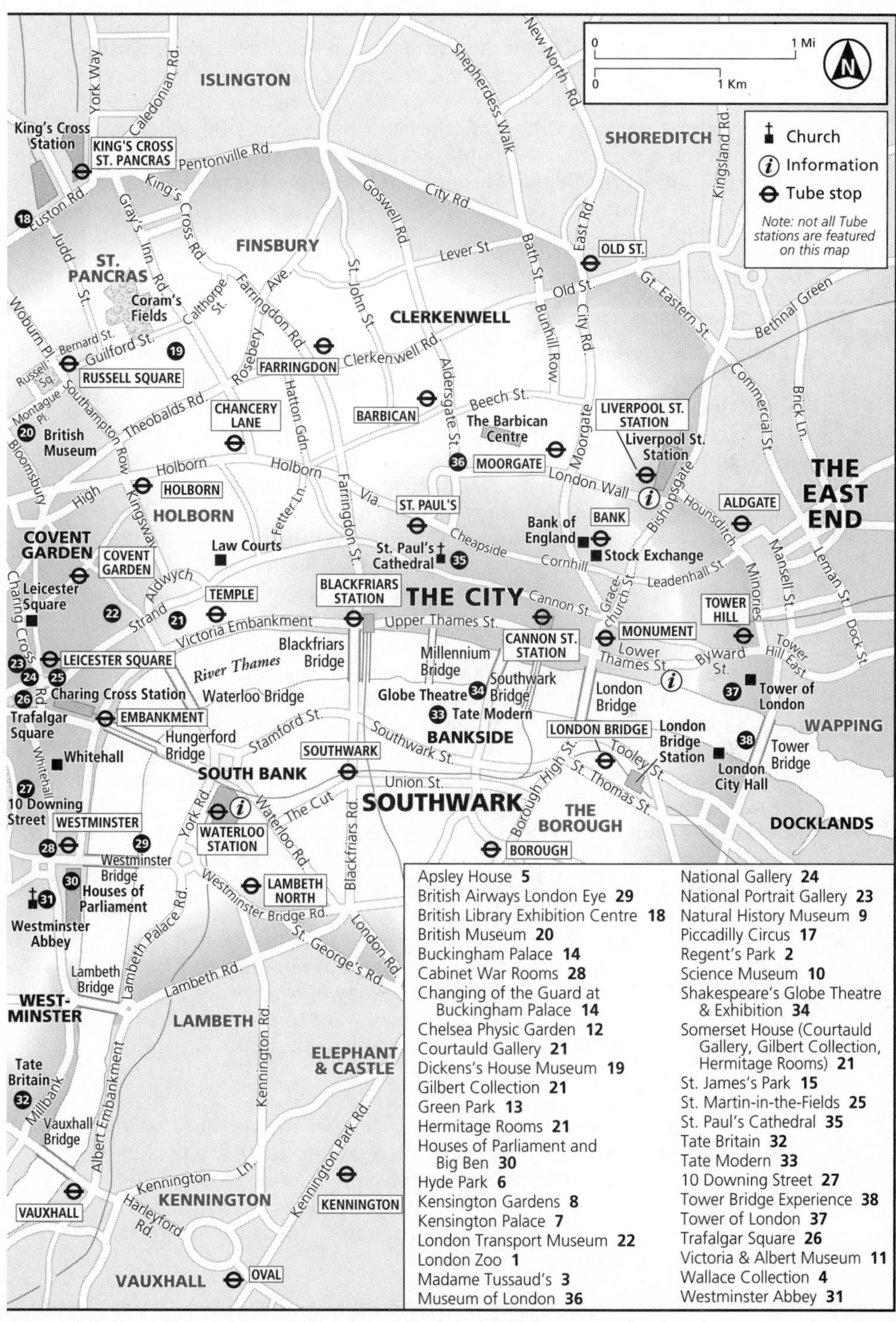

ISLINGTON
SHOREDITCH
FINSBURY
ST. PANCRAS
CLERKENWELL
HOLBORN
COVENT GARDEN
THE CITY
THE EAST END
BANKSIDE
SOUTH BANK
SOUTHWARK
THE BOROUGH
WAPPING
DOCKLANDS
WEST-MINSTER
LAMBETH
ELEPHANT & CASTLE
KENNINGTON
VAUXHALL
Church
Information
Tube stop
Note: not all Tube stations are featured on this map
Apsley House 5
British Airways London Eye 29
British Library Exhibition Centre 18
British Museum 20
Buckingham Palace 14
Cabinet War Rooms 28
Changing of the Guard at Buckingham Palace 14
Chelsea Physic Garden 12
Courtauld Gallery 21
Dickens's House Museum 19
Gilbert Collection 21
Green Park 13
Hermitage Rooms 21
Houses of Parliament and Big Ben 30
Hyde Park 6
Kensington Gardens 8
Kensington Palace 7
London Transport Museum 22
London Zoo 1
Madame Tussaud's 3
Museum of London 36
National Gallery 24
National Portrait Gallery 23
Natural History Museum 9
Piccadilly Circus 17
Regent's Park 2
Science Museum 10
Shakespeare's Globe Theatre & Exhibition 34
Somerset House (Courtauld Gallery, Gilbert Collection, Hermitage Rooms) 21
St. James's Park 15
St. Martin-in-the-Fields 25
St. Paul's Cathedral 35
Tate Britain 32
Tate Modern 33
10 Downing Street 27
Tower Bridge Experience 38
Tower of London 37
Trafalgar Square 26
Victoria & Albert Museum 11
Wallace Collection 4
Westminster Abbey 31

are my roster of the most important London attractions. For their locations, see the "London's Top Attractions" map in this chapter.

To beat the crowds, try to hit the top sights on your London list early in the day (preferably right when they open) or late in the afternoon. Westminster Abbey, to cite just one example, can receive upwards of 15,000 visitors per day. Other top tourist draws, such as Buckingham Palace (when it's open to the public during August and September), the Tower of London, the British Museum, and Madame Tussaud's can jam up as the day wears on.

British Museum

Bloomsbury

The **British Museum** ranks as the most-visited attraction in London, with a magnificent, wide-ranging collection of treasures from around the world. Wandering through its seemingly endless galleries, you can't help but be struck by humankind's enduring spirit and creativity. Permanent displays of antiquities from Egypt, Western Asia, Greece, and Rome are on view, as well as prehistoric and Romano-British, medieval, Renaissance, modern, and Oriental collections. The most famous of the countless treasures are the superb **Parthenon Sculptures** that once adorned the Parthenon in Athens — sculptures that Greece wants returned. Other must-sees are the **Rosetta Stone** (which allowed archaeologists to decipher Egyptian hieroglyphics); the **Egyptian Mummies;** the **Sutton Hoo Treasure,** an Anglo-Saxon burial ship believed to be the tomb of a seventh-century East Anglian king; and **Lindow Man,** a well-preserved ancient corpse found in a bog. In December 2000, the museum's **Great Court** reopened with a glass-and-steel roof designed by Lord Norman Foster. Inaccessible to the general public for 150 years, the Great Court is now the museum's central axis. In the center is a circular building completed in 1857 that served as the museum's famous **Reading Room.** Completely restored, this building now houses computer terminals where visitors can access images and information about the museum's vast collections. For a layout of the museum, see the "British Museum" map in this chapter.

Give yourself at least three unhurried hours in the museum. If you get hungry along the way, a cafe and a restaurant are in the Great Court, and another cafe is next to Room 12. Weekday mornings are the best times to go and avoid big crowds. You may want to pick up a *Visit Guide* (£2.50/$4), available at the information desks in the Great Court, to help you chart your way.

If you have only limited time for the British Museum, consider taking one of the **90-minute highlight tours** offered daily at 10:30 a.m. and 1 and 3 p.m.; the cost is £8 ($13). Audio tours covering some of the most important objects in the museum's collections cost £3.50 ($6). Tickets and information for both tours are available at the information desk in the Great Court.

British Museum

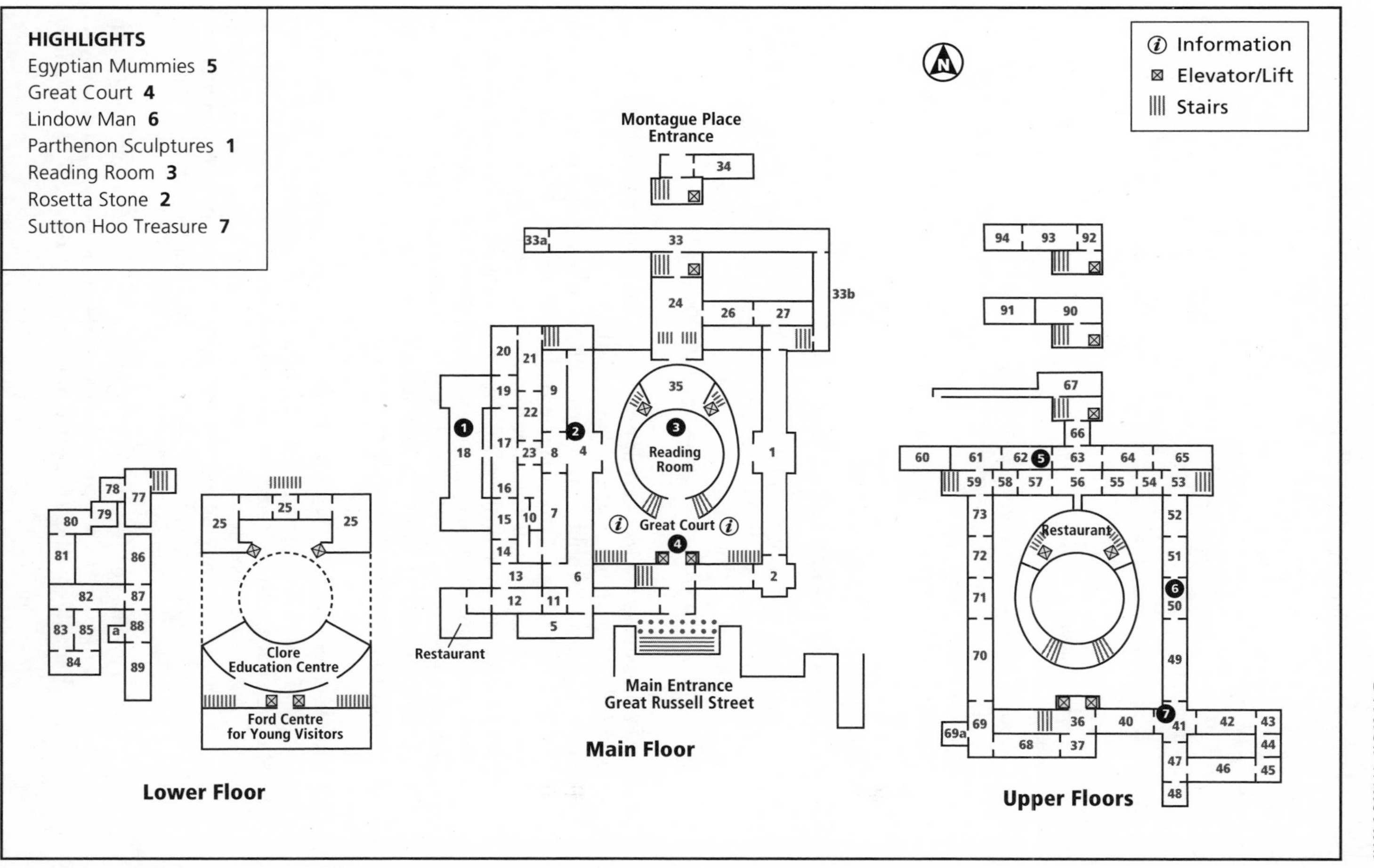
HIGHLIGHTS
Egyptian Mummies 5
Great Court 4
Lindow Man 6
Parthenon Sculptures 1
Reading Room 3
Rosetta Stone 2
Sutton Hoo Treasure 7
Information
Elevator/Lift
Stairs
Montague Place Entrance
Reading Room
Great Court
Restaurant
Main Entrance Great Russell Street
Main Floor
Clore Education Centre
Ford Centre for Young Visitors
Lower Floor
Restaurant
Upper Floors

The power of the written word

The incredible literary cache that was in the British Museum Reading Room (including its rare copy of the *Magna Carta,* the charter of liberties that was a forerunner to modern constitutions) has been moved to a remarkable new space in North London. For details, see the entry for the **British Library Exhibition Centre** later in this chapter under "Finding More Cool Things to See and Do."

Great Russell St., WC1, between Bloomsbury St. and Montgomery St. ☎ ***02076/361-555.*** *Internet:* `www.thebritishmuseum.ac.uk`*. Tube: Russell Sq. (then a five-minute walk south on Montgomery St., along the west side of Russell Square, to the museum entrance on Great Russell St.). Admission: Free. Open: Sat–Wed 10 a.m.–5:30 p.m., Thurs–Fri 10 a.m.–8:30 p.m.; closed Jan 1, Good Friday, Dec 24–26. Most of the museum has wheelchair access by elevator; call for entrance information.*

Buckingham Palace

St. James's Park and Green Park

All the pomp, majesty, scandal, intrigue, tragedy, power, wealth, and tradition associated with the British monarchy hides behind the monumental facade of **Buckingham Palace,** the London residence of the sovereign since Victoria ascended the throne in 1837.

An impressive early-18th-century structure, the palace was rebuilt in 1825 and further modified in 1913. From late July or early August (the dates change yearly) through September, when the royal family isn't in residence, you can buy a ticket to get a glimpse of the impressive staterooms used by Elizabeth II and the other royals. There isn't a guided palace tour; you wander at your own speed through 18 rooms, most of them baroque, filled with some of the world's finest artworks. In these rooms the queen receives guests on official occasions. You leave through the gardens where the queen's famous garden parties are held each summer. Budget about two hours for your visit.

On Monday through Thursday throughout the year, you can visit the **Royal Mews,** one of the finest working stables in existence, which house the magnificent Gold State Coach (used in every coronation since 1831) and other royal conveyances. The newly refurbished **Queen's Gallery,** which features changing exhibits of works from the Royal Collection, reopened early in 2002 in time for the queen's Golden Jubilee.

Buckingham Palace forms the centerpiece of **St. James's Park** and **Green Park,** two royal parks acquired by Henry VIII in the early 16th century. St James's Park, the prettier of the two, was landscaped in 1827 by John Nash in a picturesque English style with an ornamental lake and promenades. **The Mall,** a processional route between the palace and Whitehall and Horse Guards Parade, is the route used for major ceremonial occasions. **St. James's Palace,** the former London abode of Prince Charles and his two sons, and adjacent **Clarence House,** residence of the Queen Mum until her death in 2002 and now the home of Prince Charles, are between The Mall and **Pall Mall** (pronounced *Pell Mell*), a broad avenue running from Trafalgar Square to St. James's Palace. Neither residence is open to visitors.

You can charge tickets for Buckingham Palace visits by calling the **Visitor Office** at ☎ **02073/212-233.** A ticket office in Green Park is open daily July 29 to October 1 from 9 a.m. until 4 p.m. or until the last ticket has been sold. Keep in mind that every visitor is allocated a specific time for entry into the palace, which is why phoning ahead for tickets is smart. You save yourself the time and bother of *queuing* (Britspeak for standing in line) for tickets outside the palace and then having to return hours later to get in. All phone-charged tickets cost an additional £1 ($1.60).

Buckingham Palace Rd., SW1. Palace Visitor Office and Royal Mews ☎ ***02078/391-377*** *(9:30 a.m.–5:30 p.m.) or 02077/992-331 (24-hour recorded info). Internet:* `www.royal.gov.uk`. *Tube: St. James's Park (then a ten-minute walk north on Queen Anne's Gate and west on Birdcage Walk to Buckingham Gate); or Green Park (walk directly south through the park). Admission: Palace, £12 ($19) adults, £10 ($16) over 60, £6 ($10) children under 17, £30 ($48) families (2 adults, 2 children under 17). Royal Mews, £5 ($8) adults, £4 ($6) over 60, £2.50 ($4) children, £12.50 ($20) families. Queen's Gallery, £6.50 ($10) adults, £5 ($8) seniors, £3 ($4.80) children. Open: Palace, Aug 1–Oct 1 (dates may vary by a day or two) daily 9:30 a.m.–4:15 p.m. Royal Mews, daily March–July 11 a.m.–4 p.m. (last admission 3:15 p.m.); Aug–Sept 10 a.m.–5 p.m. (last admission 4:15 p.m.). Queen's Gallery, daily 10 a.m.–5:30 p.m (last admittance 4:30 p.m.). Royal Mews and Queen's Gallery closed Dec 25 and 26. Visitors with disabilities must prebook; Royal Mews and Queen's Gallery are wheelchair accessible.*

Changing of the Guard at Buckingham Palace

St. James's Park

Free of charge, you can stand outside Buckingham Palace and watch the **Changing of the Guard.** The Foot Guards of the Household Division of the Army, the queen's personal guard, carry out the ritual. The Old Guard forms in the palace forecourt before going off duty and handing everything over to the New Guard, which leaves Wellington Barracks at 11:27 a.m. precisely and marches to the palace on Birdcage Walk, usually accompanied by a band. The Guard consists of three officers and 40 men but is reduced when the queen is away. The entire ceremony takes around 40 minutes. If you can't find a spot at the front of the railings of Buckingham Palace, you can see pretty well from the Victoria Memorial in front of the palace.

More changing of the guards

If you miss the Changing of the Guard, or the event doesn't take place on the day of your visit, you can still get an eyeful of London pageantry by attending the **Mounted Guard Changing Ceremony** at the Horse Guards Building in Whitehall. The ceremony takes place daily Monday to Saturday at 11 a.m. and Sunday at 10 a.m. No ticket is required, but arrive early for a good view. To get there, take the Tube to Charing Cross and walk south from Trafalgar Square along Whitehall (about a five-minute walk); the Horse Guards Building will be on your right.

The pageantry of the Changing of the Guard is no longer a daily occurrence. The event takes place at 11:30 a.m. daily April 1 to early June, but only on alternate days at other times of the year. To avoid disappointment, make sure to call ahead or check the Web site listed in the following information.

Buckingham Palace Rd., SW1. ☎ ***02073/212-233*** *(24-hour recorded info). Internet:* `www.royal.gov.uk`. *Tube: St. James's Park (then a ten-minute walk north on Queen Anne's Gate and west on Birdcage Walk to Buckingham Gate); or Green Park (walk directly south through the park). Admission: Free.*

Houses of Parliament and Big Ben

Westminster

The **Houses of Parliament,** situated along the Thames, house the landmark clock tower containing **Big Ben,** a huge bell whose booming chime is a familiar London sound. Designed in a neo-Gothic style by Sir Charles Barry and A.W.N. Pugin, the Parliament buildings were completed in 1857. Covering approximately 8 acres, they occupy the site of an 11th-century palace of Edward the Confessor. At one end (Old Palace Yard) is the **Jewel House,** built in 1366 and the former treasury house of Edward III, who reigned from 1327 to 1377.

For most visitors, a glimpse of the exterior of the Houses of Parliament is sufficient (the best view is from Westminster Bridge). If you want to sit in the **Stranger's Gallery** to hear the rancorous debates, you can line up (pardon me, *queue*) for tickets at the St. Stephen's entrance.

Previously, overseas visitors had to go through an elaborate procedure weeks in advance of their trip in order to tour the Houses of Parliament. Now, however, **75-minute guided tours** are available in late summer and early fall (generally from the last week in July until the end of August and again from mid-September to early October). The tours cost £7 ($11), and booking in advance is recommended. The London ticket office in

Westminster Hall (at the Houses of Parliament) opens in mid-July. You can reserve by phone at ☎ **08709/063-773,** or order tickets online at www.firstcalltickets.com. For the rest of the year, the procedure for getting a tour is much more difficult. If you're interested, you can find details on the Web at www.parliament.uk.

Bridge St. and Parliament Square, SW1. ☎ ***02072/193-000;*** *02072/194-272 for the House's schedule and topics of debate. Tube: Westminster (you can see the clock tower with Big Ben directly across Bridge St. when you exit). Admission: Free. For tickets, join the line at St. Stephen's entrance. Open: Stranger's Gallery House of Commons, Mon 2:30–10:30 p.m., Tues–Wed 11:30–7:30 p.m., Thurs 11:30 a.m.–6:30 p.m., most Fridays 9:30 a.m.–3 p.m.; House of Lords, Mon–Wed 2:30–10 p.m., Thurs 10 a.m.–7:30 p.m.Parliament isn't in session late July to mid-October or on weekends.*

Kensington Gardens

Kensington

One of London's loveliest and most family-friendly parks, **Kensington Gardens** adjoins Hyde Park west of the Serpentine lake. The park was laid out during the reign of William and Mary, after they moved into Kensington Palace in 1689. Generations of children have gazed upon the famous bronze statue of **Peter Pan,** located north of the Serpentine Bridge. Commissioned in 1912 by Peter Pan's creator, J. M. Barrie, the statue marks the spot where Peter Pan (in the book *Peter Pan in Kensington Gardens*) entered the gardens to get to his home on Serpentine Island.

The park is also home to the **Albert Memorial,** an ornate neo-Gothic memorial honoring Queen Victoria's husband, Prince Albert; the lovely **Italian Gardens;** and the free **Serpentine Gallery** (☎ **020/7298-2100**), which is gaining a reputation for showing cutting-edge art and is open daily (except December 24 to 27 and January 1) 10 a.m. to 6 p.m. The **Princess Diana Memorial Playground,** which opened in 2000, is in a fenced-in area at the park's northwest corner. If the weather is fine, give yourself enough time for a leisurely stroll — at least a couple of hours.

Bounded by Kensington Palace Gardens and Palace Green on the west, Bayswater Rd. on the north, Kensington Rd. and Kensington Gore on the south. ☎ ***02072/982-100.*** *Tube: High Street Kensington (then a ten-minute walk east on Kensington High St.) or Queensway (directly across from the northwest corner of the park). Open: daily, dawn to midnight.*

Kensington Palace

Kensington

Acquired by William III in 1689 and remodeled by Sir Christopher Wren, the monarchy used **Kensington Palace** as a royal residence until 1760.

Victoria was born in the palace and was informed here, in 1837, that she was the new Queen of England (and could move to the grander Buckingham Palace). One wing of the palace was Princess Diana's London home after her divorce from Prince Charles. After her death, tens of thousands of mourners gathered in front of the palace and left a sea of floral tributes.

The palace was also the home of Princess Margaret (Queen Elizabeth's sister) until her death in 2002, and is still the home of the duke and duchess of Kent, so portions of the building are closed to visitors. But you can visit the **State Apartments.** A **free audio guide,** keyed to every room and exhibit, explains the history and background. Before reaching the State Apartments, you pass through the **Royal Ceremonial Dress Collection**'s Dressing-for-Royalty exhibit, which takes you through the process of being presented at court, from the first visit to the tailor or dressmaker to the final bow or curtsy. Dresses worn by Queen Victoria, Queen Elizabeth II, and Princess Diana are on display. Give yourself about two hours to view the dress collection and the palace's rooms.

For a pleasant and not-too-expensive tea or snack, after visiting Kensington Palace, stop in at **The Orangery** (☎ **02073/760-239**) in the gardens adjacent to the palace. The cafe is open daily noon to 6 p.m. Lunches cost about £7 ($11); from 3 p.m. you can get a good tea for £6.95 to £12.95 ($11 to $21).

The Broad Walk, Kensington Gardens, W8. ☎ ***02079/379-561.*** *Internet:* `www.hrp.org.uk`. *Tube: Queensway on the north side (then a ten-minute walk south through the park) or High Street Kensington on the southwest side (then a ten-minute walk through the park). Open: March–Oct daily 10 a.m.–5 p.m., Nov–Feb daily 10 a.m.–4 p.m. Admission: £10 ($16) adults, £7.50 ($12) seniors and children 5 to 15. Despite some stairs, the palace is accessible for visitors with disabilities; call first.*

Madame Tussaud's

Marylebone

Madame Tussaud's wax museum is a world-famous tourist attraction, and people tend to either love it or hate it. The question is: Do you want to pay the high admission price and devote the time to see lifelike wax figures? (You need at least two hours to see everything.) The original moldings of members of the French court are undeniably fascinating. Madame Tussaud had direct access to the former royals — she made molds of their heads after they were guillotined during the French Revolution. And animatronic gadgetry makes the **Spirit of London** theme ride fun. But the **Chamber of Horrors** is definitely for the ghoulish (parents with little ones may want to think twice about wandering here). This is where you can see one of Jack the Ripper's victims lying in a pool of (wax?) blood and likenesses of mass murderers, such as Gary Gilmore and Charles Manson. You can find better stars next door, at the **London Planetarium** (☎ **02079/356-861**).

Go early to beat the crowds; better still, reserve tickets by credit card (☎ **08704/003-000**) up to three days in advance, then go straight to the head of the line at your allotted time.

*Marylebone Rd., NW1. ☎ **02079/356-861.** Tube: Baker St. (then a two-minute walk east on Marylebone Rd). Admission: £14.95 ($24) adults, £11.80 ($19) over 60, £10.50 ($17) children under 16; children under 4 not admitted. Combination tickets (including the London Planetarium): £16.95 ($27) adults, £13.50 ($22) over 60, £12 ($19) children under 16. Open: June–Aug daily 9 a.m.–5:30 p.m.; Sept–May Mon–Fri 10 a.m.–5:30 p.m., Sat–Sun 9:20 a.m.–5:30 p.m. Tussaud's is wheelchair accessible by elevator, but call first, because only three chair-users are allowed in at a time.*

National Gallery

Trafalgar Square

If great art is your passion, then you may think that the **National Gallery** is paradise. The museum houses one of the world's most comprehensive collections of British and European paintings. All the major schools from the 13th to the 20th centuries are represented, but the Italians get the lion's share of wall space, with artists like Leonardo da Vinci, Botticelli, and Raphael on the roster. The French Impressionist and post-Impressionist works by Monet, Manet, Seurat, Cézanne, Degas, and van Gogh are shimmering and sublime. And because you're on English soil, check out at least a few of Turner's stunning seascapes, Constable's landscapes, and Reynolds' society portraits. And you won't want to miss the Rembrandts. Budget at least two hours here. A good restaurant for lunch, tea, or snacks is on the second floor.

Use the free **computer information center** to make the most of your time at the gallery. You can design a tour based on your artistic preferences and print out a customized tour map. You can also rent a portable **audio-tour guide** for £3 ($4.80). **Free guided tours** are offered daily at 11:30 a.m. and 2:30 p.m. with an additional tour on Wednesday at 6:30 p.m.

A £21 million revamp of the National Gallery began in 2003 and is scheduled to be completed by 2005. When work is finished, the gallery will have two new entrances in the east wing and a new shop and cafe, and a previously hidden inner courtyard will be transformed into a spacious atrium.

*Trafalgar Sq., WC2. ☎ **02077/472-885.** Tube: Charing Cross (then a two-minute walk north across Trafalgar Sq.). Admission: Free, but admission charged for special exhibits, usually around £5 ($8). Open: Thurs–Tues 10 a.m.–6 p.m., Wed 10 a.m.–9 p.m.; closed Jan. 1, Good Friday, and Dec 24–26. The entire museum is wheelchair accessible.*

National Portrait Gallery

Trafalgar Square

What do the following people have in common: Sir Walter Raleigh, Shakespeare (wearing a gold earring), Queen Elizabeth I, the Brontë sisters, Winston Churchill, Oscar Wilde, Noël Coward, Mick Jagger, and Princess Di? Their portraits hang in the **National Portrait Gallery,** a visual *Who's Who* of famous Brits. The galleries are arranged in chronological order. The earliest portraits are in the **Tudor Gallery;** portraits from the 1960s to the 1980s are displayed in the **Balcony Gallery.** The rooftop cafe provides great West End views. Plan on spending at least two hours, but getting sidetracked here is easy, so you may want more time.

St. Martin's Place (off Trafalgar Sq. behind the National Gallery), WC2. ☎ ***02073/060-055.*** *Tube: Leicester Sq. (then a two-minute walk south on Charing Cross Rd.). Admission: Free; audio tour £3 ($4.80). Open: Sat–Wed 10 a.m.–6 p.m., Thurs–Fri 10 a.m.–9 p.m. All but the landing galleries are wheelchair accessible; call first for entry instructions.*

Natural History Museum

South Kensington

Filled with magnificent specimens and exciting displays relating to natural history, this museum houses the national collections of living and fossil plants, animals, and minerals. The most popular attraction in this enormous Victorian-era museum is the huge **dinosaur exhibit,** with 14 complete skeletons, a pair of animatronic raptors, and a life-size, robotic T-Rex lunching on a freshly killed Tenontosaurus. Bug-filled **Creepy Crawlies** is another popular kid pleaser. The sparkling gems and crystals in the **Mineral Gallery** are literally dazzling, and in the **Meteorite Pavilion** you can see fragments of rock that crashed into the earth from the farthest reaches of the galaxy. The museum offers enough to keep you occupied for at least two hours.

Picture-perfect Queen Mum

The Royal Family portrait commissioned by the National Portrait Gallery to celebrate the Queen Mother's 100th birthday (in 2000) is the newest royal addition to go on display in the National Portrait Gallery. Artist John Wonnacott painted the canvas that portrays Queen Elizabeth, Prince Phillip, Prince Charles, and Princes William and Harry in conversation with the Queen Mother in the White Drawing Room in Buckingham Palace. Interestingly, Prince William — Charles' firstborn and thus the second in line to the throne — dominates the picture. The Queen Mother died in 2002.

*Cromwell Rd., SW7. ☎ **02079/425-000.** Tube: South Kensington (the Tube station is on the corner of Cromwell Rd. and Exhibition Rd., at the corner of the museum). Admission: Free. Open: Mon–Sat 10 a.m.–5:50 p.m., Sun 11 a.m.–5:50 p.m. Nearly all the galleries are flat or ramped for wheelchair users; call for instructions on entering the building.*

St. Paul's Cathedral

The City

After the Great Fire of 1666 destroyed the city's old cathedral, the great architect Christopher Wren was called upon to design **St. Paul's,** a huge and harmonious Renaissance-leaning-toward-baroque building. Nazi bombing raids wiped out the surrounding area, so Wren's masterpiece, capped by the most famous dome in London, rises majestically above a crowded sea of undistinguished office buildings. Grinling Gibbons carved the exceptionally beautiful choir stalls, which are the only impressive artworks inside.

Christopher Wren is buried in the crypt, and his epitaph, on the floor below the dome, reads LECTOR, SI MONUMENTUM REQUIRIS, CIRCUMSPICE ("Reader, if you seek his monument, look around you"). His companions in the crypt include Britain's famed national heroes: the Duke of Wellington, who defeated Napoleon at Waterloo, and Admiral Lord Nelson, who took down the French at Trafalgar during the same war. But many people want to see St. Paul's simply because Lady Diana Spencer wed Prince Charles here in what was billed as the fairy-tale wedding of the century.

You can climb up to the **Whispering Gallery** for a bit of acoustical fun or gasp your way up to the very top for a breathtaking view of London. You can see the entire cathedral in an hour or less. For an overview of the cathedral's layout, see the "St. Paul's Cathedral" map in this chapter.

The pedestrian-only **Millennium Bridge,** designed by Lord Norman Foster, links St. Paul's Cathedral to the Tate Modern art gallery on the other side of the Thames. The bridge was so shaky when it opened in 2000 that it was immediately closed for repairs. A steadier version reopened in 2001.

*St. Paul's Churchyard, Ludgate Hill, EC4. ☎ **02072/364-128.** Tube: St. Paul's (then a five-minute walk west on Ludgate to cathedral entrance on St. Paul's Churchyard). Admission: £6 ($10) adults, £5 ($8) seniors and students, £3 ($4.80) children. Guided tours: daily, £2.50 ($4) adults, £2 ($3.20) seniors, £1 ($1.60) children under 10. Audio tours (available 8:30 a.m.–3 p.m.) £3.50 ($6) adults, £2.50 ($4) seniors and students. Open: Mon–Sat 8:30 a.m.–4 p.m.; no sightseeing on Sunday (services only). The cathedral is wheelchair accessible by the service entrance near the South Transept; ring the bell for assistance.*

St. Paul's Cathedral

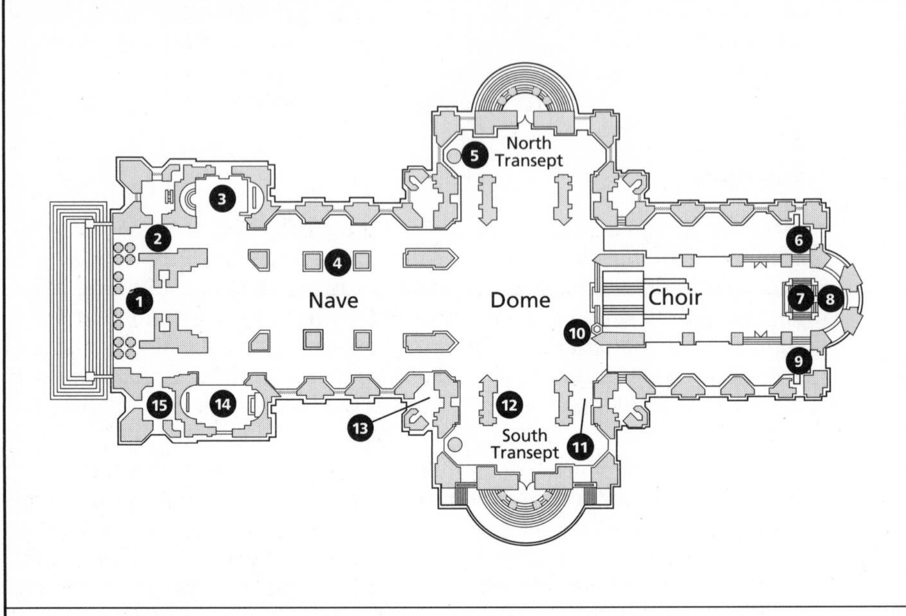

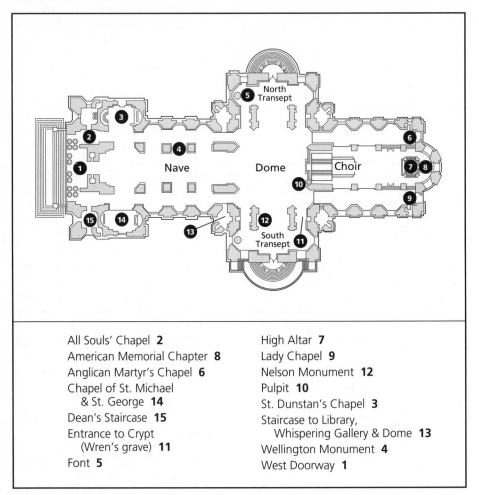

All Souls' Chapel **2**
American Memorial Chapter **8**
Anglican Martyr's Chapel **6**
Chapel of St. Michael & St. George **14**
Dean's Staircase **15**
Entrance to Crypt (Wren's grave) **11**
Font **5**
High Altar **7**
Lady Chapel **9**
Nelson Monument **12**
Pulpit **10**
St. Dunstan's Chapel **3**
Staircase to Library, Whispering Gallery & Dome **13**
Wellington Monument **4**
West Doorway **1**

Tate Britain
Pimlico

The Tate Gallery took this name to distinguish it from its new counterpart, Tate Modern, which opened in May 2000 on the South Bank. **Tate Britain** retains the older (pre-20th-century) collections of exclusively British art plus works by major British stars like David Hockney and experimental works by Brits and foreigners living in Britain. Among the masterpieces on display in a host of newly refurbished galleries are dreamy works by the British pre-Raphaelites, the celestial visions of William Blake, bawdy satirical works by William Hogarth, genteel portraits by Sir Joshua Reynolds, bucolic landscapes by John Constable, and the shimmering seascapes of J.M.W. Turner. Plan on spending at least two hours here. A restaurant and cafe are on the lower level.

*Millbank, Pimlico SW1. ☎ **02078/878-000.** Tube: Pimlico (then a ten-minute walk south on Vauxhall Bridge Rd. to the river and north on Millbank to the museum entrance). Bus: For a more scenic route, take bus 77A, which runs south along The Strand and Whitehall to the museum entrance on Millbank. Admission: Free; varying admission fees for special exhibits; audio tours £3 ($4.80). Open: daily 10 a.m.–5:50 p.m. Most galleries are wheelchair accessible, but call first for details on entry.*

Tate Modern

Bankside

The former Bankside Power Station is the setting for the fabulous **Tate Modern,** which opened in May 2000. Considered one of the top modern art museums in the world, the Tate Modern houses a collection of international 20th-century art, displaying major works by some of the most influential artists of the last century: Picasso, Matisse, Dalí, Duchamp, Moore, and Bacon among them. A gallery for the 21st-century collection exhibits new art as it's created. For fans of contemporary art and architecture, this new star on the London art scene is not to be missed. Plan on spending at least two hours. The Tate Restaurant, open for lunch and tea, offers stunning views over the Thames; definitely call first to book a table.

*25 Sumner St., SE1. ☎ **02078/878-000.** Tube: Southwark (then a ten-minute walk north along Blackfriars Rd. and east along the riverside promenade) or Blackfriars (then a ten-minute walk south across Blackfriars Bridge). Admission: Free; there may be charges for special exhibits. Open: Mon–Thurs 10 a.m.–6 p.m., Fri–Sat 10 a.m.–10 p.m.*

Tower of London

The City

The **Tower of London** offers enough to keep you captivated for a good three to four hours, but *make sure* you save time for the **Crown Jewels,** which include the world's largest diamond (the 530-carat Star of Africa) and other breathtaking gems set into royal robes, swords, sceptres, and crowns.

In 1066, William the Conqueror built the city's best-known historic site. The Tower served as his fortress and later as a prison, holding famous captives, such as Sir Walter Raleigh and Princess Elizabeth I. Ann Boleyn and Catherine Howard (two of the eight wives of Henry VIII), the nine-day queen Lady Jane Grey, and Sir Thomas More were among those who lost their heads on **Tower Green.** According to Shakespeare, the two little princes (the sons of Edward IV) were murdered in the **Bloody Tower** by henchmen of Richard III, but many modern historians refute this story. For the layout of the tower, see the "Tower of London" map in this chapter.

Huge black ravens hop around the grounds of the Tower of London. A legend says that the tower and the British Commonwealth will fall if the ravens ever leave. Their wings have been clipped as a precaution.

Tower of London

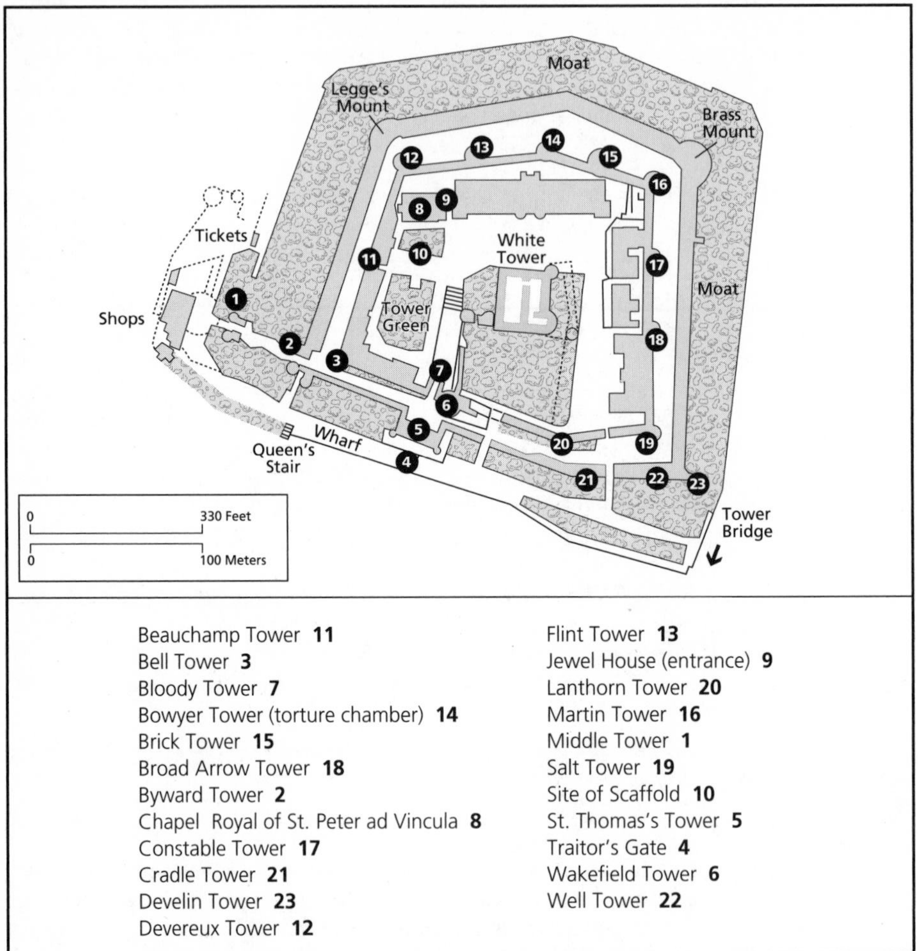

*Tower Hill, EC3. ☎ **02077/090-765.** Tube: Tower Hill (then a five-minute walk west and south on Tower Hill). Bus: Eastbound bus 25 from Marble Arch, Oxford Circus, or St. Paul's; it stops at Tower Hill, north of the entrance. Admission: £11.50 ($18) adults, £8.75 ($14) seniors and students, £7.50 ($12) children 5–15, £34 ($54) families (2 adults, 3 children). Tours: Yeoman Warders (also known as "Beefeaters") give free one-hour tours of the entire compound every half-hour, starting at 9:30 a.m. (Sunday at 10 a.m.) from the Middle Tower near the main entrance. The last guided walk starts about 3:30 p.m. in summer or 2:30 p.m. in winter (weather permitting). Open: March–Oct Mon–Sat 9 a.m.–5 p.m., Sun 10 a.m.–5 p.m.; Nov–Feb Tues–Sat 9 a.m.–4 p.m., Sun–Mon 10 a.m.–4 p.m.; closed Jan 1 and Dec 24–26. There's wheelchair access onto the grounds, but many of the historic buildings can't accommodate wheelchairs.*

Trafalgar Square

St. James's

Until very recently, **Trafalgar Square** was an island in the midst of a roaring traffic interchange surrounded by historic buildings, such as St. Martin-in-the-Fields church and the National Gallery. After a major urban redesign scheme, it reopened in 2003 with one side attached to the steps of the National Gallery, so visitors can easily get to the square without crossing any streets at all. Besides being a major tourist attraction, Trafalgar Square is the site of many large gatherings, including political demonstrations, Christmas revels, and New Year's Eve festivities. The square honors military hero Admiral Lord Nelson (1758–1805), who lost his life at the Battle of Trafalgar. **Nelson's Column,** with fountains and four bronze lions at its base, rises some 145 feet above the square. At the top, a 14-foot-high statue of Nelson (who was 5-feet, 4-inches tall in real life) looks commandingly toward **Admiralty Arch,** passed through by state and royal processions between Buckingham Palace and St. Paul's Cathedral. You don't really need more than a few minutes to take in the square. **St. Martin-in-the-Fields** (☎ **02079/300-089**), the famous neoclassical church at the northeast corner of Trafalgar Square, was designed by James Gibbs, a disciple of Christopher Wren, and completed in 1726; the 185-foot spire was added about 100 years later. The church was the precursor of dozens of similar-looking churches throughout colonial New England. **The Academy of St. Martin-in-the-Fields,** a famous musical ensemble, frequently performs here. Lunchtime concerts are held on Monday, Tuesday, and Friday at 1 p.m., and evening concerts are held Thursday to Saturday at 7:30 p.m. Concert tickets are £6 to £15 ($10 to $24). For reservations by credit card, call ☎ **02078/398-362.** The church is open Monday to Saturday 10 a.m. to 6 p.m. and Sunday from noon to 6 p.m.; admission is free.

Café-in-the-Crypt (☎ **02078/394-342**), one of the West End's most pleasant and reasonably priced self-service restaurants, is in the crypt of St. Martin-in-the-Fields. It serves traditional English home cooking Monday to Saturday from 10 a.m. to 8 p.m. and on Sunday from noon to 8 p.m. The busy crypt also contains the **London Brass Rubbing Centre** (☎ **02074/376-023**), which provides paper, metallic waxes, and instructions on how to rub your own replica of historic brasses. Prices range from £2 to £15 ($3.20 to $24), including materials and specific brasses. Kids 10 and up love this place. The center is open Monday through Saturday 10 a.m. to 6 p.m., and on Sunday noon to 6 p.m.

Bounded on the north by Trafalgar, on the west by Cockspur St., and on the east by Whitehall. Tube: Charing Cross (an exit from the Underground station leads to the square).

Victoria & Albert Museum

South Kensington

The **Victoria & Albert Museum** (known as the V&A) is the national museum of art and design. In the 145 galleries filled with fine and decorative arts from around the world, you can find superbly decorated period rooms, a fashion collection spanning 400 years of European designs, Raphael cartoons (designs for tapestries in the Sistine Chapel), the Silver Galleries, and the largest assemblages of Renaissance sculpture outside Italy and of Indian art outside India. The **Canon Photography Gallery** shows work by celebrated photographers. In November 2001, the museum opened its spectacular new British Galleries. Allow at least two hours just to cover the basics.

*Cromwell Rd., SW7. ☎ **02079/422-000.** Tube: South Kensington (the museum is across from the Underground station). Admission: Free. Open: Thurs–Tues 10 a.m.–5:45 p.m., Wed 10 a.m.–10 p.m.; closed Dec 24–26. The museum is wheelchair accessible (about 95% of the exhibits are step-free).*

Westminster Abbey

Westminster

The Gothic and grand **Westminster Abbey** is one of London's most important and venerable historic sites. The present abbey dates mostly from the 13th and 14th centuries, but a church has been on this site for more than a thousand years. Since 1066, when William the Conquerer became the first English monarch to be crowned here, every successive British sovereign save two (Edward V and Edward VIII) has sat on the **Coronation Chair** to receive the crown and sceptre. In the **Royal Chapels** you can see the **tomb of Henry VII,** with its delicate fan vaulting, and the **tomb of Queen Elizabeth I,** buried in the same vault as her Catholic half-sister, Mary I, and not far from her rival Mary Queen of Scots. In **Poets' Corner,** some of England's greatest writers (including Chaucer, Dickens, and Thomas Hardy) are interred or memorialized. Other points of interest include the College Garden, Cloisters, chapter house, and Undercroft Museum, which contains the Pyx Chamber with its display of church plate. In September 1997, the abbey was the site of Princess Diana's funeral, and in 2002, the funeral service for the Queen Mother took place here. The Abbey is within walking distance of the Houses of Parliament. For a floor plan of the Abbey, see the "Westminster Abbey" map in this chapter.

*Broad Sanctuary, SW1. ☎ **02072/227-110.** Tube: Westminster (then a three-minute walk west following Parliament Sq. to Broad Sanctuary). Bus: The 77A going south along The Strand, Whitehall, and Millbank stops near the Houses of Parliament, near the Abbey. Admission: Abbey and Royal Chapels, £6 ($10) adults, £3 ($4.80) seniors and students, £2 ($3.20) children 11–16, £12 ($19) families (2 adults, 2 children). Chapter House, Pyx Chamber, and Museum, free with tours or £2.50 ($4) adults, £1.30 ($2) children. Guided tours: Led by an Abbey Verger £3 ($4.80); call for times; tickets for tours at Enquiry Desk in the Abbey; audio tours £2 ($3.20). Open: Cathedral, Mon–Fri 9 a.m.–4:45 p.m. (last admission 3:45 p.m.), Sat 9 a.m.–2:45 p.m.;*

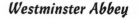

Westminster Abbey

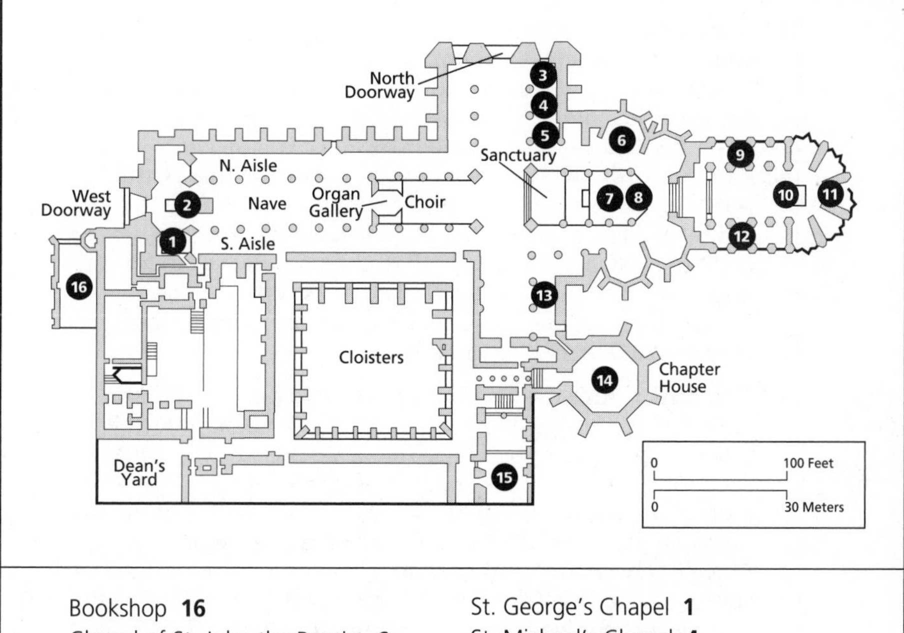

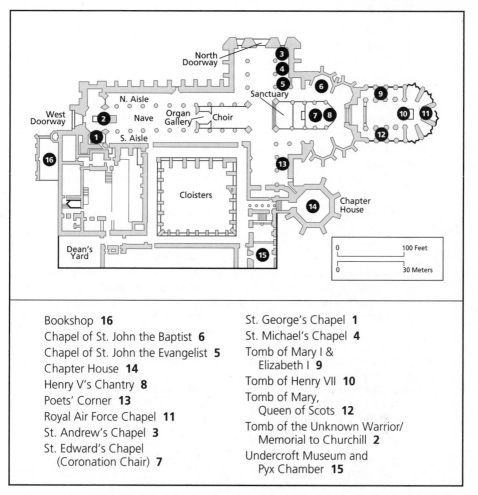

Bookshop **16**
Chapel of St. John the Baptist **6**
Chapel of St. John the Evangelist **5**
Chapter House **14**
Henry V's Chantry **8**
Poets' Corner **13**
Royal Air Force Chapel **11**
St. Andrew's Chapel **3**
St. Edward's Chapel (Coronation Chair) **7**
St. George's Chapel **1**
St. Michael's Chapel **4**
Tomb of Mary I & Elizabeth I **9**
Tomb of Henry VII **10**
Tomb of Mary, Queen of Scots **12**
Tomb of the Unknown Warrior/ Memorial to Churchill **2**
Undercroft Museum and Pyx Chamber **15**

no sightseeing on Sunday (services only). Cloisters, daily 10 a.m.–6 p.m. Chapter house, Pyx Chamber, and Undercroft Museum, daily 10 a.m.–4 p.m. College Garden, April–Sept 10 a.m.–6 p.m., Oct–March 10 a.m.–4 p.m. There's ramped wheelchair access through the Cloisters; ring the bell for assistance.

Finding More Cool Things to See and Do

London offers much more to see than the places I describe in the previous section, which includes the essential A-list sights that almost everyone who visits London wants to see. If you have more time, you can pick and choose from the following attractions to round out your visit (and don't forget to check out the side trips I describe in Chapter 13):

- **Apsley House** (Hyde Park Corner, W1; ☎ **02074/995-676;** Tube: Hyde Park Corner), an imposing neoclassical mansion designed by Robert Adam and completed in 1778, was the London residence of the first duke of Wellington, who defeated Napoleon at Waterloo in 1815. With its sumptuous interiors and treasure trove of paintings, china, swords, and military honors, the house reflects the duke's position as the most powerful commander in Europe. A **free audio guide** explains all the details on a self-guided tour that lasts about an hour. Admission is £4.50 ($7) for adults, £3 ($4.80) for seniors, and free for children under 18. The house is open Tuesday to Sunday from 11 a.m. to 5 p.m. It's closed January 1, Good Friday, May 1, and December 24 to 26.

- The **British Airways London Eye** (Bridge Road, SE1, beside Westminster Bridge on the South Bank; ☎ **08705/000-600** for advance credit-card booking; Tube: Westminster) is a 400-foot-high rotating wheel that offers unparalleled views of London from its enclosed observation pods. Each glass-sided elliptical module holds about 25 passengers; the pods are large enough so you can move freely about. Lasting about 30 minutes (equivalent to one rotation), the ride (or "flight") is remarkably smooth. The London Eye was scheduled to remain in operation through 2003 and has been such a hit that it will probably stay open into 2004. You can save time by reserving a ticket in advance. Admission is £11 ($18) for adults, £10 ($16) for seniors, and £5.50 ($9) for children under 16. The London Eye is open daily May to October from 9:30 a.m. (9 a.m. Friday through Sunday) to 8 p.m. and November to May daily from 10 a.m. to 6 p.m.

- The **British Library Exhibition Centre** (96 Euston Rd., Marylebone, NW1; ☎ **02074/127-513;** Tube: King's Cross/St. Pancras) houses the literary treasures of the British Museum. This is where you can see a copy of the *Magna Carta,* the illustrated *Lindisfarne Gospel* from Ireland, Shakespeare's first folio, and handwritten manuscripts by world-famous British authors such as Jane Austen and Thomas Hardy. Allow at least an hour, more if you love literature or literary history. Admission is free. The center is open Monday and Wednesday to Friday from 9:30 a.m. to 6 p.m., Tuesday from 9:30 a.m. to 8 p.m., Saturday from 9:30 a.m. to 5 p.m., and Sunday from 11 a.m. to 5 p.m.

- The history-laden **Cabinet War Rooms** (Clive Steps, King Charles Street, Westminster, SW1; ☎ **02079/306-961;** Tube: Westminster) are in the World War II bunker used by Winston Churchill and his chiefs of staff during "England's darkest hour." A free audio tour guides you through this labyrinth of underground rooms where Churchill and his War Cabinet planned military campaigns. It has all been meticulously preserved, right down to the cigar waiting by Churchill's bed. You can almost hear the air-raid sirens. Admission is £7 ($11) for adults, £5.50 ($9) for seniors and students, free for children under 16. The rooms are open daily April to September from 9:30 a.m. to 6 p.m., October to March from 10 a.m. to 6 p.m. (last entry 5:15 p.m.). From the Tube, walk west (staying on the north side of the street) to Parliament Street, then turn right to reach King Charles Street.

- **Chelsea Physic Garden** (Swan Walk, 66 Royal Hospital Rd., Chelsea SW3; Tube: Sloane Square, then a 15-minute walk south on Lower Sloane Street and west to the end of Royal Hospital Road), is a little-known gem of a garden on the grounds of the Royal Hospital. Set on 3½ acres, it dates to 1673 and is filled with plant species cultivated hundreds of years ago for their commercial and medicinal benefits. The garden is open from April through October Wednesday from 2 to 5 p.m. and Sunday from 2 to 6 p.m.; daily from 2 to 5 p.m. during the Chelsea Flower Show in May. A nice teahouse is on the premises. Admission is £5 ($8) adults, £3 ($4.80) students and children 5 to 15.
- The **Dickens's House Museum** (48 Doughty St., Bloomsbury, WC1; ☎ **02074/052-127;** Tube: Russell Square) was the home of the great Victorian novelist and his family from 1837 to 1839. Here the prolific Charles Dickens penned such famous works as *The Pickwick Papers, Oliver Twist,* and *Nicholas Nickleby*. The museum contains the world's most comprehensive Dickens library, portraits, illustrations, and rooms furnished as they were in Dickens' time. The admission price is £4 ($6) for adults, £3 ($4.80) for seniors, and £2 ($3.20) for children. Hours are Monday to Saturday from 10 a.m. to 5 p.m.

- **Hyde Park** (bounded by Knightsbridge to the south, Bayswater Road to the north, and Park Lane to the east; ☎ **02072/982-100;** Tube: Marble Arch or Lancaster Gate), the former private boar-and-deer-hunting domain of Henry VIII, is now the largest and most popular of the Central London parks — and one of the largest urban green spaces in the world. With adjoining Kensington Gardens, Hyde Park is 630 acres of landscaped lawns, flowerbeds, avenues of trees, and a 41-acre lake known as the Serpentine, where you can row and sail model boats. Rotten Row, the park's 300-year-old riding track, was the country's first public road to be lit at night. At the northeastern tip, near Marble Arch, is Speakers' Corner, a famous Sunday-morning-venting spot for orators. **Free band concerts** are held in the park's bandshell on Sundays and Bank Holidays from May to August, and the **Dell Restaurant** (☎ **02077/060-464**) at the east end of the Serpentine offers cafeteria-style food and drinks. It's open in summer weekdays 10 a.m. to 6 p.m., weekends 10 a.m. to 7 p.m.; in winter weekdays 10 a.m. to 4 p.m., weekends 10 a.m. to 5 p.m. The park is a pleasant place for an hour's stroll, but staying longer is always tempting. The park is open daily from dawn to midnight.

- The **London Transport Museum** (The Piazza, Covent Garden, WC2; ☎ **02073/796-344;** Tube: Covent Garden) chronicles the development of the city's famous Underground and double-decker bus system. A wonderful collection of historic vehicles is on display, including an 1829 omnibus, a horse-drawn bus, and London's first trolley bus. Interactive exhibits allow younger visitors to operate the controls of a Tube train and get their tickets punched. After two hours, you may have to drag them away. Admission is £5.95 ($10) for adults, £4.50 ($7) for seniors, free for children under 16 with adult. The museum is open Saturday to Thursday from 10 a.m. to 6 p.m., Friday from 11 a.m. to 6 p.m. (last entry at 5:15 p.m.).

- The 36-acre **London Zoo** (at the north end of Regent's Park, NW1; ☎ **02077/223-333;** Tube: Regent's Park, then bus C2 north to Delaney Street or Camden Town) is Britain's largest zoo, with about 8,000 animals in various species-specific houses. The best are the **Insect House** (bird-eating spiders); the **Reptile House** (huge monitor lizards and a 15-foot python); the **Sobell Pavilion for Apes and Monkeys;** and the **Lion Terraces.** In the Moonlight World, special lighting effects simulate night for the nocturnal creatures so you can see them in action. The newest exhibit, Web of Life, in the Millennium Conservatory, brings together special animal displays with interactive activities to show the interconnectedness and diversity of different life forms. The Children's Zoo, with interactive exhibits placed at low height, is designed for 4- to 8-year-olds. Many families budget almost an entire day for the zoo; I recommend at least three hours. Admission is £12 ($19) adults; £10 ($16) seniors, students, and visitors with disabilities; £9 ($14) children 3 to 14; £38 ($61) families (2 adults, 2 children). The zoo is open daily from March 10 to October 26 from 10 a.m. to 5:30 p.m.; October 27 to February 10 from 10 a.m. to 4 p.m., February 11 to March 9 from 10 a.m. to 4:30 p.m. The zoo is closed December 25.

- The **Museum of London** (150 London Wall, EC2, in the Barbican district near St. Paul's Cathedral; ☎ **02076/003-699;** Tube: St. Paul's), one of the most comprehensive city museums in the world, sits in the original square-mile *Londinium* of the Romans, overlooking Roman and medieval city walls. Archaeological finds; paintings and prints; social, industrial, and historical artifacts; and costumes, maps, and models trace the city's history and development from prehistoric times to the 21st century. Of special interest is the **gilt-and-scarlet Lord Mayor's Coach,** built in 1757 and weighing 3 tons. Admission is free. The museum is open Monday to Saturday from 10 a.m. to 5:50 p.m., Sunday from noon to 5:50 p.m. Closed January 1 and December 24 to 26.

- **Regent's Park** (just north of Marylebone Road, surrounded by the Outer Circle road; ☎ **02074/867-905;** Tube: Regent's Park or Baker Street) is one of London's great green spaces. Home of the **London Zoo,** the park is also where people come to play soccer, cricket, tennis, and softball; boat in the lake; visit Queen Mary's Rose

Garden; and let their kids have fun in the many playgrounds. Summer lunch and evening bandstand concerts happen here, as well as puppet shows and other children's activities on weekdays throughout August. The park's northernmost section rises to the summit of Primrose Hill, which provides fine views of Westminster and the city. The park is open from dawn to dusk.

- The state-of-the-art **Science Museum** (Exhibition Road, London SW7; ☎ **02079/424-454;** Tube: South Kensington) covers the history and development of science, medicine, and technology. On display are rarities, such as an 1813 steam locomotive, Arkwright's spinning machine, Fox Talbot's first camera, Edison's original phonograph, and the Apollo 10 space module. Kids 7 to 12 years old find the interactive displays challenging and fun. The **Garden Galleries** provide construction areas, sound-and-light shows, and games for younger kids. The Wellcome Wing, which opened in 2000, is devoted to contemporary science and has an IMAX 3-D film theater. Allow at least two hours, more if you're going to see the film. A signposted exit in the Tube station goes directly to the museum, which is open daily 10 a.m. to 6 p.m. Admission to the museum is free; the IMAX theater (☎ **08708/704-868** for advance booking) costs £14.50 ($23) for adults, £8.50 ($14) for seniors and children 5 to 15. The museum is closed December 24 to 26.
- **Shakespeare's Globe Theatre & Exhibition** (New Globe Walk, South Bank, SE1, just west of Southwark Bridge; ☎ **02079/021-500;** Tube: London Bridge) is a full-size replica of the roofless "wooden O" that served as the Bard's London theater. On **guided tours** through the oak-and-thatch theater and its workshops, you discover tons of info about Shakespeare and the London theater world of the Elizabethans. The exhibition (with theater tour) costs £8 ($13) for adults, £6.50 ($11) for seniors and students, £5.50 ($9) for children. From October to April the theater is open daily from 10 a.m. to 5 p.m.; during the May-to-September performance season, the Globe is open daily from 9 a.m. to noon.

Dinner and a show at the Globe Theatre

The Globe presents Shakespeare plays from May to September. Theatergoers sit on wooden benches under the open sky. For tickets, call ☎ **02074/019-919** within the U.K. or **02079/021-475** from overseas; you can check out the current performance schedule at `www.shakespeares-globe.org`. Ticket prices range from £5 ($8) for standing room to £27 ($43). Even if you don't plan to see a play at the Globe, you can have a snack, tea, or a full meal in the theater. No reservations are required at **The Globe Cafe,** open daily from May to September 10 a.m. to 11 p.m., and from October to April 10 a.m. to 6 p.m. If you want lunch or dinner, reserve a table in advance at **The Globe Restaurant** (☎ **02079/289-444**), which is open daily from noon to 2:30 p.m. and 5:30 to 11 p.m.

From autos to art

The late Queen Mother once remarked how sad it was that the courtyard at **Somerset House** had become an Inland Revenue car park. It was just the spur needed to restore the 1,000-room civil service palace, designed by Sir William Chambers (1724–1796), and open it to the public.

- A heady mix of high culture and street entertainment, the "new" **Somerset House** (The Strand, WC2; ☎ **02078/454-600;** www.somerset-house.org.uk; Tube: Temple, then a five-minute walk north on Arundel Street and west on The Strand), houses three noteworthy art collections. It also has a new courtyard with dancing fountains and a riverside terrace with a great summer cafe. All three galleries are open daily from 10 a.m. to 6 p.m. (last admittance 45 to 60 minutes earlier), and closed January 1 and December 24 to 26. The courtyard is open daily from 7:30 a.m. to 11 p.m. (7 p.m. in winter). Admission to Somerset House is free; each gallery charges separate admission.
    - The **Courtauld Gallery** (☎ **02078/482-526**) has been in Somerset House since 1989. Impressionist and Post-impressionist paintings are the gallery's main strength. Major works include Manet's *Bar at the Folies Bergères;* Monet's *Banks of the Seine at Argenteuil; Lady with Parasol* by Degas; *La Loge* by Renoir; Van Gogh's *Self-Portrait with Bandaged Ear;* and several Cézannes, including *The Card Players.* Admission is £5 ($8) for adults, £4 ($6) for seniors, free for children under 18 and for everyone Mon before 2 p.m.
    - The **Gilbert Collection** (☎ **02074/209-400**), in the South Building, showcases glittering gold, silver, and mosaics valued at £75 million when Arthur Gilbert donated the 800-piece collection to the nation in 1996. You see objects here from Princess Diana's old home, Althorp. Admission is £5 ($8) for adults, £4 ($6) for seniors, free for children under 18;
    - The **Hermitage Rooms** (☎ **02078/454-630**), an offshoot of the State Hermitage Museum in St. Petersburg, exhibits pieces from the Russian Imperial collections in changing shows. Half the tickets are sold in advance (☎ **02074/133-398;** www.ticketmaster.co.uk), half at the door, for half-hourly timed entry. Tickets cost £6 ($10) for adults, £4 ($6) for seniors and students, free for children under 5
- **10 Downing Street** (10 Downing St., SW1; Tube: Westminster), the residence of the prime minister, is on many London visitors' must-see list, so I'm sorry to tell you that there's nothing to see here

except a heavily guarded gate. By peering through the gate, you can get a glimpse (on the right side) of No. 10, the official residence of the British Prime Minister since 1732. The Chancellor of the Exchequer usually resides next door at No. 11 (the Blairs, with their large family, now reside there), and No. 12 serves as the office of the chief government whip, responsible for maintaining discipline and cooperation in the vociferous House of Commons. These three small brick terrace houses, built on a cul-de-sac in 1680, stand in sharp contrast to the enormous 19th-century offices lining Whitehall, the government quarter around Downing Street.

- **Tower Bridge Experience** (North Pier, Tower Bridge, SE1; ☎ **02073/781-928;** Tube: Tower Hill) lets you get inside one of the world's most famous bridges to find out why, how, and when the bridge was built. Harry, a Victorian bridge worker brought to life by animatronics, tells you the story and explains how the mechanism for raising the bridge works. The experience takes about 90 minutes, and the views up and down the Thames from the bridge's glass-enclosed walkways are magnificent. The attraction is open daily from 9:30 a.m. to 6 p.m. (last admission 75 minutes before closing). Admission is £4.50 ($7) for adults, £3 ($4.80) for seniors, students, and children 5 to 15.
- The **Wallace Collection** (Hertford House, Manchester Square, Marylebone, W1; ☎ **02079/350-687;** Tube: Baker Street) is in the palatial "town house" of the late Lady Wallace. The French works by such artists as Watteau and Fragonard are outstanding, but you also find masterworks from the Dutch (including Rembrandt), English, Spanish, and Italian schools. Vying for your attention are collections of decorative art, ornaments from 18th-century France, and European and Asian armaments. You need at least an hour just to give everything a cursory glance. The museum is open Monday to Saturday from 10 a.m. to 5 p.m. and Sunday from noon to 5 p.m. Admission is free.

Seeing London by Guided Tour

When it comes to London sightseeing tours, you're limited only by your imagination, stamina, and budget. You can tour London with an experienced guide by bus, by boat, or on foot.

Bus tours

Original London Sightseeing Tours (☎ **02088/771-722;** `www.theoriginaltour.com`) maintains a fleet of double-decker buses (many of them open on top), and offers hop-on/hop-off service at more than 90 boarding points around the city. You can choose from four tour routes. The **Original London Sightseeing Tour** lasts 90 minutes and passes every major sight in Central London and the South Bank; the tour starts from Piccadilly Circus (Tube: Piccadilly Circus) outside the Planet Hollywood restaurant on Coventry Street and departs every few minutes daily from 9 a.m. to 6 p.m. (to 9 p.m. in summer). You don't have to book any of the sightseeing tours in advance; you can pay on the bus. A ticket good for 24 hours on all routes costs £15 ($24) for adults and £7.50 ($12) for children under 16. For more information or to book online, check out the Web site.

Visitors Sightseeing Tours, Departure Lounge, Royal National Hotel, Bedford Way (☎ **02076/367-175**; www.visitorsightseeing.co.uk; Tube: Russell Square) offers the **Big Bus Tour,** which passes every major sight and offers live commentary and hop-on/hop-off service on open-top buses. The cost is £15 ($24) for adults, £6 ($10) for children. Other tours, available daily, are conducted on luxury buses with certified guides; tour prices vary according to the itinerary. On Wednesday, Friday, and Sunday at 6:50 p.m., a macabre tour, **Ghosts, Ghouls & Ancient Taverns,** explores sights associated with Jack the Ripper and the medieval plague and includes stops at a couple of pubs along the way. The cost is £17 ($27); the tour, which lasts about two hours, isn't recommended for children under 14. Call ahead to reserve a place.

Another tour company with many guided excursions is **Golden Tours,** 4 Fountain Square, 123–151 Buckingham Palace Rd. (☎ **800/456-6303** in the U.S. or 02072/337-030; www.goldentours.co.uk). Its buses are comfy and have restrooms, and the certified guides have a certifiable sense of humor. The daily **Historic & Modern London** tour is a full-day outing that includes the West End, Westminster Abbey, the Changing of the Guard (at Buckingham Palace or Horse Guards Parade), the City of London, St. Paul's Cathedral, the Tower of London, and a cruise from the Tower down to Charing Cross Pier; the price includes a pub lunch and a tea aboard ship. The cost is £58 ($93) for adults and £50 ($80) for kids under 16; all admission prices are included, so this one turns out to be a real winner in terms of what you see and how much you pay. Tours depart from the office at Buckingham Palace Road (Tube: Victoria) and other points in Central London. You can book your tickets directly or online, or you can ask your hotel concierge to do it two days in advance.

Boat tours

A cruise down the majestic Thames is a marvelous way to take in the city's sights. Sightseeing boats regularly ply the river between Westminster and the Tower of London; some continue downstream to Greenwich (site of the Prime Meridian, *Cutty Sark*, and Old Royal Observatory) and upstream to Kew Gardens and Hampton Court (see Chapter 13 for descriptions on all three). Along the way, you can see many of London's great monuments — the Houses of Parliament,

Westminster Abbey, St. Paul's Cathedral, the Tower of London, and Tower Bridge. The main departure points along the Thames are at **Westminster Pier** (Tube: Westminster), **Waterloo Pier** (Tube: Waterloo), **Embankment Pier** (Tube: Embankment), **Tower Pier** (Tube: Tower Hill), and **Greenwich Pier** (Tube: Greenwich). For recorded information on what's available, call ☎ **0839/123-432.**

Evan Evans (☎ 02079/501-777; www.evanevans.co.uk) offers three cruises. A **daily lunch cruise** departs at 12:15 p.m. from Embankment Pier aboard the *Silver Bonito;* the cost is £17.50 ($28) per person. Another daily offering starts with a guided boat tour of the Thames, includes a tour of the Tower of London, and continues by bus to The City and St. Paul's; the price is £30.50 ($46) for adults and £28.50 ($43) for children 3 to 16. A **full-day tour** offered Monday to Saturday takes in Westminster Abbey, continues to Buckingham Palace (or Horse Guards Parade) for the Changing of the Guard, includes a lunch cruise on the Thames, and returns by bus to St. Paul's Cathedral and the Tower of London. The price is £53.50 ($80) adults and £48.50 ($73) children.

Thames River Cruises (☎ 0209/304-091; www.catamaran-cruisers.co.uk) runs a fleet of boats on the Thames. A ticket from Westminster Pier to Greenwich is £7.80 ($12) adults, £6.30 ($10) seniors, £3.90 ($7) children, and £20.25 ($32) for a family (2 adults, 2 children). Daily from March through November and on weekends the rest of the year, **Circular Cruise** (☎ **02078/392-111**) offers a one-hour circular cruise from Westminster Pier (Tube: Westminster) that passes most of London's major monuments and stops at Festival Pier, Bankside Pier, London Bridge City Pier, and St. Katharine's Pier (hop on/hop-service). All the boats provide live commentary and have a fully licensed bar. The cost is £6.30 ($10) for adults, £5.30 ($8) for seniors and students, £3.15 ($5) for children, and £17.50 ($28) for families (2 adults, 3 children).

Bateaux London (☎ **02079/252-215**) offers a **nightly dinner cruise** that leaves Embankment Pier (Tube: Embankment) at 7:15 p.m. and returns at 9:45 p.m. The cruise, which includes a four-course dinner with live music and after-dinner dancing, costs £58 ($93) per person Sunday through Wednesday, £60 ($96) Thursday through Saturday. A one-hour lunch cruise with a three-course set menu and live commentary is offered Monday to Saturday for £21 ($34) per person; the boat departs from Embankment Pier at 12:15 p.m. A two-hour (three-course) Sunday lunch cruise departs from Embankment Pier at 12:15 p.m. and costs £35 ($56) per person. Advance reservations are required for all tours, and a smart-casual dress code applies (no sweatpants or running shoes).

An amphibious tour

London Frog Tours (☎ 02079/283-132; www.frogtours.com) has adapted several World War II amphibious troop carriers, known as DUKWs, to civilian comfort levels and painted them bright yellow. It runs 80-minute road-and-river trips. Tours start behind County Hall (site of the British Airways London Eye giant observation wheel). It picks up passengers on Chicheley Street (Tube: Westminster, then walk across Westminster Bridge), and then rumbles through Westminster and up to Piccadilly, gathering bemused stares as it passes many of London's major tourist sites. Then the vehicle splashes into the Thames at Vauxhall for a 30-minute cruise as far as the Houses of Parliament. The expensive ticket of £16.50 ($26) for adults, £13 ($21) for seniors, £11 ($18) for children, and £49 ($78) for families is worth its vacation-snap value alone. The ongoing commentary is hilarious.

Walking tours

A walking tour is an affordable way to see London from street level in the company of a knowledgeable guide. This type of tour is great for history, literature, and architecture buffs, and older kids generally have a good time as well. The weekly events listings in *Time Out* magazine, available at every news agent in London, include dozens of intriguing walks; a walk happens every day.

If you want to follow detailed strolls on your own, check out the 11 tours offered in *Frommer's Memorable Walks in London* by Richard Jones (Wiley Publishing, Inc.). **London Walks,** P.O. Box 1708, London NW6 4LW (☎ **02076/243-978;** `www.london.walks.com`), offers a terrific array of tours, including **Jack the Ripper's London, Christopher Wren's London, Oscar Wilde's London,** and **The Beatles' Magical Mystery Tour.** Guides lead different walks every day of the week, rain or shine; tours last about two hours and end near an Underground station. You don't need to make advance reservations. Call for schedules and departure points. A London Walk costs £5 ($8) for adults and £4 ($6) for students with ID; kids are free if accompanied by a parent.

Stepping Out, 32 Elvendon Rd. (☎ **02088/812-933;** `www.walklon.ndirect.co.uk`), offers guided walking tours of several London neighborhoods, including Southwark on the South Bank. Tours generally last from 1½ to 2 hours. **Brothels, Bishops and the Bard,** an offbeat theme walk, explores the Clink (the oldest prison in London), the Shakespeare memorial window in Southwark Cathedral, and the Globe Theatre's original site. The cost is £5 ($8) for adults and £3.50 ($5) for seniors and students.

Following My One-, Two-, and Three-Day Sightseeing Itineraries

Every London visitor faces one problem: how to see as much as possible in a limited amount of time. What do you do if you have only one, two, or three days at your disposal? The itineraries that follow are commonsense, limited-time suggestions that include the top London sights. For descriptions of each stop, see "Discovering the Top Attractions," earlier in this chapter.

If you have one day in London

Start your day with a morning visit to majestic **Westminster Abbey,** visiting the Royal Tombs and Poets' Corner. Afterward, because they're right next door, stroll around the **Houses of Parliament.** Unless you queue up to hear a debate, you won't be able to get inside, but you will have a great riverside view from Westminster Bridge. On the opposite side of the Thames is the **British Airways London Eye,** a 450-foot-high observation wheel. Reserve in advance for the trip up and over London; otherwise, you may spend at least a half-hour in line for a ticket and another hour waiting to board. You're not far from **Tate Britain;** if you're in the mood to look at great English art, head over to **Pimlico.** Renting a self-guided audio tour adds to the enjoyment.

Later in the afternoon, stroll through **Green Park** to **Buckingham Palace.** If you visit in August or September, you can reserve ahead of time and tour the State Rooms. If you're not touring the palace itself, visit the **Royal Mews,** the **Queen's Gallery,** or both. From Buckingham Palace, you can stroll down **The Mall** through **St. James's Park,** passing **Clarence House,** home of the Queen Mother until 2002 and now the official London residence of Prince Charles, and **St. James's Palace. Trafalgar Square,** London's grandest and certainly most famous plaza, is your next stop. Continue from there to nearby **Piccadilly Circus,** the teeming epicenter of London's West End. Regent Street, Piccadilly, and Jermyn Street offer great **shopping.** If you haven't already reserved a seat for a **West End show,** you may want to stop by the half-price ticket booth in **Leicester Square** to see what's available. A traditional **afternoon tea** at one of London's great hotels is a delightful way to end the afternoon. Have **dinner** in Soho before or after the show or concert.

If you have two days in London

On your second day, arrive as early as you can at the **Tower of London** and immediately hook up with one of the one-hour guided tours led by the Beefeaters. Later, you can explore the precincts on your own, making certain you allot enough time to see the Crown Jewels. From the Tower, head over to nearby **St. Paul's Cathedral,** which you can see in about a half-hour. The **British Museum,** your next stop, has enough to keep you occupied for several days; if you want to see only the highlights, allow yourself a minimum of two hours. Finish off your afternoon in Knightsbridge at **Harrods,** the most famous department store in London and perhaps the world. Knightsbridge and adjacent South

Kensington offer innumerable **dining** options. After dinner, cruise on to one of the **bars, pubs,** or **clubs** described in the "Living It Up After Dark" section later in this chapter.

If you have three days in London

Begin your third day at the **National Gallery.** Renting an audio guide helps you to discover more about your favorite paintings. You can have lunch in the **National Gallery restaurant** or cross the street and dine in the **restaurant in the crypt** of St. Martin-in-the-Fields church. Then spend a bit of time wandering through the **National Portrait Gallery,** located right behind the National Gallery, where you find the likeness of just about every famous British person you've ever heard of. Renting one of the self-guided audio tours is a good idea. From the portrait gallery you can stroll down **Charing Cross Road,** stopping in at one of the many bookstores, or easily walk to **Covent Garden Market,** where you find scores of interesting shops. Spend your afternoon strolling in **Kensington Gardens** and visiting **Kensington Palace,** formerly the London home of Princess Diana. If you don't go to the palace, you can consider visiting one of South Kensington's three great museums: the **Museum of Natural History,** the **Science Museum,** and the **Victoria & Albert.** Later, go for a traditional **English dinner** at Rules, London's oldest restaurant, or Simpson's-in-the-Strand. Are you up for a **play** or a **concert** tonight?

Shopping 'til You Drop

When you think of shopping in London, what items come to mind? Silky cashmere sweaters? Burberry raincoats? Hand-tailored suits and shirts? Tartan plaids? Irish linens? Silver spoons? Old engravings? Bone china? Books? Whatever you think of, you can find it somewhere in London, one of the world's greatest shopping cities. In addition to the major department stores, you find hundreds of small, enticing specialty shops and boutiques that delight the eye and empty the wallet.

When to shop and how to find deals

Normal **shopping hours** are Monday to Saturday 10 a.m. to 5:30 p.m., with late closing (7 or 8 p.m.) on Wednesday or Thursday. Stores may legally be open for six hours on Sunday, usually 11 a.m. to 5 p.m.

Stores in London have **two sale periods:** one in January and the other in July. Discounts can range from 25% to 50% at leading department stores. Harrods has the most famous January sale in London, but just about every other store also has a big sale at this time.

The *VAT (value-added tax)* in London and throughout England is 17.5%. The VAT is added to the price on every price tag. Anyone who isn't a resident of the European Union can get a VAT refund on retail goods, but not on restaurant and hotel bills. For the details on how to recoup as much as 15% of your shopping spree, see Chapter 9.

Where to shop and what to buy

Most of the department stores, designer shops, and *multiples* (chain stores) have their flagships in the **West End.** The key streets are **Oxford Street** for affordable shopping; **Regent Street** for fancier shops, more upscale department stores, and specialty dealers; **Piccadilly** for older established department stores; **Jermyn Street** for traditional English luxury goods; and **Bond Street** for chic upscale fashion boutiques. The **Covent Garden** area is great for all-purpose shopping. **Charing Cross Road** is known for its extraordinary number of bookstores, selling both new and old volumes.

Chelsea is famous for **King's Road** (Tube: Sloane Square), a street that became world-famous during the Swinging Sixties. King's Road is still popular with the young crowd but is becoming more and more a lineup of chain stores, markets, and *multistores* (large or small conglomerations of indoor stands, stalls, and booths within one building). The area is also known for its design-trade showrooms and stores of household wares. King's Road begins on the west side of Sloane Square tube station.

London has plenty of big department stores to choose from. **Harrods**, 87–135 Brompton Rd., SW1 (☎ **02077/301-234;** Tube: Knightsbridge), may be the world's most famous department store. As firmly entrenched in London life as Buckingham Palace, this enormous emporium has some 300 departments, delectable Food Halls, and several cafes. **Fortnum & Mason,** 181 Piccadilly, W1 (☎ **02077/348-040;** Tube: Piccadilly Circus), is a department store that serves as the queen's London grocer. In a setting of deep-red carpets and crystal chandeliers, you find everything from pâté de foie gras and Campbell's soup to bone china, crystal, leather, antiques, and stationery. Dining choices include the **Patio, St. James's,** and **The Fountain.** A Chelsea emporium founded in 1877, **Peter Jones,** Sloane Square, SW1 (☎ **02077/303-434;** Tube: Sloane Square), is known for household goods, household fabrics and trims, china, glass, soft furnishings, and linens; the linen department is one of London's best.

Bargain hunters can zero in on goods manufactured in England. At **The Filofax Centre,** 21 Conduit St., W1 (☎ **02074/990-457;** Tube: Oxford Circus), you find the entire range of Filofax inserts and books at about half the price that they are in the States. Prices at the U.K.-based **Body Shop** stores are much lower than in the States. You can stock up on their politically and environmentally correct beauty, bath, and aromatherapy products at **The Body Shop,** 375 Oxford St., W1 (☎ **02074/097-868;**

West End Shopping

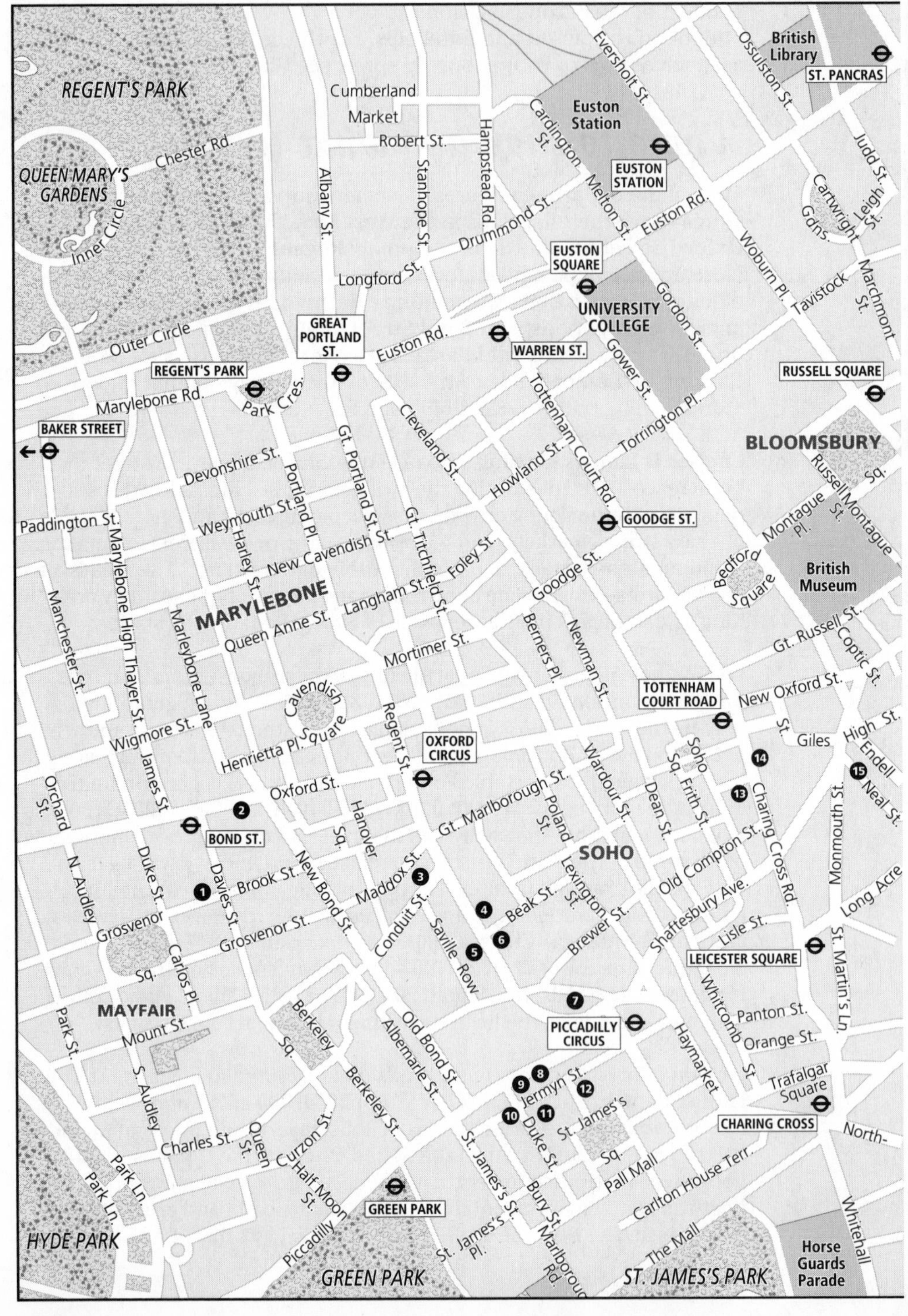

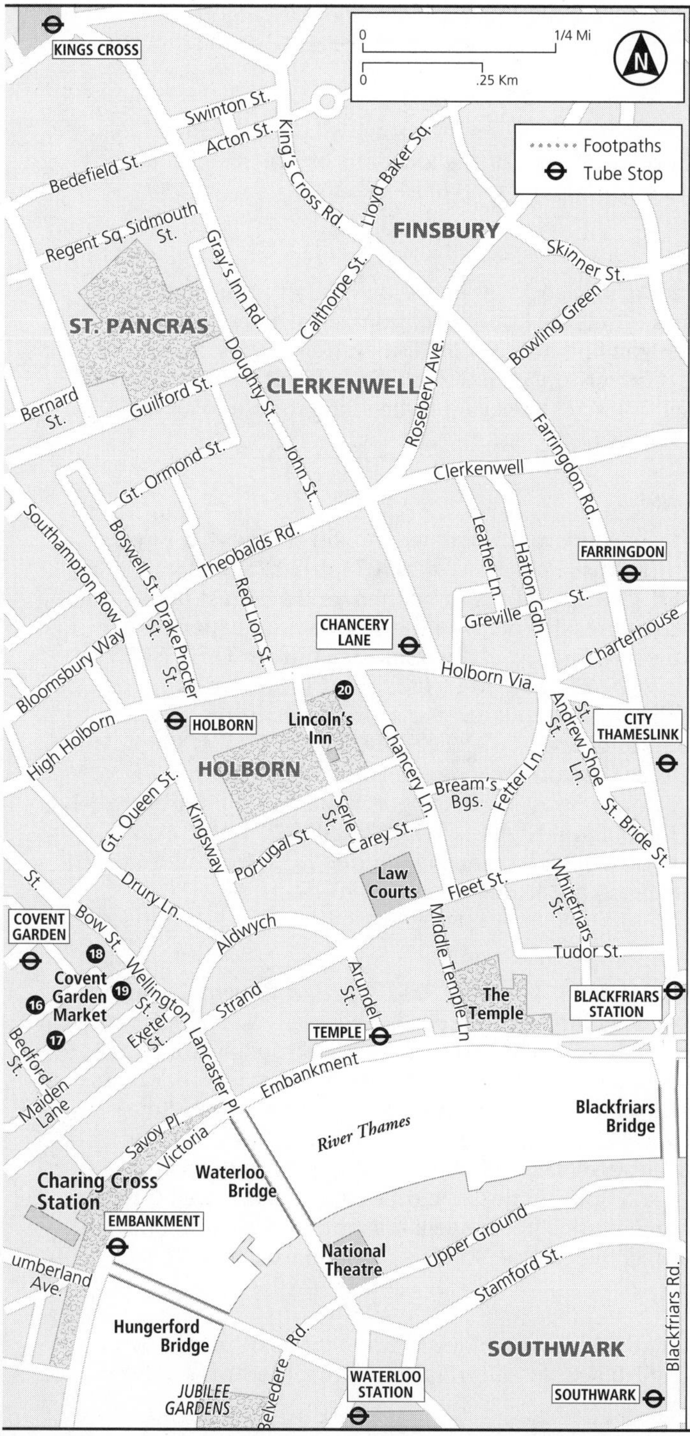

The Body Shop **2**
Burlington Arcade **5**
Church's **1**
Covent Garden Market **17**
Culpepper the Herbalist **18**
Dr. Marten's Department Store **16**
The Filofax Centre **3**
Floris **12**
Fortnum & Mason **9**
Hamleys **4**
Hatchards **8**
Hilditch & Key **10**
Irish Linen Company **5**
London Silver Vaults **20**
Murder One **14**
Neal's Yard Remedies **15**
Penhaligon's **19**
Royal Doulton Regent Street **6**
Scotch House **7**
Taylor of Old Bond Street **11**
W & G Foyle, Ltd. **13**

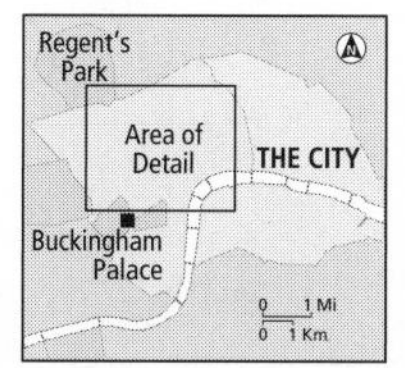

Tube: Bond St.), which has branches in every shopping zone in London. **Dr. Marten's Department Store,** 1–4 King St., WC2 (☎ **02074/971-460;** Tube: Covent Garden), is the flagship for internationally famous Doc Martens shoes. Prices are far better here than they are outside the United Kingdom.

What follows is a description of where to go and what to look for in some of London's key shopping areas. For the locations of stores in the West End, see the "West End Shopping" map in this chapter.

Bond Street

Divided into New (northern section) and Old (southern portion), Bond Street is the address for all the hot international designers. Here and on adjacent streets, you find a large conglomeration of very expensive fashion boutiques. **Church's,** 133 New Bond St., W1 (☎ **02074/931-474;** Tube: Bond St.), sells classy shoes said to be recognizable to all the snobby maîtres d'hôtel in London.

Charing Cross Road

For books, head to Charing Cross Road, where you find **W & G Foyle, Ltd.,** 113–119 Charing Cross Rd., WC2 (☎ **02074/403-225;** Tube: Tottenham Court Rd.), which claims to be the world's largest bookstore and carries an impressive array of hardcovers and paperbacks, as well as travel maps, records, and sheet music. **Murder One,** 71–73 Charing Cross Rd., WC2 (☎ **02077/343-485;** Tube: Leicester Sq.), specializes in crime, romance, science fiction, and horror books. Established in 1797, **Hatchards,** 187 Piccadilly, W1 (☎ **02074/399-921;** Tube: Piccadilly Circus), is London's most historic and atmospheric bookstore. Some distance away, in Kensington, you find the **Children's Book Centre,** 237 Kensington High St., W8 (☎ **02079/377-497;** Tube: High Street Kensington), the best place in London to go for children's books; fiction is arranged according to age, up to 16.

Covent Garden

The **Covent Garden Market** (☎ **02078/369-136;** Tube: Covent Garden), which is actually several different markets, is open daily 9 a.m. to 5 p.m. The place can be a little confusing until you dive in and explore it all. The **Apple Market** is the fun, bustling market in the courtyard where traders sell collectible nostalgia: glassware and ceramics, leather goods, toys, clothes, hats, and jewelry. On Monday, antiques dealers take over. On the backside is the **Jubilee Market** (☎ **02078/362-139**), with inexpensive crafts, clothes, and books. The **Covent Garden Market** itself (in the restored hall on The Piazza) is full of specialty shops selling fashions and herbs, gifts and toys, books and personalized dollhouses, hand-rolled cigars . . . you name it.

The Covent Garden area is a good place to find herbalists and shops selling excellent English soaps, toiletries, and aromatherapy goods.

Culpeper the Herbalist, 8 The Market, Covent Garden, WC2 (☎ **02073/796-698;** Tube: Covent Garden), sells food, bath, and aromatherapy products as well as dream pillows, candles, sachets, and many a shopper's fave: the battery-operated aromatherapy fan. **Penhaligon's,** 41 Wellington St., WC2 (☎ **02078/362-150;** Tube: Covent Garden), is an exclusive-line, Victorian perfumery dedicated to good grooming, with a large selection of perfumes, after-shaves, soaps, candles, and bath oils for women and men. **Neal's Yard Remedies,** 15 Neal's Yard (off Shorts Garden), WC2 (☎ **02073/797-222;** Tube: Covent Garden), is noted the world over for its all-natural, herbal-based bath, beauty, and aromatherapy products in cobalt-blue bottles.

Jermyn Street

Two-block-long Jermyn Street, one of St. James's most exclusive nooks, is where you find posh high-end men's haberdashers and toiletry shops, many of which have been doing business for centuries. **Taylor of Old Bond Street,** 74 Jermyn St., SW1 (☎ **02079/305-544;** Tube: Piccadilly Circus), carries the world's finest collection of men's shaving brushes, razors, and combs, plus soaps and hair lotions. **Floris,** 89 Jermyn St., SW1 (☎ **02079/302-885;** Tube: Piccadilly Circus), is a small mahogany-clad store that's been selling its own line of soaps and perfumes since 1851. For more than a century, **Hilditch & Key,** 73 Jermyn St., SW1 (☎ **02079/305-336;** Tube: Piccadilly Circus), has been selling what many people consider the finest men's shirts in the world: 100% cotton, cut by hand, with buttons fashioned from real shell.

If you're shopping in Regent Street or Jermyn Street, visit the **Burlington Arcade,** running from Regent Street to Savile Row. This famous, glass-roofed Regency passage, lit by wrought-iron lamps and decorated with clusters of ferns and flowers, is lined with intriguing shops and boutiques. The **Irish Linen Company,** 35–36 Burlington Arcade, W1 (☎ **02074/938-949;** Tube: Piccadilly Circus), carries items crafted of Irish linen, including hand-embroidered handkerchiefs and bed and table linens.

Regent Street

Curving Regent Street, just off Piccadilly Circus, is a major shopping street for all sorts of goods. If you're after English bone china, stop in at **Royal Doulton Regent Street,** 154 Regent St., W1 (☎ **02077/343-184;** Tube: Piccadilly Circus or Oxford Circus), which carries Royal Doulton, Minton, and Royal Crown Derby. **Scotch House,** 84–86 Regent St., W1 (☎ **02077/340-203;** Tube: Piccadilly Circus), has a worldwide reputation for its comprehensive selection of cashmere and wool knitwear for men, women, and children; the shop also sells tartan garments and accessories, as well as Scottish tweed classics. If you're looking for toys or children's gifts, check out **Hamleys,** 188–196 Regent St., W1 (☎ **02074/942-000;** Tube: Piccadilly Circus), which stocks more than 35,000 toys and games on seven floors.

Shopping in the vaults

If you're searching for silver, go to the **London Silver Vaults,** Chancery House, 53–63 Chancery Lane, WC2 (☎ **02072/423-844;** Tube: Chancery Lane). Here, you go into real vaults — 40 in all — filled with a staggering collection of old and new silver and silverplate, plus a collection of jewelry.

Living It Up After Dark

London by day is lovely; London by night is lively. Whatever you're looking for — grand opera, a hip-hop dance club, or a historic pub — you can find it here. As the cultural hub of the United Kingdom, London is always brimming over with possibilities for after-dark adventures.

Finding out what's happening

You can find details for all London shows, concerts, and other performances in the daily newspapers: the *Daily Telegraph,* the *Evening Standard,* the *Guardian,* the *Independent,* and the *Times.* For the most comprehensive listings of everything that's going on in London, plus thumbnail synopses of the plots and (usually scathing) critical opinion, buy a copy of the weekly magazine *Time Out.* The publication is available at London newsstands on Wednesday. You may also find the following Web sites useful:

- `www.albemarle-london.com` offers descriptions of West End shows and performing arts events as well as online ticket booking.
- `www.keithprowse.com` is an international ticket agency that sells tickets for West End shows and performing arts events in London.
- `www.londontheatre.co.uk` provides a complete listing of shows currently playing in London's West End, plus seating plans for the theaters and theater news and reviews.

Getting tickets

The following ticket agencies accept credit card bookings 24 hours a day, and all charge at least 25% commission:

- **Albemarle Booking Agency (☎ 02076/379-041;** `www.albemarle-london.com`)
- **Keith Prowse (☎ 800/669-7469** in the U.S. or 02078/369-001; `www.keithprowse.com`)
- **Ticketmaster (☎ 08706/069-999;** `www.ticketmaster.co.uk`)

You can avoid the agencies' hefty fees if you go to the box office to buy tickets or call the venue and order tickets by phone. With a credit card you can usually order tickets directly from the box office (or online in some cases) before you leave home and pick them up after you arrive in London.

Raising the curtain on performing arts and music

Planning a night out in London isn't a problem — choosing from among all the possibilities is where the difficulty lies.

Theater

When it comes to theater, London is the greatest. The **West End theater district** — or **Theatreland,** as it's called — concentrates in the area around Piccadilly Circus, Leicester Square, and Covent Garden. But the theaters at the Barbican and South Bank Arts Centre are theatrically considered West End venues as well. Tickets for even the biggest hit shows are cheaper in London than in New York; you rarely pay more than £40 ($64) for the best seats in the house. Just as important to the theatrical vitality of London are the city's many **"fringe" venues.** Fringe is the equivalent of Off or Off Off Broadway in New York. If you want to see a show, look at the following theaters' schedules:

- The prestigious **Royal Shakespeare Company** (☎ **08706/091-110;** www.rsc.org.uk) performs in the 1,156-seat **Barbican Theatre,** Silk Street, EC (Tube: Barbican); the **Gielgud Theatre,** Shaftesbury Avenue, W1 (☎ **02074/945-085;** Tube: Piccadilly Circus); and the **Theatre Royal Haymarket,** Haymarket SW1 (☎ **08709/013-356;** Tube: Piccadilly Circus).
- The **Royal National Theatre,** South Bank Arts Centre, SE1 (☎ **02074/523-000;** www.nt-online.org; Tube: Waterloo) performs Shakespeare, classic revivals, musicals, and new plays in three theaters. For information on performances, call ☎ **02074/523-400** (Monday to Saturday 10 a.m. to 11 p.m.); check the Web for information and an online booking form.
- **Shakespeare's Globe Theatre,** New Globe Walk, Bankside, SE1 (☎ **02074/019-919;** www.shakespeares-globe.org; Tube: Cannon St. or London Bridge), presents a June-to-September season of the Bard's plays in a reconstructed open-air Elizabethan theater. After a couple of hours, the benches can be a bit numbing, but you see Shakespeare performed not far from the original theater — and you're right beside the Thames.

The **Society of London Theatres** operates a **half-price ticket booth** in the clock tower building by the gardens in Leicester Square (Tube: Leicester Square). The booth doesn't have a phone info line, so you have to show up in person to see what's on sale that day. The booth is open Monday to Saturday from noon to 6:30 p.m.; it sells only matinee tickets before 2 p.m. on matinee days (Wednesday, Saturday, and Sunday). Tickets are sold only on the day of performance. Visa and MasterCard are accepted. You pay exactly half the price plus a nominal fee (under $5). The most popular shows won't be available, but you may luck out. Tickets for the English National Opera and other events are sometimes available as well. Ask for a free copy of *The Official London Theatre Guide,* which lists every show with addresses and phone numbers and includes a map of the West End theater district.

Opera, ballet, and classical music

The **Royal Opera** and **Royal Ballet** perform at the **Royal Opera House,** Covent Garden, WC2E (☎ **02073/044-000** info line; `www.royalopera.org`; Tube: Covent Garden). Ticket prices for grand opera run £10 to £150 ($16 to $240). The season runs September to August. For a summary of the opera and ballet season, check the Web site.

The **English National Opera** and **English National Ballet** perform at the **London Coliseum,** St. Martin's Lane, WC2N (☎ **02076/328-300** for box office, open 24 hours Monday through Saturday for phone bookings and from 10 a.m. to 8 p.m. to purchase tickets in person; `www.eno.org`; Tube: Leicester Square). The operas here are all sung in English. Seats run £8 to £66 ($13 to $106); 100 balcony seats at £2.50 ($4) and 37 Dress Circle seats at £27 ($43) go on sale at 10 a.m. on the day of the performance (except for Saturday evenings). The opera and ballet season runs September to July. To book online, go to the Web site.

The home base for the **London Symphony Orchestra** (`www.lso.co.uk`) is the **Barbican Hall** at the Barbican Centre, Silk Street, EC2Y (☎ **02076/388-891** for 24-hour recorded info; Tube: Barbican).

Classical music and dance concerts are held year-round in the three auditoriums of the **South Bank Centre,** South Bank, SE1 (☎ **02079/604-242;** `www.sbc.org.uk`; Tube: Waterloo). All manner of orchestras (some British, some international) perform symphonic works in the **Royal Festival Hall.** Chamber-music concerts and dance programs take place in the smaller **Queen Elizabeth Hall,** and recitals are held in the more intimate **Purcell Room.** You can get tickets and information on all three venues at the box office or online. For credit-card phone bookings, call ☎ **02079/604-242.**

The **Royal Albert Hall,** Kensington Gore, SW7 (☎ **02075/892-141** box office; Tube: High St. Kensington) is another all-purpose venue for classical music. This enormous, circular, domed concert hall has been a landmark in South Kensington since 1871. One of London's most eagerly awaited musical events is the mid-July to mid-September series of classical and pops concerts known as the **Proms.** Orchestras come from all over Europe to play.

Checking out the club and bar scenes

London is a big club town; the action doesn't really get hot until around midnight. For more options, check out the listings for music and clubs in *Time Out.* For the locations of places in this section, see the "London's Clubs, Pubs, and Bars" map in this chapter.

Jazz and other live music

London has plenty of small, smoky jazz clubs where you can groove 'til the wee hours. In Soho, **Ronnie Scott's,** 47 Frith St., W1 (☎ **02074/390-747;** Tube: Tottenham Court Rd.), has been London's preeminent jazz club for years, with dependably high-caliber performances. You have to order food (meals or snacks) on top of the £5 to £20 ($8 to $32) cover. For something trendier with fewer tourists, try Islington's **Blue Note,** 1 Hoxton Sq., N1 (☎ **02077/298-440;** Tube: Old St.), for its innovative and wide-ranging musical program. Cover ranges from £3 to £10 ($4.80 to $16).

In Earl's Court, the **606 Club,** 90 Lots Rd., SW10 (☎ **02073/525-953;** Tube: Earl's Court or Fulham Broadway), is a basement club where young British jazz musicians play. There's no cover to get in, but you have to order something to eat, and a charge of £5 ($8) is added to your bill to pay the musicians. You can find good food and diverse music (Afro-Latin jazz to rap) at the **Jazz Cafe,** 5 Parkway, NW1 (☎ **02079/166-060;** Tube: Camden Town). Admission is £12 to £18 ($19 to $29).

How about a pizza with your jazz? In Soho, try the **Pizza Express Jazz Club,** 10 Dean St., W1 (☎ **02074/398-722;** Tube: Tottenham Court Rd.), where big names from the American jazz scene regularly perform; the cover is £15 to £20 ($24 to $32). In Knightsbridge, you find **Pizza on the Park,** 11 Knightsbridge, SW1 (☎ **02072/355-273;** Tube: Hyde Park Corner), where the basement Jazz Room books mainstream jazz; admission is £16 to £18 ($26 to $29).

The **Ain't Nothing But Blues Bar,** 20 Kingly St., W1 (☎ **02072/870-514;** Tube: Oxford Circus), the only true-blue blues venue in town, features local acts and touring American bands; the cover charge is £3 to £5 ($4.80 to $8) on Friday and Saturday; you get in free before 9:30 p.m.

Dance clubs

In Islington, **The Complex,** 1–5 Parkfield St., N1 (☎ **02072/881-986;** Tube: Angel), has four floors with different dance vibes on each; open Friday and Saturday; admission is £10 to £12 ($16 to $19).

London's Clubs, Pubs, and Bars

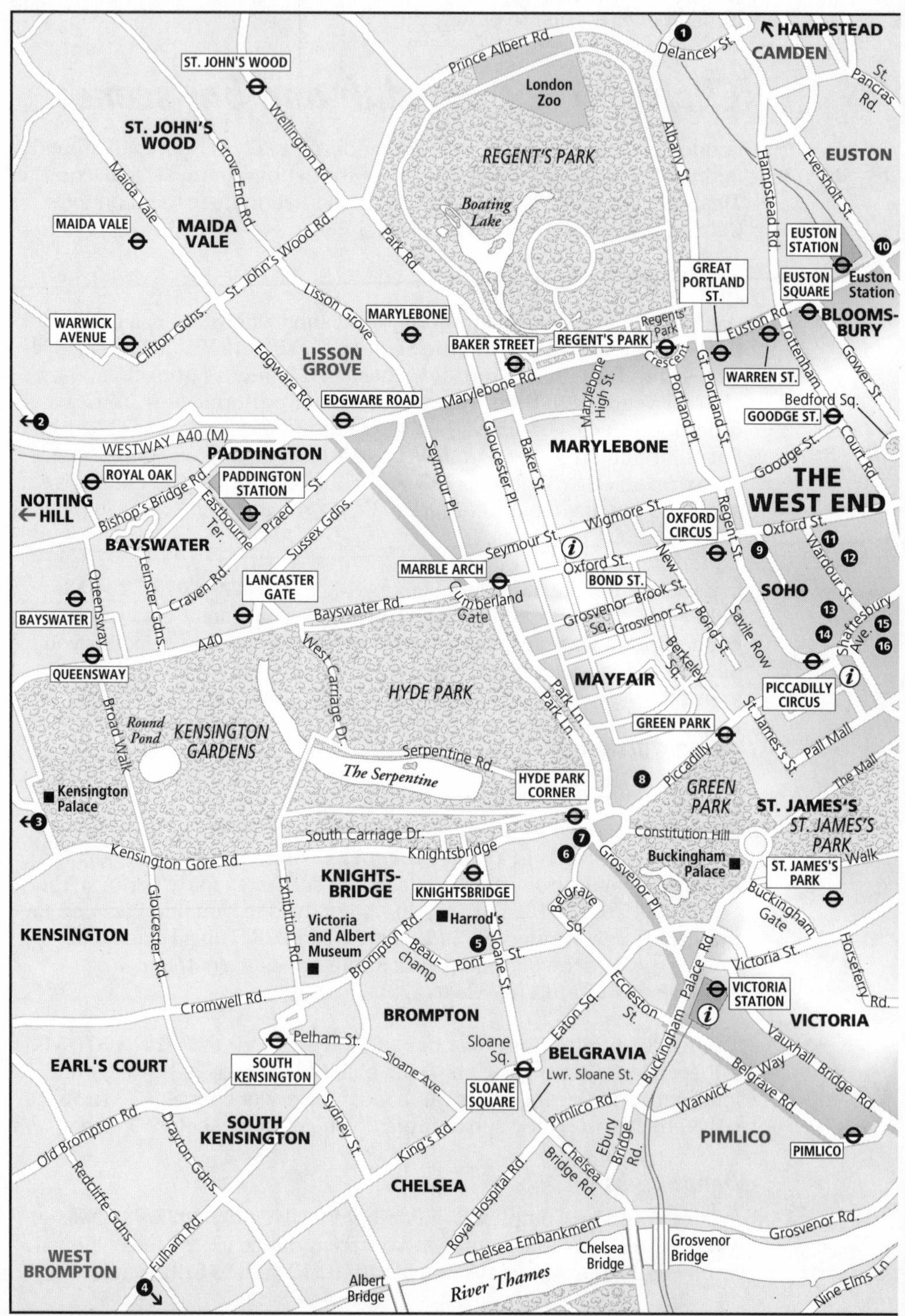

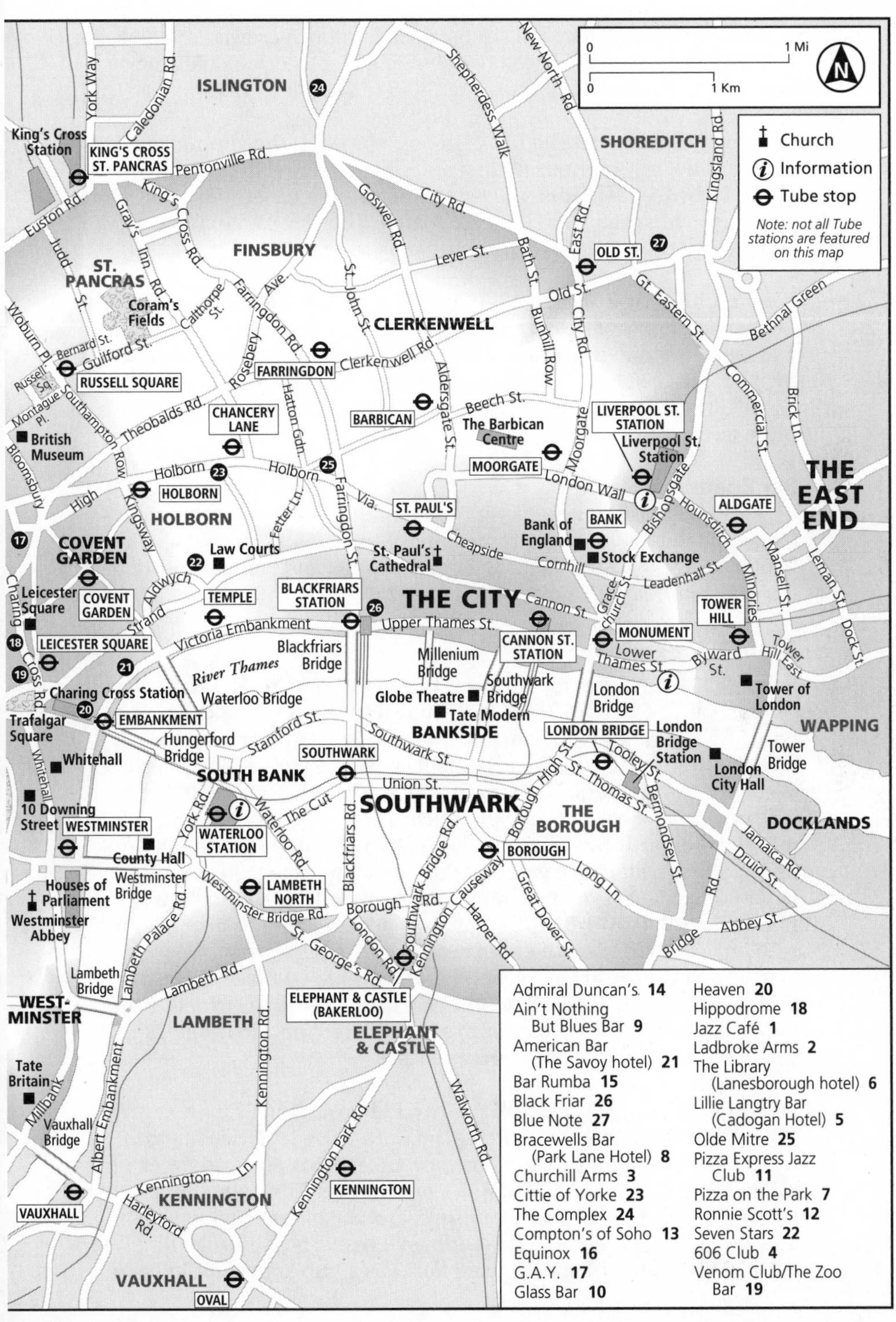

Admiral Duncan's 14
Ain't Nothing But Blues Bar 9
American Bar (The Savoy hotel) 21
Bar Rumba 15
Black Friar 26
Blue Note 27
Bracewells Bar (Park Lane Hotel) 8
Churchill Arms 3
Cittie of Yorke 23
The Complex 24
Compton's of Soho 13
Equinox 16
G.A.Y. 17
Glass Bar 10
Heaven 20
Hippodrome 18
Jazz Café 1
Ladbroke Arms 2
The Library (Lanesborough hotel) 6
Lillie Langtry Bar (Cadogan Hotel) 5
Olde Mitre 25
Pizza Express Jazz Club 11
Pizza on the Park 7
Ronnie Scott's 12
Seven Stars 22
606 Club 4
Venom Club/The Zoo Bar 19

The **Equinox,** Leicester Square, WC2 (☎ **02074/371-446;** Tube: Leicester Square), with London's largest dance floor, is a lavishly illuminated club boasting one of the largest lighting rigs in Europe. A crowd as varied as London itself dances to virtually every kind of music, including dance hall, pop, rock, and Latin. The cover is £5 to £12 ($8 to $19).

Lady Di's favorite scene in her club-hopping days, the **Hippodrome,** at the corner of Cranbourn Street and Charing Cross Road, WC2 (☎ **02074/374-311;** Tube: Leicester Square), is a cavernous place with a great sound system and lights to match. The club is tacky, touristy, and packed on weekends. The cover is £4 to £12 ($6 to $19).

Venom Club/The Zoo Bar, 13–17 Bear St., WC2 (☎ **02078/394-188;** Tube: Leicester Square), features a trendy Euro-androgynous crowd and music so loud that you have to use sign language. This club boasts the slickest, flashiest, most psychedelic decor in London. The cover is £3 to £5 ($4.80 to $8) after 10 p.m. (It's free before 10 p.m., but the place is empty.)

Bar Rumba, 36 Shaftesbury Ave., W1 (☎ **02072/872-715;** Tube: Piccadilly Circus), has a different musical theme every night: jazz fusion, phat funk, hip-hop, drum 'n' bass, soul, R&B, and swing. The minimum age for admittance is 21 on Saturday and Sunday and 18 on Monday to Friday. The cover is £3 to £12 ($4.80 to $19).

English pubs

If you're looking for a pub in The City, the **Cittie of Yorke,** 22 High Holborn, WC1 (☎ **02072/427-670;** Tube: Holborn or Chancery Lane), has the longest bar in Britain and looks like a great medieval hall, which is appropriate because a pub has existed at this location since 1430. The **Seven Stars,** 53 Carey St., WC2 (☎ **02072/428-521;** Tube: Holborn), at the back of the law courts, is tiny and modest except for its collection of Toby mugs and law-related art. Many barristers drink here, so Seven Stars is a great place to pick up some British legal jargon. The namesake of an inn built here in 1547, the **Olde Mitre,** Ely Place, EC1 (☎ **02074/054-751;** Tube: Chancery Lane), is a small pub with an eccentric assortment of customers. An Edwardian wonder of marble and bronze art nouveau, the wedge-shaped **Black Friar,** 174 Queen Victoria St., EC4, (☎ **02072/365-650;** Tube: Blackfriars), features low-relief carvings of mad monks, a low-vaulted mosaic ceiling, and seating carved out of gold marble recesses.

In West London, the **Churchill Arms,** 119 Kensington Church St., W8 (☎ **02077/274-242;** Tube: Notting Hill Gate or High St. Kensington), which is loaded with Churchill memorabilia, hosts an entire week of celebration leading up to Winston's birthday on November 30. Visitors are often welcomed like regulars here, and the overall ambience is down-to-earth and homey. The **Ladbroke Arms,** 54 Ladbroke Rd., W11 (☎ **02077/276-648;** Tube: Holland Park), is a pub known for its food.

With background jazz and rotating art prints, the place strays a bit from a traditional pub environment but makes for a pleasant stop and a good meal.

Classy bars

With surroundings far removed from the hurly-burly of London's streets, the hotel bars in this section are elegant and dressy. A jacket and tie are required for gents at the American Bar; a smart-casual dress code (no jeans, sweatpants, or tennis shoes) is in effect at the others.

The **American Bar** in The Savoy hotel, The Strand, WC2 (☎ **02078/364-343;** Tube: Charing Cross or Embankment), one of the most sophisticated gathering places in London, reputedly serves the best martini in town. With a plush decor of Chinese lacquer, comfortable sofas, and soft lighting, **Bracewells Bar** in the Park Lane Hotel, Piccadilly, W1 (☎ **02074/996-321;** Tube: Green Park or Hyde Park), is chic and nostalgic.

The Library in the Lanesborough hotel, 1 Lanesborough Place, SW1 (☎ **02072/595-599;** Tube: Hyde Park Corner), is one of London's poshest drinking retreats and boasts an unparalleled collection of cognacs.

The **Lillie Langtry Bar** in the Cadogan Hotel, Sloane Street, SW1 (☎ **02072/357-141;** Tube: Sloane Square or Knightsbridge), epitomizes the charm and elegance of the Edwardian era, when Lillie Langtry, an actress and a society beauty (and a mistress of Edward VII), lived here.

Gay and lesbian bars and dance clubs

Check the gay listings in *Time Out* to find out what's going on, because many clubs have special gay nights. You may also want to check out *Frommer's Gay & Lesbian Europe* (Wiley Publishing, Inc.) for its extensive coverage of London's gay scene.

In terms of size, central location, and continued popularity, the best gay disco in London — which is the best disco here, period — is **Heaven,** Under the Arches, Craven Street, WC2 (☎ **02079/302-020;** Tube: Charing Cross or Embankment). Hours are 10:30 p.m. to 3 a.m. on Monday and Wednesday, 10:30 p.m. to 6 a.m. on Friday, 10:30 p.m. to 5 a.m. on Saturday; admission varies from £3 to £10 ($4.80 to $16). **G.A.Y.,** London Astoria, 157 Charing Cross Rd., Soho, WC2 (☎ **09061/000-160;** Tube: Tottenham Court Rd.), is the biggest gay dance venue in Europe. Hours are Saturday 10:30 p.m. to 5 a.m.; admission is £10 ($16).

For general, where-it's-happening action, stroll along Old Compton Street (Tube: Leicester Square or Tottenham Court Road) in Soho. You may want to duck into **Admiral Duncan's,** 54 Old Compton St., W1 (☎ **02074/375-300**) or the two-floor **Compton's of Soho,** 53–55 Old Compton St., W1 (☎ **02074/797-961**). Both of these gay bar/pubs are

Soho institutions, open noon to 11 p.m. from Monday through Saturday, and noon to 10:30 p.m. on Sunday. The city's largest women-only bar is **Glass Bar,** West Lodge, Euston Square Gardens, 190 Euston Rd., NW10 (☎ **02073/876-184;** Tube: Euston). This bar on two levels has a smart-casual dress code (think khakis, not sweatpants) and is open Tuesday through Friday from 5 p.m. until late, on Saturday from 6 p.m. until late, and Sunday from 2 to 7 p.m.; admittance isn't allowed after 11:30 p.m. on Monday through Saturday.

Fast Facts: London

American Express

The main office is at 6 Haymarket, SW1 (☎ 02079/304-411; Tube: Piccadilly Circus). Full services are available Monday to Friday 9 a.m. to 5:30 p.m. and Saturday 9 a.m. to 4 p.m. At other times — Saturday 4 p.m. to 6 p.m. and Sunday 10 a.m. to 5 p.m. — only the foreign-exchange bureau is open. Other offices are at 78 Brompton Rd., Knightsbridge SW3 (☎ 02075/843-431; Tube: Knightsbridge); 84 Kensington High St., Kensington W8 (☎ 02077/958-703; Tube: High St. Kensington); 51 Great Russell St., Bloomsbury WC1 (☎ 02074/048-700; Tube: Russell Square); 1 Savoy Court, The Strand WC2 (☎ 02072/401-521; Tube: Charing Cross).

ATMs

ATMs, also called "cashpoints," are widely available at banks and in shopping areas throughout Central London.

Country Code and City Code

The country code for England is **44.** London's telephone area code is **020.** If you're calling a London number from outside the city, use **020** followed by the eight-digit number. If you're calling within London, leave off the **020** and dial only the eight-digit number.

Currency Exchange

In London, you can easily exchange cash or traveler's checks by using a currency-exchange service called a *bureaux de change.* You find these services at the major London airports, at any branch of a major bank, at all major rail and Underground stations in Central London, at post offices, and at American Express and Thomas Cook offices.

Every major bank in Central London has a foreign currency window where you can exchange traveler's checks or cash. The major banks with the most branches include Barclays Bank (☎ 02074/413-200), Midland Bank (☎ 02075/993-232), and NatWest (☎ 02073/955-500).

Doctors and Dentists

In an emergency, contact Doctor's Call at ☎ 07000/372-255. Some hotels also have physicians on call. Medical Express, 117A Harley St., W1 (☎ 02074/991-991; Tube: Oxford Circus), is a private clinic with walk-in medical service (no appointment necessary) Monday to Friday 9 a.m. to 6 p.m. and Saturday 9:30 a.m. to 2:30 p.m. Guy's Hospital, St. Thomas St., SE8 (☎ 02079/555-000; Tube: London Bridge) provides 24-hour emergency dental service.

Embassies and High Commissions

London is the capital of the United Kingdom and therefore the home of all the embassies, consulates, and high commissions. United States: 24 Grosvenor Sq., W1 (☎ 02074/999-000; Tube: Bond St.). Canada: MacDonald House, 38 Grosvenor Sq., W1 (☎ 02072/586-600; Tube: Bond St.). Ireland: 17 Grosvenor Place, SW1 (☎ 02072/352-171; Tube: Hyde Park Corner). Australia: Australia House, Strand, WC2 (☎ 02073/794-334; Tube: Charing Cross or Aldwych). New Zealand:

New Zealand House, 80 Haymarket at Pall Mall, SW1 (☎ 02079/308-422; Tube: Charing Cross or Piccadilly Circus).

Emergencies

For police, fire, or an ambulance ☎ **999.**

Hospitals

The following offer 24-hour emergency care, with the first treatment free under the National Health Service: Royal Free Hospital, Pond Street, NW3 (☎ 02077/940-500; Tube: Belsize Park), and University College Hospital, Grafton Way, WC1 (☎ 02073/879-300; Tube: Warren St. or Euston Sq.). Many other London hospitals also have accident and emergency departments.

Information

The main Tourist Information Centre, run by the London Tourist Board, is in the forecourt of Victoria Station (Tube: Victoria) and is open Monday through Saturday 8 a.m. to 7 p.m. in January and February, 9 a.m. to 8 p.m. from Easter through May and October through Easter, and 8 a.m. to 9 p.m. from June through September; Sunday year-round from 9 a.m. to 6 p.m. The center offers booking services and free literature on London attractions and entertainment. Other Tourist Information Centres are in the Liverpool Street Underground station (open Monday through Friday from 8 a.m. to 6 p.m., Saturday from 8 a.m. to 5:30 p.m., and on Sunday from 9 a.m. to 5:30 p.m.); the Arrivals Hall of the Waterloo International Terminal (open daily 8:30 a.m. to 10:30 p.m.); the Heathrow Terminal 1, 2, and 3 Underground station (open daily 8 a.m. to 6 p.m., until 7 p.m. Monday through Saturday June through September).

Internet Access

Internet Exchange, 37, The Piazza, The Market, Covent Garden (☎ 02078/368-636; Internet: `www.internet-exchange.co.uk`), with Internet access and PC rental, is open from 10 a.m. to 10 p.m. weekdays and 10 a.m. to 8 p.m. on Saturday and Sunday. Besides this convenient Covent Garden location, it has branches all over London.

Maps

The best all-around street directory, *London A to Z,* is available at most news agents and bookstores. You can obtain a bus and Underground map at any Underground station.

Newspapers/Magazines

The *Times, Telegraph, Daily Mail,* and *Evening Standard* are all dailies carrying the latest news. The *International Herald Tribune,* published in Paris, and an international edition of *USA Today* are available daily. Most newsstands also sell *Time* and *Newsweek.* The weekly magazine *Time Out* contains an abundance of useful information about the latest happenings in London. *Gay Times,* a high-quality, news-oriented magazine covering the gay and lesbian community, is available at most news agents.

Pharmacies

They're called *chemists* in the United Kingdom. Boots has outlets all over London. Bliss the Chemist, 5 Marble Arch, W1 (☎ 02077/236-116; Tube: Marble Arch), is open daily from 9 a.m. to midnight. Zafash Pharmacy, 233–235 Old Brompton Rd., SW5 (☎ 02073/732-798; Tube: Earl's Court), is London's only 24-hour pharmacy.

Police

In an emergency, dial ☎ **999** (no coin required).

Post Offices

The Main Post Office, 24 William IV St., WC2 (☎ 02079/309-580; Tube: Charing Cross), is open Monday to Saturday from 8:30 a.m. to 8 p.m. Other post offices and sub-post offices (windows in the back of news-agent stores) are open Monday to Friday from 9 a.m. to 5:30 p.m. and Saturday from 9 a.m. to 12:30 p.m. Look for red ROYAL MAIL signs outside.

Restrooms

The English often call toilets *loos.* They're marked by public-toilets signs on streets, in parks, and in a few Tube stations. You also find well-maintained lavatories that can be used by anybody in all larger public buildings, such as museums and art galleries, large department stores, and rail stations. Public lavatories are usually free, but you may need a 20p coin to get in or to use a washroom. In some places (like Leicester Square) you find coin-operated "Super Loos" that are sterilized after each use. If all else fails, duck into the nearest pub.

Safety

London is generally a safe city, both on the street and in the Underground. As in any large metropolis, use common sense and normal caution when you're in a crowded public area or walking alone at night. The area around Euston Station has more purse-snatchings than anywhere else in London.

Smoking

Most U.S. cigarette brands are available in London. Smoking is forbidden in the Underground (on the cars and the platforms) and on buses. Most restaurants have no-smoking tables, but they're sometimes separated from the smoking section by very little space. No-smoking rooms are available in more and more hotels, and some B&Bs are now entirely smoke free.

Taxes

The 17.5% value-added tax (VAT) is added to all hotel and restaurant bills and is included in the price of many items you purchase. This can be refunded if you shop at stores that participate in the Retail Export Scheme (signs are posted in the window). See Chapter 9 for more information.

Taxis

You can hail a cab from the street; if the "For Hire" light is lit, the cab is available. You can phone for a radio cab at ☎ 02072/720-272.

Tourist/Transit Assistance

The Britain Visitor Centre, 1 Regent St., Piccadilly Circus, SW1 (Tube: Piccadilly Circus), provides tourist information to walk-in visitors Monday to Friday from 9 a.m. to 6:30 p.m., Saturday and Sunday from 10 a.m. to 4 p.m. There's no phone assistance. Here you find hotel- and theater-booking agencies, a currency exchange, and plenty of free brochures on river trips, walking tours, and day trips from London.

For 24-hour information on London's Underground, buses, and ferries, call ☎ 02072/221-234.

Weather

For the daily London weather report before you go, check the Web sites listed next.

Web Sites

The Web page for the British Tourist Authority, `www.visitbritain.com`, is a good all-around resource for visitors to London and the United Kingdom in general. At `www.londontown.com`, you can browse sections on attractions, restaurants, nightlife, and hotels. For a useful list of gay and gay-friendly hotels, services, clubs, and restaurants, check out `www.gaylondon.co.uk`. Information on all London's airports is available at `www.heathrow.co.uk`. London Transport, which is in charge of all forms of public transportation in the city (Tube, buses, ferry service) is accessible at `www.londontransport.co.uk`. At `www.royal.gov.uk`, the official Royal Web site, you find history, information, and trivia about the British monarchy.

Chapter 13

Day-Tripping from London

In This Chapter

- Exploring the ancient university towns of Cambridge and Oxford
- Going upriver to Greenwich
- Discovering Hampton Court Palace
- Sniffing the roses at Kew Gardens
- Wandering through Blenheim Palace
- Visiting the royal residence at Windsor Castle

With so much to see and do in London, many visitors never leave the city. But several wonderful attractions are within easy commuting distance. You can visit any one of these places in a day and be back in London in time for dinner and an 8 o'clock curtain. For locations of the destinations, see the "Day Trips from London" map in this chapter.

Cambridge: Medieval Colleges on the River Cam

Students at Oxford refer to **Cambridge** as "the other place." Located 55 miles north of London in Cambridgeshire, Cambridge is most famous for its university. Every year about 8,000 students apply to this prestigious school, which accepts only about 1,600. The beautiful colleges, many dating from the Middle Ages, are built around quiet inner quadrangles or "quads." The River Cam runs past the colleges and is particularly beautiful in April, when daffodils line its banks. Magnificent King's College Chapel is a definite must-see in Cambridge. For the locations of my recommended attractions and restaurants, see the "Cambridge" map in this chapter.

Day Trips from London

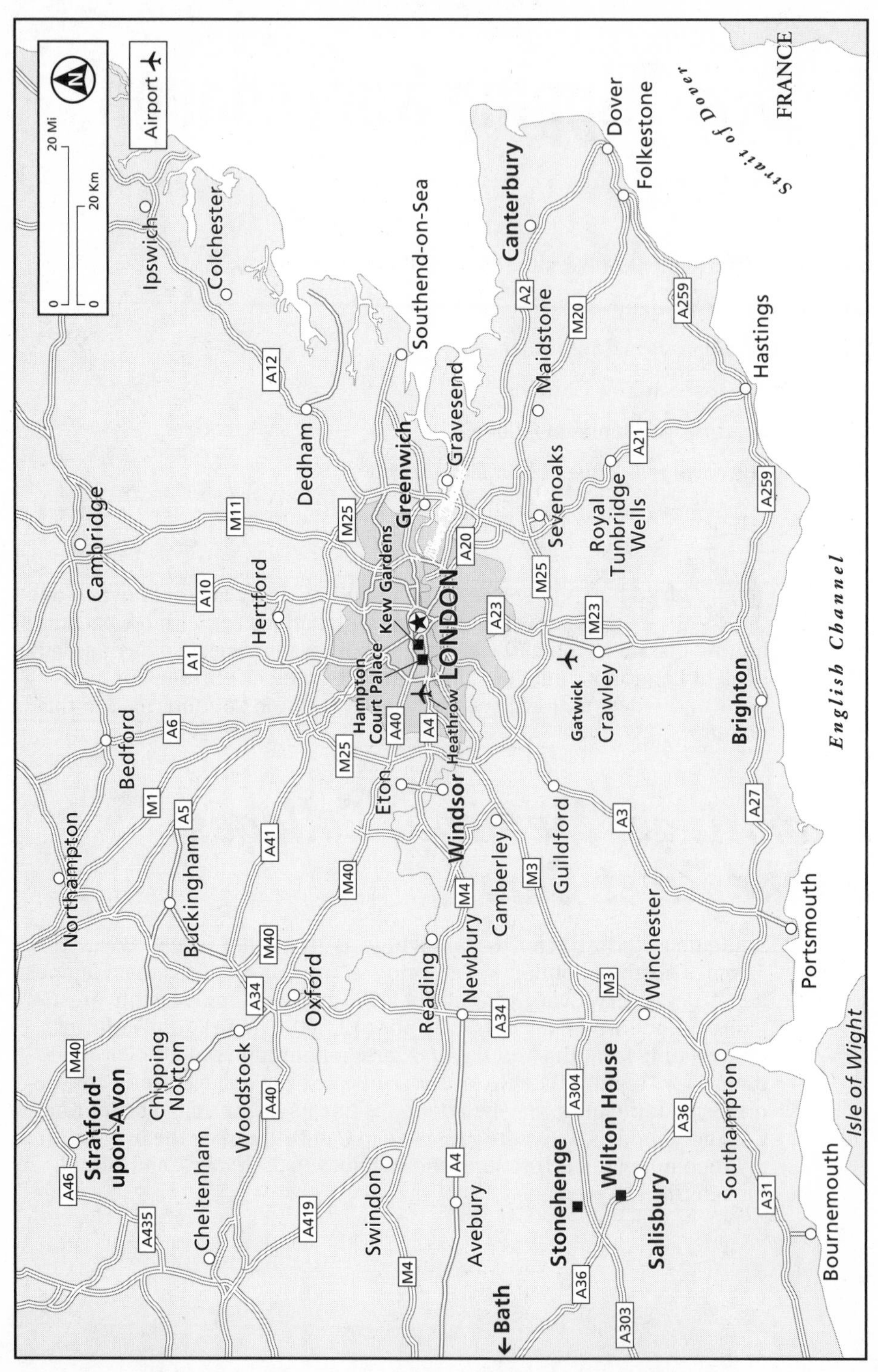

Cambridge

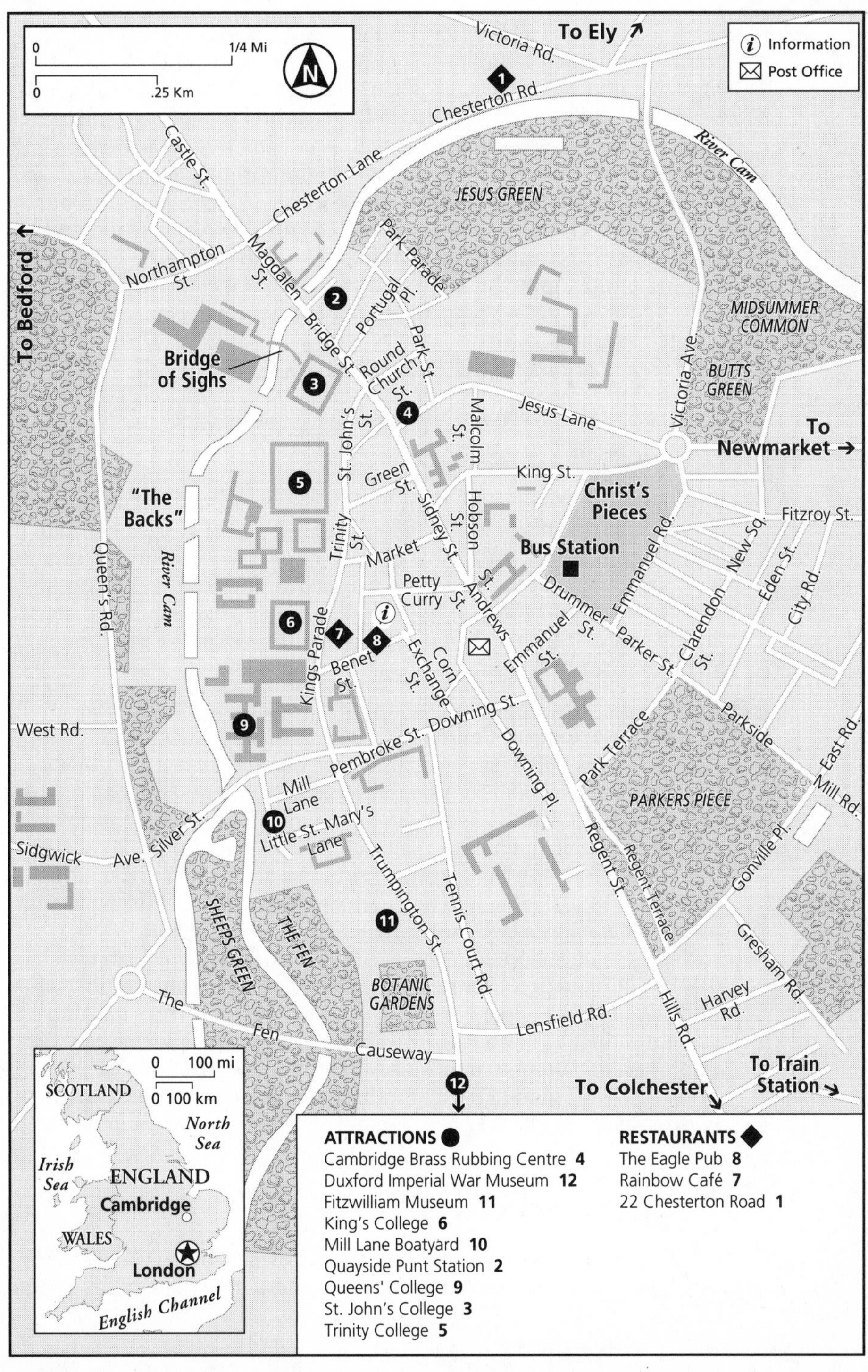

To Ely
Information
Post Office
0
1/4 Mi
0
.25 Km
Victoria Rd.
Chesterton Rd.
River Cam
Castle St.
Chesterton Lane
JESUS GREEN
To Bedford
Northampton St.
Magdalen St.
Park Parade
Portugal Pl.
MIDSUMMER COMMON
Bridge St.
Park St.
Bridge of Sighs
Round Church St.
BUTTS GREEN
Victoria Ave.
Malcolm St.
Jesus Lane
To Newmarket
St. John's St.
King St.
"The Backs"
Green St.
Christ's Pieces
Hobson St.
Sidney St.
Fitzroy St.
Trinity St.
Market
Bus Station
Emmanuel Rd.
New Sq.
Queen's Rd.
River Cam
Petty Curry
St. Andrews St.
Drummer St.
Eden St.
City Rd.
Clarendon St.
Kings Parade
Benet St.
Corn Exchange St.
Emmanuel St.
Parker St.
Parkside
West Rd.
Pembroke St.
Downing St.
Park Terrace
East Rd.
Downing Pl.
Mill Lane
PARKERS PIECE
Mill Rd.
Little St. Mary's Lane
Silver St.
Sidgwick Ave.
Trumpington St.
Regent St.
Regent Terrace
Gonville Pl.
Tennis Court Rd.
SHEEPS GREEN
THE FEN
Gresham Rd.
BOTANIC GARDENS
Hills Rd.
Harvey Rd.
The Fen Causeway
Lensfield Rd.
To Train Station
To Colchester
0
100 mi
0
100 km
SCOTLAND
North Sea
Irish Sea
ENGLAND
Cambridge
WALES
London
English Channel
ATTRACTIONS
Cambridge Brass Rubbing Centre 4
Duxford Imperial War Museum 12
Fitzwilliam Museum 11
King's College 6
Mill Lane Boatyard 10
Quayside Punt Station 2
Queens' College 9
St. John's College 3
Trinity College 5
RESTAURANTS
The Eagle Pub 8
Rainbow Café 7
22 Chesterton Road 1

Getting to Cambridge

Direct trains depart hourly from London's King's Cross Station for the 45-minute journey to Cambridge. A same-day round-trip ticket costs £15.60 ($25); all travel must take place after 9:30 a.m. For schedules, call ☎ **08457/484-950.** Going by **National Express** bus is cheaper — £9.50 ($15) for a day-return (round-trip) ticket — but the trip from Victoria Coach Station to Drummer Street Station in Cambridge takes two hours. Contact National Express (☎ **0990/808-080;** www.gobycoach.com) for schedules. I don't recommend driving to Cambridge because most of the city is closed to traffic (with parking lots on the outskirts). If you drive from London, take the M11 north; the city is well marked.

Finding information and taking a tour

You have two places to go for information in Cambridge:

- **Guide Friday Ltd.** (☎ **01223/362-444;** www.guidefriday.com) operates a tourist center right in the train station. You can book rooms and buy maps at this office and buy tickets for a one-hour **open-top bus tour** (£7.50/$12). Buses depart daily from the train station starting at 9:45 a.m. and run every 15 to 20 minutes until 3 or 4 p.m., depending on the season. Guide Friday is open daily in the summer from 9:30 a.m. to 5 p.m.; the rest of the year the center closes at 3 p.m.
- In town, on Wheeler Street behind the Guildhall, you find the **Tourist Information Centre** (☎ **0906/586-2526;** www.cambridge.gov.uk). This office has brochures on town and area attractions and can also book a room for you. The free pamphlet called *Cambridge Where to Go—What to See* is useful for its information on the colleges (and their open hours) and includes a street plan. The center is open Monday through Friday from 10 a.m. to 5:30 p.m., Saturday from 10 a.m. to 5 p.m., and Sunday from 11 a.m. to 4 p.m. This office offers a **two-hour city walking tour** (£7.85/$13) that includes colleges open to the public. The walks leave from the Tourist Information Centre at 1:30 p.m. daily throughout the year; additional walks depart at 10:30 a.m. on weekdays from mid-June to September, at 11:30 a.m. daily from April to October, and at 2:30 p.m. from mid-June to mid-August. For more information or to book a special guided tour, stop in this office or call **Blue Badge Guides** at ☎ **01223/457-574;** E-mail: Tours@cambridge.gov.uk.

Getting around Cambridge

Cambridge is a compact city, so you can walk everywhere. The distance from the train station to the city center is about a mile (20-minute walk), so hop on the No. 3 shuttle bus (80p/$1.25) running into town every few minutes from in front of the station. Taxis are available right outside the train and bus stations. Cambridge, with all its students, is a big cycling city. If you want to rent a bike, during the summer months a rental stall is right at the train station (no phone). You can also rent bikes at **Geoff's Bike Hire,** 65 Devonshire Rd. (☎ **01223/365-629**), and **Mike's Bikes,** 28 Mill Rd. (☎ **01223/312-591**). Expect to pay about £8 ($13) a day plus a refundable deposit for a standard bike.

Exploring the best of Cambridge

Cambridge has enough to keep you happily occupied for an entire day. Wandering through the ancient courtyards of the colleges is fun, but so many visitors (3½ million a year) now descend on Cambridge that several of the colleges have instituted visiting hours and admission fees.

When visiting Cambridge, keep in mind that the colleges are completely closed to visitors during exam season, from mid-April until late June. Note, too, that open hours for the colleges can be restricted during term time from September to June. Summer is the best time to visit if you want to get into the college courtyards, but it's also the busiest tourist season.

Fitzwilliam Museum

The Fitzwilliam Museum is Cambridge's best museum and one of England's oldest museums. A palatial mid-19th-century building, the museum houses the original collections bequeathed to Cambridge University in 1816 by Viscount Fitzwilliam. Typical of an upper-class gentleman, Fitzwilliam collected antiquities from Egypt and Greece (mummies, sarcophagi, vases, and so forth) and porcelain from all over Europe. You can see all this, plus an amazing assortment of later bequests — pewterware, portrait miniatures, and illuminated manuscripts — on display in the **Lower Galleries.** You find a rich and varied selection of European paintings and sculpture, including works by Picasso, Cezanne, and Renoir, in the **Upper Galleries.** Check out the rooms devoted to British painting to find important works by the poet/artist/mystic William Blake, English landscapes by Constable and Turner, satirical prints by Hogarth, and portraits by Gainsborough. The 20th-century gallery displays works by modern British artists, such as David Hockney, Lucian Freud, and Barbara Hepworth. **Guided tours** (£3/$4.80) are available on Sunday at 2:30 p.m. The museum houses a pleasant cafe for lunch or tea.

Trumpington St. (near Peterhouse College). ☎ ***01223/332-900.*** *Admission: free, but suggested donation £3 ($4.80). Open: Tues–Sat 10 a.m.–5 p.m., Sun 2:15–5 p.m.; closed Jan 1, Good Friday, May Day, and Dec 24–31.*

King's College

Henry VI founded King's College in 1441. The college encloses one of England's greatest architectural treasures: **King's College Chapel.** Located on the north side of the college's Great Court, the chapel was begun in 1446 and completed about 90 years later. The structure was built in a tall, slender, highly decorated Gothic style. The stunning interior conveys both strength and delicacy. Look up to the ceiling, and you see what many consider to be the finest fan vaulting in England. Nearly 500 years ago, Flemish glaziers made the enormous windows of richly colored stained glass that depict stories from the Old and New Testaments. A painting by Rubens, *Adoration of the Magi,* adorns the altar.

You may want to arrange your schedule so you can hear *Evensong* at King's College Chapel. In the late afternoons during term time, the chapel's famous boys' choir walks in procession across the college grounds in black and white robes to sing in the chapel (Tuesday through Saturday, 5:30 p.m.; free). You can also hear the choir during Sunday services at 10:30 a.m. and 3:30 p.m. On Christmas Day, the famous Festival of Nine Lessons and Carols (a traditional Christmas service) sung by the choir is broadcast around the world from the chapel.

*On King's Parade. ☎ **01223/331-212.** Admission (to college and chapel): £4 ($6) adults, £3 ($4.80) students and children 12–17, free for kids under 13. Open: during the school year, Mon–Sat 9:30 a.m.–3:30 p.m., Sun 1:15–2:15 p.m.; the rest of the year, Mon–Sat 9:30 a.m.–4:30 p.m., Sun 10 a.m.–5 p.m. Closed Dec 26–Jan 1.*

Queens' College

Queens' College got its name because two queens — one the wife of Henry VI, the other the wife of Edward IV — endowed the college in 1448. For many, Queens' represents the quintessential and perhaps the most picturesque of all the Cambridge colleges. Step inside to the **Old Court** and you can see a self-contained academic universe — library, chapel, hall, rooms, and kitchens, all clustered around a small green lawn. The unique sundial in Old Court dates from 1642 and is one of the country's finest. Not only can the sundial tell apparent solar time, but it also can calculate the sun's altitude, the date, the time of sunrise and sunset, and the zodiac sign. The last remaining half-timbered building in Cambridge, **President's Lodge,** is in the southeast corner of **Cloister Court.** (A half-timbered building is made of a wooden framework and has the spaces filled with plaster or brick.) Another unusual feature of Queens' is the **Mathematical Bridge** over the Cam. A copy of the original bridge built in 1749, the span was named because meticulous calculations made nails unnecessary.

*Queen's Lane. ☎ **01223/335-511.** Admission: £1 ($1.50). Open: Nov 1–March 19 daily 1:45–4:30 p.m.; March 20–May 16 and June 20–Oct 31, Mon–Fri 1:45–4:30 p.m. and Sat–Sun 10 a.m.–4:45 p.m.; closed May 17–June 19.*

Trinity greats

The largest of the Cambridge colleges, Trinity also has the longest list of illustrious alums. In addition to Isaac Newton and Lord Byron, the poets John Dryden and Alfred Lord Tennyson, the novelists William Thackeray and Vladimir Nabokov, the composer Ralph Vaughan Williams, the philosopher Ludwig Wittgenstein, kings Edward VII and George VI, and the present heir to the throne, Prince Charles, all attended Trinity.

St. John's College

Before entering St. John's College, on St. John's Street next door to Trinity, take a moment to examine its magnificent **Tudor gateway.** All the fancy carving and statuary is the heraldic "signature" of Lady Margaret Beaufort (1443–1509), mother of Henry VII and grandmother of Henry VIII. A great patron of Cambridge, Lady Margaret founded Christ's College in 1505 and died before her second project, St. John's, was completed in 1511. Inside the First Court you see the original building of St. John's College. Two more courts lie beyond, and beyond those courts you come to the famous **Bridge of Sighs,** built in 1831 over the River Cam. The covered wooden bridge is closed to the public; you can get a better view from a punt, or small boat. (For information about punt rentals, see "Finding more to see and do in Cambridge," later in this chapter.)

St. John's St. ☎ ***01223/338-600.*** *Admission: £1.75 ($2.80). Open: daily 10 a.m.–5:30 p.m.*

Trinity College

Henry VIII founded Trinity College in 1546, which is why his coat of arms decorates the **Great Gate** on Trinity Street. Beyond the gate is the **Great Court,** a vast, asymmetrical expanse of lawn surrounded by fine Tudor buildings, including a 15th-century clock tower. Rumor has it that Lord Byron (1788–1824), a Trinity student who became the most famous poet of his day, bathed naked with his pet bear in the fountain. Pass through "the screens" — a passageway between the dining hall and the kitchens — and you come to **Nevile's Court,** where Sir Isaac Newton tested his theory on the speed of sound. **Trinity College Library,** on the west side of Nevile's Court, is another famous Cambridge building. Designed by Sir Christopher Wren and begun in 1676, the library contains a treasure trove of rare books and manuscripts, many written by Trinity alums. The library's marble statue of Lord Byron, shown composing his poem *Childe Harold's Pilgrimage,* is a masterful work by the Danish sculptor Bertel Thorvaldsen. The four figures standing on the library's parapet are 17th-century representations of Divinity, Mathematics, Law, and Physics — the disciplines for which Trinity is best known.

Trinity St. ☎ ***01223/338-400.*** *Admission (college and library): £1.75 ($2.80). Open: college, daily 10 a.m.–6 p.m.; library, during the school year, Mon–Fri noon to 2 p.m. and Sat 10:30 a.m.–2:30 p.m.; library, outside of term, Mon–Fri noon to 2 p.m.*

Finding more to see and do in Cambridge

Visitors flock to Cambridge to see the historic colleges and breathe in the rarified academic atmosphere. Check out my additional suggestions for things to see and do:

- **Brass rubbing in the round church:** The Church of the Holy Sepulchre is one of England's few surviving Norman round churches. The building is no longer used for services but has taken on new life as the **Cambridge Brass Rubbing Centre (☎ 01223/871-621**). Instructions and materials are provided — all you supply is the elbow grease. The brasses are replicas, not originals. A rubbing costs £2 to £15 ($3.30 to $25). Even if you don't want to rub, step inside for a look at this unique structure with its thousand-year-old rounded Norman arches and 600-year-old oak roof. The center is open daily in winter from 1 to 4 p.m. and in summer from 10 a.m. to 5 p.m.

- **Punting on the River Cam:** Cambridge takes its name from the lovely River Cam. The most famous section of the river is called "The Backs" because many of the colleges back onto its shores. Punting on the Cam is a time-honored tradition. Floating along in one of these flat-bottomed boats looks so romantic, so delightful, so easy! Instead of oars, the punter uses a long stick and propels the boat from the rear like a Venetian gondolier. But the stick frequently gets stuck in the muddy river bottom, and the boat often just doesn't obey orders. So unless you're adept at watersports, consider a **chauffeured punt tour** along the river. If you want to try it yourself, you can rent punts, rowboats, and canoes from **Scudamore's Punting Company (☎ 01223/359-750;** `www.scudamores.com`). It has two locations: **Quayside Punt Station,** beside the Magdalene Street bridge, and **Mill Lane Boatyard,** beside the Silver Street bridge. The boatyards are open from Easter to October. The rental cost is £12 to £14 ($19 to $22) per hour, plus a refundable £40 ($64) deposit, for up to 6 people in a punt. You can arrange a chauffeured punt at these boatyards, too; the price usually comes out to about £10 ($16) per person.

- **Flying back in time:** Duxford, in the countryside about 5 miles south of Cambridge, was an important airfield during World War II. Today, with its preserved hangars, control tower, and Operations Room, the **Duxford Imperial War Museum (☎ 01223/835-000**) is one of Europe's top aviation museums. You find a major exhibition on the 1940 Battle of Britain, in which Duxford played a major role, and more than 180 historic aircraft. A collection of tanks and military vehicles, including Field Marshal Montgomery's mobile tactical headquarters, is also on display. The **American Air Museum** features American fighter planes and other artifacts. A free sightseeing train takes visitors around the 85-acre site. A self-service restaurant is on the grounds, or you can bring your own picnic. To get here, rail travelers can use the museum's free bus service, which runs hourly (9:40 a.m. to 3:40 p.m.) from the Cambridge train station. By car, drive south from Cambridge on the M11 to Junction 10. Admission is £8.50 ($14) for adults, £6.50 ($10) for seniors, £4.50 ($7) for students 16 to 18, free for children under 16. The museum is open daily March 17 to October 27 from 10 a.m. to 6 p.m., and in winter daily from 10 a.m. to 4 p.m.; closed from December 24 to 26.

Dining in Cambridge

If you're looking for good vegetarian food, try the **Rainbow Cafe** (☎ **01223/321-551**). Located at 9a King's Parade, down a narrow passageway opposite King's College Gates, this subterranean haven is noted for its excellent daily specials, spinach lasagna, and hearty Latvian potato bake with carrots, garlic, herbs, and cheese. Main courses cost £7.25($12). The cafe is open Monday through Saturday from 11 a.m. to 11 p.m. It takes MasterCard and Visa.

The Eagle Pub, 8 Benet St. (☎ **01223/505-020**), is a good choice if you're looking for a pub lunch. The pub, which dates to the 16th century, was a gathering place for both American and British pilots during World War II. You find a bit of everything on the menu, including fish and chips, sausage and mash, pasta, and beef stroganoff. Main courses cost £3.50 to £10.50 ($6 to $17). Food is served daily from noon to 2:30 p.m., but the pub is open until 11 p.m. It accepts American Express, Diners Club, MasterCard, and Visa.

22 Chesterton Road, the restaurant in a converted Victorian house at 22 Chesterton Rd. (☎ **01223/351-880**), is the place to go if you're in the mood for fine dining. This dinner-only restaurant (open Tuesday to Saturday 7 to 9:45 p.m.) is one of the best in Cambridge. The classic English cooking emphasizes local products of the highest quality. The set-price dinner is £24.50 ($39). Making reservations is a good idea. The restaurant takes MasterCard and Visa.

Greenwich: The Center of Time and Space

Time is of the essence in **Greenwich,** a town and borough of Greater London, about 4 miles east of The City. The world's clocks are set according to Greenwich Mean Time, and visitors from around the globe flock here to stand on the **Prime Meridian,** the line from which the world's longitude is measured. The main attractions in Greenwich, parts of which UNESCO has designated a World Heritage Site, are the Old Royal Observatory, the Queen's House, and the National Maritime Museum, all located in Greenwich Park, and the *Cutty Sark,* berthed on the Thames. The Royal Naval College, a grouping of historic buildings on the Thames, is one of the finest and most dramatically sited architectural and landscape ensembles in the British Isles. Greenwich offers enough to keep you fully occupied for a full day and is a great outing for kids.

Getting to Greenwich

The most interesting route to Greenwich is by **Docklands Light Rail**, which takes you past Canary Wharf and all the new Docklands development. The one-way fare is £1.50 ($2.25). To get there, ride the Tube to Tower Hill, where you connect to the DLR at its Tower Gateway station (near the Tower of London). Take the light rail to Island Gardens, and then walk through the foot tunnel beneath the Thames to Greenwich. You come out next to the *Cutty Sark*. You can also take the Jubilee Underground line to North Greenwich. **Thames River Services** (☎ **02079/304-097**) runs a fleet of boats from Westminster Pier to Greenwich Pier year-round. A round-trip ticket is £7.80 ($12) for adults, £6.30 ($10) for seniors, £3.90 ($6) for children, and £20.25 ($32) for families (2 adults, 2 children).

Finding information and taking a tour

All the attractions in Greenwich are clearly signposted, and you can easily reach them on foot. The **Greenwich Tourist Information Centre,** Pepys House, Cutty Sark Gardens (☎ **08706/082-000**), open daily from 10 a.m. to 5 p.m., offers 1½- to 2-hour **walking tours** (at 12:15 p.m. and 2:15 p.m.) of the town's principal sights for £4 ($6). Reservations aren't necessary, but calling first to verify the schedule is a good idea.

Exploring Greenwich

Cutty Sark

The majestic *Cutty Sark,* last of the tea-clipper sailing ships, was launched in 1869 and first used for the lucrative China Sea tea trade. Later, the ship carried wool from Australia, and after that (until the end of World War II) it served as a training ship. Today, the hold contains a collection of nautical instruments and paraphernalia. You can visit the ship on a self-guided tour, and see everything in about 30 minutes.

King William Walk (along the Thames). ☎ ***02088/583-445.*** *Admission: £3.95 ($6) adults, £2.95 ($5) children 5–15, £9.80 ($16) families. Open: daily 10 a.m.–5 p.m.*

National Maritime Museum

The National Maritime Museum is dedicated to Britain's seafaring past. The paintings of ships tend to be boring, but you also find sailing crafts and models and an extensive exhibit on Admiral Lord Nelson, which includes hundreds of his personal artifacts (including the coat he was wearing when he was shot at the Battle of Trafalgar in 1805). New galleries with interactive technology explore modern maritime issues. You can see the entire collection in about 30 minutes.

In Greenwich Park. ☎ ***02083/126-608.*** *Admission: free. Open: daily 10 a.m.–5 p.m.*

Old Royal Observatory

After leaving Queen's House (see the next listing), you can huff your way up the hill in the park to explore the "center of time and space." This is where you find the **Prime Meridian** (longitude zero degrees). Of particular interest inside the observatory is the collection of original 18th-century chronometers (marked H1, H2, H3, and H4), beautiful instruments that were developed to help mariners chart longitude by time instead of by the stars.

In Greenwich Park. ☎ ***02083/126-608.*** *Admission: free. Open: daily 10 a.m.–5 p.m.*

Queen's House

Adjacent to the National Maritime Museum is the splendidly restored Queen's House, designed by Inigo Jones in 1616 and later used as a model for the White House. Anne of Denmark, the wife of James I, commissoned Queen's House, the first classical building in England, and it was completed in 1635 (with later modifications). You can visit the royal apartments on a self-guided tour that takes about a half-hour; special exhibits are also held here.

In Greenwich Park. ☎ ***02083/126-608.*** *Admission: free. Open: daily 10 a.m.–5 p.m.*

Royal Naval College

Near the *Cutty Sark,* the Royal Naval College occupies the site of Greenwich Palace, which stood here from 1422 to 1620 and was the birthplace of Henry VIII, Mary I, and Elizabeth I. Badly damaged by Oliver Cromwell's troops during the Civil War in the 17th century, the palace was later torn down. In 1696, a naval hospital for retired seamen was erected in its place. The river-side buildings, designed by Sir Christopher Wren, became the Naval College in 1873 and are today a

UNESCO-designated World Heritage Site. The only rooms open to visitors are the **chapel** and the imposing **Great Hall,** with its dazzling painted ceiling; the body of Lord Nelson lay in state here in 1805.

King William Walk (along the Thames). ☎ ***02088/582-154.*** *Admission: free. Open: daily 10 a.m.–5 p.m.*

Dining in Greenwich

If you're looking for a nice spot for lunch, try the **Green Village Restaurant,** 11–13 Greenwich Church St. (☎ **02088/582-348**). This place serves several kinds of fresh fish (try the fish pie if it's available), American-style burgers, salads, and omelets. It's open daily from 11 a.m. to midnight.

Hampton Court Palace: Henry VIII's Riverside Estate

In 1514, Cardinal Thomas Wolsey, Henry VIII's Lord Chancellor, began building **Hampton Court** in East Moseley, Surrey, 13 miles west of London on the north side of the Thames. But Cardinal Wolsey got on the monarch's bad side when he opposed the king's request for a divorce from Catherine of Aragon. This provided a convenient excuse for the greedy Tudor monarch to nab Hampton Court for himself and make the property a royal residence, a status it held from 1525 until 1760. Henry's fifth wife (of six), Catherine Howard, supposedly haunts the place to this day, though you'd think the hordes of tourists would have scared her away by now.

Getting to Hampton Court

Frequent trains from London's Waterloo Station make the half-hour trip to Hampton Court Station; a round-trip (*day return* in Britspeak) fare costs about £5 ($8). The palace entrance is a two-minute walk from the station. If you have plenty of time, you can take a boat from **Westminster Pier** to Hampton Court; the journey takes almost four hours. From April to September, boats usually run at 10 a.m. and 12:45 p.m.; call **Westminster Passenger Service (☎ 02079/302-062;** `www.wpsa.co.uk`) for more information. Round-trip fares are £18 ($29) for adults, £12 ($19) for seniors, £9 ($14) for children 5 to 15, and £45 ($72) for families (2 adults, 2 children). By car, the palace is on A308 close to the A3, M3, and M25 motorways.

Ghost palace

So many people, from staff to visitors, have reported encounters with Catherine Howard's ghost in the "haunted gallery" at Hampton Court that psychologists from the University of Hertfordshire conducted an investigation to see if they could find a scientific explanation for the phenomenon. Catherine, the fifth wife of King Henry VIII, was locked up in Hampton Court prior to her beheading for adultery in 1542. One day she supposedly escaped and in desperation ran along the 40-foot gallery to pound on the king's door and beg for mercy. Sightings in this gallery of a running, screaming apparition have been reported for centuries. After weeks of research, the ghost hunters came away empty-handed.

Exploring Hampton Court

Hampton Court Palace

The **Anne Boleyn Gate,** with its 16th-century astronomical clock, and the **Great Hall,** with its hammer-beam ceiling, are remnants from Hampton Court's Tudor days. In the late 17th century, Sir Christopher Wren significantly altered the place for William and Mary. Wren also designed the famous **Maze,** where you can wander in dizzy confusion. Inside the enormous palace, something of a maze itself, you can see various state apartments and private rooms, including the King's Dressing Room, the Tudor kitchens, wooden carvings by Grinling Gibbons, Italian paintings, and guides dressed in period costumes. The manicured Thames-side gardens are lovely. A cafe and restaurant are on the grounds.

East Moseley, Surrey. ☎ ***02087/819-500.*** *Admission: £11 ($18) adults, £8.25 ($13) seniors and students, £7.25 ($12) children 5–15. Open: mid-March–mid-Oct Tues–Sun 9:30 a.m.–6 p.m., Mon 10:15 a.m.–6 p.m.; mid-Oct–mid-March Tues–Sun 9:30 a.m.–4:30 p.m., Mon 10:15 a.m.–4:30 p.m.; closed Jan 1, Dec 24–26.*

Royal Botanic Gardens (Kew Gardens): Royal Pleasure Grounds

Located 9 miles southwest of Central London, the **Royal Botanic Gardens** at Kew — more familiarly known as **Kew Gardens** — are a feast for garden lovers' eyes (and noses).

Getting to Kew Gardens

The easiest way to get here is to take the **Underground** to Kew Gardens; from the station, the entrance on Kew Road is a ten-minute walk west on Lichfield Street. If you have more time, you can take a boat. From April to late September, the **Westminster Passenger Service Association** (☎ **02079/302-062;** wpsa.co.uk) operates vessels that leave from London's Westminster Pier daily from 10:15 a.m. to 2 p.m. Round-trip fares for the 90-minute journey are £15 ($24) for adults, £10 ($16) for seniors, £7.50 ($12) for children 5 to 15, and £37.50 ($60) for families (2 adults, 2 children). The last boat from Kew back to London usually departs around 5:30 p.m. (depending on the tide).

Exploring Kew Gardens

Royal Botanic Gardens

On display in the 300-acre gardens is a marvelous array of specimens first planted in the 17th and 18th centuries. Orchids and palms are nurtured in the Victorian conservatory. Also onsite are a lake, aquatic gardens, a Chinese pagoda, and even a royal palace. **Kew Palace,** the smallest and most picturesque of the former royal compounds, is where King George III went insane. **Queen Charlotte's Cottage** was the mad king's summer retreat. Neither building is open to the public.

*Kew. ☎ **02083/325-622.** Admission: £7.50 ($12) adults, £5.50 ($9) seniors and students, children under 16 free. Tours: free 1-hr. tours daily 11 a.m. and 2 p.m. Open: daily 9:30 a.m–dusk, conservatory closes one hour before gardens.*

Oxford: Town and Gown

Oxford University, one of the world's oldest, greatest, and most revered universities, dominates the town of **Oxford,** about 54 miles northwest of London. Its skyline pierced by ancient tawny towers and spires, Oxford has been a center of learning for seven centuries (the Saxons founded the city in the tenth century). Roger Bacon, Sir Walter Raleigh, John Donne, Sir Christopher Wren, Dr. Samuel Johnson, Edward Gibbon, William Penn, John Wesley, Lewis Carroll, T. E. Lawrence, W. H. Auden, and Margaret Thatcher are just a few of the distinguished alumni who've taken degrees here. Even Bill Clinton studied at Oxford.

Although academically oriented, Oxford is far from dull. Its long sweep of a main street (High Street, known as "The High") buzzes with a cosmopolitan mix of locals, students, black-gowned dons, and foreign visitors. You can tour some of the beautiful historic colleges, each sequestered away within its own quadrangle (or quad) built around

Oxford

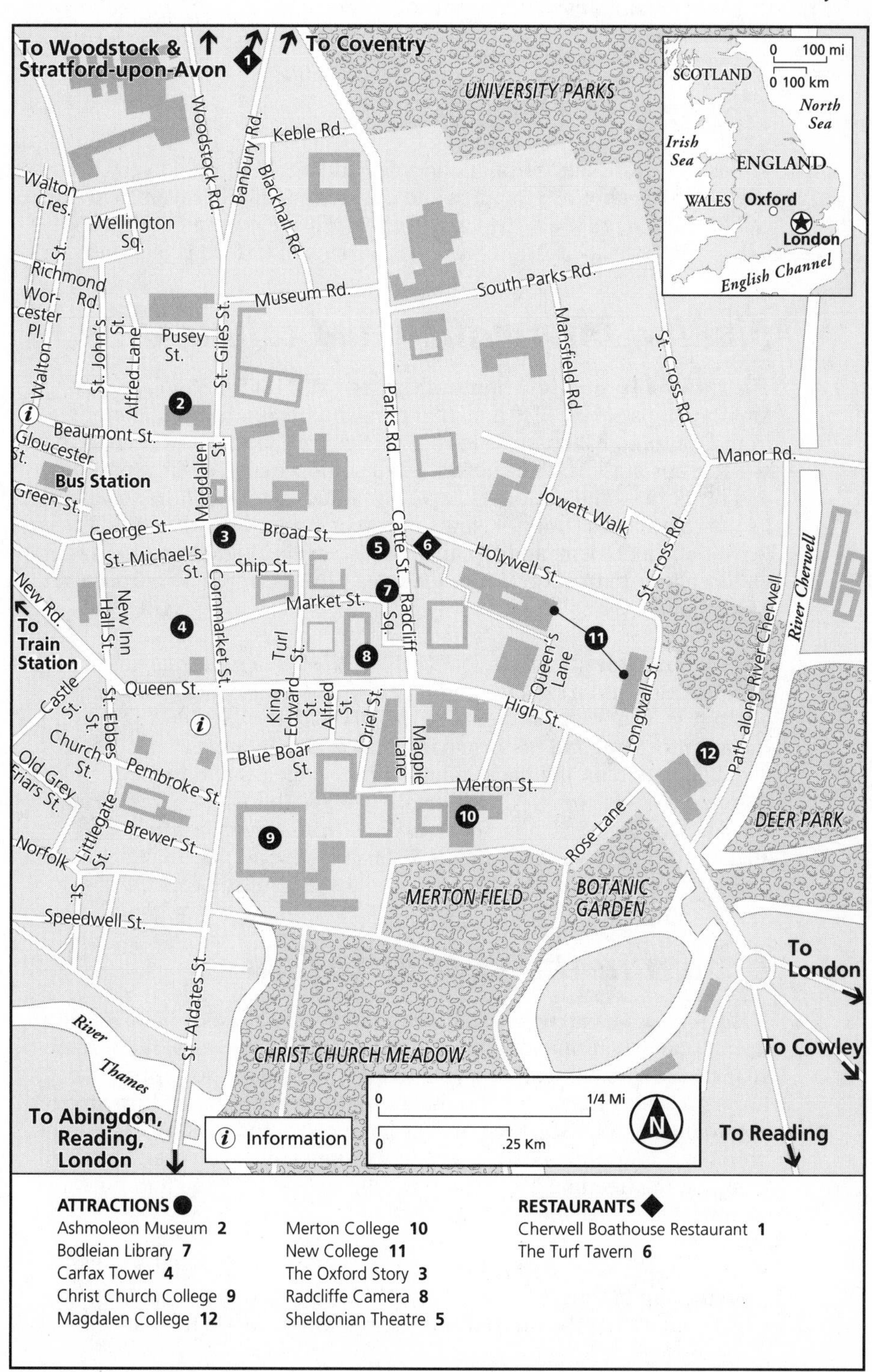

To Woodstock & Stratford-upon-Avon
To Coventry
UNIVERSITY PARKS
SCOTLAND
North Sea
Irish Sea
ENGLAND
WALES
Oxford
London
English Channel
0 100 mi
0 100 km
Keble Rd.
Woodstock Rd.
Banbury Rd.
Blackhall Rd.
Walton Cres.
Wellington Sq.
Richmond Rd.
Worcester Pl.
Museum Rd.
South Parks Rd.
St. John's St.
Alfred Lane
Pusey St.
St. Giles St.
Walton St.
Mansfield Rd.
St. Cross Rd.
Parks Rd.
Beaumont St.
Gloucester St.
Bus Station
Green St.
Magdalen St.
Manor Rd.
Jowett Walk
George St.
Broad St.
Holywell St.
St. Michael's St.
Ship St.
Catte St.
Cornmarket St.
Market St.
Radcliff Sq.
New Rd.
To Train Station
New Inn Hall St.
Turl St.
Queen's Lane
Longwall St.
Path along River Cherwell
River Cherwell
Queen St.
Castle St.
St. Ebbes St.
King Edward St.
Alfred St.
Oriel St.
High St.
Church St.
Pembroke St.
Blue Boar St.
Magpie Lane
Old Grey Friars St.
Merton St.
Brewer St.
Littlegate St.
Rose Lane
DEER PARK
Norfolk St.
MERTON FIELD
BOTANIC GARDEN
Speedwell St.
To London
St. Aldates St.
River Thames
CHRIST CHURCH MEADOW
To Cowley
To Abingdon, Reading, London
Information
0 1/4 Mi
0 .25 Km
N
To Reading
ATTRACTIONS
Ashmoleon Museum 2
Bodleian Library 7
Carfax Tower 4
Christ Church College 9
Magdalen College 12
Merton College 10
New College 11
The Oxford Story 3
Radcliffe Camera 8
Sheldonian Theatre 5
RESTAURANTS
Cherwell Boathouse Restaurant 1
The Turf Tavern 6

an interior courtyard; stroll along the lovely Cherwell River; and visit the Ashmoleon Museum. For the locations of my recommended attractions and restaurants, see the "Oxford" map in this chapter.

Getting to Oxford

Trains to Oxford leave from London's Paddington Station every hour; the trip takes about 90 minutes and costs £16 ($26). For train schedules, call (☎ **08457/484950**). By car, take the M40 west from London and follow the signs. Note, however, that parking in Oxford is a nightmare.

Finding information and taking a tour

The **Oxford Tourist Information Centre** (☎ **01865/726-871**), open Monday to Saturday 9:30 a.m. to 5 p.m. and on Sunday in summer from 10 a.m. to 3:30 p.m., is in the Old School Gloucester Green, opposite the bus station. The center sells a comprehensive range of maps and brochures and conducts two-hour **walking tours** of the town and its major colleges (but not New College or Christ Church) daily. Tours leave daily at 11 a.m. and 2 p.m. and cost £6 ($10) adults and £3 ($4.80) children 5 to 15. A special tour includes Christ Church on Saturday at 11 a.m. and 2 p.m.

The Oxford Story, 6 Broad St. (☎ **01865/790-055**), packages Oxford's complexities into a concise and entertaining **audiovisual tour.** The exhibition, spanning 800 years of the city's history, reviews some of the architectural and historical features you may otherwise miss. It also fills you in on the backgrounds of the colleges and those people who've passed through their portals. The exhibit is open daily from April to October, 9:30 a.m. to 6 p.m., and from November to March 10 a.m. to 4:30 p.m. Admission is £6.50 ($11) for adults, £5 ($8) for children 5 to 15, and £20 ($32) for families (2 adults, 2 children).

Exploring the best of Oxford

Many Americans arriving at Oxford ask: "Where's the campus?" Oxford doesn't have just one, but 39 widely dispersed colleges serving some 16,000 students. Instead of trying to see them all (impossible in a day), focus on seeing a handful of the better-known ones. Faced with an overabundance of tourists, the colleges have restricted visiting to certain hours and to groups of six or fewer; in some areas, you aren't allowed at all. Before heading off, check with the tourist office to find out when and what colleges you can visit.

A good way to start your tour is with a bird's-eye view of the colleges from the top of **Carfax Tower** (☎ **01865/792-653**) in the center of the city, just north of the information center. The tower is all that remains from St. Martin's Church, where William Shakespeare stood as godfather for a fellow playwright. The tower is open daily from November to March 10:30 a.m. to 3:30 p.m., and from April to October 10 a.m. to 5:30 p.m. Admission is £1.20 ($2) for adults and 60p ($1) for children 5 to 15.

I recommend visits to the following four colleges:

- **Christ Church College (☎ 01865/276-150)**, facing St. Aldate's Street, was begun by Cardinal Wolsey (who built Hampton Court, described earlier in the chapter) in 1525. Christ Church has the largest quadrangle of any college in Oxford and a chapel with 15th-century pillars and impressive fan vaulting. **Tom Tower** houses Great Tom, the 18,000-pound bell that rings nightly at 9:05 p.m., signaling the closing of the college gates. Several notable portraits, including works by Gainsborough and Reynolds, hang in the **Picture Gallery** and 16th-century **Great Hall.** The college and chapel are open Monday through Saturday from 9:30 a.m. to 5:30 p.m., Sunday from 11:30 a.m. to 5:30 p.m. Admission is £4 ($6) for adults, £3 ($4.80) for seniors and children 5 to 15.
- **Magdalen** (pronounced *Maud*-lin) **College** on High Street (**☎ 01865/276-000**), founded in 1458, boasts the oldest botanical garden in England and the most extensive grounds of any Oxford college; you even find a deer park. The 15th-century bell tower, one of the town's most famous landmarks, is reflected in the waters of the Cherwell River. You can cross a small footbridge and stroll through the water meadows along the path known as Addison's Walk. June to September, the college is open daily noon to 6 p.m.; off-season, it's open daily 2 to 6 p.m. Admission is £2.50 ($4) for adults and £1.25 ($2) for children 5 to 15.
- **Merton College (☎ 01865/276-310)**, dating from 1264, stands near Merton Street, the only medieval cobbled street left in Oxford. The college is noted for its 14th-century library, said to be the oldest college library in England (admission is £1/$1.60). On display is an *astrolabe* (an astronomical instrument used for measuring the altitude of the sun and stars) thought to have belonged to Chaucer. The library and college are open Monday to Friday 2 to 4 p.m., and Saturday and Sunday 10 a.m. to 4 p.m.; both close for a week at Easter and at Christmas.
- **New College (☎ 01865/279-555)**, on New College Lane, contains the first quadrangle to be built in Oxford (14th century), an architectural boilerplate for the quadrangles in many other colleges. The antechapel holds Sir Jacob Epstein's remarkable modern sculpture of Lazarus and a fine El Greco study of St. James. In the garden, you can see remants of the old city wall that used to surround Oxford. Easter to September, you can visit the college daily from 11 a.m. to 5 p.m.; off-season, the hours are 2 to 4 p.m. daily. Admission is £2 ($3.30) from Easter to October, free off-season.

Finding more to see and do in Oxford

Other attractions worth checking out include the following:

- **Architectural highlights:** East of Carfax, at the north end of Radcliffe Square, is the **Bodleian Library,** Broad Street (☎ **01865/277-000**), the world's oldest library, established in 1450. Hours are Monday to Friday from 9 a.m. to 7 p.m. and Saturday from 9 a.m. to 1 p.m. The **Radcliffe Camera,** the domed building just south of the Bodleian, is the library's reading room, dating from 1737. You can only see it on guided tours (£3.50/$5), given April through September Monday through Friday at 10:30 and 11:30 a.m. and 2 and 3 p.m., and mornings only on summer weekends and during the winter. To one side of the Bodleian is the **Sheldonian Theatre,** Broad Street (☎ **01865/277-299**), which dates from 1669 and was the first major work by Sir Christopher Wren, designed when he was an astronomy professor at Oxford. Today, the college uses the building for lectures and concerts, and you get great city views from the cupola. It's open daily 10 a.m. to 12:30 p.m. and 2 to 4:30 p.m. Admission is £1.50 ($2.40) for adults and £1 ($1.60) for children 5 to 15.
- **Ashmolean Museum:** Located on Beaumont Street (☎ **01865/278-000**), this is the oldest museum in England. A beautiful classical building from the 1840s houses the collections of the University of Oxford — European and Asian art, silver, ceramics, and antiquities from ancient Egypt, Greece, and Rome. The museum is open Tuesday to Saturday from 10 a.m. to 5 p.m. and Sunday from 2 to 5 p.m. From June through August, the museum stays open until 7:30 p.m. on Thursday and opens at noon on Sunday.

Dining in Oxford

One of the best places to eat in Oxford is the **Cherwell Boathouse Restaurant,** Bardwell Road (☎ **01865/552-746**). This place is about 2 miles outside of the city, right on the Cherwell River, and serves Modern British and French cuisine. Before dinner, you can try your hand at punting; a rental agency is on the other side of the boathouse. Main courses are £9 to £14 ($14 to $22). The restaurant is open Tuesday through Sunday from noon to 2 p.m. and Tuesday through Saturday 6 to 10 p.m.; it's closed December 24 to 30. American Express, MasterCard, and Visa are accepted.

For less expensive pub grub (salads, soups, sandwiches, beef pie, chili con carne) or a pint of beer, try **The Turf Tavern,** 4 Bath Place (☎ **01865/243-235**). Dating to the 13th century, the tavern has served the likes of Thomas Hardy, Richard Burton and Elizabeth Taylor, and Bill Clinton, who was a frequent visitor during his student days at

Oxford. You reach the pub using St. Helen's Passage, which stretches between Holywell Street and New College Lane. Main courses are £4 to £6 ($6 to $10); food is served Monday to Saturday noon to 8 p.m. The tavern accepts MasterCard and Visa.

Blenheim Palace: Ancestral Home of the Churchills

Located 8 miles north of Oxford in Woodstock, Oxfordshire, **Blenheim Palace** is one of the most beautiful country estates in England. Visiting the magnificent Baroque palace, birthplace of Sir Winston Churchill, and strolling through the magnificently landscaped grounds can take up the better part of a day, although sampling the highlights in three hours is also possible. The palace has several playgrounds and activity areas for kids.

Getting to Blenheim Palace

From Oxford, the nearest train station, you can take a taxi (about £10/ $16) or Bus No. 20 from the bus station (it stops at the palace gate and costs £3.70/$6 for a day return). If you have a car, Blenheim is a ten-minute drive from Oxford and a 45-minute drive from Stratford-upon-Avon (see Chapter 19). Approaching Oxford from the M40, take the Junction 9 turn-off and follow signs to Blenheim.

Exploring Blenheim Palace

Make the palace your first stop. To get there, you can walk or take a narrow-gauge railway from the parking lot. I recommend that you join up with a **palace tour** — they start every five to ten minutes and last about a half-hour — but you can also wander through at your own pace. Blenheim was built between 1705 and 1722 for John Churchill, First Duke of Marlborough, in recognition of his victory over the French at the Battle of Blenheim in 1704. The palace was a gift from Queen Anne, whose royal coat of arms is part of the decorations in the Great Hall. The principal architects were Sir John Vanbrugh, also responsible for Castle Howard in Yorkshire, and Nicholas Hawksmoor. Together they devised the most beautiful Baroque palace in England.

The remarkable **Great Hall** is 67 feet high, with stone carvings by Grinling Gibbons and a painted ceiling that shows Marlborough victorious at Blenheim. Sir Winston Churchill, England's prime minister during World War II, was born in a room west of the Great Hall in 1874. The **Churchill Exhibition** contains a variety of interesting exhibits, from letters to his baby curls. The **Green Drawing Room** and the two damask-covered rooms beyond it all have their original ceilings and family portraits painted by George Romney, Joshua Reynolds, John Singer Sargent, and Sir Anthony Van Dyck. A famous tapestry in the **Green Writing Room** shows Marlborough accepting Marshall Tallard's surrender at the Battle of Blenheim. In the **Saloon,** used as the state dining room, the silver-gilt dining table is laid with Minton china.

Three apartments known as the **State Rooms** display more hung tapestries showing Marlborough's victorious campaigns. The **Long Library,** famous for its extraordinary stucco decoration and two false domes, exhibits coronation robes, liveries, uniforms, and the coronets of the present Duke and Duchess. Sarah, the First Duchess, designed much of the **chapel,** which not unexpectedly pays homage to the Duke of Marlborough.

Blenheim is set in acres of beautiful parkland with a variety of gardens designed by Capability Brown and the French landscape architect Achille Duchene. In spring, daffodils and bluebells cover the grassy banks. In summer, hoops of pink roses adorn the **Rose Garden**. Brown designed the **Grand Cascade,** a picturesque waterfall. A path leads to the lake, where you can rent a rowboat. Exotic butterflies inhabit **The Butterfly House.** The **Marlborough Maze,** the world's largest symbolic hedge maze, was designed to reflect the palace's history and architecture. Cafes and restaurants are scattered about; you can have lunch, tea, or a snack during your rambles.

Woodstock, Oxfordshire. ☎ ***01993/811-325;*** *Internet:* `www.blenheimpalace.com`. *Admission: £10 ($16) adults, £8 ($13) seniors and children 16–17, £5 ($8) children 5–15, £26 ($42) family (2 adults, 2 children). Open: palace March 14–Oct daily 10 a.m.–4:45 p.m; grounds daily summer 9 a.m.–6 p.m., winter 9 a.m.–4 p.m.*

A royal pain

In June 2003, the royal family was royally freaked out when a man dressed in an Osama bin Laden costume managed to scale a wall at Windsor Castle, talk his way past security guards, and get into Prince William's 21st birthday party. The culprit, who climbed up onto the stage as William was making a speech thanking his grandmother, Queen Elizabeth II, for the costume party, turned out to be a comedian known for gate-crashing celebrity events. But the queen wasn't amused, and the security breach led to an apology from the police and a full-scale investigation.

Windsor Castle: Official Royal Residence

Located in Windsor, Berkshire, 20 miles from the center of London, **Windsor Castle** is one of the queen's official residences. Some 900 years ago, William the Conqueror constructed the castle, an imposing skyline of towers and battlements rising from the center of the 4,800-acre Great Park, which has been used as a royal residence ever since. The town is also the site of Eton College, one of the most exclusive boys' schools in the world.

Getting to Windsor Castle

Trains leave every half-hour from Waterloo Station in London for the 50-minute trip (the stop is Windsor & Eton); the round-trip fare is £6.50 ($10). If you're driving from London, take M4 west.

Exploring Windsor Castle

The **State Apartments,** open to visitors, range from the intimate chambers of Charles II to the enormous Waterloo Chamber, built to commemorate the victory over Napoléon in 1815. All are superbly furnished with important works of art from the Royal Collection. Sir Edwin Lutyens designed **Queen Mary's Dollhouse,** a marvelous palace in miniature, as a present for Queen Mary (wife of King George V) in 1921. From April through June, the **Changing of the Guard** takes place at 11 a.m. Monday through Saturday (on alternate days the rest of the year). From the ramparts of Windsor, you can look down on the playing fields of **Eton College,** where aristocrats and social climbers have been sending their boys for generations. You can explore the famous school and the charming town of **Eton** by strolling across the Thames Bridge.

*Windsor, Berkshire. ☎ **01753/868-286.** Admission: £11.50 ($18) adults, £9.50 ($15) seniors and students, £6 ($10) children under 17, £27.50 ($41) families. Open: March–Oct daily 9:45 a.m.–5:30 p.m. (last entry 4 p.m.), Nov–Feb daily 9:45 a.m.–4:15 p.m. (last entry 3 p.m.); closed Jan 1, March 28, June 16, Dec 25–26.*

Part IV
The Southeast

"He had it made after our trip to England. I give you, 'Clifford Fountain from Hever Castle'."

In this part . . .

Here, I introduce you to Kent and Sussex, the counties that form the wedge-shaped southeastern corner of England between London and the English Channel. The area is incredibly rich in history. In Chapter 14, I take you to a trio of beautiful towns. Canterbury is famous for its magnificent cathedral, a place of pilgrimage for hundreds of years. Rye is a treasure trove of ancient streets lined with half-timbered inns and Georgian shops. Brighton, with its long beach, amusement pier, and fanciful Royal Pavilion, is a seaside resort that's a favorite weekend getaway spot for Londoners. In Chapter 14, I also tell you about visiting Battle, home to one of the most hallowed spots on English soil: the site where William the Conqueror fought King Harold for the English throne in 1066.

The Kentish countryside is full of moated castles, glorious gardens, and stately homes. In Chapter 15, I guide you through Dover Castle, with its 2,000-year history that stretches back to the time of the Romans. Hever Castle is noteworthy for its associations with Anne Boleyn and its magnificent gardens. Many castle connoisseurs, including several kings and queens who lived there, consider Leeds Castle the most beautiful in England. And speaking of beautiful, you won't find a more spectacular garden anywhere than the one at Sissinghurst. For a glimpse of how the other half lived, you can visit Knole, a country estate that just happens to have 365 rooms, or Chartwell, the country home of Sir Winston Churchill.

Every place that I describe in this part can be the destination of a day trip from London. Alternatively, you can stay overnight in any of the towns in Chapter 14 and be assured of a good hotel, fine restaurants, and atmosphere galore.

Chapter 14

Kent and Sussex

In This Chapter

- Visiting Canterbury Cathedral
- Exploring the cobbled streets of Rye
- Reliving the Battle of Hastings
- Seeing the Royal Pavilion in Brighton

Kent and Sussex make up the southeast corner of England, an area that extends east and south from London to the English Channel. (See "The Southeast" map coming up in this chapter.) At its narrowest point, near Dover, the channel separating England from France is only 20 miles wide. Because of its proximity to the European mainland, this part of England has always been of prime strategic importance. Two thousand years ago, the Romans landed on these shores and began their systematic conquest of what they called *Britannia.* In 1066, William the Conqueror sailed over from Normandy and fought King Harold for the crown of England at a place now called, appropriately enough, Battle. Kent and Sussex became the scene of ferocious air battles and daring sea escapes during World War II. (Dover Castle, described in Chapter 15, played a pivotal role in the country's coastal defenses.)

Despite all the historic dramas that have played out here, the countryside has an air of calm repose. The land is lush and green, with chalk *downs* (high, open, grassy land over a chalk-limestone substrate) appearing near the coastline. Kent and Sussex (divided into West Sussex and East Sussex) are wealthy counties, favored spots for country living because of their mild climate and proximity to London.

In this chapter, I head first to Canterbury to explore the wonders of Canterbury Cathedral and the charming old town that grew up around it. From Canterbury, I travel to Rye and stroll the ancient lanes of a once-proud seaport that is, today, one of England's loveliest small towns. After exploring the battlefield and ruined abbey at Battle, I stop off in the lively resort town of Brighton for some fun beside the seaside.

The Southeast

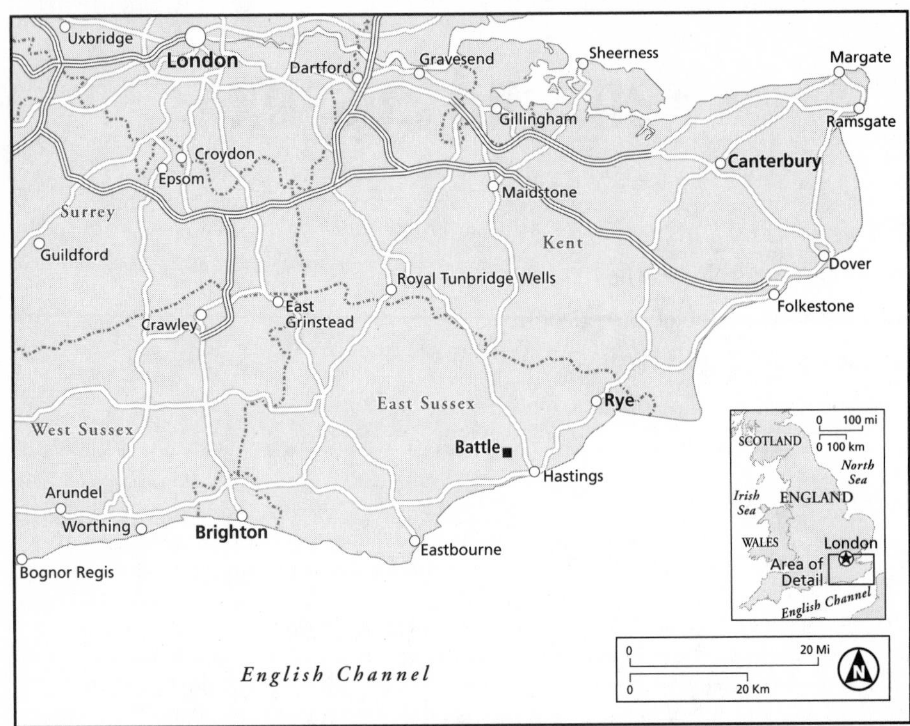

Canterbury: Tales from the Great Cathedral

Magnificent **Canterbury Cathedral** is one of England's glories. Spinning the yarns immortalized in *The Canterbury Tales,* Chaucer's pilgrims made their way here. For nearly 400 years, the devout, in search of miracles and salvation (and a bit of adventure), trekked to the cathedral's shrine of St. Thomas à Becket, archbishop of Canterbury. In 1170, Henry II's henchmen murdered him in the cathedral. The pilgrims didn't stop coming until Henry VIII had the shrine destroyed in 1538.

Modern pilgrims, called *day-trippers,* continue to pour into the Kentish city of Canterbury, on the River Stour. (See the "Canterbury" map in this chapter.) I recommend that you spend most of your time visiting the cathedral, which remains the town's greatest attraction, and exploring the picturesque semi-medieval streets that surround it. You may also want to visit some of the small but noteworthy museums and attractions that can help you to piece together an image of Canterbury through the centuries.

Canterbury

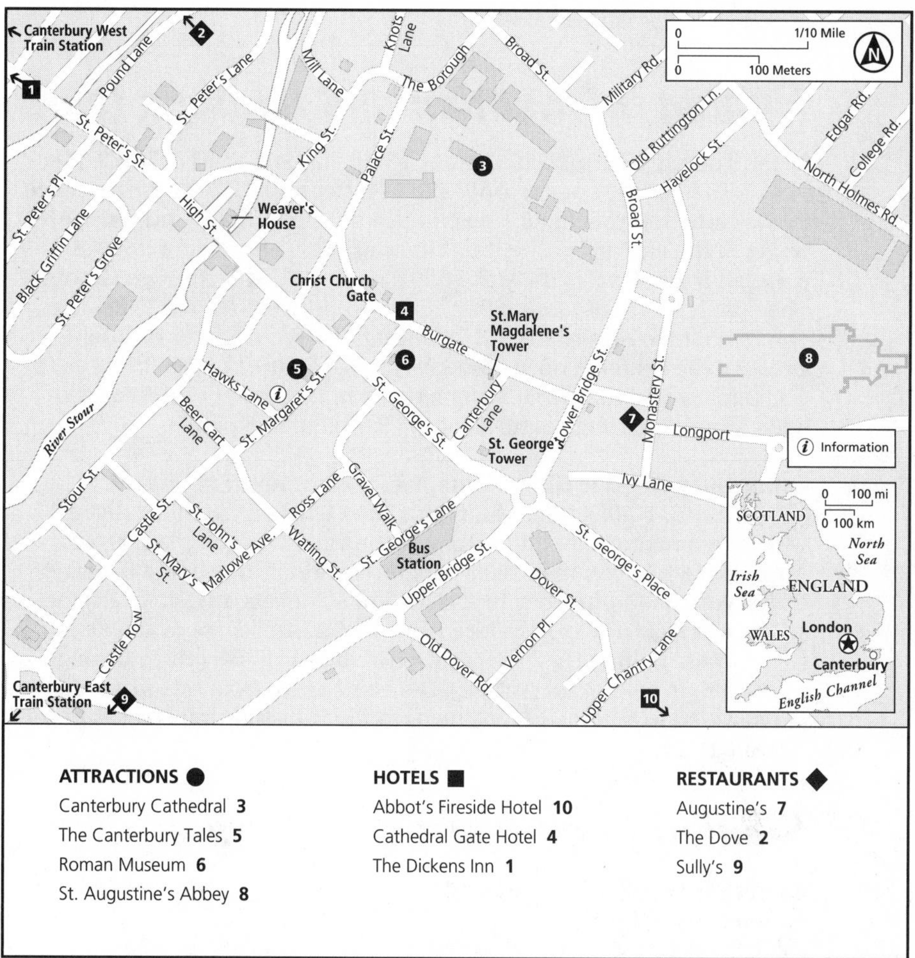

Getting to Canterbury

Canterbury, which is 62 miles (99 km) east of London, has two train stations, Canterbury East and Canterbury West — both within easy walking distance from the city center. From London's Victoria Station, trains run about every half-hour to Canterbury East. Hourly trains from London's Charing Cross stop at Canterbury West. The journey takes 1½ hours and costs £16.50 ($26) for a day return (round-trip) ticket from London. For train schedules and information, call ☎ **08457/484-950.**

National Express (☎ **0990/808-080**) offers frequent, direct bus service from London's Victoria Coach Station to Canterbury's bus station on St. George's Lane, a few minutes' walk from the cathedral. The trip takes one hour and 50 minutes; day return fare is £10.50 ($17).

To drive from London, take A2, then the M2; Canterbury is signposted all the way. The city center is closed to cars, but several parking areas are close to the cathedral.

Finding information and taking a tour

At the **Tourist Information Centre,** 12–13 Sun St. (☎ **01227/378-100;** www.canterbury.co.uk), opposite Christchurch Gate at the entrance to the cathedral precincts, you can buy tickets for **daily guided-tour walks** of the city and cathedral. The walks leave from here daily at 2 p.m. (additional walks daily at 11:30 a.m. from Easter through October). The cost is £3.75 ($6) for adults; £3.25 ($5) for seniors, students, and children under 14; and £10 ($16) for families. From Easter through October, the center is open Monday through Saturday from 9:30 a.m. to 5:30 p.m. and Sunday from 10 a.m. to 4 p.m.; the rest of the year, it's open Monday through Saturday from 9:30 a.m. to 5 p.m.

Canterbury Historic River Tours, Weaver's House, 1 St. Peter's St. (☎ **07790/534-744**), offers **half-hour boat trips** on the Stour River with a commentary on the history of the buildings you pass. From April through September, river conditions permitting, boats depart daily every half-hour from 10 a.m. to 5 p.m. Tickets are £4.80 ($8) for adults and £3.80 ($6) for children 5 to 15. Umbrellas are available in case of rain. Behind the 15th-century Weaver's House (enter through the Weaver's restaurant garden), the boats leave from the *ducking stool* (a chair tied to the end of a plank used for punishing miscreants in centuries past).

Staying in or near Canterbury

Canterbury itself has surprisingly few hotels, but other acceptable options are in the vicinity.

Abbot's Fireside Hotel

$ **Elham**

This pretty 15th-century hotel sits in the middle of Elham, a village 10 miles south of Canterbury, midway between Canterbury and Dover. The hotel is small and cozy, with only six medium-size rooms (all with private bathrooms). You find welcoming log fires, exposed beams, and a good restaurant. The staff welcomes children.

High Street, Elham (near Canterbury), Kent CT4 6TD. (By car from Canterbury: Take A2 southeast toward Dover; exit at Barham and drive through town to next village, which is Elham.) ☎ ***01303/840-265.*** *Fax: 01303/840-852. Internet:* www.abbotsfireside.com. *Rack rates: £75–£115 ($120–$180) double. Rates include English breakfast. AE, MC, V.*

Cathedral Gate Hotel

$ Canterbury

If you want to stay near the cathedral like the pilgrims of yore, you can't get any closer than this 27-room hotel adjoining Christchurch Gate (one of the gates into the cathedral precincts). Dating from 1438, the hotel has comfortable and modestly furnished rooms and an overall ambience of sloping floors, massive oak beams, and winding corridors.

36 Burgate, Canterbury, Kent CT1 2HA. ☎ ***01227/464-381.*** *Fax: 01227/462-800. Internet:* `www.cathgate.co.uk`. ***Rack rates: £46.50–£100 ($74–$160) double. Rate includes continental breakfast. AE, DC, MC, V.***

The Dickens Inn

$ Canterbury

This half-timbered Tudor inn is close to the Canterbury West train station, a five-minute walk from the town center. The inn has nine comfortable rooms, all with private bathrooms and modern amenities. A good on-site restaurant serves traditional English meals and afternoon teas.

71 St. Dunstan's St., Canterbury, Kent CT2 8BN. ☎ ***01227/472-185.*** *Fax: 01227/464-527. Internet:* `www.dickens-inn.co.uk`. ***Rack rates: £55–£75 ($88–$120) double. DC, MC, V.***

Dining in or near Canterbury

Restaurant options in and near Canterbury run the gamut from traditional to contemporary.

Augustine's

$–$$ Canterbury MODERN BRITISH

You find this fun, informal restaurant in a Georgian house just outside of the center of town, on the way to St Augustine's Abbey. This spot is a dependable neighborhood favorite that serves good cooking, including vegetarian dishes, using fresh, local ingredients. The relaxed atmosphere makes Augustine's a good spot for dining with children.

1 & 2 Longport. ☎ ***01227/453-063.*** *Fixed-price lunch: £8.95 ($14). Main courses: £12–£25 ($19–$40). MC, V. Open: Tues–Sat noon to 1:30 p.m. and 6:30–9 p.m., Sun noon to 2 p.m. Closed Jan.*

The Dove

$$–$$$ Dargate FRENCH/MEDITERRANEAN

Not many pubs serve food as good as this one, located a few miles southwest of town in the village of Dargate. The chef-owner offers a constantly changing menu that represents the best of French and Mediterranean-style cooking. A blackboard displays the daily specials. Whatever's fresh and in season appears on the menu, which may include cooked crab risotto, roast venison, grilled mackerel, braised beef; or duck.

Plumpudding Lane. (By car from Canterbury: Take A290 north to A299, turn west and exit at Dargate.) ☎ ***01227/751-360.*** *Main courses: £15–£25 ($24–$40). MC, V. Open: Tues–Sun noon to 2 p.m.; Tues–Sat 7–9 p.m.*

Sully's

$$–$$$ Canterbury TRADITIONAL BRITISH

This restaurant in the County Hotel is one of Canterbury's best. You can choose from a selection of traditional English dishes, try one of the more imaginatively conceived platters, or sample seasonal specialties, such as grilled lemon sole or roasted breast of pheasant.

County Hotel, High Street. ☎ ***01227/766-266.*** *Reservations recommended. Fixed-price lunch £17 ($27); fixed-price dinner £23–£28 ($37–$45). AE, DC, MC, V. Open: daily 12:30–2:30 p.m. and 7–10 p.m.*

Exploring Canterbury

Much of central Canterbury is a pedestrian-only zone, making it a pleasant place to stroll.

Canterbury Cathedral

Imagine how overwhelmed medieval pilgrims must have been when they first saw this massive and magnificent structure. The cathedral's origins date to A.D. 597, when St. Augustine arrived on a mission from Rome. Fire and Viking marauders destroyed the earlier church. What stands on the site today is the first cathedral in England to be built in the Gothic style. The crypt dates from about 1100 and the cathedral from the 13th century, with a central bell tower — called Bell Harry — added in the 15th century. After Archbishop Thomas à Becket was murdered in the cathedral in 1170, pilgrims from all over Europe began to flock to his shrine. Although Henry VIII destroyed Becket's shrine, its site is still marked in the **Trinity Chapel,** near the high altar. Noteworthy features of the cathedral include panels of rare **stained glass** and the medieval **royal tombs** of Henry IV and Edward the Black Prince. Give yourself at least an hour to visit the cathedral.

As you stroll the cathedral grounds, you may encounter flocks of well-behaved boys and girls wearing blazers and ties. They attend **King's School,** the oldest public school in England, housed in several fine medieval buildings (not open to the public) around the cathedral.

11 The Precincts. ☎ ***01227/762-862.*** *Admission: £4 ($6) adults, £3 ($4.80) children 5–15, students, and seniors. Open: Mon–Sat 9 a.m.–5 p.m. (Nov–March until 4:30 p.m.), Sun 12:30–2:30 p.m. and 4:30–5:30 p.m.; closed to sightseeing during services.*

The Canterbury Tales

This museum and exhibition is informative and entertaining even if you don't know a thing about Geoffrey Chaucer (1342–1400) or *The Canterbury Tales,* his spirited and sometimes bawdy stories about a group of medieval pilgrims on their way to visit Becket's shrine at Canterbury Cathedral. The pilgrimages that were so popular in Chaucer's time are re-created here in tableaux. You can hear five of Chaucer's tales and the story of St. Thomas à Becket's murder on **audio headsets.** Give yourself 45 minutes to an hour to see and hear the entire show.

23 St. Margaret's St., off High Street, in St. Margaret's Church. ☎ ***01227/454-888.*** *Admission: £6.50 ($10) adults; £5 ($8) seniors, students, and children 5–16. Open: daily Feb 19–June and Sept–Oct 10 a.m.–5 p.m.; July–Aug 9:30 a.m.–5:30 p.m; Nov–Feb 10 a.m.–4:30 p.m.*

Roman Museum

Two millennia ago, following their conquest of England, Romans lived in Canterbury, which they called *Durovernum Cantiacorum.* This small but fascinating museum, in the excavated Roman levels of the city between the cathedral and High Street, chronicles their daily lives. Allow 30 minutes.

Butchery Lane. ☎ ***01227/785-575.*** *Admission: £2.60 ($4) adults; £1.65 ($2.65) seniors, students, and children 5–15. Open: year-round Mon–Sat 10 a.m.–5 p.m.; June–Oct Sun 1:30–5 p.m.*

St. Augustine's Abbey

Although the cathedral gets the lion's share of attention in Canterbury, another Christian site predates the cathedral by about 600 years. Set in a spacious park, about a 15-minute walk east from the town center, are the atmospheric ruins of St. Augustine's Abbey, founded in A.D. 598 and one of the oldest Anglo-Saxon monastic sites in the country. You tour this World Heritage site with an **interactive audio tour.** Allow 30 minutes.

Trek another five minutes east from St. Augustine's Abbey and you encounter England's oldest parish church. No one knows for sure who founded **St. Martin's Church,** North Holmes Road (☎ **01227/459-482**), but it was already in existence when Augustine arrived from Rome to convert the Anglo-Saxon natives in A.D. 597. The tiny church was given to Queen Bertha, the French (Christian) wife of Saxon (pagan) King Ethelbert of Kent, as part of her marriage contract. The church is open daily from 9 a.m. to 5 p.m., and admission is free. Allow ten minutes at most; the church is tiny.

Longport. ☎ ***01227/767-345.*** *Admission: £3 ($4.80) adults, £2.30 ($3.70) seniors and students, £1.30 ($2.40) children under 16. Open: daily April–Oct 10 a.m.–6 p.m., Nov–Mar 10 a.m.–4 p.m.; closed Jan 1, Dec 24–26.*

Rye: Smugglers, Mermaids, and Writers

"**Rye** is like an old beautifully jewelled brooch worn at South-England's throat." So wrote Patric Dickinson, one of the many writers who have fallen under the spell of this remarkably beautiful coastal town in East Sussex. (See the "Rye" map in this chapter.) Henry James spent the last years of his life here, and E.F. Benson, author of *Mapp and Lucia*, was mayor. (Benson called the town "Tilling" in his novels.)

The town earned its official title, "The Ancient Town of Rye," nearly a millennium ago when Rye joined the federation of coastal defense towns known as the Cinque Ports. After a pleasurable stay in 1573, Queen Elizabeth I decreed that the town could use the additional title "Rye Royale." Located today about 2 miles inland from the English Channel, Rye was a powerful seaport that protected the coast from foreign marauders while carrying on a lively business in smuggling and piracy. That maritime history still clings to the cobblestone lanes threading through Rye.

Rye is small enough that you can see it all in about three hours, but so charming that you may want to spend the night. The town claims to have more historic buildings than any other town in England, and preservationists assiduously protect their appearance. As a result, you see buildings dating from the 13th century to the Victorian era, with no modern intrusions. Rye is also known for several excellent restaurants, many of which serve fresh, locally caught seafood.

Getting to Rye

Rye is 62 miles southeast of London. By train, visiting Rye is an easy day trip. Trains depart hourly from London's Charing Cross Station and require a change at Ashford International; the total trip takes about 1½ hours. The day return (round-trip) fare from London is £18.60 ($30). For train schedules, call ☎ **08457/484-950.** The easy walk from Rye train station on Cinque Ports Street to Strand Quay, a good place to start your explorations, takes about ten minutes.

Rye

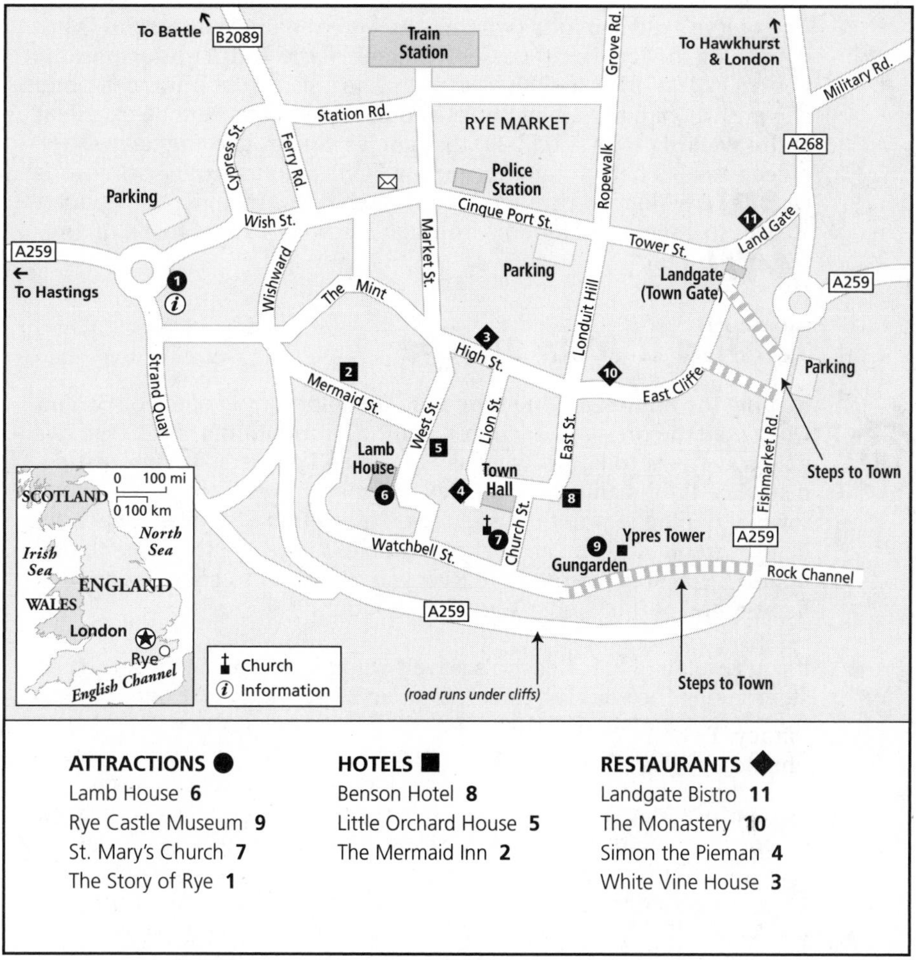

ATTRACTIONS ●
Lamb House **6**
Rye Castle Museum **9**
St. Mary's Church **7**
The Story of Rye **1**

HOTELS ■
Benson Hotel **8**
Little Orchard House **5**
The Mermaid Inn **2**

RESTAURANTS ◆
Landgate Bistro **11**
The Monastery **10**
Simon the Pieman **4**
White Vine House **3**

By car, Rye is 10 miles northeast of Hastings on A259. From London, take the M25, M26, and M20 east to Maidstone, turning southeast along A20 to Ashford; at Ashford, take A2070 south to Rye. Cars aren't allowed into the historic center, so you need to park in one of the nearby lots and walk from there. Currently, no bus service is available from London to Rye.

If you drive, you can easily combine a trip to Rye with a trip to Battle, scene of the momentous Battle of Hastings in 1066 (see "Battle: 1066 and All That," later in this chapter).

Finding information

One of Rye's old sail lofts (where sails were repaired) on Strand Quay now holds the Rye Heritage Center, home of the **Tourist Information Centre** (☎ **01797/226-696;** www.rye-tourism.co.uk). You can obtain a free town map here, buy books and postcards, and rent an excellent **audio walking tour** (£2/$3.20) that guides you around the town. The office can also help you to find a room. Office hours from April through October are Monday through Saturday from 10 a.m. to 5 p.m., Sunday 10 a.m. to 4 p.m., and Monday through Saturday 10 a.m. to 4 p.m. the rest of the year.

Taking a tour of Rye

Renting the **audio walking tour** from the information office on Strand Quay (see the previous section, "Finding information") is the best available way to get to know Rye. Easy to use and packed with interesting historical tidbits and ghost stories, the tour makes a circuit around the town, stopping to point out sights you may otherwise miss. Depending on how frequently you stop, the tour takes anywhere from one to three hours. If you stay overnight in Rye, you may want to consider an overnight rental of the "Ghost Walks" audio tour.

If you're a fan of E. F. Benson's novels set in Rye, you may want to consider taking the **walking tour "Mapp and Lucia's Rye."** Conducted by the Secretary of the E. F. Benson Society, the walk takes you past the characters' houses to the Benson memorials in St. Mary's Church and ends at Lamb House, the onetime residence of E. F. Benson. From the last week in May through September, the 90-minute walks take place on Wednesday and the first and third Saturday of the month at 2 p.m. Cost is £4.75 ($8) per person. You don't need to reserve in advance; just show up at Hilder's Cliff (the end of High Street). For more information, call ☎ **01797/223-114** or 01797/226-696. (Before coming to Rye, you may also want to watch the film versions of the books: The *Mapp and Lucia* stories, written in the 1920s and 1930s, were filmed in ten one-hour segments for television in the 1980s and are available on video.)

Staying in Rye

Rye offers any number of charming, historic places to stay, some with gardens, some with views out over Romney Marsh. Following is a sampling.

Benson Hotel

$

A former vicarage, this comfortable, three-story brick B&B sits just off High Street. The four guest rooms have four-poster beds and private bathrooms. From your room, you'll have a view over Rye's rooftops or out toward distant Romney Marsh.

East Street, Rye, East Sussex TN31 7JY. ☎ ***01797/225-131.*** *Fax: 01797/225-512. Internet:* www.bensonhotel.co.uk. ***Rack rates: £80–£94 ($121–$150) double.*** *Rates include breakfast. MC, V.*

Little Orchard House

$

This charming Georgian-era B&B is named for the romantic little orchard garden tucked behind the house. Period antiques and paintings decorate the two guest rooms; both have private bathrooms. The rate includes a generous country breakfast with many local and organic products.

West Street, Rye, East Sussex TN31 7ES. ☎ *and fax:* ***01797/223-831.*** *Internet:* www.littleorchardhouse.com. ***Rack rates: £64–£90 ($102–$144) double.*** *Rates include English breakfast. V.*

The Mermaid Inn

$$

When you enter this famous half-timbered inn, one of the oldest and loveliest in England, you're instantly wafted back to the "Olde England" of your dreams. The inn is hundreds of years old, full of ancient oak timbers, creaking floors, and huge fireplaces with log fires (plus a resident ghost or two). The 31 rooms, every one different, spread over several levels and have modern bathrooms. This is the best hotel in Rye, and has one of the best restaurants.

Mermaid Street, Rye, East Sussex TN31 7EU. ☎ ***01797/223-065.*** *Fax: 01797/225-069. Internet:* www.mermaidinn.com. ***Rack rate: £160–£200 ($256–$320) double.*** *Rates include English breakfast. Special rates with dinner available. AE, DC, MC, V.*

Rye's calendar of events

During August, Rye holds its **Medieval Weekend,** with a parade of costumed locals, a two-day fair, and a street market on High Street. In September, the town stages the **Rye Festival of Music and the Arts,** which features concerts and exhibitions. The town celebrates Guy Fawkes Night (November 5) with the **Rye Bonfire Weekend:** Bonfire societies from all over Sussex participate in a parade and torchlight procession through the darkened streets before the ceremonial bonfire and fireworks. For information about the holiday, see the sidebar "Famous failure: Guy Fawkes," later in this chapter. For more information about the celebration, contact the Tourist Information Centre at ☎ **01797/226-696**.

Dining in Rye

Rye is known for its restaurants, many of which serve fresh seafood.

Landgate Bistro

$–$$ **MODERN BRITISH**

This highly regarded bistro close to the old town gate is known for the quality of its local produce, fish, and lamb. The cooking is sophisticated but not fussy. For starters, you may have leek and Roquefort tart or wild-mushroom risotto. Main courses may include free-range chicken, wild rabbit, or "very fishy stew," which uses fresh, locally caught fish.

*Landgate. ☎ **01797/222-829.** Main courses: £9.90–£12.70 ($16–$20). AE, MC, V. Open: Tues–Sat 7:–9:30 p.m.*

The Monastery

$$ **MODERN BRITISH/FRENCH**

The Monastery, on busy High Street, is considered one of Rye's top restaurants. A sample menu may include garlic mushrooms with smoked bacon, poached salmon in white wine and dill, and lamb with red-currant jam and rosemary. In the summer, reserving a table in advance is a good idea.

*High Street. ☎ **01797/223-272.** Main courses: £12–£15 ($19–24), fixed-price dinner: £17.50 ($26). MC, V. Open: Tues–Sun noon to 2 p.m.; Tues–Sat 7–9:45 p.m.*

Simon the Pieman

$ **LIGHT FARE/AFTERNOON TEA**

At this charming tearoom in the shadow of St. Mary's Church, you can get a light lunch, cake and coffee, or an afternoon cream tea. Daily specials include homemade soups and sandwiches and an enticing selection of cakes, pies, and fudge.

*Lion St. ☎ **01797/22207.** Lunch: £3.50–£7 ($6–$12). Cream tea: £4.40 ($7). No credit cards. Open: Mon–Fri 9:30 a.m.–5 p.m., Sat 9:30 a.m.–5:30 p.m., Sun 1:30–5:30 p.m.*

Exploring Rye

Formerly a fortified island surrounded by the sea, Rye occupies a hill that now rises above the flat green expanse of Romney Marsh. From atop the former ramparts, you can see the River Rother, home to the local fishing fleet, winding its way toward the sea. Rye is a town to explore on foot (cars aren't allowed) and at your leisure. You can savor it in its entirety rather than in a specific church or museum. Rye is jam-packed with half-timbered Tudor and Elizabethan houses, handsome Georgian townhouses, secret passageways, quaint corners, cobbled lanes, windy viewpoints, enticing shops, and wonderful restaurants. (For a definition of the architectural styles mentioned in this paragraph, see Chapter 1.)

Lamb House

This dignified red-brick Georgian house is full of literary associations. The house was the last residence of the American writer Henry James, who became a British citizen at the end of his life and lived here from 1898 to 1916. In this house, James entertained many other writers, including H. G. Wells, Rudyard Kipling, and Joseph Conrad. One guest, E. F. Benson, acquired the house after James's death. Benson, who became mayor of Rye, went on to write a series of satirical novels set in the town. Visitors to Lamb House, now a National Trust property, can see some of the rooms and personal possessions used by James and Benson. The house also has a charming walled garden. You can see the house and garden in under a half-hour.

*West Street. ☎ **01892/890-651** (regional office of National Trust). Admission: £2.60 ($4.20) adults, £1.30 ($2.10) children 5–15. Open: April–Oct Wed and Sat 2–6 p.m.*

Rye Castle Museum

Rye's local history museum has two sites. The 12th-century **Ypres Tower** displays medieval pottery, ironwork, and items having to do with smuggling (for which Rye was notorious). Originally built as part of the town's defenses, the tower is one of Rye's oldest buildings. The structure survived the burning of the town by the French in the late 14th century and was later used as a prison and a mortuary. From the terrace, you can view what was once Rye's busy harbor. The **Gungarden** below the tower received its name from the small cannons mounted there for the symbolic protection of Queen Elizabeth, the Queen Mother, who made an official visit in the 1980s. (The Queen Mum was Warden of the Cinque Ports, an honorary title formerly held by Winston Churchill.) On East Street, a former bottling factory has been converted into the **East Street Gallery,** the second half of the museum. In the Gallery, you can see a splendid 18th-century fire engine, paintings and engravings of Rye, an exhibition of the famous local pottery, and maritime memorabilia. You can breeze through both of these sites in less than a half-hour.

*Pump Street (Ypres Tower) and East Street (Gallery). ☎ **01797/226-728.** Admission: joint ticket to both, £2.90 ($4.60) adults, £1.50 ($2.40) children 7–16, £5.90 ($9) families (2 adults, 2 children). Open: Apr–Oct, Mon, Thurs–Fri Tower 10 a.m.–1 p.m. and 2–5 p.m., Gallery 2–5 p.m., Sat–Sun, both 10:30 a.m.–1 p.m.; Nov–March, Tower only Sat–Sun 10:30 a.m.–3:30 p.m.*

St. Mary's Church

For almost 900 years, the parish church of St. Mary's has dominated the hill on which the old town stands. In 1377, French invaders looted the town, set it on fire, and carried the church bells off to France. The following year, men from Rye sailed to Normandy and brought the bells back. The church's turret clock, the oldest in the country, dates from 1561 and has an 18-foot-long pendulum. The church's "Quarter Boys" (bells so called because they strike the quarters but not the hours) were added in 1760. The church has several interesting stained glass windows, although none are very old. The most beautiful window, by Sir Edward Burne-Jones, dates from 1891 and can be seen in the north aisle. You can climb the church tower for a magnificent view out over the rooftops of Rye.

*Church Square. ☎ **01797/222-430.** Admission: tower, £1.50 ($2.40). Open: church and tower, daily 9 a.m.–6 p.m. (4 p.m. in winter). The tower isn't accessible to wheelchairs.*

The Story of Rye

Located in the same building as the tourist information center, this attraction uses an elaborate scale model of the town for a miniature sound-and-light show detailing highlights in Rye's long and sometimes bloody history. Kids usually enjoy the spectacle. The show lasts approximately 20 minutes and provides a good overall introduction.

*Rye Heritage Center, Strand Quay. ☎ **01797/226-696.** Admission: Adults £2.50 ($4), £1.50 ($2.40) seniors, £1 ($1.60) children 5–15. Open: daily 10 a.m.–3 p.m.*

Battle: 1066 and All That

If you ever studied English history, the year 1066 probably rings a bell. The date is important because in that year, Duke William of Normandy defeated Harold, king of England, at the Battle of Hastings. After the battle, William became known as William the Conqueror. He had himself crowned king at Westminster Abbey and Winchester and began construction of the Tower of London and other fortifications that you can still see today. William's conquest of England ended the post-Roman Anglo-Saxon era. For taxation purposes, the new monarch compiled a list of every property and building in his newly conquered land. The list became the famous *Domesday Book,* a unique record of England in the 11th century. (The original *Domesday Book,* housed in the Public Records Office in London, isn't accessible to the public. You can, however, peruse its contents on the Web at `www.domesdaybook.co.uk`.)

But all this history started with a battle, and that's where Battle comes into the viewfinder. In the town, preserved behind high brick walls, is the actual battlefield where the Saxon and Norman soldiers clashed on that fateful day in 1066. (Many people think that the Battle of Hastings took place in Hastings, but the conflict happened here, 6 miles inland.) For anyone with an interest in history, Battle is a memorable spot to visit. Basing yourself in nearby Rye or Brighton, you can come to Battle as part of a larger tour of southeast England, or you can come to Battle for a day trip from London. Local tourist associations refer to the Sussex countryside around Battle as "1066 Country."

Getting to Battle

Battle is 57 miles south of London. Direct train service is available from London's Charing Cross Station (Battle is a stop on the London-Hastings line). The trip takes about 90 minutes; a standard day return (round-trip) costs about £16 ($26). There are also train connections from Rye, about 18 miles southeast, via Hastings. The easy walk from the Battle train station to the battlefield entrance on High Street takes about ten minutes. (To get to the battlefield, turn left outside the station and right at the first main street.) For train schedules and information, call ☎ **08457/484950.**

By car, Battle is about 6 miles north of Hastings on A2100. Parking lots are near the entrance to the battlefield.

National Express (☎ **0990/808-080;** www.gobycoach.co.uk) offers evening-only bus service from London's Victoria Coach Station, but I don't recommend that you spend the night in Battle, so use this option as a last resort.

Finding information

The **Battle Tourist Information Centre,** 88 High St. (☎ **01424/773-721;** www.battletown.co.uk), across from Battle Abbey, has a free town pamphlet that includes a map. The center is open daily from 10 a.m. to 6 p.m. in summer, 10 a.m. to 4 p.m. in winter.

Dining in Battle

A plethora of restaurants and tearooms beckon travelers along High Street. For hearty and traditional home-cooked English food, try the **Gateway Restaurant,** 78 High St. (☎ **01424/772-056**), open daily from 9 a.m. to 5:30 p.m. Lunch specials usually include several old-fashioned pies: steak, ale, and mushroom; steak and kidney; and chicken, leek, and bacon. You can also get toasted sandwiches, baguettes with different fillings, an all-day brunch, or an afternoon cream tea (£4/$6). Lunch costs about £4.50 to £5.50 ($7 to $9); no credit cards are accepted.

Another atmospheric place for a simple hot lunch, snack, or afternoon tea with homemade cakes is the **Copper Kettle,** also on High Street (☎ **01424/772-727**). It's in the Almonery, a lovely, beamed medieval hall (where the Town Council meets) with a pretty, walled garden. The shop is open Monday through Saturday from 9:30 a.m. to 4:30 p.m. Lunch costs under £5 ($8); no credit cards are accepted.

Famous failure: Guy Fawkes

In the front hallway of the Almonery, the building on High Street that houses the Copper Kettle (see "Dining in Battle," in this chapter), you can see one of the oldest Guy Fawkes sculptures in the country, bearded and dressed in black and red with a pointed hat. Residents parade the figure around town before a bonfire is lit on Guy Fawkes Night, November 5.

Who, you may ask, was Guy Fawkes (1570–1606)? Guy was the most famous guy behind the Gunpowder Plot, a conspiracy of Catholic extremists to blow up Protestant King James and the Houses of Parliament. On November 4, 1605, poor Guy was caught red-handed in the Palace of Westminster. The treasonous plot, and Guy Fawkes's subsequent execution, gave rise to a popular rhyme:

Please to remember / The 5th November:

Gunpowder, Treason and Plot.

We know of no reason / Why Gunpowder Treason

Should ever be forgot.

Every year since 1605, on November 5, residents of towns, villages, and cities throughout England light bonfires, toss firecrackers, and parade or burn an effigy of Guy Fawkes to celebrate his failure to blow up the king and the Parliament. Guy Fawkes Night is perhaps the longest running tradition in England, even though the religious and royalist sentiments that inspired it have long vanished.

Exploring the 1066 Battle of Hastings Abbey and Battlefield

Make sure that you visit this site in Battle, and give yourself at least two unhurried hours to take it all in. This attraction offers a fascinating journey back in time. The preservationist organization English Heritage, which owns the site, has done a clever job of making the experience both interesting and informative. You receive an **audio guide** when you pay for your ticket.

The tour starts with an outdoor video presentation, *1066 — The Battle of Hastings,* that fills you in on the major events leading up to the battle. Next comes an exhibition, "Prelude to Battle," which uses text panels to draw you deeper into the story of the intrigues and the royal power struggle between King Harold and Duke William of Normandy. Finally, you walk onto the battlefield itself. The long (complete) tour takes about an hour; a shorter version takes about 45 minutes. Take the longer tour if you have time (and the weather is good).

Linked to your audio guide, descriptive panels line the pathway around the battlefield. The battle's unfolding events are presented as seen through the eyes of three different narrators: Aelfric, a Saxon thane; Henri, a French knight; and Edith, the wife of King Harold. As you tour the battlefield, you can follow the story and tactics used by both sides from these three perspectives. The vivid, first-hand accounts of the battle are fictional, but they bring history alive for kids of all ages.

King Henry VIII dissolved the great abbey that William had constructed to mark the spot where King Harold was slain. Today, the abbey is an atmospheric ruin, but you can explore several rooms.

Entrance at south end of High Street. ☎ ***01424/773-792.*** *Admission: £5 ($8) adult, £3.80 ($6) seniors, £2.50 ($4) children 5–15, £12.50 ($20) families (2 adults, 2 children). Open: daily April–Sept 10 a.m.–6 p.m., Oct 10 a.m.–5 p.m., Nov–March 10 a.m.–4 p.m. (last audio tour issued one hour before closing); closed Jan 1, Dec 24–26. Uneven terrain makes much of the battle site inaccessible to wheelchair users; however, a short gravel path does wind through part of the site.*

Brighton: Fun Beside the Seaside

On the Sussex coast, a mere 50 miles south of London, **Brighton** is England's most famous, and probably most popular, seaside town. (See the "Brighton" map in this chapter.) Brighton was a small fishing village until the Prince Regent, a fun-loving dandy who reigned as George IV from 1820 to 1830, became enamored of the place and had the incredible Royal Pavilion built. Where royalty moves, fashion follows, and Brighton, on the English Channel, eventually became one of Europe's most fashionable towns. (The long terraces of Georgian town homes that you see everywhere in Brighton date from that period.) Later in the 19th century, when doctors prescribed breathing sea air as a cure for everything from depression to tuberculosis, the Victorians descended in hordes. (The famous Brighton pier is from that era.) Today, Brighton is a popular place for weekend getaways. People come to hang out on the long stretch of beach, shop, stroll, and party the night away at clubs and discos. Gays and lesbians are very much a part of the local and visitor scene.

Getting to Brighton

Connex South Central runs more than 40 trains a day from London's Victoria Station. The trip takes about an hour; an off-peak (after 9:30 a.m.) round-trip ticket costs £15.10 ($24). For train schedules call **☎ 08457/484-950.**

National Express (☎ 0990/808-080; `ww.gobycoach.co.uk`) runs hourly buses from London's Victoria Coach Station. A same-day round-trip ticket for the two-hour journey costs £9 ($14). If you drive, the M23 from Central London leads to Brighton. The drive should take about one to 1½ hours, but if the roads are clogged, the trip may take twice as long.

Brighton

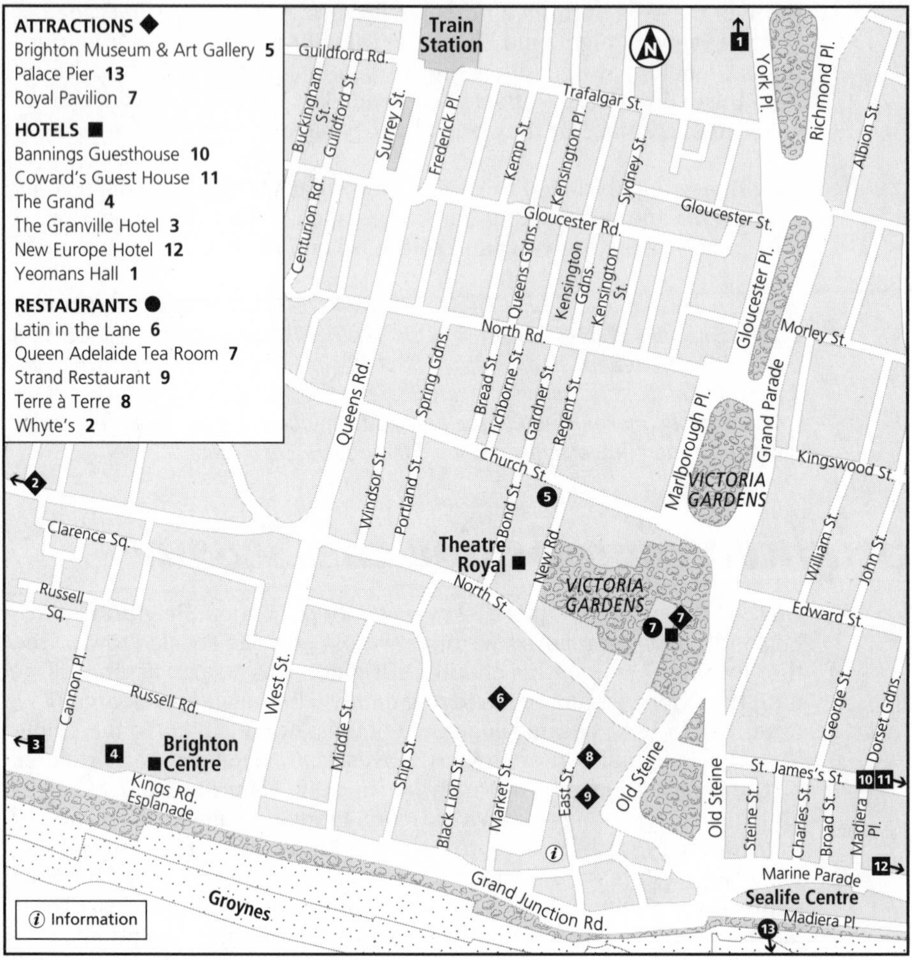

ATTRACTIONS ◆
Brighton Museum & Art Gallery **5**
Palace Pier **13**
Royal Pavilion **7**

HOTELS ■
Bannings Guesthouse **10**
Coward's Guest House **11**
The Grand **4**
The Granville Hotel **3**
New Europe Hotel **12**
Yeomans Hall **1**

RESTAURANTS ●
Latin in the Lane **6**
Queen Adelaide Tea Room **7**
Strand Restaurant **9**
Terre à Terre **8**
Whyte's **2**

ⓘ Information

Finding information

Brighton's **Tourist Information Centre,** 10 Bartholomew Sq. (☎ **0906/ 711-2255;** `www.tourism.brighton.co.uk`), is opposite the town hall, about a ten-minute walk south from the train station. The center is a good place to pick up a map and information on current events. You can also reserve a room here. The center is open Monday through Friday from 9 a.m. to 5:30 p.m., Saturday from 10 a.m. to 5 p.m., and Sunday from 10 a.m. to 4 p.m.

At the Tourist Information Centre, gay and lesbian visitors can ask for the Gay Information Sheet, which lists guesthouses, pubs, and clubs.

Getting around Brighton

Brighton is a compact town, and the easiest way to get around is on foot. While here, forget about that frantic need for sightseeing and relax. That's what Brighton is all about. This is a place for leisurely strolling, either in the town or along the seaside promenades. Brighton is small enough so you won't get lost and large enough to offer some good cultural diversions. **Brighton and Hove Bus Company** (☎ **01273/886-200**) offers frequent and efficient service; the local fare is £1.20 ($1.90). Taxis are usually available at the train station, or you can call **Streamline** (☎ **01273/747-474**) for a cab.

Staying in or near Brighton

Brighton is a favorite weekend getaway spot, and you find many hotels and B&Bs. The Tourist Information Centre, 10 Bartholomew Sq. (☎ **0906/711-2255;** `www.tourism.brighton.co.uk`), can also help you find a room.

The Grand

$$$$ **Brighton**

The grandest place to stay in Brighton is the Grand, a huge, dazzling white resort hotel built on the seafront in 1864. The Grand, the only five-star luxury hotel in Brighton, has 200 spacious and predictably gorgeous guest rooms, done mostly in blues and yellows, with big tile baths. The most expensive rooms have sea-facing balconies and floor-to-ceiling, double-glazed windows. The welcoming staff, attentive to the needs of families with children, can help arrange baby-sitting.

King's Road, Brighton, East Sussex BN1 2FW. ☎ ***01273/224-300.*** *Fax: 01273/224-321. Internet:* `www.grandbrighton.co.uk`. *Rack rates: £230–£250 ($368–$400) double. Rates include English breakfast. Lower weekend and "leisure" rates available. AE, DC, MC, V.*

The Granville Hotel

$–$$ **Brighton**

Located opposite the West Pier, Granville's is a good choice if you're looking for a smaller hotel on the sea front. A former townhouse, this place has 24 individually designed rooms, all with private bathrooms and some with four-poster beds. The hotel is completely nonsmoking and welcomes families with children.

124 Kings Rd., Brighton, East Sussex BNT 2FA. ☎ ***01273/326-302.*** *Fax: 01273/728-294. Internet:* `www.granvillehotel.co.uk`. *Rack rates: £85–£145 ($136–$232) double. Rates include breakfast. MC, V.*

Brighton's gay and lesbian hotels and B&Bs

Several hotels and B&Bs in Brighton cater to gay and lesbian visitors. **Bannings Guesthouse,** 14 Upper Rock Gardens, Brighton, Sussex BN2 1QE (☎ **01273/681-403;** www.bannings.co.uk) is a snug Georgian townhouse for women only; the guesthouse has six rooms, all with private bathrooms, which cost £45 to £50 ($72 to $80) for a double, breakfast included. **Coward's Guest House,** 12 Upper Rock Gardens, Brighton, Sussex BN2 1QE (☎ **01273/692-677**), is a dapper Regency-era townhouse that caters to men; it has six rooms with private bathrooms, which rent for £45 to £60 ($72 to $96) double, breakfast included. The **New Europe Hotel,** 31–32 Marine Parade, Brighton, Sussex BN2 1TR (☎ **01273/624-462;** Fax: 01273/624-575; www.legendsbar.co.uk), is the largest (30 rooms) gay-owned and -operated hotel in Brighton. A double room with private bathroom costs £60 to £65 ($96 to $104), breakfast included. The hotel is also the home of Legends, one of the most popular gay clubs in town.

Yeomans Hall

$ **Blackstone**

A quiet countryside alternative, this 15th-century house is 6 miles northwest of the brash bustle of Brighton in the farming village of Blackstone. Comfortably furnished, Yeomans Hall features exposed beams and inglenook fireplaces. Three guest rooms are available, two with private bathrooms.

Blackstone, near Henfield, Sussex BN5 9TB. ☎ ***01273/494-224.*** *E-mail:* stay@yeomanshall.fsnet.co.uk. *Rack rates: £48–£55 ($77–$88) double. Rates include breakfast. No credit cards.*

Dining in Brighton

Brighton is known for its restaurants. It boasts dozens of places to dine, at all levels of the culinary ladder. Here are a few of my recommended choices.

Latin in the Lane

$–$$ **ITALIAN/SEAFOOD**

At this restaurant you can sample Italian antipasti, such as melon with Parma ham or mixed salami with fresh figs, and then go on to pastas or fish, which comes fresh from the market every day. Seafood risotto with wild mushrooms, cream, and white wine is good, and so is the casserole of fresh, seasonal seafood and mussels in white wine, parsley, and garlic.

10/11 King's Rd. ☎ ***01273/328-672.*** *Main courses £6–£14 ($10–$22). AE, DC, MC, V. Open: daily noon to 2:15 p.m. and 6:30–11 p.m.*

Strand Restaurant

$–$$ MODERN BRITISH/SEAFOOD

One of the hippest (and friendliest) places for dining is the bow-fronted Strand. The ever-changing menu may include starters such as herby homemade vegetable soup, pâté, or mussels cooked with fresh cream, wine, and garlic, followed by chicken breast with leeks and blue cheese sauce, artichoke-and-pesto lasagna, or lamb chops with gravy.

6 Little East St. ☎ ***01273/747-096.*** *Main courses: £8–£15 ($13–$24). AE, DC, MC, V. Open: daily 12:30–10 p.m.*

Terre à Terre

$–$$ VEGETARIAN

Considered the best vegetarian restaurant in England, perhaps in Europe, Terre à Terre elevates meatless cuisine to the art it should be but rarely is. The food is impeccably fresh and beautifully presented. You can eat your way through the menu with the Terre à Tapas, a superb selection of the best dishes, big enough for two. On the menu, you find imaginative dishes, such as Camembert soufflé and *Chianti pomodoro bolla* (a tomato dish made with Chianti).

71 East St. ☎ ***01273/729-051.*** *Reservations essential on weekends. Main courses: £10–£11 ($16–$18). DC, MC, V. Open: Mon 6–10:30 p.m., Tues–Sat noon to 10:30 p.m., Sun 10 a.m.–10:30 p.m. (brunch 10 a.m.–1 p.m.).*

Whyte's

$$–$$$ MODERN BRITISH

The cooking at this dressy establishment, housed in a tiny bow-fronted cottage just off the seafront, is among the best in Brighton. Starters may be herbed salt cod with red pepper syrup and poached egg or wild smoked salmon strips. The main-course offerings may include succulent roast fillet of lamb or crispy roast duckling with raspberry-vinegar sauce; Whyte's also offers a daily fresh fish and vegetarian dish.

33 Western St. ☎ ***01273/776-618.*** *Reservations required. Fixed-price dinners: £17.50–£21 ($28–$34). MC, V. Open: Tues–Sat 7–10 p.m.*

Exploring Brighton

Brighton is a fun city to explore. It's compact enough that you can walk everywhere, but large enough that you can discover quiet streets off the beaten tourist track. A stroll along the seaside promenade is an essential part of any trip to Brighton.

Brighton Museum & Art Gallery

Close to the Royal Pavilion on Church Street is the city's small museum and art gallery. Here you find interesting collections of Art Nouveau and Art Deco furniture, glass, and ceramics, plus a fashion gallery. It's a good place to wile away a spare hour. After a refurbishment in 2001, the museum looks much fresher than it used to.

Church Street. ☎ ***01273/290-900.*** *Admission: free. Open: Mon–Tues and Thurs–Sat 10 a.m.–5 p.m., Sun 2–5 p.m.*

Palace Pier

The town's famous amusement area juts out into the sea just south of the Royal Pavilion. The pier was built in the late 19th century when Brighton became a major holiday resort. Today, Palace Pier looks rather tacky but is still worth visiting. At night, all lit up with twinkling lights, the pier is almost cheerily irresistible. Spend a half-hour here, but don't expect to find much more than junk food and arcade games.

Seafront. Admission: free. Open: 24 hours.

Royal Pavilion

Set in a small landscaped park, Brighton's must-see attraction is one of the most extraordinary palaces in Europe. John Nash redesigned the original farmhouse and villa on this site for George IV (when the king was still Prince Regent). The fun- and food-loving George lived here with his mistress, Lady Conyngham, until 1827. The king's brother, William IV, and their niece, Queen Victoria, also used the pavilion. Finding the accommodations too cramped and lacking a sea view, Victoria closed the Royal Pavilion, put the furnishings into storage, and moved to Osborne House on the Isle of Wight. The city of Brighton eventually got the furnishings back and opened the pavilion to the public. Give yourself about an hour for a leisurely walk-through tour.

A pier of the realm collapses

Brighton has two famous piers, but only the tacky Palace Pier is open to visitors today. The other, West Pier, was built in 1866 and reached its heyday in the 1920s, when it had a concert hall and charged admission to keep the riffraff at bay; it closed in 1975 for safety reasons. Plans to renovate West Pier, the only pier in Britain that has received the top heritage grade designation, gained urgency just before New Year's 2003, when a chunk of the ornate structure collapsed into the sea. At last report there was still no consensus on what to do with what was once the greatest piece of marine architecture in England.

Tea at the pavilion

Before you leave the Royal Pavilion, consider having lunch or a cream tea in the superbly restored **Queen Adelaide Tea Room** (**☎ 01723/292-736**), open daily 10:30 a.m. to 4:30 p.m. (to 5 p.m. in summer). Queen Adelaide, who used this suite in 1830, didn't appreciate the epicurean tastes of her husband, George IV. Dismissing his renowned French chefs, she reverted to English cuisine so dreary that Lord Dudley complained, "You now get cold pâté and hot champagne." The lunch selections range from £3 to £5 ($4.80 to $8) and cream teas from £4 to £6 ($6 to $10).

The crazily wonderful exterior is an Indian fantasy of turrets and minarets. The interior, decorated in the Chinese style, is sumptuous and fantastically extravagant. The **Long Gallery** has a color scheme of bright blues and pinks, the **Music Room** has a domed ceiling of gilded, scallop-shaped shells, and the **King's private apartments** on the upper floors epitomize the Regency lifestyle of the rich and royal.

Bounded by North Street, Church Street, Olde Steine, and New Road. ***☎ 01273/290-900.*** *Admission: £5.80 ($9) adults, £4 ($4.50) students and seniors, £3.40 ($4) children under 16, £15 ($24) families (2 adults, up to 4 children). Open: daily Oct–Mar 10 a.m.–5:15 p.m., Apr–Sept 9:30 a.m.–5:45 p.m. Closed Dec 25–26. Wheelchair users should call first.*

Seafront

Brighton and neighboring Hove stretch out along the English Channel. The entire seafront is a pebbly public beach used for swimming and sunning. If you're into sunbathing *au naturel,* Brighton has the only nude beach in England, about a mile west of Palace Pier. All along the seafront are promenades for strolling.

Shopping in Brighton

The Lanes, Brighton's original fishing village, is now a warren of narrow streets filled with small shops selling upscale goods and many tourist trinkets. **North Laines** has more interesting shops, including some trendy outfitters. **Duke's Lane** is a good place to look for men's clothing, and **Duke Street** and **Upper North Street** are good for antiques.

Shops in Brighton are generally open Monday through Saturday from 10 a.m. to 6 p.m., with a later closing on Thursday or Friday. During the summer tourist season, some shops are open on Sunday and closed on Monday.

Stepping out in Brighton, night or day

Brighton is preeminently a resort town, a place where people go to relax and have fun. The nighttime scene is a lively one, especially from April through September.

The performing arts

The **Brighton International Festival** (☎ **01273/292-950;** `www.brighton-festival.org.uk`), one of England's best-known arts festivals, happens in May and features a wide array of drama, literature, visual art, dance, and concert programs ranging from classical to hard rock. England's best actors regularly appear at the **Theatre Royal,** New Road (☎ **01273/328-488**), which presents a full season of dramatic works.

The highly regarded **Brighton Philharmonic Orchestra** (☎ **01273/622-900**) performs a season of classical concerts at **The Dome,** 29 New Rd. (adjacent to the Royal Pavilion). Built in 1803 as the stables for George IV's horses and remodeled into a concert hall in 1935, The Dome is a venue for concerts of all kinds. When internationally known performers come to town, they play at the 5,000-seat **Brighton Centre,** Russell Road (☎ **01273/202-881**).

The pub and club scene

Brighton fills up on the weekends, especially in summer, with folks looking for a good time. You find many choices for nighttime entertainment. Pick up a copy of the local entertainment weekly, *The Punter,* or look for *What's On,* a weekly events sheet posted around town, to find out what's happening. Pub hours are Monday through Saturday from 11 a.m. to 11 p.m. and Sunday from noon to 10:30 p.m. Dance clubs open later and sometimes remain open for 24-hour stretches on weekends. Clubs generally have a cover charge of £5 to £7 ($8 to $11).

Clubbers usually start their evening at a bar or pub. One good place to begin is the 100-year-old **Colonnade Bar,** New Road (☎ **01273/328-728**). An even older establishment — parts of it date to the 16th century — is **The Cricketers,** Black Lion Street (☎ **01273/329-472**). **Cuba,** 160 King's Road (☎ **01273/770-505**), is a popular beachside drinking spot. **Steamers,** King's Road (☎ **01273/775-432**), is also popular (and loud) on Friday and Saturday nights.

When you're ready to dance, one place you can try is **Event II**, Kingswest on West Street (☎ **01273/732-627**), which boasts state-of-the-art lighting and visual effects. At **Gloucester,** Gloucester Plaza (☎ **01273/699-068**), you find different music all through the week: from '70s and '80s retro hits to alternative and groove.

Gay and lesbian spots

Brighton's "Gay Village" centers on St. James's Street, east of the Royal Pavilion, and along the seafront. Ask at the tourist information center for a list of current gay and lesbian nightlife choices. All the gay pubs and bars are fairly close to one another. Pub hours are Monday through Saturday from 11 a.m. to 11 p.m. and Sunday from noon to 10:30 p.m. **Legends,** the smartly redecorated bar in the New Europe Hotel, 31–32 Marine Parade (☎ **01273/624-462**), has a cabaret area for weekly entertainment. Summer weekends are a nonstop buzz at the big new **Amsterdam** hotel bar, 11–12 Marine Parade (☎ **01723/688-825**). **The Harlequin,** 43 Providence Place (☎ **01273/620-630;** open pub hours), a cabaret bar with weekly drag shows and karaoke, has been voted the best gay bar outside London. **Marlborough,** 4 Princes St. (☎ **01273/570-028;** open pub hours), a traditional pub in the heart of town, is popular with lesbians. **Club Revenge,** 32 Old Steine St., opposite the Palace pier (☎ **01273/606-064),** spreads over two floors and holds about 700 people; the club has lasers, smoke machines, and views of the seafront. A sociable crowd packs the place.

Chapter 15

Kent's Best Castles, Stately Homes, and Gardens

In This Chapter

- Exploring Knole, one of England's largest homes
- Visiting Anne Boleyn's Hever Castle
- Calling at Chartwell, home of Winston Churchill
- Lollygagging in Leeds Castle
- Strolling through the great garden at Sissinghurst
- Viewing the White Cliffs from Dover Castle

The county of Kent is rich in castles, stately homes, and magnificent gardens. All are within about 50 miles of London, so you can visit them on day trips. Alternatively, you can incorporate Kent's most famous sights into a car tour of the Southeast. (For ideas on towns to visit, see Chapter 14.)

Kent is known as the Garden of England (see the "Kent's Castles, Stately Homes, and Gardens" map in this chapter). A mild year-round climate favors Kent, where fruit grows and hops ripen in the summer sun. Old walled orchards and conical *oast* (hops-drying) houses are still part of the landscape. Kent has more gardens open to the public than any other county in England. With the one exception of Dover Castle, the castles and stately homes that I describe in this chapter all have superbly landscaped grounds.

Don't worry about finding a meal. In every castle, home, and garden you find at least one restaurant or tea shop where you can get lunch, a snack, or tea.

Kent's Castles, Stately Homes, and Gardens

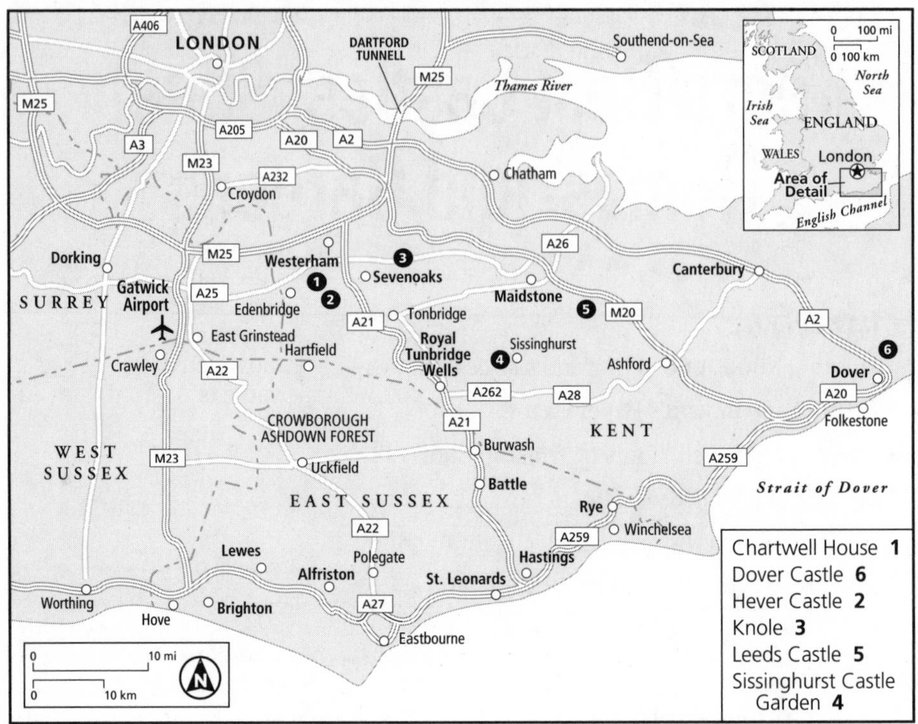

The places in this chapter are all in the country. They're near small towns with rail stations but not always within easy walking distance of the station. You can, however, visit them all by train or bus, continuing by taxi when necessary. Taxis are generally available outside the train stations. If you drive yourself, make sure that you have a good map with you. I do provide directions to each sight, but as soon as you're off the motorway and main roads, Kent is full of winding lanes. The attractions have parking on-site or in parking lots.

The Web site `www.traintaxi.co.uk` provides information about taxi service from every train station in England. The site gives you the phone numbers of local taxi companies so that you can make reservations and have a cab waiting when you arrive.

Knole: A Room for Every Day of the Year

Set in a picturesque deer park, this great country homestead houses important collections of portraits, silver, tapestries, and 17th-century furniture. What makes **Knole** so wonderfully unique is its size and the fact that the house has remained basically unaltered since 1603. A visit here is an ideal day trip from London; be sure to give yourself at least three hours to take it all in.

Getting to Knole

Frequent train service connects Sevenoaks Station, 1½ miles from the Knole, to London's Charing Cross Station. The journey takes 30 minutes and costs about £8.50 ($14) for a day-return (round-trip) ticket. Call ☎ **08457/484-950** for train schedules. From the rail station, you can walk to the park entrance in the center of Sevenoaks or take the connecting hourly bus service. You can also find cabs at the station or call **Bluebird ☎ 01732/45531** to reserve one in advance; one-way taxi fare to the entrance is about £3 ($4.80). By car, Knole is 5 miles north of Tonbridge, off A225.

Exploring Knole

With its skyline of gables, chimneys, battlements, and pinnacles, this enormous house resembles an entire village. Like a well-protected medieval community, Knole has a central gatehouse with an inner gatehouse (Bourchier's Tower). The gatehouses may conjure up visions of a traditional castle, but they are, in fact, entirely decorative.

Thomas Bourchier, Archbishop of Canterbury, purchased the land and original house at Knole in 1456. He set about transforming the fortresslike building into a home suitable for Princes of the Church (the archbishop of Canterbury, as the spiritual head of the Church of England, wielded enormous wealth and power). Four more archbishops resided at Knole before Henry VIII took possession of the house (just as he took possession of Hampton Court Palace, home of Cardinal Wolsey). Henry VIII enlarged Knole until it was suitable as a royal palace, but he never spent much time there. His daughter, Elizabeth I, presented the house and estate to her cousin Thomas Sackville, the 1st Earl of Dorset, in 1566. His descendants have lived at Knole ever since. Knole was the childhood home of Vita Sackville-West, who created the gardens at Sissinghurst Castle. (See the section, "Sissinghurst Castle Garden: Romance amongst the Roses," later in this chapter.)

In 1603, the 1st Earl enlarged and embellished what would become one of England's greatest houses. Occupying some 4 acres, Knole was built with seven courtyards, representing the days of the week, 52 staircases, one for each week of the year, and 365 rooms, one for every day of the year. The 13 state rooms open to the public are magnificent representatives of the Elizabethan and Stuart eras. Rooms that you can tour include three long galleries, each with an adjoining state bedroom, and the King's Bedroom, which has a 17th-century bed decorated with gold and silver thread and topped with ostrich feathers.

In addition to its outstanding tapestries and textiles, important portraits by Van Dyck, Gainsborough, and Reynolds fill the house. Among the house's original features are the fine plasterwork ceilings, the carved wooden screen in the Hall, and the painted walls of the staircases. The elaborate marble and alabaster chimneypiece and mantle in the Ballroom (the former living quarters of Archbishop Bouchier) stretches from floor to ceiling and is considered one of the finest works of Renaissance sculpture in England.

Large herds of fallow and Japanese deer roam the parkland surrounding the house. The private garden is open only once a month and requires separate admission. A tearoom where you can get lunch or tea is on the premises.

Tonbridge Road, Sevenoaks. ☎ ***01732/462-100*** *or 01732/450-608 (recorded information). Admission: house £5.50 ($9) adults, £2.75 ($4) children 4–15, £13.75 ($22) families (2 adults, 2 children); garden £2 ($3.20) adults, £1 ($1.60) children 4–15; deer park free to pedestrians. Open: house Mar 22–Nov 2 Wed–Sun 10:30 a.m.–5 p.m.; garden May–Sept first Wed of the month 11 a.m.–4 p.m.; park open daily; tearoom Mar 22–Nov 2 Wed–Sun 1–4.30 p.m.*

Hever Castle: Anne Boleyn Slept Here

A lovely, moated castle set amid immaculately landscaped gardens 30 miles south of London, **Hever Castle** was the childhood home of Anne Boleyn (1507–1536), the second wife of Henry VIII. Anne of Cleves, Henry's fourth wife, also lived here. In 1903, the American millionaire William Waldorf Astor bought the castle and created the beautiful gardens. Hever is a fairly easy day trip from London. Give yourself at least an hour for the house and another two hours to enjoy the gardens.

Getting to Hever Castle

From London's Victoria Station, trains depart throughout the day for two stations near Hever Castle. The trip takes an hour and costs about £10.50 ($17) for a day round-trip ticket. You must change trains at East Croyden. From **Hever Station**, it's a pretty 1-mile, 15-minute walk to the castle. Taxis aren't available at this station. **Edenbridge Town Station** is 3 miles from the castle. From the station, you can take a taxi to the castle. Booking a cab in advance is a good idea; without doing so, you may have to wait for an hour or more. Call **Rely On Cars** (☎ **01732/863-800**) or **Edenbridge Cars** (☎ **01732/864-009**); the one-way taxi fare from the train station to the castle is about £5 ($8).

On Sunday, you may have to get off at the **Edenbridge Station** and take a taxi to the castle; one-way fares are about £5 ($8). For taxi companies, see the preceding information for Edenbridge Town Station. If you're traveling to Hever Castle on a Sunday, always check to find out whether the train stops at Edenbridge Town Station or Edenbridge Station.

By car, Hever Castle is 3 miles southeast of Edenbridge, midway between Sevenoaks and East Grinstead off B2026. From London, take the M25 and exit at junction 5 or 6.

Exploring Hever Castle

Hever Castle's long and varied history stretches back over seven centuries. To experience this rich history, you can wander through the rooms in the castle at your own pace; guides can answer your questions.

The castle's stone gatehouse and outer walls were constructed in the 13th century. In about 1500, the Boleyn (or Bullen, as it was then written) family added a more comfortable Tudor manor house within the walls. In the middle of divorcing his first wife, Catharine of Aragon, Henry VIII wooed Anne Boleyn at Hever Castle.

Henry VIII's desire for Anne Boleyn helped change the course of English history. When Catharine of Aragon didn't produce a male heir, the king turned his eye to Anne. Hoping that the 25-year-old Anne would give him the successor he wanted, Henry sought to divorce Catherine. When the pope refused Henry's request, Henry broke with the Catholic Church and established the Church of England with himself as head. He then married Anne, but she also failed to deliver a male child. (Her first child was Elizabeth I, who became one of England's greatest monarchs.) Eventually, Henry had Anne arrested on trumped-up charges of adultery and incest with her brother George. Both Boleyn siblings were executed, George first and then the unfortunate Anne, who was beheaded at the Tower of London. She is sometimes known as Anne of the Thousand Days because that's how long she was queen.

After Anne's demise and the death in childbirth of his third wife, Jane Seymour, the much-married monarch gave Hever Castle to his fourth wife, Anne of Cleves, who lived there after Henry divorced her. You can view costumed likenesses of Anne, Henry, and his other five wives in the **waxwork exhibition,** "The Six Wives of Henry VIII," on the top floor of the castle.

William Waldorf Astor acquired Hever Castle in 1903 and spent a fortune restoring it. What you see today is a result of Astor's preservation efforts. Inside, splendid carving and paneling cover the castle walls. Antiques, some interesting works of art, including portraits of Anne Boleyn and her daughter, Elizabeth, and a Holbein painting of Henry VIII fill the rooms. You can also view two of Anne's prayer books. In 2003, two newly acquired portraits of Mary Queen of Scots went on display.

The **gatehouse,** which is the last room you visit, contains a grisly collection of torture instruments, including beheading axes. Anne asked for a French axe to be used on her neck — she knew French axes did a quicker, cleaner job.

Further enhancing the castle's romantic setting, Astor created the magnificent **gardens** between 1904 and 1908, which include the **Italian Garden,** filled with statuary and sculpture collected in Italy and dating from Roman to Renaissance times; the **Maze;** a 35-acre lake; and the **rose garden.** The **Tudor herb garden,** close to the castle, opened in 1994.

Two self-service restaurants serving hot lunches, snacks, and teas are on the premises.

*Edenbridge. ☎ **01732/865-224**. Admission: castle and garden £8.40 ($13) adults, £7.10 ($11) seniors, £4.60 ($7) children 5–15, £21.40 ($34) families (2 adults, 2 children). Open: April–Oct daily, gardens 11 a.m.–5 p.m., castle noon to 5 p.m.; March and Nov until 4 p.m. Closed Dec–Feb.*

Chartwell: The Private Life of a Famous Prime Minister

Chartwell House was the home of Sir Winston Churchill (1874–1965) from 1924 until he died. The home can't compare with the grandeur of Blenheim Palace (see Chapter 13), where Churchill was born, but if you're interested in the personal life of Britain's wartime prime minister and one of its great statesmen, **Chartwell** will fascinate you. Give yourself at least 1½ hours to visit the house and gardens. If you're driving, you can easily combine a visit to Chartwell with a visit to Hever Castle or Knole.

Getting to Chartwell

From London's Charing Cross Station, you can hop on frequent train service to **Sevenoaks**, 6½ miles east of Chartwell, and to **Oxted**, 6 miles west of Chartwell. The journey takes about 40 minutes and costs about £8.50 ($14) for a day-return (round-trip) ticket. Call ☎ **08457/484-950** for train schedules. From either station you can take a cab to Chartwell. To reserve a taxi from Sevenoaks, call **Bluebird** (☎ **01732-45531**); from Oxted, call **Terrys** (☎ **01883/712-623**) or **D Line** (☎ **01883/715-576**). The taxi fare is approximately £8 ($13).

By car, Chartwell is 2 miles south of Westerham; fork left off B2026 after 1½ miles.

Exploring Chartwell House

The National Trust administers Chartwell, a family home where the rooms and gardens remain much as Churchill left them. Churchill's watercolors, pictures, maps, and personal mementos are on display throughout, and you see first editions of his books (Churchill won the Nobel Prize for Literature). His energy and range of interests was prodigious: You can trace his career from his school days at Harrow to his years as a war correspondent, Chancellor of the Exchequer, parliamentarian, and prime minister. Some of his famous uniforms and hats are on display, and you can hear tapes of his speeches. In addition to the house, you can visit the beautiful terraced gardens containing the lakes he dug, the brick wall he built with his own hands, the water garden where he fed his fish, and his garden studio, which holds many of his paintings.

Westerham. ☎ ***01732/866-368.*** *Admission: house, garden, and studio £6.50 ($10) adults, £3.25 ($5) children 5–15, £16.25 ($26) families (2 adults, 2 children). Open: Mar 22–June and Sept 3–Nov 9 Wed–Sun 11 a.m.–5:30 p.m.; July–Aug Tues–Sun 11 a.m.–5:30 p.m.; Nov 12–Dec 21 Wed–Sun 10:30 a.m.–5 p.m.*

Leeds Castle: Castle of Queens, Queen of Castles

Leeds Castle, tucked away in the Kent countryside 40 miles southeast of London, is one of the world's most beautiful castles. Built on two small islands, its stone facade mirrored in a lake, this treasure trove of history has enough in its rooms and gardens to beguile you for half your day. Coming here is an easy day trip by train or bus from London, or you may want to combine a visit with an overnight trip to Canterbury or Rye (see Chapter 14).

Getting to Leeds Castle

Trains run frequently from London's Victoria Station to **Maidstone** and **Bearsted** stations; the latter is closer to the castle. **Connex (☎ 0870/603-0405;** `www.connex.co.uk`) offers an all-in-one ticket to Bearsted Station with connecting bus service to and from the castle; the cost is £21.50 ($34) for adults, £10.80 ($17) for children. **National Express (☎ 08705/808-080;** `www.nationalexpress.co.uk`) runs a "Days Out" bus-and-admission package from London's Victoria Coach Station every day that the castle is open. Buses leave at 9 a.m. and arrive at Leeds Castle at 10:30 a.m. Depending on the day you travel, the package costs £15 to £17 ($24 to $27) for adults, £10 to £12 ($16 to $19) for children. By car, from London's ring road, continue east along the M26 and M20; the castle is 4 miles east of Maidstone at the junction of A20 and the M20.

Exploring Leeds Castle

Part of Leeds' fascination lies in the stories of its various owners. The castle reflects the changing tastes and fortunes of several families and dozens of generations. The original buildings were wood, constructed in A.D. 857 during the Saxon era. After the Norman Conquest of 1066, the buildings were given to the French Crevecoeur family, who rebuilt them in stone. The castle's vineyard (still producing) is listed in the *Domesday Book,* tax records compiled in 1086. Under Edward I, in 1278, Leeds became a royal palace. During the medieval era, six queens of England lived there. Faces from many eras greet you as you walk through the castle. Look for the portrait of Catharine of Valois (it hangs near her apartments). Catherine, the widow of Henry V, eloped with Owen Tudor. Henry VIII, their great-grandson, stayed at the castle often, and added the Tudor windows.

By the mid-16th century, Leeds was no longer a royal palace. A house was built on the larger island in the early 1600s. An owner in the 18th century, the 6th Lord Fairfax, owned 5 million acres of land in Virginia and was a mentor and friend to George Washington. After several more owners, Olive Lady Baillie purchased the house in 1926 and completely transformed the inside. Her collections of medieval and Renaissance tapestries, Chinese porcelain, paintings, and furniture give Leeds Castle a sumptuous quality.

The tour of Leeds Castle begins in the **Norman Cellar,** passes through the medieval **Queen's Rooms,** and into Henry VIII's richly decorated **Banqueting Hall.** The circuit then takes you into a suite of rooms decorated in the 1920s. In the Gatehouse, where you enter, is something dog lovers won't want to miss: the **Dog Collar Museum,** with a collection that dates back to the 16th century.

Your first glimpse of Leeds Castle is from the **Wood Garden and Duckery,** which you pass through on the way to the entrance. In the spring, wood anemones carpet the banks of the stream; swans and wildfowl live here year-round. The **Culpeper Garden,** named for the castle's 17th-century owners, is a large cottage garden planted with lavenders, roses, lupins, and poppies that start blooming in early summer. The **Lady Baillie Garden** takes its inspiration from the Mediterranean. If you reach the center of the **Maze,** you're rewarded with entry into a mysterious underground grotto.

Often overlooked is the **Aviary,** which opened in 1988 and houses more than 100 species of rare and endangered birds, including parrots, toucans, cockatoos, kookaburras, and cranes.

Two restaurants serve hot meals. You also find a tearoom and snack stands throughout the grounds.

*Maidstone. ☎ **01622/765-400.** Admission: summer, £12 ($19) adults, £10.50 ($17) seniors and students, £8.50 ($13) children 4–15, £35 ($56) families (2 adults, 2 children); off-season, small discount. Open: daily Apr–Oct 10 a.m.–5 p.m, Nov–Mar 10 a.m.–3 p.m.; closed Dec 25 and on two days in June and July for classical concerts.*

Sissinghurst Castle Garden: Romance amongst the Roses

The writer Vita Sackville-West and her diplomat husband, Sir Harold Nicolson, created **Sissinghurst,** one of the world's most famous gardens. Sissinghurst Castle, an Elizabethan manor house with a central red-brick tower, was in ruins when the Nicolsons bought it in 1930. Vita, who had grown up in the huge manor house at Knole (see "Knole: A Room for Every Day of the Year," earlier in this chapter), developed a garden scheme that is like a series of small, enclosed compartments, intimate in scale, romantic in atmosphere, and filled with color year-round. Her goal was to create a garden of "profusion, extravagance, and exuberance within the confines of the utmost linear severity."

Getting to Sissinghurst Castle Garden

The nearest train station, **Staplehurst,** is 5½ miles away. Direct trains run from London's Charing Cross Station; the trip takes just under an hour and costs about £7.50 ($11) for a combined rail-bus ticket. From Staplehurst Station, take Cranbrook bus to the village of Sissinghurst; from there, the castle gardens are an easy 1¼-mile walk on pavement and through countryside. From Staplehurst Station, you can also get a cab; cost one-way to the gardens is about £7 ($11); to reserve a taxi, call **MTC** (**☎ 01580/890-003**) or **Weald** (**☎ 01850/893-650**). For train information, call **☎ 0845/484-950.** By car, the garden is 2 miles northeast of Cranbrook and 1 mile east of Sissinghurst village on A262.

Exploring Sissinghurst Castle Garden

What you see at Sissinghurst is a beautiful garden with lush plantings that soften a strict formal design. The **White Garden,** with foliage and blossoms that are entirely white or silver, is probably the most celebrated of the several "rooms" that make up Sissinghurst. Every season has its highlights. In April and May, primroses carpet the **Nuttery,** and the **Spring Garden** is full of blossoming daffodils and other bulb plants. The orchard holds an enticing **Wild Garden.** Many people come specifically to see the summer roses. Vita Sackville-West planted hundreds in every form and helped return some lost roses to cultivation. Lovely old varieties climb through trees and over walls. In June and July, a wave of fragrance ascends all over the garden from the thousands of roses blooming everywhere.

The **library** and the **tower study** where Vita worked are also open to visitors. You can have lunch or tea at the Granary Restaurant on the premises.

Note: Sissinghurst limits the number of guests in its garden at any given time. Upon your arrival, you receive a ticket that indicates your admittance time. Waiting times depend on the season and time of day. If you arrive during peak times (summer 11 a.m. to 4 p.m.), you may have to wait an hour or more for admittance; the garden is least crowded in April, September, and October, and after 4 p.m. on Tuesday to Friday year-round. If you arrive after 4 p.m. on Tuesday to Friday, you get in immediately. No wheelchairs and strollers are admitted (the paths are narrow and uneven), but baby carriers are available.

Sissinghurst, near Cranbrook. ☎ ***01580/710-700*** *or 01580/710-701 (recorded information). Admission: £6.50 ($11) adults, £3 ($4.80) children, £16 ($26) families (2 adults, 2 children). Open: March 22–Nov 2 Fri–Tues 11 a.m.–5.30 p.m., Nov 5–Dec 21 Wed–Sun 11 a.m.–4 p.m.; last admission 1 hour before closing.*

Dover Castle: Towers and Tunnels

Dover is one of the busiest Channel ports, with thousands of visitors arriving daily on ferries and hovercrafts from the Continent. Unfortunately, your first impulse upon seeing Dover may be to leave town as quickly as possible. The town is low on charm and has the transient, unfocused air of a place where people pass through but never stay. Many people want to visit Dover to see the famed white cliffs. A better reason to visit — the only reason, in my opinion — is to explore **Dover Castle.** Sitting high on a cliff top, overlooking the Channel, the castle is awash with 2,000 years of history, right through World War II. Dover Castle puts on a good show, one that everyone can enjoy. You can go there as a day trip from London or, if you're arriving in Dover by ferry, you can visit the castle before heading on to other parts of the country. I don't recommend that you stay overnight in Dover.

Getting to Dover Castle

Dover is 77 miles southeast of London, on the English Channel. Frequent train service connects London's Victoria Station to **Dover Priory Station**. The trip takes about one hour and 40 minutes; a round-trip ticket costs about £21 ($35). Call ☎ **0845/484-950** for train schedules. From the train station, you can walk through the town to the castle — about a 1½-mile trek, part of it uphill — or get a cab right outside the station (the fare will be about £5/$8). From early May through September, the daily **Guide Friday** (`www.guidefriday.com`) bus service travels from the station to the castle entrance, stopping at other attractions along the way. The sightseeing bus, which operates hourly between 10 a.m. and 4 p.m., costs £6 ($10) for adults, £5 ($8) for seniors and students, and £2.50 ($4) for children. I don't recommend traveling to Dover from London by bus as a day trip because the trip takes anywhere from two hours and 40 minutes to three hours. **National Express** (☎ **0990/808-080**) runs coaches between London's Victoria Coach Station and Dover throughout the day; return fare is £17.50 ($28). By car, the castle is on the east side of Dover, signposted from the M20 and A2.

The castle covers some 70 acres and offers plenty to see. If you don't want to walk from place to place within the compound, take the free Land Train that makes a circuit of the grounds. You can get a free map when you enter.

Exploring Dover Castle

Start with the **Secret Wartime Tunnels.** The entrance to the tunnels is near the castle's general visitor entrance. You can only visit these tunnels with a **guided tour** (allow 40 minutes), and you may have to wait on busy days, but it's well worth it. The tour takes you into the labyrinth of underground tunnels that were used during World War II as a hospital and general war office. Wartime sound and light effects accompany your visit. The rooms have been preserved as they were during the war; you see the Underground Command Center, the hospital with its operating room, and the living quarters.

The other sites within the castle compound are set up as separate attractions (all included in your ticket price). In the **Keep Yard,** you find an introductory film that you can use to help plan what you want to see. You can view a 2,000-year-old **lighthouse tower** (called "the Roman pharos") dating from the Roman occupation of Britain, and a much-restored Saxon church beside it. The **1216 Siege Experience,** an audio tour of an exhibit that includes sound and light effects, tells the story of the unsuccessful French siege of the castle. You can look out over the channel on the **Battlement Walk** and explore the **Medieval Tunnels.** Kids particularly enjoy the Secret Wartime Tunnels and the 1216 Siege Experience because of the special effects.

For a glimpse of those famed white cliffs of Dover, which are sadly turning a bit brown because of air pollution, climb the steps to **Admiralty Look-out.**

If all this clambering around makes you hungry, head to the restaurant in the Keep Yard, where you can get hot food and snacks.

Dover. ☎ ***01304/201-628.*** *Admission: £7 ($11) adults, £5.30 ($8) seniors, £3.50 ($5) children 5–15, £17.50 ($26) families (2 adults, 2 children). Open: daily April–Sept 10 a.m.–6 p.m., Oct 10 a.m.–5 p.m., Nov–March 10 a.m.–4 p.m.; closed Jan 1, Dec 24 to 26.*

Part V
The West Country

"I think I'll have the Cocoa Puffs shepherd's pie."

In this part . . .

The West Country is a bold, mysterious place. Rugged moors stretch like a spine down the center of a narrowing peninsula that begins in Hampshire and ends in Cornwall at the rocky headland called Land's End. Giant prehistoric landmarks — Stonehenge being the most famous — dot the landscape. Centuries of wind and rain have worn down the ancient Celtic crosses that stand like lonely sentinels in village churchyards. The sea beats incessantly along the peninsula's north and south coasts. The West Country also happens to have England's mildest climate, with spring coming earlier and autumn lingering later than in the rest of the country. The area is also one of the most appealing regions to visit.

In Chapter 16, I introduce you to the best places in Hampshire and Wiltshire. Bucolic Hampshire was part of the ancient Saxon kingdom of Wessex. Winchester, the kingdom's most beautiful city, is a two-hour train ride from London. The landscape starts to change in Wiltshire, where Stonehenge, that great silent challenge to modern sensibilities, stands on the flat expanse of Salisbury Plain.

I devote Chapter 17 to Devon, home to the cathedral city of Exeter and enormous Dartmoor National Park, one of the most unspoiled natural landscapes in England. In Chapter 18, I take you to Cornwall. Penzance on the south coast and St. Ives on the north make good bases for exploring Land's End and other special places in this westernmost county in the West Country.

Chapter 16

Hampshire and Wiltshire: Old Wessex and New Sarum

In This Chapter

- Wending your way through Winchester
- Sauntering through Salisbury
- Visiting Stonehenge

The Hampshire countryside has a bit of everything: marshland and heath, traditional farms and quiet villages with thatched-roof cottages, ancient woodlands, rolling hills, narrow lanes, and *chalk downs* (high, open, grassy land over a chalk-limestone substrate). Hampshire is basically an agricultural county known for special crops, such as watercress, strawberries, and hops, with large-scale farming appearing on the scene more recently. Along its south coast is the naval town of Portsmouth, with the Isle of Wight lying across the channel known as The Solent.

Wiltshire, adjoining Hampshire to the west, is a fertile county characterized by undulating chalk downs and stretches of woodland. Over the centuries, farmers and herders have used much of the county for sheep grazing. The flat and mostly treeless expanse of Salisbury Plain, an area well known to prehistoric inhabitants of England, dominates the central part of Wiltshire. The Ridgeway, the oldest known path in England, crosses the plain, and it was here that ancient peoples erected mysterious stone-circle monuments like Stonehenge. Salisbury is a good place to headquarter if you want to explore the Wiltshire countryside. Wilton House, one of England's finest stately homes, is close by, as are the magnificent gardens at Stourhead, one of the oldest and most famous landscape gardens in England.

For an overview, see the "Hampshire and Wiltshire" map in this chapter.

Hampshire and Wiltshire

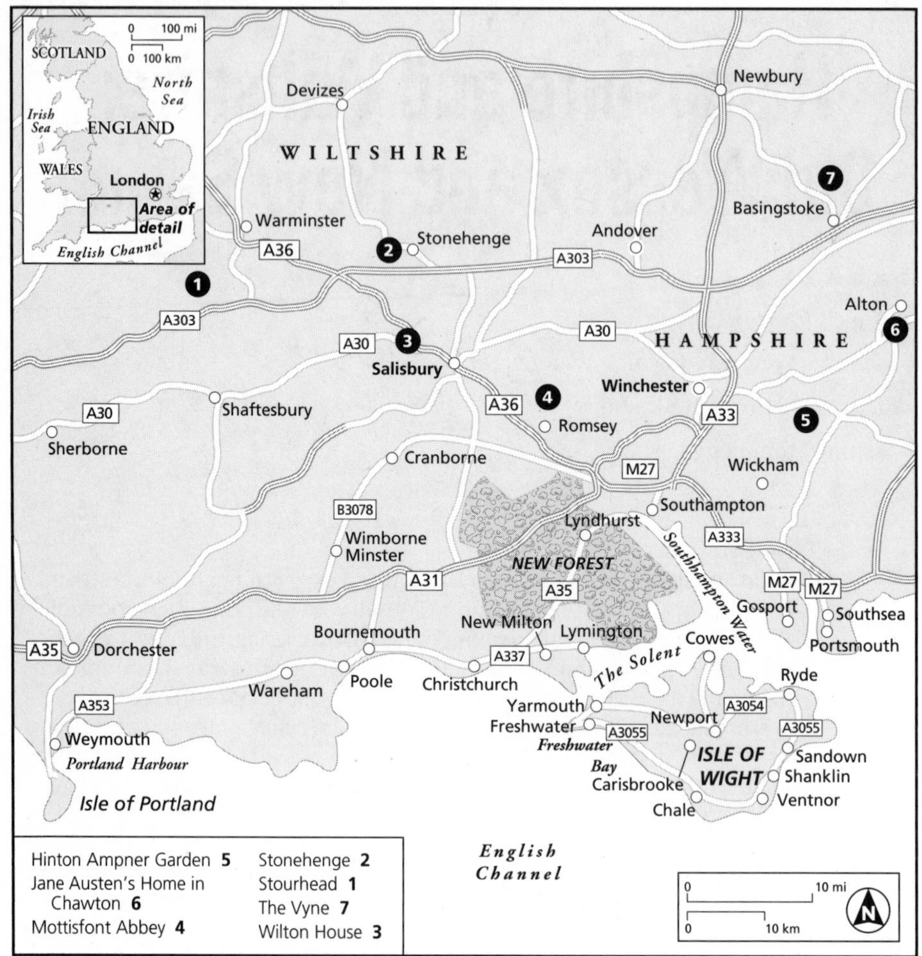

Welcome to Wessex

Hampshire, along with Wiltshire and several other counties in southern England, was part of the ancient kingdom of Wessex formed by Saxons in the fifth century, following the withdrawal of Roman troops from England. Winchester, the Hampshire town of most interest to visitors, was the capital of this ancient kingdom. The countryside around Winchester is home to some famous manor houses and gardens.

Winchester: King Alfred Meets Jane Austen

King Alfred and Jane Austen didn't really meet, of course, because they lived almost a thousand years apart. But Alfred (849–899), the great Saxon king of Wessex, and Jane Austen (1775–1817), the brilliant novelist, are the most prominent personalities associated with Winchester, the capital of the ancient kingdom of Wessex. Elusive, legendary King Arthur has a spot of honor, too — King Arthur's Round Table has been on display here for more than 600 years. Another famous visitor was William the Conqueror, who came to Winchester to claim his crown after the Battle of Hastings (see Chapter 14). William founded the present cathedral, and in Winchester he ordered the compiling of his inventory of England, the *Domesday Book*. But long before Arthur, Alfred, William, or Jane, the Romans were here — Winchester's High Street was their east-west route through the city.

I recommend that you visit **Winchester** as a day trip from London (see the "Winchester" map in this chapter). Reaching Winchester and exploring the city is easy. One of the best-kept and prettiest small cities in England, it evokes its ancient heritage with pride. The cathedral alone is worth a trip. With a walk, lunch, and afternoon tea, you can spend a very pleasant day indeed in the old capital of Wessex.

Getting to Winchester

Frequent, direct train service (☎ **08457/484-950**) goes from London's Waterloo Station to Winchester. The trip takes about one hour; a same-day return (round-trip) ticket costs £19.40 ($31). The center of town is about a half-mile from the station. To get there, you can easily walk (ten minutes), hop on a white park-and-ride bus (15p/30¢), or take a taxi (about £3.50/$6) from the rank outside the station. **National Express** (☎ **0990/808-080**) runs several buses a day from London's Victoria Coach Station; the fastest trip takes two hours (the longest, more than four hours); a round-trip ticket costs £12 ($19). The bus lets you off on Broadway, in the center of town. If you're driving from London, take the M3 to Junction 9. You can't drive in the town center; you find parking lots on the roads coming into the city.

Finding information and taking a tour

The ultra-helpful **Tourist Information Centre,** in the Guildhall on Broadway (☎ **01962/840-500;** `www.winchester.gov.uk`), has loads of local info and a free, **self-guided walking tour** booklet. You can also buy tickets for guided walking tours that make a 1½-hour circuit

Winchester

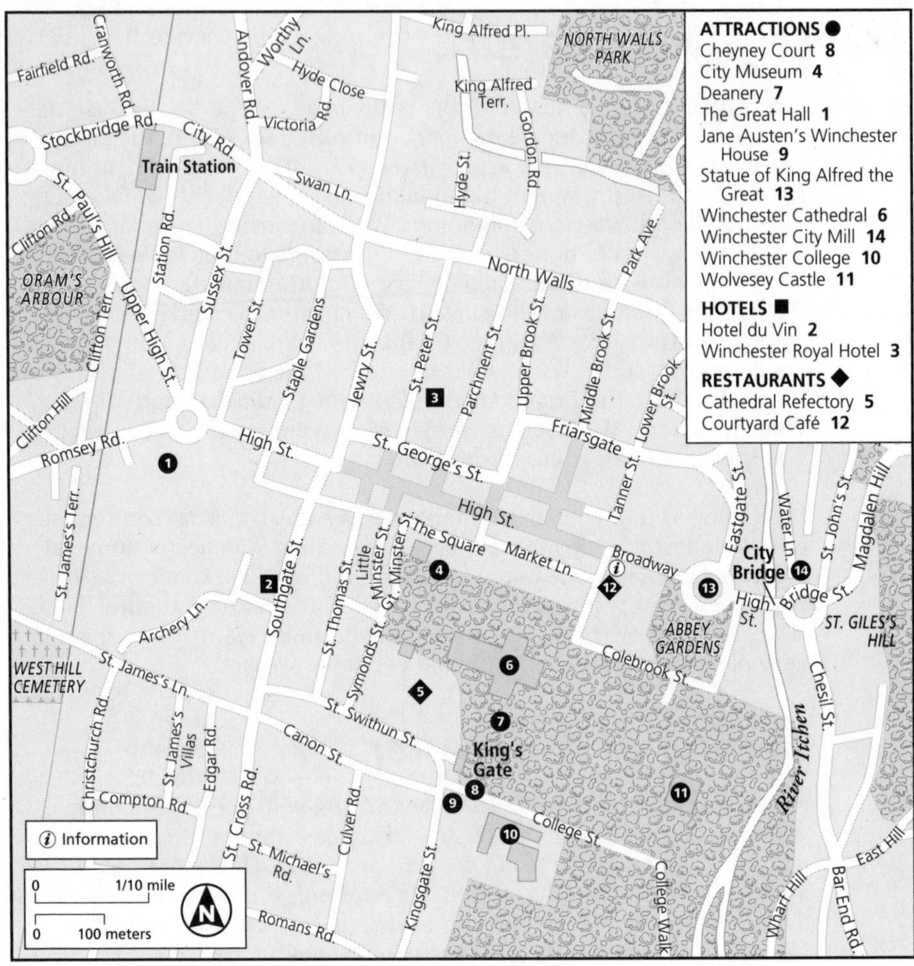

around this fascinating city. Tours leave the center January through March on Saturday at 11 a.m. and 2:30 p.m.; in April Monday through Friday at 11 a.m. and Saturday at 11 a.m. and 2:30 p.m.; in May and June Monday through Friday at 11 a.m., Saturday at 11 a.m. and 2:30 p.m., and Sunday at 2:30 p.m.; in July and August Monday through Saturday at 11 a.m. and 2:30 p.m. and Sunday at 2:30 p.m.; in October Monday through Saturday at 11 a.m. and 2:30 p.m.; and in November and December on Saturday at 11 a.m. Tour price is £3 ($4.80) for adults, free for kids. The center is open June through September Monday through Saturday from 11 a.m. to 6 p.m. and Sunday from 11 a.m. to 2 p.m.; October through May Monday through Saturday from 11 a.m. to 5 p.m.

Staying in Winchester

The Tourist Information Centre has a hotel-booking service. If you want to spend the night, I recommend the following hotels:

- **Hotel du Vin,** Southgate Street, Winchester, Hants SO23 9EF (☎ **01962/841-414;** Fax: 01962/842-458; www.hotelduvin.com), is a stylish townhouse hotel with a good bistro. Double with breakfast from £105 to £185 ($168 to $296).
- **Winchester Royal Hotel,** St. Peter Street, Winchester, Hants SO23 8BS (☎ **01962/840-840;** www.marstonhotels.com), is comfortable, full of character, and close to the cathedral. Doubles with breakfast £150 ($240).

Finding lunch or a spot of tea

The **Courtyard Cafe** (☎ **01962/622-177**), in the Winchester Guildhall right behind the Tourist Information Centre, is a great, informal spot for a morning cappuccino; homemade soups, salads, and sandwiches at lunchtime; or an afternoon tea. Lunch costs about £5 to £7 ($8 to $11). The cafe is also a gallery; prints and photographs line its walls. The cafe is open daily from 9:30 a.m. to 5 p.m.

The **Cathedral Refectory,** Inner Close (☎ **01962/853-224**), is behind a medieval wall next to the cathedral. This spot specializes in desserts and meals made from fresh local ingredients. Lunch costs about £6 to £10 ($10 to $16). Hours are Monday through Saturday from 9:30 a.m. to 5 p.m. and Sunday from 10 a.m. to 5 p.m.

Exploring Winchester and the surrounding area

The main attraction in Winchester is the ancient cathedral. After viewing the cathedral, stroll through the town using the walking tour I describe in this section. Jane Austen fans can visit her former homes in Winchester and in the nearby village of Chawton, but the latter requires at least two additional hours if you rely on public transportation.

Visiting the top attraction: Winchester Cathedral

Nine-hundred-year-old Winchester Cathedral occupies the heart of the city and is the repository of many historic treasures. In all, 12 English kings lie here, indicative of Winchester's long reign as capital of Wessex and England after the Norman Conquest. The cathedral you see today was begun in 1079, after the Conquest, and has the longest *nave* (the long central hall of a church) in Europe. **Jane Austen's grave** is a simple, stone-floor marker in the north aisle. A few feet farther along is a **12th-century font** made of Tournai marble carved with stories of St. Nicholas (patron saint of pawnbrokers long before he became known as Old Saint Nick). Above and on either side of the **Great Screen,** an elaborate carving completed in 1476, you see **mortuary chests** containing the remains of Saxon kings and bishops. The beautiful **choir stalls** were carved in about 1308. Check out the **Winchester Bible,** an extraordinary illuminated manuscript, in the library. For a leisurely stroll through the cathedral, give yourself about 45 minutes.

The world-famous **Winchester Cathedral Choir** sings at all main services, including *Evensong* (a service in which part of the liturgy is sung), held Monday though Saturday at 5:30 p.m. and Sunday at 3:30 p.m. Visitors are welcome to attend.

Winchester (in the town center). ☎ ***01962/853-224.*** *Admission: £3.50 ($6) suggested donation. Open: daily 7:15 a.m.–6 p.m. Tours: Mon–Sat free 50-minute tours of cathedral 11 a.m. and 3 p.m.*

Strolling through Winchester: A walking tour

Winchester is a walking city par excellence, with all sorts of fascinating corners in which you can poke around. What follows is a walking tour that takes about two hours, or longer if you linger:

1. **Winchester Cathedral and Precincts:** Begin your tour at Winchester Cathedral, one of Europe's greatest cathedrals. See "Visiting the top attraction: Winchester Cathedral" the preceding section, for the cathedral's highlights. After exploring the interior, step outside. Adjacent to the cathedral is the **Deanery,** formed from 13th-century buildings that had belonged to the Priory of St. Swithin (which stood here before Henry VIII dissolved all the monasteries in 1539). **Cheyney Court,** the picturesque half-timbered porter's lodge beside the ancient priory gate (King's Gate) was formerly the Bishop of Winchester's courthouse. The Deanery and Cheyney Court buildings aren't open to the public.
2. **Jane Austen's Winchester house:** Walk through King's Gate and turn left onto College Street. Almost immediately you come to a private house with a plaque on it. This is where Austen died on July 18, 1817, aged 42. Austen scholars believe she died of Addison's disease, a malfunctioning of the adrenal glands. The ailing writer came to Winchester from the nearby village of Chawton so she could be close to her doctor. She is buried in Winchester Cathedral. Farther down Queen Street are the buildings of **Winchester College,** the oldest public school in England, founded in 1382. There's no public access to the Austen house or the college.
3. **Winchester City Mill** and **Statue of King Alfred the Great:** Follow College Street to the end and turn left. Then take the short, lovely walk along the narrow River Itchen, which served as part of the Roman defense system. To your left are the remains of **Wolvesey**

Castle, a 12th-century bishop's palace destroyed during the Civil War of 1642 to 1649. At the end of Bridge Street, you come to the City Bridge, an 1813 reconstruction of a Saxon span built 1,000 years earlier. On the opposite side of the bridge is the **Winchester City Mill** (☎ **01962/870-057**). You can stop in to have a look at the mill's restored machinery, an exhibition on the history and surroundings, and a pretty island garden that's home to kingfishers, otters, and water voles. The mill is open 11 a.m. to 5 p.m. Saturday and Sunday in March; Wednesday through Sunday from April to the end of June and from September through October; daily in July and August. Admission is £2 ($3.20).

Turn left on Bridge Street and you see the famous bronze **statue of King Alfred the Great** holding aloft his sword. What, you ask, made Alfred so great? Probably that he was an enlightened man in the Dark Ages, and drove off the marauding Danes. A soldier, statesman, and scholar, he made Winchester the capital of his southern England kingdom, called Wessex. Winchester remained as powerful and prosperous as London even after the Norman Conquest of 1066.

4. **City Museum:** Walk down Broadway to The Square and you find the small, attractive **City Museum** (☎ **01962/863-064**). Upstairs you come upon a room devoted to Roman Winchester, with a fine Roman mosaic centerpiece. You can see everything in about 15 minutes. Admission is free. Hours are Monday through Saturday from 10 a.m. to 5 p.m., Sunday from noon to 5 p.m. (November through March until 4 p.m. and closed Monday).
5. **King Arthur's Round Table** and **The Great Hall:** Continue down High Street and turn left (south) through the Westgate, a fortified medieval gateway. All that remains of once-mighty Winchester Castle is the **Great Hall** (☎ **01962/846-476**) on Castle Avenue. The stone hall is famous for displaying something that isn't what legend claims it is: the Round Table of King Arthur and his knights. Looking like a giant Wheel of Fortune, the painted wooden table has hung here for some 600 years. King Arthur, if he ever existed, was probably a Romano-British chieftain of the fifth century. (Do the math.) The hall is open daily 10 a.m. to 5 p.m. (until 4 p.m. on winter weekends). Admission is free.

Taking a side trip to Chawton

Jane Austen's house in Chawton is about 17 miles northeast of Winchester. **Stagecoach Hampshire Bus** (☎ **01256/464-501**) No. X64 runs from Winchester Bus Station to Chawton at 10 minutes past each hour Monday through Saturday; on Sunday and holidays, bus no. 64 leaves at 20 minutes past the hour starting at 10:20 a.m. and every two hours thereafter. The trip takes about 30 minutes. Ask the driver to drop you at the Alton Butts stop, the one closest to the Austen house. From the bus stop, walk toward the railway bridge, cross the busy road, and continue, passing a brown tourist sign and following the road beneath an underpass. The walk from the bus stop to the house takes about 15 minutes. For more information, inquire at the Tourist Information Centre in Winchester. If you drive from Winchester, take A31 northeast; you'll see a signed turnoff to the house from the roundabout junction with A32.

Jane Austen's House in Chawton

Jane Austen's novels have been in print since they were first published nearly 200 years ago. Television and movie adaptations in the last few decades have made her work even more popular. The witty, eagle-eyed novelist did more than sleep in this sturdy red-brick Georgian house, where she lived with her mother and sister Cassandra from 1809 until 1817. Here, on a small round table in the parlor, she dipped her quill and revised her earlier novels, *Pride and Prejudice* and *Sense and Sensibility*, and wrote *Mansfield Park* and *Emma*. Creatively, this was where she spent the most productive years of her life. When she wasn't writing, she made patchwork quilts (one is on display in her bedroom) and jaunted around in her donkey carriage (on view in the old bakehouse). Austen family memorabilia spreads throughout the house, which has a charm and modesty evidently not unlike the great author herself. Allow a half-hour.

Chawton (northeast of Winchester). ☎ ***01420/83262.*** *Admission: £4 ($6) adult, £3 ($4.80) seniors and students. Open: March–Nov daily 11 a.m.–4 p.m.; Dec–Feb Sat–Sun 11 a.m.–4 p.m. Wheelchair access is very limited in the house.*

Touring more of the region's historic sights

The National Trust maintains several interesting properties in Hampshire. Among the best are

- **Hinton Ampner Garden,** Bramdean, Alresford (☎ **01962/771-305**), features a 20th-century shrub garden with scented plants, overflowing borders, and spring-flowering bulbs and fruit trees. To get there from Winchester, drive east on A272.
- **Mottisfont Abbey,** Mottisfont, Romsey (☎ **01794/340-757**), is a delightful estate on the River Test with ruins of a 12th-century monastery and walled gardens containing the National Collection of Old-Fashioned Roses. The abbey is a few miles west of Winchester.
- **The Vyne,** Sherborne St. John, Basingstoke (☎ **01256/883-858**), is a 16th-century manor with a Tudor chapel and lovely gardens. The manor is north of the village of Basingstoke, northeast of Winchester, off A339.

Salisbury: High-Spire Act

The tall, slender spire of Salisbury Cathedral rises up from the plains of Wiltshire like a finger pointing toward heaven. **Salisbury,** or New

Salisbury

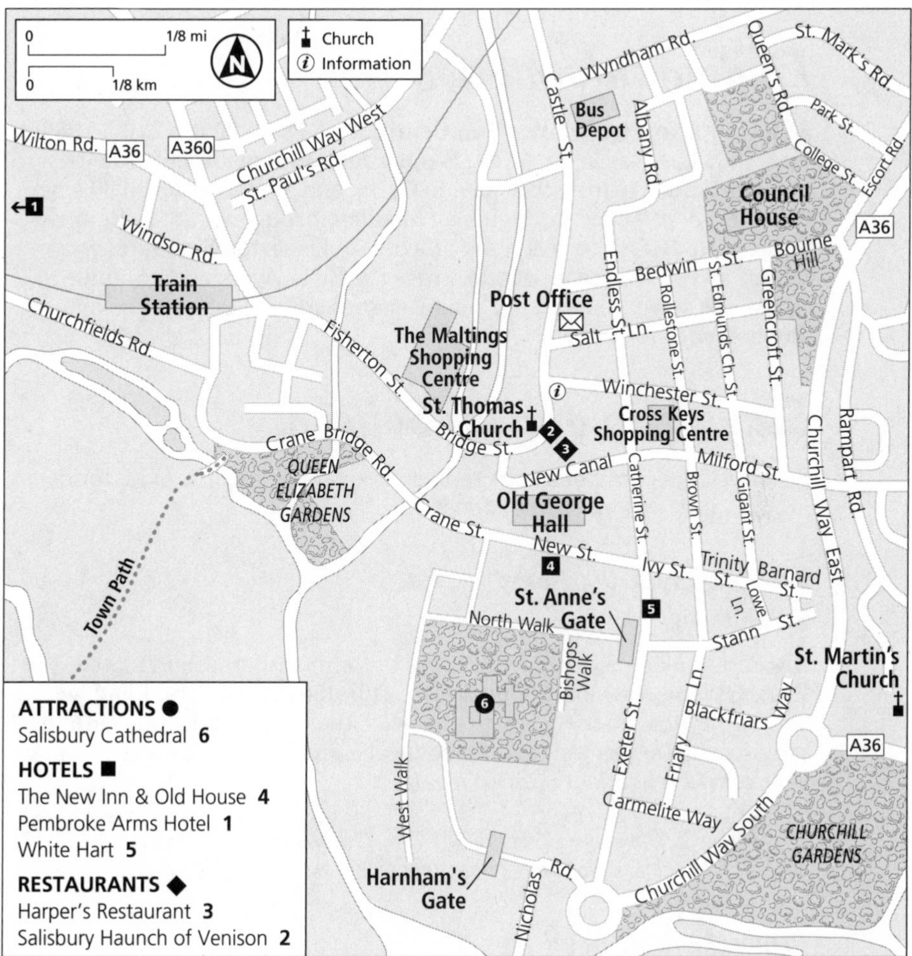

Sarum as it was once called, lies in the valley of the River Avon, 90 miles southwest of London and about 30 miles west of Winchester (see the "Salisbury" map in this chapter). Filled with Tudor inns and tearooms and dominated by its beautiful cathedral, this old market town is often overlooked by visitors eager to see Stonehenge, about 9 miles away.

Getting to Salisbury

Hourly **Network Express** trains travel from London's Waterloo Station to Salisbury (pronounced *Sauls*-bury); the journey takes about 1½ hours and costs about £23 ($37) for a same-day round-trip ticket. For information and schedules, call ☎ **08457/484-950. National Express** (☎ **0990/808-080**) has direct bus service from London's Victoria Coach Station.

If you drive from London, head west on the M3 to the end of the run, continuing the rest of the way on A30.

Finding information

Salisbury's **Tourist Information Centre,** Fish Row (☎ **01722/334-956;** www.visitsalisburyuk.com) is open June through August Monday through Saturday from 9:30 a.m. to 6 p.m. and Sunday from 10:30 a.m. to 4 p.m.; September through May Monday through Saturday from 9:30 a.m. to 5 p.m. To reach the office, take Fisherton Street, on your far left as you leave the station, cross the River Avon, and continue to follow the street; the street changes names several times and eventually becomes Fish Row.

Staying in or near Salisbury

Salisbury's accommodations represent an appealing mix of historic architecture and modern comforts.

The New Inn & Old House

$ **Salisbury**

If you're looking for an inexpensive but atmospheric (and smoke-free) B&B, try The New Inn & Old House. This 15th-century building, with a walled garden backing up to the wall that surrounds the cathedral grounds, has seven well-appointed oak-beamed guest rooms. The restaurant serves reasonably priced meals.

39–47 New St., Salisbury, Wiltshire SP1 2PH. ☎ ***01722/327-679.*** *Rack rates: £50–£70 ($80–$112) double. Rates include continental breakfast. AE, MC, V.*

Pembroke Arms Hotel

$ **Wilton**

This elegant little eight-room hotel in Wilton, northwest of Salisbury off the A36, sits in a large garden opposite Wilton House, one of Wiltshire's most famous stately homes, and not far from Stonehenge. The en-suite double rooms are fairly spacious and traditionally furnished. The hotel is known for its restaurant. The only way to book a room, however, is online; the Pembroke Arms doesn't maintain a reservations number.

Minster St. Wilton, Salisbury, Wiltshire SP2 0BH. Internet: www.pembrokearmshotel.activehotels.com. *Rack rates: £70–£90 ($112–$144) double. Rates include breakfast. MC, V.*

White Hart

$$–$$$ Salisbury

A Salisbury landmark since Georgian times, the White Hart offers accommodations in the older section of the building or in a new motel-like section in the rear. The 68-room hotel was completely refurbished in 1995 and has a good restaurant. The rooms are nicely furnished, although some of the bathrooms are small. Some rooms are large enough for families, and the staff can help arrange baby-sitting.

1 St. John St., Salisbury, Wiltshire SP1 2SD. ☎ ***0870/400-8125.*** *Internet:* `www.whitehart-salisbury.co.uk`. *Rack rates: £110–£160 ($176–$256) double. Rates include continental breakfast. AE, MC, V.*

Dining in Salisbury

Salisbury has many good restaurants. Here are some of my choices.

Harper's Restaurant

$ MODERN BRITISH

For homemade, uncomplicated, wholesome food in the center of Salisbury, go to Harper's. You can order from two menus, one featuring cost-conscious bistro-style platters and the other a longer slate of all-vegetarian pasta dishes.

6–7 Ox Row, Market Place. ☎ ***01722/333-118.*** *Reservations recommended. Main courses: £8.50–£12.50 ($14–$20), fixed-price lunch £8 ($13), fixed-price dinner £13 ($21). AE, MC, V. Open: Mon–Sat noon to 2 p.m. and 6:30–9:30 p.m.*

Salisbury Haunch of Venison

$ TRADITIONAL ENGLISH

This creaky-timbered, wonderfully atmospheric 1320 chophouse and pub served old-fashioned English roasts and grills until 2003. The trendy new menu at the third-floor restaurant, now called One Minster Street, isn't always successful but does feature some good dishes, such as cassoulet of venison sausage and fish pie. Do check out the ancient pub rooms even if you don't dine here.

1 Minster St. ☎ ***01722/322-024****). Main courses: £7–£10 ($12–$16). Fixed-price menu £7.50 ($12); served noon–1 p.m., 6–7 p.m., and 9–10 p.m. AE, MC, V. Open: food served daily noon to 2:30 p.m. and Mon–Sat 6:00–9:30 p.m. Pub open Mon–Sat 11 a.m.–11 p.m., Sun noon to 10:30 p.m.*

Exploring Salisbury and the surrounding area

In many ways, Salisbury is a quintessential English country town, bustling during the day and quiet at night. Make a stroll around the quiet confines of the Cathedral Close part of your exploration. Within the old cathedral gates are several streets with 18th- and 19th-century houses; it's the largest cathedral close in England. If you follow the Town Path through the water meadows west of the cathedral, you'll see views of Salisbury Cathedral that have changed little since the days of John Constable (1776–1837), who painted the scene many times.

Salisbury Cathedral

Salisbury

Despite an ill-conceived renovation in the 18th century, this 13th-century structure remains the best example in England of Perpendicular Gothic, an architectural style in which vertical lines predominate (see Chapter 1 for more on architecture). At 404 feet, the cathedral's spire is the tallest in the country. The cathedral's beautiful 13th-century octagonal **chapter house** possesses one of the four surviving original texts of the *Magna Carta*. Adding to the serene beauty of the cathedral are the **cloisters** and an exceptionally large ***close*** (the enclosed precinct surrounding a cathedral), comprising about 75 historic buildings. Allow about an hour.

The Close, Salisbury. ☎ ***01722/555-120.*** *Suggested donation £3.80 ($6) adults, £2 ($3.20) children, £8.50 ($14) families. Open: daily June–Aug Mon–Sat 7:15 a.m.–7:15 p.m., Sept–May 7:15 a.m.–6:15 p.m.*

Stourhead

Stourton

Stourhead is a world-famous 18th-century landscape garden. The Palladian-style villa (see Chapter 1, for a discussion of architectural styles), with its early Chippendale furniture and art treasures, was built in 1722 for a merchant banker, Henry Hoare. The gardens, laid out in 1741, represent a dramatic change in English garden design. Until the early 18th century, English gardens generally followed the formal, geometrical French style. At Stourhead, the landscape was fashioned to look more natural and more picturesque, with small temples, monuments, rare trees, flowering shrubs, and plants set around a beautiful lake. With its tranquil walks and long vistas, Stourhead is pleasant to visit any time of year, but May and June are the prime months for blossoms.

Stourton (from Salisbury, take A36 northwest to A303 west to Mere [about 25 miles total]; Stourton is 3 miles northwest of Mere off B3092). ☎ ***01747/841-152.*** *Admission: house and garden £8.90 ($14) adults, £4.30 ($7) children 5–15, £21.20 ($34) families (2 adults, 2 children). Open: garden year-round daily 9 a.m.–7 p.m.; house April–Nov Fri–Tues 11 a.m.–5 p.m.*

Wilton House

Wilton

Wilton is one of England's great country estates. The home of the earls of Pembroke, the house is noted for its 17th-century state rooms by the celebrated architect Inigo Jones and for the historic events that took place here. Shakespeare's troupe may have entertained in Wilton House. Several centuries later, General Dwight Eisenhower and his advisers made preparations here for the D-Day landings at Normandy. Beautifully maintained furnishings and paintings by Van Dyck, Rubens, Brueghel, and Reynolds fill the house. You can visit the reconstructed **Tudor kitchen** and **Victorian laundry,** and see the **Wareham Bears,** a collection of some 200 miniature dressed teddy bears. The 21-acre grounds include **rose and water gardens**, **riverside and woodland walks,** and a huge adventure **playground** for children.

If you're without wheels, take the bus that stops on New Canal, a ten-minute walk north of Salisbury train station, to Wilton House; check with the tourist office for schedules (see "Finding information," earlier in this section).

Wilton (3 miles west of Salisbury on A30; follow signs). ☎ ***01722/746-729.*** *Admission: £9.25 ($15) adults, £7.50 ($12) seniors and students, £5 ($8) children 5–15, £22 ($35) families (2 adults, 2 children). Open: April 11–Oct 26 daily 10:30 a.m.–5:30 p.m.*

Stonehenge: Visiting the Standing Stones

About 9 miles north of Salisbury is one of the world's most renowned prehistoric sites, the giant stone circle of Stonehenge, one of England's most popular attractions. Recognizing its importance, UNESCO designated Stonehenge a World Heritage Site.

The crowds can reach epidemic proportions as the day wears on, so I recommend that you come here as early as possible in the day.

Getting to Stonehenge

Hourly **Network Express** trains travel from London's Waterloo Station to Salisbury; the journey takes about 1½ hours and costs about £23 ($37) for an off-peak (after 9:30 a.m.) round-trip ticket. For information and schedules, call ☎ **08457/484-950.** From the station, take a Wilts & Dorset bus to Stonehenge; buses depart daily October through April from 11 a.m. to 2 p.m.; May through September from 10 a.m. to 5 p.m. The bus trip takes about 40 minutes, and the round-trip fare is about

£5 ($8). **National Express** (☎ **0990/808-080**) has direct bus service from London's Victoria Coach Station to Salisbury; the bus terminal in Salisbury is about a ten-minute walk east of the train station. If you drive from London, head west on the M3 to the end of the run, continuing the rest of the way on A30 to Salisbury. From there, take A338 north to A303, and then head east to the turn-off on A360.

Exploring Stonehenge

Believed to be 3,500 to 5,000 years old, Stonehenge is a stone circle of megalithic pillars and lintels built on the flat Salisbury Plain. Many folks are disappointed when they actually see the site, which isn't as huge as modern-day megasensibilities expect. (A path surrounds the site and keeps visitors 50 feet from the stones.) Keep in mind, however, what a remarkable achievement, in terms of design and engineering skills Stonehenge represents. Many of the stones, which weigh several tons, were mined and moved from distant sites in a time before fork-lifts, trucks, and dynamite. Such a feat indicates a high level of skill, dedication, and manpower.

Who built it and what does it all mean? The old belief that the Druids built Stonehenge has been discredited (the site is probably older than the Celtic Druids). Because Stonehenge is aligned to the summer equinox and capable of predicting eclipses, a popular theory maintains that the site was an astronomical observatory. Whatever its purpose, Stonehenge was an important shrine or ceremonial gathering place of some kind. But in an age that thinks it knows everything, Stonehenge still keeps its tantalizing mysteries to itself.

*9 miles north of Salisbury. (☎ **01980/624-715**). Admission: £5 ($8) adults, £3.80 ($6) students and seniors, £2.50 ($4) children (5–15). Admission includes audio guide. Open: daily March 16–May and Sept–Oct 15 9:30 a.m.–6 p.m., June–Aug 9 a.m.–7 p.m., and Oct 16–March 15 9:30 a.m.–4 p.m.*

Chapter 17

Devon: Moors, Tors, and Sandy Shores

In This Chapter

- Examining Exeter
- Exploring Dartmoor National Park
- Touring Torquay and the English Riviera
- Seeing where the Pilgrims set sail in Plymouth

Traveling westward from London through Wiltshire, you enter Devon, a scenically diverse county with a windy, unspoiled north coast, a popular south coast, and a giant national park in between. (See "Devon" map in this chapter.) If you're looking for outdoor adventures in England, Devon is a good place to visit. You can go walking or pony trekking across Dartmoor National Park, with its high, open moorland and giant granite rock formations known as *tors.* You can go swimming along the south coast, with its clean, sandy beaches. Or you can relax in laid-back Torquay, taking leisurely boat rides or drives in an area known as the English Riviera. Devon's cities and villages are loaded with history. Exeter's magnificent cathedral dates from the 12th century, and Plymouth was where the Pilgrims set sail for the New World in 1620.

You can easily get to Exeter, Torquay, and Plymouth by train from London. Devon's good public transportation system lets you explore without a car by using local buses, small rail lines, and boats. If you want to see more of the countryside, consider renting a car in Exeter.

Devon, like neighboring Cornwall, has long been associated with the cream tea, which is available in the afternoon at just about every restaurant and teashop throughout the county. Devonshire clotted cream, a version of what the French call *crème fraîche,* is "silvery" as opposed to Cornish cream's "golden" hue. A cream tea should be served with a scone (made without baking soda) and strawberry preserves.

Devon

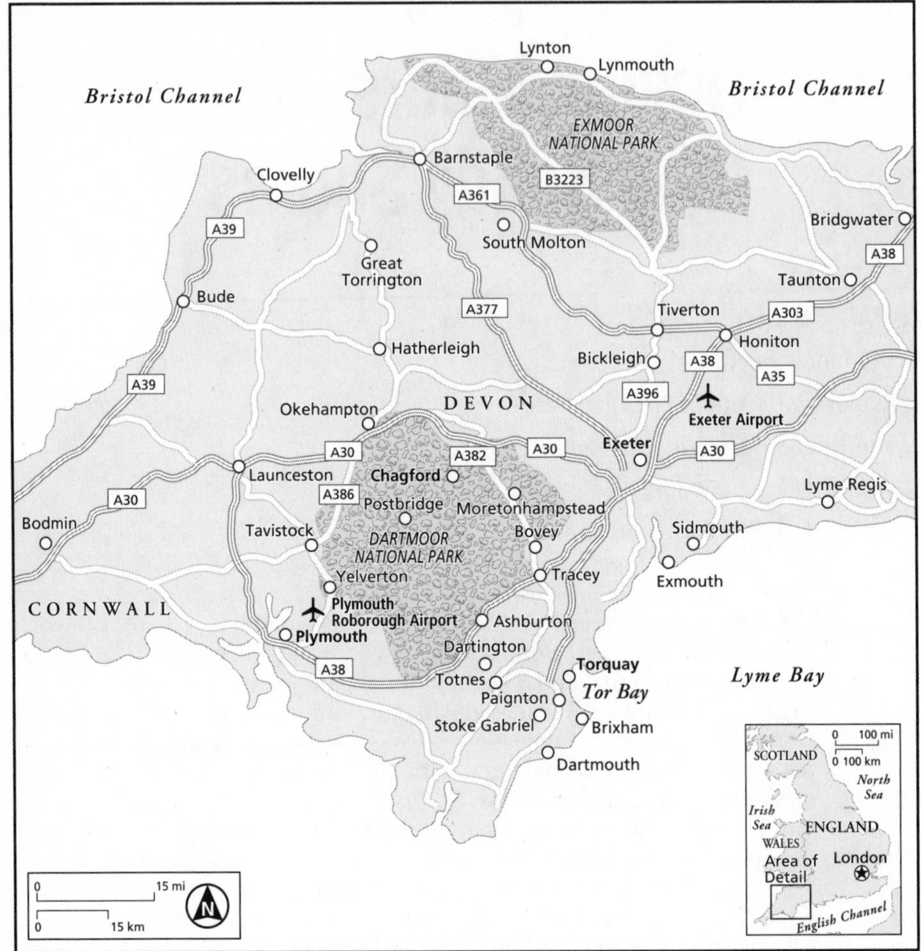

Exeter: Sea Captains and Silversmiths

Exeter, one of England's oldest cities, began as the most westerly outpost of the Roman Empire (see "Exeter" map in this chapter). Saxon King Alfred the Great refounded Exeter in the ninth century. By the 11th century, the time of the Norman Conquest, Exeter was one of England's largest towns. The English wool trade, which made villages in the Cotswolds (see Chapter 20) so prosperous during the Tudor era, also sustained Exeter until the 18th century. During World War II, the Germans bombed the center of the city. Much of Exeter's medieval core was gutted, but luckily the city's greatest treasure, its magnificent Norman cathedral, wasn't destroyed. As a result of the bombing and subsequent rebuilding, Exeter (like Plymouth) has a somewhat

Exeter

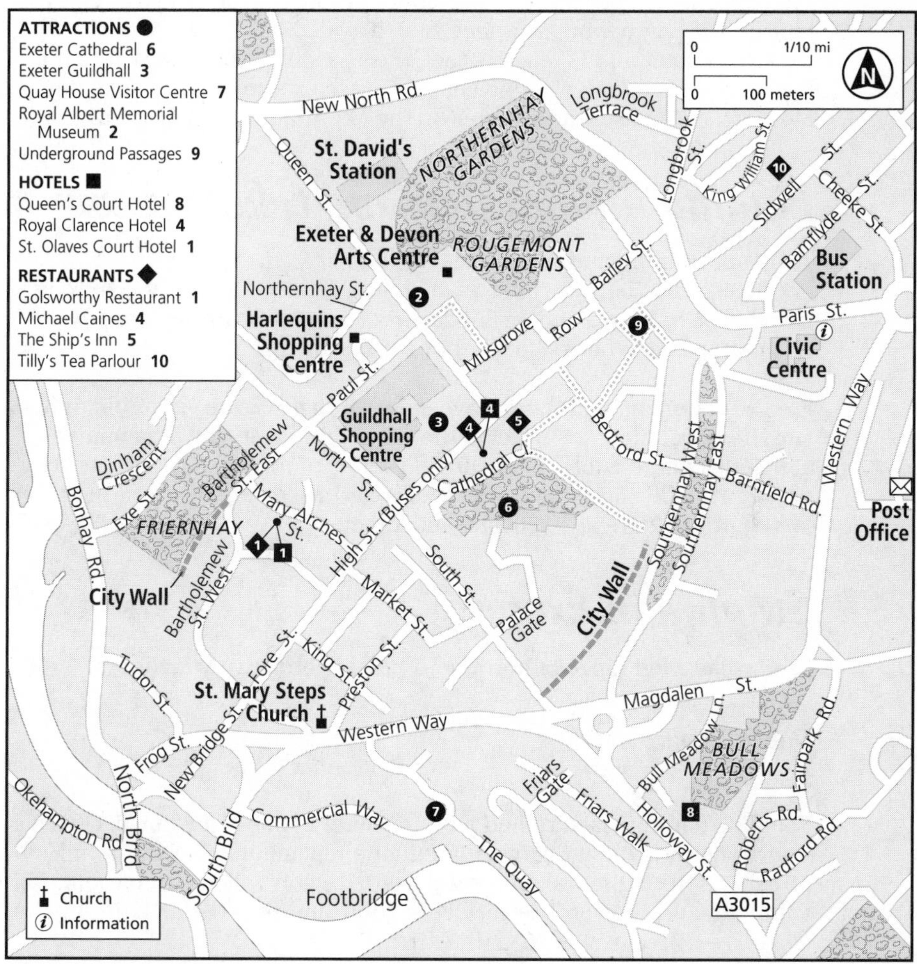

piecemeal look. The most picturesque part of town is the area around the cathedral; you also find a newly redeveloped area along the River Exe that's good for strolling and shopping. You may want to stay overnight in Exeter or just stay long enough to see the cathedral and other sights. From the cathedral, you can easily hop in a car and explore Dartmoor National Park, just a few miles to the west.

Getting to Exeter

Trains from London's Paddington Station depart hourly for the 2½-hour journey to Exeter's **St. David's** Station (the cheapest round-trip supersaver fare is £43/$69); local trains connect St. David's to **Exeter Central,** closer to the town center. For train schedules, call ☎ **08457/484-950.**

National Express (☎ **0990/808-080**) buses depart from London's Victoria Coach Station every two hours during the day; the trip takes four hours. Frequent bus service is also available for the one-hour trip between Exeter and Plymouth. (See the section "Plymouth: Where the Pilgrims Set Sail," later in this chapter.) By car from London, take the M4 west, cutting south to Exeter on the M5 (junction near Bristol).

Finding information and taking a tour

The **Tourist Information Centre,** in the Civic Centre, Paris Street (☎ **01392/265-700;** www.exeter.gov.uk), is open Monday to Saturday from 9 a.m. to 5 p.m., and on Sunday from June through October 10 a.m. to 4 p.m. You can book a hotel room at this center.

Free 90-minute guided tours leave daily throughout the year from opposite the Royal Clarence Hotel in the Cathedral Close, the area immediately adjacent to Exeter Cathedral. From April through October, tours depart at 10:30 and 11 a.m. and 2, 2:30, and 7 p.m. From November to March, tours leave at 10:30 a.m. and 2 p.m.

Staying in Exeter

Exeter has a full range of hotels and B&Bs. Here are my favorites.

Queen's Court Hotel

$

You'd be hard pressed to find a better hotel in this price range. Queen's Court sits on a quiet, leafy square just a few minutes' stroll from High Street and the cathedral. The hotel has 18 freshly redecorated rooms, all with bath and shower. The service is good, and so is the restaurant, The Olive Tree. Breakfast is £6 ($10) extra.

6–8 Bystock Terrace, Exeter, Devon EX4 4HY. ☎ ***01392/272-709.*** *Fax: 01392/491-390. Internet:* www.queenscourt-hotel.co.uk. ***Rack rates: £64–£74 ($102–$118)*** *double. AE, MC, V.*

Exeter's arts festival

The two-week Exeter Festival, held from late June to mid-July, features candlelit classical music concerts in the cathedral, plus jazz, rock, theater, and opera performances throughout the city. For information, call the **Exeter Festival Office** (☎ **01392/265-198**).

Royal Clarence Hotel

$$–$$$

This well-known, well-maintained, Georgian-era hotel opposite the cathedral is the nicest place to stay in the city. The 56 rooms are decorated in a mixture of period styles; the rooms in front look out onto the cathedral. Some units are big enough for families, and the hotel can help arrange baby-sitting. Breakfast is an additional £9.50 ($13.75). Michael Caines, the hotel restaurant, is one of Exeter's top dining spots (see "Dining in Exeter," later in this chapter).

Cathedral Yard, Exeter, Devon EX1 1HD. ☎ ***01392/319-955.*** *Fax: 01392/439-423. Internet:* `www.regalhotels.co.uk/royalclarence`. ***Rack rates: £130–£155 ($208–$248) double. AE, DC, MC, V.***

St. Olaves Court Hotel

$$

Set in its own walled garden close to the cathedral, this intimate hotel was created from a townhouse built in 1827. An original spiral staircase runs to many of its 15 guest rooms. Furnished with antiques, the rooms have period charm and decent-size bathrooms with new showers. The standards are high throughout. You can dine on excellent gourmet cuisine in the hotel's Golsworthy Restaurant.

Mary Arches St. (off High St.), Exeter, Devon EX4 3AZ. ☎ ***800/544-9993*** *in U.S. or 01392/217-736. Fax: 01392/413-054. Internet:* `www.olaves.co.uk`. ***Rack rates: £115–145 ($184–$232) double. Rates include continental breakfast. AE, DC, MC, V.***

Dining in Exeter

From Modern British cuisine to simple pub fare, Exeter has a restaurant to suit every taste. Here are some that I like.

Golsworthy Restaurant

$$ **CONTINENTAL**

The restaurant in this Georgian townhouse hotel is a favorite with locals and visitors because of its reliably high standards of cooking. For starters, you may find confit of duck terrine, with rack of lamb, filet of veal, or baked scallop of salmon to follow. The desserts are wonderful.

In the St. Olaves Court Hotel, Mary Arches St. ☎ ***01392/217-736.*** *Reservations recommended. Main courses: £14.50–£19.50 ($23–$31); fixed-price lunch £15 ($24), fixed-price dinner £19–£23 ($30–$37). AE, DC, MC, V. Open: daily noon to 2 p.m., 6:30–9:30 p.m.*

Michael Caines

$$ MODERN BRITISH

This classy, smoke-free, hotel restaurant is one of Exeter's dining hot spots. Many of the dishes are made with local, organically grown products. The menu changes all the time, but you may find lentil and foie gras soup or seafood risotto as a starter, with main courses featuring fresh fish, lamb, venison, or chicken with interesting accompaniments. There's a special children's menu, and kids under 5 eat free. Michael Caines Cafe, adjacent to the restaurant, is less fancy in cuisine and decor, but also a great place to dine. Don't confuse chef Michael Caines, who presides over the kitchen at Gidleigh Park (see "Staying in Dartmoor National Park," later in this chapter) with Michael Caine the actor.

In the Royal Clarence Hotel, Cathedral Yard. ☎ ***01392/310-031.*** *Reservations recommended. Main courses: restaurant £13–£16.50 ($21–$26), fixed-price lunch £15–£18 ($24–$29); cafe £7.25–£15.60 ($12–$25). AE, DC, MC, V. Open: daily noon to 2:30 p.m. and 7–10 p.m.*

The Ship's Inn

$ TRADITIONAL ENGLISH/PUB

For an atmospheric, inexpensive pub lunch, try this restaurant. The Ship's Inn is the oldest pub in Exeter; Francis Drake and Sir Walter Raleigh frequented the place more than 400 years ago. The menu has plenty of simple offerings, like soups and sandwiches, but you can also get homemade steak and kidney or chicken and mushroom pie and good fish and chips.

St. Martin's Lane. ☎ ***01392/272-040.*** *Main courses: £5.95–£6.95 ($10–$11). MC, V. Open: meals served Sun–Mon noon to 3 p.m., Tues–Thurs noon to 9 p.m., Fri noon to 6 p.m., Sat 11 a.m.–6 p.m. Pub open Mon–Sat 11 a.m.–11 p.m., Sun noon to 10:30 p.m.*

Tilly's Tea Parlour

$ TEAS/LIGHT FARE

Pop into Tilly's if you want an old-fashioned cream tea with rich Devonshire cream and home-baked scones. You can also get breakfast and lunch; daily specials are posted. Kids enjoy the relaxed atmosphere and the dessert selection.

48 Sidwell St. ☎ ***01392/213-633.*** *Main courses: £2–£5 ($3.20–$8). No credit cards. Open: daily 9 a.m.–5:30 p.m.*

Exploring Exeter

You can see the noteworthy sights in Exeter in a couple of hours, and on foot.

Exeter Cathedral

The cathedral's twin towers are of Norman origin, built in the 12th century. The west front is remarkable for its rows of sculptured saints and kings, the largest surviving array of 14th-century sculpture in England. The original Norman interior was remodeled in the 13th century, in a soaring Decorated Gothic style. The remarkable fan-vaulted roof is the longest of its kind in the world. The cathedral's astronomical clock is reputedly the source of the "Hickory Dickory Dock" nursery rhyme. Allow 30 minutes.

1 The Cloisters. ☎ ***01392/255-573.*** *Suggestion donation £2 ($3.20). Open: Mon–Fri 7:30 a.m.–6:15 p.m., Sat 7:30 a.m.–5 p.m., Sun 8 a.m.–7:30 p.m.*

Exeter Guildhall

One of England's oldest municipal buildings, the Guildhall was referred to in surviving documents as far back as 1160. Its colonnaded front was a Tudor addition of 1593. Inside, you find a display of silver; the city has long been known for its silverwork.

The Guildhall closed in 2003 for repairs and is expected to reopen sometime in 2004.

High St. ☎ ***01392/265-500.*** *Admission: free. Open: Mon–Fri 10:30 a.m.–1 p.m. and 2–4pm.*

Quay House Visitor Centre

Start your walk along Exeter's revamped Quayside area. Just south of the town center, you come across a small port to which seagoing ships have access by means of a 5½-mile-long canal dug in the 16th century. The Visitor Centre provides an **audio-visual program** that fills you in on key events in Exeter's 2,000-year history.

Quayside. ☎ ***01392/265-213.*** *Admission: free. Open: daily Easter–Oct 10 a.m.–5.p.m., Sat–Sun 11 a.m.–4 p.m.*

Royal Albert Memorial Museum

The city's large Victorian-era museum has collections of paintings, local glassware, clocks and watches, silver, and Roman artifacts. The Royal Albert also administers St. Nicholas Priory (off Fore Street), the guest wing of a 700-year-old Benedictine Priory that later became an Elizabethan merchant's home.

Paul St. ☎ ***01392/665-858.*** *Admission: free. Open: Mon–Sat 10 a.m.–5 p.m.*

Underground Passages

This is a labyrinth of vaulted underground tunnels dug beneath High Street during the medieval era to bring fresh water to the city. An **introductory video and a tour** relate the tunnels' history. Kids love the tour, which explores the ancient tunnels.

Boots Corner, off High St. ☎ ***01392/265-887.*** *Admission: £3.75 ($5) adults, £2.75 ($3.75) children 5–15. Open: Easter–Sept Mon–Sat 10 a.m.–5 p.m.; Oct–Easter Tues–Fri 2–5 p.m., Sat 10 a.m.–5 p.m. Access is very limited for wheelchair users.*

Shopping for Exeter silver

Exeter is known for its silver, identifiable by the three-castle mark stamped onto the article. At **Burford,** 1 Bedford St. (☎ **01392/254-901**), you can find spoons that date from the 18th century and earlier. Ten dealers share space in **The Quay Gallery Antiques Emporium,** on the Quay off Western Way (☎ **01392/213-283**), selling furniture, porcelain, metal ware, and collectibles.

Dartmoor National Park: Back to Nature

A protected national park since 1951, **Dartmoor** is one of England's unique natural landscapes (see "Dartmoor National Park" map in this chapter). Dartmoor National Park's eastern boundary is only 13 miles west of Exeter. Dartmoor encompasses some 368 square miles (953 sq. km) of high, open moorland covered with yellow-flowering *gorse* (a spiny, yellow-flowered shrub), purple heather, and windswept granite outcroppings called *tors*. Moorland rivers with small waterfalls rush down green, wooded valleys. The last unspoiled landscape in England, Dartmoor is home to wild ponies and many other kinds of wildlife. More than 500 miles of public footpaths and bridle paths crisscross this remarkably atmospheric landscape. Although a national park, the land in Dartmoor is privately owned, and about 33,000 people live and work in the area.

Scattered throughout Dartmoor are grand country hotels, cozy village inns, and countryside B&Bs. The ancient village of **Chagford,** about 20 miles west of Exeter, makes a good base for touring. Open moors with high granite tors surround the town, which overlooks the River Teign in its deep valley. In addition to enjoying the splendid countryside, you can visit Dartmoor's two historic houses: **Buckland Abbey,** near Plymouth, was the home of Sir Francis Drake, and **Castle Drogo,** just a mile from Chagford, was the last castle built in England.

Dartmoor National Park

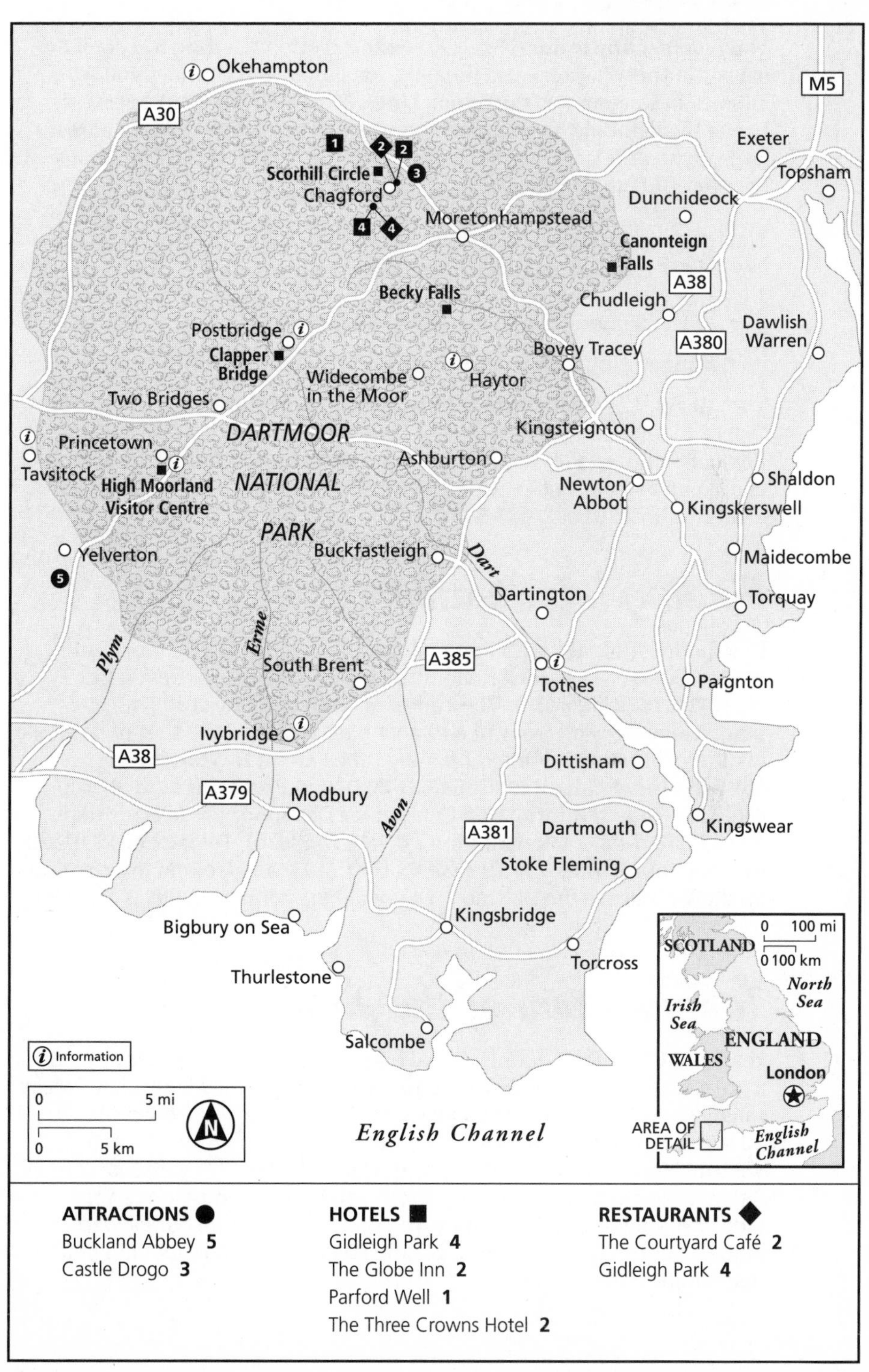

ATTRACTIONS ●
Buckland Abbey **5**
Castle Drogo **3**

HOTELS ■
Gidleigh Park **4**
The Globe Inn **2**
Parford Well **1**
The Three Crowns Hotel **2**

RESTAURANTS ◆
The Courtyard Café **2**
Gidleigh Park **4**

Getting to the park

You can take the train to Exeter (see the section "Getting to Exeter," earlier in this chapter) and then use local buses to connect you with villages in Dartmoor. **Transmoor Link** (☎ **01392/382-800**) operates buses throughout the summer. If you're driving, Exeter is the nearest large city to the park. From Exeter, continue west on B3212 to Chagford or other Dartmoor villages.

You may want to take the train to Exeter and then rent a car. The following car-rental companies have offices in Exeter:

- **Avis,** 29 Marsh Green Rd. (☎ **01392/259-713**)
- **Budget,** Unit 2 Grace Rd. Central (☎ **01392/496-555**)
- **Hertz,** 12 Marsh Barton Rd. (☎ **01392/207-207**)

The car-rental agencies cluster in the Marsh Barton industrial area, a couple miles south of Exeter's town center. To get there, you can call a local taxi at ☎ **01392/433-433.**

Finding information

Dartmoor National Park's main information hub is **High Moorland Visitor Centre,** Tavistock Road, Princetown, Yelverton, Devon PL20 6QF (☎ **01822/890-414**). The center is open daily from 10 a.m. to 5 p.m. in summer and from 10 a.m. to 4 p.m. in winter. Smaller park information centers with limited opening times are in **Haytor** (☎ 01364/661-520), **Newbridge** (☎ 01364/631-303), and **Postbridge** (☎ 01822/880-272). Tourist Information Centres for Dartmoor are in **Ivybridge** ☎ 01752/897-035). **Okehampton** (☎ 01837/53020), **Tavistock** (☎ 01822-612-938), and **Totnes** (☎ 01803/863-168). You can also find information on the Web site of the Dartmoor National Park Authority: `www.dartmoor-npa.gov.uk`.

Taking a tour of the park

Year-round, the Dartmoor National Park Authority offers **guided walks** — a great way to introduce yourself to Dartmoor's special landscape. Walks range from easy 1½-hour village strolls to six-hour treks covering 9 to 12 miles of moorland. Details are available from the High Moorland Visitor Centre (see preceding paragraph). The cost for walks is £2 to £4 ($3.20 to $6), depending on duration. You don't need to make a reservation, just show up at the departure point. Going to the park's Web site at `www.dartmoor-npa.gov.uk` is the fastest means of obtaining information about the walks.

Staying in Dartmoor National Park

Dartmoor is a special world, with unspoiled countryside that's still wild in parts. Several old villages lie within the area Dartmoor National Park covers. Chagford is one of the most convenient.

Gidleigh Park

$$$$$ Near Chagford

Staying at this marvelous country-house hotel is an unforgettable experience. Located two miles outside of Chagford, Gidleigh Park was built in 1929 on 45 acres of beautifully landscaped gardens with a river running through the property. The standards are impeccably high, but the hotel isn't fussy or formal. The 15 enormous guest rooms have fine marble baths and a wonderfully old-fashioned English ambience. The hotel is famous throughout the West Country for its cuisine (see "Dining in Dartmoor National Park," later in this chapter), and the room rate includes a sumptuous four-course dinner. If you're looking for a splurge, this hotel is it.

Gidleigh Rd., Chagford, Devon TQ13 8HH. ☎ ***01647/432-367.*** *Fax: 01647/432-574. Internet:* `www.gidleigh.com`. ***Rack rates: £420–£550 ($672–$880) double. Rates include English breakfast, morning tea, and dinner. MC, V.***

The Globe Inn

$ Chagford

A 16th-century stone inn that served stagecoaches, The Globe Inn sits in the center of charming Chagford. Downstairs, you find two bars and a restaurant serving traditional English dishes and daily specials. Upstairs are nicely furnished guest rooms with private bathrooms. The inn can pack a picnic lunch for you on request.

High St., Chagford, Devon TQ13 8AJ. ☎ ***01647/433-485.*** *Rack rates: £45–£60 ($72–$96) double. Rates include English breakfast. V.*

Parford Well

$ Near Chagford

This professionally run B&B is wonderfully attuned to guests' needs (including privacy). Tim Daniel, the owner, worked as a hotelier in London before starting this country retreat. The modern house, set within a walled garden, holds three guest rooms decorated with an understated English elegance. The rooms are quiet, comfortable, and very cozy.

Sandy Park, Devon TQ13 8JW. ☎ ***01647/433-353.*** *Internet:* `www.parfordwell.co.uk`. ***Rack rates: £56–£72 ($90–$115) double. Rates include English breakfast. No credit cards.***

The Three Crowns Hotel

$ Chagford

The Three Crowns Hotel is in a 13th-century granite building that was formerly the home of the Wyddons, an important local family. Over the years, the home was renovated into a comfortable hotel with rooms that have modern amenities and private bathrooms. With its mullioned windows, massive oak beams, and open fireplace, the downstairs lounge is a good spot for a drink. On the premises is a restaurant that serves traditional English cuisine; main courses are £10 to £13 ($16 to $21). Kids usually enjoy the hotel's atmosphere and village setting.

High St., Chagford, Devon TQ13 8AJ. ☎ ***01647/433-444.*** *Fax: 01647/433-117. Internet:* `www.chagford-accom.co.uk`. *Rack rates: £70 ($112) double. Rates include English breakfast. MC, V.*

Dining in Dartmoor National Park

The restaurant at Gidleigh Park is one of the culinary highlights of England, but you also find simple pubs and country cafes in the Dartmoor villages.

The Courtyard Cafe

$ Chagford VEGETARIAN

Part of a local store dedicated to all things organic and sustainable, this cafe makes a good spot for a vegetarian lunch. Consider the menu's homemade soup, vegetarian pizzas and quiches, and fresh salads. One of the specialties is local Devonshire ice cream.

76 The Square. ☎ ***01647/432-571.*** *Main courses: £4–£7 ($6–$11). No credit cards. Open: Mon–Sat lunch noon to 3 p.m.; tea or snacks 9 a.m.–5:30 p.m.*

Gidleigh Park

$$$$ Near Chagford ENGLISH/INTERNATIONAL

Even if you're not staying at Gidleigh Park, you may want to consider eating there. The cooking has been acknowledged with a raft of awards and honors, including two Michelin stars, and chef Michael Caines opened another restaurant in the Royal Clarence Hotel in Exeter (see "Staying in Exeter," earlier in this chapter). The seven-course tasting menu changes weekly, but may include such delicacies as Jerusalem artichoke and truffle soup, duck confit risotto with fennel, dill wild mushrooms with Parmesan, and braised turbot and scallops with chive butter sauce. You can choose from various fixed-price menus at lunch and dinner; nothing will disappoint you.

Gidleigh Rd. ☎ ***01647/432-367.*** *Fax: 01647/432-574. Internet:* `www.gidleigh.com`. *Reservations essential. Fixed-price dinner £67.50–£72.50 ($108–$116); fixed-price lunch £27–£41 ($43–$67). Open: daily 12:30–2 p.m. and 7–9 p.m.*

Exploring in and around Dartmoor National Park

Dartmoor is home to some of England's wildest and windiest expanses, where wild ponies still graze, giant tors rise among fields of bracken, and streams rush through forested valleys. Dartmoor has been settled for centuries, and small villages are part of its timeless landscape.

Buckland Abbey

Yelverton

Tucked away in its own secluded valley above the River Tavy, 3 miles west of Yelverton, Buckland was originally a small but influential Cistercian monastery. Parts of the abbey date from around 1278, but the main parts of the house were built in the 16th century when Sir Richard Grenville remodeled the dissolved abbey into a noble residence. The tower over the church's crossing and many other original features of Buckland Abbey are still visible.

The great Elizabethan navigator Sir Francis Drake bought Buckland in 1581, shortly after circumnavigating the world. The house, today a National Trust property, displays memorabilia of Drake and Grenville. Behind the house is a monastic tithe barn, where the monks stored the food that the farmers were required to give them. On the estate grounds, you find an herb garden and some delightful walks. Give yourself at least an hour to see everything.

3 miles west of Yelverton off A386. ☎ ***01822/853-607.*** *Admission: £5 ($8) adults, £2.50 ($4) children 5–15, £12.50 ($20) families (2 adults, 2 children). Open: April 12–Nov 2 Fri–Wed 10:30 a.m.–5:30 p.m., Nov 3–Dec 21 and Feb 14–March Sat–Sun 2–5 p.m. (dates vary yearly). Most of the house and grounds are accessible to wheelchair users; call in advance to make arrangements.*

Castle Drogo

Drewsteignton

The architect Sir Edwin Lutyens designed this granite castle, which was built for a self-made millionaire, Julius Drewe, between 1910 and 1930. Perched on a rocky cliff above the Teign River, the castle commands panoramic views of Fingle Gorge and Dartmoor. Drewe wanted his dream house — the last castle built in England — to combine the grandeur of a medieval castle with the comforts of the 20th century. Designed for easy, elegant living, the interior includes a kitchen, a scullery, and elaborately appointed bathrooms. Go outside to see the terraced formal garden with roses and herbaceous borders, as well as woodlands with flowers in spring. You can see the house and gardens in about an hour.

4 miles northeast of Chagford, or 6 miles south of Exeter-Okehampton Rd. (A30). ☎ ***01647/433-306.*** *Admission: castle and grounds, £5.90 ($10) adults, £2.90 ($4.60) children, £14.70 ($23) families (2 adults, 2 children). Open: castle, March 29–Nov 2 Wed–Mon 11 a.m.–5.30 p.m.; garden daily year-round 10.30 a.m.–5:30 p.m. Most of the castle is accessible to visitors in wheelchairs; call in advance to make arrangements.*

Dartmoor National Park

You can find more remains of prehistoric huts, enclosures, burial monuments, stone rows, and stone circles in Dartmoor National Park than anywhere else in Europe. You need a detailed ordnance survey map to find these ancient sites (you can buy maps at the visitor centers). **Scorhill Circle,** 4 miles west of Chagford, is a prehistoric stone circle. Near **Postbridge,** a village about 14 miles south of Chagford, you can see a legacy of Dartmoor's medieval past in the form of a clapper bridge, a giant slab of flat rock spanning the East Dart River.

Dartmoor is popular walking country, but don't attempt any long-distance hikes without taking sensible precautions. Always have an ordnance survey map of the area and be prepared for sudden changes in the weather.

If you're not a walker, you can explore Dartmoor by car. Two main roads cross the open moorland. B3212 enters and crosses the eastern side of the high moor through the best area of heather moorland, which is at its peak bloom in late August. B3357 cuts through the center, sometimes running alongside the West Dart River and passing the tors. From the villages, smaller lanes lead off into the moorland.

Torquay: Relaxing on the English Riviera

Torquay (pronounced Tor-*key*), 23 miles southeast of Exeter, lies on sheltered Tor Bay, an inlet of the English Channel, in an area known as the English Riviera. The area isn't like the French Riviera, except that the temperature is mild, the days are often sunny, and you're close to the sea. Victorian health-seekers made the town a popular spot. The pre–jet set crowd that brought Torquay a touch of British glamour from the 1950s to the 1970s has long since departed on cheap flights to more exotic locales.

Torquay is now essentially a resort town for honeymooners, retirees, and families. It's a place for hanging out and taking it easy. Torquay and the neighboring towns of **Brixham** and **Paignton** form **Torbay,** a cluster of resorts around **Tor Bay.** You find several safe, sandy beaches, parks, seaside promenades, and gardens along Torbay, which is a center for yachting and watersports. At night, concerts, productions from London's West End, vaudeville shows, and ballroom dancing keep the vacationers entertained. I don't suggest that you go out of your way to visit Torquay, but it does make for a good overnight if you're touring the West Country.

Getting to Torquay

Trains run throughout the day from London's Paddington and Waterloo stations to Torquay, whose station is in the town center on the seafront. The trip takes three hours, 15 minutes to four hours, 15 minutes. You can also take direct service from Exeter's St. David's Station; the trip takes only 40 minutes. For train schedules and fares, call ☎ **08457/484-950. National Express** (☎ **0990/808-080**) buses leave from London's Victoria Coach Station every couple of hours during the day. The trip takes five to six hours and costs £32.50 ($52) round-trip. From Exeter, the bus journey takes less than an hour and costs £6.25 ($10) round-trip. If you're driving from Exeter, take A38 south and continue on A380.

Getting around and touring Torquay

If you're without a car, you can make local excursions by boat. From May through October, the **Brixham Ferry** provides daily service between Torquay and Brixham for £4 ($6) round-trip. **Neptune Cruises** runs a daily 11 a.m. excursion cruise from Torquay up the Dart River to Dartmouth, returning at 4:45 p.m.; the cost is £8.50 ($14). You can buy tickets at the kiosk on the quay or at the Stagecoach Travel office, Vaughn Parade. For more information, contact the Tourist Information Centre (see the next section).

Finding information

The **Tourist Information Centre**, Vaughan Parade (☎ **01803/297-428**), is open Monday through Saturday from 9 a.m. to 5 p.m. It has plenty of information on local attractions and a hotel-finding service.

Staying and dining in Torquay

If you're going to stay in Torquay, I recommend that you find a seafront hotel with a good restaurant and rooms with views over Tor Bay. Try the following, which all have good restaurants, evening entertainment, and recreational facilities, and offer special short-break rates for two or more nights:

- **The Imperial Hotel,** 1 Park Hill Road, Torquay, Devon TQ1 2DG (☎ **01803/294-301;** Fax 01803/298-293; E-mail: `imperialtorquay@paramount-hotels.co.uk`), overlooks Tor Bay and is the dowager empress of Torquay luxury resort hotels. Doubles start at £170 ($272) with breakfast.
- **Livermead Cliff Hotel,** Sea Front, Torquay, Devon TQ2 6RQ (☎ **01803/299-666;** Fax: 01803/294-496; `www.livermeadcliff.co.uk`), sits right on the water's edge with steps down to a beach. Doubles with sea views go for £147 to £169 ($235 to $270) with breakfast and dinner.
- **The Livermead House,** Sea Front, Torquay, Devon TQ2 8QJ (☎ **01803/294-361;** Fax: 01803/200-758; `www.livermeadhouse.co.uk`), with its heated swimming pool and sun patio, is another good choice on the sea front. Doubles with sea views go for £122 to £1150 ($195 to $240) with breakfast and dinner.
- **Osborne Hotel,** Hesketh Crescent, Meadfoot, Torquay, Devon TQ1 2LL (☎ **01803/213-311;** Fax: 01803/296-788; `www.osborne-torquay.co.uk`), part of a beautiful Regency building, has sea-facing doubles with breakfast from £124 to £168 ($198 to $269).

Exploring Torquay

Torquay's only nonaquatic tourist attraction of note is **Torre Abbey,** The Kings Drive (☎ **01803/293-593**), about a quarter-mile east of the town center. A prosperous abbey founded in 1196, Torre was later converted to a luxurious private residence. It has painting galleries, furnished period rooms, ancient cellars, and gardens. The Agatha Christie Memorial Room displays the personal possessions, paintings, books, and original manuscripts of the famous mystery writer, who was born in Torquay. Admission is £3 ($4.80) for adults, £2.50 ($4) for students and seniors, £1.50 ($2.40) for children 8 to 15. The abbey is open daily from Easter to November 9:30 a.m. to 6 p.m.

The English Riviera coastline stretches some 22 miles, from Torquay to the family resort town of Paignton and the harbor and fishing town of Brixham. In 1874, Isaac Singer, founder of the sewing machine empire, built the **Oldway Mansion** (☎ **01803/201-201**), which is on Torquay Road in Paignton, a short drive south of Torquay. His son Paris enhanced the mansion's decor and had a rehearsal space and performance hall built for his mistress, the dancer Isadora Duncan. The house is open year-round Monday to Saturday from 9 a.m. to 5 p.m., plus Sunday 9 a.m. to 4 p.m. from June through September. Admission is free.

Plymouth: Where the Pilgrims Set Sail

Many Americans want to visit **Plymouth** because the Pilgrims set sail from this port on the Mayflower in 1620. They landed 66 days later in Massachusetts. Don't go to Plymouth expecting to find a quaint Elizabethan city. During World War II, German bombs gutted the ancient town, and the way the town has been rebuilt isn't what you would call picturesque. I don't recommend staying in Plymouth, but you may want to stop off here as part of your exploration of the West Country. I suggest that you give yourself a couple of hours here, have a cream tea, and head out to someplace more scenic, perhaps Dartmoor or neighboring Cornwall.

Getting to Plymouth

Frequent direct trains leave from London's Paddington Station for the 3½- to 4-hour journey to Plymouth. There's also direct service from Exeter's St. David's Station (one hour) and from Torquay (one hour) to Plymouth. For train fares and schedules, call **☎ 08457/484-950.** Plymouth Train Station is on North Road, north of the town center. Western National Bus No. 83/84 runs from the station into the heart of town. **National Express** (**☎ 0990/808-080**) runs buses from London's Victoria Coach Station; the trip takes five to nine hours and costs £35 ($56) round trip. Buses also run directly to Plymouth from Exeter and from Torquay. Driving from Exeter, head southwest (skirting around Dartmoor National Park) on A38. From Torquay, head west on A385 and continue southwest on A38.

The **Plymouth Discoverer** (**☎ 01752/222-221**) bus runs year-round in Plymouth, making a circuit from the railway station to the Barbican, the seafront, and back.

Taking a tour or cruise in Plymouth

From April through October, **Guide Friday** (**☎ 01752/222-221;** `www.guidefriday.com`) offers an **open-top bus tour,** a good way to see the sights. The tour makes a circuit of Plymouth's principle attractions; it takes about an hour if you stay on the bus, but you're free to get on and off as often as you like. The cost is £6.50 ($11) for adults, £5.50 ($9) for seniors and students, £2 ($3) for children, and £13 ($21) for families (2 adults, 2 children).

If you're feeling seaworthy, you may want to take a **boat tour** of Plymouth Sound. **Plymouth Boat Cruises** (**☎ 01752/822-797**) offer a **one-hour Grand Circular cruise** that passes the Mayflower Steps, commercial docks, and nuclear submarine base, and continues to the Tamar River. Boats depart daily from April through September every 30 minutes from 10:45 a.m. through the afternoon; the fare is £5 ($8) for adults, £4.50 ($7) for seniors, £2.50 ($4) for children 5 to 15, and £11 ($18) for families (2 adults, 3 children). They also have **four-hour cruises** up the Tamar River and **two-hour sea cruises**. Departures are from Phoenix Wharf, a short walk south from the Barbican. You can purchase tickets from the Tourist Information Office, the National Marine Aquarium, or the kiosk at Phoenix Wharf.

Finding information

The **Tourist Information Centre** is at Island House, the Barbican (☎ **0870/225-4950;** `www.visitplymouth.co.uk`). A second information center, **Plymouth Discovery Centre,** is at Crabtree Marsh Mills. Both are open from Easter through September, Monday through Saturday 9 a.m. to 5 p.m., Sunday 10 a.m. to 4 p.m.; winter hours are Monday through Friday 9 a.m. to 5 p.m., Saturday from 10 a.m. to 4 p.m.

Locating a spot for lunch or tea

Tudor Rose Tea Rooms, 36 New St. (☎ **01752/255-502**), dating from 1640, is a convenient and inexpensive little tearoom and lunch spot with an outdoor garden; it's close to the Mayflower Steps but away from the crowds on the quay. Tudor Rose serves traditional home-cooked English food and afternoon cream teas. A sandwich or a cream tea costs about £3 ($4.80). Hours are Tuesday through Saturday from 10 a.m. to 5:30 p.m. No credit cards.

Exploring Plymouth

Plymouth was badly bombed in World War II, and the area around Plymouth Harbor is the only part of town where you'll probably want to spend any time.

The Barbican

This small segment of the Elizabethan town of Plymouth, reconstructed around the harbor, is where you want to spend most of your time. Today's tourist attractions and mall-like atmosphere make imagining Plymouth as it was difficult, but in Elizabethan days, this was one of England's greatest ports. Sir Francis Drake, whose house you can see near Dartmoor (see "Exploring in and around Dartmoor National Park," earlier in this chapter), became Plymouth's mayor after he made his famous round-the-world voyage on the *Golden Hinde*. Drake left Plymouth in 1577 from a quay in the Barbican area, and was gone for three years.

On Plymouth Harbor.

Plymouth: Departure point for the U.S.

The Pilgrims may have been the earliest and most famous emigrants to leave Plymouth, England, for Plymouth, Massachusetts, but they were hardly the last. During the 19th century, estimates show that more emigrant ships bound for the United States left from Plymouth than from anywhere else in Europe. More than 100 towns in New England are named after places in Devon.

The Hoe

If you walk south from the Barbican, you come to the Hoe, a promontory overlooking Plymouth Sound, an inlet of the English Channel. Flowing into the Sound from the west is the River Tamar, the age-old boundary between Devon and Cornwall and a Royal Navy anchorage for more than 400 years. To the east is the River Plym, from which Plymouth takes its name. On the Hoe, you can see 17th-century ramparts surrounding a citadel and an 18th-century lighthouse, Smeatons Tower.

South of the Barbican.

Mayflower Steps

To commemorate the spot from which the *Mayflower* sailed for the New World, a neoclassical stone archway was erected in 1934 at the base of West Pier in the Barbican. The flags of the United States and the United Kingdom fly above the spot, but otherwise little distinguishes it. A full list of the names of all who sailed is on the side of Island House, now the Barbican's Tourist Information Centre. Some of the Pilgrims reputedly lodged at the house before setting sail. The new **Plymouth Mayflower Centre** (**☎ 01752/306-330**), with exhibits relating to the Barbican, the Pilgrims, and later emigrants, opened on Barbican Quay, a few steps from the Steps, in 2002. It's open daily from 10 a.m. to 5 p.m.; admission is £4 ($6.40) for adults, £2 ($3.20) for children, and £10 ($16) for families (2 adults, 2 children).

On Plymouth Harbor in the Barbican.

National Marine Aquarium

This popular and well-designed aquarium gives you insight into the lives of the aquatic creatures that inhabit the rivers of Devon and the waters of Plymouth Sound. The exhibits start with the watery environment of a moorland stream on Dartmoor, continue on to a river, and then move down an estuary and beyond, from the shoreline to the continental shelf. You see fish, anemones, corals, sea horses, jellyfish, and sharks. The large tanks and variety of fish inevitably fascinate children.

Rope Walk, Coxside (follow signs from the Barbican). ☎ ***01752/600-301.*** *Admission: £8 ($13) adults, £6.50 ($10) seniors, £4.75 ($8) children 5–15, £23 ($37) families (2 adults, 2 children) Open: daily 10 a.m.–6 p.m. (until 5 p.m. Nov–March).*

Plymouth Gin Distillery

The former Black Friars priory was turned into a gin distillery in 1793 and has been in continuous operation ever since. The distillery makes the only English gin with an *appelation contrôlée,* which means this brand can only be made here. The gin is still made with water from Dartmoor, in the original copper stills.

60 Southside St. ☎ ***01752/665-292.*** *Admission (including 1–1/2-hr. tour): £2.75 ($4.40) adults, £2.25 ($3.40) seniors and students over 17. People under 18 not admitted. Distillery tours offered March–Dec daily 10:30 a.m.–4:45 p.m., Jan–Feb Sat 10:30 a.m.–4:45 p.m.*

Chapter 18

Cornwall: Saints, Salts, Sea, and Sun

In This Chapter

- Pausing in Penzance
- Looking out to sea at Land's End
- Strolling the quaint streets of St. Ives
- Frolicking in Fowey
- Stopping in at Cornwall's best houses and gardens

The Tamar River west of Plymouth is the age-old boundary between Devon and Cornwall. (See "Cornwall" map in this chapter.) At one time, the river was also a kind of dividing line between Cornwall and the rest of "civilized" England. The Cornish, who spoke their own language until the 18th century, were always considered a race apart. Their land, Cornwall, jutting like a toe out into the Atlantic, was a place of myth and mystery, associated with legendary figures, such as Tristan and Isolde and King Arthur.

Cornwall has a special mystique that comes from its rocky landscape, its warm, buttery light, and the windy blue seascapes that you encounter at every turn. A history that stretches back more than 3,000 years to a time when Phoenician traders sailed up the Cornish coast to trade for the tin that was mined here haunts Cornwall. In Cornish churchyards, you can see ancient Celtic crosses from the fifth and sixth centuries, the time when men and women known as "saints" (they were missionaries from Ireland and Wales) first brought Christianity to this pagan land. Many Cornish places are named for these early saints. Along the Cornish coast, you find picturesque stone-built fishing villages huddled alongside small, sheltered harbors. The former haunts of fishermen and sea salts, and more than a few pirates and smugglers, they're a reminder of Cornwall's strong seafaring traditions.

Cornwall

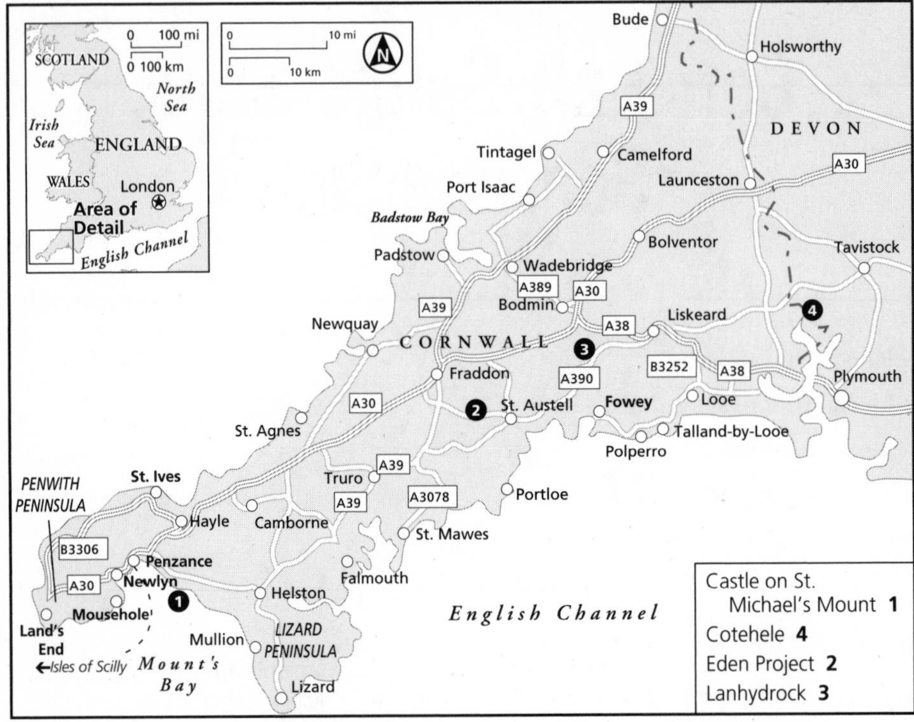

Today, tourism keeps Cornwall afloat. In summer, the warm, often sunny climate draws hordes of vacationers. In this chapter, I take you first to the lively market town of Penzance, the end of the line as far as train travel goes. The major attraction in Penzance is St. Michael's Mount, a castle that began life as a monastery. From Penzance, you can easily reach Land's End, the westernmost point in England, exploring the south coast fishing villages of Newlyn and Mousehole on the way. The picturesque village of St. Ives on the north coast (a few miles from Penzance) became an artists' colony in the early 20th century. Today, with a branch of the Tate Museum and plenty of good hotels and restaurants, St. Ives is one of the nicest spots to stay in Cornwall. In this chapter, I also point you in the direction of other worthwhile sights — from major tourist attractions, such as the Eden Project, to historic houses and special gardens — scattered throughout Cornwall.

Princely perks: The Duchy of Cornwall

In his redistribution of English lands, William the Conqueror gave Cornwall to one of his relatives. In the 14th century, Edward III created the Duchy of Cornwall as an estate for the eldest sons of the monarch. Cornwall, through 24 dukes, has remained a Duchy ever since. Prince Charles, the oldest son of Queen Elizabeth II, is the present Duke of Cornwall. Income from the Duchy of Cornwall, in leased lands and estates, amounts to tens of millions of pounds every year, and is a "nice little earner" for Charlie.

Penzance: As in "The Pirates of . . . "

Penzance, 77 miles southwest of Plymouth, is the most westerly town in England and a good base for exploring Land's End and western Cornwall. Penzance is the end of the line for mainline trains from London, 280 miles to the northeast. Built on hills overlooking Mount's Bay, Penzance is temperate enough to grow palm trees and plants that can't survive elsewhere in England.

Gilbert and Sullivan made Penzance famous in their operetta *The Pirates of Penzance,* but the town doesn't trade on that musical connection. In reality, Penzance has survived several major calamities: Barbary pirates raided the town, Spaniards sacked and burned it in the 16th century, Cromwell partially destroyed it during the 17th-century Civil War, and the Germans bombed it in the 1940s. Despite all that, Penzance is an unusually friendly town. This is the only part of England where you may hear yourself addressed as "my love."

Getting to Penzance

Express InterCity trains depart throughout the day from London's Paddington Station for the 5½-hour journey to Penzance. The round-trip advance-purchase supersaver fare is £58 ($93). For train schedules, call ☎ **08457/484-950** or check online at `www.railtrack.co.uk`. **National Express** (☎ **0990/808-080**) operates daily bus service from London's Victoria Coach Station. The trip takes 7½ to nine hours; round-trip fare is £39.50 ($63). If you're driving, the fastest route is A30, which cuts across Devon and Cornwall from Exeter.

Good train service connects London to Penzance and St. Ives, the two places I recommend as touring headquarters in Cornwall. If you're without a car, excellent local bus service serves towns throughout the county; for more information, contact **Western National** (☎ **01208/79898;** Internet: `www.firstwesternnational.co.uk`). If you want to rent a car, the following car-rental agencies have offices in Penzance:

- **Economy Hire,** Heliport Garage (☎ **01736/366-636**)
- **Enterprise,** The Forecourt, Longrock (☎ **01736/332-000**)
- **Europcar,** Station yard (☎ **01736/360-078**)

Finding information and taking a tour

The **Tourist Information Centre,** Station Road, (☎ **01736/362-207;** `www.penzance.co.uk`), is open Monday through Friday from 9 a.m. to 5 p.m., Saturday 9 a.m. to 4 p.m. (until 1 p.m. October through May), and Sunday 10 a.m. to 1 p.m. (June through September only).

Belerion Walks, Avon House, 13 Penare Rd. (☎ **01736/362-452**), offers year-round **guided walks** of the town; tours last about 90 minutes and cost £3.75 ($6). Call to reserve a spot. **Harry Safari** (☎ **01736/711-427;** `www.harrysafari.co.uk`) runs a **four-hour guided tour,** which is one of the best ways to see this part of Cornwall. Guides drive you through the area in a minivan to all sorts of hidden corners and scenic spots. The tour costs £15 ($24); you can be picked up in Penzance or St. Ives.

A cruise around Mounts Bay, passing St. Michael's Mount and local coastal beauty spots where you may see seals or dolphins, makes for a fun excursion. **MVS Mermaid & Viking** (☎ **01736/368-565**) operates two-hour coastal cruises at 3 p.m. (most days); the cost is £8 ($13) adults, £6.50 ($10) children 5 to 15. Boats leave from the marina area.

Exchanging money and finding an ATM

Penzance has several banks. Try the following: **Barclays,** 9 Market Jew St. (☎ **01736/362-271**); **HSBC,** The Greenmarket (☎ **01736/361-619**); and **Lloyds,** Market Place (☎ **01736/360-633**).

Staying in Penzance

Penzance is a holiday town with many hotels and B&Bs. Here are a few of my faves.

The Abbey

$$

The Abbey, in a 17th-century building overlooking Penzance harbor, is the most stylish guesthouse in Penzance. Owned by Jean Shrimpton, a famous British model in the 1960s, and her husband, Michael Cox, the hotel uses bold colors and antiques to convey an atmosphere of over-stuffed English elegance. It's like staying in a small, luxuriously appointed house. The nine guest rooms are lovely, and so are the bathrooms. You can arrange to have dinner in the hotel, or you may prefer the equally stylish Abbey Restaurant next door (see "Dining in Penzance," later in the chapter).

Abbey St., Penzance, Cornwall TR18 4AR. ☎ ***01736/366-906.*** *Fax: 01736/351-163. Rack rates: £110–£140 ($176–$224) double. Rates include breakfast. AE, DC, MC, V.*

The Georgian House Hotel

$

This 18th-century Georgian building, formerly the house of a mayor of Penzance, reputedly has a resident ghost. But the real spirit of the 11-room B&B is modern art: The dining room, where you're served breakfast, is painted with murals inspired by Picasso and Matisse. Guest rooms are comfortable and well equipped, and a nice lounge and bar are on the premises. The hotel is right on Chapel Street, the most interesting street in town.

20 Chapel Street, Penzance, Cornwall TR18 4AW. ☎ ***01736/365-664.*** *Fax: 01736/365-664. Rack rates: £55–£70 ($88–$112) double. Rates include breakfast. AE, MC, V.*

Mount Prospect Hotel

$–$$

This 21-room hotel overlooking Mounts Bay and the town is one of the best places to stay in Penzance. Impeccably maintained, the hotel features comfortable, well-furnished rooms, many with sea views, and good-size bathrooms (most with bath and shower). Kids enjoy the on-site pool. A special rate, which includes dinner at the hotel's fine restaurant, is a noteworthy bargain. Nonguests can also dine here on Modern British cuisine; dinner is served nightly from 7 to 8:30 p.m.

Britons Hill, Penzance, Cornwall TR18 3AE. ☎ ***01736/363-117.*** *Fax: 01736/350-970. Internet:* `www.hotelpenzance.com`*. Rack rates: £70–£115 ($112–$184) double with English breakfast; £100–£145 ($160–$232) double with dinner and English breakfast. AE, MC, V.*

Special events in Penzance

Daphne du Maurier, whose famous novel *Rebecca* is set in Cornwall, lived in Bodinnick in nearby Fowey (see "Fowey and the Saint's Way: River Town and Holy Track," later in this chapter). Every year in May, Penzance sponsors the **Daphne du Maurier Festival of Arts and Literature,** featuring all kinds of performers and events. For information, call the box office ☎ **01726/223-535** or check out the town's Web site at `www.penzance.co.uk`.

Dining in Penzance

You won't lack dining options in Penzance. Many of the restaurants feature fresh seafood.

Abbey Restaurant

$–$$$ MODERN EUROPEAN

At this stylish restaurant next to the Abbey Hotel, you enter a luscious red womb of a bar-lounge and walk up to an airy dining room with views out over Penzance harbor. Chef-owner Ben Tunnicliffe cooks in a modern European style that makes use of fresh local fish, meat, and produce. For starters, try pan-fried foie gras or crab cakes with cucumber chutney. Main courses change often but may include wild seabass with fettuccine, pancetta, and artichokes or end of lamb. The wine list is excellent.

*Abbey St. ☎ **01736/330-680.** Reservations recommended. Main courses: £5.75–£17.50 ($9–$28). MC, V. Open: Fri–Sat noon to 2 p.m.; Tues–Sun 7–10 p.m.*

Harris's Restaurant

$$–$$$ MODERN BRITISH/FRENCH

For a restaurant to stay in business for more than 30 years, it must be doing something right. This well-established restaurant, located down a narrow cobbled lane off Market Jew Street, is one of Penzance's best and most highly regarded. The cooking emphasizes fresh, local produce and seafood, with dishes such as crab Florentine and poached lobster.

*46 New Street. ☎ **01736/364-408.** Reservations recommended. Main courses: £10–£21.95 ($16–$35). AE, MC, V. Open: Tues–Sat noon to 2 p.m. and 7–10 p.m.; closed three weeks in winter.*

The Summer House Restaurant with Rooms

$$ ITALIAN

This restaurant-inn in a Regency-era house just off the promenade is a good choice if you're in the mood for innovative Mediterranean-style food. The set-price menus change daily, depending on what's fresh in the market, and an interesting Italian wine list is available. In the summer, you can dine by candlelight in the beautiful walled garden. If you want to stay here, there are five large, stylishly furnished rooms with private bathrooms; a double with breakfast goes for £75 to £95 ($120 to $152), a double with dinner and breakfast costs £122 to £145 ($195 to $232).

*Cornwall Terrace, Penzance, Cornwall TR18 4HL. ☎ **01736/363-744.** Fax: 01736/360-959. Internet:* `www.summerhouse-cornwall.com`*. Reservations required. Fixed-price dinner £23.50 ($38). MC, V. Open: restaurant April–Oct Tues–Sun 7–10 p.m.; hotel closed Oct–March.*

Sylvester's Restaurant

$ CONTINENTAL

In a historic wharf building next to the Wharfside Shopping Centre, Sylvester's is an informal restaurant that catches plenty of tourist trade. The place serves good, inexpensive, home-cooked meals, including local seafood dishes, with minimum fuss.

Wharf Road. ☎ ***01736/366-888.*** *Main courses: Lunch £5–£8 ($8–$13); fixed-price dinner £15 ($24). AE, MC, V. Open: Easter–Oct daily 10:30 a.m.–9:30 p.m.; Nov–Easter Mon–Thurs 10:30 a.m.–5:30 p.m., Fri–Sat 10:30 a.m.–9:30 p.m.*

The Turks Head

$ INTERNATIONAL/PUB

The atmospheric, low-ceilinged Turks Head claims to be the oldest tavern in town because an inn on this spot has been welcoming travelers since the 13th century. You get good, hearty food, everything from fisherman's pie and seafood platters to ratatouille and chicken tikka masala, a spicy Indian dish.

49 Chapel St. ☎ ***01736/363-093.*** *Main courses: £6–£10 ($10–$16); bar snacks £2.50–£5 ($4–$8). MC, V. Open: food served daily 11 a.m.–2:30 p.m. and 6–10 p.m.; pub open Mon–Sat 11 a.m.–11 p.m., Sun 11 a.m.–10:30 p.m.*

Exploring in and around Penzance

St. Michael's Mount is the must-see attraction in Penzance. The town itself doesn't offer a lot in the way of special interest or tourist attractions, though Chapel Street has some interesting buildings. Garden lovers will enjoy visiting Trengwainton Garden outside of town.

Castle on St. Michael's Mount

Mount's Bay

For nearly 350 years, this amazing island-castle in Mount's Bay has been the home of the St. Aubyn family. Connected to the mainland by a 500-foot-long causeway, the castle incorporates parts of an earlier 12th-century Benedictine priory that was founded as the daughter house of Mont St. Michel in Normandy. Later, in the 16th and 17th centuries, St. Michael's Mount was an important fortress to protect the coastline from foreign attack. (The beacon on top of the church tower was lit to warn of the approach of the Spanish Armada in 1588.) A royalist stronghold during the Civil War, the fort was forced to surrender after a long siege. The St. Aubyn family still inhabits part of the castle and has lived there since 1659.

Visitors enter through the **West Door,** above which hangs the St. Aubyn family crest. The **Entrance Hall,** altered in the 19th century, was the living area for the Captain of the Mount in the 16th and 17th centuries. The little adjacent chamber, known as **Sir John's Room,** is the owner's private sitting room. Sporting weapons and war memorabilia hang in the **Armoury.** The snug **Library** is in the oldest (12th century) part of the castle, as is the dining room, which served as the monks' refectory. The **Priory Church** on the island's summit has beautiful rose windows. In a newer section of the castle are the elegant rococo-style **Blue Drawing Rooms.**

St. Michael's Mount is one of the most visited National Trust properties in Britain. Give yourself at least three hours for a visit, and be aware that you'll have to climb many stairs to reach the castle. If the tide is in, boatmen known as "hobblers" will ferry you over or back. On the island are two restaurants, open April to October only, where you can have lunch or tea. Lunch costs about £4 to £8 ($6 to $13), a cream tea about £4 ($6).

To get here by bus, take bus No. 20 or 22 from Penzance to Marazion, the town opposite St. Michael's Mount.

On St. Michael's Mount, Mount's Bay (take A30 from Penzance). ☎ ***01736/710-507.*** *Internet:* `www.stmichaelsmount.co.uk`*. Admission: £4.80 ($8) adults, £13 ($21) families (2 adults, 2 children). Open: April–Oct Mon–Fri 10:30 a.m.–5:30 (last admission 4:45 p.m.), and most weekends in summer; Nov–March usually Mon, Wed, and Fri by conducted tour only at 11 a.m., noon, 2 and 3 p.m.; call to verify.*

Chapel Street

Penzance

Chapel Street, running north-south from St. Mary's Church near the waterfront up to Parade Street, is the most architecturally significant street in Penzance. Strolling the length takes only a few minutes, and doing so gives you a glimpse of the Penzance of yore. Chapel Street has always been a mixture of residential and commercial buildings. Facades that look Georgian (that is, from the late 18th and early 19th centuries) often hide much older buildings. Two hundred years ago, the **Union Hotel** with its Assembly Rooms was the center of the town's social activities. Across the road from the Union Hotel is the **Egyptian House,** built in 1835 with Egyptian motifs and ornamentation. Other houses on the street belonged to mayors, mariners, and traders. Just below the Regent Hotel is the **Old Custom House,** a fine building whose interior retains many original 18th-century features (it's now a shop selling antiques, crystal, and German Christmas ornaments). Farther down is the **Turks Head,** which claims to be the oldest inn in Penzance. Across from the inn is the austere **Wesleyan Chapel** of 1814. Nearby, marked by a blue plaque, is the home of Maria Branwell, the beloved "Aunt Branwell" who moved to Yorkshire to raise Charlotte, Emily, Anne, and Branwell Brontë after their mother died. Chapel Street's most impressive building is **St. Mary's Church,** rebuilt in the 1830s on the site of an earlier medieval chapel.

Penlee House Gallery & Museum

Penzance

Built as a private residence in 1865, Penlee House is now Penzance's art gallery and museum. The painting collection focuses on the Newlyn School of artists, mostly landscape painters active in the area between 1880 and 1930. The museum has exhibits ranging from Stone Age to the present day. You can tour the entire museum in about 30 minutes. The Orangery Cafe is a nice spot for tea or a light lunch.

Morrab Road. ☎ ***01736/363-625.*** *Admission: £2 ($3.20) adults, free for children 5–15. Open: Mon–Sat 10 a.m.–5 p.m., (until 4:30 p.m. Oct–April).*

Trengwainton Garden

West of Penzance

Nowhere else on mainland Britain will you find a garden with plants as exotic as the ones grown here. Trengwainton (pronounced as it's spelled, Treng-*wain*-ton), which means the "House of the Spring" in Cornish, is set in the granite hills behind Penzance and commands panoramic views of Mount's Bay and the Lizard Peninsula. The first walled gardens were constructed in the 18th century, but the plantings didn't really flourish until the late 1920s, under Sir Edward Bolitho. Several species of rhododendrons, which Bolitho planted from seeds collected in Asia, flowered for the first time outside their native habitat in this garden. You see color throughout the year, from camellias and magnolias in early spring to acres of blue hydrangea in late summer. You can have lunch or a Cornish cream tea in the tea house. The garden is a National Trust property. Give yourself at least an hour to enjoy it.

To get here by bus, take the First National bus No. 10/A from Penzance to St. Just; ask the driver to let you off along the way at the stop nearest Trengwainton. (Check with the Tourist Information Centre for bus schedules.)

2 miles west of Penzance, ½ mile west of Heamoor off Penzance-Morvah Rd. (B3312). ☎ ***01736/362-297*** *or 01637/875-404. Admission: £4 ($6) adults, £10 ($16) families (2 adults, 2 children). Open: Feb 16–Nov 2 Sun–Thurs 10 a.m.–5 p.m. (until 5:30 p.m. April–Sept).*

The Penwith Peninsula: A Driving Tour from Penzance to Land's End

On a map, the **Penwith Peninsula** west of Penzance looks like a giant toe dipping into the Atlantic. This area is a great place for a driving tour, which I outline in this section. B3315 follows the peninsula's southern coastline past the fishing villages of Newlyn and Mousehole — good places to stop and explore for an hour or so — to famous Land's End, where you can pick up the fast A30 back to Penzance. The distances here aren't that great; driving this loop without stopping takes about an hour, but the trip makes a pleasant half- or full-day excursion from Penzance or St. Ives. If you're without a car, bus service runs from Penzance to Newlyn, Mousehole, and Land's End. For times and schedules, check with the tourist office or the local bus service, **First Western National** (☎ **01209/719-988;** www.firstwesternnational.co.uk).

Stop #1: Newlyn

Just a couple of miles south of Penzance lies the port of Newlyn, home of England's second-largest fishing fleet. Chances are that any fresh fish or lobster that you eat in Penzance or even St. Ives was landed in the waters near Newlyn. *Pilchards* (mature sardines) have traditionally been the biggest catch off these shores. In general, though, the pilchard fishing industry that was the mainstay of Cornwall's coastal villages from the medieval era until the early part of the 20th century is now a tiny fragment of what it was. **The Pilchard Works Museum and Factory,** The Coombe (☎ **01736/332-112**), is the last remaining salt pilchard factory in England; the factory has a small adjunct museum that explains the process of curing pilchards; for almost a hundred years, this factory has supplied salt (cured) pilchards to the same Italian company. The museum is open weekdays Easter through October from 10 a.m. to 6 p.m.

The seascapes and the quality of light along this part of the Cornish coast lured several artists to the area in the late Victorian era. You can see the paintings of the Newlyn School in Penzance at Penlee House. (See "Exploring in and around Penzance," earlier in this chapter.) The **Newlyn Art Gallery,** Newlyn Green (☎ **01736/363-715**), has a small collection of the distinctive Arts and Crafts copper work that was produced in Newlyn from 1890 to 1950. The free museum is open Monday to Saturday from 10 a.m. to 5 p.m.

If the sea air has you feeling *peckish* (hungry), you'll find the best fish and chips in town at the **Tolcarne Inn,** Tolcarne Place (☎ **01736/365-074**). Or you may want to try fresh crab or Newlyn fish pie: white and smoked fish and prawns in white wine sauce, topped with cheese and breadcrumbs. Meals (lunch and dinner daily) are served in a pub-like room with a beamed ceiling. Main courses go for £5 to £9.25 ($8 to $15); MasterCard and Visa are accepted.

Stop #2: Mousehole

A few miles south of Newlyn lies the former fishing village of Mousehole (pronounced *Muz*-zle). With its curving quay, its small, protected harbor, and its quaint stone cottages, Mousehole is a pretty place. The town attracts many tourists who come for lunch or tea and a look around. The town itself is the attraction here.

One good restaurant to try is **Cornish Range,** 6 Chapel St. (☎ **01736/731-488**), open daily in the summer and Wednesday to Saturday in the winter for lunch and dinner. On the menu, you find fish soup, crab Florentine, roasted cod and mullet, and many other fresh fish dishes. Main courses go for £10.95 to £15 ($18 to $24). MasterCard and Visa are accepted. If you're looking for a good, unfussy Cornish cream tea, pop into **Pam's Pantry,** 3 Mill Lane (☎ **01736/731-532**), open daily February to November 9:30 a.m. to 6:30 p.m. This cash-only hole–in-the-wall also serves Newlyn crab in soups, sandwiches, and salads. A cream tea is under £4 ($6), and main courses go for £5 to £8 ($8 to $13).

Stop #3: The Minack Theatre

The oceanside **Minack Theatre** (☎ **01736/810-694**) was carved out of a rocky hillside in Porthcurno, a village 9 miles southwest of Penzance (from Mousehole, continue south on B3315 and follow signs). The theater is legendary because of its outdoor setting, overlooking the ocean. If you stay in Penzance or St. Ives, an evening here makes for a memorable experience. From May to September, theater companies from all over England stage performances of everything from Shakespeare to musical comedies, a tradition dating to 1932. Bring a cushion (if you have one), a sweater, and a raincoat just in case. You can check out the Visitor Centre even if you're not seeing a play. Theater tickets cost £6.50 ($11) for adults and £3.25 ($5) for children age 5 to 15. The exhibition hall, which has information on the theater's history, is open daily from 9:30 a.m. to 5:30 p.m. (10 a.m. to 4 p.m. October through March). The theater presents evening performances Monday through Friday at 8 p.m. and matinees on Wednesday and Friday at 2 p.m. from the end of May to mid-September.

Stop #4: Land's End

Atlantic-facing Land's End, where high granite cliffs plunge down to the roaring sea, is one of the country's most famous and dramatic landmarks. But a theme-park development that you have to pass through to reach the headland mars the grandeur of this windy point, the westernmost on mainland Britain. A well-marked path leads out to an observation point, and you can follow other coastal paths if the day is fine. The British-owned Scilly Isles are 28 miles out to sea; otherwise, nothing lies between England and the eastern coast of North America.

St. Ives: Artists' Haven by the Sea

Understanding why this former fishing village on the north coast of Cornwall attracts artists is easy. The sea at **St. Ives** changes color like a jewel shimmering in the sunlight. The town's whitewashed stone cottages and painted stucco villas stretch along rocky coves and a long, curving sand beach. A relaxing place to stay, St. Ives is much smaller than Penzance. A branch of London's Tate museum commemorates a group of local artists, including Barbara Hepworth and Ben Nicholson, who lived and worked in the town. The town is still a favorite hangout for artists and craftspeople. You find dozens of small galleries for browsing, in addition to plenty of good restaurants specializing in locally caught seafood.

Getting to St. Ives

Trains run throughout the day from London's Paddington Station to the area. For St. Ives, you change trains at St. Erth on the main line to Penzance, or you can take a train direct from Penzance. The total trip is about 5½ to six hours. For train information, call ☎ **08457/484-950.** Long-distance buses from London's Victoria Coach Station take up to nine hours; call **National Express** (☎ **0990/808-080**) for more information. Driving from Penzance, you can take A30 northeast to its junction with A3074 and follow A3074 north.

For information about renting a car in Penzance, see the section "Getting to Penzance," earlier in this chapter.

Finding information

The **Tourist Information Centre** in the Guildhall, Street-an-Pol (☎ **01736/796-297**), is open Monday through Friday from 9:30 a.m. to 5:30 p.m.; Saturday from April to mid-May 10 a.m. to 1 p.m. and from mid-May through August 9:30 a.m. to 5:30 p.m.; Sunday from mid-May through September 10 a.m. to 1 p.m. The center dispenses information on the area, stocks brochures on local attractions, and operates a room-finding service.

Staying in St. Ives

St. Ives draws visitors year-round but is particularly busy in the warm summer months. You find dozens of hotels and B&Bs in this small Cornish town. Here are my recommended choices.

Garrack Hotel & Restaurant

$$–$$$

This hotel is renowned for its restaurant and has special rates that include dinner. The Garrack is in a traffic-free area of St. Ives with views looking out over the gardens to the sea. Some of the 18 guest rooms are in a former private house, the others in a modern wing and separate cottage. All have private bathrooms. The indoor pool is great for kids. The romantic sea-view restaurant serves fresh fish and lobster from Newlyn; organic beef, lamb, and venison; and produce from its own garden. A four-course fixed-price meal is £24.50 ($39). Even if you stay elsewhere, you may want to eat here (reservations required).

Burthallan Lane, St. Ives, Cornwall TR26 3AA. ☎ ***01736/796-199.*** *Internet:* `www.garrack.com`. *Rack rates: £110–£162 ($176–$259) double with English breakfast; £150–£204 ($240–$326) double with dinner and breakfast. AE, DC, MC, V.*

Pedn-Olva Hotel

$$–$$$

Located right on the edge of a commanding cliff, this hotel was stylishly refurbished in 2001 and has 30 rooms with the best sea views in St. Ives. Most of the rooms (and bathrooms) are smallish, but the panoramic views are mesmerizing. There's a fine restaurant, sunny terraces, and a pool, and you're a 2-minute walk to the center of town or the beach. It's a light, bright, airy hotel with lots of nice features.

Porthminster Beach, St. Ives, Cornwall TR26 2EA. ☎ ***01736/796-222.*** *Fax: 01736-797-710. Internet:* `www.walterhickshotels.co.uk`. *Rack rates: £110–£136 ($176–$217) double. Rates include English breakfast. AE, DC, MC, V.*

Tregony

$

This well-maintained, nonsmoking B&B in a pretty, bay-fronted Victorian house sits just above the Tate St. Ives and Porthmeor Beach. The B&B has five guest rooms, two of them with sea views and all with private bathrooms with showers. This B&B's staff welcomes families with children.

Clodgy View, St. Ives, Cornwall TR26 1JG. ☎ ***01736/795-884.*** *Fax: 01736/798-942. Internet:* `www.tregony.com`. *Rack rates: £50–£58 ($80–$93) double. Rate includes English breakfast. MC, V.*

Dining in St. Ives

As you might expect, fresh seafood is on the menu in many St. Ives restaurants. Here are my dining choices.

Josephs

$ **SEAFOOD/INTERNATIONAL**

This small, smart cafe-restaurant overlooking the harbor specializes in seafood, with four or five choices daily. You can also get duck, chicken, and steak. Pastas are served at lunchtime. Try the seafood spaghetti made with scallops and prawns.

*39a Fore St. ☎ **01736/796-514.** Reservations recommended for dinner. Main courses: £8.50–£14 ($14–$22). MC, V. Open: daily 10 a.m.–4:30 p.m. and 6:30–9:45 p.m.*

Porthminster Beach Cafe

$$–$$$ **MODERN BRITISH/INTERNATIONAL**

This pleasant cafe on Porthminster Beach overlooking St. Ives Bay serves some interesting dishes. The offerings emphasize fresh fish, but tasty vegetarian options are always on the menu. A meal may consist of prosciutto and charred artichokes with Cornish Brie and spiced pears, or John Dory (a type of fish) on a risotto cake made with sun-dried tomatoes.

*Porthminster Beach. ☎ **01736/795-352.** Reservations recommended for dinner. Fixed-price lunch £8 ($13), fixed-price dinner £25 ($40). MC, V. Open: April–Oct daily 11 a.m.–4 p.m. and 7–10 p.m.*

Russets Restaurant

$$ **SEAFOOD/INTERNATIONAL**

This intimate restaurant, a favorite with both locals and visitors, wisely specializes in fresh seafood. Don't pass up crab soup if it's available. Or you may want to try fish stew with *aioli* (a cold sauce made with crushed garlic, egg yolks, olive oil, and lemon). If you're not into fish, you can choose from breast of duck, chicken, and lamb.

*18a Fore St. ☎ **01736/794-700.** Reservations recommended for dinner. Main courses: lunch £5–£15 ($8–$24), dinner £10–£30 ($16–$48). AE, DC, MC, V. Open: daily noon to 2 p.m., 7–10 p.m. (closed Mon Nov–Mar).*

Exploring St. Ives

Over a century ago, artists started coming to St. Ives for the wonderful light and atmosphere. The sculptor Barbara Hepworth was one who stayed, and her house is one of the town's most magical places to visit. Tate St. Ives is the biggest tourist draw. The sandy beaches and high headlands with views of the sea make for great walks.

Barbara Hepworth Museum and Sculpture Garden

This wonderful adjunct of the Tate St. Ives (just a couple of minutes' walk from that museum) gives remarkable insight into the work of Dame Barbara Hepworth, one of the great sculptors of the 20th century. What you see is Hepworth's actual studio and sculpture garden. She lived here from 1949 until her death in 1975 at age 72. On the lower level, you find an informative exhibit on her life and career. Then you go upstairs to a marvelous living area and from there out into the **sculpture garden.** On display throughout are about 47 sculptures and drawings from 1928 to 1974, photos, working tools, and Hepworth memorabilia.

Barnoon Hill. ☎ ***01736/796-226.*** *Admission: £3.95 ($6) adults, £2.25 ($3.60) seniors and students. Combined ticket with Tate St. Ives £6.95 ($11) adults, £3.90 ($6) seniors and students. Open: Mar–Oct daily 10 a.m.–5:30 p.m.; Nov–Feb Tues–Sun 10 a.m.–4:30 p.m.*

Tate St. Ives

A branch of the Tate museum in London, Tate St. Ives opened in 1993 and quickly became the town's biggest attraction. The museum is devoted exclusively to modern art, and particularly to the works of artists who lived in Cornwall. St. Ives itself has been an artists' colony since 1928. Personally, I think the building, which sits on the site of old town gasworks, is ungainly and confusing, although the spaces are filled with light and have some fine seaward views. The museum has no permanent collection, but presents changing exhibitions four times a year; the paintings, sculptures, and ceramics on display are chosen from works in the Tate's vast collection (the British National Collection of Modern Art). You also find works by contemporary artists. A pleasant cafe where you can have lunch or a snack is on the premises. The Gallery also manages the nearby Barbara Hepworth Museum and Sculpture Garden (see the preceding information on that museum).

Porthmeor Beach. ☎ ***01736/796-226.*** *Admission: £4.25 ($7) adults, free for seniors and children under 18. Combined ticket with Barbara Hepworth Museum £6.95 ($11) adults, £3.90 ($6) students. Open: Mar–Oct daily 10 a.m.–5:30 p.m.; Nov–Feb Tues–Sun 10 a.m.–4:30 p.m.*

Finding more to see near St. Ives

Cornwall, like Wiltshire and Devon, is full of prehistoric sites, although nothing as grand as Stonehenge. What follows are descriptions of three ancient sites near St. Ives that you may want to check out; before you set out, I recommend that you stop at the Tourist Information Centre for more exact directions:

- **Chysauster** (*Kie*-sis-ter) is the remains of a remarkable Iron Age village with four pairs of houses each fronting a village street. Each house is oval in plan, but the roughly circular rooms are set in thick walls, and all open to a central courtyard. Now open to the sky, the rooms were apparently roofed with stone or thatch, although the courtyards were open. During the excavation, archaeologists discovered hearths, pottery, and other domestic debris lying on the paved floors. Each house also had a stone-fenced back garden. From St. Ives, drive south on B3311, turning west toward New Mill and the marked site.
- **Lanyon Quoit** is a huge granite slab, 17 feet by 9 feet, and 18 inches thick, resting on three upright stones. This is all that remains of a Neolithic tomb. From St. Ives, drive west on B3306 to a signposted

turn-off just before Morvah. Trengwainton Garden (see the preceding section, "Exploring in and around Penzance") is a couple of miles farther south.

- **Zennor Quoit** (also called Mulfra Quoit) is an unusual type of Early Bronze Age megalithic tomb, which originated in Brittany and is found in the Penwith area of Cornwall. Divided into chamber and antechamber, a large round *cairn* (a heap of stones used as a marker) originally covered the tomb, but all trace of this has disappeared, leaving the internal structure standing free. From St. Ives, drive west on B3306 to the signposted turnoff. Be prepared for a 15-minute walk on a path that is often wet and overgrown.

Fowey and the Saint's Way: River Town and Holy Track

Located on the south coast, about midway between Plymouth and Penzance, **Fowey** (pronounced *Foy*) is a small, scenic harbor town with several historic buildings and an interesting past. The town stretches along the green, wooded banks of the River Fowey, a shipping channel that empties into St. Austell Bay. The river is a favorite spot for pleasure boats of all kinds. A car-ferry service runs between Fowey to Bodinnick, on the east side of the river. Daphne du Maurier, who used Cornwall as a setting for her most famous novel, *Rebecca,* grew up in Bodinnick, part of Fowey. You can pick up a free map and guide to the town and surrounding villages at Fowey's **Tourist Information Centre,** The Ticket Shop, 4 Custom House Hill (☎ **01726/833-616**). The center is open daily from Easter through September (Monday to Friday from 9 a.m. to 5:30 p.m., Saturday 9 a.m. to 5 p.m., Sunday 10 a.m. to 5 p.m.); the center closes on Sundays in the off-season.

If you want lunch or tea in Fowey, **The Toll Bar,** Lostwithiel Street (☎ **01726/833-001**) has a nice outdoor terrace overlooking the river and sea. The **Marina Hotel & Waterside Restaurant,** Esplanade, Fowey, Cornwall PL23 1HY (☎ **01726/833-315;** fax 01726/832-779; www.themarinahotel.co.uk) has 12 lovely rooms, most of them overlooking the river, and a fine-dining restaurant. A double room with breakfast goes for £100 to £188 ($160 to $301).

This has been great walking country for thousands of years. The 26-mile-long **Saint's Way** begins at Padstow on the north coast, crosses the moors of central Cornwall, and ends at Fowey. During the Bronze Age and Iron Age, Saint's Way was a coast-to-coast trading route that avoided the treacherous waters off Land's End. Later, Saint's Way became the route for missionaries and pilgrims crossing from Ireland to take ships from Fowey to France and on to Rome or Santiago de Compostela in Spain. You see hill forts, granite Celtic crosses, holy wells, and ancient churches all along the route.

Cotehele, Eden Project, and Lanhydrock: Three Great Cornish Gardens

Cornwall, blessed with the mildest climate in England, is equally blessed with magnificent gardens. Check out these three places where plant lovers can revel in nature. Two of them are former estates with fascinating houses; the third is new.

Cotehele

Set on the steep, wooded slopes of the River Tamar, west of Plymouth, **Cotehele** (pronounced *Co*-teel; ☎ **01579/351-346**) is a marvelous manor house with magnificent gardens. This is one of the least altered medieval houses in England. Built in granite and slate, Cotehele blends in naturally with the landscape. The rooms inside, unlit by electricity, display a wonderful collection of ancient furniture, textiles, and tapestries. The chapel contains the oldest working domestic clock in England, still in its original place. Formal gardens, terraces, and a daffodil meadow surround the house, situated near the top of the valley. The steep valley gardens below contain many species of exotic plants that thrive in Cornwall's mild climate. The house is a National Trust property. A good restaurant is in the nearby medieval barn. You need at least two hours to see everything. Admission is £6.60 ($10), £16.50 ($26) for families (2 adults, 2 children). From March 23 to November 2, the house is open Saturday through Thursday from 11 a.m. to 5 p.m. (in October and November until 4:30 p.m.); the gardens are open year-round from 10:30 a.m. to dusk. To get there from Plymouth, take A38 northwest, then A388, turning east on A390 and south at Harrowbarrow.

Eden Project

A few miles west of Fowey, overlooking St. Austell Bay, is a major tourist attraction called **Eden Project** (☎ **01726/811-911;** `www.edenproject.com`), which opened in March 2001. The Eden Project is both an educational resource and an environmental showcase. The site comprises two gigantic geodesic conservatories, one devoted to the rainforest, the other to the fruits and flowers of the Mediterranean, South Africa, and California. Sunflowers, lavender, and hemp are among the plants that grow outside on the acres of landscaped grounds. Plants from all sorts of different terrains are grown in microhabitats. Eden Project is intriguing and definitely worth a couple of hours. A trip here is a fun way to introduce kids to plants and environmental issues. Admission is £10 ($16) for adults, £7.50 ($12) for seniors, £4 ($6) for children 5 to 15, and £25 ($40) for families (2 adults, 3 children). The attraction is open daily from 9:30 a.m. to 6 p.m. (November through February until 5 p.m.). St. Austell is the nearest town. The Eden Project is signposted from A390, A30, and A391.

Lanhydrock

Set in a beautiful landscape overlooking the valley of the Fowey River, **Lanhydrock** (Lan-*hi*-druck) is one of the grandest homes in Cornwall. The magnificent Long Gallery, with its 17th-century plaster ceiling depicting scenes from the Old Testament, is one of few rooms that survived a disastrous fire in 1881. You can view approximately 50 rooms that reflect the organization and lifestyles in a rich Victorian household that depended on servants to keep it running efficiently. Lanhydrock reveals the other side of grand living: the kitchens, sculleries, and larders where the staff toiled.

Different kinds of gardens — from Victorian *parterres* (ornamental gardens with paths between the beds) to woodland gardens with camellias, magnolias, and rhododendrons — surround the house on all sides. An avenue of ancient beech and sycamore trees runs from the 17th-century gatehouse down to a medieval bridge across the Fowey. The National Trust manages the property. You need at least two hours to take it all in. Admission is £7.20 ($12), £18 ($29) for families (2 adults, 2 children). The house is open April through September Tuesday to Sunday from 11 a.m. to 5:30 p.m. and in October from 11 a.m. to 5 p.m. The garden is open daily year-round from 10 a.m. to 6 p.m. Lanhydrock is about 10 miles north of Fowey and 2½ miles east of Bodmin; the home is signposted from A30, A38, and B3268.

Part VI
England's Heartland

"I appreciate that our room looks out onto several Regency fountains, but I had to get up 6 times last night to go to the bathroom."

In this part . . .

Central England encompasses many more counties than the two I describe in this part. But the bordering counties of Warwickshire and Gloucestershire are, to my mind, the heart of England's heartland. William Shakespeare, whose words have become a permanent part of the English language, was born and died in Warwickshire. And Gloucestershire can boast some of the most beautiful countryside and villages in England.

In Chapter 19, I take you through Shakespeare's hometown, Stratford-upon-Avon, where you can visit the houses that the great poet and playwright called home. From Stratford, you can make an easy day trip to mighty Warwick Castle, the most impressive castle in this piece of central England. Chapter 20 begins with the Regency spa town of Bath, a place that epitomizes the graceful, glamorous world of Jane Austen and Georgian England. From Bath, you can head to Cheltenham, a smaller spa town in Gloucestershire, or tour the Cotswolds, where picturesque medieval market towns of honey-colored stone stand as proud reminders of the days when the wool trade brought long-lived prosperity to the region.

Chapter 19

Stratford-upon-Avon and Warwick Castle

In This Chapter

- Visiting Shakespeare's hometown
- Spending time in mighty Warwick Castle

William Shakespeare is the one name that people around the world associate with England. Shakespeare (1564–1616) was a universal genius: His plays and poems transcend geographical boundaries and strike a chord common in all humanity. It's no wonder, then, that **Stratford-upon-Avon,** the town where he was born and died, is one of the most visited places in England. **Warwick Castle** is only a few miles away and easily accessible by train from Stratford, so you may want to visit both when in the area. Bath and the Cotswolds are also nearby (see Chapter 20). For an overview of the area, see the "England's Heartland" map in this chapter.

Stratford-upon-Avon: In the Bard's Footsteps

Do I need to tell you whose spirit pervades this market town on the River Avon, 91 miles northwest of London? Stratford-upon-Avon is a shrine to the world's greatest playwright, William Shakespeare, who was born, lived much of his life, and is buried here. In summer, crowds of international tourists overrun the town, which hustles its Shakespeare connection in every conceivable way.

Stratford boasts many fine Elizabethan and Jacobean buildings, but it's not really a quaint village anymore. (See the "Stratford-upon-Avon" map in this chapter.) If you arrive by train, your first glimpse will be of a vast parking lot across from the station. Don't let this put you off. The charms of Stratford's formerly bucolic setting haven't been completely lost — you'll find plenty of charming corners as you explore. Besides the literary pilgrimage sights, the top draw in Stratford is the **Royal Shakespeare Theatre,** where Britain's foremost actors perform.

England's Heartland

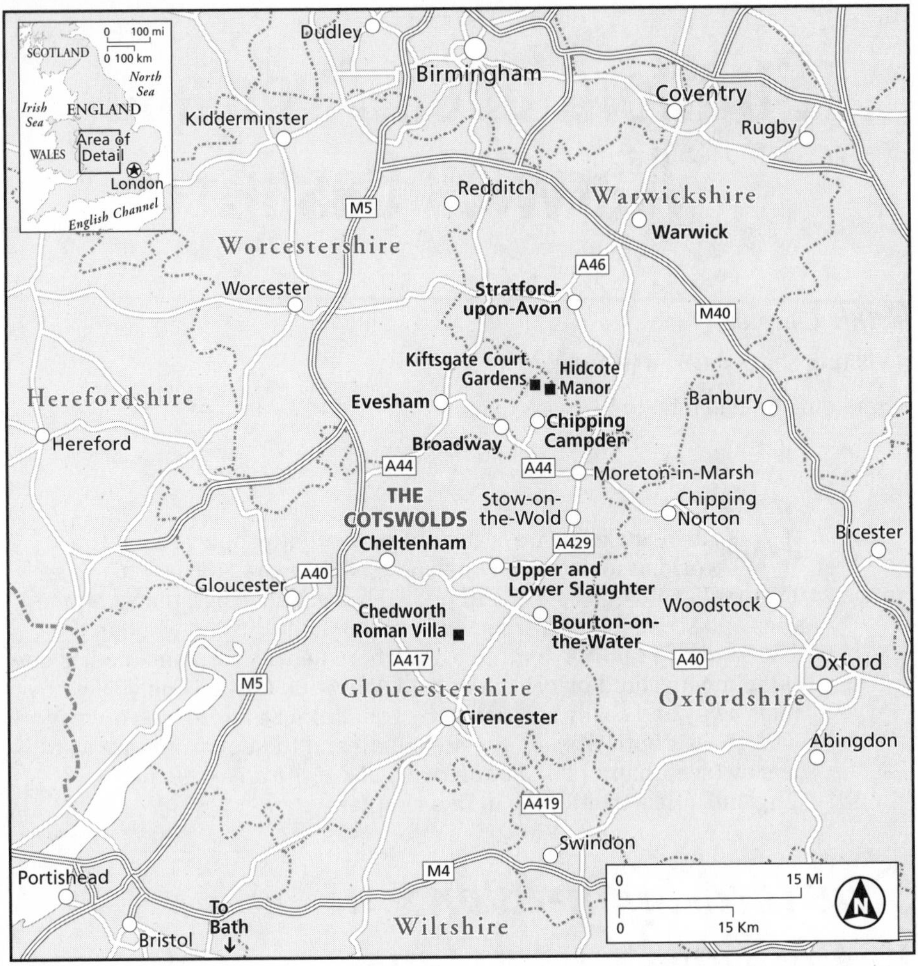

Stratford has much to see and enjoy. I recommend that you spend at least a day here. Consider an overnight stay if you're a theater lover, but make sure that you book your theater seat in advance. (See the section "Seeing a play in Stratford-upon-Avon,"" later in this chapter.)

Getting to Stratford-upon-Avon

Direct trains leave frequently from London's Paddington Station; the journey takes about two hours and costs £23 ($37) for a standard-class round-trip ticket. Call ☎ **08457/484-950** for information and schedules. **National Express** (☎ **0990/808-080**) offers daily bus service from London's Victoria Coach Station; the trip lasts a little more than three hours and costs £17 ($27) for a round-trip ticket. By car from London, take the M40 toward Oxford and continue to Stratford-upon-Avon on A34.

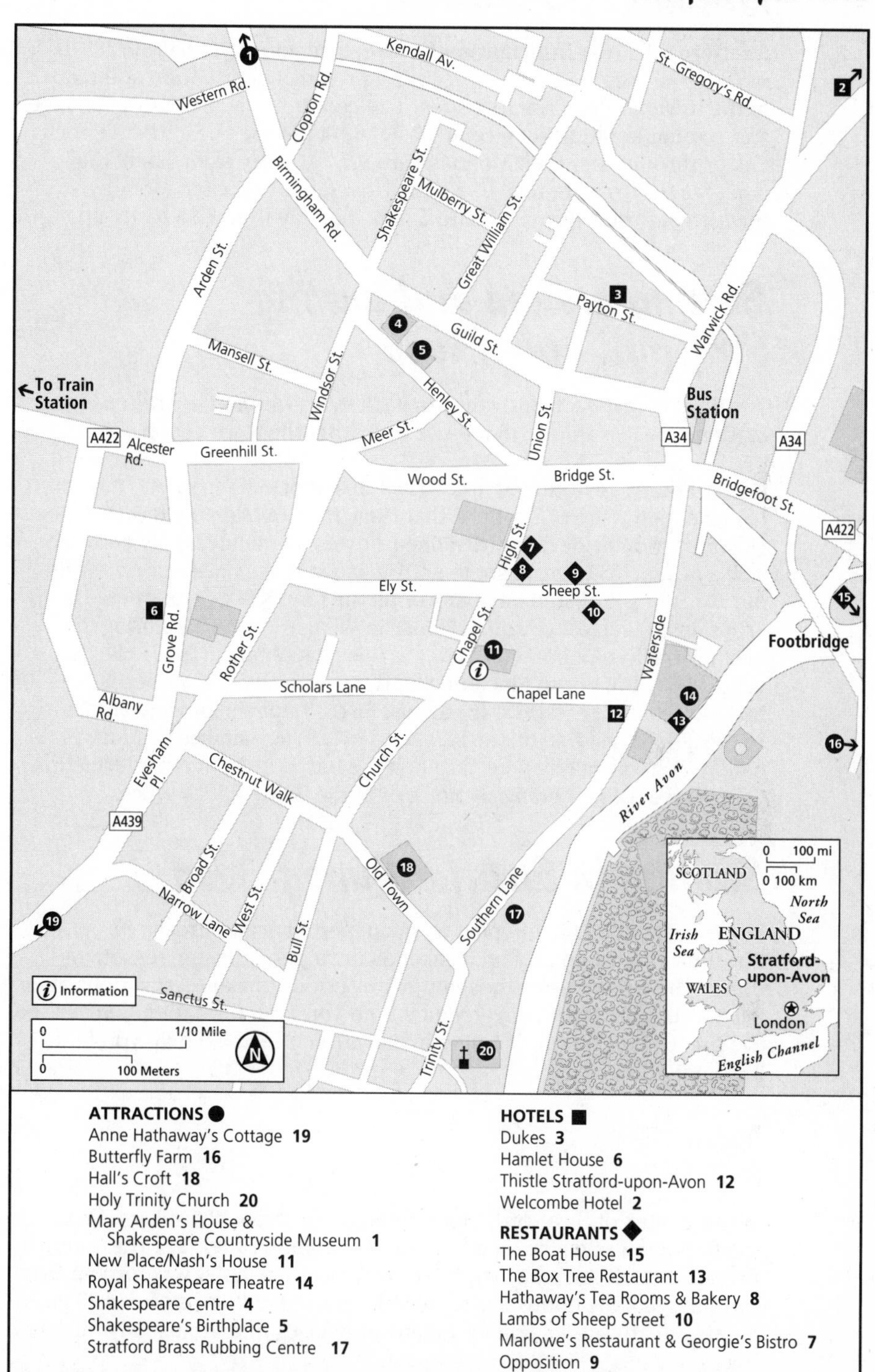
Stratford-upon-Avon
Kendall Av.
St. Gregory's Rd.
Western Rd.
Clopton Rd.
Birmingham Rd.
Shakespeare St.
Mulberry St.
Great William St.
Arden St.
Payton St.
Guild St.
Warwick Rd.
Mansell St.
Windsor St.
Henley St.
To Train Station
Bus Station
Meer St.
Union St.
A422
Alcester Rd.
Greenhill St.
A34
A34
Wood St.
Bridge St.
Bridgefoot St.
A422
High St.
Ely St.
Sheep St.
Grove Rd.
Rother St.
Chapel St.
Waterside
Footbridge
Albany Rd.
Scholars Lane
Chapel Lane
Evesham Pl.
Chestnut Walk
Church St.
River Avon
A439
Broad St.
Old Town
Narrow Lane
West St.
Bull St.
Southern Lane
Information
Sanctus St.
0 1/10 Mile
0 100 Meters
Trinity St.
SCOTLAND
0 100 mi
0 100 km
North Sea
Irish Sea
ENGLAND
Stratford-upon-Avon
WALES
London
English Channel
ATTRACTIONS ●
Anne Hathaway's Cottage 19
Butterfly Farm 16
Hall's Croft 18
Holy Trinity Church 20
Mary Arden's House & Shakespeare Countryside Museum 1
New Place/Nash's House 11
Royal Shakespeare Theatre 14
Shakespeare Centre 4
Shakespeare's Birthplace 5
Stratford Brass Rubbing Centre 17
HOTELS ■
Dukes 3
Hamlet House 6
Thistle Stratford-upon-Avon 12
Welcombe Hotel 2
RESTAURANTS ◆
The Boat House 15
The Box Tree Restaurant 13
Hathaway's Tea Rooms & Bakery 8
Lambs of Sheep Street 10
Marlowe's Restaurant & Georgie's Bistro 7
Opposition 9

Finding information

Stratford's **Tourist Information Centre,** Bridgefoot (☎ **01789/293-127;** www.shakespeare-country.co.uk), provides information and maps of the town and its principal sites. The center has a currency exchange and a **room-booking service** at ☎ **01789/415-061.** The center is open Easter through October, Monday through Saturday from 9 a.m. to 6 p.m., Sunday from 11 a.m. to 5 p.m.; November to Easter, Monday through Saturday from 9 a.m. to 5 p.m., Sunday from 11 a.m. to 4 p.m.

Getting around and touring Stratford-upon-Avon

Stratford is compact, and you can walk everywhere. The train and bus stations are less than a 15-minute walk from the town center.

Guide Friday, 14 Rother St. (☎ **01789/294-466;** www.guidefriday.com), offers guided tours of Stratford that leave from outside the tourist office. Open-top, double-decker buses depart every 15 minutes daily between 9:30 a.m. and 5:30 p.m. in summer. You can take the one-hour ride without stops or get off and on at any or all the town's five Shakespeare properties, including Mary Arden's House in Wilmcote (see "Exploring the best of Stratford-upon-Avon," later in this chapter). The tour ticket is valid all day but doesn't include admission into any of the houses. The bus tour cost is £7.50 ($12) for adults, £6 ($10) for seniors and students, £3 ($4.80) for children under 12, and £18 ($29) for families (2 adults, 4 children). You can buy your ticket on the bus, at the Tourist Information Centre (see the preceding section), or at the Guide Friday office.

Staying in Stratford-upon-Avon

Make reservations if you plan to sleep, perchance to dream, in Stratford — particularly on weekends during the theater season and during the summer. For those popular periods, make reservations at least a couple of weeks in advance. The Tourist Information Centre (see the preceding section, "Finding information") can also help you find accommodations.

Dukes

$

In the center of Stratford, close to Shakespeare's birthplace, Dukes is smaller and less glamorous than the Welcombe Hotel (see the listing in this section), but it's charming for the price. The hotel was formed from two Georgian townhouses. The nicely restored public areas and 22 guest rooms are attractive. You find many amenities that are usually found in more expensive hotels here, and the hotel's restaurant serves good English and Continental cuisine.

Payton Street, Stratford-upon-Avon, Warwickshire CV37 6UA. ☎ ***01789/269-300.*** *Fax: 01789/414-700. Rack rates: £65–£100 ($104–$160) double. Rates include English breakfast. AE, MC, V.*

Hamlet House

$

This unpretentious, well-maintained B&B in a Victorian townhouse is a convenient three-minute walk from the train station and close to everything else in Stratford. Two of its five guest rooms have private bathrooms; the others share a toilet and shower. Yvonne and Paul, the owners, are helpful, hospitable, and welcome children. The breakfast is hearty.

52 Grove Rd., Stratford-upon-Avon, Warwickshire CV37 6PB. ☎ ***01789/204-386.*** *Internet:* `www.hamlethouse.com`. *Rack rates: £40–£56 ($64–$90) double. Rates include English breakfast. No credit cards.*

Thistle Stratford-upon-Avon

$$–$$$

If this hotel were any closer to the Royal Shakespeare Festival theaters, the guests would be on stage. Thistle is a British chain of upscale full-service hotels, offering well-decorated rooms (63 of them in this hotel) with an abundance of amenities. The building dates to 1791 and has been decorated to look like a traditional Georgian townhouse. Bards Restaurant serves fine English and Continental cuisine.

Waterside, Stratford-upon-Avon, Warwickshire CV37 6BA. ☎ ***800/847-4358*** *in U.S. and Canada or* ***01789/294-949.*** *Fax: 01789/415-874. Internet:* `www.thistlehotels.com`. *Rack rates: £128–£185 ($205–$296) double. AE, DC, MC, V.*

Welcombe Hotel

$$$

This is the place to stay if you're wanting to feel manor born. Located 1½ miles northeast of the town center, Welcombe Hotel is in one of the county's great Victorian (Jacobean-style) houses. An 18-hole golf course and 157 acres of grounds surround this luxurious full-service hotel. The largest of the 68 guest rooms are big enough for tennis matches.

Warwick Road, Stratford-upon-Avon, Warwickshire CV37 0NR. ☎ ***01789/295-252.*** *Fax: 01789/414-666. Internet:* `www.welcombe.co.uk`. *Rack rates: £175–£205 ($280–$328) double. Rates include English breakfast. DC, MC, V.*

Dining in Stratford-upon-Avon

As you might expect in a town that attracts visitors from around the globe, Stratford-upon-Avon is not lacking in restaurants. Here are my dining choices.

The Boat House

$–$$ MODERN BRITISH/INTERNATIONAL

This chic bistro above a boathouse on the River Avon is a fun and flavorful place to dine. The inventive menu is international in scope, and the food never loses out in the translation. You may find spicy Thai spring rolls, Szechuan-style tuna, roast halibut with tomato risotto, or spinach lasagna. The decor's nautical theme features wooden tables, bare floorboards, and rope.

Swan's Nest Lane (on the river between Clopton Bridge and footbridge). ☎ ***01789/297-733.*** *Reservations recommended for dinner. Main courses: £9–£15 ($14–$22), fixed-price lunch £10.95 ($18). MC, V. Open: Wed–Sat noon to 2 p.m., Mon–Sat 6–11 p.m.*

The Box Tree Restaurant

$$$$ BRITISH/CONTINENTAL

This lovely restaurant in the Royal Shakespeare Theatre looks out on the River Avon with its gliding white swans. The menu offers a bit of everything — French, Italian, and English dishes. You can dine by candlelight after a performance. Use a special phone in the theater's lobby to make a reservation here.

In the Royal Shakespeare Theatre. ☎ ***01789/293-226.*** *Reservations required. Fixed-price matinee lunch £16 ($29); 3-course fixed-price dinners £26–£27 ($39–$40) AE, MC, V. Open: noon to 2:30 p.m. on matinee days (call for schedule) and Mon–Sat 5:45 p.m. to midnight.*

Hathaway's Tea Rooms & Bakery

$ TEAS/LIGHT FARE

If you enjoy afternoon tea in atmospheric surroundings, this place is great. The tea rooms are on the second floor of a building that dates from 1610. Cream tea comes with homemade fruit scones, clotted cream, and jam, and high tea includes a variety of sandwiches. You can also get an English breakfast and light meals through the day.

19 High St. ☎ ***01789/292-404.*** *Cream teas £3.90 ($6); high teas £5.95 ($10). No credit cards. Open: daily 9 a.m.–5:30 p.m.*

Lambs of Sheep Street

$–$$ **MODERN BRITISH**

Although it's in one of Stratford's oldest buildings, with low ceilings and timber framing, Lamb's serves modern British cooking with flair. Typical menu offerings include pan-fried pork with sage prosciutto, chargrilled ribeye steak, breast of chicken roasted in mango with lime butter, and vegetarian dishes such as tomato risotto with grilled vegetables and pesto.

12 Sheep St. ☎ ***01789/292-554.*** *Reservations recommended. Main courses: £11.95–£13.50 ($19–$22); fixed-price lunch and dinner £11.50–£14 ($18–$22). AE, MC, V. Open: daily noon to 2 p.m.; Mon–Sat 5–10 p.m., Sun 6–9:30 p.m.*

Marlowe's Restaurant & Georgie's Bistro

$–$$ **BRITISH/MODERN BRITISH**

An Elizabethan townhouse is the setting for these adjoining eateries. Marlowe's is the classier "silver service" restaurant. The bar, where a fire blazes in winter, leads to an oak-paneled dining room where you can sample specialties such as Drunken Duck (duck marinated in gin, red wine, cracked pepper, and juniper berries). In summer, you can dine on the patio. Georgie's, the bistro area, is great for a relaxed, informal meal. Try fish and chips or pork and leek sausages.

18 High St. ☎ ***01789/204-999.*** *Reservations required for Marlowe's. Main courses: Marlowe's £9–£15 ($14–$24); Georgie's £6–£8 ($10–13). Fixed-price lunch and dinner at Marlowe's £19.75–£22.50 ($32–$36). AE, MC, V. Open: daily noon to 2 p.m. and 5:45–11:00 p.m.*

Opposition

$ **BRITISH/INTERNATIONAL**

This cozy, oak-beamed restaurant in a 16th-century building in the heart of Stratford serves good bistro fare. Lunch and dinner choices are a mix of traditional and Modern British cuisine, with some pasta dishes and Cajun breast of chicken. For dessert, you may want to try *Eton mess,* a concoction of strawberries, meringue, and cream.

13 Sheep St. ☎ ***01789/269-980.*** *Reservations recommended. Main courses: £7–£16 ($11–$26). MC, V. Open: daily noon to 2 p.m. and 5–11 p.m.*

Exploring the best of Stratford-upon-Avon

You can easily spend the better part of a day visiting the Shakespeare sights in Stratford. They are what most visitors come to see.

One ticket gets you into the five sites administered by the **Shakespeare Birthplace Trust (☎ 01789/201-807;** www.shakespeare.org.uk): Anne Hathaway's Cottage, Hall's Croft, Mary Arden's House, New Place/Nash's House, and Shakespeare's Birthplace. You can pick up the ticket at your first stop. This five-in-one ticket costs £13 ($21) for adults, £12 ($19) for seniors and students, £6.50 ($10) for children 5 to 15, and £29 ($46) for families (2 adults, 3 children). All the Shakespeare sites have access limitations, so visitors in wheelchairs are advised to call ahead for more information.

To follow Shakespeare's life from birth to death, I recommend that you visit the sights in this section in the following order: Shakespeare's Birthplace, Anne Hathaway's Cottage, New Place/Nash's House, Hall's Croft, Holy Trinity Church, and Mary Arden's House & Shakespeare Countryside Museum.

Shakespeare's Birthplace

Stratford-upon-Avon

The Bard, son of a glover and wool merchant, first saw the light of day on April 23, 1564, in this house, the logical place to begin your tour. You enter through the modern **Shakespeare Centre,** where you can spend a few minutes browsing the exhibits that illustrate his life and times. The house, filled with Shakespeare memorabilia, is actually two 16th-century half-timbered houses joined together: His father's shop was on one side and the family residence on the other. After visiting the bedroom where wee Willie was (probably) born, the Elizabethan kitchen, and other rooms, you can walk through the garden. You need at least 30 to 60 minutes for a thorough visit; be prepared for crowds.

Henley Street. ***☎ 01789/204-016.*** *Admission: £6.50 ($10) adults, £5.50 ($9) seniors and students, £2.50 ($4) children 5–15, £15 ($24) families (2 adults, 3 children). Open: daily April–May and Sept–Oct Mon–Sat 10 a.m.–5 p.m., Sun 10:30 a.m.–5 p.m.; June–Aug Mon–Sat 9 a.m.–5 p.m., Sun 9:30 a.m.–5 p.m., Nov–Mar Mon–Sat 10 a.m.–4 p.m., Sun 10:30 a.m.–4 p.m.; closed Dec 24–26.*

Anne Hathaway's Cottage

Shottery

Anne Hathaway, who came from a family of *yeoman* farmers (farmers who owned and worked their own land), lived in this lovely thatched cottage until 1582, the year she married 18-year-old Shakespeare. (Anne was 7 years older than Will.) Many original 16th-century furnishings, including the courting *settle* (a type of bench that courting couples sat on), are preserved inside the house, which Anne's descendents occupied until 1892. Before leaving, stroll through the beautiful garden and orchard. Allow about 30 minutes.

To visit the cottage, located about a mile south of Stratford, take a bus from Bridge Street or, better still, walk there along the well-marked country path from Evesham Place.

*Cottage Lane, Shottery. ☎ **01789/204-016.** Admission: £5 ($8) adults, £4 ($6) seniors and students, £2 ($3.20) children 5–15, £12 ($19) families (2 adults, 3 children). Open: April–May Mon–Sat 10 a.m.–5 p.m., Sun 10:30 a.m.–5 p.m.; June–Aug Mon–Sat 9 a.m.–5 p.m., Sun 9:30 a.m.–5 p.m.; Sept–Oct Mon–Sat 9:30 a.m.–5 p.m., Sun 10 a.m.–5 p.m.; Nov–Mar Mon–Sat 10 a.m.–4 p.m., Sun 10:30 a.m.–4 p.m.; closed Jan 1, Good Friday, Dec 24–26.*

New Place/Nash's House

Stratford-upon-Avon

In 1610, Shakespeare was a relatively prosperous man whose plays had been seen by Queen Elizabeth. He retired to New Place, a Stratford house he purchased a few years earlier, and where he died in 1616. The house was later torn down. Of New Place, only the garden remains. You enter the garden through Nash's House, which belonged to Thomas Nash, husband of Shakespeare's granddaughter. The house contains 16th-century period rooms and an exhibit illustrating Stratford's history. A knot garden landscaped in an Elizabethan style with clipped boxwood borders adjoins the house. You can see the house and garden in 15 to 30 minutes.

To reach the site from Anne Hathaway's Cottage, retrace your steps back to Shakespeare's Birthplace and then walk east on Henley Street and south on High Street, which becomes Chapel Street.

*Chapel Street. ☎ **01789/204-016.** Admission: £3.50 ($6) adults, £3 ($4.80) seniors and students, £1.70 ($2.70) children 5–15, £9 ($14) families (2 adults, 3 children). Open: Apr–May and Sept–Oct daily 11 a.m.–5 p.m.; June–Aug Mon–Sat 9:30 a.m.–5 p.m., Sun 10 a.m.–5 p.m.; Nov–Mar Mon–Sat 11 a.m.–4 p.m., Sun 10 a.m.–4 p.m.; opens at 1:30 p.m. Jan 1 and Good Friday; closed Dec 24–26.*

Hall's Croft

Stratford-upon-Avon

Shakespeare's daughter Susanna probably lived with her husband, Dr. John Hall, in this magnificent Tudor house with a walled garden. The house is furnished in the style of a middle-class 17th-century home. You can view exhibits illustrating the theory and practice of medicine in Dr. Hall's time. The word *croft,* by the way, means a small farm. You can see Hall's Croft in less than a half-hour.

To get here from New Place, travel south on Chapel and Church streets and turn east on Old Town.

You can take a convenient break from your Shakespeare pilgrimage at **Drucker's Cafe,** Old Town (☎ **01789/292-107**), a cozy informal eatery attached to Hall's Croft. Sandwiches and homemade soup cost about £2.50 ($4), and a pot of tea is £1 ($1.60). The cafe is open daily from 10 a.m. to 5 p.m. in summer, until 4 p.m. in winter.

Old Town. ☎ ***01789/292-107.*** *Admission: £3.50 ($6) adults, £3 ($4.80) seniors and students, £1.70 ($2.70) children 5–15, £9 ($14) families (2 adults, 3 children). Open: Apr–May and Sept–Oct daily 11 a.m.–5 p.m.; June–Aug Mon–Sat 9:30 a.m.–5 p.m., Sun 10 a.m.–5 p.m.; Nov–Mar daily 11 a.m.–4 p.m.; closed Dec 24–26.*

Holy Trinity Church

Stratford-upon-Avon

Shakespeare died on his birthday (April 23), aged 52, and is buried in this beautiful parish church near the River Avon. His wife, Anne, his daughter Susanna, and Susanna's husband, John Hall, lie beside him in front of the altar. A bust of the immortal bard looks down on the gravesite. For a man who wrote some of the world's most enduring lines, his tomb's inscription is little more than trivial verse, ending with "and curst be he who moves my bones." Obviously, Shakespeare didn't want to leave Stratford — ever. You can visit the entire church in about 15 minutes.

To reach the church from Hall's Croft, walk south to Southern Lane, which runs beside the River Avon, and follow it south to Trinity Street, where you find a path to the church.

Old Town. ☎ ***01789/266-316.*** *Admission: church free, Shakespeare's tomb £1 ($1.60). Open: March–Oct Mon–Sat 8:30 a.m.–6 p.m., Nov–Feb Mon–Sat 8:30 a.m.–4 p.m.; Sun year-round 2–5 p.m.*

Mary Arden's House & Shakespeare Countryside Museum

Wilmcote

For more than 200 years, Palmers Farm, a Tudor farmstead with an old stone dovecote and outbuildings, was identified as the girlhood home of Mary Arden, Shakespeare's mother. Recent evidence revealed, however, that Mary Arden actually lived in the house next door, at Glebe Farm. In 2000, the house at Glebe Farm was officially designated the Mary Arden House. Dating from 1514, this house contains country furniture and domestic utensils; in the barns, stable, cowshed, and farmyard is an extensive collection of farm implements illustrating life and work in the local countryside from Shakespeare's time to the present.

For a leisurely look at everything, give yourself about 45 minutes.

To reach this last Shakespeare shrine, drive north to Wilmcote on A34. The house is also a stop on the Guide Friday bus tour (see "Getting around and touring Stratford-upon-Avon," earlier in this chapter).

Wilmcote (about 3½ miles north of Stratford on A34). ☎ ***01789/204-016.*** *Admission: £5.50 ($9) adults, £5 ($8) seniors and students, £2.50 ($4) children 5–15, £13.50 ($22) families (2 adults, 3 children). Open: Apr–May Mon–Sat 10 a.m.–5 p.m., Sun 10:30 a.m.–5 p.m.; June–Aug Mon–Sat 9:30 a.m.–5 p.m., Sun 10 a.m.–5 p.m.; Sept–Mar Mon–Sat 10 a.m.–4 p.m., Sun 10:30 a.m.–4 p.m.; closed Dec 24–26.*

Finding more to see and do in Stratford-upon-Avon

Most people come to Stratford to see the Shakespeare sites. If you have the kids with you and old houses bore them silly, here are a couple of alternative attractions that they can enjoy:

- **Butterfly Farm,** Tramway Walk, Swan's Nest Lane (☎ **01789/299-288**), is an enclosed greenhouse filled with hundreds of colorful, free-flying butterflies. You can discover various insect displays amid the tropical plants and flowers of a re-created rainforest. Besides the butterflies, kids enjoy seeing forest insects and spiders. Admission is £4.25 ($7) for adults, £3.75 ($6) for seniors and students, £3.25 ($5) for children 5 to 15, and £12.50 ($19) for families (2 adults, 2 children). The farm is open daily 10 a.m. to 6 p.m. in the summer and from 10 a.m. to dusk in the winter.

- **Stratford Brass Rubbing Centre,** Avon Bank Gardens, Southern Lane (☎ **01789/297-671**), has dozens of interesting replica brasses from English churches and provides all the materials you need to make an on-the-spot rubbing for £1 to £20 ($1.60 to $32). Creating a brass rubbing is fun and easy even for nonartistic kids (and adults). To make a brass rubbing, all you do is rub a hard wax crayon over paper covering the memorial brass; the impression you obtain is the rubbing. The center is open daily from 10 a.m. to 6 p.m. in the summer and Saturday and Sunday from 11 a.m. to 4 p.m. in the winter.

Seeing a play in Stratford-upon-Avon

The **Royal Shakespeare Theatre,** Waterside, Stratford-upon-Avon CV37 6BB (☎ **01789/403-403;** `www.rsc.org.uk`), is the home of the **Royal Shakespeare Company,** which typically stages five Shakespeare plays during a season running from November to September. The company performs the plays in the Festival Theatre, which has a proscenium stage (a traditional stage), or in The Swan, a thrust stage (a stage that extends into the audience) with side galleries. Although demand depends on the play, I recommend that you order your tickets at least two to three weeks in advance. The theater always holds a few tickets for sale on the day of a performance, but you may not get a good seat at this time. The box office is open Monday through Saturday from 9 a.m. to 8 p.m., but closes at 6 p.m. on days when there are no performances. Ticket prices are £8 to £42 ($13 to $67). You can book tickets online through the Royal Shakespeare Company Web site.

Shopping in Stratford-upon-Avon

Stratford's weekly **Market**, held on Friday, dates back more than 800 years. The **Shakespeare Bookshop,** in the Shakespeare Centre, Henley Street (☎ **01789/201-819**), is the region's best bookshop for Shakespeare-related material. The nearby **Pickwick Gallery,** 32 Henley St. (☎ **01789/294-861**), carries a wide variety of old and new engravings. **Elaine Rippon Craft Gallery,** Shakespeare Craft Yard off Henley Street (☎ **01789/415-481**), designs, creates, and sells sumptuous silk and velvet accessories and carries fine British contemporary crafts.

Warwick Castle: Warlords and Ladies

The ancient county town of Warwick (pronounced *War*-ick) is situated on a rocky hill on the north side of the River Avon, about 8 miles northeast of Stratford. Although you can explore some intriguing old streets in the town, most visitors come here with one goal in mind: to visit mighty Warwick Castle, one of England's most popular tourist attractions. Dramatically sited above the river on the town's south side, the castle is a splendid example of a medieval fortress that's been adapted over the centuries to reflect its inhabitants' tastes and ambitions.

Give yourself at least three hours to visit the castle and the lovely gardens and parkland around it; if you want to wander through the town, add an hour or two.

Warwick Castle was built as a medieval fortress and, as such, has a large number of steps and narrow doorways, which present limitations for mobility-restricted visitors. Travelers with disabilities are encouraged to call first or check the Web site, `www.warwick-castle.co.uk`, for more information.

Getting to Warwick Castle and taking a tour

The castle sits right in the center of Warwick, a 15-minute walk from the train or bus station. Trains run direct to Warwick from Stratford-upon-Avon; contact **Chiltern Railways** (☎ **08705/165-165**) for information. Direct trains go to Warwick from London's Marylebone station; the trip takes one hour and 45 minutes and costs about £24 ($38) for a round trip. **National Express** (☎ **0990/808-080**) offers daily bus service between Victoria Coach Station in London and Warwick; the two–hour-and-45-minute trip costs £17 ($27) round trip. National Express also runs buses to Warwick from Riverside bus station in Stratford-upon-Avon; the 15-minute journey costs £2 ($3.20) round trip. By car from Stratford, take junction 15 off the M40 and continue for 2 miles.

Bus tours of Warwick Castle from Stratford-upon-Avon are available through **Guide Friday** (☎ **01789/294-466;** `www.guidefriday.com`).

Dining at Warwick Castle

Being robbed by a highwayman wasn't an uncommon experience for travelers 200 years ago. At Warwick Castle's **Highwayman's Supper,** guests hear the highwayman's side of the story. The themed event's setting is the castle in the 18th century on a night when the Earl of Warwick is away and the castle housekeeper gives the guests a private viewing of the staterooms. Afterward, in the coach house, a five-course meal is served (with unlimited wine, ale, or soft drinks) accompanied by 18th-century music, dancing, and bawdy tall tales. A Highwayman's Supper is held most Fridays and Saturdays throughout the year and nightly (except Sunday) in December until Christmas. The cost is £37 ($53) per person (slightly higher during December). For reservations and further information, call ☎ **01926/406-602** or fax 01926/406-611.

Note: This event is unsuitable for guests under 18 years of age.

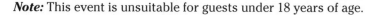

History and architecture of Warwick Castle

Warwick Castle reflects more than a thousand years of turbulent English history. The castle was the ancestral home of the earls of Warwick, key players in medieval England's brutal political conflicts — not the sort of guys you'd want messing with you. One of them, Richard Neville (known as "the Kingmaker"), was so powerful that he helped depose both Henry VI and Edward IV. Another earl of Warwick executed Joan of Arc.

For their family stronghold, the earliest earls chose a strategic site first fortified by the Saxons and later, in 1068, by the Normans. About three centuries later, the 11th Earl of Warwick expanded the Norman stronghold into the enormous walled and turreted fortress that visitors see today. When James I granted the castle to Sir Fulke Greville in 1604, the new owner spent a fortune converting the inner buildings into a luxurious mansion. Extensive restorations were made after a disastrous fire in 1871. Lord Brooke, the most recent owner, sold the ancestral mansion to the owners of Madame Tussaud's wax museum, who have added some entertainment features.

Architecturally, the castle marks the transitional period between the formidable but dreary strongholds of medieval England and the more domestic fortified houses that replaced them. The massive outer walls and defense towers date to the 14th century. From the Porter's Lodge (1800), a winding path cut in the solid rock leads to a double gateway between two massive towers. In the grassy inner court, the Bear and Clarence Towers are on the right, a castle-mound (all that's left from Norman times) rises in front, and the domestic buildings are on the left.

Exploring Warwick Castle

The entire castle complex is open for exploration, but save most of your time — at least one hour — to wander through the **Private Apartments.** In these rooms, you encounter lifelike figures that are part of an exhibition known as the Royal Weekend Party. In 1898, the Countess of Warwick hosted a weekend party for Edward, Prince of Wales, later Edward VII. A century later, the wax artists at Madame Tussaud's created likenesses of the guests, including a twenty-something Winston Churchill (seen leafing through a book in the **Library**), and the Duke of York, later George V, who is seen lighting a cigarette in the **Card Room.** Upstairs, their hostess (known to her friends as Daisy) is dressing for dinner, and so are some of her guests, including Consuelo, Duchess of Marlborough (a member of the Vanderbilt family), Lord Curzon (Viceroy of India) and the Countess' special guest, the future King Edward VII. All the room settings are meticulous re-creations employing original furniture in use at the time of the party. The **Chapel** and **State Rooms** are next to the Private Apartments. The 16th-century **Great Hall** is the longest (330 feet) and largest of the rooms on view. The hall overlooks the river and has a collection of arms and armor. The other rooms were mostly decorated from 1770 to 1790. The **Cedar Room** has Van Dyke portraits, and paintings by Velasquez and Rubens hang in the Red Drawing Room.

Several exhibitions use sound and light effects and wax figures to tell stories about the castle. **Death or Glory** is about former resident Richard Neville, "the Kingmaker," preparing for battle. Another, in the **Ghost Tower,** tells of Fulke Greville's murder. After visiting the very depressing **dungeon,** you may want to walk along the castle **ramparts** for a breath of fresh air. The castle overlooks beautiful parkland and **gardens** laid out by Capability Brown, one of the greatest landscape gardeners of 18th-century England. Peacocks roam freely through the grounds, and the River Avon runs through them.

Warwick. ☎ ***0870/442-2000.*** *Admission (price varies by season and day of the week): £11.25–£13.50 ($18–$22) adults, £8–£9.75 ($13–$16) seniors, £8.50–£10 ($14–$16) students, £6.95–£8 ($11–$13) children 5–15, £32–£36 ($51–$58) families (2 adults, 2 children). Open: daily Apr–July and Sept 10 a.m.–6 p.m.; Aug 10 a.m.–7 p.m.; Oct–March 10 a.m.–5 p.m.*

Finding more to see and do in Warwick

I don't recommend staying overnight in Warwick, but you may want to stroll through town to check out a few of the following buildings:

- **Lord Leycester Hospital** (☎ **01926/491-422**), established in 1571 by Robert Dudley, earl of Leicester (a favorite of Queen Elizabeth I), is a marvelous grouping of half-timbered almshouses leaning against the old West Gate. The hospital buildings, some dating from around 1400, give you a good picture of what buildings in the town looked like before a fire destroyed most of them in 1694. If you spot someone wearing a black cape with a silver pendant in the shape of a boar, it's one of the "Brethren" (retired servicemen) who live at the hospital and welcome visitors. Inside, you can visit the beautiful galleried **courtyard,** the **Great Hall** and magnificent **Guildhall,** and the **Chaplains' Dining Hall.** In the wonderfully atmospheric Brethren's Kitchen, with stone floors and exposed oak beams, you can get a good afternoon tea for about £4 ($6). The hospital is open Tuesday through Sunday from 10 a.m. to 4 p.m. (5 p.m. in winter); admission is £3.20 ($5), £2.70 ($4.30) seniors, and £2.20 ($3.50) children. To get to the hospital from Warwick Castle, follow Castle Street up the hill to High Street and turn left.

- **St. Mary's Church** (☎ **01926/403-940**), on Church Street, had to rebuild its tower and nave after the great fire of 1694. Spared by the fire was the **Beauchamp Chantry,** the location of a famous gilded bronze tomb effigy of Richard Beauchamp, a powerful earl of Warwick who died in 1439. (A *chantry,* by the way, is a chapel endowed by a family for the chanting of Masses, usually for the chapel's principle founder.) The tomb of Robert Dudley is against the north wall. The church, less than a five-minute walk from Warwick Castle, is open daily from 10 a.m. to 6 p.m. (November to March until 4 p.m.).

Chapter 20

Bath and the Best of the Cotswolds

In This Chapter

- Basking in Bath
- Checking out Cheltenham
- Exploring charming Cotswolds villages
- Strolling through Cirencester

The Cotswold Hills occupy a region in central England that's been inhabited for some 6,000 years. Tucked into this gentle landscape are prehistoric mounds, the remains of Roman villas, magnificent gardens, old manor houses, and amazingly preserved towns that grew rich on Cotswold wool during the Middle Ages. For hundreds of years, merchants came from London and as far away as Florence to buy Cotswold fleeces for shipment around the world.

This area of grassy limestone hills, woodlands, cool green ravines, and high open plateaus (known as *wolds*) is roughly bordered by Bath to the south, Oxford to the east, Stratford-upon-Avon to the north, and Cheltenham to the west. This area isn't large: From north to south, the Cotswolds stretch some 78 miles. More than 80% of the land is still farmland; a network of distinctive dry stone walls marks the fields.

The Cotswolds are a popular touring region. Many people visit the medieval villages just to stroll around, shop (the Cotswolds have more antiques stores than anywhere else in England), and have an afternoon cream tea. Although the region has many lovely villages, in this chapter I include the ones that hold the most interest for casual village-hoppers: **Bourton-on-the-Water, Upper and Lower Slaughter, Broadway,** and **Chipping Campden. Bath,** which starts this chapter, is a must-see city even if you don't plan to tour the Cotswolds. Other worthwhile stops are the smaller cities of **Cheltenham** and **Cirencester.**

Public transportation options in the Cotswolds aren't very useful for visitors on a tight schedule. You can best explore this area by car. Otherwise, getting from one village to the next is difficult.

Bath: Hot Mineral Springs and Cool Georgian Splendor

Bath, 115 miles west of London, sits on the doorstep of the Cotswolds but not quite in them (see the "Bath" map in this chapter). This beautiful spa town on the River Avon is worth at least a day and makes a good base for exploring the region. Bath can also be a day trip from London.

In ancient times, the area was known far and wide for its hot mineral springs, which drew the Celts and later the Romans, who settled here in A.D. 75 and built a huge bath complex to soak their weary bones. Centuries later, in 1702, Queen Anne dipped her royal bod into the soothing sulfurous waters and sparked a trend that transformed Bath into an ultra-fashionable spa. Aristocrats, socialites, social climbers, and flamboyant dandies, like Beau Nash, held sway. Jane Austen, a demure visitor, used Bath as an upwardly genteel setting for her class-conscious novels.

Filled with remarkable curving *crescents* (row houses built in a long, curving line) and classically inspired buildings built of toffee-colored stone, the town you see today is a fabulous legacy from the Georgian era. Its architectural legacy is so important that UNESCO named Bath a World Heritage Site. For more on the city's architecture, see the sidebar, "Building blocks of history: Bath," in this chapter.

Getting to Bath

Trains for Bath leave from London's Paddington Station every 30 minutes, and the trip lasts about 90 minutes. Standard round-trip fare is £33 ($53) on weekdays, and £39.70 ($64) on weekends. **National Express** (☎ **08705/808-080**) runs frequent buses from London's Victoria Coach Station. Depending on departure time, the trip takes three to four hours; round-trip fare is £10.50 ($17). By car, take the M4 to Junction 18, and then drive a few miles south on A46.

Bath is one of the most convenient places for renting a car to tour the Cotswolds. Several car-rental agencies in town are

- **Arrows Self-Drive Hire,** Claverton Buildings, Widecombe, ☎ **01225/422-262**
- **Avis,** Riverside Business Park, ☎ **01225/446-680**
- **Enterprise,** Riverside Business Park, ☎ **01225/443-311**

Bath

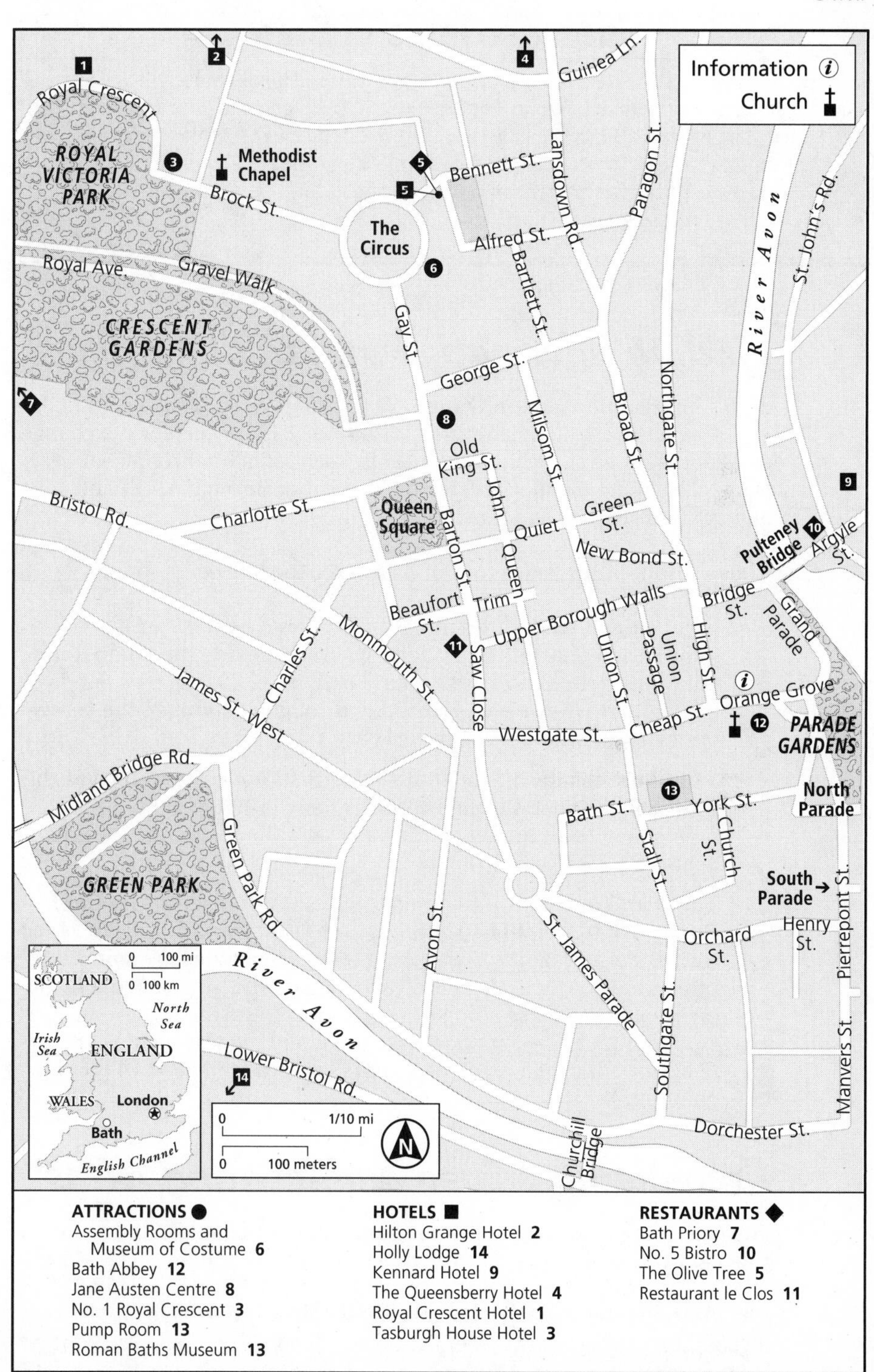
Information
Church
Royal Crescent
ROYAL VICTORIA PARK
Methodist Chapel
Brock St.
Bennett St.
Guinea Ln.
Lansdown Rd.
Paragon St.
The Circus
Alfred St.
Bartlett St.
Royal Ave.
Gravel Walk
CRESCENT GARDENS
Gay St.
George St.
Milsom St.
Broad St.
Northgate St.
River Avon
St. John's Rd.
Old King St.
John St.
Queen Square
Bristol Rd.
Charlotte St.
Barton St.
Quiet St.
Queen St.
Green St.
New Bond St.
Pulteney Bridge
Argyle St.
Beaufort St.
Trim St.
Upper Borough Walls
Bridge St.
Grand Parade
Monmouth St.
Charles St.
Saw Close
Union St.
Union Passage
High St.
James St. West
Orange Grove
Westgate St.
Cheap St.
PARADE GARDENS
Midland Bridge Rd.
Bath St.
York St.
North Parade
Church St.
Stall St.
Green Park Rd.
GREEN PARK
South Parade
Avon St.
St. James Parade
Orchard St.
Henry St.
Pierrepont St.
Southgate St.
Manvers St.
Lower Bristol Rd.
Dorchester St.
Churchill Bridge
0 100 mi
0 100 km
SCOTLAND
North Sea
Irish Sea
ENGLAND
WALES
London
Bath
English Channel
0 1/10 mi
0 100 meters
N
ATTRACTIONS
Assembly Rooms and Museum of Costume 6
Bath Abbey 12
Jane Austen Centre 8
No. 1 Royal Crescent 3
Pump Room 13
Roman Baths Museum 13
HOTELS
Hilton Grange Hotel 2
Holly Lodge 14
Kennard Hotel 9
The Queensberry Hotel 4
Royal Crescent Hotel 1
Tasburgh House Hotel 3
RESTAURANTS
Bath Priory 7
No. 5 Bistro 10
The Olive Tree 5
Restaurant le Clos 11

Special events in Bath

Bath's Regency (1714–1830) buildings provide wonderful settings for performances during the **International Music Festival** in mid-May and the **Mozartfest** in November. In March, the city hosts a well-known **Literature Festival.** For information on these events, contact the **Bath Festival's Box Office,** 2 Church St., Abbey Green, Bath BA1 1NL (☎ **01225/463-362**) or check out the city's Web site at www.visitbath.co.uk.

Finding information and taking a tour

Bath's **Tourist Information Centre** (☎ **01225/477-101;** www.visitbath.co.uk), on town square in front of Bath Abbey, has a currency exchange and room-finding service. The center is open Monday through Saturday from 9:30 a.m. to 6 p.m. (until 5 p.m. November through April) and Sunday from 10 a.m. to 4 p.m.

Those who want to take a tour of Bath have the following options:

- **Free, guided walks** around Bath are offered by the Tourist Information Centre. The walks leave from outside the Pump Room, adjacent to the center, year-round daily at 10:30 a.m. plus Sunday through Friday at 2 p.m. From May through September, the center offers an additional evening walk at 7 p.m.
- **Jane Austen's Bath:** The Tourist Information Centre also gives this walk, and it departs from the center daily at 1:30 p.m. in July and August and on Saturday and Sunday only the rest of the year. The cost is £3.50 ($6).
- **The Bath Tour:** This is an open-top bus tour presented by **Guide Friday** (☎ **01225/444-102;** www.guidefriday.com). The hour-long tour departs from the bus station every 15 minutes in summer, otherwise hourly. Tickets are valid all day, and you can get off and on to explore places along the route. The tour starts at the bus station but can be joined at any stop along the way; cost is £8 ($12) for adults, £6 ($10) for seniors and students, and £4 ($6) for children.

Exchanging money and locating ATMs

You can change money at the **Tourist Information Centre** in the center of town (☎ **01225/477-101**); at **American Express,** 5 Bridge St. (☎ **01225/444-767**); and at **Marks & Spencer,** 16–19 Stall St. (☎ **01225/462-591**). The following banks have 24-hour cash machines: **Barclays** on Manvers Street, **Lloyds** on Milson Street, **HSBC** on Milson Street, and **NatWest** on High Street.

Staying in and around Bath

Beautiful Bath has plenty of hotels and B&Bs. Here are my recommended choices.

Hinton Grange Hotel

$$–$$$ Hinton

This hotel appeals to romantics looking for a special hideaway in the southern Cotswolds countryside. A 15th-century farmhouse, barns, and stables were converted to make this classy hotel, situated on six acres of parkland. With low beams, stone walls, blazing fires, and candlelight in the lounges and dining rooms, the atmosphere is Olde English all the way. Most of the 19 guest rooms are large, with open coal fires, beamed ceilings, Victorian bathing alcoves, antique decor, and terraces opening into the grounds.

Hinton, near Dyrham (from Bath, take A46 north to Dyrham exit), Somerset SN14 8HG. ☎ ***0117/937-2916.*** *Fax: 0117/937-3285. Internet:* `www.hintongrange.co.uk`. *Rack rates: £119–£225 ($190–$360) double. Rates include English breakfast. AE, DC, MC, V. No children under 14.*

Holly Lodge

$–$$ Bath

This skillfully converted townhouse B&B has plenty of charm. All seven cozy, nonsmoking bedrooms have private bathrooms. Each one is individually furnished, and two have four-poster beds. Breakfast is served in a pretty conservatory.

8 Upper Oldfield Park, Bath, Somerset BA2 3J2. ☎ ***01225/424-042.*** *Fax: 01225/481-138. Internet:* `www.hollylodge.co.uk`. *Rack rates: £79–£97 ($126–$155) double. Rates include English breakfast. AE, DC, MC, V.*

Kennard Hotel

$–$$ Bath

On the east side of Pulteney Bridge, within walking distance of everything in Bath, this elegant hotel with 13 guest rooms occupies a beautifully restored Georgian townhouse from 1794. All the rooms are individually furnished to a high standard, have their own bathrooms, and offer an abundance of amenities

11 Henrietta St., Bath, Somerset BA2 6LL. ☎ ***01225/310-472.*** *Fax: 01225/460-054. Internet:* `www.kennard.co.uk`. *Rack rates: £98–£118 ($157–$189) double. Rates include English breakfast. AE, MC, V.*

The Queensberry Hotel

$$–$$$ **Bath**

A large Georgian townhouse built in 1772, the Queensberry occupies a prime position near the Assembly Rooms and the Royal Crescent, two major attractions. The 29 rooms in this stylish boutique hotel are decorated with flair and comfort. For information on the hotel's award-winning restaurant, The Olive Tree, see "Dining in Bath," later in this chapter.

Russel St., Bath, Somerset BA1 2QF. ☎ ***01225/447-928.*** *Fax: 01225/446-065. Internet:* `www.bathqueensberry.com`. ***Rack rates: £120–£185 ($192–$296) double. Rates include continental breakfast. AE, DC, MC, V.***

Royal Crescent Hotel

$$$–$$$$ **Bath**

"Sumptuous" is the only word to describe this hotel, which occupies part of Bath's most famous crescent. Every room is different, and all have been furnished in an elegant style that's in keeping with the building's historical character. You can visit an on-site spa with a heated pool, and an award-winning restaurant, Pimpernel's, for fine dining. If you want to splurge in Bath, this hotel is your best choice.

16 Royal Crescent, Bath, Somerset BA1 2LS. ☎ ***01225/823-333.*** *Fax: 01225/339-401. Internet:* `www.royalcrescent.co.uk`. ***Rack rates: £170–£340 ($272–$544) double. AE, DC, MC, V.***

Tasburgh House Hotel

$$ **Outside Bath**

On seven acres of landscaped grounds with views out over the Avon Valley, this Victorian guesthouse is a half-mile from the city center on A46 Warminster Road. The 13 rooms are nicely furnished with much attention to detail; all have private bathrooms. The garden adjoins the Kennet and Avon canal towpath, which makes for a nice walk into the countryside or town.

Warminster Road, Bath, Somerset BA2 6SH. ☎ ***01225/425-096.*** *Fax: 01225/463-842. Internet:* `www.bathtasburgh.co.uk`. ***Rack rates: £110–£125 ($176–$200) double. Rates include English breakfast. AE, DC, MC, V.***

Dining in Bath

Bath's sophisticated dining scene features many cuisines. Here are my favorite places to eat.

Bath Priory

$$$–$$$$ MODERN BRITISH

The restaurant in this hotel is a gourmet's delight. Your starter may be ravioli with crab and ginger with lobster sauce or wild mushroom tart. Typical main courses include honey-glazed breast of duck, sautéed or pan-fried fish, roast lamb, and pasta. The dining room looks out into pretty gardens.

Bath Priory Hotel, Weston Rd. (west side of Victoria Park). ☎ ***01225/331-922.*** *Reservations required for dinner. Fixed-price lunch £25 ($40), fixed-price dinner £47.50 ($76). AE, MC, V. Open: daily noon to 1:45 p.m. and 7:00–9:30 p.m.*

No. 5 Bistro

$$ FRENCH

This pleasant, smoke-free bistro in the city center has polished elm floors, bright prints, many plants, and candles. The chef produces mouth-watering dishes cooked to order from a varied menu. Lighter meals are served at lunch. The seasonally adjusted evening menu features daily specials, which may include Provençal fish soup, chargrilled loin of lamb, or vegetarian dishes such as roast stuffed peppers and vegetable gratin. Wednesdays are devoted to fresh fish.

5 Argyle St. ☎ ***01225/444-499.*** *Reservations recommended. Main courses: £13–£14 ($21–$22), fixed-price dinner £23 ($37). AE, MC, V. Open: Mon–Sat noon to 2:30 p.m. and 6:30–10 p.m.*

The Olive Tree

$$ INTERNATIONAL

This popular hotel restaurant has a Mediterranean ambience and a menu drawn from all over the globe. A delicious fish ragout is usually available, but you also find dishes such as asparagus, sun-dried tomato, and herb risotto cakes, and roast pork loin. For dessert, try almond and cherry steamed sponge cake.

Queensberry Hotel, Russel St. (just north of Assembly Rooms). ☎ ***01225/447-928.*** *Reservations recommended. Main courses: £9–£16 ($14–$26); fixed-price lunch £16.50 ($26), fixed-price dinner £28 ($45). AE, DC, MC, V. Open: Mon–Sat noon to 2 p.m.; daily 7–10 p.m.*

Restaurant le Clos

$$ BRITISH MODERN/FRENCH

This semicircular restaurant provides good food and great city views. You find some surprising touches, such as breast of duck with kumquat confit and Grand Marnier sauce, but the sauces never overburden the fish or meat. Vegetarian diners always have one or two good items to choose from.

1 Seven Dials Saw Close. ☎ ***01225/444-450.*** *Reservations recommended. Main courses: £8–£17 ($13–$27), fixed-price lunch £15.95 ($26), fixed-price dinner £21.50 ($34). AE, MC, V. Open: daily noon to 2:30 p.m. and 6–10 p.m.*

Exploring Bath

Bath's legacy of architecture from the Regency era (1811–1830) is so important that the city is a UNESCO World Heritage Site. To view the historic buildings and visit the sights, you can easily walk everywhere in this compact town. If you're interested in guided walks or a bus tour, see the section "Finding information and taking a tour," earlier in this chapter.

Assembly Rooms and Museum of Costume

A classic building worth visiting is the Assembly Rooms, the site of all the grand balls and social climbing in 18th-century Bath. The complex houses the excellent Museum of Costume, where you can see just what those dandies and their ladies wore. You can see the Assembly Rooms in 15 minutes; allow an hour if you're also visiting the Museum of Costume.

Bennett Street. ☎ ***01225/477-785.*** *Admission: Assembly Rooms free, Museum £5 ($8) adults; £4 ($6) seniors, students, children 6–18; £14 ($22) families (2 adults, 2 children). Open: daily 10 a.m.–5 p.m.; closed Dec 25 and 26.*

Bath Abbey

The 18th-century abbey dominates the adjacent square. Step inside for a look at the graceful fan vaulting, the great east window, and the unexpectedly simple memorial to Beau Nash, the most flamboyant of the dandies who frequented Bath in its heyday.

Abbey Church Yard. ☎ ***01225/422-462.*** *Free admission, but donations encouraged. Open: Mon–Sat 9 a.m.–6 p.m. (Nov–March until 4:30 p.m.); Sun 1–2:30 p.m. and 4:30–5:30pm.*

Bridges, Crescents, Circuses, and Parades

Bath was built for promenading. Filled with beautiful squares and sweeping residential crescents, it remains a wonderful town for walking. Stroll along the **North Parade** and the **South Parade, Queen Square** (where Jane Austen lived), and **The Circus.** Built in 1770 and inspired by Florence's Ponte Vecchio, **Pulteney Bridge** spans the River Avon a few blocks south of the Assembly Rooms. Pulteney Bridge is one of the few bridges in Europe lined with shops and restaurants.

Building blocks of history: Bath

Queen Anne sparked the royal enthusiasm for Bath's healing waters, but it wasn't until a few years later, during the Georgian and Regency eras (1714–1830) that Bath became one of the social hot spots of England. In about 100 years, what had been a small provincial spa town was transformed into one of Europe's most elegant cities. The extraordinary building boom created Bath's famous curving crescents of sumptuous townhouses, garden squares, and dozens of beautifully proportioned detached homes and public buildings. This period's architecture was unusually restrained (unlike many of the personalities); it's based on classical models and motifs that present harmonious and well-proportioned facades.

If you're interested in the architecture, stop in and spend an hour or so at the **Building of Bath Museum,** The Countess of Huntingdon's Chapel, The Vineyard (off Paragon St.; ☎ **01225/333-895**). The museum examines the city's Georgian and Regency architecture and interiors. Exhibits detail the crafts used in the course of construction and introduce the architects who contributed to Bath's remarkable development. The museum is open Tuesday through Sunday from 10:30 a.m. to 5 p.m. (also on Monday in July and August). Admission is £4 ($6) for adults, £3 ($4.80) for seniors and students, and £1.50 ($2.40) for children 5 to 15. To reach the museum from the Assembly Rooms, head east on Alfred Street and north on Paragon Street; the museum will be on your left.

Jane Austen Centre

Bath's newest attraction is in a Georgian townhouse on an elegant street where Miss Austen of Chawton (see Chapter 16) lived. Truth be told, Jane Austen didn't really like Bath very much, but she was a keen observer and drew on it for her witty portraits of 18th-century society. Text-heavy exhibits and a video tell you more about the life and times of this brilliant daughter of a country pastor and convey a sense of what life was like in Bath during the Regency period. If you're an Austen fan, allow about an hour for your visit. If you're not a fan, this place won't convert you.

*40 Gay Street. ☎ **01225/443-000.** Admission: £3.95 ($6) adults, £3.45 ($6) seniors and students, £2.45 ($4) children, £11.45 ($18) families (2 adults, 2 children). **Open:** Mon–Sat 10 a.m.–5:30 p.m., Sun 10:30 a.m.–5:30 p.m.*

No. 1 Royal Crescent

The Royal Crescent is a magnificent, curving row of 30 townhouses regarded as the epitome of England's Palladian style (a classical style incorporating elements from ancient Greek and Roman buildings). John Wood the Younger designed the crescent in 1767. No. 1 Royal Crescent is a gorgeously restored 18th-century house with period furnishings. A tour of the interior gives you a vivid picture of how the elite lived during the Regency era. Allow about 30 minutes.

Royal Crescent. ☎ ***01225/428-126.*** *Admission: £4 ($6) adults; £3.50 ($6) seniors, students, children 6–16; £10 ($16) families (2 adults, 2 children). Open: mid-Feb–Oct Tues–Sun 10:30 a.m.–5 p.m., Nov Tues–Sun 10:30 a.m.–4 p.m.*

Pump Room

Overlooking the Roman baths is the late-18th-century Pump Room, where the fashionable congregated to sip the waters. You can enter and taste the supposedly healthful liquid for yourself (but it's not Perrier). The Pump Room is an amusingly old-fashioned place for *elevenses* (morning coffee or tea), lunch, or afternoon tea, usually with live musical accompaniment. Main courses go for £9 to £10 ($14 to $16); afternoon tea is £6 to £8 ($10 to $13).

Stall Street ☎ ***01225/477-785.*** *Admission: free. Open: daily March–June 9:30 a.m.–5 p.m., July–Aug 9:30 a.m.–10 p.m., Sept–Oct 9:30 a.m.–5 p.m.; Nov–Feb 10 a.m.–4:30 p.m.*

Roman Baths Museum

Ancient British tribes considered the hot, healing waters of Bath's mineral springs sacred, but the Romans built the enormous complex that forms the nucleus of this subterranean museum, one of Bath's most important attractions. Upon entering, you take a portable, self-guided audio tour keyed to everything on display, including the original Roman baths and heating system; the tour is informative, well done, and fun for children and adults. Give yourself about one hour to see the museum.

In July and August, you can visit the atmospheric Roman Baths Museum at night with a *torch* (Britspeak for flashlight).

Pump Room, Stall Street (beside Bath Abbey). ☎ ***01225/477-785.*** *Admission: £8 ($13) adults, £7 ($11) seniors and students, £5 ($8) children 6–18, £20 ($32) families (2 adults, 2 children). Open: daily Jan–Feb and Nov–Dec 9:30 a.m.–4:30 p.m., Mar–June and Sept–Oct 9:30 a.m.–5 p.m., July–Aug 9 a.m.–9 p.m.*

Cheltenham: A Little Bath

Like Bath, its more glamorous neighbor 40 miles to the south, Cheltenham was a spa town. Mineral springs were discovered in 1716, and people came to sip the healthy but not very tasty water. The first pump room was installed in 1742, but Cheltenham didn't become fashionable until 1788, when George III came to take a five-week "course" of the waters. The town still has its wide, leafy promenades, public gardens, and pretty Regency-era architecture. Although technically falling just outside the boundaries of the Cotswolds, Cheltenham is a good town in which to base yourself. Here you find plenty of hotels, cafes, and some fine restaurants, plus good shopping, and far fewer tourists than in Bath. Considered the cultural center of the Cotswolds, Cheltenham hosts two major international events: the **Cheltenham Festival of Literature** (☎ **01242/227-979;** www.cheltenhamfestivals.co.uk) in May and the **International Festival of Music** (☎ **01242/227-979**) in early July.

Getting to Cheltenham

Trains run frequently from London's Paddington Station to Cheltenham Spa, Cheltenham's small train station. Some trains run direct; others require a change at Swindon or Bristol Parkway. The trip on a direct train takes two hours and costs about £30 ($48) round trip. For train information, call ☎ **08457/484-950. National Express** (☎ **08705/808-080**) runs several buses a day from Victoria Coach Station in London to the Royal Well bus station in the center of Cheltenham. The trip takes two hours and 45 minutes to three hours and 15 minutes; round-trip fare is £21 ($34). National Express also runs buses to Cheltenham from Oxford (a 90-minute trip) and Stratford-upon-Avon (a one-hour trip). If you come by car, Cheltenham is close to Junction 11 of the M5; the town is 41 miles west of Oxford on A40.

Traveling among the local villages

You can get from Cheltenham to several of the Cotswolds villages on buses; ask for the pamphlet "Getting There by Public Transportation" in the Cheltenham tourist office (see the next paragraph). **Pulhams Coaches** (☎ **01451/820-369**) is the area's most useful bus service, running daily between Cheltenham and Bourton-on-the-Water (see "Bourton-on-the-Water: Bridges on the Windrush," later in this chapter).

Finding information and taking a tour

The **Tourist Information Centre,** 77 Promenade (☎ **01242/522-878;** www.visitcheltenham.gov.uk) has many useful brochures on the town and Cotswolds region. You can book accommodations in the office or by calling ☎ **01242/517-110.** The center is open year-round Monday to Saturday from 9:30 a.m. to 5:15 p.m.

From about June 12 through September 12, the Tourist Information Centre offers guided walking tours of Regency-era Cheltenham, pointing out the best of the town's fine architecture and floral decorations. The tours depart at 11 a.m. Monday to Friday, last about 1¼ hours, and cost £2.50 ($4).

The train station is about 1 mile from the town center. You can walk everywhere or call a taxi (☎ **01242/580-580).**

Staying in Cheltenham

Here are my recommended choices for staying in Cheltenham.

Hotel on the Park

$$ Pittville Park

I highly recommend this immaculate hotel overlooking Pittville Park just north of the town center. The hotel is in a beautifully restored 1830s villa, and each of the 12 guest rooms has been carefully designed and furnished. The feeling throughout is intimate and opulent but not at all stuffy.

*38 Evesham Rd., Cheltenham, Glos GL52 2AH. ☎ **01242/518-898.** Internet:* `www.hotelonthepark.co.uk`. *Rack rates: £108–£133 ($173–$213) double. AE, DC, MC, V.*

Lawn Hotel

$ Pittville Park

Located just inside the iron gates leading to Pittville Park, this nonsmoking B&B caters to vegetarians and vegans. The B&B has nine high-ceilinged rooms, four with private bathrooms and one with a four-poster bed. The house dates from the 1840s and has many nice touches.

*5 Pittville Lawn, Cheltenham, Glos GL52 2BE. ☎ and fax: **01242/526-638.** Rack rates: £45–£50 ($72–$80) double. No credit cards.*

Parkview

$ Town center

This friendly B&B is in a row of Regency townhouses off Albert Road. The B&B has three large guest rooms, but only one has a private bathroom (with shower). The other two rooms share a bathroom with an enormous tub and shower. Families with children are welcome.

*4 Pittville Crescent, Cheltenham, Glos GL52 2QZ. ☎ **01242/575-567.** E-mail:* `jospa@R250.freeserve.co.uk`. *Rack rates: £45–£55 ($72–$88) double. Rates include English breakfast. No credit cards.*

Dining in Cheltenham

Cheltenham has several good restaurants. Here are three of them.

The Daffodil

$$ MODERN BRITISH

This very hip restaurant was created from an Art Deco movie palace and looks like the gleaming set of a Busby Berkeley musical. The food is good but not surprising, and sometimes the ambience trumps the meal. For main courses, you can find steak, kidney, and Guinness (stout) pie topped with an oyster, roasted rack of lamb, and Mediterranean vegetable tart.

18–20 Suffolk Parade. ☎ ***01242/700-088.*** *Reservations recommended for dinner. Main courses: £10.50–£16.95 ($17–$27); fixed-price meals: £15–£18 ($24–£29). AE, DC, MC, V. Open: Mon–Sat noon to 2:30 p.m. and 6:30–10:30 p.m.*

Le Petit Blanc

$$ FRENCH

A stylish restaurant that welcomes kids, Le Petit Blanc has steel tables offset by vibrant fabrics. The nice bar menu includes items such as pea and ham soup with baguette, or you can order scones and jam. For a main course, try fish soup, tomato risotto, herb pancakes, roast rabbit, or confit of guinea fowl, wild mushrooms, and Madeira *jus* (the juices from cooking meat mixed with Madeira wine).

In the Queen's Hotel, The Promenade. ☎ ***01242/266-800.*** *Reservations required weekends. Main courses: £8.25–£15 ($13–$24), fixed-price lunch or dinner £15 ($24). AE, DC, MC, V. Open: daily noon to 3 p.m.; Mon–Sat 6–10:30 p.m., Sun 6–10 p.m.*

The Retreat

$ INTERNATIONAL

The Retreat's been around since 1981 and is one of the most popular spots in town for lunch (the restaurant becomes a bar at night). You can order a simple sandwich or something much more substantial from a menu that changes every day. Fish, pasta, and steak are always available; nothing is fat-fried. The place also has a nice courtyard garden.

10–11 Suffolk Parade. ☎ ***01242/235-436.*** *Main courses: £6–£13 ($10–$21). AE, DC, MC, V. Open: Mon–Sat noon to 2:15 p.m.*

Exploring Cheltenham

The main sights in Cheltenham are mostly pleasant reminders of a genteel, bygone era. Nothing truly extraordinary is here, however, so you may want to save your valuable time for exploring the nearby Cotswolds villages, such as Bourton-on-the-Water, Upper and Lower Slaughter, Broadway, or Chipping Campden. (I detail all later in this chapter.) In less than two hours, you can see Cheltenham's main sights, all free, including:

- **Cheltenham Art Gallery and Museum,** Clarence St. (☎ **01242/237-431**), is notable for its collection of 19th-century Arts and Crafts furniture, silver, jewelry, ceramics, carvings, and textiles. (Cheltenham was a center of the Arts and Crafts movement started by William Morris.) You also find exhibits on local history and a small 20th-century gallery with a Stanley Spencer painting. The gallery and museum is open Monday through Saturday from 10 a.m. to 5:20 p.m. and Sunday from 2 to 4 p.m.

- Cheltenham's **Imperial Gardens** often win first place in the national "Britain in Bloom" contest. The gardens are in an open square and seasonally planted. To reach them, walk south from the Tourist Information Centre on Promenade until the street becomes Montpellier Walk.
- The **Pittville Pump Room,** Pittville Park (☎ **01242/523-852**), which opened in 1830, is a remnant of spa days, when health-conscious people came to Cheltenham to sip the alkaline water (for the digestion), take carriage rides (for the air), and promenade (for the exercise). Inside, the Pump Room is a ballroom and an area where you can taste the water (the only natural, consumable alkaline waters in Great Britain). On Sunday from the end of May until the end of September, the Pump Room is open for lunch and afternoon cream teas, accompanied by classical music.

Shopping in Cheltenham

Cheltenham is a regional hub, so you find many appealing shops. Antique stores cluster in the **Suffolk quarter** along Suffolk Road, Great Norwood Street, and Suffolk Parade. You can find boutiques, art galleries, and crafts and specialty shops in the **Montpellier quarter** along Montpellier Walk and the Promenade.

Bourton-on-the-Water: Bridges on the Windrush

Like other villages in the Cotswolds, Bourton-on-the-Water grew rich from the wool trade during the medieval era. But its history actually dates to Roman times, when the town served as an outpost along the Fosse Way, a strategic Roman road that cut across England from the North Sea to St. George's Channel. (Today the road is A429.) The "water" in the village's name is the River Windrush, which flows gently through the village's heart, its narrow channel lined with low, graceful stone bridges. Virtually all the village buildings are made of a local honey-colored stone that gives off a soft, mellow glow. When the wool trade ended, Bourton became a forgotten backwater, which helped to preserve its wealth of medieval buildings. Today, this town, with an almost endless succession of shops, tearooms, and tourist attractions, is perhaps the most commercialized of the Cotswolds villages. The best times to visit are spring and fall, avoiding the summer influx of tourists. The **Tourist Information Centre** is on Victoria Street (☎ **01451/820-211**).

Getting to Bourton-on-the-Water

By car from Cheltenham, 15 miles to the southeast, take A40. The village doesn't have parking; you find *car parks* (Britspeak for parking lots) on Station Road and Rissington Road. Trains run from London's Paddington Station to Moreton-in-Marsh; from there, you can take a **Pulhams Coaches** (☎ **01451/820-369**) coach 6 miles to Bourton. The same company runs about four buses a day from Cheltenham.

Stopping for a spot of tea

The **Mad Hatter Tearoom,** Victoria Street (☎ **01451/821-508**), serves hot meals all day, including fish and chips for £5.50 ($9); cream teas cost £3.25 ($5).

Exploring Bourton-on-the-Water

Many people come here just to stroll leisurely through the village, shop, and have an afternoon cream tea. If you're looking for additional activities, check out the following:

- **St. Lawrence's Church,** in the center of the village, was constructed in the 12th century. The tower dates from 1784.

- Housed in an 18th-century water mill, **Cotswold Motoring Museum and Toy Collection,** The Old Mill (☎ **01451/821-255**), displays a collection of vintage cars, toys, motorbikes, and advertising signs. It's open daily February to November from 10 a.m. to 6 p.m. Admission is £2.50 ($4) for adults, £1.50 ($2.40) for children.
- **The Cotswold Perfumery,** Victoria Street (☎ **01451/820-698**), is a perfume shop with an exhibition on the history of perfume, a perfume garden, and a video about perfume; if the smell of perfume gives you a headache, steer clear. The perfumery is open daily from 9:30 a.m. to 5:30 p.m. (Sunday from 10:30 a.m.) and costs £2 ($3.20) for adults, £1.75 ($2.80) for seniors and children under 15.

- **The Model Village at the Old New Inn,** High Street (☎ **01451/820-467**), has been around for some 70-odd years and is the town's most popular attraction. Local stone was used to re-create the entire village in miniature; you walk through and see everything at one-ninth its actual height. Kids get a kick out of feeling like a giant. Summer hours are daily from 9 a.m. to 5:45 p.m.; in winter, it's open daily from 10 a.m. to 4 p.m. Admission is £2.75 ($4.40) for adults, £2 ($3.20) for children.

- **Birdland,** Rissington Road (☎ **01451/820-480**), is a series of aviaries with more than 350 species of some 1,200 birds, including penguins, cranes, storks, and waterfowl. You find a picnic area, a cafe, and a children's playground. Birdland is open daily April through October from 10 a.m. to 6 p.m. and November through March from 10 a.m. to 4 p.m. Admission is £4.60 ($7) for adults, £3.60 ($6) for seniors, and £2.60 ($4) for children 4 to 14.

- **The Cotswold Pottery,** Clapton Row (☎ **01451/820-173**), is a small country pottery that exhibits and sells hand-thrown pots of exceptional quality. Hours are Monday through Saturday from 10 a.m. to 5 p.m. and Sunday from 10:30 a.m. to 4 p.m.

Upper Slaughter and Lower Slaughter: Quiet and Atmospheric

Just 1½ miles northwest of Bourton-on-the-Water is **Lower Slaughter,** the prettiest village in the Cotswolds. With the River Eye running through it, Lower Slaughter is a picture of quiet, commercial-free elegance. There's really nothing to "do" here except stroll through the peaceful country lanes with their stone houses. You can stop in at **The Old Mill,** a working mill on Mill Lane (☎ **01451/820-052**), and have tea in its riverside tearoom. The mill is open daily from 10 a.m. to 6 p.m. in the summer and until 4 p.m. in the winter.

If you fall under the spell of Lower Slaughter, you can stay here — in a pretty place that costs a pretty penny. A double room at **The Washbourne Court Hotel,** Lower Slaughter, Gloucestershire GL54 2HS (☎ **01451/822-143;** `www.washbournecourt.co.uk`), goes for £120 to £230 ($192 to $368).

A 1-mile country footpath known as Warden's Way connects Lower Slaughter with **Upper Slaughter,** the next village. A leisurely walk between the two takes about an hour each way. The well-marked footpath skirts the edge of the River Eye, passing meadows with grazing sheep and old cottages surrounded by gardens. (The trail actually begins in Bourton-on-the-Water, along the ancient Roman footpath known as the Fosse Way.) Upper Slaughter is a small, peaceful, commercial-free village where you can stroll and savor the Olde English atmosphere.

Broadway: Village Shopping

Located 18 miles northeast of Cheltenham, Broadway is another picture-perfect Cotswold village. Saxons first settled the village in the sixth century. In the 16th century, Broadway became an important stagecoach stop. During the Victorian age, Broadway's charm and tranquility drew painters and writers. Today, visitors come to bask in the ambience of the golden-yellow stone buildings, which mostly date from the 16th century through Georgian times. Broadway doesn't have the kind of tourist attractions that Bourton-on-the-Water has, but day-trippers still pack the village during the summer tourist season. Visitors come here to stroll, shop, and have lunch or afternoon tea. High Street has so many upscale shops that it's sometimes called "the Bond Street of the Cotswolds" (a reference to London's chic shopping street).

Getting to Broadway

Broadway is 58 miles north of Bath and 15 miles southwest of Stratford-upon-Avon. Trains run daily from London's Paddington Station to Moreton-in-Marsh, 8 miles away; call ☎ **08457/484-950** for train information. **National Express** (☎ **0990/808-080**) runs one bus a day from London's Victoria Coach Station to Broadway; the trip takes 2½ hours. By car from Cheltenham, take B4632 northeast; from Bourton-on-the-Water, take A429 northeast to Moreton-in-Marsh and then head northwest on A44.

Finding information

The small **Tourist Information Centre,** 1 Cotswold Court (☎ **01386/852-937**), is open February through December, Monday through Saturday from 10 a.m. to 1 p.m. and 2 to 5 p.m.

Staying in Broadway

One lodging option in the village is the 16th-century **Lygon Arms,** High Street, Broadway, Worcestershire WR12 7DU (☎ **01386/852-255;** `www.thelygonarms.co.uk`). Doubles in this full-service luxury hotel go for £179 to £239 ($286 to $382). The 69-room hotel has acres of grounds, a health spa, and every amenity you can think of.

If you want to stay in an exceptionally beautiful house in the Cotswold countryside, try **Mill Hay,** Snowshill Road, Broadway, Worcestershire WR12 7JS (☎ **01386/852-498;** `www.broadway-cotswolds.co.uk/millhay.html`). The house, with only three guest rooms, is a spacious, golden-stoned Queen Anne with three acres of superlative gardens. Doubles with English breakfast go for £120 to £160 ($192 to $256).

Stopping for a spot of tea

For an informal lunch or old-fashioned cream tea in Broadway, try **Small Talk,** 32 High St. (☎ **01386/853-676;** `www.broadway-cotswolds.co.uk/smtalk.html`), adjacent to the Lygon Arms hotel. The cafe is open daily from 9 a.m. to 5 p.m. Lunch is a reasonable £5 to £8 ($8 to $12); a cream tea with homemade scones is £4.50 ($7). Sandwiches are available if you want to have a picnic. Small Talk rents out six charming guest rooms, all with private bathrooms; prices start at £50 ($80).

Exploring Broadway and Vicinity

Soak up the atmosphere of this Cotswold village by taking a leisurely stroll along **High Street.** Along the way, you pass little antiques shops, boutiques, galleries, and pubs. You may want to spend a few minutes looking at the antique toys and 100-year-old teddy bears on display in the **Broadway Teddy Bear Museum,** 76 High St. (☎ **01386/858-323**). In an 18th-century shop called "Broadway Bears and Dolls," the museum is open Tuesday through Sunday and costs £2.50 ($4) for adults, £1.75 ($2.80) for seniors and children under 14.

If you want to savor a bit of Elizabethan ambience, stop in for a meal, a drink, or afternoon tea at the half-timbered **Lygon Arms** (☎ **01386/852-255;** see the section "Staying in Broadway," earlier in this chapter). This wonderfully atmospheric hotel, in business since 1532, has crackling fires, exposed beams, and paneled lounges.

On Snowshill Road, 1 mile south of town, is **St. Eadburgha's,** a lovely medieval church built of the characteristic local stone. Another half-mile brings you to a local landmark and one of England's outstanding viewpoints: **Broadway Tower** (☎ **01386/852-390**) was built in the early 19th century as a *folly* (a picturesque building evoking an earlier age) high atop Broadway Hill. From the hilltop, you can see 12 surrounding counties. The tower and surrounding land is now a country park. In the tower, you find exhibits connected with its past as a retreat for William Morris, founder of the Arts and Crafts movement; the grounds are home to red deer and Cotswold sheep, and children can visit an animal park and playground. A restaurant is on the premises, or you can bring a picnic. Tower and park are open daily from April through October from 10:30 a.m. to 5 p.m.; winter hours are daily 11 a.m. to 3 p.m. Admission to the tower is £3 ($4.80) for adults and £1.50 ($2.40) for children; the animal park costs £2.95($4.70) for adults, £2 ($3.20) for children.

The countryside to the northwest of Broadway, near the town of Evesham, is known as the **Vale of Evesham.** The area has some of England's most productive fruit-growing land. For a few weeks between mid-March and mid-May, the roadsides are ablaze with the soft pinks of cherry, apple, and pear blossoms, and the white of flowering plums.

Chipping Campden: Picture Perfect

Have your camera ready as you enter this village, because you'll see a picture everywhere you turn. Chipping Campden was a wool town in the Middle Ages. Here you find thatched-roof cottages with walls of mellow yellow Cotswold stone and a beautiful High Street with Tudor and Elizabethan buildings.

The **Tourist Information Centre,** 2 Rosary Court, High St. (☎ **01386/841-206**), is open daily from 10 a.m. to 5 p.m.

Getting to Chipping Campden

By car from Broadway, take B463 east 4 miles; from Cheltenham, 20 miles to the west, head north on A435 and A46, and then turn southeast on A44. The closest train service is from London's Paddington Station to Moreton-in-Marsh, 7 miles away; from there you can take a taxi to Chipping Campden; call **Bourton** (☎ **01481/820-972**) to reserve a cab.

Staying and dining in Chipping Campden

The best choice for a fine meal and a comfortable bed is the **Noel Arms Hotel,** High Street, Chipping Campden, Gloucestershire GL55 6AT (☎ **01386/840-317;** `www.cotswold-inns-hotels.co.uk`). This 14th-century coaching inn has a modern wing, but the original section retains many original features, such as stone fireplaces and beamed ceilings. A double room with full English breakfast is £120 ($192). Reservations are recommended for the restaurant, which offers a classy international menu with meat, fish, and vegetarian choices. Fixed-price lunches are £14.95 to £16.95 ($24 to $27), fixed-price dinners are £22 to £25 ($35 to $40); a sumptuous afternoon cream tea served in one of the lounges is £18.50 ($30).

For good, unfancy lunches and teas, try **The Bantam Tea Rooms,** also on High Street (☎ **01386/840-386;** `www.thebantam.co.uk`). A traditional lunch of cottage pie or steak and kidney pie costs about £6 ($10), and a cream tea is under £4 ($6). The place is open Wednesday through Monday from 11:30 a.m. to 4:30 p.m. The Bantam also rents out charming, inexpensive rooms nestled up under the eaves, all with private bathrooms; doubles cost £65 to £70 ($104 to $112), full English breakfast included.

Exploring Chipping Campden

You can walk through the village and see everything in about 30 minutes. First, at the north end of town, visit **St. James's Church,** which prosperous wool merchants built in the 15th century. The church is a fine example of the Perpendicular Gothic style, a medieval building style in which vertical lines dominate. Nearby is a grouping of medieval **almshouses,** built to house six poor men and six poor women. High Street contains many beautiful Cotswold stone buildings dating from the 14th to the 17th centuries. The imposing **Market Hall** was built in 1627 for the town's local produce market.

Kiftsgate Court and Hidcote Manor Gardens

The Cotswolds are blessed with many beautiful gardens, two of which, near Chipping Campden and Broadway, you'll want to see if you're at all interested in English gardens. The two gardens, Kiftsgate Court and Hidcote Manor, are only about a mile apart.

Just east of the village of Mickleton off the B4632 from Broadway, **Kiftsgate Court Gardens** (**☎ 01386/438-777**) is the creation of three generations of women gardeners. Heather Muir started Kiftsgate in the 1920s. Her daughter Diany Binny added to the gardens in the 1950s. Diany's daughter Anne now looks after them. Kiftsgate was designed as a series of connecting gardens, each with its own distinct character. The newest addition is a contemporary water garden. Light lunches and homemade teas are served from June to August. In April, May, August, and September, the garden is open Wednesday, Thursday, and Sunday from 2 p.m. to 6 p.m. In June and July, it's open Wednesday, Thursday, Saturday, and Sunday from noon to 6 p.m. Admission is £4.50 ($7) for adults, £1 ($1.60) for children under 16. Allow at least an hour.

One of the great gardens of England, **Hidcote Manor** (**☎ 01386/438-333**), lies 4 miles northeast of Chipping Campden and 9 miles south of Stratford-upon-Avon. Set on 10 acres, Hidcote Manor is comparable in beauty, skill, and ingenuity to Sissinghurst in Kent (see Chapter 15). In 1907, Major Lawrence Johnstone began to create a series of hedged outdoor rooms linked by the corridors of its main vista. The rooms are furnished with all sorts of topiary and an amazing variety of plantings that add color, texture, and contrast. Give yourself at least an hour to see this garden, a National Trust property. A restaurant serves lunch from noon to 2:30 p.m. and teas from 3 to 5:30 p.m. The gardens are open March 23 through May and in September Saturday through Wednesday from 10:30 a.m. to 5:30 p.m.; daily from 10:30 a.m. to 5:30 p.m. in June and July; Saturday through Wednesday from 10:30 a.m. to 4:30 p.m. October through November 3. Admission is £5.80 ($9) for adults, £2.90 ($4.60) for children 5–15, and £14.50 ($23) for families (2 adults, 2 children). Access for visitors with disabilities is limited in parts.

Cirencester: Market Town with a Roman Past

Regarded as the unofficial capital of the Cotswolds, Cirencester (pronounced *Sih*-ren-*ses*-ter) is a bustling market town 16 miles south of Cheltenham. During the Middle Ages, Cirencester was a center of the great Cotswold wool industry. But long before that, in Roman times, Cirencester was the second-largest town in Britain. Known then as *Corinium Dobunnorum,* the town stood at the crossroads of five major roads. Like Bath and Cheltenham, Cirencester makes for a good touring base in the Cotswolds. Londoners in search of weekend and summer homes in the Cotswolds have recently "discovered" the town, and many good restaurants and quality shops have opened.

Getting to Cirencester

The nearest train station is at Kemble, 4 miles to the southwest. Trains run from London's Paddington Station; it's an 80-minute trip, which may involve a transfer at Swindon depending on the train you take. For train information, call ☎ **08457/484-950**). A bus (no. 51) runs to Cirencester from Cheltenham via Stroud Valley Monday through Saturday. **National Express** (☎ **0990/808-080**) offers direct service from London's Victoria Coach Station.

Finding information

The **Tourist Information Centre,** Corn Hall, Market Place (☎ **01285/654-180**), sells an inexpensive town map with a walking tour. The center also has a room-booking service. From April through September, the center is open Monday from 9:45 a.m. to 5 p.m. and Tuesday through Saturday from 9:30 a.m. to 5 p.m.

You can exchange money at Lloyds Bank on Castle Street.

Staying in Cirencester

Cirencester doesn't offer many hotel or B&B choices. Here are two options.

Corinium Hotel

$ **Cirencester**

This pleasant, family-owned hotel with a walled garden was a wool merchant's house in Elizabethan days. The hotel was later refaced with mellow Cotswold stone, and the stables and coach house were converted into a restaurant and bar. The guest rooms, all with private bathrooms, are fresh and comfortable.

12 Gloucester St., Cirencester, Gloucestershire GL7 2DG. ☎ ***01285/885-807.*** *Fax: 01285/885-807. Internet:* `www.coriniumhotel.co.uk`. *Rack rates: £75–£95 ($120–$152) double. Rates include English breakfast. AE, MC, V.*

Smerrill Barns

$ **Outside Cirencester**

Located 2 miles southwest of town (off A429), near the village of Kemble, this country guesthouse is in an 18th-century Cotswold stone barn. Converted in 1992, the hotel is completely up-to-date, nicely decorated, quietly comfortable, and smoke-free.

Near Kemble, Cirencester, Gloucestershire GL7 6BW. ☎ ***01285/770-907.*** *Fax: 01285/770-706. Internet:* `www.smerrillbarns.com`*.* ***Rack rates: £60 ($96) double.*** *Rates include English breakfast. MC, V.*

Dining in Cirencester

Now that Londoners, many of whom have country homes in the Cotswolds, have "discovered" Cirencester, the number and variety of restaurants has increased. Here are my recommendations.

Ann's Pantry

$ **TRADITIONAL**

This old-fashioned lunch and tea room is upstairs at the rear of an intriguing antiques shop. You can get a sandwich or a daily lunch special, which may be mussels with leeks, duck, or chicken curry. The cream tea with Cornish clotted cream is very good.

Cirencester Arcade, 25 Market Place. ☎ ***01285/644-214.*** *Main courses: £4–£7 ($6–$11), cream tea £3.50 ($6). AE, MC, V. Open: Mon–Fri 9:30 a.m.–5 p.m., Sat 9:30–5:30 p.m., Sun 11 a.m.–5 p.m.*

Harry Hare's Restaurant & Brasserie

$ **INTERNATIONAL**

You find English, Italian, French, and vegetarian dishes at this cheerful, informal restaurant, and a kids' menu, too. Harry Hare's has a country Gothic look with plank floors, an old fireplace, and wicker chairs. The food is good, and there's an ample wine list.

3 Gosditch St. ☎ ***01285/652-375.*** *Main courses: £5–£10 ($8–$16). AE, MC, V. Open: daily 10:30 a.m.–10:30 p.m.*

Slug and Lettuce

$ **PUB/TRADITIONAL**

This friendly pub restaurant is part of a national chain. You can get a good ribeye steak, beef and Guinness stout sausages, smoked haddock fishcakes, and other traditional dishes.

17 West Market Place. ☎ ***01285/653-206.*** *Main courses: £6–£8.50 ($10–$14). MC, V. Open: Mon–Sat 11 a.m.–11 p.m., Sun noon to 10:30 p.m.; food served Sun–Thurs until 9 p.m., Fri–Sat until 8 p.m.*

Swan Yard Cafe

$ **TRADITIONAL**

This is a great, informal, all-purpose cafe, where you can order a sandwich, quiche, or homemade soup. If it's available, try Homity pie, a traditional dish made with mashed potatoes, onions, and garlic — like shepherd's pie without the meat. The cafe is in Swan's Yard, which is to your left as you face the parish church.

West Market Place. ☎ ***01285/641-300.*** *Main courses: £3–£5 ($4.80–$8). MC, V. Open: Mon–Sat 9:30 a.m.–5p.m., Sun 11 a.m.–4 p.m.*

Tatyan's

$–$$ CHINESE

This well-known Chinese restaurant serves Peking, Hunan, and spicy Szechuan dishes. On the menu you find dishes such as sizzling prawns, chicken with ginger, and sweet and sour pork.

27 Castle St. ☎ ***01285/653-529.*** *Main courses £5.50–£16 ($9–$26), fixed-price lunch £10.50 ($17), fixed-price dinner £14.50 ($23). AE, MC, V. Open: Mon–Sat noon to 2 p.m. and 7–9 p.m.*

Exploring Cirencester

Two millennia ago, only London was larger and more powerful than Cirencester, then called *Corinium Dobunnorum*. The town was a Roman administrative center for the area around the southern Cotswold hills, one of the most prosperous regions in Roman Britain. You can still see the remains of the **Roman amphitheatre,** constructed in the second century A.D. to accommodate some 8,000 spectators. The entrance is on Cotswold Avenue, on the south side of town (free admission).

The **Corinium Museum,** Park Street (☎ **01285/655-611**), is one of England's best small museums. The museum is devoted entirely to the history of Cirencester from the Iron Age through the medieval wool era. In the antiquities on display, the Roman era predominates. You find an outstanding collection of mosaic floors and re-created Roman-era interiors. You can easily while away an hour here. The museum is open Monday through Saturday from 10 a.m. to 5 p.m. and Sunday from 2 to 5 p.m. Admission is £2.50 ($3.75) for adults, £1 ($1.50) for students, and 80p ($1.20) for children. *Note:* At press time, the museum was closed for a complete refurbishment and scheduled to reopen in late summer 2004.

If you look south across Park Street from the museum, you see an enormous **yew hedge,** reputedly the highest in Europe. Planted in 1720, the hedge is now 40 feet high. The yew hedge is part of **Cirencester Park,** the Earl of Bathurst's 3,000-acre estate designed by the poet Alexander Pope. The park is open to the public; use the entrance gates on Cecily Hill.

Cirencester's importance as a wool town during the Middle Ages is reflected in the size of its **Parish Church of St. John the Baptist** (☎ **01285/653-142**), which dominates the Market Place. The church isn't quite as large as a cathedral, but it comes close. Special details include the fan-vaulted porch and a rare 15th-century pre-Reformation pulpit. A silver-gilt cup made for Anne Boleyn in 1535 is on display.

Shopping in Cirencester

Cirencester is a local market town, which means that people come from miles around to do their shopping. A **street market,** one of the oldest in the country, is held on Monday and Friday in the central Market Place in front of the parish church. On Friday, you can shop in an **antiques market** in Corn Hall next to the Tourist Information Centre; on Saturday, you find a **crafts market** in the same space.

If you're looking for antiques or local crafts, you can also try the following:

- At **Brewery Arts Centre,** Brewery Court, (☎ **01285/657-181**), resident craft workers sell everything from baskets to handmade porcelain, glass, jewelry, and leather goods. A good cafe is on the premises.
- **Rankine Taylor Antiques,** 34 Dollar St., (☎ **01285/652-529**), sells silver, 17th- to 19th-century glass, and furniture.
- **William H. Stokes,** The Cloister, 6/8 Dollar St. (☎ **01285/653-907**), specializes in furniture, tapestries, and items from the 16th and 17th centuries.

If you need to pick up some swanky groceries, head to the **Cirencester Waitrose,** an upscale supermarket on Sheep Street. Gloucestershire Royals, such as Princess Anne (who lives in the countryside nearby) and Princess Michael of Kent, have been seen stocking up in this store.

Chedworth Roman Villa

The remains of one of the largest and finest Roman villas in Britain are about a half-hour's drive from Cirencester. The villa is at the end of a green, wooded valley. The National Trust administers the site, which includes the excavated remains of a water shrine, two bathhouses, and even a lavatory. Shedlike roofs protect fine fourth-century mosaics. Start your tour with the short introductory video, and then wander at will. No one knows if this complex of buildings was a religious center or a giant Roman farm. Maybe it was both. You can see the entire site in under an hour.

Admission is £3.90 ($6) for adults, £2 ($3.20) for children 5 to 15, and £9.80 ($16) for families (2 adults, 2 children). The site is open April to October 26, Tuesday through Sunday from 10 a.m. to 5 p.m.; in March and from October 28 to November 16 it's open from 11 a.m. to 4 p.m. Call ☎ **01242/890-250** for more information. To get there from Cirencester, head north on A429, turn west at Fossebridge, and follow the signs for 3 miles to Chedworth.

Part VII
Way Up North

"It says, children are forbidden from running, touching objects, or appearing bored during the tour."

In this part . . .

This part introduces you to Yorkshire and Cumbria, large counties "way up north," close to Scotland. Scenically, the region is quite different in its appeal from central and southern England, which are softer and greener. Gray-stone villages and mile upon mile of open moorland, rocky shoreline, small lakes, and treeless mountains fill the flinty northern landscape. Yorkshire and Cumbria are places of rugged character and independence. Local accents are sometimes closer to Scots than to the "Oxbridge" accents heard in the south.

Chapter 21 covers Yorkshire in the northeast. York, with its vast cathedral and medieval walls, is one of England's great cities. Magnificent Castle Howard and Scarborough, a fun-loving resort town on the North Sea, are close by. In Chapter 21, I also tell you about Yorkshire's two national parks: North York Moors, extending over a vast tract of heather-covered moorland and North Sea coastline, and Yorkshire Dales, a peaceful world of rolling farmland and traditional villages. Many people forever associate the Yorkshire moors with the novels *Wuthering Heights* and *Jane Eyre*. Haworth, where you can visit the home of the authors Emily and Charlotte Brontë, is a literary shrine second only to Stratford-upon-Avon.

Chapter 22 visits Cumbria, also known as the Lake District, in the northwest corner of England. Lake District National Park, which encompasses the entire county, protects a hauntingly beautiful world of lakes, bracken-covered mountains, and lovely stone villages. Tourists from around the world come to this remote part of England to hike, boat on Lake Windermere, bask in the glorious scenery, and visit the homes of William Wordsworth in Grasmere and Beatrix Potter near Lake Windermere. Keswick, on a pretty lake called Derwentwater, is another Lake District town that's well worth visiting.

Chapter 21

Yorkshire

In This Chapter

- Visiting York and its great cathedral
- Having some fun in Scarborough
- Seeing North York Moors and Yorkshire Dales National Parks
- Stopping in at the Brontë Parsonage Museum in Haworth

Yorkshire, a land of great and varied contrasts, is blessed with some of the most dramatic landscapes in England, and some of the most tranquil. (See the "Yorkshire" map in this chapter.) This northern region's windswept moors, sheltered dales, and rushing streams — or *becks,* as people call them up north — draw walkers from around the world to the countryside. But Yorkshire was an industrial powerhouse during the 19th century, and many of its cities and towns are pretty grim reminders of those Industrial Revolution days. (Don't worry. I'm not taking you to any industrial heritage towns.) In Yorkshire, you can attune your ears to the broad, Scots-like accents of the North.

I begin this chapter with **York,** Yorkshire's most visited city. Ringed by medieval walls, with a stupendous cathedral and winding medieval streets, York is one of the most beautiful and fascinating cities in England. From York, you can make an easy trip by train and taxi to the splendor of **Castle Howard** and the haunting **Eden Camp,** a World War II prisoner-of-war camp. **Scarborough,** on the 100-mile stretch of Yorkshire coast, is a resort town on the North Sea, also easily accessible by train from York. If you want to explore Yorkshire's two national parks and the Brontë country in and around Haworth, you may want to rent a car in York rather than depend on public transportation. **North York Moors National Park** is known for its unspoiled coastline and vast stretches of heather-crowned moorland. Farther inland to the west is **Yorkshire Dales National Park,** with its old stone villages, rolling farmland, and dramatic limestone formations. This chapter ends in **Haworth,** where the Brontës created their evocative masterpieces of moorland passion, *Wuthering Heights* and *Jane Eyre.*

Yorkshire

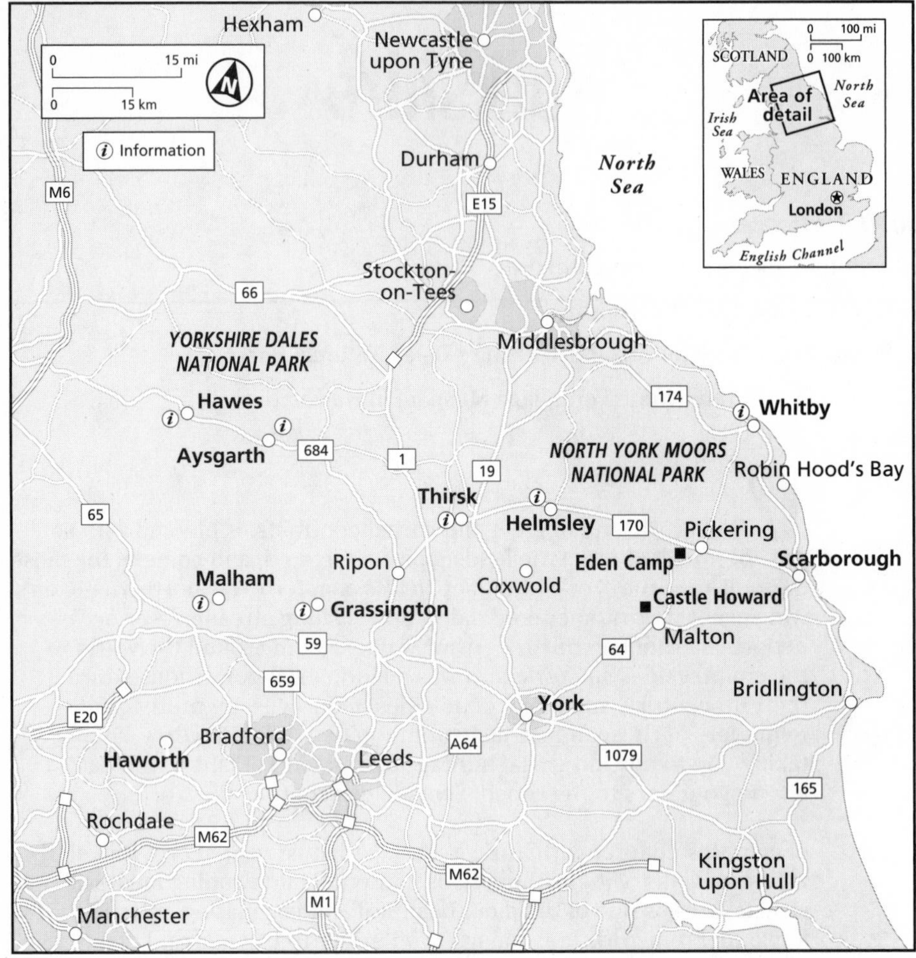

York: Ancient Walls and Snickelways

York is only 195 miles north of London, close enough for a day trip but worlds apart in character. York is the capital of the North and one of England's most historic cities. Under the Romans, who built a major fort here, the city was known as *Eboracum.* For hundreds of years after that, York was a thriving Viking settlement called Jorvik. And finally, after the Norman conquest, it became York, queen of the North.

Interesting museums, historic buildings of all kinds, good hotels, excellent shops, and fine restaurants make York a popular tourist city, and rightly so. Enormous York Minster, the largest Gothic structure north of the Alps, dominates the city. And, amazingly, the old town's 800-year-old walls and fortified gateways still girdle the old town center.

York

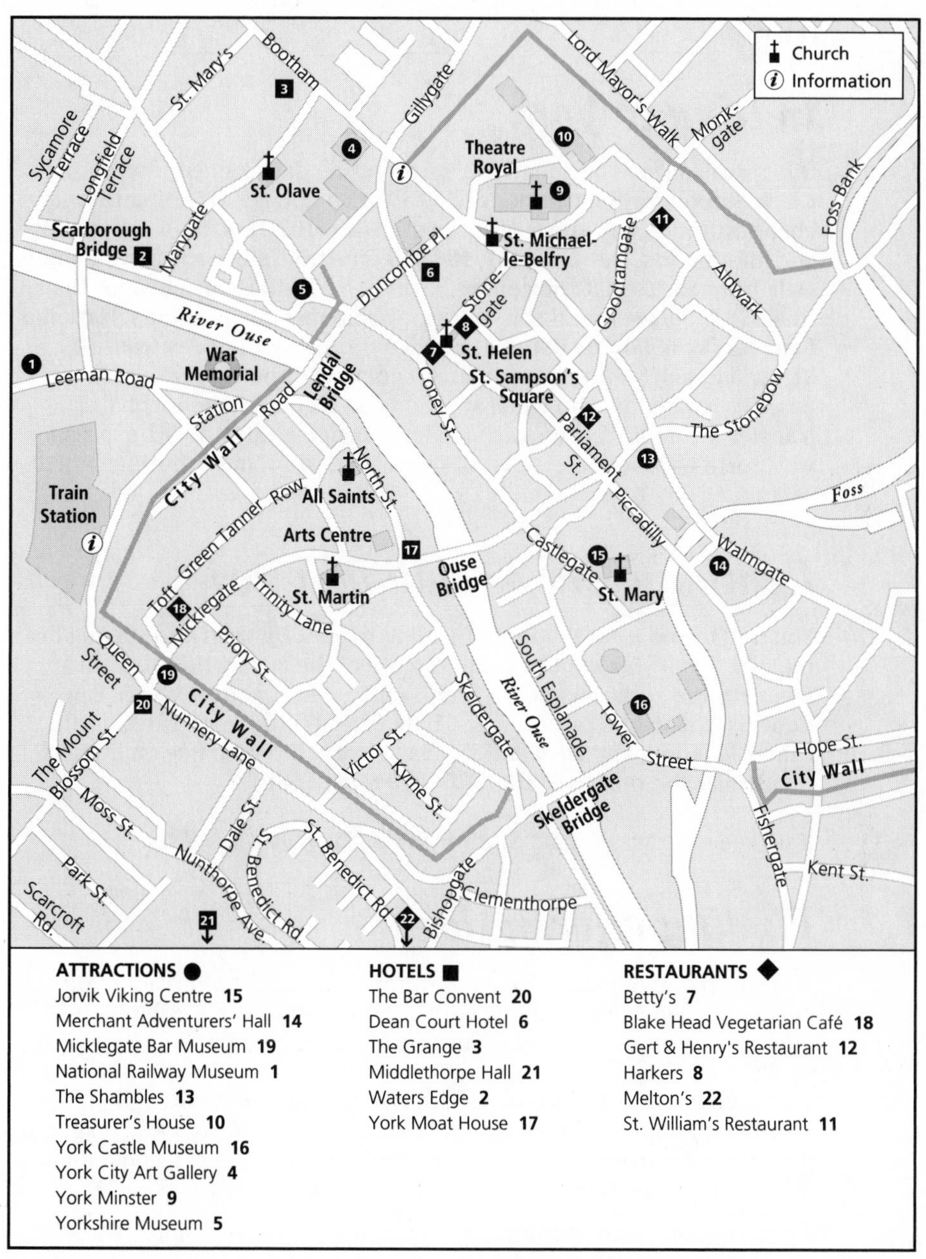

York is considered the best-preserved medieval walled city in England. (A bloody history reputedly makes York the most haunted city in England, too.) You can soak up the city's history while exploring its maze of ancient streets and *snickelways* (hidden alleyways). You can get everywhere on foot and see many attractions in just a day. York makes a good base for exploring the rest of Yorkshire. A few miles east is Castle.

Getting to York

Direct trains leave frequently throughout the day from London's King's Cross Station for the two-hour trip to York's Rougier Street Station. The cheapest round-trip supersaver fare is £64 ($102). For train schedules and information, call ☎ **08457/484-950.** The train station is a five-minute walk from York's historic center. Buses are considerably cheaper than trains (£27.50/$44 round-trip) but take a minimum of five hours. **National Express** (☎ **0990/808-080**) has service throughout the day from Victoria Coach Station in London. I recommend that you take a direct bus; otherwise, the trip can last as long as six hours and involve a transfer in Leeds. If you're driving from London, take the M1 expressway north to junction 45, east of Leeds, and from there continue northeast on A64 to York.

Renting a car or calling a taxi

You don't need a car if you're traveling to York by train and staying in the city. But if you want to explore more of the fascinating Yorkshire countryside, York is a good place to rent a car. **Practical Car & Van Rental** (☎ **01904/624-277;** Fax: 01904/658-647) has good rates, a city center location, and weekend specials. **Hertz** has an office on Station Road, near the railway station (☎ **01904/612-586**).

If you need a taxi, contact **Station Taxis** (☎ **01904/623-332**).

Finding information

You can visit two places for information in York. At both places you can get an inexpensive guidebook with a map, book a room, and obtain information on guided tours. The two places include

- A convenient branch of the **Tourist Information Centre** (no phone) is right in the train station. The office is open Monday through Saturday from 9:30 a.m. to 5 p.m. (6 p.m. in summer), and Sunday from 10 a.m. to 4 p.m. (4:30 p.m. in summer).
- The main **Tourist Information Centre,** De Grey Rooms, Exhibition Square (☎ **01904/621-756;** `www.york-tourism.co.uk`.), is open Monday through Saturday from 9 a.m. to 5 p.m. (6 p.m. in summer), and Sunday from 10 a.m. to 4 p.m. (5 p.m. in summer). This branch is near York Minster, just beyond the Royal Theatre.

Special events in York

York celebrates its Viking heritage with feasts, music, and pageantry during the **Jorvik Viking Festival** (☎ **01904/636-668**), held in mid-February. The acclaimed **York Early Music Festival** (☎ **01904/632-220;** www.ncem.co.uk) has special programs at Easter and in July. York has one of Europe's most prestigious horseracing courses; **York Racecourse** (☎ **01904/620-911;** www.yorkracecourse.co.uk) holds meets from May to October.

Exchanging money and locating ATMs

Both Tourist Information Centres have a currency exchange. You can also try **American Express,** 6 Stonegate (☎ **01904/670-030); HSBC,** 13 Parliament St. (☎ **01904/884-001**); and **Royal Bank of Scotland,** 6 Nessgate (☎ **01904/642-961**).

Taking a tour in York

More guided tours are offered in York than in just about any other city in England, excluding London. You can explore the city by foot, bus, or boat. The city is small enough that you can easily get around and see everything by yourself, but a guided tour is useful because you'll see parts of the town that you may otherwise miss.

During the summer, you can hire a horse-drawn carriage in front of the Dean Court Hotel near York Minster. A 15-minute ride around the cathedral *close* (the walled precinct surrounding the cathedral) costs about £5 ($8) per person.

Boat tours

What could be more fun than cruising down the River Ouse through the middle of England's most historic walled city? Departing from the pier below Lendal Bridge, **York Boat** (☎ **01904/647-204;** www.yorkboat.co.uk) provides a 45-minute tour with live commentary that nicely complements a walking tour. From February 9 through November 24 at least four boats depart each day; you can buy your ticket on board. The cost is £6 ($10) for adults, £5.50 ($9) for seniors, and £3 ($4.80) for children 5 to 15.

Bus tours

Guide Friday (☎ **01904/625-618;** www.guidefriday.com) runs open-top, double-decker tour buses on a circuit of all the main sights in York (one hour total). The ticket, valid all day so you can hop on and off as you want, costs £7.50 ($12) for adults, £5 ($8) for students, £3 ($4.80) for children 5 to 15, and £15 ($24) for families (2 adults, 2 children). The buses run year-round from about 9:30 a.m. to 5 p.m.; you can get on at the train station and buy your ticket from the driver.

Walking tours

Thumbs up to the **York Association of Voluntary Guides (☎ 01904/640-780)** for its free two-hour guided tours of the city. The tours depart daily at 10:15 a.m. year-round from Exhibition Square in the city center. Additional tours start at 2:15 and 6:45 p.m. in summer. You don't need to make a reservation; just show up.

Yorkwalk (☎ 01904/622-303; `www.yorkwalk.co.uk`) offers a series of two-hour walks on intriguing subjects on different days of the week. All walks start at the Museum Gardens Gates on Museum Street just north of Lendal Bridge; the cost is £5 ($8) for adults, £2 ($3.20) for children. Essential York, Roman York, Romantic York, and the Jewish Heritage Walk are some of the offerings; I'm sorry I didn't have time for the Historic Toilet Tour. Call or visit the Web site to find out times and topics, or pick up their leaflet at the Tourist Information Centre.

Staying in York

The largest city in northern England, York has a fine array of hotels and B&Bs. Following are my recommended choices.

The Bar Convent

$

This former convent is an inexpensive, unusual, and convenient place to stay. The accommodations are in a Georgian building on the corner of Nunnery Lane and Blossom Street, a five-minute walk from the train station. The 15 rooms are comfortable but nothing fancy; only one has a private bathroom. The convent, which houses a neoclassical chapel, was founded in 1686 and was active as a school until 1985.

17 Blossom Street, York YO24 1AQ. ☎ ***01904/643-238.*** *Fax: 01904/631-792. Internet:* `www.bar-convent.org.uk`. ***Rack rates: £46–£48 ($74–$77) double with shared bathroom, £54–£58 ($86–$93) double with bathroom.*** *Rates include continental breakfast. MC, V.*

Dean Court Hotel

$$–$$$

You can't get any closer to York Minster than this full-service hotel almost directly beneath the towers. The building, originally used to house clergy, dates from 1850 and was converted into a 39-room hotel after World War I. The rooms are comfortable, although some are quite small, and decorated with many traditional patterned fabrics and wallpapers. The restaurant serves traditional English and international fare at lunch and dinner.

*Duncombe Place, York YO1 2EF. ☎ **800/528-1234** in the U.S. or 01904/625-082. Fax: 01904/620-305. Internet:* `www.deancourt-york.co.uk`. *Rack rates: £115–£170 ($184–$272) double. Rates include English breakfast. AE, DC, MC, V.*

The Grange

$$$–$$$$

Created from a classical Regency brick townhouse, The Grange is a small, elegant hotel close to the city walls and a few minutes' walk from York Minster. The individually designed rooms use antique furniture and plenty of English chintz. Bathrooms are nicely done. The hotel offers room service and three good restaurants: The Ivy, serving classic French and Modern British cuisine, is considered one of the best restaurants in York; the Dom Ruinart Seafood Bar serves fresh fish, seafood, and champagne; and the Brasserie offers informal dining in the old brick vaulted cellars.

*1 Clifton, York YO30 6AA. ☎ **01904/644-744.** Fax: 01904/612-453. Internet:* `www.grangehotel.co.uk`. *Rack rates: £140–£200 ($224–$320) double. Rates include English breakfast. AE, MC, V.*

Middlethorpe Hall

$$$ **South of York**

One of the country's finest hotels is in a 26-acre park, 1½ miles south of town. Middlethorpe Hall is an elegant country house that was built in 1699. It was the residence of Lady Mary Wortley Montagu, a famous diarist of the early 18th century. The hotel offers a high standard of personal service and comfort and features beautifully restored rooms, lovely gardens (with a 350-year-old cedar tree), a health spa, and a fine restaurant. Some of the 30 guest rooms are in the main house, others are in the remodeled stable house. The furnishings are traditional, and each roomy bathroom has a tub and shower. An English breakfast costs £14.95 ($24). At dinner, men are requested to wear a jacket and tie.

*Bishopthorpe Road, York YO23 2GB. ☎ **800/260-8338** in U.S., or 01904/641-241. Fax: 01904/620-176. Internet:* `www.middlethorpe.com`. *Rack rates: £160–£210 ($256–$336) double. AE, MC, V.*

Waters Edge

$

If you're looking for a small B&B, check out this guesthouse in two side-by-side Victorian houses overlooking the river. Waters Edge is close to everything in town and has five nicely furnished bedrooms, all with private bathrooms. The B&B is completely nonsmoking. Children are welcome.

*5 Earlsborough Terrace, Marygate, York YO30 7BQ. ☎ **01904/644-625.** Fax: 01904/731-516. Internet:* `www.watersedgeyork.co.uk`. ***Rack rates: £50–£60 ($80–$96)*** *double. Rates include English breakfast. MC, V.*

York Moat House

$$

This modern 200-room hotel within the city walls overlooking the River Ouse has a pleasant waterside restaurant and bar. This property is part of a British chain that caters to business travelers. The rooms are nicely decorated and have decent-size bathrooms. A health and fitness center is on the premises.

*North St., York YO1 1JF. ☎ **01904/459-988.** Fax 01904/641-793. Internet:* `www.moathousehotels.com`. *£150 ($240) double. Rates include English breakfast. Parking £6 ($10). AE, DC, MC, V.*

Dining in York

York suffers no shortage of good restaurants. Here are my recommendations.

Betty's

$ **TRADITIONAL ENGLISH/SWISS/TEAS**

Founded in 1919, Betty's is a wonderfully old-fashioned Art Nouveau tearoom-pâtisserie-restaurant. A dozen or so hot dishes, both fish and meat, are available. Specialties include smoked salmon muffins, pasta with leeks and bacon, and haddock and prawns in white-wine cream sauce. The pastries, all made according to secret recipes, are superb. At the shop in front, you can buy specialties such as Yorkshire fat rascals: warm scones with citrus peels, almonds, and cherries.

*6–8 St. Helen's Square. ☎ **01904/659-142.** Main courses: £6–£8 ($10–$13); cream tea £5.50 ($9). AE, MC, V. Open: daily 9 a.m.–9 p.m.*

Blake Head Vegetarian Cafe

$ **VEGETARIAN/VEGAN**

This conservatory-style cafe dedicated to vegetarian and vegan cuisine is tucked away at the back of a bookshop. You can order a hearty mixed-grill breakfast, filled baguettes, quiche, great salads (including goat's cheese), and Welsh rarebit, a blend of cheddar cheese, Yorkshire ale, and mustard grilled on toast. The relaxed atmosphere makes it a good place to bring kids.

*104 Micklegate. ☎ **01904/623-767.** Breakfast £2.95–£5.95 ($4.75–$10), lunch £3.50–£5.75 ($6–$9). MC, V. Open: Mon–Sat 9:30 a.m.–5 p.m., Sun 10 a.m.–5 p.m.*

Gert & Henry's Restaurant

$–$$ ENGLISH

This cozy, comfortable, unpretentious restaurant in a half-timbered building is a good choice for a casual dinner, and it's open on Sunday night, when many other restaurants in York close. The menu sticks pretty much to traditional English dishes and seafood (including fish and chips) but also offers good salads and a few pastas.

Jubbergate, The Market. ☎ ***01904/621-445.*** *Main courses £5.95–£14.95 ($10–$24). MC, V. Open: daily 10 a.m.–2:30 p.m. and 4–10 p.m.*

Harkers

$ ENGLISH/PUB FOOD

Harkers is a good place to stop in for a simple lunch from the bar menu, or for tapas. It can become something of a mob scene after work, but that makes it more fun. The bar-restaurant is in the former Yorkshire Insurance Company building dating from 1824. Rumors of a makeover were circulating recently, so the name may have changed.

St. Helen's Sq. ☎ ***01904/672-795.*** *Main courses £3–£8.95 ($4.80–$14). MC, V. Open: daily noon to 4 p.m. (lunch) and 4–8 p.m. (tapas).*

Melton's

$$ MODERN BRITISH/INTERNATIONAL

Melton's has an à la carte menu, but the fixed-price meals offer good value. This stylishly informal restaurant is hard to categorize — except to say that the cooking is wonderful and the staff welcomes children. The menu changes according to season and availability of produce. You may find pistachio soup, grilled seabass stuffed with herbs, Yorkshire sirloin, or braised lamb.

7 Scarcroft Rd. ☎ ***01904/634-341.*** *Reservations recommended. Main courses £11.50–£17 ($18–$27), fixed-price lunch and early dinner £17 ($27),. MC, V. Open: Tues–Sun noon to 2 p.m. and Mon–Sat 5:30–10:30 p.m.*

St. William's Restaurant

$ TRADITIONAL/MODERN BRITISH

For an affordable lunch, dinner, or tea, check out this small, attractive restaurant in front of St. William's College at the east end of York Minster. The menu changes daily but always has some delicious choices, such as wild mushroom and leek risotto, pork loin wrapped in Cumbrian ham, or roast loin of venison. This spot is good for a simple cappuccino or an afternoon cream tea with scones and cakes.

3 College St. ☎ ***01904/634-830.*** *Lunch buffet £7.95 ($13), fixed-price dinner £14.50–£17.50 ($23–$28). AE, DC, MC, V. Open: daily 10 a.m.–5 p.m. and 6:30 p.m.–9:30 p.m.*

Exploring York

York is a delightful city to explore, full of old streets, lanes, *snickelways* (alleyways), and many tourist attractions. Keep a map with you, because it's easy to get lost on the city's medieval streets.

The City Walls and Micklegate Bar Museum

Almost 3 miles of medieval walls enclose the center of York. Fortified gateways (or "bars") still serve as entrances to the old part of town. A path (open daily 8 a.m. to dusk) runs along the top of the walls, with plenty of great views along the way. You find stairways up to the top of the walls at the four gates.

A good place to start a wall walk is at Micklegate, the southern entry used by royalty. Housed in the 800-year-old fortified tower is the tiny **Micklegate Bar Museum (☎ 01904/634-436)**, which looks at the social history of the gate in a quirky, humorous light. From February through October the museum is open daily from 9 a.m. to 5 p.m.; in November and December it's open weekends 9 a.m. to dusk (closed in January). Admission is £1.50 ($2.40) for adults, £1 ($1.60) for seniors and students, and 50p (80¢) for children 5 to 15. You can see it all in about 15 minutes.

Jorvik Viking Centre

If you want to revisit the Viking Age, hop into one of the time cars here to be transported back to A.D. 948, when Eric Bloodaxe was king and York was *Jorvik,* a thriving Viking port and trading town. The scenes you see — of village life, market stalls, crowded houses, and the wharf — are meticulous re-creations based on archaeological finds in this area; even the heads and faces of the animatronic characters you see were modeled on Viking skulls. Artifacts unearthed on this site are on display. Give yourself at least an hour.

Coppergate. ***☎ 01904/643-211.*** *Admission: £6.95 ($11) adults, £6.10 ($10) seniors and students, £5.10 ($8) children 5–15. Open: April–Oct daily 9 a.m.–5:30 p.m.; Nov–March daily 9 a.m.–4:30 p.m.*

Merchant Adventurers' Hall

In the medieval era, guilds ran English towns. This 14th-century stone and half-timbered guildhall belonged to York's most powerful guild, the Merchant Adventurers (they controlled trade into and out of the city). This building, one of the largest and best-preserved guildhalls in the country, has a great hall for business, a hospital for charitable work, and a chapel for worship. Allow 15 minutes.

Fossgate. ***☎ 01904/654-818.*** *Admission: £2 ($3.20) adults, £1.70 ($2.75) seniors and students, 70p ($1.10) children 5–15. Open: Apr–Sept Mon–Thurs 9 a.m.–5 p.m., Fri–Sat 9 a.m.–3 p.m., Sun noon to 4 p.m.; Oct–Mar Mon–Sat 9 a.m.–3 p.m.*

Shrine in The Shambles

No. 35 The Shambles is a shrine to St. Margaret Clitheroe, a butcher's wife who was executed during the Reformation for hiding Catholic priests in her attic. She was martyred by being crushed to death beneath a wooden door weighted down with rocks. She was canonized in 1970.

National Railway Museum

As you probably guessed, this museum is devoted to England's railroad system. The great exhibits appeal to both adults and children. The earliest train cars on display date from the 1840s and look like stagecoaches on tracks. You can peek into the windows of private royal coaches, from Queen Victoria's of 1869 with its bulky furniture (the engineer had to stop when the queen wanted to move from one car to the next) to Queen Elizabeth's streamlined, functional carriage, used until 1977. You see a replica of the first steam locomotive (1830) and a display of the new Eurostar high-speed train. It's fascinating (now, if they could just get the trains outside to run on time). You need at least an hour for a thorough visit. On some trains, kids can climb up into the engineer's area.

Leeman Road. ☎ ***01904/621-261.*** *Admission: free. Open: daily 10 a.m.–6 p.m. Closed Dec 24–26.*

The Shambles

Until 150 years ago, The Shambles was a street where butchers displayed their finest cuts in open windows on wide shelves called *shammels.* Today, this narrow, winding lane with buildings so close that they shut out the light is England's most famous medieval street. Gift shops have replaced the butcher shops, so you can get in a bit of retail therapy as you stroll down the street.

Treasurer's House

This elegant town house in Minster Yard housed the York Minster's treasures. Built in 1620, the house was extensively remodeled during the Victorian era. Inside are beautiful period rooms with collections of 17th- and 18th-century furniture, glass, and china. You can see the entire collection in about 30 minutes. A nice tearoom is on the premises.

Minster Yard. ☎ ***01904/624-247.*** *Admission: £3.50 ($6) adults, £1.75 ($2.80) children 5–15. Open: April–Oct Sat–Thurs 10:30 a.m.–5 p.m.; closed Nov–March.*

York Castle Museum

You can see 400 years of social history at York's top museum, which happens to be England's most popular folk museum. Using a treasure trove of now-vanished everyday objects, the exhibitions recreate slices of life from past historical epochs. The museum is in York's 200-year-old prison buildings, with graffiti still on the walls of the dingy cells. You can walk down a reconstruction of Kirkgate, a cobbled Victorian shopping street; see a Jacobean dining room; visit a moorland cottage and a gypsy caravan; and call in at a Victorian police station and an Edwardian pub. The Jane Austen Costume Collection is a haberdashery of fashion and fabrics. Kids love the giant dolls' houses. Allow at least an hour.

Eye of York (near Clifford's Tower). ☎ ***01904/653-611.*** *Admission: £6 ($10) adults, £3.50 ($6) children 5–15, £16 ($26) families (2 adults, 2 children). Open: daily 9:30 a.m.–5 p.m.*

York City Art Gallery

The gallery is in an Italian Renaissance-style building completed in 1879. The collections on view span seven centuries of Western European painting and include pictures by Parmigianino and Bellotto, Lely, and Reynolds. You can also view an outstanding collection of 20th-century studio pottery. You can see the entire collection in less than an hour.

Exhibition Square (city center). ☎ ***01904/551-861.*** *Admission: free. Open: daily 10 a.m.–5 p.m. Closed Jan 1, Dec 25 and 26.*

York Minster

Awesome York Minster, the largest Gothic cathedral in northern Europe, was built between 1220 and 1472. Architecturally, it spans the entire range of Gothic style: Early English (1220–1260), Decorated (1280–1350), and Perpendicular (1361–1472). The chief cathedral in the North of England, York Minster contains half of all the medieval stained glass in the country. The **Five Sisters' Window** from 1260 is the oldest complete window in the Minster. (*Minster,* by the way, is a term used for a church, usually with cathedral status, attached to a monastery.) The **Great West Window,** painted in 1338 and set in heart-shaped tracery, is known as the "Heart of Yorkshire."

Above the south door, a magnificent **Rose Window** (1500) commemorates the union of the royal houses of Lancaster and York. Painted in 1310, the **Jesse Window** in the south nave depicts Jesus's family tree. The Minster's Decorated Gothic **Nave** (the main central space in the interior), begun in 1291 and finished in the 1350s, is one of Europe's widest. A 15th-century **Choir Screen** decorated with statues of 15 kings of England, from William I (the Conqueror) to Henry VI, separates the nave from the choir. In the south transept, you can descend into the ***Undercroft*** (the rooms under the church), where excavations have revealed the Roman *basilica* (an assembly hall, not a Christian church) that stood here nearly 2,000 years ago. You can take a well-designed "time

York Minster

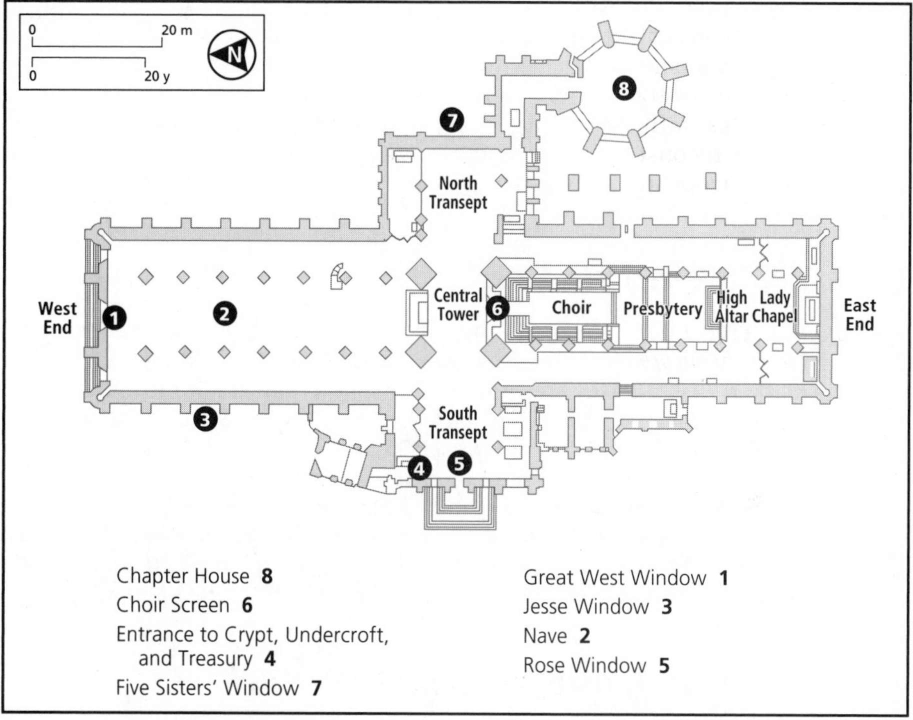

walk" to see Roman, Anglo-Saxon, and Norman remains. The walk leads to the 12th-century **Crypt** and the **Treasury,** where silver plate and other church treasures are on display. From the nave, a separate entrance leads to the 13th-century **Chapter House,** filled with fine stone carvings and medieval glass. Give yourself at least one hour to see everything in the cathedral.

Minster Yard. ☎ ***01904/557-216.*** *Admission: free for minster and chapter house, but suggested donation £3 ($4.80) adults, £1 ($1.60) children; crypt, undercroft, and treasury £3.80 ($6) adults, £1.80 ($2.90) children 5–15. Open: Minster and chapter house daily Nov–Mar 7 a.m.–6 p.m. (to 6:30 p.m. in Apr, 7:30 p.m. in May, 8:30 p.m. June–Aug, 8 p.m. in Sept, 7 p.m. in Oct); crypt, undercroft, treasury, and tower Mon–Sat 10 a.m.–4 p.m., later in summer).*

Yorkshire Museum

The Yorkshire Museum is somewhat old-fashioned and heavy on the text panels, but if you start in the Roman section and walk through to the end, you get a sound presentation of Yorkshire's history from two millennia ago through the 16th century. You can view elegant Roman jewelry, mosaics, and Anglo-Saxon silver. Viking treasures include swords and battle-axes. The Middleham Jewel, a 15th-century pendant decorated with a large sapphire, was found in 1985 in North Yorkshire. The museum lies in 10 acres of landscaped gardens amid the ruins of St Mary's Abbey, formerly the North's wealthiest abbey. On the grounds is a 15th-century timber-framed building known as The Hospitium. Give this museum about an hour.

Museum Gardens (in the center of York). ☎ ***01904/551-800.*** *Admission: £4 ($6) adult, £2.50 ($4) children 5–15, £10 ($16) families (2 adults, 2 children). Open: daily 10 a.m.–5 p.m. Closed Jan 1, Dec 25 and 26.*

Shopping in York

High-end shops, including designer clothes boutiques and fine jewelry, are on **Swinegate,** a street that was once — you guessed it — a hog market. The **Quarter** area around Swinegate is known for its independent, one-of-a-kind shops. **Newgate Market,** between Parliament Street and The Shambles (☎ **01904/551-355**), is York's biggest open-air market, open daily with more than 100 stalls selling crafts, clothes, candles — you name it. If you're looking for antiques, head over to **The Red House Antiques Centre,** 1 Duncombe Place (the street runs south from York Minster; ☎ **01904/637-000**), where more than 60 dealers sell quality, time-touched merchandise in a beautiful Georgian building.

Stepping out at night in York

York is busy at night as well as during the day, especially during the summer, when the air is warmer and the light lingers longer. You may want to take a special nighttime tour or head out to a pub.

Ghost walks

Apparently plenty of supernatural activity takes place in York, which some claim is England's most haunted city. Evening ghost walks, with entertaining commentary and sometimes a bit of spookery thrown in, are a regular year-round industry. You have several tours from which to choose. You can buy your tickets (all tours are £3/$5 for adults, £2.50/$4 for seniors, and £2/$3 for children 5 to 15) on the spot:

- **Original Ghost Walk of York** (☎ **01759/373-090**), which began in 1973, explores folklore, legend, and dreams. This walk features really good storytelling. Walks leave nightly year-round at 8 p.m. from The King's Arms Pub, Ouse Bridge.
- Traditional ghost-storytelling is what you get on the **Haunted Walk** (☎ **01904/621-003**), which departs at 8 p.m. from Exhibition Square.
- **The Ghost Hunt of York** (☎ **01904/608-700**), the most popular of the walks, is a fun, one-hour walk and performance led by "Andy Dextrous," ghost hunter. Walks leave nightly at 7:30 p.m. from The Shambles, York's medieval street.

- You get more traditional ghost-storytelling on **The Ghost Trail** (☎ **01904/633-276**), which leaves nightly at 7:30 p.m. from the front entrance of York Minster.

The best pubs

The Cross Keys, Goodramgate (☎ **01904/686-941**), close to York Minster, is a popular pub with a beer garden and live music. Also on Goodramgate is **Old White Swan** (☎ **01904/540-911**), with a warm-weather courtyard, three bars, and home-cooked food. **The Punchbowl,** 7 Stonegate (☎ **01904/615-491**), is a 300-year-old pub serving traditional Yorkshire ales and filling pub food. The half-timbered **Black Swan,** Peasholme Green (☎ **01904/686-911**), dates from the 15th century and is known for its folk music performances.

Performing arts

Theatre Royal, St. Leonard's Place (☎ **01904/623-568;** `www.theatre-royal-york.co.uk`), and the **Grand Opera House,** Cumberland Street (☎ **01904/671-818;** `www.york-operahouse.co.uk`), offer a year-round schedule of plays and concerts.

Day-tripping from York: Castle Howard and Eden Camp

If you're staying in York or the vicinity, you may want to visit Castle Howard and Eden Camp, both easily accessible from York by car, train, or taxi. The two places are close to one another but worlds apart: Castle Howard gives you a glimpse of the wealth and power of the English aristocracy, and Eden Camp tells the story of ordinary men and women living under extraordinary circumstances.

Getting to Castle Howard

Castle Howard is 15 miles north of York off A64 (20 minutes by car). From York, you can get a train to Malton (local Scarborough line), and then take a taxi (about £10/$16) 9 miles to the castle; to reserve a taxi, call **Station** ☎ **01653/696-969. Coastliner Coaches** (☎ **01653/692-556**) operates buses from York and Scarborough.

Exploring Castle Howard

You can visit enormous Castle Howard on a self-guided tour. The grounds of the castle are well worth exploring, too.

Set against a backdrop of North Yorkshire's Howardian Hills, Castle Howard is instantly recognizable to anyone who's seen the television series *Brideshead Revisited.* The castle is a truly magnificent sight: not really a castle, but certainly one of England's grandest stately homes. The largest house in Yorkshire, Castle Howard has been the home of the Howard family since the 17th century.

Sir John Vanbrugh designed Castle Howard (assisted by Nicholas Hawksmoor) and built it for the 3rd Earl of Carlisle. The castle was Vanbrugh's first project; his second was Blenheim Palace (see Chapter 13). The facade is a showcase of elegant architectural details, including statues, long arched windows, and a beautiful cupola crowning the center of the house.

The castle doesn't offer any guided tours; you're free to walk through at your own pace. Guides staff every room and can fill you in on the history. The marble entrance hall, lit by the dome, is particularly impressive, as is the Long Gallery, but the house has many superb rooms, all filled with fine furniture, statues, and china. The collection of paintings includes works by Rubens, Tintoretto, Van Dyke, Canaletto, and Reynolds, as well as a famous portrait of Henry VIII by Hans Holbein. *Brideshead* memorabilia fills one room.

The 1,000-acre park is landscaped with lakes and fountains, rose gardens, and shady woodland gardens. On the grounds, at the end of a short walk, is Vanbrugh's classically inspired Temple of the Four Winds, and a circular mausoleum by Hawksmoor. There are three restaurants: **The Hayloft Cafe** in the Stable Courtyard and **The Fitzroy Room** in the main house, both open daily 10 a.m. to 5 p.m., and **The Lakeside Cafe,** open weekends and holidays only, near the Great Lake. To see the house and gardens, you need a minimum of two hours, preferably three.

Malton. ☎ ***01653/648-333.*** *Open: Feb 14–Nov 2 daily 11 a.m.–4 p.m. (grounds open at 10 a.m.). Admission: £9 ($14) adults, £8 ($13) seniors, £6 ($10) children 5–15.*

Getting to Eden Camp

Eden Camp is just north of the Malton train station, 5 miles east of Castle Howard off A64 York-Scarborough Road at the junction of A169 to Pickering. From York, take a train to Malton (local Scarborough line), and then take a taxi (about £10/$16) to Eden Camp; to reserve a taxi at the Malton train station, call **Station** (☎ **01653/696-969**).

Exploring Eden Camp

Eden Camp spreads over several acres. The various buildings left from that period explore different aspects of World War II.

In 1942, Malton became the site of a prisoner-of-war camp. The first inmates, 250 Italians captured in North Africa, worked constructing the 35 wooden huts that you see today. The Italians left in 1944 and were followed by Germans, who remained until 1948. While at the camp, the prisoners worked on local farms under the control of the War Agriculture Officer.

Eden Camp's huts have now been re-equipped to tell about life in Britain during World War II (1939–1945). Realistic tableaux, sounds, and smells have been created to help you imagine life at a time when food was strictly rationed, blackouts were a nightly occurrence, and 80,000 civilians were killed in bombing raids over England. Each hut covers a different aspect of the story, starting with the rise of the Nazi Party, Hitler, and the outbreak of war. The sound of Vera Lynne singing "We'll Meet Again" is a haunting reminder of a time when people didn't know what the next day would bring. Eden Camp has much to see, so give yourself at least two to three hours.

Old Malton. ☎ ***01653/697-777.*** *Admission: £4 ($6) adults, £3 ($4.80) seniors and children 5–15. Open: daily 10 a.m.–5 p.m. Closed Dec 24 to mid-Jan.*

Scarborough: Cliffs and Arcades

The first and largest resort town on the Yorkshire coast, Scarborough is famous for its giant curving swath of sandy beach on the North Sea. The town clusters around two splendid bays (North Bay and South Bay) with a headland in between. South Cliff, the neighborhood around South Bay and the harbor with its Esplanade, is the main part of town. Scarborough is a fun place to visit for a day or to stay overnight if you're exploring North York Moors National Park (see "Yorkshire's Two National Parks: Moors and Dales," later in this chapter).

The seafront in Scarborough is a gaudy hodgepodge of noisy arcades, fish and chips shops, and tourist traps; its cheesiness is part of what makes the area fun. The town that covers the cliffs and hills above is more Victorian in character. Victorian-era cliff lifts still convey people up and down from the cliffs to the beach, just as they did when Scarborough was a pre-eminent Victorian spa town (people came to drink the mineral waters and to swim in the sea). In the end, Scarborough isn't a town where you go for heavy doses of culture. Popular with families, Scarborough is for hanging out on the beach, breathing the fresh sea air, and having a good time.

Getting to Scarborough

Scarborough is 35 miles northeast of York and 253 miles north of London. Local trains run all day between York and Scarborough. Trains leave London's Victoria Station almost every hour for York, where you change trains for the one-hour trip to Scarborough. For train information, call **☎ 08457/484-950. Yorkshire Coastliner (☎ 01653/692-556;** `www.yorkshire-coastline.co.uk`) operates two to four buses a day from York to Scarborough. By car from York, take A64 northeast.

Getting around Scarborough

The town is small enough that you can walk everywhere, but the hills from beach to town can make for a steep climb. For taxi service, call **Streamline Taxis** (☎ **01904/638-833**) or **Station Taxis** (☎ **01904/366-366**).

Finding information and taking a tour

The main **Tourist Information Centre,** across from the train station on Valley Bridge Road (☎ **01723/373-333;** www.scarborough.gov.uk), has maps, a room-booking service, and information on local attractions. The center is open daily May to September from 9:30 a.m. to 6 p.m.; Monday through Saturday from October to April, 10 a.m. to 4:30 p.m. A smaller **Tourist Information Centre** (no phone) is along the beach at Harborside; this center is open from 10 a.m. to 5 p.m. daily from May to September, and on Sunday only from November to April.

Step Back in Time (☎ **01723/355-682;** www.ScarboroughGuidedTours.ic24.net) is a local guide service that conducts guided walks on request (£4/$6).

Staying in Scarborough

Scarborough has plenty of hotels and B&Bs to choose from. Following are my recommended choices.

Bradley Court Hotel

$$ South Cliff

Bradley Court Hotel is a good, moderately priced hotel without sea views but within walking distance to town and beach. The 40-room hotel is Victorian with somewhat dowdy English modern furnishings. You find some nice connected rooms that are good for families up in the former attics, and a few larger "premiere" rooms. All rooms have private bathrooms with tubs and showers. The breakfast is good. Request a room in back if traffic noise bothers you.

Filey Road, Scarborough, YO11 2SE. ☎ ***01723/360-476.*** *Fax: 01723/376-661. E-mail:* info@bradleycourthotel.co.uk. *Rack rates: £50–£75 ($80–$120) double. Rates include English breakfast. MC, V.*

Biederbecke's Hotel

$$ Town center

Biederbecke's, in an 1835 building at the end of a Victorian *crescent* (a row house built in a long, curving line), is Scarborough's most stylish hotel. The 27 guest rooms are comfortable and well furnished, with good-size tiled bathrooms (most with tub-shower combinations and bidets). Even if you don't stay here, stop in for a drink at the **Red Square Cocktail Bar,** with its blue and orange walls, contemporary furniture, and giant poster of Lenin. The bar is the hippest hangout in town. I describe the hotel restaurant, **Marmalade's,** later in this chapter under "Dining in Scarborough."

*1–3 The Crescent, Scarborough YO11 2PW. ☎ **01723/365-766.** Fax: 01723/367-433. Internet:* `www.beiderbeckes.com`. *Rack rates: £110–£130 ($176–$208) double. Rates include English breakfast. AE, MC, V.*

The Esplanade

$$ Town center

If you want a spacious room that has a big bathroom with tub and shower and panoramic sea views, you can't beat The Esplanade. The hotel is a large and rather old-fashioned place, created a century ago from three mid-19th-century houses on the top of the South Cliff above The Esplanade. A wonderful roof terrace overlooks South Bay and the town below.

*Belmont Road, Scarborough YO11 2AA. ☎ **01723/360-382.** Fax: 01723/376-137. Rack rates: £95 ($152) double. Rates include English breakfast. AE, V.*

Granville Lodge

$ South Cliff

This pretty, well-maintained hotel is in a Victorian building close to the town center. All 40 rooms have private bathrooms, and some have four-poster beds. The lodge has a good restaurant; ask about special rates that include dinner.

*Belmont Road. ☎ **01723/367-668.** Fax: 01723/363-089. Internet:* `www.granville.scarborough.co.uk`. *Rack rates: £52–£58 ($84–$93) double. Rates include English breakfast. MC, V.*

Dining in Scarborough

The restaurant scene in Scarborough has improved in recent years. Here are my recommended choices for dining.

Cafe Italia

$ COFFEE/LIGHT FARE

This small, atmospheric Italian coffee bar sits on a street over to one side of the Grand Hotel. Come here for good coffee, focaccia sandwiches, and ice cream.

*36 St. Nicholas Cliff (near the Grand Hotel). ☎ **01723/501-975.** Lunch: £4–£7 ($6–$11). No credit cards. Open: Mon–Sat 10 a.m.–4 p.m.*

Marmalade's

$$ INTERNATIONAL

This is Scarborough's liveliest and most sophisticated restaurant. The large, varied menu includes vegetarian offerings such as Thai vegetable curry. Carnivores can choose from steak, chicken, rack of lamb, seared venison, and veal dishes, all served with intriguing sauces and side dishes. Fresh fish is also on the menu; the crab and fish chowder is worth trying. For simpler, cheaper fare, like fish and chips or meat and potato pie, eat in the bar.

1–3 The Crescent (in Biederbecke's Hotel). ☎ ***01723/365-766.*** *Reservations recommended weekend dinner. Main courses: restaurant £10.75–£14.75 ($18–$24); bar £6 ($10). AE, MC, V. Open: daily 11 a.m.–3 p.m.; Mon–Sat 6–10 p.m., Sun 6–9 p.m.*

Mother Hubbard's

$ FISH AND CHIPS

On the second floor of a building near the Tourist Information Centre, this family-style fish restaurant serves the best fish and chips in town. You're not paying for decor or frills here, although the dining room is pleasant and cheery. Go for the haddock and chips; the batter is light and crispy. You can also get fresh cod or lemon sole.

43 Westborough. ☎ ***01723/376-109.*** *Meals: £5.50–£7 ($9–$11). No credit cards. Open: Mon–Sat 11:30 a.m.–6:45 p.m.*

Exploring Scarborough

Scarborough consists of an upper town and a lower area beside the beach. The town has always been more about enjoying the pleasures of the seaside than anything else.

Art Gallery

Scarborough's small art gallery is next to Wood End Museum (see listing later in this chapter). The most interesting works on display relate to the Scarborough area during the Victorian age. You can see everything in about 15 minutes.

The Crescent. ☎ ***01723/374-753.*** *Admission (includes Rotunda Museum and Wood End Museum): £2 ($3.20) adults, £1.50 ($2.40) seniors and children 5–15, £5 ($8) families (2 adults, 2 children). Open: June–Sept Tues–Sun 10 a.m.–5 p.m., Oct–May Thurs–Sat 11 a.m.–4 p.m.*

Rotunda Museum

The history and architecture of this small, circular museum are more interesting than its collections. Built in 1829 to contain the rock collections of William Smith (known as the father of English geology), it was one of England's first purpose-built museums. You don't need more than a few minutes to wander through; the second floor, with its original painted frieze and curving wall cabinets, remains intact. Your ticket allows admission to Wood End and the Art Gallery (I describe both in this section).

Vernon Rd. ☎ ***01723/374-839.*** *Admission (includes Art Gallery and Wood End Museum): £2 ($3.20) adults, £1.50 ($2.40) seniors and children 5–15, £5 ($8) families (2 adults, 2 children). Open: June–Sept Tues–Sun 10 a.m.–5 p.m.; Oct–May Tues, Sat–Sun 11 a.m.–4 p.m.*

Scarborough Castle

The headland between Scarborough's North and South bays was originally the site of a fourth-century Roman signal station. The castle here, built in the 12th century, is partially in ruins, but you get panoramic views of the coastline from its battlemented walls. An audio tour (included in the admission price) fills you in on the castle's turbulent history. Give yourself an hour, but add more time if you want to enjoy the headland walks.

Castle Road. ☎ ***01723/372-451.*** *Admission: £3 ($4.80) adults, £2.20 ($3.50) seniors, £1.50 ($2.40) children 5–15. Open: April–Sept daily 10 a.m.–6 p.m., Oct daily 10 a.m.–5 p.m., Nov–March Wed–Sun 10 a.m.–4 p.m.*

Scarborough Sea Life & Marine Sanctuary

Northeast England's leading marine animal rescue center, this place also operates as an aquarium, with fish, seals, sea otters, sea turtles, and other denizens of the deep. More than 30 multilevel viewing areas allow you to get close to various sea creatures, from sharks to shrimps. Kids enjoy the touch pools, where they can pick up velvet crabs, starfish, and anemones. You can watch feeding demonstrations and many marine-themed presentations.

Scalby Mills, North Bay. ☎ ***01723/376-125.*** *Admission: £6.50 ($10) adults, £4.75 ($8) children 5–15, £21 ($34) families (2 adults, 2 children). Open: Oct–June daily 10 a.m.–5 p.m., July–Sept 10 a.m. –8 p.m.*

Wood End Museum

Wood End was the childhood vacation home of the miserable Sitwell siblings, Edith, Osbert, and Sacheverell, who went on to become literary figures. The Victorian house now contains a library of their works and a pretty boring collection of stuffed animals (the real kind) from the Museum of Natural History. This museum is of interest only to fans of the Sitwells and requires about 10 minutes to see.

The Crescent. ☎ ***01723/367-326.*** *Admission (includes Art Gallery and Rotunda Museum): £2 ($3.20) adults, £1.50 ($2.40) seniors and children 5–15, £5 ($8) families (2 adults, 2 children). Open: June–Sept Tues–Sun 10 a.m.–5 p.m.; Oct–May Wed, Sat–Sun 11 a.m.–4 p.m.*

The fishing village of Whitby

The old fishing, whaling, and smuggling village of Whitby, with its quaint cobbled streets and picturesque houses, is 20 miles up the Yorkshire coast from Scarborough, in North York Moors National Park. Smaller and less touristy than Scarborough, Whitby makes a pleasant day trip from York or Scarborough. The port at Whitby has been in use for more than 1,000 years. Nowadays, people come to stroll the town's winding maze of streets and enjoy the coastal scenery, with its cliffs, coves, and bays. (The beaches are clean, but the North Sea is pretty cold for swimming, or "bathing," as the Brits call it.)

The River Esk divides the town into east and west sections. From Tate Hill Pier on the east side, Church Lane climbs up to the 199 steps leading to the **Church of St. Mary,** whose churchyard was one of the inspirations for Bram Stoker's *Dracula*. The imposing ruins of **Whitby Abbey,** founded in the seventh century, dominate the cliff top above. On the beachfront on the west side of town you find a **monument to Captain Cook,** who left Whitby in locally made ships for his circumnavigation of the globe. (It was Cook who claimed Australia and New Zealand for Great Britain.)

You can see all the sights in Whitby on **The Whitby Tour** (☎ **0191/521-0202**), a 50-minute open-top bus tour that operates daily from April to October. The cost is £4.50 ($7) for adults and £3 ($4.80) for seniors and students. Tours begin at about 10 a.m. (from Langborne Road, near the Tourist Information Centre) and depart hourly until 4 p.m.

For a map and more information, stop in at the **Tourist Information Centre,** Langborne Road (☎ **01947/602-674**), open daily from 9:30 a.m. to 4:30 p.m. (until 6 p.m. in summer). Daily bus service goes from Scarborough to Whitby, but no easy train connections are available. The Tourist Information Centre in Scarborough can give you up-to-the-minute bus schedules. If you're driving from Scarborough, take A171 north.

Seeing the performing arts in Scarborough

The **Stephen Joseph Theatre** (☎ **01723/370-541;** `www.sjt.uk.com`), opposite the train station on the corner of Westborough and Valley Bridge Road, was created from an Art Deco movie theater. The space is known as "Alan Ayckborne's theatre" because the British playwright-director opens his plays here before doing so in London. Troupes from around the country present a full season of offerings. The **theater restaurant** (☎ **01723/368-463**), a good place for a pre-show meal, serves traditional and British Modern main courses, salads, and desserts.

Yorkshire's Two National Parks: Moors and Dales

Two national parks have helped to preserve Yorkshire's famous moors, dales, and coastline. Using York or Scarborough as a base, you may want to explore the vast heather-covered moors and Yorkshire coastline that make up North York Moors National Park. York also makes a good base for touring Yorkshire Dales National Park, as does Windermere in Cumbria (see Chapter 22), at the park's northwestern corner. Both parks attract hordes of summer ramblers and long-distance hikers. Visitors on a limited schedule can rent a car in York (see "Renting a car or calling a taxi" in the preceding section on York) for touring one or both of the parks.

North York Moors National Park

Vast stretches of heather moorland — the largest expanses in England and Wales — makes the North York Moors unique. In late summer, the countryside turns into a great flowing sea of purple. Wonderful views cut across *dales* (rich farmland, where people have worked for centuries) and sweep out to the North Sea. Old crosses and standing stones remind you of the moorland's ancient human heart. The 554-square-mile park is also an important protected area for birds and wildlife.

From Scalby Mills near Scarborough to Saltburn in the north, picturesque, cliff-clinging villages, such as Whitby (see "The fishing village of Whitby" sidebar in this chapter) where fishing boats tie up at the harbors below, dot the coastal section. Commercial development along the coast and throughout the moors has been limited, so the area retains much of its rugged, down-to-earth character.

Getting to North York Moors National Park

Motorways encircle the park: A170 skirts the southern boundary, A19 and A172 traverse the western edge, and A171 follows the eastern coastline, and then cuts across the park's northern boundary. The only major road through the park is A169. Within the park, you otherwise find small roads, so having a good map is essential (you can pick one up at a visitor center). If you're traveling by car from York, head northeast on A64; you can cut north on A169 at Malton to the Visitor Centre at Pickering, or continue on A64 to Scarborough, and there pick up A171, the coastal road. See "Getting to York" and "Getting to Scarborough," earlier in this chapter, for train and bus information from London.

Getting around North York Moors National Park

The popular **North Yorkshire Moors Steam Railway (☎ 01751/472-508;** www.northyorkshiremoorsrailway.com) chugs along a wonderfully scenic 18-mile route through the heart of the park between the village of Grosmont (near Whitby) and the market town of Pickering. All-day Return Rover tickets let you hop off at any of the train's five restored stations for a walk through a village or the surrounding moors. The ticket costs £12 ($19) for adults, £10.50 ($17) for seniors, and £6 ($10) for children 5 to 15. Trains run daily from April through October.

Walking is the best way to discover this area's beauty. More than 2,000 miles of public paths allow you to explore even the remotest parts of the countryside. If you do go walking (or even if you drive), make sure you get Ordnance Survey Outdoor Leisure maps 26 and 27, which show every path and road. The National Park publishes *Walks around . . .* booklets for various sections of the park, including Robin Hood's Bay, The Moors Centre, Goathland, Rosedale, and Sutton Bank. The maps and the booklets are available at the park information centers (see the next paragraph).

Finding information

Information about the park is available from the **North York Moors National Park Authority,** Head Office, The Old Vicarage, Bondgate, Helmsley, York YO62 5BP (**☎ 01439/770-657;** www.northyorkmoors-npa.gov.uk); **The Moors Centre,** Danby, Whitby (**☎ 01287/660-654**); or **Sutton Bank National Park Centre,** Sutton Bank, Thirsk (**☎ 01845/597-426**). They're open daily in March, November, and December from 11 a.m. to 4 p.m., April through October daily from 10 a.m. to 5 p.m., and in January and February on Saturday and Sunday from 11 a.m. to 4 p.m.

Exploring North York Moors National Park

North York Moors National Park was home to three great medieval religious houses. At **Mount Grace Priory,** near Osmotherley off A19, you can see how the Carthusian monks lived, each with his own cell and garden. Farther south, between Thirsk and Helmsley off A170, is **Byland Abbey,** which was the home of a Cistercian Order. The majestic ruins of **Rievaulx Abbey,** oldest and most famous of the three, housed more than 600 monks. This National Trust property is located in the southwest section of the park, 2 miles west of Helmsley off B1257. All these sites are easy day trips from York, if you have a car.

The patchwork of fields and open moorland in the **Esk Valley** exudes an aura of timelessness. Near **Lealholm** and **Glaisdale,** old stone tracks mark the routes walked by generations of farmers and travelers. The watermill in the farming hamlet of **Danby** was the village's most important building; the mill is more than 350 years old and still working. Nearby are the ruins of **Danby Castle,** built in the 14th century as a fortified home. A short stroll down to the river takes you to **Duck Bridge,** first used 600 years ago. For the locations of all these sights, consult Ordnance Survey Outdoor Leisure maps 26 and 27 or the booklet *Walks around . . .*, both available at the park information centers (see the preceding section).

Yorkshire Dales National Park

Covering some 700 square miles, Yorkshire Dales National Park is home to a collection of varied landscapes: heather-capped moors, swift moorland rivers, colorful hay meadows, and rugged limestone crags. Bustling market towns and traditional sandstone villages nestle among fields and rolling farmland dotted with stone barns and stacked, drystone walls. Yorkshire Dales has different moods, wild and windswept in one place, quietly pastoral and rustic in another.

Getting to Yorkshire Dales National Park

The A1 to the east, A66 to the north, and the M6 to the west flank Yorkshire Dales National Park. Although driving is the easiest way to explore the park, you can also take public transportation. For information on local bus service, call ☎ **0113/245-676.** The nearest railway stations are Darlington and Northallerton; for train information, call ☎ **08457/484-950. National Express** (☎ **0990/808-080**) runs buses to Darlington.

Finding information

You can obtain information at the park's Web site, `www.yorkshiredales.org`. You can get maps, general information, and help with accommodations at **National Park Centres** in the following towns: **Aysgarth** (☎ **01969/663-424**), open daily April to October; **Grassington** (☎ **01756/752-774**), open daily from Easter through October; **Hawes** (☎ **01969/667-165**), open year-round; and **Malham** (☎ **01729/830-363**), open daily from April through October and on Saturday and Sunday the rest of the year.

Exploring Yorkshire Dales National Park

The Yorkshire Dales are a favorite walking area — paths crisscross the entire park. Among the best walking areas and towns to explore are the following (for maps and information, visit the National Park Centres, listed in the previous paragraph):

- **Aysgarth,** where the river cascades down a series of waterfalls, is one of the park's scenic highlights.
- **Dales Way,** a popular footpath, passes through the village of **Grassington,** in the scenic Upper Wharfedale section.

- **Hawes,** in Upper Wharfedale, is said to be the highest market town in England. Hawes is a lively place where you find shops selling local crafts and famous Wensleydale cheese. Hawes's old train station, next to the National Park Centre, is now the **Dales Countryside Museum** (☎ **01969/667-494**), where you can find out more about the 10,000-year human history of the Yorkshire Dales.
- **Malham,** the town closest to the park's remarkable limestone formations, has more good hiking. During the summer, up to half a million visitors swamp this 200-person village.

Haworth: On the Trail of the Brontës

Emily Brontë's *Wuthering Heights* or Charlotte Brontë's *Jane Eyre* may have sparked your interest in Yorkshire and the moors. Emily and Charlotte lived with a third sister, Anne, also a novelist *(The Tenant of Wildfell Hall)*, and their brother Branwell in the West Yorkshire town of Haworth, 45 miles southwest of York. Grim industrial cities (such as Leeds, Bradford, Halifax, and Keighley) surround Haworth, which wouldn't be on anyone's radar if it weren't for the Brontë clan. For more than a century now, people from around the world have trekked up the cobbled Main Street of Haworth to see the house where these three women, daughters of a local parson, wrote their compellingly passionate novels. Although Branwell's failed career as a portrait painter led him to drink and drugs, he did paint the famous portrait of Charlotte, Emily, and Anne that now hangs in London's National Portrait Gallery.

Getting to Haworth

The nearest train station with service from a major city is Leeds. From Leeds, you can take the West Yorkshire Metrotrain to Keighley, 3 miles south of Haworth. The Keighley and Worth Valley Railway runs steam trains between Keighley and Haworth (year-round on the weekends and daily from late June to early September). There's regular bus service to Haworth from Keighley and Bradford (8 miles away). For local train and bus information, call ☎ **01535/645-214;** for national train information, call ☎ **08457/484-950.** If you're driving from York, take A64 west to Leeds and A6120 to Shipley; from there, take A650 to Keighley and B6142 to Haworth.

Finding information and taking a tour

For information on the town, stop at the **Tourist Information Centre,** 2–4 West Lane (☎ **01535/642-329**), open daily from 9:30 a.m. to 5:30 p.m. (until 5 p.m. November through March; closed December 24 to

26). Well-marked walks lead from the town into the heather-covered moors so memorably evoked in the Brontë sisters' works. You can pick up a leaflet describing the most popular walks from the center.

Dining in Haworth

If you want a well-prepared dinner, try **Weaver's Restaurant,** 15 West Lane (☎ **01535/643-822**). Making reservations is essential because this restaurant is the best in town. The cooking is both traditional and modern British. Main courses go for £9 to £16 ($14 to $26), and a set-price lunch or dinner costs £15.50 ($25). The restaurant is open Tuesday through Sunday from 11:30 a.m. to 2:30 p.m. and Tuesday through Saturday from 7 to 9:30 p.m. If you want a casual lunch, check out the offerings — pubs, tearooms, and cafes — lining Main Street and West Lane. A pub lunch averages around £8 to £10 ($13 to $16).

Exploring Haworth

Haworth really should rename itself Brontëville, because the Brontë name is on everything from tea shops to trinket outlets. The one must-see literary shrine is the **Brontë Parsonage Museum** (☎ **01535/642-323;** `www.bronte.org.uk`), the house where the literary-minded siblings spent most of their lives. Built in 1778 at the top of the village behind the parish church, the house is furnished much as it would have been when the Brontës lived there. You find a collection of personal memorabilia, manuscripts, and even some of Charlotte's clothes (she was tiny). The museum is open daily February through December from 10 a.m. to 5:30 p.m., daily from 11 a.m. to 5 p.m. in January; closed December 24 to 27. Admission is £4.80 ($8) for adults, £3.50 ($6) for seniors and students, £1.50 ($2.40) for children age 5 to 15, and £10.50 ($17) for families (2 adults, 3 children). Depending on your interest, allow 30 to 60 minutes to visit the museum.

After visiting the house, you can stop in at the **parish church,** which is much altered since the Brontë sisters' days. Charlotte, the only one to wed, was married here in 1854 and buried here a year later, aged 39. Emily, who died in 1848 at age 30, is also in the family vault. Anne died in Scarborough at age 29 and is buried there.

Chapter 22

The Lake District

In This Chapter

- Enjoying the scenery at Lake Windermere
- Visiting Hill Top, home of Beatrix Potter
- Touring Dove Cottage, Wordsworth's home in Grasmere
- Savoring the spectacular countryside around Keswick

In 1974, the counties of Cumberland and Westmorland joined with a bit of Lancashire to officially create **Cumbria** in the northwest corner of England. But actually, Cumbria existed about 1,000 years before that as an ancient Celtic kingdom. And before that, about 5,000 years ago, the region was the home of Neolithic tribes that manufactured stone axes and erected stone circles. Today, this area, roughly 270 miles northwest of London and covering some 885 square miles, is protected as the **Lake District National Park.** The largest national park in the United Kingdom, it's also one of the most popular.

If you can, give yourself at least a couple of days in the Lake District. I cover three towns and lakes in this chapter: **Bowness** on Lake Windermere, **Grasmere** on the lake of the same name, and **Keswick** on Derwentwater. You find good hotels and restaurants in all three, and all are convenient for exploring this fascinating region, which stretches from Lancashire north to the Scottish border, east to the counties of Yorkshire, Durham, and Northumberland, and west to the Irish Sea. (See "The Lake District" map in this chapter.)

Odes and bunny rabbits

The Lake District's two most famous residents were the poet William Wordsworth and Beatrix Potter, who wrote and illustrated children's books. The landscape inspired both writers, and they used it in their work. Wordsworth composed his poetry outdoors, often in the area around Grasmere. Potter used Lakeland settings for her tales about Peter Rabbit and Jemima Puddleduck.

The Lake District

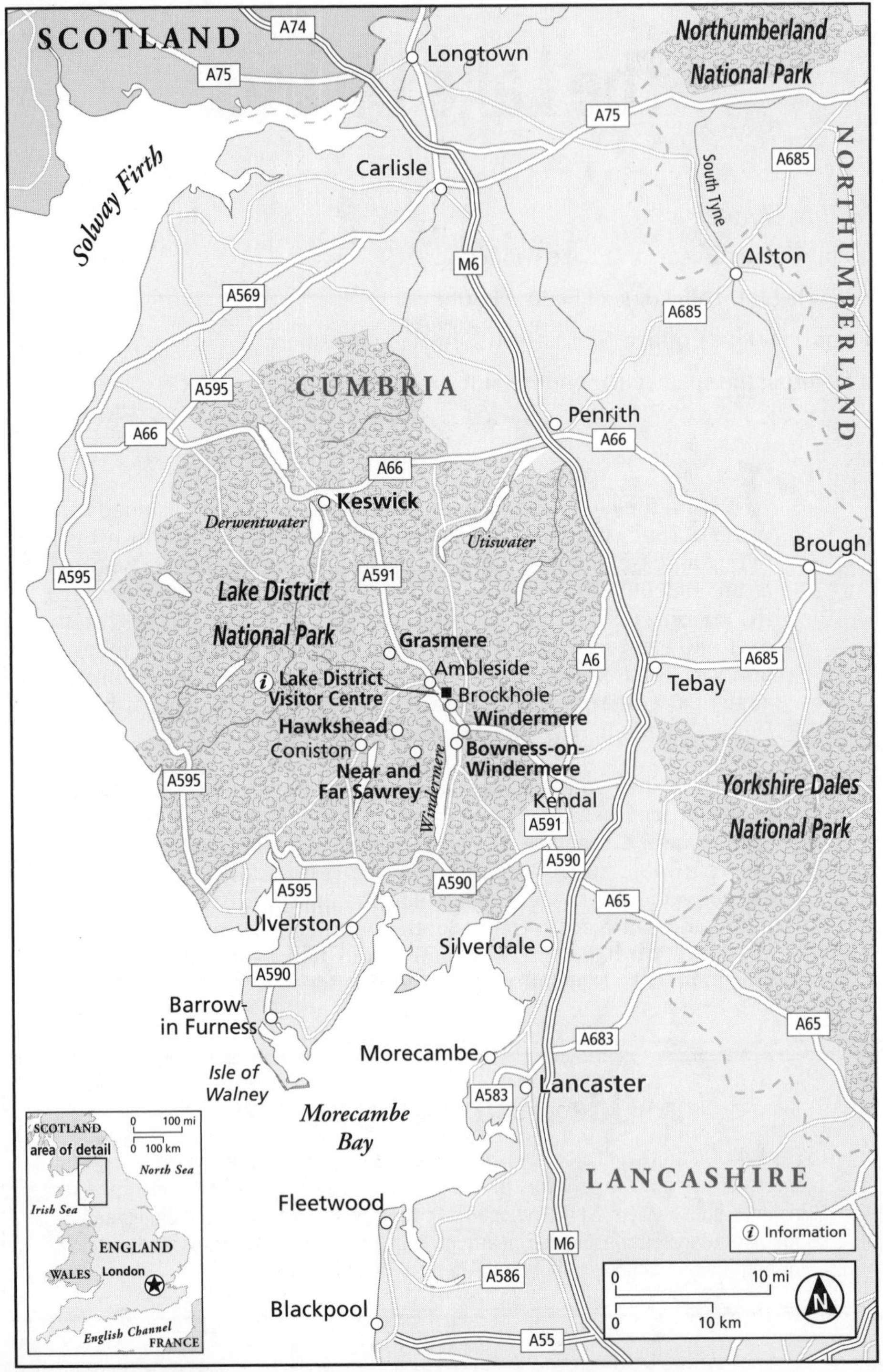

The Lake District: Natural Beauty and Literary Treasures

The Lake District, or Lakeland as it's also called, is a hauntingly beautiful place with a distinct personality. Treeless peaks covered with *bracken* (large, coarse ferns) surround a series of tranquil, jewel-like lakes radiating like spokes around 3,210-foot-high Scafell Pike, England's highest mountain. Having a sense of wide-open spaces is rare in England, and that's why the Lake District is so popular with hikers. Wonderful hiking trails lace the entire region, passing fern-fringed streams, stands of purple foxglove, hedgerows bursting with dog roses, ancient stone circles, and cottages made of gray-green Lakeland slate.

The weather in the Lake District is unpredictable — squalls can suddenly appear. Be prepared for fine, thin rains, vapory mists, and blustery winds. If you're thinking about hiking, bring waterproof boots and rain gear. To check on the rapidly changing weather conditions, call the **Weatherline** at **☎ 01787/75757.**

Getting to the Lake District

Bowness-on-Windermere, Grasmere, and Keswick all make good bases for exploring the region. **Virgin** (**☎ 0345/222-333**) operates trains between London and Oxenholme, the nearest main-line station to Lake Windermere. The trip takes about five hours and costs £60 ($96) for an advance-purchase round-trip ticket. From Oxenholme, local train service runs to Windermere. **National Express** (**☎ 08705/808-080**) runs buses from London's Victoria Coach Station to Windermere, but travel time is more than 6½ hours. The closest airports are Manchester, Leeds, and Newcastle. Driving from London, the fastest route is the M1 to Birmingham, where you pick up the M6 heading north. From the M6, take A590 and then A591 northwest to Windermere.

Lake District lingo

The Lake District and northern England in general are unique in their topography. Nowhere else in the country can you find the mixture of mountains, lakes, and streams that characterize this area. These natural features even have special names. Here are a few words that you may encounter:

- A *tarn* is a steep-banked mountain lake or pool.
- A *beck* is a mountain stream.
- A *mere* is a small, still lake.
- *Fells* are mountains.

Getting around the Lake District

Having a car opens up the entire region, but traffic in the summer is heavy and sometimes aggravating. You may want to rent a car in York (see Chapter 21) and drive west through Yorkshire Dales National Park to the Lake District. (Otherwise you can rent a car in Leeds or Manchester.) But boats and local buses (train service is unavailable in this area) can get you to all the towns and tourist sites that I describe without too much difficulty. The distances aren't great; in some cases, you can even walk. For all public transport questions — to, from, and within Cumbria — call the **Cumbria Traveline ☎ 0870/608-2608** (7 a.m. to 8 p.m. daily). You can also check the district's Web site: www.travelcumbria.co.uk.

Stagecoach Cumbria (☎ 0870/606-2608; www.stagecoachbus.co.uk) operates buses between all the towns I describe in the following sections. A one-day **Explorer pass,** good for unlimited travel, is £7.50 ($12) for adults and £5.25 ($8) for children 5 to 15; a **four-day pass** is £17 ($27) for adults and £12.50 ($20) for children 5 to 15. You can buy tickets on the bus or at any tourist information center (see the "Finding information" sections in this chapter for locations).

Taking a tour of the Lake District

If you're without a car, why not consider taking a guided tour of the Lake District? You have many options, including the following:

- **Countrywide Holidays,** Miry Lane, Wigan, Lancashire WN3 4AG (**☎ 01942/823-456;** www.countrywidewalking.com), offers safe and sociable walks led by experienced guides from different Lakeland locales; prices vary according to the walk you choose.
- **Cumbrian Discoveries,** Mickle Bower, Temple, Sowerby, Penrith CA10 1RA (**☎ 01768/362-201;** Internet: www.cumbria.com/discovery), arranges tailor-made tours on foot, by car, and by minibus. Prices depend on your itinerary.
- **Lakeland Safari Tours,** 23 Fisherbeck Park, Ambleside LA22 0A (**☎ 01539/433-904;** www.lakesafari.co.uk), offers full- and half-day tours in a luxury six-seater for £22 ($35; half-day) to £33 ($53; full day).
- **Lakes Supertours,** 1 High St., Windermere LA23 1AF (**☎ 01539/442-751;** www.lakes-supertours.co.uk), picks you up at your hotel for minibus trips to Beatrix Potter's house, Wordsworth's Dove Cottage, and Lakeland beauty spots. Prices depend on the type and duration of your tour.

Lake Windermere: Largest Lake in England

Glinting like a long, thin blade within its surrounding fells, 10-mile-long Windermere is England's longest lake. Windermere is also the region's most popular lake, a center for sailing, rowing, and yachting. (You can swim here, too, but the water's pretty brisk.) The town of **Windermere** (right around the train station) blends into **Bowness-on-Windermere** (also called Bowness) on the lake's eastern shore. Both towns are busy tourist-resort centers and good central spots to base yourself. You can walk from Windermere to Bowness in about 15 minutes; a local bus runs frequently from the train station at Windermere to Bowness Pier, a departure point for lake cruises. People come to Lake Windermere to hike, take boat trips, and visit the sites associated with Beatrix Potter.

Finding information and exchanging money

A few steps from the train station, Windermere's **Tourist Information Centre,** Victoria Street (☎ **015394/46490;** `www.cumbria-the-lake-district.co.uk`), sells maps and local guides and has a hotel-booking service. The center is open daily from 9 a.m. to 5 p.m. (from April through September until 6 p.m. and in July and August until 7:30 p.m.). A **National Park Information Centre** (with a bureaux de change) is at Bowness Bay (☎ **015394/42895**), next to the boat landing. See also the listing for the Lake District Visitor Centre in "Exploring around Lake Windermere," later in this chapter.

Barclays, Crescent Road, Windermere (☎ **015394/46111**), changes money weekdays from 9:30 a.m. to 4:30 p.m. and has an ATM.

Touring by boat or foot

Exploring the lake and the dramatically beautiful countryside around it is relatively easy — and you don't need a car to do it. In the two sections that follow, I tell you how to see the highlights of Lake Windermere by land and water.

Lake cruises

Various boat trips are available year-round on Lake Windermere. From the piers at Bowness, ferries make regular trips to Waterhead (near Ambleside) on the north shore and Lakeside on the southern end. The boats are fitted out for sightseeing, with big windows and open decks. From mid-May to mid-August, you can also take an evening wine cruise. A round trip from Bowness to Ambleside is £6.40 ($10) for adults, £3.30 ($50) for children 5 to 15, and £17.50 ($28) for families (2 adults, 2 children). For more information, contact **Windermere Lake Cruises** (☎ **01539/531-188;** www.windermere-lakecruises.co.uk).

Windermere Ferry (☎ **0860/813-427**), which shuttles passengers, cyclists, and cars between Bowness and Far Sawrey, on the western shore, is the cheapest way to get across the lake. Ferries depart about every 30 minutes throughout the day from Ferry Nab, south of the excursion-boat piers. The one-way passenger fare is 40p (60¢); a car costs £2 ($3.20).

A **Freedom of the Lake pass** is valid on all scheduled boats — including Windermere Lake Cruises and Windermere Ferry — on Lake Windermere for 24 hours. The cost is £11.50 ($18) for adults, £6.25 ($10) for children 5 to 15, and £28 ($45) for families (2 adults, 2 children).

Walks and rides

You won't find much solitude around Lake Windermere during the summer months, but some good, nonstrenuous walks provide memorable views. One of the easiest, and a good choice if you have older kids in tow, is the 2½-mile-round-trip trail from the Windermere Tourist Information Centre on Victoria Street to Orrest Head (784 feet). The trail gives you plenty of photo-op panoramas of the lake and the villages along the shore.

The Lake District is wonderful biking country, but be aware that cars can jam the local roads during the summer. You can rent bikes at **Country Lanes Cycle Centre** (☎ **015394/44544**), in the Windermere railroad station. It's open daily from 9 a.m. to 5 p.m. Easter through October. Bike rental is £17 ($28) plus deposit.

Staying near Lake Windermere

Lake Windermere is one of England's premier tourist attractions, so you'll have no problem finding a hotel or B&B. Here are my choices.

Linthwaite House

$$$–$$$$ **Bowness**

This large Victorian house overlooking Lake Windermere offers high-quality accommodations and wonderful service. The 26 rooms, all with private bathrooms, are appealingly decorated in a variety of styles that combine elegance and upscale comfort. The hotel has its own small tarn and can provide tackle for fly fishing.

Crook Road, Bowness-on-Windermere, Cumbria LA23 3JA. ☎ ***015394/88600.*** *Fax: 015394/88601. Internet:* www.linthwaite.com. *Rack rates: £99–£231 ($158–$370) double. Rates include English breakfast. AE, MC, V.*

Miller Howe Hotel

$$$–$$$$ Windermere

Miller Howe is one of those great country-house hotels that can turn a holiday into heaven. The hotel sits on a hill amid acres of landscaped gardens and enjoys a spectacular view of Lake Windermere. The restaurant is one of the most famous in the country, and guests come specifically to dine here. (The rates look high, but if you figure in the cost of the masterful six-course dinner that comes with the room, it's actually pretty reasonable.) The house is warm and sumptuous, with fires, cozy lounges, and pampering service. The spacious and beautifully furnished rooms (12 in all) have big bathrooms with tubs and showers. If you don't stay, consider dining here.

Rayrigg Road, Windermere, Cumbria LA23 1EY. ☎ ***015394/42536.*** *Fax: 015394/45664. Internet:* `www.millerhowe.com`. *Rack rates: £170–£270 ($272–$432) double. Rates include dinner and English breakfast. AE, DC, MC, V.*

The Old England

$$–$$$ Bowness-on-Windermere

This well-appointed hotel is for people who want to stay right on the water's edge. The hotel is just steps from Bowness Pier, and gardens lead down to the hotel's own jetties. Originally built as a lakeside mansion in the Victorian era, the hotel has grand-size public rooms and 76 comfy guest rooms with private bathrooms. In the summer, the hotel has a heated outdoor pool, a favorite with kids. The restaurant, overlooking the water, is a good place for lunch or dinner.

Bowness-on-Windermere, Cumbria LA23 3DF. ☎ ***0870/400-8130.*** *Fax 01539/443-432. Internet:* `www.heritage-hotels.com`. *Rack rates: £100–£170 ($160–$272) double. Rates include English breakfast. AE, MC, V.*

Dining near Lake Windermere

Windermere is a busy tourist center, so it has plenty of restaurants. In this section, I list my favorites.

Aunty Val's Tea Rooms

$ Bowness-on-Windermere TEAS/TRADITIONAL ENGLISH

Here's a good, quiet spot for an inexpensive lunch or tea. You can get homemade soup, toasted sandwiches, and a couple of hot main courses, such as steak and kidney pie, meat and potato pie, or a *Cornish pasty* (usually meat and onions baked in a crust). If you've never had hot sticky toffee pudding with cream, try it here. You can also choose from an assortment of homemade pastries.

Church Street, Bowness-on-Windermere. ☎ ***015394/88211.*** *Main courses: £3.50–£6 ($6–$10). No credit cards. Open: daily 11 a.m.–5 p.m.; closed Fri Nov and May.*

The Hole in't Wall

$ Bowness-on-Windermere PUB/INTERNATIONAL

Back in 1612, one side of this building was an ale house (it still is), and the other was a blacksmith. A hole in the wall connected the two. Now the place has a dark, wood-paneled interior with a fireplace. The food runs the gamut from whole roast pheasant to fisherman's pie, a daily curry, and daily specials listed on the blackboard. The menu always includes something that kids can enjoy. Set off a bit from the main tourist track in Bowness, it's an atmospheric spot to sample Cumbrian ales.

Lowside, Bowness-on-Windermere. ☎ ***015394/43488.*** *Main courses: £5.50–£10 ($9–$16). MC, V. Open: Mon–Sat 11 a.m.–11 p.m., Sun noon to 10:30 p.m.*

Miller Howe Cafe

$ Windermere MODERN BRITISH

Lakeland Ltd., right behind the Windermere train station, is one of England's largest retailers of creative kitchenware and food-related paraphernalia. The store contains this good cafe, where you can get a well-prepared lunch or tea. Options include homemade soups, sandwiches, salads, and quiches. Many families with children come here for lunch. You may want to stop in for some shopping even if you don't eat here — plenty of gift possibilities. (The cafe isn't related to the gourmet restaurant in the Miller Howe Hotel.)

Lakeland Ltd., Station Precincts, Windermere. ☎ ***015394/88100.*** *Main courses: £5–£8 ($8–$13). MC, V. Open: Mon–Fri 9 a.m.–6 p.m., Sat 9 a.m.–5 p.m., Sun 11 a.m.–4 p.m.*

Miller Howe Hotel Restaurant

$$$$ Windermere MODERN BRITISH

Dinner at this fine hotel restaurant is a somewhat ritualistic affair. It has only one seating, at 8 p.m., and the six-course menu is the same for everyone (with a la carte options). A typical meal may start with a trio of canapés (with áballontine of foie gras) and advance to a first course of seared scallops wrapped in cabbage followed by champagne sorbet. The main course may be local lamb in red-wine-rosemary sauce, with vegetables, followed by dessert. The elegant, two-tiered, candlelit dining room overlooks Lake Windermere, which is definitely a culinary high point of the Lake District. If you're staying at the hotel, your room rate includes dinner.

In the Miller Howe Hotel, Rayrigg Road, Windermere. ☎ ***015394/42536.*** *Reservations required. Six-course fixed-price dinner £39.50 ($63), 3-course fixed-price lunch £17.50 ($28). AE, DC, MC, V. Open: lunch and dinner daily.*

From Peter Rabbit to preservation

You can thank the creator of Peter Rabbit for some of the beautiful landscapes you see in the Lake District today. Beatrix Potter treasured the beautiful scenery and invested the earnings from her best-selling children's books in buying parcels of land and ensuring its preservation when she bequeathed it to the National Trust.

Exploring around Lake Windermere

You probably won't want to spend too much time in the town of Windermere itself. The lake and surrounding countryside are what make this part of England so special.

Beatrix Potter Gallery

Hawkshead

Beatrix Potter's skills as an illustrator of her own children's stories are amply displayed in this National Trust collection of her original drawings and watercolors. You also find an exhibition about Potter's life. The gallery is in what was the office of Potter's husband, a local attorney. After visiting the gallery, spend a little time wandering around Hawkshead, one of the region's prettiest villages. If you're a Potter fan, allow at least 45 minutes; add another 30 minutes if you want to wander around Hawkshead.

The poet William Wordsworth was a student at **Hawkshead Grammar School,** founded in 1585 (no phone). It's open Easter through October Monday through Saturday 10 a.m. to 1 p.m. and 2 to 5 p.m.; admission is £2 ($3.20) for adults, 50p (80¢) for children.

Main Street, Hawkshead. ☎ ***015394/36355.*** *Admission: £3 ($4.80) adult, £1.50 ($2.40) children 5–15, £7.50 ($12) family (2 adults, 2 children). Open: Mar 24–Oct Sun–Thurs 10:30 a.m.–4:30 p.m.*

Hill Top

Near Sawrey

Beatrix Potter wrote and illustrated many of her famous children's tales in this 17th-century stone cottage. She was born in London but spent summer holidays in the Lake District with her family. The international success of *The Tale of Peter Rabbit* allowed her to buy this small, pretty house and move permanently to the Lakeland village of Near Sawrey. Potter deeded her house to the National Trust before she died in 1943, and the interior remains as she left it, complete with her furniture, bone china, and garden. Because the house is so small, only a certain number of visitors are allowed in at any one time. Hill Top uses a timed-entry admission policy, which may keep you waiting in the summer. After you go inside, allow about 15 minutes to visit the house. You can get a pub lunch at the **Tower Bank Arms** (☎ **015394/36336**) in front of the house.

Windermere Lake Cruises (☎ **015395/31188**) runs a convenient boat and bus shuttle from Bowness's Pier 3 that connects at Hawkshead with a minibus to Hill Top. Round-trip fares are £6 ($10) for adults and £3.50 ($6) for children 5 to 15. Between April and October, you can also take Bus No. 505 or 506 from the train station in Windermere to Hill Top.

Near Sawrey, Ambleside (west side of Lake Windermere, 2 miles south of Hawkshead). ☎ ***015394/36269.*** *Admission: £4.50 ($7) adults, £1 ($1.60) children 5–15, £10 ($16) families (2 adults, 2 children). Open: April–Oct Sat–Wed 10:30 a.m.–4:30 p.m.*

The Lake District Visitor Centre

Brockhole

Housed in a lakeside mansion with terraced gardens, this visitor center presents an extensive overview of the national park and its special features. It offers all sorts of activities: An adventure playground is available for kids; visitors can enjoy interactive exhibits and daily guided walks, too. The gardens and grounds, with views down to Lake Windermere and beyond, are home to a wide variety of unusual shrubs and plants. **The Cafe,** which specializes in traditional Cumbrian recipes, serves meals daily from noon to 2 p.m. From the visitor center's jetty, you can hop on one of Windermere Lake Cruises' circular cruises (see "Touring by boat or foot," earlier in this chapter). From April to October, a boat from Bowness can take you to the Lake District Visitor Centre.

Brockhole, Windermere (between Windermere and Ambleside on A591). ☎ ***015394/46601.*** *Internet:* `www.lake-district.gov.uk`. *Admission: free. Parking: £4 ($6) per car. Open: building Mar 23–Oct daily 10 a.m.–5 p.m.; grounds daily year-round.*

Windermere Steamboat Centre

Windermere

A unique collection of boats used on Lake Windermere during the last 150 years is on display in this small lakeside museum. The oldest boat is a steam launch from 1850. You also find exhibits on the history of boating and racing on the lake. You can see the boats and displays in under 30 minutes. The center offers a fun, 50-minute cruise around Belle Isle (an island in Lake Windermere) in an Edwardian steam launch; call ahead to reserve a seat. The cost for the cruise is £5 ($8) for adults and £2.50 ($4) for children 5 to 15.

Rayrigg Road, Windermere. ☎ ***015394/45565.*** *Admission: £3.50 ($6) adult, £2 ($3.20) child 5–15, £8.50 ($14) family (2 adults, 3 children). Open: daily mid-March–Oct 10 a.m.–5 p.m.*

The World of Beatrix Potter
Bowness-on-Windermere

If you grew up on Beatrix Potter stories and think that her illustrations are cute, then you'll enjoy this miniature theme park — having a child along helps, too. The attraction is a series of small, skillfully recreated tableaux related to those famous Potter characters, Peter Rabbit and Jemima Puddleduck. You can have tea in the Tailor of Gloucester (another Potter story) tearoom, and of course you can shop for Potter-inspired merchandise. You can see everything in under an hour.

The Old Laundry, Bowness-on-Windermere. ☎ ***015394/88444.*** *Admission: £3.75 ($6) adults, £2.50 ($4) children. Open: daily year-round 10 a.m.–4:30 p.m. (summer until 5:30 p.m.)*

Grasmere: Wordsworth Territory

Grasmere Village draws fans of William Wordsworth in the way that Near Sawrey draws Beatrix Potterholics. High fells surround this lovely Lakeland village with the River Rothay running through it. The village is 8 miles north of Windermere on its own jewel of a lake, Lake Grasmere. Wordsworth called the area "the loveliest spot that man hath ever found." By bus, the trip from Windermere to Grasmere Village takes less than 30 minutes. You can also take the ferry to Ambleside, at the north end of Lake Windermere (the stop is called Waterside), and continue by bus. Keep in mind that this is an extremely popular tourist route, and summer traffic includes tour buses. Grasmere Village is about a quarter-mile from Dove Cottage and Lake Grasmere.

Rydal, the village where Wordsworth lived out his final years in relative affluence as England's Poet Laureate, is about midway between Ambleside and Grasmere.

Finding information

The Lake District National Park Authority's **Waterhead Information Centre** (**☎ 015394/32729**), next to the ferry landing at Waterhead, has books and maps and can advise you on good walks in the area. The center is open daily from April through September 9:30 a.m. to 5:30 p.m. **Grasmere Information Centre** (**☎ 015394/35245**), across from the parish church and behind the Grasmere Garden Centre, is another good resource for local information. Both have a bureaux de change.

Touring on foot

Several pleasant short walks begin in Grasmere. Check with the Grasmere Information Centre (see the preceding section) for maps and suggestions. More experienced hikers may want to tackle the

3½-mile round-trip trail to the rocky summit of Helm Crag; the walk takes about two hours. You can also walk east on Easedale Road to the nearby peaks known as "The Lion and the Lamb" and "The Lady at the Organ."

Staying in and around Grasmere

Grasmere is a small village with a good selection of accommodations. My recommended choices follow.

Harwood Hotel

$ Grasmere

Located right in the center of Grasmere, this small hotel built of traditional Lakeland stone dates to the 1850s and was operated as a temperance guest house. The house is now a comfortable B&B with eight nicely decorated rooms, two of them with four-poster beds. Four of the rooms have en-suite bathrooms, and the others have private bathrooms outside the room. A nice coffee lounge and Newby's Bakery & Deli, which serves local specialties (and can pack you a picnic lunch), are part of the hotel.

Red Lion Square, Grasmere, Ambleside, Cumbria LA22 9SP. ☎ ***015394/35248.*** *Fax: 015394/35545. Internet:* `www.harwoodhotel.co.uk`. ***Rack rates: £39–£59 ($62–$94) double. Rates include English breakfast. AE, MC, V.***

How Foot Lodge

$ Grasmere

This 1843 Victorian villa, now a B&B, is practically on the doorstep of Dove Cottage and Lake Grasmere, and it's only a five-minute walk to town. The lodge has six large guest rooms, all with private bathrooms. One room is a suite with its own sunroom — great if you're traveling with children. On chilly mornings, you find a log fire burning in the lounge.

Town End, Grasmere, Cumbria LA22 9SQ. ☎ ***015394/35366.*** *Fax: 015394/35268. Internet:* `www.howfoot.co.uk`. ***Rack rates: £52–£56 ($83–$90) double. Rates include English breakfast. MC, V.***

White Moss House

$$–$$$ Rydal Water

This Lakeland villa built in 1730 overlooking Rydal Water and the surrounding fells was the home of William Wordsworth and his family. The villa is now a small, sumptuous country-house hotel with just seven guest rooms and a separate cottage suite on the hillside. All the rooms are individually decorated in a traditional country-house style. The room rate includes a memorable five-course dinner prepared by Peter Dixon, a Master Chef of Great Britain. His Modern English cooking makes use of local free-range and organic products; the restaurant has an exemplary wine cellar.

*Rydal Water (off A591, 1½ miles south of Grasmere), Grasmere, Cumbria LA22 9SE. ☎ **015394/35295.** Internet: `www.whitemoss.com`. Rack rates: £156–£184 ($250–$294) double. Rates include five-course dinner and English breakfast. AE, MC, V.*

Wordsworth Hotel

$$$$ Grasmere

This hotel in the heart of the village is the poshest place in town. Set on two acres of landscaped grounds, with a heated indoor pool and sauna and an upscale country ambience throughout, the Wordsworth Hotel features 35 individually decorated rooms that have large, modern bathrooms (with tubs and showers) and luxury-hotel amenities, such as room service and nightly shoeshines. The room rate includes a multicourse dinner served in The Prelude restaurant.

*Grasmere, Ambleside, Cumbria LA22 9SW. ☎ **015394/355-592.** Fax: 015394/35765. Rack rates: £210–£250 ($336–$400) double. Rates include dinner and English breakfast. AE, DC, MC, V.*

Dining in Grasmere

Here are my restaurant choices for Grasmere.

Dove Cottage Tea Rooms and Restaurant

$ MODERN BRITISH/CONTINENTAL

This roadside restaurant is close to Dove Cottage, the main tourist attraction in Grasmere. It's not the most atmospheric spot, but it serves good home-cooked food and afternoon teas. You can get a lunch special of soup, a main course, and dessert, or sandwiches and pastas. Dinner choices are a la carte and may include roasted salmon, lamb, duck, or sirloin steak. Kids enjoy the casual atmosphere and simple foods.

*Town End, Grasmere. ☎ **015394/35268.** Main courses: £4.50–£6.50 ($7–$10), lunch specials £7.50–£8.50 ($12–$14). MC, V. Open: Mon–Sat 10 a.m.–4:30 p.m., Wed–Sat 6:45–9 p.m.*

Lamb Inn

$ TRADITIONAL ENGLISH/PUB

If you want a good pub meal in nice, nonfancy surroundings, this is a good choice. You can get a bowl of homemade soup, sandwiches, roast lamb, or spicy Cumberland sausages. Other offerings include fish and chips, Yorkshire puddings, and vegetarian dishes. Kids enjoy the casual atmosphere and can usually find something on the menu they like.

*In the Red Lion Hotel, Red Lion Square, Grasmere. ☎ **015394/35456.** Main courses: £5.50–£10.50 ($9–$17). AE, MC, V. Open: pub Mon–Sat 11 a.m.–11 p.m., Sun noon to 10:30 p.m.; food served daily noon to 2:30 p.m. and 5:30–9 p.m.*

Wordsworth: The silent nightingale

William Wordsworth is considered one of England's great poets. The sights and scenes of the Lake Country, where he was born, spent most of his mature years, and died, influenced much of his poetry. Traveling in France after his graduation from Cambridge, Wordsworth fell in love with Annette Vallon, who gave birth to his daughter Caroline. He never married Annette, apparently because the French Revolution prevented his return to France.

In 1798, Wordsworth co-authored *Lyrical Ballads,* a volume that included "Tintern Abbey," the work that introduced Romanticism, with its love of nature, to England. In this poem, Wordsworth extolled not the great but the ordinary man: "That best portion of a good man's life, / His little, nameless, unremembered acts / Of kindness and of love."

In 1802, the poet married Mary Hutchinson, an old school friend. With Mary, he had five children. *The Prelude,* completed in 1805, is a long autobiographical poem. Some of his other famous poems include "Daffodils" and "Intimations of Immortality" ("Though nothing can buy back the hour / Of splendour in the grass, of glory in the flower"). From 1847 until his death in 1850, Wordsworth was England's Poet Laureate, appointed by Queen Victoria. He was called "the silent nightingale" because during those years he never composed a poem.

The Prelude

$$$ **MODERN BRITISH**

The restaurant in the posh Wordsworth Hotel is a dress-up kind of place with fine food and attentive service. You choose from a fixed-price menu that changes daily. Starters may include a salad of sweet-and-sour seared rabbit or potato pancakes stacked with locally smoked trout. The Prelude also offers a fresh fish dish of the day. Main courses may include Scotch beef with poached pear, grilled calves' liver, breast of duck, or vegetarian couscous and Indian special vegetable pie.

Wordsworth Hotel. ☎ ***015394/355-592.*** *Reservations required. Fixed-price dinner £30 ($48) for 3 courses, £32.50 ($52) 4 courses. AE, DC, MC, V. Open: daily for lunch and dinner.*

Exploring in and around Grasmere

William Wordsworth made the small village of Grasmere famous, and his two homes draw the lion's share of tourists. The village itself is so small that you can see everything in it in less than an hour.

Dove Cottage and The Wordsworth Museum

South of Grasmere

Picturesque 400-year-old Dove Cottage was the home of William Wordsworth (1770–1850), one of England's most famous Romantic poets and the one most identified with the Lake District. Wordsworth composed most of his greatest poems in Dove Cottage, where he lived between 1799 and 1808 with his wife, children, and his sister Dorothy, whose journals chronicle their daily lives. A guide takes you through the entire house, which has been altered little over the years. You can view some of the family's personal possessions. Tours are limited to about 20 people at a time, so you may have to wait. A few steps away is the Wordsworth Museum, which documents the poet's life and works with manuscripts, books, and paintings. You need about 20 minutes for the tour and another 30 minutes for the museum — twice that if you're a Wordsworth fan.

On A591 (¼ mile south of Grasmere Village). ☎ ***015394/35544.*** *Admission: £5.50 ($9) adults, £4.90 ($8) seniors, £2.50 ($4) children 5–15, £13 ($21) families (2 adults, 2 children). Open: daily 9:30 a.m.–5:30 p.m.; closed last three weeks in Jan, Dec 24–26.*

The Grasmere Gingerbread Shop

Grasmere

You smell this place before you see it, and I recommend that you stop in. This famous shop, in a tiny cottage next to the parish church, sells a marvelous gingerbread made from a 150-year-old secret recipe developed by Sarah Nelson and kept in a local bank vault. You can buy the gingerbread fresh or in sealed packs (a great gift idea). The shop also sells Kendal Mint Cakes, a super-sweet mint bar that Sir Edmund Hilary used to raise his blood sugar while climbing Mt. Everest.

Church Cottage, Grasmere, next to the parish church. ☎ ***015394/35428.*** *Internet:* `www.gingerbread.co.uk`. *Open: Apr–Oct Mon–Sat 9:15 a.m.–5:30 p.m., Sun 12:30–5:30 p.m.; Nov–Mar Mon–Sat 9:30 a.m.–4:30 p.m., Sun 12:30–5:30 p.m.*

Grasmere Parish Church

Grasmere

Grasmere's parish church is dedicated to St. Oswald, the seventh-century King of Northumbria. The oldest part of the gray stone church dates from the 13th century. The building has an attractive interior, much altered in later centuries. The Wordsworths worshipped here and are buried in the churchyard beside the river, close to eight yew trees planted by the poet. You can visit the church and churchyard in 15 minutes.

Grasmere. ☎ ***015394/35428.*** *Open: daily 9 a.m.–5 p.m.*

Rydal Mount

South of Grasmere

In 1813, Wordsworth moved his family to Rydal Mount, a much grander house between Ambleside and Grasmere. From here, the man who immortalized the Lake District countryside had commanding views of Lake Windermere, Rydal Water, and the surrounding fells. The house still belongs to the poet's descendants, but much of it is open, and you can wander through the dining room, drawing room, family bedrooms, and study. Take time to stroll through the gardens he designed; Dora's Garden, ablaze with daffodils in the spring, was planted in memory of his daughter Dora. You can easily spend 30 minutes here, longer if you wander in the garden.

On A591 (2½ miles south of Grasmere and 1½ miles north of Ambleside). ☎ ***015394/33002.*** *Admission: £4 ($6) adults, £1.25 ($2) children. Open: March–Oct daily 9:30 a.m.–5 p.m.; Nov–Feb Wed–Mon 10 a.m.–4p.m.; closed Jan 10–31.*

Keswick: Lakeland Central

Compared to tiny Grasmere, Keswick (pronounced *Kes*-ick) is a large, bustling market town. Situated on a lovely lake (Derwentwater), Keswick is a lively regional hub that turns into a busy resort on weekends and during the summer (see the "Keswick" map in this chapter). The town, with its narrow streets and sturdy gray stone buildings, stands on the banks of the River Greta beneath the slopes of the Skiddaw Range. Some of the most beautiful walking country in England lies around Keswick.

Getting to Keswick

Keswick is located about 20 miles north of Lake Windermere and 11 miles north of Grasmere. Cumbria Stagecoach Bus No. 555 departs from Grasmere several times a day; the trip takes about 30 minutes. The bus drops you off just a couple of blocks from Main Street, and you can walk everywhere from there. Taxis wait right at the bus stop, or you can call **Davies Taxis** at ☎ **017687/72676.**

Finding information and exchanging money

The **National Park Information Centre,** Moot Hall, Market Square (☎ **017687/72645**), is open daily from 9:30 a.m. to 5:30 p.m. (until 4:30 p.m. in winter). The center has maps, guidebooks, local information, and a bureaux de change. The staff sells detailed leaflets on the best local walks. You can also find visitor information on the Web at `www.keswick.org`.

Keswick

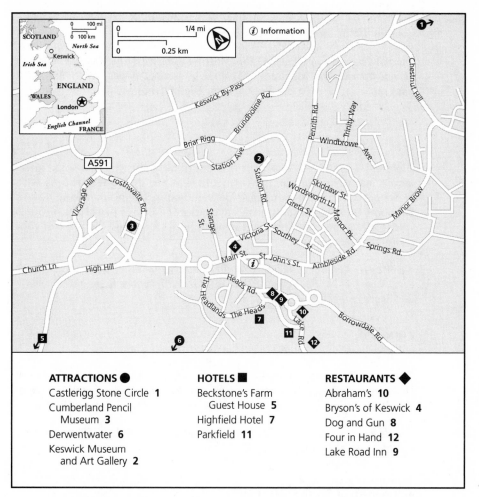

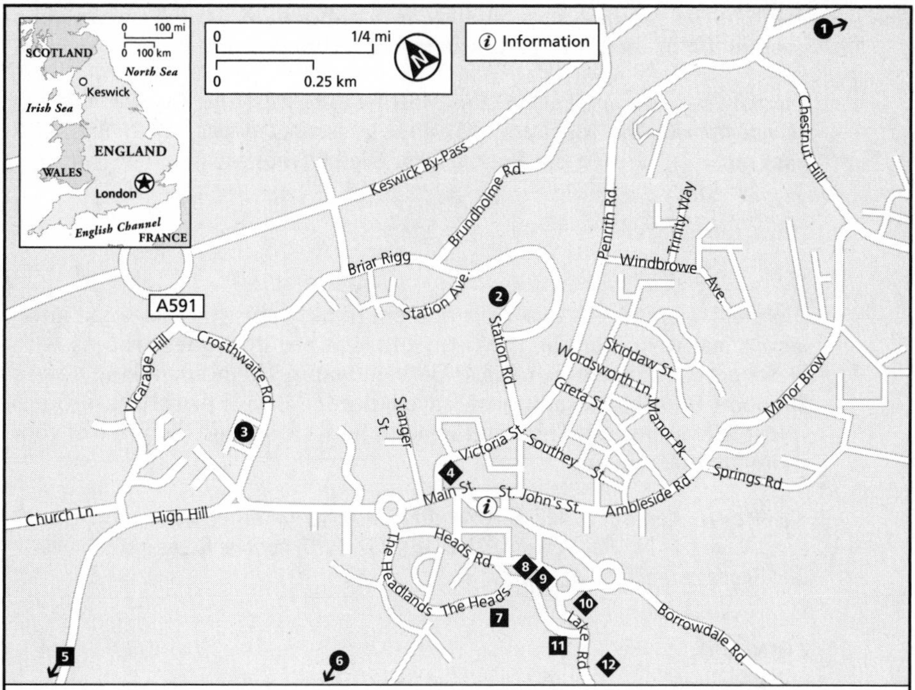

ATTRACTIONS ●

- Castlerigg Stone Circle **1**
- Cumberland Pencil Museum **3**
- Derwentwater **6**
- Keswick Museum and Art Gallery **2**

HOTELS ■

- Beckstone's Farm Guest House **5**
- Highfield Hotel **7**
- Parkfield **11**

RESTAURANTS ◆

- Abraham's **10**
- Bryson's of Keswick **4**
- Dog and Gun **8**
- Four in Hand **12**
- Lake Road Inn **9**

National Westminster Bank, 28 Main St. (☎ **01768/72091**), is open weekdays from 9 a.m. to 5 p.m. and has a bureaux de change and an ATM.

Staying in or near Keswick

Here are my recommended choices for staying in or near Keswick.

Beckstone's Farm Guest House

$ West of Keswick

Nature lovers revel in the scenery that surrounds this Georgian farmhouse in the Derwent Valley 7 miles from Keswick. Kids find plenty to explore right outside the inn's door. Most of the rooms have panoramic views toward the Skiddaw range of mountains. The inn has five comfy bedrooms with private bathrooms (three with tubs, two with showers). Some of the rooms are in an attached, remodeled barn. You can get a good lunch or dinner at the Swan Hotel, right across the road.

Thornthwaite, Keswick, Cumbria CA12 5SQ (take A66 west from Keswick; local bus service from Keswick stops at The Swan Hotel across the road). ☎ ***017687/78510.*** *Rack rates: £48 ($77) double. Rate includes English breakfast. No credit cards.*

Highfield Hotel

$–$$ Keswick

Highfield was built as two Victorian-era houses and still has some interesting features, including two turrets that are now guest rooms with views across Hope Park toward Derwentwater. The nonsmoking hotel's 20 roomy units have traditional English decor. All have private bathrooms (most with showers). The hotel is noted for its food, and the price of your room includes dinner.

The Heads, Keswick CA12 5ER. ☎ ***017687/72508.*** *Internet:* `www.highfieldkeswick.co.uk`. *Rack rates: £98–£116 ($157–$187) double. Rates include dinner and English breakfast. AE, MC, V.*

Parkfield

$ Keswick

This friendly, nonsmoking B&B has a great location right at the head of Derwentwater, steps away from Keswick's theater and shopping street. Here you find eight nicely furnished rooms, all with shower and toilet.

The Heads, Keswick CA12 5ES. ☎ ***017687/72328.*** *Rack rates: £54 ($86) double. Rate includes English breakfast. AE, MC, V.*

Dining in Keswick

Simple, hearty meals are the order of the day in Keswick. You can get a good meal at the following places.

Abraham's

$ VEGETARIAN/TRADITIONAL ENGLISH

This nonsmoking tearoom is a great place for a filling breakfast, a light, healthy lunch, or a rich dessert. The informal atmosphere makes it a popular spot for families. The salad menu usually includes dishes such as vegetarian flan; chicken, ham and chestnut pie; or prawns. The homemade soup is always vegetarian. The blackboard lists daily specials.

Third floor of George Fisher Ltd. Outdoor Equipment Store, 2 Borrowdale Road. ☎ ***017687/71333.*** *Main courses: £5–£7 ($8–$11). No credit cards. Open: daily 10:30 a.m.–5:30 p.m. (5 p.m. in winter).*

Bryson's of Keswick

$ TRADITIONAL ENGLISH/TEAS

The first floor is a wonderful bakery where you can buy apple and black-currant pies, tarts, cakes, muffins, and breads — great treats for kids of all ages. The second floor serves meals, concentrating on local specialties, such as spicy Cumberland sausage, Cumbrian ham, and locally caught trout. You can get an excellent cream tea here, too.

42 Main St. ☎ ***017687/72257.*** *Main courses: £6–£7 ($10–$11). No credit cards. Open: Mon–Sat 9 a.m.–5:30 p.m., Sun 9 a.m.–5 p.m.*

Dog and Gun

$ TRADITIONAL ENGLISH/PUB

This pub serves some good traditional dishes. You may want to try home-made lamb curry, roast beef and Yorkshire pudding, goulash, or steak and kidney pie.

Lake Road (just off the market square). ☎ ***017687/73463.*** *Main courses: £5–£6 ($8–$10). MC, V. Open: pub Mon–Sat 11 a.m.–11 p.m., Sun noon to 10:30 p.m.; food served daily noon to 2:30 p.m. and 5:30–9 p.m.*

Four in Hand

$–$$ MODERN BRITISH

This old coaching inn has an attractive dining room (with fireplace) that serves top-end bar food. A house specialty is lamb steak cooked in rich red-wine and onion sauce. Fish dishes typically include poached salmon with cream and dill sauce. Also available are hearty local favorites, such as Cumberland sausage and vegetarian offerings, such as mushroom stroganoff.

Lake Road. ☎ ***017687/72665.*** *Main courses: £7.50–£13 ($12–$21). MC, V. Open: winter Mon–Sat noon to 3 p.m. and 5–11 p.m. (Sun until 10:30 p.m.); summer Mon–Sat 11 a.m.–11 p.m., Sun noon to 10:30 p.m.*

Lake Road Inn

$ TRADITIONAL ENGLISH/PUB

This cozy, old-fashioned pub, near the Dog and Gun, serves such staples as homemade soup, roast chicken, lasagna, braised shoulder of lamb, and locally caught trout with white-wine-and-parsley sauce. You may want to stop in to sample a Cumbrian ale.

Lake Road (head south from the tourist office on Borrowdale Road and turn right on Lake Road, about a 2-minute walk). ☎ ***017687/72404.*** *Main courses: £4.75–£8.25 ($8–$13). MC, V. Open: Easter–Oct pub Mon–Sat 11 a.m.–11 p.m., Sun noon to 10:30 p.m.; food served daily noon to 2:30 p.m. and 5:30–9 p.m. Closed Nov–Easter.*

Exploring in and around Keswick

The indoor tourist attractions in and around Keswick are interesting but not all that important. The landscape itself makes the place so special and invites walks and boat rides.

Castlerigg Stone Circle

Near Keswick

If you have time for only one walk in the Lake District, make it this one, which appeals to older kids as much as to adults. The walk leads to the best preserved of the 40 or so prehistoric stone circles found throughout Cumbria. The circle's unrivaled setting, on the flat top of a low hill above Keswick, surrounded by high fells, adds greatly to its appeal. Castlerigg consists of 33 standing stones forming a circle, with another 10 stones arranged as a rectangular enclosure. The circle was probably constructed about 3000 B.C. No one can say definitively what its purpose was, but it may have served as the focal point for a scattered tribe of Neolithic people involved in making stone axes. Although much smaller than Stonehenge (and lacking the lintels that cap the stones there), Castlerigg conveys the same sense of timeless mystery.

From the National Park Information Centre in Keswick, follow the signposted trail that leads 1½ miles east along A591 to Castlerigg Stone Circle; walking to the circle and back takes about 2½ hours. You can drive here following A591; a parking lot is across from the stones.

Cumberland Pencil Museum

Keswick

This museum devoted to the humble pencil is worth 30 minutes of your time. The exhibits inevitably pique the interest of children and their parents. Discovered near Keswick in the early 1500s, the Elizabethans used pure graphite to make cannonball molds, and local farmers used it to mark their sheep. In 1832, the precious carbon became the source of lead for a thriving local pencil industry. After watching an introductory video, you wander past the displays (oldest pencils in the world and so on) and discover the answer to that burning question: How do they get the lead into the pencil? If you're looking for high-quality colored pencils, the shop is an excellent source.

Southey Lane (take Main Street north to Southey Lane). ☎ ***017687/73626.*** *Admission: £2.50 ($4) adults, £1.25 ($2) seniors and children 5–15, £6.25 ($10) families (2 adults, 2 children). Open: daily 9:30 a.m.–4 p.m.*

Derwentwater

Southwest of Keswick

Many folks consider Derwentwater, studded with islands and enfolded in a landscape of low, bare hills with craggy peaks, the prettiest of all the lakes. The lake is about 3 miles long, 72 feet deep. At its northern end, closest to Keswick, is a popular park. **Keswick Launch (☎ 017687/72263;** `www.keswick-launch.co.uk`), located at the lake's north end, operates daily 50-minute cruises starting at 10 a.m. from Easter through November (Saturday and Sunday only from December to mid-March). The small launches make a circuit of the lake and stop at several docks where you can get out and walk. The cost is £5.40 ($9) for adults, £2 ($3.20) for children 5 to 15, and £10.90 ($18) for a family (2 adults, 3 children). During the summer, an evening wine cruise is available.

Keswick Museum and Art Gallery

Keswick

This small Victorian museum has nothing of major importance, but a look at the paintings, manuscripts, crystals, and bric-a-brac collected over the years is fun. The most famous exhibit is a 500-year-old mummified cat found in the roof of Clifton Church, Penrith, in 1842; this desiccated feline is absolutely fascinating to kids.

Fitz Park, Station Road. ***☎ 017687/73263.*** *Admission: £1 ($1.60) adults, 50p (80¢) children 5–15. Open: Easter–Oct Tues–Wed 10 a.m.–4 p.m., Thurs 10 a.m.–7 p.m.*

Shopping in Keswick

My favorite shop in Keswick is **Ye Olde Friars,** 6–8 Market Square (**☎ 017687/72234**), an old-fashioned candy store that sells black treacle and butter toffee and other locally made sweets. **George Fisher Ltd.,** 2 Borrowdale Rd. (**☎ 017687/72178**), is one of the largest specialist outdoor clothing and equipment stores in the country. **The Tea Pottery,** Central Car Park (**☎ 017687/73983**), sells goofy and expensive handmade teapots.

Discovering Keswick's performing arts

Theatre by the Lake, Lakeside (**☎ 017687/74411;** `www.theatrebythelake.com`), is a new 400-seat theater with a year-round repertory of plays, films, dance, concerts, and theatrical events.

Part VIII

The Part of Tens

"Douglas, I'd like to talk to you about the souvenirs you brought back from our trip to England."

In this part . . .

Everything in this part is extra. You can have a great time in England without reading a word of it. But if you do read this part, I'll turn you on to some extra-special places that you may otherwise miss. I also describe everything in this part elsewhere in the guide. These top ten lists are just a way to give added focus to some special-interest areas that you may want to explore further.

Literature is one of the great links between England and other parts of the world. So, in Chapter 23, I give you the lowdown on ten famous English writers, from William Shakespeare to Beatrix Potter, and tell you how you can visit places where they lived and worked. Then, because more and more people are interested in gardens and gardening, in Chapter 24, I introduce you to ten great English gardens that you can visit. Finally, in Chapter 25, I point out some magnificent English cathedrals and churches that you may want to include on your itinerary.

Chapter 23

Ten Writers and the Places They Lived

In This Chapter

- Seeing the England of Austen, the Brontës, and Henry James
- Visiting the London museum of Dickens
- Discovering the Lake District of Wordsworth and Beatrix Potter
- Venturing into the gardens of Vita Sackville-West
- Making a literary pilgrimage to Shakespeare's Stratford-upon-Avon

I don't know about you, but some of my earliest memories of England came from literature. Long before I ever visited the Lake District, I had seen the distinctive landscape in Beatrix Potter's illustrated children's tales. Peter Pan, who lived in Kensington Gardens, made me curious about London. As I grew older, I read English novels and went to plays written by Shakespeare. If you're literary minded, you can track down several places in England associated with your favorite authors. Even if you stay in London for your entire trip, you can do some literary sleuthing. Blue plaques on London buildings identify the abodes of famous writers and artists. Some of England's most famous poets, novelists, and playwrights are buried or commemorated in Poets' Corner, Westminster Abbey (see Chapter 12).

Jane Austen

One of England's most enduringly popular writers is Jane Austen (1775–1817). Her highly polished novels are depictions of social and domestic life in Regency England — that is, the period just before Dickens and the Victorians. Austen's fictional world is full of wit and romance. She never married. When she was 21, her father, a minister, retired and moved his family to **Bath,** where you can see the house she lived in and visit the **Jane Austen Centre,** a museum dedicated to her life and times.

After her father's death, Austen lived in the quiet village of **Chawton** with her mother and sister Cassandra. The **Jane Austen House,** which you can visit, is a small red-brick dwelling that her wealthy brother Edward gave her. In this house, she began revising her earlier drafts of *Sense and Sensibility* (published in 1811) and *Pride and Prejudice* (published in 1813). Austen continued writing and publishing novels until 1817, when illness forced her to move to **Winchester** for medical help. You can pay your respects at Austen's grave in **Winchester Cathedral.** Information on all the Jane Austen sites is in Chapter 16.

Charlotte, Emily, and Anne Brontë

A trip to **Haworth** in Yorkshire (Chapter 21) brings you to the **Brontë Parsonage Museum,** home of that trio of sibling scribes, Charlotte (1816–1855), Emily (1818–1848), and Anne (1820–1849) Brontë. The windswept moors that figure so prominently in Emily's *Wuthering Heights* and Charlotte's *Jane Eyre* surround the town, which markets the Brontë name in every conceivable way. Like Jane Austen, the Brontës were the children of a minister. They were educated (in grim schools, like the one called Lowood in *Jane Eyre*) but had no independent means of support, so all three had to work as governesses. (Anne's *The Tenant of Wildfell Hall* and Charlotte's *Jane Eyre* both have governess heroines.)

Charlotte and Emily spent a brief time at a school in Brussels (where Charlotte fell in love with her married teacher), but otherwise the Brontës stayed close to the parsonage, writing the novels that would make them famous. Tragedy struck when Anne, 29, and Emily, 30, died in quick succession of tuberculosis. Charlotte eventually married one of her father's curates but died at age 39.

Charles Dickens

Charles Dickens (1812–1870) was one of the most prolific and best-loved novelists of the Victorian era. When Dickens was a boy, his father was thrown into debtor's prison, and young Charles was forced to work in a factory. His subsequent rise to fame as a reporter, editor, and novelist is as remarkable as anything in his fiction. *David Copperfield* is Dickens's most autobiographical novel.

Dickens was a writer who didn't flinch at exposing the horrors of the day and tackling social issues, such as child labor and London's teeming slums. Some of his characters (Ebenezer Scrooge in *A Christmas Carol,* to cite just one example) have become as famous as Shakespeare's. Dickens moved around constantly, but in London you can visit the **Dickens's House Museum,** where he penned *Oliver Twist, The Pickwick Papers,* and *Nicholas Nickleby.* The museum contains the world's most comprehensive Dickens library, plus portraits, illustrations, and rooms furnished as they were in his lifetime. See Chapter 12 for more details on the museum.

Henry James (and E. F. Benson)

Novelist Henry James (1843–1916) was an American, but he loved England so much that he became a British citizen. In his long career, James wrote 20 novels, 112 stories, 12 plays, and literary criticism. The son of one of the best-known intellectuals in mid-19th-century America, he grew up in Manhattan. (William James, his brother, was one of the earliest psychologists.)

An Irish grandfather provided the wealth that endowed the family with the privileges of culture, travel, education, and social affluence — attributes found in Henry James's fictional characters, many of whom are Americans living in England or Italy. After living in Paris, James moved to England, living first in London and then in Sussex. **Lamb House,** his last home, is just one of many reasons to visit the beautiful Sussex town of **Rye.** (E. F. Benson, who wrote the *Mapp and Lucia* novels, later owned Lamb House.) For more on Rye, see Chapter 14.

Beatrix Potter

The life of famed children's book writer and illustrator Beatrix Potter (1866–1943) is singularly lacking in drama and tragedy. Born in South Kensington, London, she was an only and lonely child, but had many pets that she carefully observed and sketched. When Beatrix was 16, her parents rented a summer house in the Lake District. They returned every year afterward, and Beatrix fell in love with the beautiful countryside.

Many years later, when *The Tale of Peter Rabbit,* her first published book, sold 50,000 copies, she bought **Hill Top,** her house in **Near Sawrey,** close to Lake Windermere. The house is now open to the public. Potter's illustrations and watercolors are on display at the **Beatrix Potter Gallery** in nearby **Hawkshead.** The gallery is in a building that held the law offices of William Heelis, whom she married when she was 47. Over the years, Beatrix Potter used her earnings to buy thousands of acres in the Lake District (and became a prize-winning sheep farmer). She wanted the countryside that had so inspired her to be preserved for future generations, and she left it all to the National Trust. You can read more about the Lake District and these Potter sites in Chapter 22.

Vita Sackville-West

Not many people read the novels and poems of Vita Sackville-West (1892–1962) anymore, but many people know about her life. She was born at **Knole,** an enormous house in Kent, and she later wrote an entertaining book called *Knole and the Sackvilles*. Virginia Woolf (1882–1941) used Vita as the inspiration for the gender-bending hero/heroine in her brilliant novel *Orlando,* which also has Knole as a setting. Vita, famous for her lesbian affairs, married the diplomat Harold Nicholson and had two children. Nigel Nicholson, one of their sons, wrote about his parents in *Portrait of a Marriage,* later filmed for television. Vita and Harold worked together to create the magnificent gardens at **Sissinghurst Castle,** now one of the world's most famous gardens. Check out Chapter 15 for more on Knole and Sissinghurst. Vita's garden books still sell; her best novel is *The Edwardians.*

William Shakespeare

England's most famous literary pilgrimage site is **Stratford-upon-Avon,** where you can visit the homes occupied by William Shakespeare (1564–1616) and his family. Before visiting **Shakespeare's Birthplace,** on Henley Street, spend a few minutes in the adjacent **Shakespeare Centre,** where exhibits illustrate the life and times of this Elizabethan genius. **Anne Hathaway's Cottage,** about a mile south of Stratford, was the home of the woman Shakespeare married when he was 18 and she was 25.

A relatively prosperous Shakespeare retired to **New Place** on Chapel Street; all that remains of it is the garden. **Nash's House,** next door, belonged to Thomas Nash, husband of Shakespeare's granddaughter. Nearby **Hall's Croft** is a magnificent Tudor house where Shakespeare's daughter Susanna probably lived with her husband, Dr. John Hall. Shakespeare and his family are buried in **Holy Trinity Church.** About 3½ miles north of Stratford is **Mary Arden's House.** For decades, this Tudor farmstead was assumed to be the girlhood home of Shakespeare's mother, but scholars have recently suggested that Shakespeare's mum probably lived in the house next door. I cover Stratford-upon-Avon in Chapter 19.

William Wordsworth

When William Wordsworth died in 1850 at the age of 80, he was Poet Laureate of England and perhaps the world's most famous poet. His fame rests on the poems in *Lyrical Ballads* and *The Prelude*. A champion of the Romantic Movement, which emphasized imagination and emotion and extolled nature, Wordsworth is closely associated with the **Lake District,** where he lived most of his life.

Born in Cumberland (today's Cumbria) in 1770, Wordsworth was the son of a lawyer. He attended **Hawkshead Grammar School** in the village of **Hawkshead** (also the location of the Beatrix Potter Gallery), and studied at Cambridge. Most of Wordsworth's greatest poems were composed in **Dove Cottage,** Grasmere, where he lived between 1799 and 1808 with his wife, children, and his sister Dorothy, whose journals chronicle their daily lives. In 1813, Wordsworth moved his family to **Rydal Mount,** a much grander house between Ambleside and Grasmere. He and other family members are buried in the churchyard of **Grasmere Parish Church.** For more details on all these sites, see Chapter 22.

Chapter 24

Ten Great English Gardens

In This Chapter

- Visiting ten glorious English gardens
- Discovering what makes each garden unique

England is famous for its spectacular gardens. You don't need to be a specialized or even knowledgeable gardener to appreciate and enjoy these wonderful creations. Gardens are living art forms meant to beguile your senses and refresh your spirit. Most, but not all of the gardens I describe in this chapter are planted around grand stately homes and castles, which may be part of your visit. Four of the gardens are in or near London, and the rest are scattered throughout the country.

If you plan to visit gardens on your trip, May and June are probably the prime months, but the flowering season continues into September. "Britain's Gardens," a map with brief descriptions of 100 gardens in England, Scotland, Wales, and Ireland, is available free from VisitBritain. (See the Appendix for an address.)

Castle Howard

Gardens are never static. Plants grow and die, styles change, and new owners make their own marks on the landscape. The 1,000-acre park at Castle Howard in Yorkshire is an example of how a garden can change over time.

The castle is famous for its 18th-century landscape, dotted with ornamental temples and *follies* (ornamental buildings that serve as focal points in a landscape). John Vanbrugh's classically inspired Temple of the Four Winds and the circular mausoleum by Nicholas Hawksmoor are particularly notable. When the South Parterre was laid out between 1715 and 1725, the house's architectural drama was extended into the surrounding landscape with obelisks, urns, statues, and a 50-foot column.

Most of that visual drama was removed in the 1850s, when the Atlas Fountain and a *parterre* (an ornamental garden with paths between its beds) of boxwood, plants, and gravel were installed. In the late 19th century, grass and yew hedges replaced the parterre. The walled Rose

Garden and Ray Wood, full of rare rhododendrons and plants that survive in their own protected microclimate, were planted only in the last half-century. And the work goes on today, allowing visitors to stroll through fields and woodland, over bridges, and beside lakes. Castle Howard is an easy day trip from York; see Chapter 21 for more information.

Chelsea Physic Garden

This 3½-acre gem, hidden behind the high brick walls surrounding Chelsea Royal Hospital, is the second-oldest botanical garden in England. When the Worshipful Society of Apothecaries founded the garden in 1673, *physic* referred to medicine and medicinal agents. The goal of the apothecaries was to develop medicinal and commercial plant species. Seeds from this garden, for example, were used to start the cotton industry in the British colony of Georgia, first settled in 1733. Planted in the garden are some 7,000 exotic herbs, shrubs, trees, and flowers. This garden also boasts England's earliest rock garden. See Chapter 12 for more details.

Eden Project

Located on the south coast of Cornwall, the Eden Project is a garden of the 21st century. It's not an old-fashioned pleasure ground like the other gardens I mention in this chapter, but rather an intriguing educational showcase meant to stimulate an awareness of the Earth and humanity's dependence on plants and all living things. Already a major tourist attraction, the Eden Project consists of two giant geodesic conservatories sunk in deep craters. One dome covers the rainforest, and the other dome features the fruits and flowers of the Mediterranean, South Africa, and California. Outside, on the acres of landscaped grounds, plants from all sorts of terrains grow in specially created microhabitats. You find more information in Chapter 18.

Hever Castle

In the early 16th century, when Anne Boleyn was growing up at Hever Castle, the grounds looked nothing like they do today. The superb landscaping was created about a century ago, after the American millionaire William Astor bought Hever in 1903. Astor, who'd been American ambassador to Italy, created the castle's magnificent Italian Garden between 1904 and 1908. This garden combines the formal structure and design elements of Italian Renaissance gardens with English plantings. A remarkable collection of Roman to Renaissance statuary and sculpture collected in Italy fills Astor's creation.

In other parts of the grounds, you find a maze, a 35-acre lake, and the obligatory English rose garden. The Tudor herb garden, built close to the castle in 1994, gives you an idea of what gardens were like in Anne Boleyn's day. You can visit this garden as a day trip from London; see Chapter 15.

Hidcote Manor

When you see a garden such as Hidcote Manor's, you have to marvel at the patience and love that went into creating it. An American officer, Lawrence Johnstone, bought the Cotswold estate in 1907. What this amazing gardener did with a high, windswept limestone scarp is nothing short of amazing. Johnston created a series of terraces and planted unusual hedges (as windbreaks) to form compartments off a long central axis. Rare and exotic plants — including rhododendrons, camellias, and magnolias that are lime intolerant — are planted in beds of sawdust. Hidcote is in some ways the forerunner of Sissinghurst because it comprises a variety of garden "rooms." Stopping here is a must for anyone touring the Cotswolds. For more information on Hidcote, see Chapter 20.

Kew Gardens

The Royal Botanic Gardens at Kew — more commonly known as Kew Gardens — are perfect for a half-day trip from London. (Getting there takes about a half-hour on the Underground.) The 300-acre gardens date to 1730, when Frederick, Prince of Wales, leased the property and helped lay out the grounds. His widow, Augusta, and his son George III really developed Kew. They enlisted botanists who began to bring plants from all over the world. Capability Brown later redesigned the gardens and destroyed many of the earlier buildings, but the 163-foot-high Chinese pagoda remains. The Palm House, a great glass house conservatory, was completed in 1848. On the grounds are picturesque Kew Palace, used by King George III (who went temporarily insane) and Queen Charlotte's Cottage, a royal summer retreat. From April through September, you can reach Kew by boat from London's Westminster Pier. See Chapter 13 for more details on Kew Gardens.

Lanhydrock

Gardens are usually meant to beautify and set off a house. The beautiful gardens of Lanhydrock surround one of the largest stately homes in Cornwall. Here, different kinds of gardens — from Victorian parterres to woodland gardens where camellias, magnolias, and rhododendrons grow in dappled shade — embellish the great house and overlook the Fowey River valley below. An avenue of ancient beech and sycamore trees runs from the 17th-century gatehouse down to a medieval bridge across the Fowey. You find details about Lanhydrock in Chapter 18.

Sissinghurst Castle Garden

This world-famous garden in Kent represents what many people consider the most beautiful example of an English garden. The sheer profusion and abundance of plants gives Sissinghurst a romance uniquely its own. The writer Vita Sackville-West and her diplomat husband, Sir Harold Nicolson, bought the ruined castle in 1930 and jointly created the gardens. Harold designed the various "compartments" or "rooms" of the garden, and Vita "furnished" them with plants, trees, and shrubs that provide color all year round. See Chapter 23 for more on Vita Sackville-West.

The White Garden, with foliage and blossoms that are entirely white or silver, is the most famous garden area at Sissinghurst. Typical English plants, such as primroses and daffodils, are extensively used. Roses, many of them fragrant old varieties that were nearly lost, were planted by the hundreds and now climb through trees and over walls. You can visit Sissinghurst as a day trip from London, but be aware that entrance is by timed ticket; see Chapter 15 for more information.

Stourhead

Stourhead in Wiltshire represents a new kind of gardening style that swept through England starting in the early 1700s. Before that, the wealthy based their show-off gardens on French models, with designs that were strictly geometric and pretty low to the ground. The new style favored a natural look, with flowing, irregular lines, plantings of trees and shrubs, and ornamental lakes instead of giant fountains.

The architect Henry Flitcroft laid out the gardens at Stourhead in 1741 for Henry Hoare, a wealthy merchant banker who'd already built a mansion on the site in the *Palladian style* (a classical style incorporating elements from ancient Greek and Roman buildings). Flitcroft transformed small ponds into lakes spanned by a bridge and used classically inspired buildings as architectural ornaments along the edges. Picturesque views and tranquil vistas are what Stourhead is all about. For more details on Stourhead, see Chapter 16.

Warwick Castle

Lancelot "Capability" Brown (1716–1783) was one of the most famous landscape gardeners in 18th-century England. In the 1750s, Brown introduced what has since become known as the English landscape garden, which is meant to look like an enhanced and perfected natural landscape. You can see his work in the park at Warwick Castle in Warwickshire. The grounds, sloping down to the River Avon, have winding paths and are planted with giant trees. One unusual feature at Warwick is the peacock-shaped topiary in front of the conservatory where a flock of peacocks freely roams. See Chapter 19 for details on visiting the castle.

Chapter 25

Ten (Or So) Great English Churches

In This Chapter

- Visiting England's most important churches and cathedrals
- Discovering the unique qualities of these sacred places

Churches and cathedrals are special places where you can come in direct contact with England's long history. Enter a church in just about any village, no matter how quiet and tiny, and you're in the place where countless generations have gathered to worship, celebrate, and grieve. Within the church, you may find a 900-year-old baptismal font, elaborate tombs with reclining figures, memorial stones, medieval brasses, ancient stained glass, and medieval carved figures and ornaments in wood and stone.

Over the centuries, even the smallest churches become fascinating almanacs of changing styles. The country is also blessed with an amazing assortment of magnificent cathedrals, huge places where monarchs have been crowned and famous people are buried. No matter how great or small, England's churches are architectural treasures, and I urge you to visit some of those I describe in this chapter.

Canterbury Cathedral: Pilgrim Central

Throughout the Middle Ages, pilgrims from throughout Europe flocked to this great cathedral in Kent. Their goal: To see the shrine of Saint Thomas à Becket, an archbishop killed in the cathedral in 1170 by henchmen of Henry II. (People believed if they prayed at the shrine, they would receive special indulgences after death.) The popularity of Becket's shrine, which added enormous wealth to the monastery at Canterbury, rankled the absolutist monarch Henry VIII (who reigned from 1509–1547). Becket's shrine was destroyed when Henry abolished all monasteries. Declaring himself the head of the Church of England, Henry VIII outlawed loyalty to the Pope as the head of the church, and monasteries were closed, destroyed, or converted.

In the cathedral, you can still see where the shrine stood, behind the high altar. In Canterbury, you can also visit **St. Martin's,** which may be the oldest church in England, and the ruins of **St. Augustine's Abbey,** established in A.D. 597. For more on Canterbury, see Chapter 14.

Exeter Cathedral: A Medieval Sculpture Gallery

The twin towers of Exeter Cathedral in Devon date from Norman times (12th century), but the entire church was remodeled in the 14th century. The ornamentation and architectural detailing both outside and in is representative of the aptly named Decorated Gothic style. The cathedral's most remarkable exterior feature is the image screen on the west end. The screen contains row upon row of niches filled with wonderfully carved figures of saints and kings dating from the late 14th and early 15th century. This screen is the largest collection of medieval sculpture in the entire country. Inside, the cathedral's 300 feet of uninterrupted fan vaulting is the longest in England. More information on Exeter Cathedral appears in Chapter 17.

King's College Chapel: Unparalleled Lightness

When entering this tall, thin church in Cambridge, you immediately notice how light and airy it feels. The building's style, called Perpendicular Gothic, emphasizes verticality, carrying the eyes upward to a roof of beautiful fan vaulting. Enormous windows, glowing with stained glass, add to the sense of lightness. Hearing the famed King's College boys' choir sing in this chapel is an unforgettable experience. For more information, see Chapter 13.

St. Martin-in-the-Fields: West End Landmark

St. Martin-in-the-Fields is a London landmark. Prominently sited on Trafalgar Square, the 18th-century neoclassical church with its raised portico and graceful steeple served as the prototype for dozens of churches in New England. St. Martin's is a lively social center in the West End. The crypt holds a popular cafe and a brass rubbing center, and the church itself hosts weekly concerts by the Academy of St. Martin-in-the-Fields. See Chapter 12 for more details.

St. Paul's Cathedral: Wren's Crowning Achievement

When the old St. Paul's burned down in London's Great Fire of 1666, the architect Christopher Wren designed a new cathedral on the same site. Wren was responsible for dozens of churches throughout the city, but none so grand as St. Paul's. Started in 1673 and completed in 1711, the cathedral is considered his masterpiece, and he's buried in the crypt along with national heroes like the Duke of Wellington and Admiral Lord Nelson. German bombers blitzed the entire area during World War II, but St. Paul's survived with only minor damage. In 1981, the cathedral was the site of the wedding of Prince Charles and Lady Diana Spencer. Today the mighty dome of St. Paul's, a famous London landmark, rises high above a sea of bland office buildings. You can find details on visiting St. Paul's in Chapter 12.

Salisbury Cathedral: High in the Sky

Rising some 404 feet, the spire of Salisbury Cathedral in Wiltshire is the tallest in England. The cathedral is unique in that the structure was planned and built as a single unit. In other cathedrals, building usually went on for centuries, often incorporating portions of earlier structures and changing styles along the way. But at Salisbury, the work began in 1220 and was completed just 40 years later. (The one exception was the spire, added in 1334.) As a result, Salisbury Cathedral is probably the most beautiful and harmonious example of the Early English style. See Chapter 16 for details.

Westminster Abbey: England's Crowning Glory

London's Westminster Abbey holds a hallowed place in English history, because nearly all the kings and queens of England since William the Conqueror have been crowned there. The Coronation Chair, made of English oak, has been used since 1307. The present cathedral, begun under Henry III in the 13th century, was built in French Gothic style. One architectural highlight is the Henry VII Chapel, raised above the general level of the abbey and roofed with intricate fan vaulting; the Florentine sculptor Torrigiani created Henry VII's black-and-white touchstone tomb. The abbey is also the final resting place of Queen Elizabeth I, her Catholic half-sister Mary Tudor, and Mary Queen of Scots, Elizabeth's one-time rival for the throne.

Approximately 3,300 people are buried in Westminster Abbey, including the poet Geoffrey Chaucer, the writer Dr. Samuel Johnson, the scientists Charles Darwin and Sir Isaac Newton, the composers George Frederic Handel and Henry Purcell, and the actor Sir Laurence Olivier. For more information on Westminster Abbey, refer to Chapter 12.

Winchester Cathedral: Saxon Power Base

Winchester was the capital of England before William of Normandy arrived in 1066 and won the English throne. Before 1066, Saxon kings were crowned not in London but in Winchester Cathedral, a tradition that William continued — although he had himself crowned in London's Westminster Abbey as well. To this day, the caskets of some of the pre-Conquest Saxon rulers of England rest in Winchester Cathedral. This is also where you find the grave of the early-19th-century novelist Jane Austen.

Winchester Cathedral boasts the longest *nave* (the main, central space in the interior) in Europe at 556 feet, but its massive foundations were built on nothing more than a raft of logs laid on a bog. By 1900, the building was sinking. William Walker, an underwater diver, worked beneath the foundations for five years (in water so black he couldn't see his hands), removing the decayed wood handful by handful so that the cathedral could be underpinned with concrete. For more on Winchester Cathedral, see Chapter 16.

York Minster: England's Largest Gothic Church

When missionaries from Rome arrived in the late sixth century to convert England, York in the north, like Canterbury in the south, was established as an archbishopric. The importance of York as a city is reflected in the overwhelming size of its church. The largest Gothic church in England, York Minster has more rare medieval stained glass than any other church in the country. Many English cathedrals are built on the sites of earlier churches, but York Minster was built over a Roman military headquarters. If you visit, go down into the *undercroft* (the rooms below the church), where excavations have revealed Roman walls and streets. I describe York and its magnificent church in more detail in Chapter 21.

Appendix

Quick Concierge

American Express

The main London office is at 6 Haymarket, SW1 (☎ 020/7930-4411; Tube: Piccadilly Circus). Branch offices are in Bath, 5 Bridge St. (☎ 01225/ 447-256); Brighton, 82 North St. (☎ 01273/712-905); Cambridge, 25 Sidney St. (☎ 01223/345-203); Oxford, 4 Queen St. (☎ 01865/207-105); Plymouth, 139 Armada Way (☎ 01752/502-705); Salisbury, 34 Catherine St. (☎ 01722/411-200); and York, 6 Stonegate (☎ 01904/676505).

Area/City Codes

Every U.K. telephone number in this book begins with a zero, followed by a city or area code, followed by a slash and the local number. You must dial the zero and area or city code only if you're calling from outside the area of the local number but within the United Kingdom. For information on calling the United Kingdom from outside the country, see "Telephone," later in this section.

ATMs

ATMs, sometimes called *cashpoints,* are widely available in cities and towns throughout the country. Your bank or credit card must have a special PIN (personal identification number) to operate in overseas ATMs. You can obtain this PIN from your bank before you leave on your trip.

Business Hours

Banks are usually open Monday through Friday 9:30 a.m. to 3:30 p.m.

Business offices are open Monday through Friday 9 a.m. to 5 p.m.; the lunch break lasts an hour, but most places stay open during that time. Pubs are allowed to stay open Monday through Saturday 11 a.m. to 11 p.m. and Sunday noon to 10:30 p.m. Some bars stay open past midnight. London stores generally open at 9 a.m. and close at 5:30 p.m. Monday through Saturday, staying open until 7 p.m. on Wednesday or Thursday. Elsewhere in the country, stores may be open for half-day on Saturday. Larger stores in London and in heavily touristed areas may be open on Sunday as well.

Credit Cards

American Express, Diners Club, MasterCard, and Visa are widely accepted in London and throughout the United Kingdom. If your card gets lost or stolen in England, call the following U.K. numbers: Visa ☎ 01604/230-230 (☎ 800/645-6556 in the U.S. for Citicorp Visa); American Express ☎ 01273/696-933 (☎ 800/221-7282 in the U.S.); MasterCard ☎ 01702/362-988 (☎ 800/307-7309 in the U.S.); Diners Club ☎ 0800/460-800 (☎ 800/ 525-7376 in the U.S.).

Currency Exchange

You find currency exchanges (called *bureaux de change*) in railway stations, at most post offices, and in many tourist information centers. See Chapter 9 for more on currency exchange.

Customs

If you're a United States citizen, you may bring home $800 worth of goods duty-free, providing you've been out of the country at least 48 hours and haven't used the exemption in the past 30 days. This limit includes not more than one liter of an alcoholic beverage,

200 cigarettes, and 100 cigars. Antiques more than 100 years old and works of art are exempt from the $800 limit, as is anything you mail home from abroad. You may mail up to $200 worth of goods to yourself (marked "for personal use") and up to $100 worth to others (marked "unsolicited gift") once each day, as long as the package doesn't include alcohol or tobacco products. You have to pay an import duty on anything over these limits. You'll be charged a flat rate of 10% duty on the next $1,000 worth of purchases. For more specific guidance, download the free pamphlet *Know Before You Go* from the Customs Department Web site (www.customs. ustreas.gov) or contact the U.S. Customs Service, 1300 Pennsylvania Ave., NW, Washington, DC 20229 (☎ 877/287-8867), and request it.

Returning Canadian citizens are allowed a $750 exemption and can bring back duty-free 200 cigarettes, 2.2 pounds of tobacco, 40 imperial ounces (1.2 qt.) of liquor, and 50 cigars. All valuables that you're taking with you to the U.K., such as expensive cameras, should be declared on form Y-38 before departure from Canada. For a clear summary of Canadian rules, request the booklet *Declare,* issued by the Canada Customs and Revenue Agency (☎ 800/461-9999 in Canada, or 204/983-3500; Internet: www.ccra-adrc.gc.ca).

Australian citizens are allowed an exemption of $400 or, if under 18, $200. Personal property mailed back home should be marked *Australian Goods Returned* to avoid payment of duty. On returning to Australia, you can bring in 250 cigarettes or 250 grams of loose tobacco, and 1,125 ml of alcohol. If you're returning with valuable goods you already own, such as foreign-made cameras, you should file form B263. A helpful brochure, *Know Before You Go,* is available from Australian consulates or Customs offices. For more information, contact the Australian Customs Service (☎ 1300/363-263; www.customs.gov.au).

New Zealand citizens have a duty-free allowance of $700. If you're older than 17, you can bring in 200 cigarettes, 50 cigars, or 250 grams of tobacco (or a mix of all three if the combined weight doesn't exceed 250 grams), plus 4.5 liters of wine and beer, or 1.125 liters of liquor. New Zealand currency doesn't carry import or export restrictions. Fill out a certificate of export, listing the valuables you're taking out of the country. (That way you can bring them back without paying duty.) You can find the answers to most of your questions in *New Zealand Customs Guide for Travelers Notice No. 4,* a free pamphlet available at New Zealand consulates and Customs offices. For more information, contact New Zealand Customs, The Customhouse, 17–21 Whitmore St., Box 2218, Wellington (☎ 04/473-6099 or 0800/428-786; www.customs.govt.nz).

Doctors

See "Hospitals" later in this section. For a doctor in London, see "Doctors and Dentists" in the "Fast Facts" section of Chapter 12.

Electricity

British current is 240 volts, AC cycle, roughly twice the voltage of North American current, which is 115–120 volts, AC cycle. You won't be able to plug the flat pins of your appliance's plugs into the holes of British wall outlets without suitable converters or adapters (available from an electrical supply shop). Be forewarned that you'll destroy the inner workings of your appliance (and possibly start a fire) if you plug an American appliance directly into a European electrical outlet without a transformer.

Embassies and High Commissions

All embassies, consulates, and high commissions are in London, the capital of the U.K. In case you lose your passport or have some other emergency, here's a list of addresses and phone numbers:

Australia: The high commission is at Australia House, Strand, WC2 (☎ 02073/794-334; Tube: Charing Cross), open Monday through Friday 10 a.m. to 4 p.m.

Canada: The high commission is at MacDonald House, 38 Grosvenor Square, W1 (☎ 02072/586-600; Tube: Bond St.), open Monday through Friday 8 a.m. to 11 a.m.

Ireland: The embassy is at 17 Grosvenor Place, SW1 (☎ 02072/352-171; Tube: Hyde Park Corner), open Monday through Friday 9:30 a.m. to 1 p.m. and 2:15 to 5 p.m.

New Zealand: The high commission is at New Zealand House, 80 Haymarket at Pall Mall, SW1 (☎ 02079/308-422; Tube: Charing Cross or Piccadilly Circus), open Monday through Friday 9 a.m. to 5 p.m.

United States: The embassy is at 24 Grosvenor Square, W1 (☎ 02074/999-000; Tube: Bond Street), open Monday through Friday from 8:30 a.m. to noon and 2 to 4 p.m. (there are no afternoon hours on Tuesday).

Emergencies

For police, fire, or an ambulance, dial ☎ **999.**

Holidays

Americans may be unfamiliar with some British holidays, particularly the spring and summer Bank Holidays (the last Monday in May and in August), when everyone takes off for a long weekend. Most banks and many shops, museums, historic houses, and other places of interest are closed on Bank Holidays, and public transport services are reduced. The same holds true for other major British holidays: New Year's Day, Good Friday, Easter Monday, May Day (the first Monday in May), Christmas, and Boxing Day (December 26). London crowds swell during school holidays: mid-July to early September, three weeks at Christmas and at Easter, and a week in mid-October and in mid-February.

Hospitals

Visitors to the U.K. are entitled to free *emergency* care in Emergency Outpatient Centers of National Health hospitals; visitors must pay for any inpatient or follow-up care. Check with your insurance company or HMO to see if medical expenses are covered while you're out of the country. If you require a doctor, ask your hotel, consulate, or embassy to recommend one. If the situation is a life-threatening emergency, dial ☎ **999** for an ambulance. For a list of hospitals offering 24-hour emergency care in London, see "Hospitals" in the "Fast Facts" section of Chapter 12. See Chapter 10 for insurance and medical matters.

Information

See "Where to Get More Information," later in this Appendix, to find out where to get visitor information before you leave home.

Internet Access and Cybercafes

For Internet access in London, see the "Fast Facts" section of Chapter 12. For the rest of the country, check at local Tourist Information Centres to find out if public Internet access is available. Usually cybercafes are only in larger cities; public libraries in smaller towns often have Internet access.

Liquor Laws

No alcohol is served to anyone under 18. Children under 16 aren't allowed in pubs, except in certain rooms, and then only when accompanied by a parent or guardian. Restaurants are allowed to serve liquor during the same hours as pubs (see "Business Hours" earlier in this section for these hours); however, only people who are eating a meal on the premises can be served a drink. In hotels, liquor may be served 11 a.m. to 11 p.m. to both guests and nonguests; after 11 p.m., only guests may be served.

Mail

At press time, an airmail letter to North America cost 47p (75¢) for 10 grams, and postcards require a 42p (67¢) stamp; letters generally take seven to ten days to arrive from the United States. Travel time for letters to the United States from the United

Kingdom varies wildly, but usually takes between seven and ten days as well. Mail within the United Kingdom can be sent first or second class. See "Post Offices" later in this section.

Maps

London A to Z, available in various formats from news agents and bookstores, is the best street directory to London. You can obtain a London bus and Underground map at any Underground station. If you drive through England, the best road atlases are the large-format maps produced by the Automobile Association (AA), Royal Automobile Club (RAC), Collins, and Ordnance Survey. The best maps for walkers are the detailed Ordnance Survey maps; check out their selection, including digital maps, online at www.ordsvy.gov.uk. London's Stanfords, 12–14 Long Acre, WC2 (☎ 02078/361-321; Tube: Leicester Sq.), is the world's largest map shop.

Newspapers/Magazines

The *Times, Daily Telegraph, Daily Mail, Guardian,* and *Evening Standard* are all dailies carrying the latest news. The *International Herald Tribune,* published in Paris, and an international edition of *USA Today,* beamed via satellite, are available daily. Copies of *Time* and *Newsweek* are also sold at most newsstands.

Pharmacies

Pharmacies are called *chemists* in the United Kingdom. Boots is a chain of chemists with outlets all over the country. Any prescriptions you bring with you should be generic, not brand names. For a list of pharmacies in London, see "Pharmacies" in the Fast Facts section of Chapter 12.

Police

In an emergency, dial ☎ **999** (no coin required).

Post Offices

In London, the Main Post Office, 24 William IV St., WC2 (☎ 02079/309-580; Tube: Charing Cross), is open Monday through Saturday 8:30 a.m. to 8 p.m. Other post offices and subpost offices (windows in the back of news agent stores) throughout the country are open Monday through Friday 9 a.m. to 5:30 p.m. and Saturday 9 a.m. to 12:30 p.m. Many subpost offices and some main post offices close for an hour at lunchtime. A red sign identifies post offices.

Restrooms

The English often call toilets *loos.* In London, they're marked by PUBLIC TOILETS signs on streets, parks, and tube stations. You also find well-maintained lavatories that can be used by anybody in all larger public buildings, such as museums and art galleries, large department stores, and rail stations. Toilets are always available at major tourist attractions. Public lavatories are usually free, but you may need a 20p coin to get in or to use a proper washroom. In some places (like Leicester Square in London), you find coin-operated toilets that are sterilized after each use.

Safety

England is a very safe country. In London, as in any large metropolis, use common sense and normal caution when you're in a crowded public area or walking alone at night.

Smoking

Most U.S. cigarette brands are available in England. Smoking is strictly forbidden in the London Underground (in the cars and on the platforms) and on buses, and it's increasingly frowned on in many other places. Most restaurants have nonsmoking tables, but they're usually in the same room with smokers. Nonsmoking rooms are available in more and more hotels, and some B&Bs are now entirely smoke-free.

Taxes

The 17.5% value-added tax (VAT) is added to all hotel and restaurant bills and will be included in the price of most items you purchase. You can get a refund if you shop at stores that participate in the Duty-Free

Shopping scheme (signs are posted in the window). See Chapter 9 for details on getting your VAT refunded.

Taxis

In London, you can hail a cab from the street; if the "For Hire" light is lit, it means the cab is available. You can phone for a London radio cab at ☎ 02072/720-272. Elsewhere, you can often find taxis waiting outside train and bus stations, although it's a good idea to reserve a taxi in advance at smaller stations in the country.

Telephone

For directory assistance, dial ☎ 192. The country code for the United Kingdom is **44.** To call England from the United States, dial **011-44,** the area or city code, and then the 6, 7, or 8-digit phone number. If you're in England and dialing a number within the same area code, the local number is all you need.

Three types of public pay phones are available: those that take only coins, those that accept only phone cards, and those that take coins, phone cards, and credit cards. Phone cards are available in four values — £2 ($3.20), £4 ($6), £10 ($16), and £20 ($32) — and are reusable until the total value has expired. You can buy the cards from newsstands and post offices. At coin-operated phones, insert your coins before dialing. The minimum charge is 20p (32¢). The credit-call pay phone operates on credit cards — Access (which is interchangeable with MasterCard), Visa, American Express, and Diners Club — and is most commonly found at airports and large rail stations.

To make an international call from England, dial the international access code (00), then the country code, then the area code, and finally the local number. Or call through one of the following long-distance access codes: AT&T USA Direct (☎ 0800/890-011), Canada Direct (☎ 0800-/890-016), Australia (☎ 0800/890-061), and New Zealand (☎ 0800/890-064). Common country codes are: USA and Canada, **1;** Australia, **61;** and New Zealand, **64.**

Time Zone

England follows Greenwich mean time (five hours ahead of eastern standard time). Clocks move forward one hour on the last Sunday in March and back one hour on the last Sunday in October. Most of the year, including summer, Britain is five hours ahead of the time observed on the East Coast of the United States. Because the United States and Britain observe daylight saving time at slightly different times of year, there's a brief period (about a week) in autumn when Britain is only four hours ahead of New York and a brief period in spring when it's six hours ahead of New York.

Tipping

In restaurants, service charges of 15% to 20% are often added to the bill. Sometimes this tip is clearly marked; other times it isn't. When in doubt, ask. If service isn't included, adding 15% to the bill is customary. Sommeliers get about £1 ($1.60) per bottle of wine served. Tipping in pubs isn't done, but in cocktail bars the server usually gets about £1 ($1.60) per round of drinks. Tipping taxi drivers 10% to 15% of the fare is standard. Barbers and hairdressers expect 10% to 15%. Tour guides expect £2 ($3.20), although this tip isn't mandatory. Theater ushers aren't tipped.

Train Information

For information on train schedules and departure stations, call ☎ 08457/484950 24 hours. You can also find info online at `www.railtrack.co.uk`.

Weather Updates

Weather information for the United Kingdom is available online at `http://weather.yahoo.com/region/Europe/United_Kingdom.html`. You can also dial Weathercall at ☎ 0891/500-401 for regional weather reports that are mostly geared to drivers.

Toll-Free Numbers and Web Sites

Major airlines serving England

Air Canada
☎ 888/247-2262
www.aircanada.ca

Air New Zealand
☎ 800/262-2468 (U.S.)
☎ 0800/737-767 (New Zealand)
www.airnewzealand.com

American Airlines
☎ 800/433-7300
www.im.aa.com

British Airways
☎ 800/247-9297 (U.S.)
☎ 0345/222-111 (U.K.)
www.british-airways.com

British Midland
☎ 0800/788-0555 (U.K.)
www.britishmidland.com

Continental Airlines
☎ 800/625-0280
www.continental.com

Delta Air Lines
☎ 800/221-1212
www.delta.com

Icelandair
☎ 800/223-5500
www.icelandair.is

Northwest Airlines
☎ 800/225-2525
www.nwa.com

Qantas
☎ 800/227-4500 (U.S.)
☎ 612/9691-3636 (Australia)
www.qantas.com

United Airlines
☎ 800/241-6522
www.united.com

Virgin Atlantic Airways
☎ 800/862-8621 (Continental U.S.)
☎ 0293/747-747 (U.K.)
www.virgin-atlantic.com

Major car-rental agencies operating in England

Alamo
☎ 800/327-9633 (U.S.)
☎ 0800/272-200 (U.K.)
www.goalamo.com

Avis
☎ 800/331-1212 (Continental U.S.)
☎ 0990/900-500 (U.K.)
www.avis.com

Budget
☎ 800/527-0700 (U.S.)
☎ 0541/565-656 (U.K.)
www.budgetrentacar.com

Hertz
☎ 800/654-3131 (U.S.)
☎ 0990/6699 (U.K.)
www.hertz.com

National
☎ 800/CAR-RENT (U.S.)
☎ 0990/565-656 (U.K.)
www.nationalcar.com

Major hotel chains in England

Forte & Meridien Hotels & Resorts
☎ 800/225-5843
www.forte-hotels.com
www.lemeridien-hotels.com

Heritage Hotels
☎ 0870/400-8855 (U.K.)
www.heritage-hotels.com

Hilton Hotels
☎ 800/HILTONS
www.hilton.com

Hyatt Hotels & Resorts
☎ 800/228-9000
www.hyatt.com

Inter-Continental Hotels & Resorts
☎ 888/567-8725
www.interconti.com

Moat House Hotels
☎ 800/641-0300
www.moathousehotels.com

Relais & Chateaux
☎ 800/735-2478
www.relaischateaux.fr

Sheraton Hotels & Resorts
☎ 800/325-3535
www.sheraton.com

Thistle Hotels Worldwide
☎ 800/847-4358
www.thistlehotels.com

Where to Get More Information

For more information on England, you can visit the tourist offices and Web sites listed in this section.

Locating tourist offices

For general information about London, contact an office of VisitBritain (formerly the British Tourist Authority) at one of the following addresses or on the Web at www.visitbritain.com:

- **In the United States:** The main BTA office for North America is at 551 Fifth Ave., Suite 701, New York, NY 10176-0799 (☎ 800/462-2748; Fax: 212/986-1188).
- **In Australia:** University Centre, 8th floor, 210 Clarence St., Sydney NSW 2000 (☎ 02/267-4555; Fax: 02/267-4442).
- **In New Zealand:** Suite 305, Dilworth Building, Queen and Customs streets, Auckland 1 (☎ 09/303-1446; Fax: 09/377-6965).

For more specific information on particular regions, contact the following regional tourist boards:

- **Cumbria Tourist Board** (the Lake District), Ashleigh, Holly Rd., Windermere, Cumbria LA23 2AQ (☎ 01539/44444).
- **East of England Tourist Board,** Toppesfield Hall, Hadleigh, Suffolk IP7 5DN (☎ 01473/822-922).
- **Heart of England Tourist Board,** Woodside, Larkhill Rd., Worcester WR5 2E2 (☎ 01905/763-436).
- **North West England Tourist Board,** Swan House, Swan Meadow Road, Wigan Pier, Wigan WN3 5BB (☎ 01942/821-222).
- **South East England Tourist Board,** The Old Brew House, Warwick Park, Tunbridge Wells, Kent TN2 5TU (☎ 01892/540-766).
- **Southern England Tourist Board,** 40 Chamberlayne Rd., Eastleigh, Hampshire SO50 5JH (☎ 01703/620-006).
- **West Country Tourist Board,** 60 St. David's Hill, Exeter, Devon EX4 4SY (☎ 01392/425-426).
- **Yorkshire Tourist Board,** 312 Tadcaster Rd., York YO24 1GS (☎ 01904/707-961).

Surfing the Net

You find useful and quite specific Web sites scattered throughout this guide. In this section, I point you toward some of the best of them.

Tourist info on England

For general information on all of England, try these sites for starters:

- `www.visitbritain.com`. The Web page for the official British travel agency is a good resource for visitors to London and the United Kingdom in general.
- `www.travelengland.org.uk`. The English Tourist Board's official site has information on cities and regions throughout the country.
- `www.knowhere.co.uk`. On this site, local residents provide a mish-mash of insider information for cities and towns throughout the United Kingdom.
- `www.backpackers.co.uk`. Travelers who want to backpack through England find useful information, including hostels and inexpensive accommodations, at this site.

General info on specific cities

The following tourist information center Web sites provide directories for hotels, restaurants, and attractions in cities throughout England:

- **Bath:** www.bathnes.gov.uk or www.heritagecities.co.uk
- **Brighton:** www.tourism.brighton.co.uk
- **Cambridge:** www.cambridge.gov.uk
- **Canterbury:** www.canterbury.co.uk
- **Dover:** www.dover.gov.uk
- **Greenwich:** www.greenwich.gov.uk
- **Oxford:** www.oxford.gov.uk/tourism
- **Penzance:** www.penzance.co.uk
- **Plymouth:** www.plymouthcity.co.uk
- **Salisbury:** www.salisbury.gov.uk/tourism
- **Stratford-upon-Avon:** www.shakespeare-country.co.uk or www.heritagecities.co.uk
- **Winchester:** www.winchester.gov.uk
- **Windsor:** www.rbwm.gov.uk

Visitor info for counties, regions, and national parks

The following sites give you general information on specific counties, regions, and national parks in England:

- **Cornwall:** www.cornwall-calling.co.uk, www.cornwall-online.co.uk, or www.chycor.co.uk
- **Cotswolds, Gloucestershire:** www.visit-glos.org.uk
- **Dartmoor National Park:** www.dartmoor-npa.gov.uk
- **Devon, English Riviera:** www.english-riviera.com
- **Lake District:** www.cumbria-the-lake-district.co.uk
- **North York Moors National Park:** www.northyorkmoors-npa.gov.uk
- **South Kent:** www.whitecliffscountry.org.uk
- **Warwickshire around Stratford:** www.shakespeare-country.co.uk
- **Yorkshire:** www.ytb.org.uk
- **Yorkshire Dales National Park:** www.yorkshiredales.org.uk

News on daily events, transportation, and the royals

If you're looking for news about daily events or royal happenings, log on the following Web sites:

- www.guardian.co.uk. The *Daily Guardian,* a daily newspaper, provides up-to-the minute online news coverage.
- www.Sunday-times.co.uk. The *London Times,* the oldest and most traditional of London daily papers, is a good source for general news and culture.
- www.railtrack.co.uk. This site provides information on train schedules.
- www.pti.org.uk. This very useful site (especially if you don't have a car) provides information on all forms of public transportation throughout the country.
- www.royal.gov.uk. If you want to read history, information, and trivia about the Windsors and the British monarchy in general, check out the official Royal Web site.

Online sites for London

For tourism, cultural, entertainment, or transportation information on London, check out the following sites:

- www.londontown.com. The London Tourist Board's site features special offers on hotels, B&Bs, and theater tickets.
- www.timeout.com. The weekly listings magazine *Time Out* gives you the lowdown on London's cultural events, entertainment, restaurants, and nightlife.
- www.gaylondon.co.uk. This is a useful list of gay and gay-friendly hotels, services, clubs, and restaurants.
- www.baa.co.uk. Information on London's airports is available on this site.
- www.londontransport.co.uk. This is the Web site for London Transport, which is in charge of all forms of public transportation in the city: Tube, buses, ferry service, and so on.

Making Dollars and Sense of It

Expense	Daily cost	x	Number of days	=	Total
Airfare					
Local transportation					
Car rental					
Lodging (with tax)					
Parking					
Breakfast					
Lunch					
Dinner					
Snacks					
Entertainment					
Babysitting					
Attractions					
Gifts & souvenirs					
Tips					
Other					
Grand Total					

Fare Game: Choosing an Airline

When looking for the best airfare, you should cover all your bases — 1) consult a trusted travel agent; 2) contact the airline directly, via the airline's toll-free number and/or Web site; 3) check out one of the travel-planning Web sites, such as www.frommers.com.

Travel Agency____________________ Phone____________________

Agent's Name____________________ Quoted fare____________________

Airline 1____________________ Quoted fare____________________

Toll-free number/Internet____________________

Airline 2____________________ Quoted fare____________________

Toll-free number/Internet____________________

Web site 1____________________ Quoted fare____________________

Web site 2____________________ Quoted fare____________________

Departure Schedule & Flight Information

Airline____________________ Flight #__________ Confirmation #__________

Departs____________________ Date__________ Time__________ a.m./p.m.

Arrives____________________ Date__________ Time__________ a.m./p.m.

Connecting Flight (if any)

Amount of time between flights__________ hours/mins

Airline____________________ Flight #__________ Confirmation #__________

Departs____________________ Date__________ Time__________ a.m./p.m.

Arrives____________________ Date__________ Time__________ a.m./p.m.

Return Trip Schedule & Flight Information

Airline____________________ Flight #__________ Confirmation #__________

Departs____________________ Date__________ Time__________ a.m./p.m.

Arrives____________________ Date__________ Time__________ a.m./p.m.

Connecting Flight (if any)

Amount of time between flights__________ hours/mins

Airline____________________ Flight #__________ Confirmation #__________

Departs____________________ Date__________ Time__________ a.m./p.m.

Arrives____________________ Date__________ Time__________ a.m./p.m.

All Aboard: Booking Your Train Travel

Travel Agency____________________ Phone________________

Agent's Name____________________

Web Site____________________

Departure Schedule & Train Information

Train #__________ Confirmation #__________ Seat reservation #______

Departs____________ Date________ Time________ a.m./p.m.

Arrives____________ Date________ Time________ a.m./p.m.

Quoted fare__________ First class __________ Second class

Departure Schedule & Train Information

Train #__________ Confirmation #__________ Seat reservation #______

Departs____________ Date________ Time________ a.m./p.m.

Arrives____________ Date________ Time________ a.m./p.m.

Quoted fare__________ First class __________ Second class

Departure Schedule & Train Information

Train #__________ Confirmation #__________ Seat reservation #______

Departs____________ Date________ Time________ a.m./p.m.

Arrives____________ Date________ Time________ a.m./p.m.

Quoted fare__________ First class __________ Second class

Departure Schedule & Train Information

Train #__________ Confirmation #__________ Seat reservation #______

Departs____________ Date________ Time________ a.m./p.m.

Arrives____________ Date________ Time________ a.m./p.m.

Quoted fare__________ First class __________ Second class

Sweet Dreams: Choosing Your Hotel

Make a list of all the hotels where you'd like to stay and then check online and call the local and toll-free numbers to get the best price. You should also check with a travel agent, who may be able to get you a better rate.

Hotel & page	Location	Internet	Tel. (local)	Tel. (Toll-free)	Quoted rate

Hotel Checklist

Here's a checklist of things to inquire about when booking your room, depending on your needs and preferences.

- ❑ Smoking/smoke-free room
- ❑ Noise (if you prefer a quiet room, ask about proximity to elevator, bar/restaurant, pool, meeting facilities, renovations, and street)
- ❑ View
- ❑ Facilities for children (crib, roll-away cot, baby-sitting services)
- ❑ Facilities for travelers with disabilities
- ❑ Number and size of bed(s) (king, queen, double/full-size)
- ❑ Is breakfast included? (buffet, continental, or sit-down?)
- ❑ In-room amenities (hair dryer, iron/board, minibar, and so on)
- ❑ Other ____________________

Index

• Numerics •

• A •

• D •

• E •

• F •

• G •

• H •

• K •

• L •

• M •

• N •

• O •

• R •

• S •

• U •

• Z •